THE COMPLETE IDIOT'S TRAVEL GUIDE™ TO

Mexico's Beach Resorts

by Edie Jarolim

Macmillan Travel   Alpha Books
Divisions of Macmillan Reference USA
A Simon & Schuster Macmillan Company
1633 Broadway, New York, NY 10019-6785

ISBN 0-02-862579-X
ISSN 1097-1882

Editor: Margot Weiss
Special thanks to Neil Schlecht and Leslie Wiggins
Production Editor: Michael Thomas
Photo Editor: Richard Fox
Page layout: Jena Brandt & Eric Brinkman
Proofreader: David Faust
Design by designLab
Digital Cartography by Raffaele Degennaro & John Decamillis
Illustrations by Kevin Spear

Special Sales

Bulk purchases (10+ copies) of Frommer's and selected Macmillan travel guides are available to corporations, organizations, mail-order catalogs, institutions, and charities at special discounts, and can be customized to suit individual needs. For more information write to: Special Sales, Macmillan General Reference, 1633 Broadway, New York, NY 10019.

Manufactured in the United States of America

Contents

Maps

About the Author

Edie Jarolim was a senior editor at Frommer's in New York before moving to Tucson to fulfill her Southwest fantasies—which she did in several unexpected ways, such as becoming the restaurant critic for *Tucson Monthly* magazine. She's the author of the *Frommer's Guide to San Antonio & Austin,* and her freelance articles on Mexico and the Southwest have appeared in publications ranging from *Arizona Highways* and *Bride's* magazine to the *New York Times Book Review* and *The Wall Street Journal.* She has a Ph.D. in American literature from NYU—which in no way prevented her from acting like a complete idiot the first time she went to Mexico.

An Invitation to the Reader

In researching this book, I discovered many wonderful places—hotels, restaurants, shops, and more. I'm sure you'll find others. Please tell me about them, so I can share the information with your fellow travelers in upcoming editions. If you were disappointed with a recommendation, I'd love to know that, too. Please write to:

The Complete Idiot's Travel Guide™ to Mexico's Beach Resorts
Macmillan Travel
1633 Broadway
New York, NY 10019

An Additional Note

Please be advised that travel information is subject to change at any time—and this is especially true of prices. We therefore suggest that you write or call ahead for confirmation when making your travel plans. The author, editor, and publisher cannot be held responsible for the experiences of readers while traveling. Your safety is important to us, however, so we encourage you to stay alert and be aware of your surroundings. Keep a close eye on cameras, purses, and wallets, all favorite targets of thieves and pickpockets.

The following abbreviations are used for credit cards:

AE	American Express	EURO	Eurocard
CB	Carte Blanche	JCB	Japan Credit Bank
DC	Diners Club	MC	MasterCard
DISC	Discover	V	Visa
ER	enRoute		

Introduction

No doubt about it: Mexico's beaches have mystique. Say the names "Cancún" or "Acapulco" and you'll conjure up a picture of bodies bronzing in a sandy paradise, frosty margaritas in tow.

But not all south-of-the-border beach towns are equally evocative. Most people can barely pronounce "Zihuatanejo," much less tell you exactly where it is. And the word "Mexico" itself may bring to mind negative images, many of them bred by unfamiliarity.

Clearing up misconceptions is what travel guides are for—and this one goes the extra mile. It's designed not only to give you the lowdown on what you can expect to encounter in general, but also, more than any other book you'll come across, to help you decide precisely which of Mexico's top beach towns is right for you.

As it happens, this is a great time to visit Mexico. The peso is still low in comparison with the dollar, but the Mexican economy is rebounding. You can get some great bargains while taking advantage of tourism facilities being created especially to appeal to you. Sparkling new resorts, golf courses, scuba centers, and more are competing for your *yanqui* dollar—which means it'll go a lot farther.

With all the variables to contend with—different beach resorts, different times of year to travel, different types of accommodations to choose from, to name just a few—the last thing you need is a complicated tome that just drops the (beach) ball back in your lap. This book will take you through the process of sorting out what's best for you in a well-organized, step-by-step fashion.

Part 1 introduces you to Mexico's top beach resorts and helps you decide exactly where and when to go.

Part 2 helps you with all the nitty-gritty details—everything from searching the Web for more information to choosing the best airfare and hotel, to figuring out exactly what you'll need to pack.

Part 3 gives you the inside scoop on Mexico's customs (including Customs). It'll get you from the airport to the beach, with stops for history, food, and language lessons in between.

Parts 4–11 each cover one of Mexico's top beach resorts. Part 4 is Cancún; Part 5, Cozumel; Part 6, Acapulco; Part 7, Ixtapa/Zihuatanejo; Part 8, Manzanillo; Part 9, Puerto Vallarta; Part 10, Mazatlán; and Part 11, Los Cabos.

In each of these sections you'll find a chapter describing the top hotels; a chapter with all the information you need to get around; a chapter chock-a-block with activities, both on shore and off, including shopping and nightlife; and finally a chapter that introduces you to some of the best restaurants for all budgets in that destination.

Extras

This book has several special features you won't find in other guidebooks, which will help you make better use of the information provided and do it faster.

Indexes at the end of each hotel and dining chapter cross-reference the information in ways that let you see at a glance what your options are in a particular subcategory—moderately priced restaurants, hotels in a certain area, and so on.

I've also sectioned off little tidbits of useful information in **sidebars,** which come in five types:

Yo, Gringo!

These words to the wise may not stop you from looking like a tourist, but their no-nonsense warnings and up-to-the-minute insider tips will keep you from acting like one.

Bet You Didn't Know

These boxes offer you trivia and tasty tidbits on all things Mexicano.

Time-Savers

Here, you'll find ways to avoid lines and hassles and streamline the business of traveling.

Dollars & Sense

Here, you'll find tips on saving money and cutting corners to make your trip both enjoyable and affordable.

Extra! Extra!

Check out the the handy facts, hints, and "extra" information in these boxes.

Sometimes the best way to fix something in your mind is to write it down, and with that in mind, I've provided **worksheets** in several chapters, as well as in Appendix A, to help you focus your thinking and make your decisions. (Underlining or highlighting as you read along isn't a bad idea, either.) These worksheets will help you feel more in control of your vacation and comfortable with your plans.

 A **kid-friendly icon** is used throughout the book to identify activities, attractions, hotels, and restaurants that are especially suited to people traveling with children.

Appendices at the back of the book include worksheets to help you choose a hotel and a listing of Mexico facts you'll need to know.

Acknowledgements

There are a few folks who know that writing this book involved a bit more than sampling margaritas and hopping on Waverunners. I would like to thank all the people at Burson-Marsteller, New York, and Burson-Marsteller, Mexico City, who helped arrange my research trips, especially Giada Bresaola and Verónica Palavicini. John Jones, of AeroLitoral, went above and beyond the call of duty to get my tickets to me on time (and those small planes were great, John!). The staff of the tourist offices in all the destinations I covered were extremely helpful, but I would like to tip my sombrero especially to Lilian Lobato in Acapulco, Luis Aguilar in Mazatlán, and Ana Laura Acevedo in Manzanillo, not only for their extensive on-site assistance, but also for answering my numerous follow-up queries thoroughly and promptly.

My gratitude for research help also goes to Patricia Alisau and Terri Haag, and for sympathy and pizza (when he thought I was holed up starving—not likely!) to Victor Goordman. Finally, I'd like to say muchas gracias to Macmillan Travel's Margot Weiss, the supportive, nurturing editor every writer fantasizes about—but rarely finds.

Part 1

The Big Decisions: Where & When to Go

So you've decided to treat yourself to a stay at a Mexican resort. ¡Bueno! You couldn't have picked a country with more spectacular beaches, nicer people, or a bigger bang for the American buck.

Pat yourself on the back for making a smart choice—and then consider what it is exactly you're looking for in a vacation. A quiet, romantic retreat? A family affair? A wild singles scene? Some serious sportsfishing? An infusion of another culture? The comforts of home with only a slight foreign accent? Mexico's got them all, and often in the same place. But if all you know about Mexico is burritos and beaches how can you decide where to go?

There's also the question of how you want to travel. Is this going to be a big splurge? A budget getaway? And what's the best time to visit Mexico? Maybe there are special festivals you want be in on. Or maybe you have strong feelings about the weather.

Didn't know so much was involved in figuring out how to hit the sand? Relax. By the time you finish reading through the chapters in this section, you'll be able to make quick and easy decisions about which beach resort is right for you, how much time you'll need to enjoy it, and exactly when you should go.

Chapter 1

Weighing Your Options: Which of Mexico's Beach Resorts Is Right for Me?

In This Chapter

➤ A brief description of each of Mexico's beach resorts

➤ A quiz to help you prioritize your vacation needs and make a decision on where to go

---

A beach is a beach, even if it's got a Mexican accent, right? Wrong. Although you can depend on some givens—gorgeous stretches of sand, plenty of sun (at least unless you're unlucky and run into a patch of rainy weather), great seafood—Mexico's prime vacation resorts are as different from one another as Miami is from, say, Kennebunkport, Maine. I'll get into the nitty-gritty details in the sections devoted to each of the beach towns, but in the meantime, here are some snapshots to help you focus on the resort that's exactly right for you.

Introducing Cancún

You won't have to worry about culture shock in this most gringo-ized of the resort towns, where many fast food franchises and upscale hotel chains say "Made in the U.S.A." There's a joke

Say It in Español

Cancún: Kan-KOON

Cozumel: KOH-zoo-mel

Acapulco: Ah-kah-PULL-koh

Ixtapa/Zihuatanejo: Eeks-TAH-pah/ Zee-wah-teh-NAY-hoe

Manzanillo: Man-zuh-NEE-yo

Puerto Vallarta: Pwer-toh Vah-YAHR-tuh

Mazatlán: MAH-zaht-lahn

Los Cabos: Lohs KAH-bohs

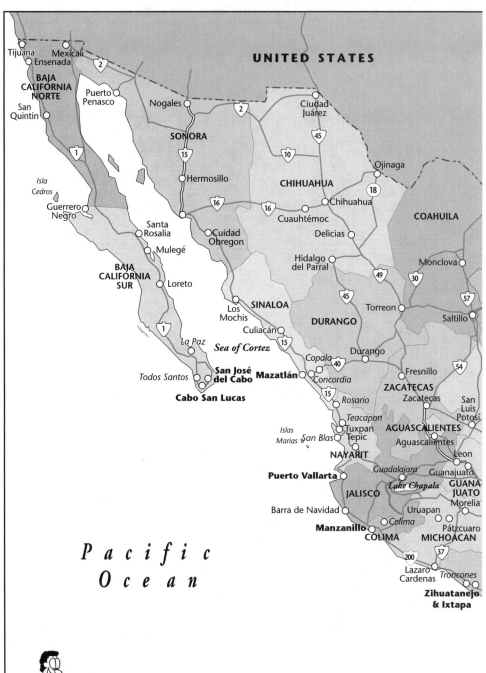

UNITED STATES

Tijuana
Mexicali
Ensenada
2

BAJA CALIFORNIA NORTE

Puerto Penasco

San Quintin

Nogales
2
Ciudad Juárez

45

SONORA

15

10

Ojinaga

Hermosillo

CHIHUAHUA

18

Isla Cedros

Guerrero Negro

16

16

Chihuahua

Cuauhtémoc

COAHUILA

Santa Rosalia

Cuidad Obregon

Delicias

Mulegé

Hidalgo del Parral

Monclova

BAJA CALIFORNIA SUR

Loreto

49

30

45

57

Los Mochis

SINALOA

Torreon

Saltillo

1

La Paz

Culiacán

DURANGO

15

Todos Santos

Sea of Cortez

Durango

San José del Cabo

Copala

40

Fresnillo

54

Mazatlán

Concordia

ZACATECAS

Cabo San Lucas

15

Rosario

Zacatecas

San Luis Potosí

Teacapon

Islas Marias

San Blas

Tuxpan
Tepic

AGUASCALIENTES

Aguascalientes

NAYARIT

Leon

Puerto Vallarta

Guadalajara

Guanajuato

Lake Chapala

GUANA-JUATO

JALISCO

Morelia

Barra de Navidad

Uruapan

Colima

Pátzcuaro

Manzanillo

COLIMA

MICHOACAN

200

37

P a c i f i c

O c e a n

Lazaro Cardenas

Troncones

Zihuatanejo & Ixtapa

Mexico

0		100 m
0		161 Km

UNITED STATES

Piedras Negras

Nuevo Laredo

85D

Matamoros

Monterrey
**NUEVO
LEON**
85

180

TAMAULIPAS

Ciudad Victoria

Gulf of Mexico

Ciudad Mante
Tampico

**SAN LUIS
POTOSÍ**
San Miguel
de Allende
QUERÉTARO
Queretaro
HIDALGO
Pachuca
Mexico City
Toluca
TLAXCALA
Cúernavaca
MORELOS
Taxco
95
GUERRERO
Chilpancingo
*Barra
de Potosi*
Acapulco
200

Tuxpan
Poza Rica
180

Jalapa
Tlaxcala
Puebla
PUEBLA
Tehuacán
190D
175
Oaxaca
OAXACA
Puerto Escondido
Puerto Angel

Veracruz
Orizaba
VERACRUZ
Coatzacoalcos
186
Salina
Cruz
Huatulco

*Bay of
Campeche*
Catemaco

*Gulf of
Tehuantepec*

Río Lagartos
Progreso
Valladolid
180
Celestún
Merida
*Playa del
Carmen*
YUCATÁN
Campeche
**QUINTANA
ROO**
CAMPECHE
Bacalar
261
Escarcega
Chetumal
TABASCO
Villahermosa
186
Tuxtla
Gutierrez
San Cristóbal de las Casas
CHIAPAS
Comitan
Tapachula
200

*Isla
Mujeres*
Cancún
Cozumel
Xel-Há
Punta
Allen
Xcalak
Peninsula

Caribbean Sea

BELIZE

GUATEMALA

HONDURAS

**EL
SALVADOR**

making the rounds in Mexico: Q: What's the difference between Miami and Cancún? A: In Miami, they speak Spanish. Expect prices to be comparable to—or higher than—those at home.

Bet You Didn't Know

The Maya (or Palancar) Reef, extending 1,800 miles along Mexico's Caribbean coast down to Guatemala, Belize, and Honduras, is second only in length to Australia's Great Barrier Reef.

But there's a reason for the astounding success this newcomer on the resort scene has had in the past 3 decades (created from scratch in 1974, it's now Mexico's Numero Uno tourist destination): Superb white-sand beaches on an azure Caribbean sea, and fun, fun, fun. Unless, to cut costs, you forgo immediate beach access and sleep in land-locked downtown, you'll emerge from your glitzy hotel room to miles of air-conditioned malls, sophisticated seaside restaurants, wild all-night bars and discos, and oceans of splashy pursuits.

Should you feel the need to take a break from relentless hedonism to get a culture fix, Cancún's there for you, too. A prime location at the tip of the Yucatán Peninsula means easy access to some of the Mayan civilization's most impressive monuments. The stunning seaside temples of Tulum are at your doorstep, and the famous ruins of Chichén Itzá and Uxmal are just an unforgettable overnight excursion away.

Cancún in a nutshell . . .

➤ No need to worry about using your halting Spanish in this English language–friendly resort.

➤ Beautiful white-sand beaches.

➤ Tons of activities and all-night parties.

but . . .

➤ With prices as high or higher than those at home, your wallet may not notice you've left the country.

➤ You won't feel as though you're in authentic Mexico.

➤ You're not the only one who wants to visit.

Introducing Cozumel

Geographically speaking, Cozumel is close to Cancún—lots of tropical fish fetishists ferry over for a day of snorkeling—but in nearly every other way, it's a universe apart. For one thing, you don't have to worry about destroying your budget here. Cozumel has plenty of reasonable beachside lodgings, although high-maintanence luxury digs are available, too. At mealtimes, your options span the spectrum from inexpensive mom-and-pop—make that madre-y-padre—places to more upscale marine-view dining rooms.

During the day, the dazzling Caribbean Sea is your playground, and you've got ringside seats at the best underwater show in Mexico, as diver Jacques Cousteau discovered in the 1960s. When you're ready to come up for air, you'll find the shopping is fine, too: Cozumel is Mexico's largest cruise ship port, and to keep those big-boat passengers happily spending, crafts come in from all over the country. But at night it's far quieter here than it is in Cancún—and in many of the other resort towns, for that matter. You'll also find a number of quiet, solitary beaches on the southeast shore and the rugged west coast.

Bet You Didn't Know

An abundance of chicle, used to make chewing gum, brought prosperity to Cozumel at the turn of the century.

Because Cozumel is considerably older than Cancún—okay, that's not saying much—you don't have to leave the island to take in some history (in fact, this is where the Spanish conquistadors first landed, although you won't see any signs). The island's only town, San Miguel, has a charming Old Mexico ambience and several small Mayan ruins worth exploring.

Cozumel in a nutshell . . .

➤ Beaches where you can truly get away from it all.

➤ Dazzling underwater life.

➤ Easy access to Mexican historical and cultural sights.

but . . .

➤ There's not much in the way of nightlife.

➤ The dinner scene is pretty casual; nowhere to show off those drop-dead duds.

➤ The cruise shippers crowd the markets when they come in.

Introducing Acapulco

An oldie but a goodie. The southernmost of the Pacific Coast resorts, Acapulco has long been in the visitor-pleasing business, and it shows. Although Old Acapulco, or downtown, has lost the sheen of its Hollywood heyday, you can still see traditional holidays being celebrated at its *zóca-*

Best Snorkeling Beaches

Playa Chankanaab, Cozumel

Deer Island Beach, Mazatlán

Playa Varadero, Ixtapa Island, Ixtapa

Marietas Islands, north of Puerto Vallarta

lo (main square), buy vegetables or love potions at the municipal market, or visit the historical museum in the fortress that once guarded the settlement from pirates.

Best Beaches for Water Sports

Playa Condesa, Acapulco

Playa Medano, Los Cabos

Playa Los Muertos, Puerto Vallarta

Playa Las Hadas, Manzanillo

These days, it's a battalion of high-rise hotels that stands guard over the stretch of wide, sandy beaches that straddle Acapulco Bay. The Costera, as this tourist strip is called, is where you stay if you like being in the thick of things. If it's seclusion you're after, Acapulco's got that too, in the tony Acapulco Diamante area where all the glitterati now gather.

Cancún may have almost as many discos, but in Acapulco, Mexico City escapees, rather than gringos, set the tone—which means these vast dance palaces are often filled to the gills with drop-dead glamorous outfits. Mexicans also like to party late, so no matter what time you retire your dancing shoes, you'll find something to eat (even McDonald's sometimes stays open 24 hours). Of course, there are classier restaurants, too, including what may be the largest number of romantic bay-view eateries in the country.

Acapulco in a nutshell . . .

➤ A destination that has something for everyone, from a traditional Mexican downtown to luxurious resorts.

➤ Dining that spans all tastes and budgets, from fast food to romantic bayside restaurants.

➤ Fantastic nightlife.

but . . .

➤ The seclusion in Acapulco Diamante doesn't come cheap.

➤ The action on the Costera can be relentless.

➤ The resort doesn't have the Hollywood cachet it once had.

Introducing Ixtapa/Zihuatanejo

Double your pleasure, double your fun: Ixtapa and Zihuatanejo have something for everyone. Practically Siamese twins—they're less than 4 miles from one another—the two Pacific Coast resorts nevertheless have very distinct personalities, although you'll find good local markets in both.

Zihuatanejo is the introvert, a village where the catch of the day is still displayed on the small dock at dawn and ranchero bands play on Sunday in the town square. No longer the well-kept secret it once was—sophisticated restaurants and boutiques and exclusive small hotels have sprung up here in recent years—it's managed to hold on to its considerable local color. Great beaches, especially Playa la Ropa and Playa Los Gatos, also keep many visitors firmly rooted to this side of the hilly divide between the two towns.

Created, like Cancún, by the Mexican government in the 1970s—although not as overgrown or garrulous as its Caribbean counterpart by a long shot—Ixtapa is the outgoing new kid on the block. The fairy godmother assigned to the twin resorts granted Ixtapa the designer golf courses, the modern marina, the high-rise hotels, and the fashionable restaurants, and laid them out along Playa Palmar, a creamy, wide stretch of sand. She may already have blown her charm quota on Zihuatanejo, but still managed to put the kibosh on overdevelopment in Ixtapa, decreeing that large amounts of land be set aside for nature preserves.

Best Beaches for Experiencing Local Color

Check out these beaches at either sunrise or sunset to see fishermen ply their nets:

Playa Municipal, Zihuatenejo (sunrise)

Playa Los Pinos, southern end of Playa Norte, Mazatlán (sunrise)

Playa Salagua, Manzanillo (sunset)

Ixtapa/Zihuatanejo in a nutshell . . .

➤ Ixtapa + Zihutenejo = Two unique resort towns for the price of one.

➤ Quiet escapes and great local color in Zihutenejo.

➤ Fashionable restaurants and a modern marina in Ixtapa.

but . . .

➤ Zihuatanejo's been "discovered"—you can't claim you're boldly going where no one has gone before.

➤ Ixtapa doesn't have a great deal of personality.

➤ Zihuatanejo doesn't have much to offer after dark.

Introducing Manzanillo

Halfway between Mazatlán and Acapulco on the Pacific Coast, Manzanillo tends to keep a low profile—except when it takes to creating fantastic resorts like Las Hadas, featured in the movie *10*. As anyone who saw the film might recall, the city drapes itself around a gorgeous set of twin bays, whose shorelines lend themselves to a splashy array of activities, especially sportsfishing. And if you're a duffer, you can tee-off at some of Mexico's best golf courses.

Greater Manzanillo is very spread out, however, and its attractions and visitors tend to be concentrated in isolated little enclaves. And the city's

industrial heart, Mexico's largest commercial port, has never grabbed the attention of the dance-until-dawn contingent.

As a result, the resort's strengths lie in its warm hospitality and in its lodgings. You can be as economical as you wanna be—there are plenty of long- and short-term places with kitchens by the beach—or as upscale (the new Grand Bay Resort in Barra de Navidad, to the north, is a prime example). Most popular, however, are the mid-range all-inclusives, perpetual motion centers that keep guests in Energizer Bunny mode well into the wee hours. Some honeymooners hide out in the glamour spots, and singles and younger couples often book the all-inclusives, but in general families and older adults dominate.

> ## Best Swimming Beaches
>
> Playa Caracol, Cancún
>
> Playa Las Brisas, Manzanillo
>
> Playa la Ropa, Zihuatenejo

Manzanillo in a nutshell . . .

➤ A quiet, warmly welcoming vacation spot that's good for families and older adults.

➤ All-inclusives offer a whirlwind of activities for the actively inclined, at a set price.

➤ Easy on the wallet

but . . .

➤ There's not a whole lot going on at night.

➤ No single concentrated section of tourist activities.

➤ The commercial port area isn't especially scenic.

Introducing Puerto Vallarta

You've got the complete crowd-pleaser here, a resort that rolls up the greatest variety of Mexican experiences—and price ranges—into a single, sparkly package. Poised against a backdrop of lush jungle and the foothills of the Sierra Madre, the largest bay on Mexico's Pacific Coast draws everyone from aging hippies, who used to hang out with Bob Dylan on the remote beach of Yelapa, to the international yachting set, who like to dock at the tony new Marina Vallarta complex.

Although it's grown enormously since the filming of "The Movie" (as the *Night of the Iguana,* which put the town on the tourist map, is often referred to), Vallarta still has central-casting-cute cobblestone streets and the sure-footed donkeys to trot along them. A continuing Hollywood presence, a contingent of culinarily savvy expats, and a slew of Europeans on charter flights have inspired some of the best restaurants you're likely to find outside

Cliff Diving in Acapulco.
(Photo credit: Cliff Hollenbeck Photography)

Lovers' Beach in Cabo San Lucas. *(Photo credit: Cliff Hollenbeck Photography)*

Horseback Riding in Ixtapa. *(Photo credit: Dave G. Houser/Corbis)*

Shoreside Palm Trees in Cancun. (Photo credit: Robert Landau)

Mango & Papaya Crepe with Tequila Butterscotch Sauce.
(Photo credit: Bob Krist)

Statue of Chac-Mool, Temple of Warriors, Chichen Itza.
(Photo credit: Bob Krist)

Playa Sábalo on Mazatlán. *(Photo credit: Cliff Hollenbeck Photography)*

Fisherman Throws a Net on Manzanillo. *(Photo credit: Richard Bickel/Corbis)*

Painted Wooden Fish in Puerto Vallarta. *(Photo credit: Cliff Hollenbeck Photography)*

Golfers at La Mantarraya in Manzanillo. (Photo credit: Tony Roberts/Corbis)

of Mexico City. In dozens of galleries and boutiques, colorful folk art from all over Mexico competes with the work of local painters and sculptors for your attention. Although nightlife may not be as wild as in places like Cancún or Acapulco, you won't have any problem finding a place to boogie—whatever that might mean to you.

Puerto Vallarta in a nutshell . . .

➤ The biggest variety of Mexican experiences, from local color to raucous nightlife.

➤ Some of the best restaurants outside Mexico City.

➤ Great shopping includes local crafts and galleries.

but . . .

➤ It's not as quiet as it once was, so you've got to share all the good spots.

➤ You're in danger of maxing out your credit cards in the stores.

➤ It's not on the very top of the night-action list.

Introducing Mazatlán

Unlike some of the beach towns whose economies depend on tourism, Mazatlán doesn't need to get a life, thank you. The northernmost of the Pacific Coast resorts, this city of half a million has a thriving commercial fishing industry. As a result,

Bet You Didn't Know

Mazatlán is the jumbo shrimp capital of the world.

you'll be able to savor the "real" Mexico here, especially in downtown where a bustling city market and newly restored blocks of gracious 19th-century buildings invite strolling, and where seaside cafes that haven't changed for decades let you linger over a Pacifico—made by the local brewery—into the late afternoon.

This is not to suggest Mazatlán has no modern resort attractions—far from it. The thriving Golden and Platinum tourist zones north of downtown sparkle with hotels, shops, restaurants, and sports toy–filled shores. At their far end, the modern El Cid Marina serves as a jumping-off point for a slew of nautical adventures. If you're seeking seclusion, you'll enjoy the miles of peaceful beaches, some on uninhabited offshore islands.

Easiest Romantic Escapes

Playa del Rey, Cancún

Playa Cerritos, Mazatlán

Playa de Amor, Los Cabos

However, don't come here looking for glamour and the high life. Mazatlán is a low-key kind of place, a magnet for retirees and snowbirds, who flock to its RV parks and long-term rental units. If you don't mind turning down the volume a bit—although you can always opt for great discos like Valentino's and gonzo beach volleyball bars if you're a party animal—this is a great place to find a Mexican vacation bargain.

Mazatlán in a nutshell . . .

➤ A low-key way to experience the "real" Mexico.

➤ A vacation bargain.

➤ Secluded beaches and offshore islands.

but . . .

➤ Restaurants, like the town, tend to be traditional rather than exciting.

➤ Nightlife is not as top-notch as in other places.

➤ Young people won't find as many peers as in the other resorts.

Best Surfing Beaches

Playa Bruja, Mazatlán

Playa Costa Azul, Los Cabos

Introducing Los Cabos

Of the three very different destinations that Los Cabos (literally, "The Capes") encompasses, the one most people are talking about when they say they're going to "Cabo" is the town of Cabo San Lucas.

It's party central for West Coasters for whom it's also, literally, the end of the road—keep driving south from California until you can't go any farther and Cabo is where you'll end up. But Cabo San Lucas has a much more sedate sibling, San Jose del Cabo, a sleepy Mexican town that pretty much shuts down after dark. The two are connected by the Corridor, a long stretch of highway lined—at very discrete distances, naturally—with gorgeous resorts, magnificent golf courses, and sophisticated restaurants.

Bet You Didn't Know

Cows in Los Cabos wore fluorescent collars for a while to keep them from getting hit by cars at night. The experiment ended because the cows wouldn't always cooperate by facing the oncoming vehicles head first.

After Cancún, this is the costliest of the Mexican beach destinations, and the most Americanized. Why come? Stunning scenery that you won't encounter at any of the other resorts, as this is where the desert meets the sea. Two seas, in fact: the Pacific and the Sea of Cortez—which also makes Los Cabos a mecca for sportsfishers. The big-name designer golf courses rank among the best in Mexico. And, of course, there's that gigantic beach bash at Cabo San Lucas, which starts at midday and rages until it's time for your huevos rancheros the next morning. If you want an excuse to let your hair down, this is the place.

Los Cabos in a nutshell . . .

➤ Stunning desert-meets-sea scenery.

➤ Great sportsfishing and some of the best golf in Mexico.

➤ A three-in-one destination, with something for everyone.

but . . .

➤ The most Americanized and costliest resort after Cancún.

➤ Because it's spread out, hard to get from one town to the other.

➤ You can't turn the party action off in Cabo San Lucas.

Quiz: Creating Your Dream Vacation

Okay, now that I've given you a little background for starters, it's your turn to figure out which Mexican beach town is best suited to your personality and purse.

Is This a Test? And What Happens if I Don't Pass?

You can't fail—it isn't that kind of quiz. Instead, it's a foolproof way of figuring out exactly which resort town is the best destination for you. You'll rate each place based on your own interests, and get to know the ones you're leaning toward a little better in the process. By the time you finish this short quiz, you should know exactly where you're headed.

Here's how you do it:

Step #1: The "Rate the Resorts" Scorecard

Your scorecard has a column for each beach town, and a row for each category that I've rated the towns on.

You'll use this scorecard to compile a score for each of the resorts based on the special-interest categories that follow. Each resort will get a predetermined 1 to 5 points, based on how suited it is to the interest or activity in that category. Five points is the highest rating, one the lowest. If a resort isn't listed, assume it scores a zero in that particular category. *Note:* The last three categories deal with ease of travel from various points within the United States and list only three resorts each.

Step #2: Score the Resorts Based on Your Interests & Needs

Go through the categories below. Stop only at those categories that interest you. For example, if you're not interested in deep-sea exploration, skip over the diving category altogether, and don't plug in points for any of the resorts into the "Diving" row above. (For example, Cozumel shouldn't earn 5 points for diving because its beautiful reefs aren't important to you.)

If you are into the nightlife scene, stop at "If you want to party all night long. . ." Insert each resort's score (5 points for Cancún, 3 points for Los Cabos, and so on) into your scorecard above.

Move on to the next category that interests you, and insert the scores into the appropriate row in your scorecard. Keep going until you've reviewed all the categories and given each resort town a score for each category that interests you.

1) If you want to party all night long . . .

Rating	Resort	Rationale
5 points	**Cancún**	Tons of options for staying up 'till sunrise. Live music, disco, fine dining, and dancing.
5 points	**Acapulco**	A tie. There's as much to do after dark as in Cancún, and older night owls as well as young ones can boogie all night long.
4 points	**Puerto Vallarta**	Mariachi hot spots and all-night discos. Jazz, dancing, and drinking—even a gay cabaret.
3 points	**Los Cabos**	Not much in the way of discos or quiet entertainment, but the bar scene can't be beat.
2 points	**Mazatlán**	A traditional port, but a terrific Carnaval scene as well as good beach bars and Valentino's, one of the best-known discos in the country.
1 point	**Ixtapa/ Zihuatanejo**	Smaller and lower-key: Check out the happy hours, Christine's disco, and colorful fiestas.

The "Rate the Resorts" Scorecard

POINTS FOR:	Cancún	Cozumel	Acapulco	Ixtapa/ Zihuatanejo	Manzanillo	Puerto Vallarta	Mazatlán	Los Cabos
Partying								
Fishing								
Snorkeling/Diving								
Golfing								
Shopping								
Dining								
Easy Traveling								
Luxury								
Kid-friendliness								
Retiree-friendliness								
Solitude								
Local Color								
Romance								
Singles Scene								
Great Sidetrips								
Bargain Prices								
Peace and Quiet								
West Coast Convenience								
Midwest Convenience								
East Coast Convenience								
TOTALS:								

2) If you want to catch the big one . . .

Rating	Resort	Rationale
5 points	**Los Cabos**	Formerly known as "Marlin Alley," Los Cabos is the big time for sportsfishing. Here, the Sea of Cortez and the Pacific Ocean meet—a fisherman's paradise.
4 points	**Cozumel**	Before it was known for diving, Cozumel was known for its world-record-size billfish, and they haven't gotten any smaller—or less hungry.
3 points	**Mazatlán**	The Sea of Cortez and the Pacific also get together here, if not quite as dramatically as in Los Cabos. The fish don't care about the scenery—they like the convergence of currents.
2 points	**Ixtapa/ Zihuatanejo**	A better kept secret than the others, but Anglo anglers have been coming for years for the abundant blue and black marlin and Pacific sailfish.
1 point	**Manzanillo**	As the huge hauls at annual sportsfishing tournaments held here since 1954 attest, this is a great place for bringing in the big ones.

3) If you want to plumb the depths (or skim the surface) . . .

Rating	Resort	Rationale
5 points	**Cozumel**	One of the top five dive destinations in the world, with the world's second-largest reef system at its doorstep. Divers and snorkelers get the island's undivided attention.
4 points	**Cancún**	Good by association—it's an hour by boat from Cozumel.
3 points	**Ixtapa/ Zihuatanejo**	Warm water, great visibility, and the convergence of two major currents—not to mention those tales of sunken Spanish treasure—make for a primo underwater show.
3 points	**Los Cabos**	A tie. The water's not quite as warm year-round, but that meeting between the Sea of Cortez and the Pacific Ocean resulted in several truly spectacular dive sites.

continues

Rating	Resort	Rationale
2 points	**Puerto Vallarta**	With visibility of up to 130 feet in summer and lots of remote spots seething with sea life, Puerto Vallarta's a fine place to take the plunge.
1 point	**Manzanillo**	A commercial port, but you can see some rare species and have lots of little-explored areas all to yourselves.

4) If you want to get teed off . . .

Rating	Resort	Rationale
5 points	**Los Cabos**	Several world-renowned golf designers have already put their signatures on the courses in the Corridor and more are on the way. Unbeatable desert-meets-sea scenery.
4 points	**Manzanillo**	You'll have to do a bit of traveling, but three challenging and stunning courses (Grand Bay, El Tamarindo, and La Mantarraya) are in the vicinity.
3 points	**Acapulco**	The tony east side of the city has become golf heaven, with four prestigious courses laid out and promises of a green(s) future.
2 points	**Ixtapa/ Zihuatanejo**	Two excellent courses abut the tourist zone— and, for excitement, it's hard to match the live alligators in the water traps.
1 point	**Mazatlán**	The 27-hole El Cid course is getting spiffed up, a John Jacobs golf school has arrived, and the buzz about the new Estrella del Mar course is all good.

Time-Savers

Although some resorts allow only nonguests to book tee times on the same day, others are less strict off season. Call as early as you possibly can if you don't want to get stuck playing in the midday heat.

5) If you want to shop 'til you drop . . .

Rating	Resort	Rationale
5 points	**Puerto Vallarta**	A magnet for crafts from around the country as well as for artists, Puerto Vallarta may have the most galleries per capita in Mexico. Clothing, jewelry, home furnishings—you name it, they've got it, and it's high quality, too.
4 points	**Ixtapa/ Zihuatanejo**	Spanish village–style shopping centers in Ixtapa for sportswear and contemporary crafts. Good tourist markets in both towns, and Zihuatanejo has a terrific "real people's" market.
3 points	**Cancún**	Miles of air-conditioned malls selling decent crafts (although at often indecent prices) as well as some of the only duty-free goods in Mexico. You can get some bargains at the downtown stalls, if you don't mind plowing through all those onyx ashtrays.
2 points	**Cozumel**	If they come on cruise ships, they will shop. Lots of appealing boutiques in San Miguel, and easy access to the high-quality shops of Playa del Carmen.
1 point	**Acapulco**	An authentic downtown market, tony boutiques at several hotels, malls with great sportswear—and the silver-jewelry mecca of Taxco just a day trip away.

6) If great food is numero uno . . .

Rating	Resort	Rationale
5 points	**Puerto Vallarta**	One of the most cosmopolitan restaurant towns in Mexico. Everything from schnitzel to sushi—not to mention great Mexican food—and it doesn't cost an arm and a leg.
4 points	**Acapulco**	They aim to please sophisticated Mexico City visitors as well as hungry gringos. A great range of options—and dazzling bay views.
3 points	**Cancún**	Lots of top-notch chefs, especially at the tony hotels, but expect to shell out plenty of pesos. Tons of places that are so much fun you won't notice what you're eating.
2 points	**Ixtapa/ Zihuatanejo**	A tacqueria that's been written up in *Gourmet* magazine, authentic Italian dining by a romantic marina . . . You can go as upscale or as funky as you like and find some pretty impressive middle ground, too.
1 point	**Cozumel**	Competing for the *yanqui* dollar of the cruise ship crowd has been good for Cozumel's restaurant scene. Unpretentious Yucatecan eateries, atmospheric seafood spots, and fine international dining rooms.

7) If your Spanish is limited to "Una Corona, por favor" . . .

Rating	Resort	Rationale
5 points	**Cancún**	In a place where you can use dollars on a bus, being Spanish-challenged is no great hindrance.
4 points	**Los Cabos**	Welcome to California south. In Cabo San Lucas, the only thing you might have trouble understanding is surfer lingo—and beer-slurred words.
3 points	**Puerto Vallarta**	A part of town is called "Gringo Gulch," and Hollywood put Puerto Vallarta on the map. They speak American film here.
2 points	**Mazatlán**	The closest beach town to the U.S., Mazatlán has been making *norteamericanos* feel at home for half a century.
2 points	**Acapulco**	A tie. Acapulco has an equally long history of hospitality, and the Hollywood contingent made a lasting impression in the 1940s and '50s.
1 point	**Cozumel**	English being the cruise ship and diver lingua franca, most Cozumeleños have got it down.

8) If you're looking for luxury . . .

Rating	Resort	Rationale
5 points	**Cancún**	A vast array of hotel-zone resorts that scramble to outdo each other in the glitz department; there's even a Ritz-Carlton here.
4 points	**Los Cabos**	The Corridor section of Los Cabos is filthy with rich properties, from exclusive boutique hotels to high-rises, and they just keep on coming.
3 points	**Puerto Vallarta**	The yachty set and world-cruiser wannabes like the Marina Vallarta complex, and hotels to the north and south of town are also ports-of-call for the pampered.
2 points	**Acapulco**	The high-tone resort action is in Acapulco Diamante, where Sylvester Stallone and other Hollywood types have homes.
1 point	**Ixtapa/ Zihuatanejo**	Ixtapa has a couple of beauties, but it's sleepy Zihuatanejo that boasts several intimate, world-class hotels.

9) If you're traveling with kids . . .

Rating	Resort	Rationale
5 points	**Manzanillo**	Family-oriented all-inclusives, lots of lodgings with kitchens—practical and fun.
4 points	**Acapulco**	Reasonably priced properties with children's programs, a couple of kiddie water parks, and an overall family-friendly attitude.
3 points	**Cancún**	If you can afford it: Lots of resorts with organized pip-squeak activities, plus kid-pleasers such as water parks and—on a day trip—Xcaret park.
2 points	**Mazatlán**	Plenty of economical places to stay, including several with cooking facilities. The aquarium's a plus, too.
1 point	**Puerto Vallarta**	A good selection of properties that cater to kids. They love the parrots at the "jungle" restaurants.

10) If you're the retiring type . . .

Rating	Resort	Rationale
5 points	**Mazatlán**	Great fishing, good golf, easy to get around, and very little pressure on the wallet—perfect!
4 points	**Manzanillo**	More spread out and with pricier golf, but otherwise similar in perks to Mazatlán.
3 points	**Los Cabos**	You do like to golf and fish, don't you? It'll cost a pretty peso, but you can't beat the scenery.
2 points	**Acapulco**	Lots of old-style Hollywood glamour, plenty of places to rekindle an old flame without breaking the budget. (And the golf's not bad, either.)
1 point	**Puerto Vallarta**	Art, cooking, and language classes, plus galleries galore—ideal for leisure pursuits that you can take home with you (but watch those cobblestones).

11) If you're seeking secluded beaches . . .

Rating	Resort	Rationale
5 points	**Cozumel**	A surprising number of escape routes; head for the southeast shore or the rugged west coast and you'll be pretty much on your own.
4 points	**Puerto Vallarta**	When the tour boats leave, Las Animas, Quimixto, and Yelapa are idyllic beaches; more of the same up north, sans crowds.

continues

Rating	Resort	Rationale
3 points	**Mazatlán**	Amazingly quiet northern town beaches accessible by frequent public transport, plus two uninhabited offshore islands and a nearby peninsula with miles of untouched shore.
2 points	**Ixtapa/ Zihuatanejo**	Zihuatanejo's Playa Los Gatas is usually fairly serene, and you can claim plenty of stretches of sand for your own on Ixtapa Island.
1 point	**Los Cabos**	Not easy to get to without a car, but many beaches along the Corridor are secluded—and spectacular.

12) If you like local color . . .

Rating	Resort	Rationale
5 points	**Ixtapa/ Zihuatanejo**	Zihuatanejo's the quintessential sleepy fishing village; small boats bob in the bay, and everyone knows everyone else's name.
4 points	**Puerto Vallarta**	Donkeys carry loads down cobblestone streets; women wash clothes in the river. Tourists? What tourists?
3 points	**Cozumel**	The Mayan language is alive and well, and many townspeople wear traditional Yucatecan garb.
2 points	**Mazatlán**	Atmospheric seaside cafes in Olas Altas, where locals gather to gossip and conduct business as they have for ages.
1 point	**Manzanillo**	A major commercial port that feels like a small town. Visitors—that means you—are welcomed as friends.

13) If you're ready for romance . . .

Rating	Resort	Rationale
5 points	**Puerto Vallarta**	Stroll along the *malecón,* sit in a Río Cuale cafe, watch the sun descend over the water—you'll know just why Liz and Dick lost control here.
4 points	**Acapulco**	Those dazzling bay-view restaurants, the lobby bars' Latin beat, that sultry year-round heat . . .
3 points	**Cancún**	Several places to dance cheek-to-cheek, and plenty of tequila sunrises and sunsets.
2 points	**Los Cabos**	It's got Playa de Amor, the Beach of Love. Need I say more?
1 point	**Ixtapa/ Zihuatanejo**	Quiet evenings with starry skies, marina and bay vistas, and boutique hotel hideaways.

14) If you want a singles mingle . . .

Rating	Resort	Rationale
5 points	**Cancún**	So many bars, so little time.
4 points	**Los Cabos**	Cabo San Lucas's theme song: "Will you still love me tomorrow?"
3 points	**Acapulco**	Nice to see young people so devoted to improving U.S./Latin American relations.
2 points	**Puerto Vallarta**	Lots of poolside action, and if by day you don't succeed, the night's always young.
1 point	**Mazatlán**	Some serious beach bars—then splendor in the sand?

15) If you want an easy escape to authentic Mexico . . .

Rating	Resort	Rationale
5 points	**Mazatlán**	Near several former silver-mining towns and an idyllic fishing village.
4 points	**Manzanillo**	Also close to a sleepy fishing village, and to the appealing state capital, Colima.
3 points	**Acapulco**	A day trip away, colonial Taxco has great charm—and great silver jewelry.
2 points	**Puerto Vallarta**	It's a rush job, but you can get a taste of Guadalajara from here.
1 point	**Cancún**	There's surprisingly little (geographic) distance between spanking new Cancún and many ancient Mayan villages and archaeological sites.

16) If you need to pinch pesos (but still want to be on the beach) . . .

Rating	Resort	Rationale
5 points	**Manzanillo**	Economical seaside all-inclusives and lodgings with kitchens, reasonable restaurants—and not much shopping to break your budget.
4 points	**Mazatlán**	The next best rates for nice beachside digs (plenty with kitchens); bargain meals and activities.
3 points	**Acapulco**	Forgo the gloss and you can get great deals on bay-front rooms; lots of inexpensive eateries, too.
2 points	**Ixtapa/ Zihuatanejo**	Some good, low-rent options on Madero and la Ropa beaches in Zihuatanejo as well as low-rent restaurants in town.
1 point	**Puerto Vallarta**	The downtown beachside digs aren't serene, but they're low-cost and near all the action.

17) If you're craving peace and quiet . . .

Rating	Resort	Rationale
5 points	**Ixtapa/ Zihuatanejo**	Zihuatanejo is low-key and sleepy, an escape from the contemporary crush.
4 points	**Cozumel**	San Miguel, the only town, gets laid back when the cruise ships leave. Plenty of isolated beaches to retreat to, too.
3 points	**Manzanillo**	A commercial center, but with lots of traditional neighborhoods and a miminum of cynical people.
2 points	**Puerto Vallarta**	Nuevo Vallarta has eerily quiet beaches and miles of untouched jungle.
1 point	**Los Cabos**	There's a serene, small-town feel to much of San Jose del Cabo—not to be confused with its out-going sibling, Cabo San Lucas.

18) Easiest to reach if you live in the western U.S. . . .

Rating	Resort	Rationale
3 points	**Los Cabos**	Just a zip down south; lots of direct flights from the coast and the Southwest. California's most packaged Mexico destination.
2 points	**Puerto Vallarta**	Frequent direct flights from L.A. and other coastal towns; Phoenix, Houston, and Dallas see a lot of air and package play, too.
1 point	**Acapulco**	Many of the direct flights are from the Southwest, but every West Coast tour operator runs charters.

19) Easiest to reach if you live in the Midwest . . .

Rating	Resort	Rationale
3 points	**Cancún**	Mexico's premier destination; getting here from there is no problemo.
2 points	**Puerto Vallarta**	TWA likes Puerto Vallarta—and so do the central states the airline serves.
1 point	**Acapulco**	Northwest and Continental connections, and several charters.

20) If you live in the eastern U.S. . . .

Rating	Resort	Rationale
3 points	**Cancún**	Closest to the East Coast—flights, packages, and discounts out the wazoo.
2 points	**Cozumel**	No direct flights, but an hour's puddle-jump from Cancún. Plenty of packages, too.
1 point	**Puerto Vallarta**	Popularity breeds specials.

Step #3: Tally the Scores to Determine Your Top Destination(s)

After you're done reviewing the categories and plugging scores into your scorecard as appropriate, tally each resort's score.

The winner—the resort town with the highest total score—should be your destination and truly reflect your interests and needs. Scores really close? Don't agonize. Flip a coin and vow to hit the other resort on your next vacation.

Is One Enough?

As should be abundantly clear by now, not all beach towns are created equal, but that doesn't mean you should spend your time and money hopping from one to another if you're feeling indecisive. You need to take just a gander at the map of Mexico inside this book's back cover to comprendo that the distances between most of the resorts are considerable.

Sure, if you're partied out in Cancún, you may want to ferry over to Cozumel to chill; you can take a day trip from Ixtapa/Zihuatanejo to Acapulco, too, if you're up for more action. But those are the exceptions. Although the focus in this chapter has been on what distinguishes the beach towns from each other, they're all multi-faceted. If you're suffering from bar burnout in Cabo San Lucas, say, there's no need to board a puddle jumper to Mazatlán when you can just cab it over to laid-back San José del Cabo. And if you need some glamour in down-to-earth Manzanillo, don your best duds and head for a fancy hotel like Las Hadas.

Moreover, another beach resort will only give you more beaches, when what you're probably looking for is something completely different. If you start coveting Puerto Vallarta's culture when you've ridden one too many Waverunners in Acapulco, it's far more practical—and rewarding—to book a day trip to Taxco than to spend hundreds of dollars on a flight north. And when you're tired of tanning in Mazatlán, why not strike out for one of the nearby mining towns instead of taking an 18-hour ferry ride to Baja California?

Chapter 2

When Should I Go?

In This Chapter

➤ A resort-by-resort weather report

➤ Times to avoid

➤ Festivals and special events

You may want to get away from it all when the weather at home is bad—but in putting together a trip to Mexico you also need to consider what you'll find when you get there. In this chapter, I'll give you a rundown of important factors to take into account when planning your Mexican vacation—everything from climate and crowds to high seasons and major celebrations.

Precipitation Anticipation

If you don't mind a little rain—you *were* planning to get wet, weren't you?—you'll get a much better deal if you visit Mexico during the rainy season, which usually consists only of a daily brief shower or two, followed by sunshine. Not surprisingly, the wet season is also when the tropical flowers are at their most glorious. Of course, nothing's guaranteed, least of all perfect weather. It's always possible to have a week of overcast skies and rain.

Sunshine on Your Shoulders

In general, Mexico has two main seasons: rainy, from mid-May to mid-October, and dry, for the rest of the year. September and early October may see some tropical storms, too. On the Pacific Coast, where most of Mexico's resorts are, full-blown hurricanes are rare. Cancún and Cozumel, on the Caribbean coast, get a share of the major storms, but they're not in the prime hurricane path.

As for the temperature, you can pretty much expect it to be warm whenever you go—it's just a question of, um, degree. It should come as no suprise that the beach towns get hotter the closer they are to the equator, which makes Zihuatanejo toastier than Mazatlán.

Weather obsessive *and* plugged in? A dangerous combination—the following Web sites can keep you occupied for a long, long time.

➤ **www.usa.today.com/weather** gives you weather charts of Acapulco, Cancún, Mazatlán, and Puerto Vallarta, including monthly temperature averages; the highest and lowest temps ever recorded during that month; average number of wet days; and more. You can get a pretty good idea of Cozumel's weather by looking at Cancún's chart; Ixtapa/Zihuatanejo data approximates Acapulco's; and Manzanillo is close to Puerto Vallarta. Sorry, if you're going to Los Cabos, you're out of luck—nothing from southern Baja California is posted.

➤ The even more comprehensive **www.weatherpost.com**, brought to you by the *Washington Post*, gives a 5-day forecast for every one of the resort cities, plus historical charts of the weather for most of them, including Cabo San Lucas; this time only Ixtapa/Zihuatanejo is excluded (again, Acapulco is a good gauge). Neither dew point nor precipitation are charted, but you get average wind speed and average morning and afternoon relative humidity.

➤ Type in **asp1.sbs.ohio-state.edu/text/wxascii/roundup/ ASUS45.KSAT**—whew!—to get the current weather in all of Mexico's beach resorts.

➤ Worried about tropical storms? **www.solar.ifa.hawaii.edu/tropical** gives you the scoop on whether any are coming the way you're thinking of going.

Resort by Resort: What's Up & What's Coming Down

➤ **Cancún** enjoys typical tropical weather. The water is warm enough for swimming year-round, and breezes from the sea keep things comfortable at night. September is the rainiest month, with the average rainfall at 9 inches, followed by October (8.6 inches) and June (7 inches); in March and April, precipitation is at a low—around 1.6 inches a month.

On the other hand, Cancún is not immune to Caribbean hurricanes, which tend to arrive in September and October; the island was particularly hard hit by Gilbert in 1988.

➤ **Cozumel** is less than an hour by sea from Cancún, so it's not surprising that it should have similarly balmy weather. Note, however, that winds are strongest in November and December, making conditions less than optimum for diving.

➤ **Acapulco's** year-round average daily temperature of 88°F means it's always swimming weather. The wettest month is September, with 15 inches of rain on average, followed by August and June, tied at 10.4 inches. December through April, the town gets less than half an inch a month (about one-tenth of an inch in February, March, and April).

Although Acapulco isn't frequently affected by hurricanes, the 1990s have been unkind to the city: Boris stopped by in 1996, and Pauline came to visit in 1997.

➤ **Ixtapa/Zihuatanejo** is just 150 miles north of Acapulco, and has essentially the same weather as its larger resort neighbor, but it feels slightly cooler—perhaps because there are far fewer people and far less concrete. It's also situated so that it isn't as severely affected by hurricanes; neither Boris nor Pauline blew in for a visit.

Dollars & Sense

Okay, so it's a bit like being an ambulance chaser, but if you don't mind following in the wake of a disaster, you can get some great deals. When Hurricane Pauline hit Acapulco in late 1997, for example, there was very little damage to the tourist areas but, because of the bad press, visitors stayed away in droves. The resorts were practically giving rooms away and airlines dropped their rates—all this during high season. If you're willing to do a little research on whether the actual circumstances warrant the media panic, you can do some major looting—legally.

➤ **Manzanillo** has weather similar to that in Puerto Vallarta, less than 200 miles away. May is the most humid month, building up to the rainy season, which starts in June. During June, July, and August and the first half of September, it rains most days—usually at night or late afternoon, for 1 to 2 hours—and then clears. Hurricanes generally bypass Manzanillo; there was a major earthquake, however, in 1995, which affected Puerto Vallarta, too, but less severely.

➤ **Puerto Vallarta** enjoys an idyllic winter, with warm days and cooler nights, but by the end of May, which is hot and humid in anticipation of the rains, things begin looking a bit parched. The rainy season begins in earnest in mid-June, with an average of 10 wet days that month, 15 apiece in July and August, and 14 in September; precipitation tends to be confined to the late afternoon. August and September are the most uncomfortable months—many restaurants close for general revamps, to clean up, and to give employees a vaction before the high season. Puerto Vallarta has escaped hurricanes so consistently that it's been designated a "hurricane hole" by marine insurers.

➤ **Mazatlán** is the northernmost of the Pacific Coast resorts, and as such avoids the high temperatures of the more southern towns, making it ideal for people who like to be warm but not hot. The mercury rarely rises into the 90s, except in August. The downside is that it can be too cool for ocean swimming in winter; late October and November are ideal both in terms of water temperature and lack of rain. The rainy season runs from July to mid-October, and it's humid from July to September. Hurricane season is September and October, but Mazatlán isn't often affected.

➤ **Los Cabos** tends toward different and often more extreme weather patterns than its Pacific and Caribbean cousins. A combination of desert and tropics means higher humidity than is characteristic in arid regions, and greater temperature drops at night than are typical in the tropics. In June, the heat begins to get uncomfortable; it's not all that rare for temperatures to reach above 100°F. The height of the rainy season runs from August through early October; September is the worst month, very hot and sticky. It can be unpredictably cool from January through March, and sometimes too windy for fishing. April and May, and late September through December, are the best times to visit.

Average High and Low Temperatures

	January		June	
	Average High	Average Low	Average High	Average Low
Cancún & Cozumel	82°F	67°F	90°F	76°F
Ixtapa/Zihuatanejo & Acapulco	86°F	72°F	90°F	76°F
Manzanillo & Puerto Vallarta	83°F	65°F	89°F	76°F
Mazatlán	74°F	63°F	86°F	77°F
Los Cabos	73°F	54°F	94°F	66°F

Seasons in the Sun

In general, prices and crowds are most intense in what is known as high season, running roughly from mid-December through Easter week; not surprisingly, this is the time of year that coincides with the best weather. The rest of the year, considered low season, brings discounts ranging from 10% to 60%, although not necessarily crowd abatement because most Mexicans take their vacations the last week of July and the first 3 weeks of August. You may have a little more difficulty in finding a room during that period, although prices usually remain low. In general, November is one of the best months to travel—the weather's decent almost everywhere, and the crowds are at a minimum.

Crowd Control

December to March   High season for foreign tourism (except the 2 weeks around Christmas week, when Mexicans travel)

The week before Easter   High season for domestic tourism

Spring Break   Open season for American youth

July to August   High season for domestic tourism

May to June & September to November   Low season

When Shouldn't I Go?

Two words: Spring Break—unless of course, you're a high-hormone undergrad and/or have no problem sleeping through the sounds of furniture breaking and people retching. When school's out for the semester, the crowds are at their most concentrated—and madding—and the prices are at their highest. If you don't feel like paying an arm and a leg to see American youth behaving badly, avoid this week like the plague. Christmas and Easter weeks also run high in terms of both prices and crowds—rates are at the second yearly peak, and Mexicans often leave their jobs and head to the beach towns—but they draw more families and couples to resorts than young revelers.

Planning for Fiesta—Not Siesta—ville

Mexicans throw great public parties, so you might want to head south when the country is celebrating one of its many colorful national or religious holidays. Water sports enthusiasts might consider planning their trips around the regattas and sportsfishing festivals held at many of the resorts.

Although popular culture festivals in Mexico are well worth seeing, having your vacation coincide with one may take quite a bit of advance planning because hotels get solidly booked at some of these times. The following are the major holidays, celebrated throughout Mexico to general hoopla. In addition, I'll give you a short list of special events—including sporting competitions—particular to the various resort towns. If you want additional general information about one of these festivals or holidays, phone the Mexico Hotline (☎ **800/44-MEXICO**). To get more details about all of them, the fax-connected can contact Fax-Me Mexico (☎ **541/385-9282**) and punch in a request for document number 308. To find out how an event is celebrated in the beach resort you're interested in visiting, you'll need to get in touch with the local tourism office (see the individual resort chapters).

Extra, Extra

The beach resorts aren't necessarily the ideal places to view traditional holiday observances—except for Mazatlán's Carnaval, none of the celebrations is nationally renowned—but you'll still get a taste for the Mexican spirit at all of them. In general, Mazatlán, Acapulco, Cozumel, and Puerto Vallarta rank the highest in terms of local color.

National Holidays

Note: Christmas and New Year's are pretty much celebrated the same way they are in the United States, although Christmas tends to be more religious, and Santa doesn't put in too many appearances in Mexico ("Pedro" Claus does turn up at some of the more gringoized resorts).

January/February/March

➤ **El Día de los Reyes (Three Kings Day** or **Epiphany**) is celebrated on **January 6** in commemoration of the Three Kings' visit to the Christ child, and is when Mexican children receive many of their gifts. It's also when everyone dives into a large fruitcake shaped like a donut into which a little clay doll has been baked. The person who gets the piece with the doll has to throw a party on Día de Candaleria, which falls on February 2.

➤ **Día de la Constitucion (Constitution Day)** on **February 5** may not be as exciting as a holiday celebrating saints or revolutions, but

Closed Doors

All banks and most businesses close January 1, February 5, March 21, May 1, May 5, September 1 (the president delivers the annual state of the nation address, similar to our state of the union), September 16, October 12 (yep, Columbus Day, or Día de la Raza), November 30, and December 25.

there are lots of official speeches and ceremonies held to honor the 1857 and 1917 constitutions.

➤ **Natalicio de Benito Juárez** on **March 21** is a two-fer: The birthday of Mexico's reformist leader, Benito Juárez (he's often called the "Abraham Lincoln of Mexico") and the spring equinox are celebrated together with major processions and pig-outs.

April/May/June
➤ The processions and celebrations held during **Semana Santa (Holy Week),** the week before Domingo Santa (Easter Sunday) are often fairly somber, but they're very moving and colorful.

➤ **Día del Trabajo (Labor Day)** on **May 1** is a big deal in a country prone to peoples' revolutions. Everything closes down and the crowds turn out to cheer the workers' parades.

➤ **Cinco de Mayo (the Fifth of May),** one of Mexico's biggest civic holidays, marks the Mexican defeat of the French at the Battle of Puebla in 1862. It's celebrated with foodfests and parades.

July/August/September
➤ **Día de la Independencia (Independence Day)**   It's hard to describe the "grito," or shout, for freedom made on September 15, 1810 by Father Miguel Hidalgo as a wake-up call to Spain that Mexico wanted them out—NOW. But if you're here for this holiday on **September 15 to 16,** be prepared to hear lots of people bellowing. A variety of events that celebrate the start of this revolution are kicked off in this way.

October/November/December
➤ **Día de los Muertos (Day of the Dead)**   Mexicans have a much friendlier attitude toward the dead than *Norteamericano*s do; they assume that just because you shed your mortal shell, it doesn't mean you can't enjoy a good meal occasionally. On **November 1 to 2,** families prepare the favorite foods of the departed and bring them along to the graveside for a major picnic. At night it's the kids' turn to dress up in costumes and masks—thus the frequent comparison to Halloween, to which this holiday bears only a superficial resemblance.

➤ **Aniversario de la Revolucíon (Anniversary of the Revolution)** marks the 1910 rebellion against Mexican dictator Porfirio Diaz. Francisco Madero, Emiliano Zapata, and Pancho Villa were the most famous of the leaders of this revolt, which is commemorated on **November 20** by everything from parades and patriotic speeches to ride-'em-out rodeos.

➤ **Día de la Virgen de Guadalupe (Day of the Virgin of Guadalupe)** on **December 12** is the biggest religious holiday in the country, the blow-out for Mexico's patron saint. She's honored with processions, street fairs, dancing, fireworks—you name it. Masses are held constantly and the churches are filled with flowers. It's a wonderful time to be in Mexico.

➤ **Posadas** celebrates the Holy Family's attempt to find a room at the *posada* (inn) from **December 16 to 24** with various pageants; their ultimate success is then celebrated. Each office has a party, of course, but individuals have them too, so that every night for a week most Mexicans are invited to something that involves loud music and large quantites of food (and you thought you were having a hard time dieting in the States!).

Town-by-Town Calendar

For more details about the various celebrations, including where to call for more information, see the A to Z sections of the individual resort chapters.

Cancún
Memorial Day Weekend   The Cancún Jazz Festival, started in 1991, features international jazz greats

Cozumel
Late February/Early March   Carnaval (3 days before Ash Wednesday)
Early May   International Sportsfishing Tournament

Acapulco
Late February/Early March   Carnaval (3 days before Ash Wednesday)
November   French Film Festival
July   Black Film Festival
Note: These are both fairly new festivals. Dates are likely to change.
December 12   Day of the Virgin of Guadalupe

Ixtapa/Zihuatanejo
January   The Ixtapa/Zihuatanejo Billfish Classic
May   International Sailfish Tournament

Manzanillo
February   International Billfishing Tournament
November   National Billfishing Competition

Puerto Vallarta
November   Two-week Fiesta del Mar (includes the only boat show in Latin America; a sailfishing tournment; a gastronomic festival; and an arts festival)
November 22   Feast of Santa Cecilia, patron saint of mariachis

Mazatlán
Late February/early March   Carnaval—one of the largest Mardi Gras celebrations in the world (held the weekdays preceding Ash Wednesday)
Early June   International Billfish Tournament
November   The Billfish Classic (the larger event of the two competitions)

Los Cabos
March 19   Feast of the patron saint of San José del Cabo
October   The Bisbee International Marlin Fishing Tournament
October 18   Feast of the patron saint of Cabo San Lucas

Lost in the Land of the Look-alike Brochures: How to Make Sense of It All & Plan the Trip That's Right for You

So now you're pretty sure you know which of Mexico's resorts you want to visit. Time to face the next major question: What's the best way to get there? It's all well and good to have tons of information, but knowing what to do with it is another enchilada entirely. The following section not only lays the best resources on the line (including many that are online), but also helps you sort through them.

These chapters operate under two assumptions: that you all want to get the best deal possible, but that no two of you are otherwise alike. You'll be traveling from different parts of the country, for one thing, and have different budgets and travel needs. By the time you finish reading through this part of the book, you should have a good idea of the best way to get to Mexico—for you.

THINGS YOU MAY WANT TO TAKE
1) UNDERWEAR
2) AIRLINE TICKETS
3) WALLET

Chapter 3

Getting Started

In This Chapter

➤ Where to go for information

➤ Surfing the Web

➤ Using a travel agent

Naturally, I'm going to try to tell you every little thing you need to know about Mexico's resorts in this book. But if you're an insatiable information hound, Web addict, brochure hoarder—or any combination thereof— I wouldn't want to deprive you of any fun, so grab a pencil, phone, fax, and modem, and get ready. I'll also clue you in here to the pros and cons of putting yourself in the hands of a travel agent when it comes to arranging your vacation.

Information, *Por Favor*

The **Mexico Hotline** (☎ **800/44-MEXICO**) is a good source for general information, including brochures and answers to the most commonly asked questions. Keep in mind, however, that hotels and other concessions spend a fair amount of money on photographers and writers, so their brochures are often like hearing about your blind date in advance: Don't be surprised if everything isn't exactly as advertised. They can be useful, however, for putting you in the picture—albeit one shot through a rose-colored lens.

The **U.S. State Department** offers a consular information sheet on Mexico with a summary of safety, medical, driving, and general travel information taken from official State Department offices reports. Write or call and ask for

Overseas Citizens Services, U.S. Department of State, Room 2201 Sea St. NW, Washington, DC 20520 (☎ **202/647-5225**).

A fax machine nets you the **Fax-Me Mexico** line operated by the Mexican Ministry of Tourism (☎ **541/385-9282**). Start out by leaving your fax number on the automated system and requesting the list of topics; there are more than 100, ranging from general tips about food, money, and accommodations to specific information about various destinations, including all the beach resorts. Pick the topic(s) you're interested in—no more than three at a time—phone again, and punch the appropriate numbers into the system. (Beware: This is a good, but addicting, resource. You can spend lots of time and end up with piles of faxes.)

You can also get a broad sprectrum of information from the following **Mexican Goverment Tourist Office** branches:

➤ **In the United States:** 300 N. Michigan Ave., 4th Floor, Chicago, Il 60601 (☎ **312/606-9015**); 10440 W. Office Dr., Houston, TX 77042 (☎ **713 780-3740**); 2401 W. 6th St., 5th Floor, Los Angeles, CA 90057 (☎ **213/351-2069**); 2333 Ponce de León Blvd., Suite 710, Coral Gables, FL 33134 (☎ **305/443-9160**); 405 Park Ave., Suite 1401, New York, NY 10022 (☎ **212/755-7261**); and the Mexican Embassy Tourism Delegate, 1911 Pennsylvania Ave. NW, Washington, DC 20006 (☎ **202/728-1750**).

➤ **In Canada:** One place Ville-Marie, Suite 1526, Montreal, PQ H3B 2B5 (☎ **514/871-1052**); 2 Bloor St. W., Suite 1801, Toronto, ON M4W 3E2 (☎ **416/925-1876**); 999 W. Hastings, No. 1610, Vancouver, BC V6C 2W2 (☎ **604/669-2845**).

Surfing the Web Before Snoozing on the Sand: Online Information Sources

For a country not universally known for technological advancements, Mexico is surprisingly well plugged in. Any good search engine will dump thousands of listings onto your desktop, so to save you time, I've compiled some of the best ones I found. In addition to the following Web sites, I'll be providing you with other, more specific ones throughout the book.

Just the Facts

The best Web site by far for both general and specific information about Mexico is *!@migo¡* at **www.mexonline.com**. This site has everything from a mini-telephone directory with the numbers of such diverse organizations as the Mexican Wildlife Office, which gives you hunting information, and the Missing Persons Hotline (presumably there's no connection between the two), as well as foreign embassies and consulates, banks, and organizations with ready information about the country and its services. It also has an excellent state-by-state guide to popular cities.

Mexico Travel Guide at **www.go2mexico.com/navigate/html** gives a good general introduction to various Mexican destinations, including all the beach resorts, but only goes into detail—glowing, of course—about sponsoring hotels, restaurants, and so forth.

Tour By Mexico (www.tourbymexico. com) offers a map of the country, state-by-state descriptions, very basic information on the culture, as well as some offbeat takes on such topics as the electrical current, national holidays, and cargo shipping. It also has links to specific resort towns, with short takes on local beaches, scenic outlooks, wildlife refuges, archaeological sites, and shopping. The grammar is charmingly goofy (I know, let's see me try to write a Web site in Spanish . . .).

> **Caveat Browser**
>
> Most sites are as ad- (or sponsor-) driven as any glossy brochures you might send for, and many are not updated regularly. You may want to cross-reference information with another source.

Hotel Sites

Try **www.mexicohotels.com** for hotel information in the most popular resort towns. Also good for Mexico hotel information is **www.hotelstravel. com/mexico.html**. Look up the region that interests you, and then scroll to the town you want to visit. Most of the popular hotels are listed.

The Camino Real chain is prevalent throughout Mexico. The site **www. caminoreal.com** gives you a brief tour of its properties throughout the country, including those in Mazatlán, Acapulco, Cancún, Puerto Vallarta, and Manzanillo.

Welcoming you in four languages, Hyatt's offering, **www.hyatt.com**, takes you on a cybertour of its Mexican resorts in places such as Cozumel, Cancún, and Acapulco.

Destination-Specific Information

www.travelfile.com/go takes you to many cities in Mexico for a closer look at sponsoring companies in those localities. Type in the name of the destination you're interested in exploring further (say, Cancún, Mexico) and you'll get (sketchy) information about dive-boat charters, accommodations, restaurants, and so on, as well as passport and visa information.

The Travelocity home page, **ps.worldview.travelocity.com/**, lets you peruse a list of cities in Mexico and then explore local options for shopping, cultural events, monetary exchange, transportation, restaurants, hotels, and so forth.

Separate from the other sites (although you can link to it from various places) is Puerto Vallarta's Web site, **www.puerto-vallarta.com**. The information on hotels, home rentals, tour operators, restaurants, and so forth is as commercial as you might expect, but it's also more up-to-date, complete, and better-translated than most of the material you'll find on foreign cities' Web pages.

The California-based *Los Cabos* magazine also has an excellent Web site at **www.loscabosguide.com**, with good maps, informative articles on local activities, and useful links to its various advertisers.

Travel Agent: Friend, Fiend, or In-Between?

A good travel agent is like a good mechanic or a good plumber: hard to find, but invaluable once you've located the right one. The best way to find a good travel agent is the same way you find a good plumber or mechanic or doctor—word of mouth.

To make sure you get the most out of your travel agent, do a little homework. Read about your destination (you've already made a sound decision by buying this book), and pick out some accommodations and attractions you think you like. If necessary, get a more comprehensive travel guide, such as *Frommer's*. If you have access to the Internet, check airfare prices on the Web yourself in advance (see chapter 5, "Fighting—and Winning—the Airfare Wars," for more information on how to do that) so you can do a little prodding. Then take your guidebook and Web information to the travel agent and ask him or her to make the arrangements for you. Because they have access to more resources than even the most complete Web travel site, travel agents should be able to get you a better price than you could get by yourself, and they can issue your tickets and vouchers right there. If they can't get you into the hotel of your choice, they can recommend an alternative, and you can look for an objective review in your guidebook right there and then.

Remember, too, that things change rapidly in the travel business, so if your agent visited a city 5 or 6 years ago, his or her information could be woefully out of date. Therefore, it's a good idea to clue your travel agent in *after* you return from your trip—what was good, what was not-so-good, and so on, so that future travelers to the same place will benefit from your experiences.

In the past 2 years, some airlines and resorts have begun limiting or eliminating travel agent commissions altogether. The immediate result has been that travel agents don't bother booking these services unless the customer specifically requests them. However, some travel industry analysts predict that if other airlines and accommodations throughout the industry follow suit, travel agents might have to start charging customers for their services. When that day arrives, the best agents should prove even harder to find.

Chapter 4

The Pros & Cons of Package Tours

In This Chapter

➤ Package tours to Mexico's resorts: the lowdown

➤ Finding the best deals

➤ Specialty packages

➤ Package Comparison Worksheet

Say the words "package tour," and many people automatically feel as though they're being forced to choose: Your money or your lifestyle. It ain't necessarily so. Most Mexican packages let you have both your independence *and* your in-the-black bank account balance. This chapter will help you decide if a package is right for you—and where to find the most suitable one if it is.

If you decide that the available package vacations just don't meet your needs—you have your heart set on staying at a hotel that isn't offered as part of a package, say, or you want to use frequent-flier miles for your airline tickets, or you're a control freak (like me) who'd rather just handle everything yourself—that doesn't mean that you'll get stuck paying top peso for everything. See the remaining chapters in part 2 for tips on do-it-yourself savings.

What Is a Package Tour?

Package tours are not the same thing as escorted tours. They are simply a way of buying your airfare, accommodations, and other pieces of your trip (usually airport transfers, and sometimes meals and activities) at the same time.

For popular destinations like Mexico, they're often the smart way to go because they can save you a ton of money. In many cases, a package that includes airfare, hotel, and transportation to and from the airport will cost you less than just the hotel alone if you booked it yourself. That's because packages are sold in bulk to tour operators, who resell them to the public. It's kind of like buying your vacation at Sam's Club, except that it's the tour operator who buys the 1,000-count box of garbage bags and resells them 10 at a time at a cost that undercuts what you'd pay at your average neighborhood supermarket.

Dollars & Sense

You can buy a package at any time of the year, but the best deals usually coincide with low season—May through early December—when room rates and airfares plunge. You may be a bit more limited in your flight dates because airlines cut back on their schedules during the slow season, but if you're flexible and don't mind a little rain for part of the day, you can get some great bargains.

What's the Catch?

Packages vary as much as garbage bags, too. Some packages offer a better class of hotels than others. Some offer the same hotels for lower prices. Some offer flights on scheduled airlines while others book charters. In some packages, your choices of accommodations and travel days may be limited.

Each destination usually has some packagers that are better than the rest because they buy in even bigger bulk. Not only can that mean better prices, but it can also mean more choices—a packager that just dabbles in Mexico may have only a half-dozen or so hotels for you to choose from, but a packager that focuses much of its energy on south-of-the-border vacations could have dozens of hotels for you to choose from, with a good selection in every price range.

Get your priorities down and then shop around. The time you invest will yield high returns.

How to Tell the Deals from the Duds

When you start delving into the wide world of packages, you may be overwhelmed—but you don't have to be. Here are a few tips to help you distinguish one deal from the other and figure out which is right for you.

> ➤ **Do a little homework.** Read through this guide, decide which resort you want to go to, and pick some accommodations you think you'll like. Compare the rack rates published in this book to the discounted

rates being offered by the packagers to see if you're actually being offered a substantial savings, or if they've just gussied up the rack rates to make their full-fare offer *sound* like a deal.

➤ **Read the fine print.** Make sure you know *exactly* what's included in the price you're being quoted, and what's not. Don't assume anything: Some packagers include everything but the kitchen sink—including discounts on activities and restaurants—while others don't even include airfare. Believe it or not, lots of airline packages don't include flights in their published prices—they know better than anybody how fares can fluctuate, and they don't want to get locked into a yearlong airfare promise.

➤ **Don't compare apples and oranges.** When you're looking over different packagers, compare the deals they're offering on similar properties. Most packagers can offer bigger savings on some hotels than others.

➤ **Know what you're getting yourself into—and if you can get yourself out of it.** Before you commit to a package, make sure you know how much flexibility you have; some packagers require iron-clad commitments, while others go with the flow, maybe charging minimal fees for changes or cancellations. Spin out as many worst-case scenarios as you can think of—go ahead, give your paranoia full reign—and ask questions based on them: What happens if my kid gets sick at the last minute and we can't go? What if the office calls me home 3 days into my vacation? What if my sister decides to marry that jerk after all and we have to adjust our schedule to attend the wedding?

➤ **Use your best judgement.** Stay away from fly-by-nights and shady packagers. If a package appears to be too good to be true, it probably is. Go with a reputable firm with a proven track record; the ones I list in this chapter are a good place to start. This is where your travel agent can come in handy. He or she should be knowledgeable about different packagers, the deals they offer, and the general rate of customer satisfaction; if not, move on to a different travel agent.

Dollars & Sense

If you want more flexibility, consider buying travel insurance that covers trip cancellation; most of the tour operators offer it for anywhere from $29 to $49. That way, if you need to axe your trip, you won't have to pay for it. (But see the "Travel Insurance: Better Safe Than Sorry?" section of chapter 9, "Tying Up the Loose Ends," so you won't end up with more—or less—coverage than you need.)

The Pick of the Packager Crop

If you go to more than one local travel agent to gather brochures, you're likely to get a good selection (you don't have to stop for long; just do a quick "I'm in a hurry, but I'll come back when I've had time to look these over" whirlwind). Another good source of information is the travel section of your local Sunday newspaper. Also check the ads in the back of national travel magazines, such as *Travel & Leisure, National Geographic Traveler,* and *Condé Nast Traveler.*

But, hey, I'm not going to make you do *all* the work. The following, in alphabetical order, are the top Mexico experts, the packagers who cover the most beach resorts in the most comprehensive fashion and from the most cities in the United States. You may not always get much in the way of service with the busier tour operators, but you will get a good deal.

Time-Savers

For one-stop shopping on the Web, go to **www.vacationpackager.com**, an extensive Web search engine that can link you up with various package-tour operators—more than 30 offering Mexican beach vacations at press time—and even let you custom-design your own package. Click on "Mexico" and then "beaches" to get plugged in.

If www.vacationpackager.com sounds like too much for you, point your browser to **www.2travel.com** and click on the Mexico icon when you get to the home page; you'll get sent over to a page with links to a number of the big-name Mexico packagers, including several listed here.

AeroMéxico Vacations

Not surprisingly, Mexico's major airline has comprehensive coverage of the country. You can get year-round packages for Acapulco, Cancún, Cozumel, Ixtapa/Zihuatanejo, Los Cabos, and Puerto Vallarta. AeroMéxico has a large selection of resorts in these destinations (39 in Cancún, 11 in Cozumel, 12 in Ixtapa/Zihuatanejo, 14 in Los Cabos, 21 in Puerto Vallarta) in a variety of price ranges. The best deals are from Houston, Dallas, San Diego, Los Angeles, Miami, and New York, in that order. For example, if you fly from Los Angeles to Puerto Vallarta in high season, you might pay $1,237 for two people, including air, 4 nights at the Westin Puerto Vallarta (a hotel with a rack rate of $185 a night), transfers, and taxes (☎ **800/245-8585;** www.aeromexico.com).

American Airlines Vacations

American has seasonal packages to Acapulco and year-round deals for Cancún, Cozumel, Los Cabos, and Puerto Vallarta. You don't have to fly with

American if you can get a better deal on another airline; land-only packages include hotel, airport transfers, and hotel room tax. American's hubs to Mexico are Dallas/Fort Worth, Chicago, and Miami,
so you're likely to get the best prices—and the most direct flights—if you live near those cities (☎ **800/321-2121;** www. americanair.com).

Sun & Culture

Want to mix capital sightseeing with capital tanning? AeroMéxico's Sun-Brero packages give you 3 nights in Mexico City and your choice of 4 nights in Acapulco, Cancún, Puerto Vallarta, or Ixtapa/Zihuatanejo plus a half-day city tour of Mexico's major city. Mexico City/Acapulco prices range from $359 to $599 per person; Mexico City/Cancún $459 to $729, Mexico City/Puerto Vallarta $409 to $569; and Mexico City/Ixtapa run from $389 to $649. All prices are for land only. You get to choose the hotel category—standard, superior, and deluxe—but have no options within those parameters.

Apple Vacations

Apple offers inclusive packages to all the beach resorts, and has the largest choice of hotels: 16 in Acapulco, 48 in Cancún, 17 in Cozumel, 13 in Ixtapa, 14 in Los Cabos, 6 in Manzanillo, 12 in Mazatlán, and 31 in Puerto Vallarta. Scheduled carriers booked for the air portion include American, United, Mexicana, Delta, TWA, American, US Airways, Reno Air, Alaska Airlines, AeroCalifornia, AeroMéxico; because Apple books blocks of seats, it gets discounts on the air that it passes along to you. The company also charters flights for its most popular runs, but you always have a choice of going with a name-brand airline if you feel more comfortable with that. Apple perks include baggage handling and the services of an Apple representative at the major hotels (☎ **800/365-2775**).

Hey, Mr. Taxman

Depending on your destination, you can save more or less by having your room taxes included. The added accommodation tariffs in Los Cabos, Cancún, and Cozumel are 12%, but in the rest of the resorts, they're a whopping 17%.

Continental Vacations

With Continental, you've got to buy air from the carrier if you want to book a room. The airline has year-round packages available to Cancún, Cozumel, Puerto Vallarta, Cabo San Lucas, Acapulco, Ixtapa, and Mazatlán, and the best deals are from Houston, Newark, NJ, and Cleveland. In high season, for example, you might pay $1,559 for two people, including round-trip airfare for both, from Newark to Cancún, and 4 nights at the Calinda Beach & Spa, a budget hotel (for Cancún) with rack rates that start at $195 per night. The price includes transfers and room taxes (☎ **800/634-5555;** www.flycontinental.com).

To Tour or Not To Tour?

Several packagers offer side trips from the beach resorts—to the Mayan ruins if you're going to Cancún, say, or to Taxco from Acapulco. Sunset cruises, city tours, and a variety of other excursions may also be on the menu.

My advice? Wait until you get to your destination to decide what you want to do. You're not going to save any money if you book from the United States, and you may lock yourself into something you later decide you don't want to do—or that you decide you want to do independently. Many of the packagers that offer tours have on-site reps; if you find you don't get a better deal from a local travel agent, you can always sign on for a trip with the packager after you get there.

Friendly Holidays

This major player in the Mexico field is based in upstate NY, but also has offices in California and Houston, so it has its bases covered. It offers trips to all the resorts covered in this guide. Although it doesn't have the largest variety of hotels to choose, the ones it works with are high quality; in Acapulco, for example, it has the Continental Plaza, Hyatt Regency, Acapulco Princess, and Las Brisas, all of which I recommend in the Acapulco chapter. In addition, its Web site is very user-friendly, listing both a starting price for 3 nights' hotel room and a figure for air add-ons—to Acapulco from New York, it's $425; from Houston, $257; from Los Angeles, $338; Chicago, $510; Miami, $338; and San Francisco, $612—so at least you have a rough idea of what your trip is likely to cost you (☎ **800/344-5687;** www.2travel.com/friendly/mexico.html).

Book Early & Save

Lots of packagers like to have their ducks lined up in advance—and will give you a bonus if you help them do that. Booking your package just 2 to 3 months in advance might save you up to $50 per person on airfare.

Book Late and Save

In addition to their regular packages, lots of airlines post last-minute specials on the Internet. For example, a week before it went into effect, Continental listed a Latin American C.O.O.L. Travel Special good for travel departing on Tuesday or Wednesday and returning a week later (Saturday night stay required). The round-trip fare was $189 from Houston to Los Cabos, and you could get a room at the Fiesta Inn San José del Cabo for $98 (double occupancy) a night, including breakfast for two. But be sure to check restrictions; changing your flights may be expensive to impossible.

Funjet Vacations

One of the largest vacation packagers in the United States, Funjet has packages to Cancún, Cozumel, Los Cabos, Mazatlán, Ixtapa, and Puerto Vallarta. You can choose a charter or fly on American, Continental, Delta, AeroMéxico, US Airways, Alaska Airlines, TWA, or United. Packages include round-trip hotel transfers and all associated taxes and hotel service charges. Funjet packages can be booked through travel agents or online at www.funjet.com.

Funjet's online booking service lets you design your own vacation. Choose a departure date, the number of people you're traveling with, and the city you want to leave from, and various options flash up in front of you. For example, a 3-night package from Chicago to Los Cabos flying on a charter and staying at the all-inclusive Presidente Inter-Continental Los Cabos cost $765 per person—not bad when you consider the rack rate at the Presidente is $155 per person, before tax.

Extra! Extra!

Given a group of packagers with a decent selection of hotels to choose from, it's the price and directness of your flight rather than the cost of your hotel room that's likely to clinch your decision to go with one rather than another. Accommodation prices tend to be competitive, but a recent sampling of packaged airfares from Chicago to Acapulco varied greatly. Friendly was the cheapest, at $419 per person via Mexicana airlines with a stop in Mexico City. Next was Apple's direct flight with Reno Air for $527. Finally, AeroMéxico Vacations charged $605 for a flight that stopped in Atlanta and changed planes in Mexico City.

Some Runners-Up

Even if an airline doesn't have a wide range of choices, it may have just the one you're looking for. Also, some packagers are bigger in some sections of the country than in others. Here are a few alternatives that might work for you.

Airlines—Free Flying?

Many airlines that include Mexico on their routes offer packages. The advantage of booking with an airline is that you can choose one that has frequent service to your hometown and one on which you accumulate frequent flyer miles (in fact, some carriers offer mileage bonuses if you buy a hotel package). Airlines don't include flights in the published price of their packages because of the frequent fluctuations in fares, and you're not always required to fly with the carrier you buy your rooms from. However, you can usually get an excellent deal on the air part of the deal if you do. Buying your package through the airlines is a safe bet—you can be pretty sure the company will still be in business when your departure date arrives.

➤ **Alaska Airlines Vacations** sells packages to Los Cabos, Puerto Vallarta, and, in high season, to Ixtapa/Zihuatanejo. Alaska flies direct to Mexico from Los Angeles, San Diego, San Jose, San Francisco, Seattle, Vancouver, Anchorage, and Fairbanks (☎ **800/396-4371,** www.alaskair.com).

Transfer, Please

For some resorts, having transfers included in the price of your package is a bigger deal than for others. Following are some typical transfer costs, representing the one-way fare from the airport to the most popular hotel zones for the different resorts. The collective van prices are per person; the taxi prices are typically for up to four people. *Note:* Because of airport taxi union restrictions, it often costs less to get *to* the airport by taxi, but few places offer collective van service for the airport return.

Cancún: Collective van $7.50; taxi $27.50.

Cozumel: Collective van $5; private van $20.

Acapulco: Collective van $6.50; taxi $21.

Ixtapa/Zihuatanejo: Collective van to Zihuatanejo $3.50, taxi $12.50; collective van to Ixtapa $4.50, taxi $16.50.

Manzanillo: Collective van $6; taxi $15.

Puerto Vallarta: Collective van $4; taxi $6.

Mazatlán: Collective van $4; taxi $17.

Los Cabos: Collective van to San José del Cabo $7; taxi $45; collective van to Corridor $10, taxi $50 to $55; collective van to Cabo San Lucas $12; taxi $60.

➤ **America West Vacations** has deals to Mazatlán, Manzanillo, Los Cabos, and Puerto Vallarta, mostly from its Phoenix gateway (☎ **800/ 356-6611,** www.americawest.com).

➤ **Delta Vacations** has year-round packages to Acapulco, Cancún, Cozumel, and Ixtapa/Zihuatanejo. Atlanta is the hub, so expect the best prices from there (☎ **800/872-7786,** www.delta-air.com).

➤ **Mexicana Vacations (or MexSeaSun Vacations)** offers getaways to all the resorts except Manzanillo, buttressed by Mexicana's daily direct flights from Los Angeles to Los Cabos, Mazatlán, Cancún, Puerto Vallarta, and Ixtapa/Zihuatanejo (☎ **800/531-9321,** www. mexicana.com).

➤ **TWA Vacations** runs seasonal deals to Puerto Vallarta and year-round packages to Cancún (☎ **800/438-292,** www.twa.com).

Dollars & Sense

Look out for TWA's occasional Mexico getaway specials on the Internet or in your newspaper. For example, one advertised a round-trip economy airfare, 2 nights at the Westin Regina Puerto Vallarta, and airport transfers—plus 2,000 bonus miles in addition to actual miles earned—for $329 from St. Louis; $395 from Nashville, Cedar Rapids, Des Moines, Detroit, Indianapolis, Little Rock, Kansas City, Omaha, and Chicago; $449 from Cleveland, Cincinnati, Dayton, Columbus, Sioux Falls, Lincoln, Milwaukee, and Minneapolis; and $485 from Atlanta, Hartford, Boston, Baltimore, Charlotte, Washington D.C., Newark, New York, Philadelphia, and Pittsburgh. Now that's comprehensive coverage!

➤ **US Airways Vacations** features Cancún in its year-round Mexico packages, departing from most major U.S. cities (☎ **800/455-0123,** www.usairways.com).

There Is a Fare There: Regional Packagers

➤ **From the East Coast, Liberty Travel** frequently runs Mexico specials. The best bet is to check the ads in your newspaper's Sunday travel section or go to a Liberty rep near you. It has no central phone number, but many local offices.

➤ **From the West Coast, Sunquest Holidays** is one of the largest packagers, arranging regular charters to Cancún, Cozumel, Los Cabos, and Puerto Vallarta from Los Angeles paired with a large selection of hotels (☎ **800/357-2400,** or 888/888-5028 for departures within 14 days).

➤ **From the Southwest, Town and Country** packages regular deals to Los Cabos, Mazatlán, Puerto Vallarta, Ixtapa, Manzanillo, Cancún, Cozumel, and Acapulco with America West from the airline's Phoenix and Las Vegas gateways. These packages can be booked through travel agents.

Kids Pint-Sized Deals

Sunquest (☎ 800/357-2400) offers free tagalongs for kids up to 18 years of age: Subject to availability and only at certain hotels, two full-paying adults can get their child's airfare and hotel stay (in the same room) at no extra cost. There are reduced rates for a second child, too, who pays airfare plus $30.

All-Inclusives: Food for Nought?

Almost all tour operators have all-inclusive resorts on their roster of available accommodations; book one of these and you'll have all meals and drinks as well as activities sewn up (see the "All-Inclusives" section of chapter 6, "The Lowdown on Accommodations in Mexico," for details). Most other packages are for rooms only, but certain hotels run seasonal specials that include food (usually just breakfast and dinner). If you don't mind committing yourself to hotel fare, you can get some good buys; inquire with the packager.

And a Last Resort . . .

The biggest hotel chains and resorts also sell packages. The Mexican-owned Fiesta Americana/Fiesta Inns, for example, runs **Fiesta Break** deals that include airfare from New York, Los Angeles, Dallas, or Houston; airport transfers; optional meal plans; and more. Call ☎ **800/9BREAK9** for details.

Playful Packages

Although airfare and hotels eat the largest chunk of most people's vacation budgets, some folks are so dedicated to a particular sport that they can rack up major charges by indulging in it to their heart's content. Anglers, golfers, and divers find Mexico especially addicting—and some hotels and even airlines are happy to facilitate their habits.

It's a Dive Deal

Given that they're two of Mexico's best underwater destinations, it's not surprising that Cozumel and Zihuatanejo have the most diving deals. In the accommodations sections of those resort chapters, I've noted the hotels that run dive specials, including the Puerto Mio and the Hotel Paraiso in Zihuatanejo, and the Hotel Safari Inn and the La Ceiba Beach Hotel in Cozumel. Several other Cozumel properties are in deep with dive operators, too; it always pays to check.

Golfing Bargains, Par None

If you're a duffer, you know how easy it is to spend a fortune teeing off. Several resorts—mostly the tony properties, such as the Grand Bay near Manzanillo, the Acapulco Princess, and the Palmilla in Los Cabos—have play-and-stay deals; they tend to be expensive, even with a discount, but the courses are top-notch and prices are lower than they would be if you paid à la (golf) carte.

You don't necessarily have to tee-off at the priciest courses to get a good deal, however. As its name suggests, **Best Golf** (☎ **888/817-GOLF**) is in the business of arranging golf vacations of all types. "Create-your-own" packages of 2 to 7 nights, including air, hotel, and confirmed advance tee-times, are available to Manzanillo, Los Cabos, Cancún, Puerto Vallarta, Ixtapa, Mazatlán, and Acapulco. **AeroMéxico Vacations** also offers golf vacation packages to Cancún and Ixtapa. There's a 4-night minimum, with unlimited golf during those days.

Ask & Ye Shall Receive

If you see that a hotel has the sport—or, on occasion, spa—of your dreams listed among its facilities, when you call to make reservations, ask if it offers any specials involving that activity. Sometimes deals are unadvertised, and sometimes you can get the best ones by phoning the hotel directly in Mexico (those on site know best how busy their golf course or massage center is). Naturally, you have the highest odds of getting some major discounts in low season.

Fishing for Bargains

Los Cabos reels in the most sportsfishing packages, but Mazatlán and Ixtapa also have some seaworthy deals. In Los Cabos, the Hotel Solmar, with a fleet of 20 cabin cruisers, and the Best Western Posada Real are among the many properties that use discounts to hook anglers. The El Cid Mega Resort in Mazatlán also boasts a flotilla of sportsfishing boats and its own marina, and it likes to play let's make a deal, too. AeroMéxico Holidays books air/land sportsfishing vacations with the Doubletree and the Dorado Pacifico in Ixtapa and with the Meliá Cabo Real and Meliá San Lucas in Los Cabos; there's a 4-day minimum, and the fishing is limited.

Tennis, Anyone?

Resorts with tennis courts sometimes offer all-you-want access as part of a package. Unlike the other sports reviewed in this section, however, tennis is a serious-sweat activity. Unless you go in the height of winter (which is low season for packages) or are committed to playing in the early morning, you might not want to shell out any extra for this netscape.

Love on the Cheap

Everyone loves a lover, including hotels. Several "romance" specials cater to honeymooners, couples renewing their vows, dangerous liasoners . . . basically, anyone who wants to spend lots of time holed up together in a hotel room. In low season, for example, Los Cabos's Palmilla throws in dinner with a bottle of wine served on your private patio with its discounted rates for an oceanfront junior suite.

Other places, however, reward only those who have just tied the knot—and can prove it. Hotels such as the Paradisus in Nuevo Vallarta will upgrade you from a garden to an ocean view; others, including all those you book through AeroMéxico Vacations "Honeymoon Holidays Special," will send a free bottle of bubbly up to your room. Be prepared to produce your "just-married" certificate, however.

Worksheet: Good Things CAN Come in Small Packages—So, Which One Is Right for You?

When you're looking into a package tour, you need to take two things into consideration: Is it really a bargain, and does it give me everything I want? A package can look like a deal—until you get the tab for the room tax and extra-person supplement. And one with a higher price tag could be well worth the extra money if it includes a hotel that gives you everything you've always wanted on a Mexico vacation—and guarantees you a water view. Maybe you don't care if there's a tour rep on site, or maybe you feel better knowing there'll be someone around to help out if things go wrong. Perhaps one packager offers a better deal for your kids than others do. And if you're terrified of flying on a no-name charter, no amount of savings is going to make the trip feel good to you.

That's where this handy checklist comes in. Use it not only to compare prices of the packages you've investigated, but also to make sure that what you want is what you're paying for—and that you're paying for what you want.

Packager:

Contact Name/Number: _____

Number of days _____ nights _____

Name of Hotel(s):

Costs

Per-person price: _____

Restrictions (if any): _____

_____

_____

What's Included (check all that apply):

☐ Airfare to/from Mexico

☐ Airport transfers

☐ Baggage transfer

☐ Hotel room(s)

☐ Taxes

    ☐ Room tax

    ☐ Airport tax

☐ Tips

☐ Cost of cancellation insurance

Food & Drink

☐ Breakfast (How many? _____)

☐ Lunch (How many? _____)

☐ Dinner (How many? _____)

☐ Non-alcoholic drinks

☐ Wine and/or beer with dinner

(continued on next page)

Kid Stuff

☐ Activities (Which? _____)

☐ Baby-sitting

Other _____

Features:

Airline

☐ Scheduled airline

☐ One on which I get frequent flyer miles

☐ Charter

☐ Number of stops (How many? _____)

☐ Number of plane changes (How many? _____)

Hotel

☐ Ocean view

☐ Directly on the beach

☐ Tennis

☐ Golf

☐ Spa

☐ Fishing

☐ Diving

☐ On-site tour representative

Other _____

Other _____

_____

_____

Chapter 5

Fighting—and Winning—the Airfare Wars

In This Chapter

➤ Which airlines fly where

➤ Resources for getting a fair deal

It's no good deciding that you want to go to a particular beach resort in Mexico, only to discover that getting there is going to require changing planes six times and cost you an arm and a leg to boot. Here's where I help you take a hard look at your airline options, a major factor in deciding where you're going to vacation. When you've come up with a geographically desirable destination, I'll also help you figure out how to cut your air costs.

Who Flies Where?

I've broken this one down for you in two ways: resort by resort, so you can tell how easy—or difficult—it'll be for you to get to the destination you're interested in; and airline by airline, in case you've got a favorite carrier and/or have some frequent-flier miles racked up on one of them.

I've listed information about direct flights only (which are not necessarily nonstops—that is, you might touch down once or maybe even twice, but you won't have to change planes). Depending on where you live, getting to your favorite resort might be a bit more complicated. Also, I was able to provide only a rough sketch of what's available at press time. Flight schedules change constantly. For more details, phone the airlines directly or check their Web sites.

➤ **FLYING TO CANCÚN** AeroMéxico has direct flights from **New York's JFK** 6 days a week. American Airlines has daily direct flights from **Dallas/Fort Worth** and **Miami.** Continental has daily direct flights from **Newark, N.J.,** and from **Houston.** Delta Airlines has direct flights weekly from **Atlanta.** Mexicana has daily direct flights from **Los Angeles.** Northwest has direct, seasonal flights from **Minneapolis/St. Paul** and/or **Memphis** and some from **Detroit.** TWA has direct, nonstop flights seasonally from **St. Louis.** United Airlines has direct flights 4 to 5 days a week from **Los Angeles.** US Airways has direct flights weekly from **Charlotte, N.C.,** and once a week from **Philadelphia.**

➤ **FLYING TO COZUMEL** Continental has daily direct flights to Cozumel from Houston.

➤ **FLYING TO ACAPULCO** American has daily direct flights from **Dallas/Fort Worth.** Continental has daily direct flights from **Houston.** Northwest has direct, seasonal flights from **Minneapolis/St. Paul** and/or **Memphis** and some from **Detroit.** America West has direct nonstop flights from **Phoenix.**

➤ **FLYING TO IXTAPA/ZIHUATANEJO** Alaska Airlines has direct flights from **Los Angeles, San Diego, San Jose, San Francisco, Seattle, Vancouver, Anchorage,** and **Fairbanks.** America West has direct nonstop flights from **Phoenix.** Continental has daily direct flights from **Houston.** Mexicana has daily direct flights from **Los Angeles.** Northwest has direct, seasonal flights from **Minneapolis/St. Paul** and/or **Memphis** and some from **Detroit.**

Smoke Gets in My Eyes

Not all flights on Mexican airlines are nonsmoking, especially those within the country. Always check ahead. If you think it's worth the savings or convenience to put up with some smoke for a few hours, make sure you get a seat as far to the front as possible; at least you won't get the most direct fumes from the smoking rows, which are in the back.

➤ **FLYING TO MANZANILLO** Both AeroCalifornia and AeroMéxico have daily direct flights from **Los Angeles.** America West has direct nonstop flights from **Phoenix.**

➤ **FLYING TO PUERTO VALLARTA** Alaska Airlines has direct flights from **Los Angeles, San Diego, San Jose, San Francisco, Seattle,**

Vancouver, Anchorage, and **Fairbanks.** American has daily direct flights from **Dallas/Fort Worth.** America West has direct nonstop flights from **Phoenix.** Continental has daily direct flights from **Houston.** Mexicana has daily direct flights from **Los Angeles.** TWA has direct, nonstop flights seasonally from **St. Louis.**

➤ **FLYING TO MAZATLÁN**   Both AeroCalifornia and Mexicana have daily direct flights from **Los Angeles.** America West has direct nonstop flights from **Phoenix.** Continental has daily direct flights from **Houston.**

➤ **FLYING TO LOS CABOS**   Both AeroCalifornia and Mexicana offer daily direct flights from **Los Angeles.** Alaska Airlines has direct flights from **Los Angeles, San Diego, San Jose, San Francisco, Seattle, Vancouver, Anchorage,** and **Fairbanks.** America West has direct nonstop flights from **Phoenix.** Continental has daily direct flights from **Houston.** Northwest has direct, seasonal flights from **Minneapolis/St. Paul** and/or **Memphis** and some from **Detroit.** United Airlines has direct flights 4 to 5 days a week from **Denver.**

Leaving on a Jetplane—But Which One?

➤ **AeroMéxico (☎ 800/237-6639)**   Daily direct flights from Los Angeles to Puerto Vallarta. Direct flights from New York's JFK 6 days a week to Cancún.

➤ **AeroCalifornia (☎ 800/237-6225)**   Daily direct flights from Los Angeles to Cabo San Lucas, Mazatlán, and Manzanillo.

➤ **Alaska Airlines (☎ 800/426-0333)**   Direct flights from Los Angeles, San Diego, San Jose, San Francisco, Seattle, Vancouver, Anchorage, and Fairbanks to Los Cabos, Mazatlán, Ixtapa/Zihuatanejo, and Puerto Vallarta.

➤ **America West (☎ 800/363-2597)**   Direct nonstop flights from Phoenix to Ixtapa/Zihuatanejo, Los Cabos, Mazatlán, Acapulco, Manzanillo, and Puerto Vallarta.

➤ **American Airlines (☎ 800/433-7300)**   Daily direct flights from Dallas/Fort Worth to Puerto Vallarta, Acapulco, and Cancún, and from Miami to Cancún.

➤ **Continental (☎ 800/231-0856)**   Daily direct flights from Newark, N.J., to Cancún, and from Houston to Cozumel, Cancún, Ixtapa/Zihuatanejo, Puerto Vallarta, Los Cabos, Acapulco, and Mazatlán.

➤ **Delta Airlines (☎ 800/221-1212)**   Direct flights weekly from Atlanta to Cancún.

➤ **Mexicana (☎ 800/531-7921)**   Daily direct flights from Los Angeles to Los Cabos, Mazatlán, Cancún, Puerto Vallarta, and Ixtapa/Zihuatanejo.

➤ **Northwest (☎ 800/225-2525)**   Direct, seasonal flights from Minneapolis/St. Paul and/or Memphis and some from Detroit to Cabo San Lucas, Cancún, Acapulco, and Ixtapa/Zihuatanejo.

➤ **TWA (☎ 800/892-4141)**   Direct, nonstop flights seasonally from St. Louis to Puerto Vallarta and Cancún.

➤ **United Airlines (☎ 800/241-6522)**   Direct flights 4 to 5 days a week from Denver to Cabo San Lucas, and from Los Angeles to Cancún.

➤ **US Airways (☎ 800/428-4322)**   Direct flights weekly from Charlotte, N.C., to Cancún and once a week from Philadelphia to Cancún.

Happy Landings: Going to Mexico Without Going Broke

Airfares are capitalism at its purest. Passengers in the same cabin on an airplane rarely pay the same fare. Rather, they pay what the market will bear.

Business travelers, who need the flexibility to purchase their tickets at the last minute or change their itinerary at a moment's notice, or who want to get home before the weekend, pay the premium rate, known as the full fare. Passengers who can book their tickets long in advance, who don't mind staying over Saturday night, or who are willing to travel on a Tuesday, Wednesday, or Thursday pay the least, usually a fraction of the full fare. It pays to plan ahead.

The airlines also periodically hold **sales,** in which they lower the prices on their most popular routes. These fares have advance purchase requirements and date of travel restrictions, but you can't beat the prices. Keep your eyes open as you're planning your vacation, and then pounce as soon as you see a sale. The sales tend to take place in seasons of low travel volume—you'll almost never find any airfare bargains around the peak Mexico winter vacation months of December through March.

If you don't want to deal with checking for sales, booking far in advance, phoning consolidators, or searching the Web—options I discuss below—there's always your travel agent to turn to: It's his or her job to find you the absolute lowest fare (but see chapter 3, "Getting Started," for advice). Just don't give your travel agent less than 2 weeks' notice and then expect a great flight bargain.

Fares: A Cancún Sampler

A typical 7-day advance purchase fare on major carriers from Los Angeles to Cancún runs around $433 per person, round-trip. From Chicago to Cancún, expect to pay around $378, and from New York to Cancún, $338. For less than 7 days' notice, the amount can double or even triple.

The APEX Vortex: Some Restrictions May Apply

APEX, or Advance Purchase Excursion fares, are those purchased anywhere from 21 days to 90 days in advance. Not all airlines have them—and not all have them for all the destinations in Mexico, or not at all times of the year.

If you do manage to find one for the destination you're interested in, you may be able to save lots of money. On the other hand, you'll be locked into taking your trip at a particular time; rarely, if ever, can you get your money back if you can't go as scheduled. At the very least, you'll have to pay a penalty for changing your mind.

Time-Savers

When you phone a consolidator, be sure you have some alternatives to your preferred travel date in mind. Discount fares for your number one choice might not be available, and by the time you think about it and call back, those seats could be long gone. Have your credit card in hand and be prepared to commit yourself to booking your trip at the time you make the phone call or suffer the "you snooze, you lose" syndrome.

Just What Are Bucket Shops, Anyway—and What Can They Do for Me?

You don't have to be all wet to want to buy your ticket through a bucket shop, which is just another name for a consolidator—which, in turn, is a large travel agency that gets discounts for buying in bulk and passes some of the savings on to you. Use a reliable bucket shop and everybody wins in the end: They got your business, and you got a cheaper airfare than if you bought directly from the airline or from a travel agent that doesn't act as a consolidator.

If a consolidator can save me 200 bucks on the same Continental flight my travel agent can get me, why haven't consolidators taken over the travel world? Here's the catch: Using a consolidator can be *very* time-consuming. Once you finally get past the busy signal, plan on being on hold for a good while before you get to an agent—and then he or she may take your name and number and take some good sweet time getting back to you. When you finally do get to discuss your travel wish list with an actual human being, you may discover the consolidator doesn't have any flights going your way at the moment, and you'll have to start the process all over again. Moreover, there are *no* refunds, no substitutions, and no means of recourse if you book with a consolidator and you can't go.

You can often locate consolidators by ads in small boxes at the bottom of the page in your newspaper's Sunday travel section. Two of the most reliable ones are ☎ **800/FLY-4-LESS** and ☎ **800/FLY-CHEAP** (the latter is slightly easier to get through to than the former).

Finding Bargain Fares on the Web

Another way to find the cheapest fare is by using the Internet to do your searching for you. After all, that's what computers do best: Search through millions of pieces of data and return information in rank order. The number of virtual travel agents on the Internet has increased exponentially in recent years. Agencies now compete the way locksmiths do in the Yellow Pages for the first alphabetical listing. At this writing, 007Travel, 1st Choice Travel, and 1Travel.com all preceded A Plus Travel in an alphabetical listing of online travel agents.

www.waycheapflights.com

AeroMéxico:
www.aeromexico.com

Alaska Airlines:
www.alaskair.com

America West: www.
americawest.com

American: www.
americanair.com

Continental: www.
flycontinental.com

Delta: www.delta-air.com

Mexicana: www.
mexicana.com.

Northwest: www.nwa.com

TWA: www.twa.com

United: www.ual.com

US Airways: www.
usairways.com.

There are too many companies now to mention, but a few of the best-regarded ones are **Travelocity (www. travelocity.com)**, **Microsoft Expedia (www.expedia.com)**, and **Yahoo's Flifo Global (travel.yahoo.com/ travel/)**. Each has its own little quirks— Travelocity, for example, requires you to register with them—but they all provide variations of the same service. Just enter the dates you want to fly and the cities you want to visit, and the computer looks for the lowest fares. The Yahoo site has a feature called "Fare Beater," which checks flights on other airlines or at different times or dates in hopes of finding an even cheaper fare. Expedia's site will e-mail you the best airfare deal once a week if you so choose. Travelocity uses the SABRE computer reservations system that most travel agents use and has a "Last Minute Deals" database that advertises really cheap fares for those who can get away at a moment's notice.

Great last-minute deals are also available directly from the airlines themselves through a free e-mail service called **E-savers.** Each week, the airline sends you a list of discounted flights, usually leaving the upcoming Friday or Saturday and returning the following Monday or Tuesday. You can sign up for all the major airlines at once by logging on to **Epicurious Travel (http://travel.epicurious.com/travel/c_planning/02_airfares/ email/signup.html)**, or go to each individual airline's Web site. See the "Extra! Extra!" sidebar "www.waycheapflights.com" for these addresses.

Chapter 6

The Lowdown on Accommodations in Mexico

In This Chapter

➤ The lowdown on lodging options

➤ Strategies for saving money and traveling with kids.

If you haven't gone with a package deal (see chapter 5, "Fighting—and Winning—the Airfare Wars"), getting a room is a crucial part of your vacation planning. Unless you *really* eat a lot—and only at the poshest of places—lodging is going to be your second greatest expense after airfare. That's why it's critical to decide on the type of place that's best for you—and why I'm going to help you iron out all the details, such as getting the best rates and getting the best rooms, whether you're traveling with a friend or your own personal brat pack.

Figuring Out What Kind of Place Is Right for You

Except for bed-and-breakfasts, which haven't really caught on in the beach towns, you can find pretty much any kind of accommodation you like at the Mexican resorts, although not necessarily at the price you'd prefer, especially if you're traveling during high season (late December through April; see chapter 2, "When Should I Go?," for more details).

In the chapters devoted to the individual beach towns, you'll find recommendations for specific places to stay. I've tried to provide the widest range of options possible, while always keeping comfort levels in mind: Unless they were truly exceptional—or had great ocean breezes—I avoided including spots that didn't have air-conditioning, for example, and never listed places where you wouldn't want to be alone with your fellow guests on the elevator. I also checked out properties that were popular with package tour operators, so I could pass along any good news I found. Ultimately, I chose what I considered the cream of the crop, based on value for money. If I touted a high-priced resort, it's because it was well worth the splurge.

Here are the major lodging categories:

Lighting Up

You're not going to find it easy to locate nonsmoking rooms (or even nonsmoking areas) in Mexico; they're definitely the exception rather than the rule. The big resorts are your best bet when it comes to finding lodgings completely unadulterated by nicotine residue. The good news is most rooms in the Mexican resorts and hotels have balconies, or at least windows that open.

Resorts

Large by definition, resorts are the most popular option, in part because they're what's offered with package deals. You get all the modern in-room amenities, including cable TV and, usually, room service, plus a flotilla of restaurants, pools, sports facilities, shops, and travel services at your disposal. They tend to be the most expensive type of accommodation, but also offer the most discount possibilities because most resorts are affiliated with large chains.

Hotels

Hotels are smaller than resorts and have fewer facilities. They can run the gamut from colonial-design villas with lush gardens, utilitarian all-suite properties, and ultra-stylish boutique hotels to bustling seaside playgrounds. You can expect every hotel at a beach town in Mexico to have at least a small swimming pool; several have almost as many facilities as resorts (travel desks, gift shops, hair salons, and so forth), but offer the advantage of being less impersonal.

All-Inclusives

In Mexico, all-inclusives are big and getting bigger. As the name implies, these properties wrap almost everything—rooms, meals, booze, entertainment, often even tips—into a single, frequently economical, price package. They serve up a menu of daytime activities, such as water aerobics, beach volleyball, or scuba lessons in the pool; excursions to other beaches or towns are sometimes offered, too. Most all-inclusives keep water toys like kayaks on hand for guests' use, gratis, but charge extra for motorized sports such as jet skiing. If they don't have their own nightclubs or discos (although many do), you can depend on some kind of evening entertainment, be it a theme night buffet, costume party, or contest. As for the food—well, you'll never go hungry, but you're unlikely to go gourmet.

Most all-inclusives tend to be fairly low-glitz, but there are some high-tone ones on the market, too. Expect to pay accordingly.

Condos, Apartments & Villas

You'll come across a mind-boggling assortment of condos, apartments, and villas,
better for long-term stays than for short
ones. Some come with housekeepers;
others also include cooks (friends of mine
lucked into one who liked offering them
different flavored tequila Jello shooters
every night), but others require that you
do all the domestic chores yourself. Naturally, there's a direct correlation between
the price you pay and the time you're
going to have to spend washing dishes.

With these types of accommodations, it's
hard to know what you're getting in
advance. If you live in the West or
Southwest, you may find ads for vacation
homes in the travel section of your local
newspaper—the *L.A. Times* runs lots of them, for example. Also, several sites
on the Internet cater to people interested in home exchanges. If you're going
to find a place on your own in this way, however, it's essential that you
check references and get a picture (yes, it's likely to be airbrushed or decep-
tively angled, but at least you'll be able to spot that orange shag rug or velvet
painting of Elvis).

Yo, Gringo!

The people who own and
rent out condos, apartments,
and villas often buy them so
they can enjoy Mexican
weather at its prime, so you
may not find the cream of
the crop available during
high season—or you'll pay
through the nose for a good
place.

Because of the uncertainty of knowing what you're getting in advance, this
type of lodging is often best for second-time trips: If you end up loving the
destination you've chosen, it's worth checking out apartments, condos, or
villas for your next visit while you're there. If you do decide to book one of
these places cold, however, travel agents are generally the best sources of
information. It's in their best interest to work with reputable local Realtors
because they stand to catch hell from you if things don't pan out.

In a nutshell . . .

➤ No muss, no fuss—everything's taken care of and organized.

➤ You'll have an instant social circle.

➤ You won't have to deal with going out for meals or nighttime
entertainment.

➤ You'll avoid the temptations of multiple shopping sprees.

but . . .

➤ The food's better at local restaurants.

➤ The nightlife's more varied outside the resort.

➤ You might pig out—and regret it—just because you already paid for it.

➤ You're going to have to pay extra for activities like windsurfing, waterskiing, and horseback riding.

Is the Price Right?

The **rack rate** is the maximum rate that a resort or hotel charges for a room. It's the rate you'd get if you walked in off the street and asked for a room for the night—and the one that is first quoted to you over the phone when you call the 800 numbers for the resorts. In Mexico, this rate is posted on the sign board at smaller hotels.

Dollars & Sense

I phoned the Krystal Hotel in Puerto Vallarta and asked how much a double room would cost for 2 nights at the end of March, which is high season. The reservations agent quoted me a price of $188. When I asked if she had any-thing cheaper, she immediately came up with a "commercial" rate of $124. Any strings attached? Nope. I just needed to secure that rate with a credit card as soon as possible.

Hotels are happy to charge you the rack rate, but you don't have to pay it! Hardly anybody does. Perhaps the best way to avoid paying the rack rate is surprisingly simple: Just ask for a cheaper or discounted rate. You may be pleasantly surprised.

Hailing a Hotel

Relying on a taxi driver to find you a hotel is iffy. Put yourself in a cabbie's hands and you might end up at a dive owned by his cousin. He'll get the kick-back; you'll get the bedbugs.

That said, owners of reputable hotels often give cab drivers a commission if they bring in customers. If you specify what you're looking for in a hotel (price range, location, and so forth), and check your room carefully before you sign on, you and your cabbie can enjoy a beautiful relationship: He'll drive you around until you find something that satisfies you—he won't earn his commis-sion if you don't stay. Just make sure you've got the rules straight up front; otherwise, you could get stuck at that cousin's dive, frantically trying to get another cab.

In all but the smallest accommodations, the price you pay for a room depends on many factors, not the least of which is how you make your reservation. A travel agent may be able to negotiate a better price with certain hotels than you could get by yourself. (That's because the hotel gives the agent a discount in exchange for steering his or her business toward that hotel.) Reserving a room through the hotel's 800 number might also result in a lower rate than if you called the hotel directly. On the other hand, the central reservations number may not know about discount rates at specific locations. For example, local franchises may offer a special group rate for a wedding or family reunion, but they might neglect to tell the central booking line. If you know which property you're interested in, your best bet is to call both the local number and the 800 number and see which one gives you a better deal (you wouldn't want to do this too often, of course, as your phone bill to Mexico could eat up any savings you might achieve).

Room rates also change with the season and as occupancy rates rise and fall. If a hotel is close to full, it is less likely to extend discount rates; if it's close to empty, it'll almost certainly be willing to negotiate. Resorts are most crowded on weekends, and usually offer discounted rates for midweek stays. Room prices are subject to change without notice, so even the rates quoted in this book may be different from the actual rate you get when you make your reservation. Be sure to mention membership in frequent flyer programs and any other corporate rewards program when you make your reservation with the large hotel chains. American chains might also recognize such things as AARP membership, although that discount is unknown in Mexico. Ask about anything you can think of. You never know when it might be worth a few dollars off your room rate.

Dollars & Sense

Always inquire about activity/theme packages. If you don't manage to get a reduction in the room rate, you might get a bunch of extras thrown in. Golf packages often give considerable savings on greens fees, for example; romance packages can net you a free bottle of champagne and breakfast in bed, and so forth.

Hotel Strategies for Families Traveling with Kids

Mexican families are very close-knit, so no one in the country would expect you to shell out for a separate room for your kids. Many U.S. hotel chains don't charge extra for children who stay in their parents' room, although the cutoff age for what defines a child can vary anywhere from 6 to 18. Some even offer free, or at least cut-rate, breakfasts for kids. Always check in advance when you call to make a reservation.

Rollaway beds, at no extra charge, are common in Mexico, but you'll have a hard time finding cribs there. Take that into consideration before you travel with an infant.

Dollars & Sense

To keep food costs down, book a room with a kitchen; they're especially easy to find in low-key towns like Mazatlán and Manzanillo. Even if you don't want to spend the whole time cooking, doing it occasionally can help your budget considerably. You can store extra drinks and snacks in the fridge, too.

If you want to have some time on your own, check to see if there is a children's program at the hotel you're considering. They're quite common—all the members of the Westin and the Camino Real chains have them, for example—but at a price. An all-inclusive property (see above) may be perfect for you if you're traveling with children, as they're specifically designed to keep people of all ages occupied all the time.

Money Matters

I know. This is the scary chapter, the one where reality rears its ugly head and you have to think about actually putting cash on the line for your fantasies, and where you need to contemplate unpleasant things like the possibility of losing your credit card. Take a deep breath and get out your pencil and pocket calculator: I'll walk you through the bad parts, and show you that an affordable trip is well within your reach—if you plan carefully.

A Pocket Full of Pesos

Mexico underwent a severe economic downturn in 1994—referred to as *La Crisis*—resulting in the devaluation of the peso. Four years ago, a dollar was worth less than 5 pesos; now a single greenback buys you about 8½ of 'em. Keep in mind that most hotels and attractions list prices in dollars, so if you stay on the road well traveled and touristy, the value of the peso won't affect your pocketbook greatly. However, if you visit places where pesos are accepted, you'll be able to take advantage of the strong dollar.

The raising of prices to adjust for the devaluation lowered the standard of living for many middle-class Mexicans, who found themselves suddenly unable to afford items once well within their reach because their wages didn't go up accordingly.

As far as you're concerned, this means that Mexico is more of a bargain in general, although less so in places largely dependent on tourism—such as the beach towns. Knowing about *La Crisis* should also give you some perspective on the pressure people are under to sell you everything from trinkets to time shares. It's a sad fact that your need to have an unhassled vacation experience often clashes with the locals' need to make a living, especially in the resorts, where food prices are unnaturally inflated.

What's in an Exchange?

Everyone has his or her preferred way of handling currency exchanges. Some people like to use travelers' checks for safety (see below). Others prefer to monitor fluctuating exchange rates, waiting until the peso goes down by a tenth of a point and then triumphantly swanning over to the bank or *casas de cambio* (exchange houses) to change money.

As far as I'm concerned, time is money. I like to get my Mexican moolah in one fell swoop at the beginning of a trip—keeping in mind, too, that there's a charge for many transactions, although some are more easily absorbed than others.

Because it's costly to change money back, I gauge in advance what I'm likely to need for a trip—that's what the worksheet at the end of this chapter is for—and take it from there.

Yo, Gringo!

Peso coins come in denominations of $1, $2, $5, and $10; bills, in denominations of $10, $20, $50, $100, $200, and $500. It's hard to get change for the larger bills, which ATMs almost always give you. Try to exchange them for smaller ones at your hotel as soon as possible.

Dollars & Sense

ATMs offer the best exchange rate—the one American banks use, and thus the most favorable to you. Mexican banks offer the next best (and there's no commission), and *casas de cambio* the best after that, although they sometimes charge a small fee for the transaction. You lose the most every time you exchange your money at a hotel front desk.

Unless (and this is not always the case) there's an ATM at the airport, my strategy is to get enough pesos at the airport's money exchange to get me to my hotel and through one evening and then head for an ATM the next morning. (In the chapters devoted to the individual resort sections, I'll be telling you the best places to locate them.) I always bring along some U.S. cash just in case I can't find a working ATM right away, so I can easily get some money the next morning at a bank or a *casa de cambio,* the money exchange booths you'll see all over the city.

Time-Savers

It often takes a long time to exchange money at Mexican banks. There are forms to fill out, and different lines to shuffle over to—and exchange hours are limited (usually from 10am to noon or 1pm, Monday through Friday). *Casas de cambio* are open longer hours, offer similiar exchange rates, and involve far less hassle.

Thus peso fortified, I use my charge card whenever possible; that way, I'm billed with the best exchange rate available on the day the transaction goes through.

Yo, Gringo!

Dollars and pesos are both indicated by $ signs—something to keep in mind before you go into sticker shock. Always ask if you're not sure, however; some high-end tourist places do in fact mark their goods in U.S. dollars. (You'll sometimes see *USD*—for "U.S. dollars"—following a price tag, too.)

Should I Carry Travelers' Checks or the Green Stuff?

Travelers' checks are something of an anachronism from the days when people used to write personal checks all the time instead of going to the ATM. In those days, travelers could not be sure of finding a place that would cash a check for them on vacation. Because they could be replaced if lost or stolen, travelers' checks were a sound alternative to filling your wallet with cash at the beginning of a trip.

Here an ATM, There an ATM

These days, travelers' checks are less necessary because most cities have 24-hour ATMs linked to an international network that most likely includes your bank at home. **Cirrus, PLUS, Visa,** and **MasterCard** are the most popular ones in Mexico; check the back of your ATM card to see which network your bank belongs to. It's not possible to get locations of specific Mexican ATMs from these companies' 800 numbers as you can in the United States, but you shouldn't have much trouble locating them once you get there (I'll be helping you along in the A to Z sections for each resort). Although many banks have begun to impose a fee ranging from 50¢ to $3 every time you use an ATM in a different city, the convenience and the exchange rate advantage more than compensate.

Check It Out

Still, if you feel you need the security of travelers' checks and don't mind the hassle of showing identification every time you want to cash a check, you can get them at almost any bank. **American Express** offers checks in denominations of $10, $20, $50, $100, $500, and $1,000. You'll pay a service charge ranging from 1% to 4%—and you're likely to pay another when you exchange them in Mexico, and/or get a lower exchange rate—although AAA members can get checks without a fee at most AAA offices. You can also get American Express travelers' checks over the phone by calling ☎ **800/ 221-7282;** American Express gold and platinum cardholders who call this number are exempt from the 1% fee.

Keep in mind, however, that travelers' checks are not easy to cash anywhere besides banks or exchange houses, and frequently, only American Express checks are recognized.

Plastic

Credit cards are invaluable when traveling. They are a safe way to carry money and provide a convenient record of all your travel expenses when you arrive home. Although merchants in some shops pass along the high fees they pay to the credit card companies and you'll get a better deal if you buy your souvenirs with pesos, in almost every other instance, using plastic is the way to go. You get the best exchange rate available on the day the transaction goes through without the hassle of having to find an ATM.

MasterCard and Visa are accepted at most hotels, restaurants, and shops, American Express a little less so, Diner's Club occasionally, and Discover not at all.

You can also get **cash advances** with your MasterCard ("Carnet" in Mexico) or Visa (Bancomer) at the appropriate bank, although you'll start paying interest on the advance the moment you receive the cash, and you won't get frequent-flyer miles on an airline credit card.

Time-Savers

It's often difficult to get advances inside banks in Mexico; you can spend hours being shifted from line to line, only to discover at the end that the bank can't complete the transaction for you after all.

There's usually no problem getting a cash advance from a bank ATM, as long as you know your secret code. Be sure to take your PIN along (if you don't know it, call the 800 number on the back of your card and find out how to locate it at least a week before you leave).

Stop, Thief! What Do I Do if My Money Gets Stolen?

Almost every credit card company has an emergency 800 number you can call if your wallet or purse is stolen. They may be able to wire you a cash advance from your credit card, although actually getting it from a Mexican bank could take a while. The issuing bank's 800 number is usually on the back of the credit card. (But that doesn't help you much if the card was stolen, does it? So just call 800 information—that's ☎ **800/555-1212**—to find out the number.) From Mexico, **Citicorp Visa's** toll-free U.S. emergency number is ☎ **95-800/645-6556;** it accepts collect calls at ☎ **605/335-2222. American Express** cardholders and traveler's check holders should call ☎ **95-800/221-7282** for all money emergencies. **MasterCard** holders need to dial ☎ **95-800/307-7309.**

Yo, Gringo!

As in the States, it's always best to use ATMs during business hours, when it's light and there are lots of people around—and when you have access to a real live bank clerk in case the machine decides to eat your card. You can get only $1,500 pesos (a little more than $200) a day from these mechanical money vendors.

If you opt to carry travelers' checks, be sure to keep a record of their serial numbers so you can handle just such an emergency.

Odds are that if your wallet is gone, you've seen the last of it, and the police aren't likely to recover it for you. However, after you realize that it's out of your hands and you cancel your credit cards, it's still worth a visit to the police station to inform the authorities because you may need the police report number for credit card or insurance purposes later. Be prepared, however, to spend some long, frustrating hours going through this process; the bureaucracy in most Mexican police stations is even more complex than that in the States and your difficulties will be compounded by a language barrier. Try to get someone bilingual to come along with you to act as an interpreter, if possible.

What Will This Trip Cost?

By now, I'm assuming you've already decided the basics: which beach resort you want to go to, how you're going to get there, and what type of accommodation you're going to be staying in when you arrive. If you've chosen a package deal, your calculations may be limited to figuring out the extras; if not, it's higher math—okay, advanced addition—time for you.

As should be clear from the previous chapters, your budget will be greatly affected by your choice of beach resort. A room in Cancún, say, is going to cost a lot more than one in Mazatlán—and ditto for all the other expenses down the line. For that reason, in order to come up with a final figure for your trip's cost, you'll have to consult the relevant sections of the individual resort chapters, but you can get a rough idea of your expenses by reading on.

When you've thought about what you want to do, and eliminated all the nonessentials, turn to the Budget Worksheet at the end of this chapter, and put it all on paper.

Air Transportation

Figure airfare is going to be your greatest expense, even after you've used all the tips in chapter 5, "Fighting—and Winning—the Airfare Wars," to cut costs as much as possible.

Airfares fluctuate year-round, what with cut-rate specials and prices hiked up for holidays, and of course, they vary widely depending on your point of origin and your destination. If you live in Los Angeles, you can expect to pay anywhere from $170 to $270 to fly round-trip to Los Cabos. The price range for those departing from the New York City area to Cancún might typically range from $330 to $450 round-trip.

Lodging

If you haven't booked a package that combines the costs of airfare and a room (see chapter 4, "The Pros & Cons of Package Tours," for details), lodging is going vie with flying as the priciest part of your trip. As noted above, you can expect to shell out a lot more for a room in some resorts than in others. In Mazatlán, for example, you can get a casual beachside place (including kitchen facilities) for less than $60 in high season, and the most upscale room on the shore won't run you more than $150. In Cancún, on the other hand, you won't find anything on the beach for less than $170, and most seaside rooms hover in the $300 range. In all the resorts, if you're willing to forgo direct access to the sand and surf, you can cut your costs by more than half—even Cancún has city rooms for under $70.

Dining

Meals are next in line as potential budget breakers, although they run a distant third to airfare and lodging. You can dine inexpensively in almost all of the Mexican resorts, although, again, it's easier to find cheap eats in some places than in others. Lots of hotels lay on all-you-can-eat breakfast buffets, which generally run from about $7 to $12 and keep you well fortified for a good part of the day. If you want to go local, you can also get some great lunch deals: At the more Mexicano of the resorts, many restaurants offer a daily *comida corrida,* or set-price menu. Ranging anywhere from $3 to $6, it generally includes soup, a main course, dessert, and coffee. If you want to stay on the beach, it's easy to get a light seafood meal for maybe a dollar or two more. Dinners are the big danger, especially if you're someplace pricey like Los Cabos, where it's easy to run up a tab of $30 per person in a hotel dining room or a sea-view restaurant; you'll pay considerably less to look out on the water in Manzanillo—perhaps $20 each for a similar meal. In all the resorts, however, there are plenty of casual places to chow down in the dark;

go for a plate of enchiladas and a Corona, and you shouldn't have to pay more than 10 bucks each.

If you're traveling with kids, fast food is always an option. Chains such as McDonald's, KFC, and Dairy Queen, the most popular of those to be found in Mexico, charge about as much south of the border as they do in the United States.

Transportation

For most of the resorts, your getting-around costs should be relatively low, especially if you take my advice in chapter 9 and pass on the rented auto. You can rack up taxi fares fairly quickly, even in an inexpensive resort like Manzanillo, where attractions are spread out, but if you're willing to take buses at least part of the time, you can easily keep your transportation costs down. Fares for city buses run no higher than 50¢, no matter where you are.

The two exceptions to this rule are Los Cabos and Cozumel, where it makes sense to rent a car because there's no public transportation system, and you can't get to the isolated beaches if you don't have wheels. Figure that an automatic plus insurance will run you about $70 a day—but one day, or at the most two, of renting a car should suffice.

Sightseeing, Activities & Entertainment

If you're just going to bake in the sun during the day and gaze up at the stars after dinner, you won't have to budget much for this category. If, on the other hand, you're thinking of being a bit more exploratory, you'll have to factor in some additional costs.

Sightseeing tours vary with the destination, the amount of time you're going to be traveling, and the extras included (for example, meals and snacks), but there are some fairly typical ranges you can use as a guideline. If you want to take a city tour, for example, it will probably run you between $10 and $20, not including food; it's $15 to be shown around Mazatlán, for example. Half-day excursions, which might cover either breakfast or lunch, typically fall into the $25 to $40 range—say, the $33 tour from Ixtapa/Zihuatenejo to Barra de Potosi. Most full-day bus tours run anywhere from $45 to $70; a travel agency trip from Acapulco to Taxco costs about $60. If you want to go the distance and airfare is part of the costs, it'll be a minumum of $200 per person. Day trips via small aircraft from Puerto Vallarta to Guadalajara, for example, cost approximately $230 per person, including guided tours, but no meals.

If you're committed to pursuing pricey activities such as golf, diving, or deep-sea fishing, you're going to have to pay a pretty peso, too, although in some cases the bite is going to be less painful than in others. Greens fees at the Marina Ixtapa Golf Club are $55, for example, but at El Tamarindo, north of Manzanillo, they're exactly double that: $110. With diving, the range isn't quite as great. You can expect to pay anywhere from $50 for a two-tank expedition in Cozumel to $70 in Ixtapa/Zihuatenejo for a similar arrangement. There are lots of variables involved in calculating the costs of deep-sea fishing—such as if you want your own boat, or if you're willing to share with strangers—but assuming you don't mind mingling your lines with people you haven't met before, you're likely to pay out anywhere from $50 to $75 per person, including bait, fishing license, and ice.

Nightlife expenses are, again, largely dependent on your style: If you want to check out a different disco every evening, you'll have to calculate in cover charges, which can be considerable—they can run as high as $20 in Acapulco, for example, although they tend to be less for women. You'll probably want to take in at least one Mexican fiesta; the average cost for them is about $25.

Shopping

Shopping, as always, is the wild card. You can easily get away with buying a few inexpensive souvenirs at the market (a woven straw bag for about $5, or a pair of tinwork candlesticks for $7.50)—or decide to refurnish your house with Mexican folk art and rack up bills in the thousands of dollars. Only you know how much you can afford. But I suggest you keep a firm figure in mind and stick to it, even if it means speaking sharply to yourself in public (but no hand-slapping, please, unless you want the locals to think you're really loco).

Tips on Tipping

For the most part, tipping is not that different in Mexico than in it is in the United States (except that no one in Mexico would be so rude as to question the amount you choose to give). Figure 15% of the bill in a restaurant, $1 per bag to a bellhop, and $2 per night for a maid in a resort (less if the hotel is less expensive). Taxi drivers don't get tips (once you've agreed on a price, it's the one you'll pay). If you're going to the airport, cabbies will help you put your luggage into the taxi, but they're not allowed to help you past the curb with your bags because that's the job of the baggage handlers, who should get about $1, total, for taking your gear over to the check-in counter.

Dollars & Sense

Bring along lots of U.S. singles. They come in handy when you need change for a tip and don't have any small-denomination pesos—a common problem. Otherwise, you're likely to end up giving a much larger tip than the situation calls for—or stiffing someone, which is not good for foreign relations.

What if I'm Worried I Can't Afford It? Keeping the Bill in Check

If you plan wisely, you'll see that you can arrange a trip to fit your budget, no matter how tight that is. In addition, I've included affordable options throughout the book, and for extra pointers on trimming costs, you can check out the "Dollars & Sense" boxes. For right now, here's a quick list of some top moneysavers.

➤ **Go off-season.** If you can travel at nonpeak times (generally, May through November), you'll find hotel prices as much as half what they are during peak months.

➤ **Travel on off days of the week so you can save on airfare.** If you can travel on a Tuesday, Wednesday, or Thursday, you may find cheaper flights to your destination. When you inquire about airfares, ask if it's cheaper to fly on a different day.

Low-Season Discounts

Not all low-season discounts are created equal; some resorts lower their rates more than others during their slack periods. The following gives a rough approximation of how much you can expect prices to be slashed in the various beach towns:

Cancún: 15% to 45%

Cozumel: 10% to 20% (biggest markdowns at the luxury beach resorts; many smaller, more modest lodgings in the town of San Miguel keep the same tariffs year-round)

Acapulco: 25% to 60%

Ixtapa/Zihuatanejo: 15% to 40%

Manzanillo: 20% to 50%

Puerto Vallarta: 20% to 50%

Mazatlán: 20% to 50%

Los Cabos: 25% to 33%

➤ **Try a package tour.** For many destinations, you can book airfare, hotel, ground transportation, and even some sightseeing just by making one call to a travel agent or packager, for a lot less than if you tried to put the trip together yourself. (See chapter 4 for some specific suggestions.)

➤ **Reserve a hotel room with a kitchen and do your own cooking.** It might not feel like as much of a vacation if you still have to wash dishes, but you'll save a lot of money by not eating in restaurants three times a day. Even if you make only breakfast and an occasional bag lunch in the kitchen, you'll still save in the long run, and you'll never be shocked by a hefty room service bill.

➤ **Always ask for discount rates.** Membership in AAA, frequent-flyer plans, trade unions, AARP, or other groups may qualify you for discounted rates on plane tickets and hotel rooms if you book them in the United States. In Mexico, you may be able to bargain for everything from moped rentals to rooms if you go off-season. Just ask; you could be pleasantly surprised.

➤ **Find out if your kids can stay in your room with you.** (That's usually the norm rather than the exception in Mexico.) A room with two double beds usually doesn't cost any more than one with a queen-size bed, and many hotels won't charge you extra if the additional person is pint-sized and related to you. Even if you have to pay $10 or $15 for a rollaway bed (which is rare in Mexico), you'll save hundreds by not taking two rooms.

➤ **Use public transportation whenever possible.** Not only will you save taxi fare, but you'll also feel super-savvy when you see how easily you can master getting around in a foreign country. Two additional bonuses: You'll get to know your destination more intimately, as buses tend to travel at a slower pace, and you'll get to interact with, or at least observe, the locals.

➤ **Cut down on the souvenirs.** It's too much to expect you to return home without *any* local trinkets, but think hard about whether that carved wooden chandelier is really going to fit in with your Danish modern living room decor.

➤ **Substitute less expensive activities for pricey ones.** Waverunners can be fun, but they cost a lot, and the ride doesn't last that long. You might be better off spending a few hours snorkeling instead.

Eating Well without Gobbling Up Your Dollars

Following just a few of these simple tips—not all apply equally to each resort—will help you spare your wallet (and maybe your waistline).

➤ **Fill up at the breakfast buffet laid on by your hotel.** If you eat late and eat well, you'll eliminate the need for a big lunch, expecially if all you're going to be doing is lazing on the beach.

➤ **Share.** Portions are rarely skimpy. At the least, why not split appetizers and desserts? Those little extras can add up.

➤ **Drink local.** Bars often use an import sticker as an excuse to jack prices way up. You're here for the tequila and Mexican beer anyway, right?

➤ **Follow Mexican custom and have lunch as your main meal.** If the restaurant of your dreams is open only for dinner, save that one for last, and chow down at less expensive places the rest of the week.

➤ **Skimp on the shrimp and lobster.** They're the priciest items on the menu. The less expensive local fish is often just as good or better.

➤ **Buy Mexican bottled water.** It's as good as the imports and about half the price.

➤ **Try expensive restaurants at lunch instead of dinner.** Lunch tabs are usually a fraction of what dinner would cost at most top restaurants, and the menu often includes many of the same specialties.

➤ **Avoid your minibar,** or use it to stash the less expensive drinks and snacks that you buy elsewhere.

➤ **Eat somewhere other than where you've gone for happy hour.** It's easy to order a lot more food than you need when you've got those drunken munchies.

Budget Worksheet: You Can Afford This Trip	
Expense	**Amount**
Airfare (× no. of people traveling)	
Car Rental (if you absolutely insist)	
Lodging (× no. of nights)	
Breakfast *may be included in your room rate* (× no. of nights)	
Lunch (× no. of nights)	
Dinner (× no. of nights)	
Baby-sitting (× no. of hours)	
Activities (water sports, tours, nightlife, and so on)	
Transportation (cabs, buses, and so on)	
Souvenirs (T-shirts, postcards, that Mexican pottery you just gotta have)	
Tips (think 15% of your meal total plus $1 a bag every time a bellhop moves your luggage, plus $2 for the maid per room night)	
Don't forget the cost of getting to and from the airport in your home town, plus long-term parking (× no. of nights)	
Grand Total	

What About Me? Tailoring Your Trip

If you have special needs—and almost everyone does—it's your turn to grab some attention. It's all well and good to ferret out the best airfare, but if you don't know how to fit in—or even whether you can—after you arrive, it's not going to matter how cheaply you travel to Mexico. In this chapter, I'll clue you in on what to expect, offer some useful tips, and, whenever possible, steer you to experts in your particular circumstances.

We Are Family: How to Travel Successfully with Kids in Tow

Mexicans dote on children. If you're traveling with kids, you'll never get "The Look"—you know, the scary one directed at you by childless (or child-free) Americans that says, "I'm just waiting for that little monster to make a wrong move." Be prepared to have your kids catered to—even spoiled.

Although Mexico generally adores kids, kids don't universally adore a foreign country. Strange food, a strange language, strange beds—not to mention travel fatigue—can crank up even the most angelic of offspring. In addition to the tips I've outlined below, check chapter 10, "Crossing the Border & What to Expect on the Other Side," for precautions you can take to ensure a healthy vacation for your kids—and a less stressful one for you.

Some Kiddie Travel Strategies

➤ To help them feel at home, take along a few of your children's favorite toys, even if it makes packing a little bulkier (but don't bring any expensive electronic gizmos that could get stolen). If they encounter foreign kids at the hotel who have never seen those playthings before, the toys could make good conversation starters.

➤ Have them study a little Spanish before the trip (the phrases on the tear-out card at the front of this book are a good place to start). Most children are amazingly quick with languages. They'll be excited to try out their new words—and you'll probably end up using them as translators.

➤ If they're old enough, have them read up on whatever aspects of Mexico—or of your specific destination—they may be interested in. Plenty of books about the country are available on all levels. They'll feel more engaged with the destination that way.

➤ Don't overwhelm them with activities. Kids get sore muscles, too. Swimming, going on a tour, and playing in the sand all in one day might be too much. Plan activities that suit your child's age, physical condition, and attention span.

Kid-Friendly Hotels

You don't have to deal with everything on your own. Many hotels have special children's programs, some more elaborate than others. They might include language learning, pottery painting, piñata breaking, and other culture-related activities, in addition to the typical supervised swimming and sandcastle building. Any guilt you might feel about dropping your darlings off is likely to evaporate when you see how hard it is to drag them away at the end of the day.

Even if a hotel doesn't have a special program, many offer playgrounds, special play areas, or pint-sized swimming pools. Some hotels have birds or other tropical animals on the premises that kids can be endlessly entertained by; a few even offer ecological programs, such as sea turtle rescues, that children can get involved with. I've noted these programs in the hotel reviews.

Child's Play

The **Krystal** (☎ 800/231-9860), **Westin** (☎ 800/228-3000), **Camino Real** (☎ 800/7-CAMINO), and **Fiesta Americana/Fiesta Inn** (☎ 800/FIESTA1) chains all have children's programs, some just in high season, others year-round.

You might also consider vacationing at an all-inclusive hotel; they have non-stop activities for kids—and open bars for adults, which makes it easy to remain even-tempered when your little charmers are being whiny. See chapter 6, "The Lowdown on Accommodations in Mexico," for more details about all-inclusive resorts, and for additional information on family-related hotel discounts.

In each of the individual resort chapters I've indicated lodgings that are particularly friendly to families—either because they have supervised programs or facilities that will keep children happy—with a kid-friendly icon **Kids** .

Time-Savers

If you want to arrange baby-sitting through your hotel, plan in advance by giving the front desk or concierge 24 hours' notice.

Finally, when you need a strictly grown-up evening out, you should have no trouble making arrangements at your hotel for your children to be watched. Many maids moonlight as baby-sitters. They may not speak English well, but they'll take good care of your kids.

Small Fries: Eating with Kids

You shouldn't have problems finding food your kids will eat, even if they're picky. Chicken, hamburgers, and spaghetti are on almost all Mexican menus and most of the resorts I'm covering have American fast food chains—I've indicated which ones in the individual resort sections. I've also noted places that teenagers will take to—franchises such as the Hard Rock Cafe, Planet Hollywood, or the Mexican Carlos Anderson chain, for example—and marked family-friendly restaurants with the soon-to-be familiar **Kids** .

For infants, dry cereals, powdered formulas, and baby bottles are available in Mexican grocery stores and minimarts.

Extra! Extra!

You might want to bring along small, zip-locked plastic bags of peanut butter and jelly, already mixed. It's lighter than packing a jar and you can squeeze the stuff out, eliminating the need for spoons. PB&J and locally supplied bread, crackers, or even tortillas should carry you and them through midnight snacks, airport delays, and other "Mom, I HATE enchiladas" travel traumas.

On a related topic, don't forget those moist towelettes and wipes.

Tips for the Senior Set

Seniors get a lot of respect in Mexico. Families are close-knit, and elderly matriarchs and patriarchs are generally deferred to—or at least consulted—on major decisions. Few people in Mexico assume there's a correlation between gray hair and mental deterioration (if they do, they don't make it obvious, anyway). However, the bonuses for golden-agers traveling in Mexico are psychological rather than financial; you'll get no cash rewards south of the border for having made it to a certain age.

Extra! Extra!

Many travel agencies that focus on senior travel are of the tour bus variety, with free trips thrown in for those who organize groups of 20 or more. Seniors seeking more independent travel should probably consult a regular travel agent.

You can, however, take advantage of senior discounts on the U.S. end. If you're not a member of **AARP (American Association of Retired Persons),** 601 E St. NW, Washington, DC 20049 (☎ **202/434-AARP**), do yourself a favor and join; everyone over 50 years old is eligible. AARP members traveling to Mexico can get reduced room rates at all Holiday Inn, Howard Johnson, Sheraton, and Best Western properties. Be sure to mention AARP membership when you make your reservations, however, because like everything in the travel industry, availability can be seasonal.

A free, helpful publication containing general touring information is *101 Tips for the Mature Traveler,* available from Grand Circle Travel, 347 Congress St., Suite 3A, Boston, MA 02210 (☎ **800/221-2610** or 617/350-7500; fax 617/350-6206). Grand Circle Travel is also one of the literally hundreds of travel agencies specializing in vacations for seniors.

Advice for Travelers with Disabilities

Uneven streets, steps between rooms, platform beds, narrow entryways—Mexico abounds in these accessibility nightmares. Although those who use wheelchairs or have other mobility problems will be assisted with great solicitude, independent travel for people with disabilities is an unfamiliar concept in Mexico, and few tourist facilities are equipped to deal with special needs.

Having a disability shouldn't stop you from traveling in Mexico, however. You just need to be super-prepared. *A World of Options,* a 658-page book of resources for disabled travelers, covers everything from biking trips to scuba outfitters. It costs $45 and is available from **Mobility International USA,** P.O. Box 10767, Eugene, OR 97440 (☎ **541/343-1284,** voice and TDD; www.miusa.org). *Note:* This not a recreational travel company; rather, it's a nonprofit organization involved in promoting travel awareness for people with disabilities.

> ## Extra! Extra!
>
> If you're plugged in, **Access-Able Travel Source, www.access-able.com**, is an all-purpose online resource. You can get information here on travel agents who have tours or can plan trips for special needs; links to other Web sites on disabilities and travel; lists of disability organizations, magazines, and newsletters; and more. Click on "Mexico" at this site's destination box and you can read about accessible villas in Los Cabos, say, or an accessible submarine tour in Cancún.

Travel companies that specialize in trips for people with disabilities of all types include **Access Travel Service,** 198 Morgan St., Barberton, OH 44203 (☎ **888/767-0673** or 330/753-3758; fax 330/753-7060; e-mail: bbkw08a@ prodigy.com); **Accessible Journeys,** 35 W. Sellers Ave., Ridley Park, PA 19078 (☎ **800/TINGLES** or 610/521-0339 TTY; fax 610/521-6959; e-mail: sales@disabilitytravel.com); **Custom Travel Care,** 4502 Centerview, Suite 133, San Antonio, TX 78228 (☎ **800 498-6454** or 210/738-0033 TTY; fax 210/736-4325; e-mail: custom@friendsintravel.com); and **Easy Access Travel,** 5386 Arlington Ave., Riverside, CA 92504 (☎ **800/920-8989** or 909/372-9595 TTY; fax 909/372-9596; e-mail: ezaccess@earthlink.net).

Easy-Access Accommodations

In general, the larger hotel chains are hip to the idea that some folks just can't hop (up steps, in and out of tubs, and so forth). The following chains all advertise wheelchair accessibility at the noted destinations:

> ## Extra! Extra!
>
> Cancún gets my nod for "Most Accessible Resort"— not only because it has the greatest number of hotel rooms that are maneuverable, but also because the hotel zone streets are wide and modern, making them much easier to navigate than those in older towns such as, say, Puerto Vallarta.

➤ **Camino Real** (Acapulco, Puerto Vallarta), ☎ **800/722-6466**

➤ **Fiesta Americana/Fiesta Inn** (Cancún, Cozumel, Los Cabos), ☎ **800/223-2332**

➤ **Holiday Inn** (Puerto Vallarta), ☎ **800/465-4329**

➤ **Hyatt Regency** (Cancún), ☎ **800/ 228-9000**

➤ **Omni** (Cancún), ☎ **800/843-6664**

➤ **Mariott** (Cancún, Puerto Vallarta), ☎ **800/228-9290**

- ➤ **Sheraton** (Acapulco), ☎ 800/325-3535

- ➤ **Westin** (Cancún, Puerto Vallarta), ☎ 800/228-3000

Other large hotels in these destinations are also accessible—the **Acapulco Princess** (☎ 800/223-1818), for example—and the chains noted above may also have other accessible locations.

Yo, Gringo!

Your hotel room may be accessible—but your hotel might not be. Some properties don't have ramps or elevators wide enough to accommodate a wheelchair. Be sure to ask hard questions when you make your reservation, and don't part with your credit card number until you get satisfactory answers.

Advice for Gay & Lesbian Travelers

"Don't ask, don't tell" is, generally, the way to go in Mexico, which is a conservative Catholic country. If you don't flaunt your sexuality by holding hands, kissing, or otherwise behaving as though you're in San Francisco, no one is going to ask why you and your same-sex partner want to share a room—or a bed (but best to specify the one-bed preference in advance when you make your reservation to avoid awkwardness at check-in).

Still, certain resorts are more gay-friendly than others, and Puerto Vallarta, Acapulco, and Cancún (in that order) all fall into that category.

The most comprehensive source of information on the subject is the recently published ***Gay Mexico,*** by Richard Black. If you can't find it at your local bookstore, you can order it by phoning Ferrari Publications (☎ **800/ 962-2912**). Ferrari also publishes *Gay Travel A to Z* and other handy guides for getting around the world with gay abandon.

If you're Web-connected, plug into the online travel magazine ***Out and About*** at **www.outandabout.com**. It has great links to other gay travel sites and lists the names and phone numbers of more than 80 tour operators specializing in gay travel.

R.S.V.P., 2800 University Ave. SE, Minneapolis, MN 55414 (☎ **800/ 328-7787** or 612/379-4697; www.rsvp.net), organizes gay cruises and resort vacations and can direct you to gay-friendly travel agencies in your neck of the woods.

Extra! Extra!

If you like safety in numbers, a good resource for gay scheduled group trips is **Envoy Travel, Inc.,** 740 N. Rush St., Suite 609, Chicago, IL 60611 (☎ **800/ 44-ENVOY** or 312/787-2400; fax 312/787-7109; www.envoytravel.com). The rainbow page of their Web site lists dozens of travel options, tours, cruises, a month-by-month events calendar, and advice on destinations in Mexico.

Or, according to Richard Klein, an Envoy travel counselor, just skip the boring research and head straight for Puerto Vallarta, the "hottest gay and lesbian destination in Mexico." Besides being a great restaurant city, it's one of the most welcoming places in Mexico for people of all persuasions.

One all-gay Puerto Vallarta hotel with an Envoy recommendation is **Paco Paco Descanso del Sol** (☎ **011-52-322/218-99**). This property has 22 rooms and organizes all-gay cruises, snorkeling expeditions, and more. (Paco Paco's gay bar is detailed in the Puerto Vallarta nightlife section of this guidebook.) Also, check out The Blue Chairs, a restaurant and bar on the gay section of Los Muertos Beach, recognizable by—what else?—the blue lounge chairs in the sand.

For gay-friendly Acapulco digs, contact **Las Palmas** at ☎ **011-52-748- 70843** or e-mail them at bobbyjoe@acapulco-laspalmas.com.

Going Solo

It's probably safer for women to travel on their own in Mexico, especially in the tourist-oriented resort cities, than it is for them to tour solo in the United States. Middle- and upper-class Mexican women often visit family members in different parts of the country, so it's not unusual to see women going around alone. True, you're likely to come across men (say, taxi drivers or waiters) who are curious about what you're up to if you're unaccompanied. I usually just say I'm traveling with my husband or boyfriend—a large person who happens to be sleeping off a professional boxing bout in our hotel room—and that our children are home with the nanny.

And bring your common sense along with your sunscreen. You wouldn't go wandering alone on the beach at night if you were drinking in the States, and it's an equally dumb thing to do in Mexico.

Yo, Gringo!

If you have to go into a *farmacia* and ask for condoms, the word is *preservativo*.

A Journey of One's Own, by Thalia Zepatos, is a very readable guide for solo voyagers and lists several singles resources in the back. If you can't find it in the bookstores, you can order it through Eight Mountain Press (☎ **503/233-3936**).

Dollars & Sense

You may be independent-minded, but not independently weathy. Hotels that offer discounts for singles are rarer than original come-on lines at pick-up bars. If you don't want to shell out for a room for two, consider finding someone to share costs through the **Travel Companion Exchange,** P.O. Box 833, Amityville, NY 11701 (☎ **800/392-1256** or 516/454-0880; fax 516/454-0170). If you join—it's $99 for 6 months, $159 for a year—you'll get a newsletter that lists other members' profiles and travel interests. If you spot someone who seems compatible, the organization can enable you to contact them directly, so you can get to know them before deciding to take up close quarters. There are no restrictions, incidently. If you want to travel with someone of the opposite gender, ain't nobody's business but your own.

The newsletter also offers other types of travel information for singles, including safety tips. If you're not looking for a roomie, you can pay $48 a year for the publication alone.

Chapter 9

Tying Up the Loose Ends

In This Chapter

➤ Car rentals

➤ Trip insurance

➤ Packing guidelines

Okay, so you've made the big decisions—like when and where and how you want to go to Mexico. Now it's time to deal with those last little niggling details that can make or break your trip.

Do I Need to Rent a Car in Mexico?

For the most part, NO, a thousand times no. Driving a car in Mexico can be a surreal, out-of-body experience. While Mexicans drive on the right side of the road and in theory have traffic laws and practices similar to those in the United States, in reality, anything goes. It's not uncommon to see a semi-tractor-trailer rig pass a bus on a mountainous blind curve, going 70 m.p.h. Macho drivers—and there are many, many of them on the road—disdain such things as traffic lights, stop signs, speed limits, and anyone who gets in their way.

In addition, there are no cattle guards and few barbed-wire fences to contain farm animals. If you hit a cow, goat, or other cash-producing creature, you can expect to pay a very hefty sum to compensate its owner.

Moreover, Napoleonic code dictates that you're guilty before proven innocent in case of an accident—which means if you're on a federal road or the pileup is sufficiently serious, you could be thrown in jail along with the other driver while blame is being assigned. And authorities can take their sweet time to decide.

Convinced you yet? In short, in most of the resorts, there's absolutely no reason to subject yourself to this kind of road stress. Buses or cabs are by far the better way to go.

Two cases, however, are an exception to this general rule: Cozumel and Los Cabos. In Cozumel, there's no public transportion, and in Los Cabos, virtually none. To get to the more deserted beaches, you'll need wheels, but see the "How to Get from Here to There (and How Not To)" sections of the "Finding Your Way Around Cozumel/Los Cabos" chapters for some destination-specific advice.

Mexican Car Insurance

You won't be able to fall back on your U.S. credit card insurance once you're out of this country. Mexican insurance, which adds about $20 to the rental car price per day, is mandatory. You wouldn't want to be without it, anyway. If you get into an accident, your insurance company representative is your ticket out of the pokey, should it come to that.

Yo, Gringo!

Be sure to point out every ding and dent and missing items (such as gas caps) on your rental car before you sign off on it. Otherwise, odds are, you're going to get blamed—and charged an arm and a leg—for them.

Travel Insurance: Better Safe Than Sorry?

There are three basic kinds of travel insurance: medical insurance, lost luggage insurance, and trip cancellation insurance, all of which may be covered under a comprehensive trip plan. Before you shell out for any of them, make sure you need the coverage. Check the policies you already have, think hard about the travel disaster scenarios you fear, and then tailor your insurance purchases from there.

Medical Insurance

Your existing health insurance may cover you if you get sick while on vacation, but not necessarily if you travel abroad—especially if you belong to an HMO. Some hospitals in Mexico's resorts accept Mexican insurance, but not all do.

For the ultimate in foreign-travel health insurance, check out **Traveler's Emergency Network (TEN),** 3100 Tower Blvd., Suite 1000B, Durham, NC 27707 (☎ **800/275-4836** or 919/490-6065), a plan that provides for emergency air evacuation in virtually any country in the world, including Mexico. The cost, an affordable $75 per year, is a must for divers and other thrillseekers, as well as a good idea for the less adrenaline-addicted and the infirm.

Wallach & Company, 107 W. Federal St., Box 480, Middleburg, VA 20118 (☎ **800/237-6615** or 540/687-3166), provides up to $250,000 medical coverage with a $100 deductible in Mexico for only $4 per person, per day.

Lost Luggage Insurance

Your homeowner's insurance may cover stolen luggage if you have an off-premises theft, but not necessarily if it occurs out of the country.

Most airlines are responsible for $1,250 on domestic flights if they lose your luggage, but rates on Mexican airlines and international carriers into Mexico differ. For instance, America West's lost luggage reimbursement rate for international travel is $9.07 per pound up to 70 pounds of checked baggage. If you plan to check baggage containing great-grandmama's diamond tiara, however, you can declare excess value for that luggage and pay anywhere from $2 to $5 per $100 of excess value over $1,250. The airline will reimburse up to a maximum of $5,000.

Perhaps you should leave that tiara in the safe at home, but if you can't avoid checking wildly expensive items, call your carrier for its exact policy.

Comprehensive Insurance

Some credit cards (American Express and certain gold and platinum Visa and MasterCards, for example) offer automatic flight insurance against death or dismemberment in case of an airplane crash; that may be all the insurance you want. Don't pay for more than you need—if you need only trip cancellation insurance, don't pay extra to cover lost or stolen property. Trip cancellation insurance alone can cost as much as 6% to 8% of the total value of your vacation if you just take your regular insurance agent's word for it.

Dollars & Sense

Always read the fine print in any contract or insurance policy, especially concerning trip cancellation by a provider. You might otherwise make incorrect—and expensive—assumptions.

When you're not sure exactly what kind of coverage you need, it's a good idea to check with a company that takes care of all eventualities. Just make sure to figure out your requirements beforehand and focus in on them.

Access America, 6600 W. Broad St., Richmond, VA 23230 (☎ **800/284-8300**), one of the best companies for comprehensive travel insurance, pretty much does it all, from lost luggage and trip cancellation and interruption insurance, to "trip inconvenience" benefits—say, if you're unavoidably delayed for more than 24 hours or if your scuba gear is shipped to Switzerland by mistake. The company also offers an emergency medical transportation service from anywhere in Mexico to the nearest appropriate facility. You choose how much coverage you need, and then consult a table for the per person rate (children under 18 are included free).

Other reputable issuers of general travel insurance include **Mutual of Omaha,** Mutual of Omaha Plaza, Omaha, NE 68175 (☎ **800/228-9792**); **Travel Guard International,** 1145 Clark St., Stevens Point, WI 54481 (☎ **800/826-1300**); and **Travel Insured International, Inc.,** P.O. Box 280568, East Hartford, CT 06128 (☎ **800/243-3174**).

Pack It Up

Start your packing by taking everything you think you'll need and laying it out on the bed. Then get rid of half of it.

I don't say this because the airlines won't let you take it all—they will, with some limits—but because you don't want to get a hernia from lugging half your house around with you. Suitcase straps can be particularly painful to sunburned shoulders.

Some essentials: comfortable walking shoes, a camera, a versatile sweater and/or jacket, a belt, toiletries and medications (pack these in your carry-on bag so you'll have them if the airline loses your luggage), and something to sleep in. Unless you'll be attending a board meeting, a funeral, or (rare at the resorts) one of the city's finest restaurants, you probably won't need a suit or a fancy dress. You'll get much more use out of a pair of jeans or khakis and a comfortable sweater. (See the packing list below for other essential packing advice.)

You're allowed two pieces of carry-on luggage, both of which must fit in the overhead compartment or under the seat in front of you. They should contain a book, any breakable items you don't want to put in your suitcase, a personal headphone stereo, a snack in case you don't like the airline food, your medications, sunglasses, any vital documents you don't want to lose in your luggage (like your return tickets, passport, wallet, and so on), and some empty space for the sweater or jacket you won't want to be wearing once you arrive at your warm, sunny destination.

Home Alone 4: An Essential To-Do-Before-You-Go Checklist

☐ Cancel your newspapers

☐ Hold the mail

☐ Send an itinerary to a family member

☐ Note down your travelers' check numbers and PINs for ATM cards

☐ Photocopy your passport, driver's license, and any other hard-to-replace official documents

☐ Make arrangements for neighbors to water your plants, feed your pets, and check on your house while you're away

---

A Packing Checklist: Don't Forget Your Toothbrush!

☐ Socks

☐ Underwear

☐ Shoes (try to keep this to two or three pairs; you'll likely be living in sandals, so be sure to bring along a pair that are comfortable to walk in)

☐ Lightweight slacks and/or skirts

☐ Short-sleeved or sleeveless shirts or blouses

☐ A nice shirt and tie or a dress (only if you plan to go out on the town in the evening)

☐ A sweater or jacket (mostly for your return trip home; at the resorts, you'll rarely need a cover-up, even at night)

☐ One or two sundresses

☐ A belt

☐ Shorts

☐ Two bathing suits (and a beach towel, if you're planning to stay at a real budget hotel)

☐ Workout clothes (if you're staying at one of the larger resorts)

☐ Toiletries (don't forget a razor, a toothbrush, a comb, deodorant, makeup, contact lens solutions, a hair dryer, an extra pair of glasses, and a sewing kit)

☐ Sunscreen

☐ Camera (don't forget the film; it can be very expensive when you're traveling)

☐ Sports equipment (golf clubs, snorkel, mask and fins, tennis racket, proof of diving certification)

☐ Medications (pack these in a carry-on bag so you'll have them even if you lose your luggage)

☐ Sunglasses (take an extra pair if they're prescription, or clip-ons to put over your glasses)

☐ Travel alarm (even some of the fanciest resorts don't have clocks)

☐ Insect repellent

☐ Flashlight (not only for negotiating paths in spread out, dimly lit resorts, but also to compensate for the inadequate reading lights in many hotels)

☐ Lightweight bag if you're planning to take an overnight excursion (also good for carrying purchases)

Culture Shock: Surviving in a Foreign Country

Trade agreements and proximity to the United States notwithstanding, Mexico is still terra incognita, *a foreign country with different laws, customs, and cultural assumptions. Part 3 is where I'll give you the inside scoop on such serious matters as how to stay healthy, keep out of jail, and avoid offending your Mexican hosts—and also clue you in on the important frivolities, such as the various forms in which you might encounter tequila and the correct time to turn up at a disco.*

Chapter 10

Crossing the Border & What to Expect on the Other Side

In This Chapter

➤ Customs and Immigration

➤ Electricity and telephones

➤ Traveling in Mexico: Getting around, staying well, and being safe

This one's an emotional roller coaster: First I get you nervous by telling you about all the things you hadn't even considered worrying about until I mentioned them—and then I calm your fears by letting you know how to deal with (and/or prevent) them.

The Paper Trail

You'll need a birth certificate or a passport to enter Mexico. If you're relying on a birth certificate, make sure that it's an original, not a copy, and that it's an official, government-issued birth certificate from a city, county, or state agency, as opposed to one issued by the hospital or a church. A birth certificate must be accompanied by a photo ID (such as a driver's license).

Documentation for the Kids

If you're traveling with your child who is not included on your passport, he or she

Extra! Extra!

It's a good idea to make two copies of the issuing page of your passport (the one with your picture on it). Carry one copy in a separate part of your luggage and leave another at home with a responsible person. This way, if your passport should get lost or stolen, it'll be far easier for you to get a replacement.

needs an original birth certificate as well. If both parents are not accompanying the child, the absent parent must sign a notarized letter stating that the child has permission to go to Mexico with the accompanying parent. Include the destination in Mexico, the duration of the visit, and the name, address, and phone number of the parent staying behind. Be sure to date the document.

If you're traveling with children other than your own, in addition to an original birth certificate, each child also needs a notarized letter from his or her parents stating that it is okay for you to bring the child to Mexico. The letter must include duration of visit, destination, name of accompanying adults, parents' home address, telephone, and so forth, as mentioned above. A picture of the child must be attached to this letter.

If you're planning to drive—under the special circumstances I described in chapter 9, "Tying Up the Loose Ends"—don't forget a driver's license (your U.S. one will do you fine).

Nobody Expects the Spanish Inquisition

Usually red tape, long lines, and forms to fill out are a few of the things you can expect. However, going back and forth between Mexico and the States (provided you're contraband-free) is usually a piece of cake.

Mexican Customs

On the plane, you're issued a form to fill out, asking for your address in Mexico, the purpose of your visit, and so forth. You are also asked to declare any unusual goods you're bringing into the country. You're permitted two cartons of cigarettes or 50 cigars, two 1-liter bottles of spirits, and 12 rolls of film. You're not allowed to import any produce, so eat that last banana before you get off the plane.

This declaration document, when stamped, turns into your **tourist card.** Hang on to it carefully—you might even want to make a copy of it, to be kept in a separate place, when you reach your hotel.

As soon as you get into the airport, you're directed to a Customs line, where your passport is checked and your tourist card stamped. After you pick up your luggage and head for the terminal, you pass what looks like a traffic light. Just press the button. Odds are the light will turn green and you'll be free to keep walking. It's rare to get a red light, which means a luggage search. If you're not smuggling in guns, huge quantities of cash, or any quantity of illegal drugs, you've got nothing to worry about.

When you leave Mexico, the airline ticket clerk examines your passport and collects your tourist card. Although you won't be able to leave the country—or enter the United States—if you don't have your passport, tourist card loss is a far less drastic problem, dire warnings in most guidebooks notwithstanding.

Because these books never spell out exactly what happens if you do misplace it, I'd always imagined there was a special airport pokey where people with lost tourist cards languished. Until I lost my tourist card. Twice. (For research purposes only, of course.) The first time I had to go to the immigration section of the airport and pay a fine of $10 to get a new tourist card; the second time, the clerk at the airline departure counter filled out a short replacement form for me, gratis.

I'm not suggesting you lose your tourist card. Just don't panic if you do. Come to the airport an hour earlier than you're supposed to if you've discovered the problem, and be very contrite and polite. But don't waste an entire day of your vacation trying to track down a new one—and don't say you heard any of this from me.

U.S. Customs
Federal law allows you to bring up to $400 in purchases, duty-free, if you've been away from the country at least 48 hours and haven't brought in any other stuff in the past 30 days. The first $1,000 over the $400 is taxed at 10%, and it goes up from there. Art—and that includes folk art—isn't subject to tariffs. You won't get taxed if you take back a single carton of cigarettes, 50 cigars (no Cubans, please), or a liter of booze (wine, beer, or the hard stuff).

Extra! Extra!
To replace a lost passport, contact your embassy or nearest consular agency (see the A to Z sections in the resort chapters for addresses).

It's rare for people returning on commercial flights from the beach resorts to get more than a cursory luggage search. If you're wearing bright colors, peeling, and otherwise look like a tourist, you shouldn't have a problem. You never know what's going to set the Customs inspectors off, however—and those drug-sniffing pooches are always waiting in the wings. Don't even think about trying to import anything illegal.

Getting Plugged In & Connected
If you have dreadful visions of various adapters bristling with oddly shaped prongs dancing in your brain, don't worry—you won't be in for any horrendous shocks in Mexico as long as you keep the following in mind.

Will My Hair Dryer Work?
Yes. The voltage in Mexico is 110, same as in the United States. If you have three-pronged appliances, however, you'll need an adapter. The outlets in most hotel rooms have only two slots, and in some older hotels, the plugs with one larger prong won't fit.

How Will Ma Bell Treat Me in Mexico?
In a word, badly. Phone service may have been improved, as everyone will assure you, but it's often an annoyance—and always an expense—to call home from Mexico.

If you're phoning from your hotel room, you're likely to get slapped with a hefty surcharge (ranging from $1.50 to $5) just to get connected to an operator who can enable you to bill the call to your credit card or to the person on the other end of the line. If you're lucky. Not every hotel operator can connect you directly with your long distance company (AT&T is still the most common). Be sure to take your company's access code (usually an 800 number) from Mexico with you before you go on this trip so you can dial the number yourself if necessary. Here are a few of the biggest carriers: **AT&T** (☎ **001/800-462-4240**), **Sprint** (☎ **001/800-877-8000**), and **MCI** (☎ **001/800-674-7000**). If you're phoning from outside your hotel room; you'll need to use a LATADEL pay phone to access these numbers. If that doesn't work, insist on talking to an international operator (**04**), who should be able to help you reach your long-distance carrier.

Yo, Gringo!

Be wary of private telephones in tourist hotels, airports, and shops advertising "Long Distance to the U.S.A. Collect and Credit Card" calls; they often tack on exorbitant service charges. Always check with the operator for the rates before you give out your credit card number or the number of the party to whom you're placing the collect call.

Never, ever make an international call directly from your hotel room. It can cost you anywhere from 75% to a whopping 400% more than it would if you charged it to your credit card or called collect.

Unless you're in Mexico on business—which is a whole other book—you'll probably have little reason to make local phone calls. If you want to reserve a restaurant table or make other tourist-related arrangements but you're not really fluent in Spanish, it's a good idea to enlist the help of the concierge or front-desk clerk. (You'd be surprised how much harder it is to communicate when you don't have body language to rely on.) Should you want to phone on your own from your room, however, ask in advance about the cost of local calls; they're generally free, but it never hurts to check.

Dollars & Sense

If you know you're going to want to check in with someone in the States, arrange a time that you're going to be in your room—and have them phone you.

Because few pay phones accept coins anymore, if you need to make a call when you're away from your hotel, you'll have to buy a **LATADEL phone card,** available in most grocery or department stores (ask at your hotel for the nearest place to find one). These cards come in denominations of 20 to 100 pesos (about $2.50 to $12.50) and are reusable; the longer you talk on each call, the more money is electronically deducted from the card (a display tells you how much time you have left. You can use your LATADEL card to call the States directly, but you won't have much time to talk, even if you buy the largest denomination card. If you need to contact a long-distance operator to place a collect or credit card call from a phone booth, however, the card is indispensable.

To call long distance (abbreviated *lada*) within Mexico, dial 01 and then the area code (one, two, or three digits) and the number. Area codes are listed before all phone numbers in this book.

International long-distance calls to the United States or Canada are accessed by dialing 001, and then the area code and seven-digit number. For other international dialing codes, dial the operator at **04.**

In Sickness & in Health

There's a lot of hysteria about health disasters awaiting the unwary tourist to Mexico—largely the result of decades of bad jokes about "Montezuma's revenge." Use common sense and follow the suggestions below, and you shouldn't have any problems. (Mexican tourists to the United States have their own jokes about our water, incidentally, since traveler's diarrhea often has more to do with encountering unfamiliar organisms than it does with encountering harmful ones.)

What to Do—& Who to Call—Before You Go

You don't need any special immunizations to travel in Mexico. Of course, it never hurts—okay, only for a second—to get a tetanus booster if you haven't had one in a long time (tetanus shots are effective for 10 years).

If you're the worrying kind, you can contact the **Center for Disease Control (CDC) Hotline** (☎ **404/332-4559**). An automated system tells you how to get information via fax or mail, or directs you to the CDC Web site (**www.cdc.gov**).

Immunization and other health information is also available from the non-profit **International Association of Medical Assistance to Travellers,** 417 Center St., Lewiston, NY 14092 (☎ **716/754-4883;** www.sentex.net/~iamat). Membership, which also entitles you to a list of approved English-speaking physicians in Mexico, is free, although donations are gratefully accepted.

If you suffer from a chronic illness, talk to your doctor before taking the trip. For such conditions as epilepsy, diabetes, or a heart condition, wear a Medic Alert Identification Tag, which immediately alerts doctors anywhere in the world to your condition and gives them access to your medical records through a 24-hour hotline. (Don't worry about whether someone there will speak Spanish, or even Uzbek, for that matter—this service includes 24-hour multilingual translators.) The Medic Alert ID tag costs $35 for the stainless steel version, more for silver or gold. After that, you're billed a $15 annual fee. Contact the **Medic Alert Foundation,** P.O. Box 819008, Turlock, CA 95381-9008 (☎ **800/825-3785**).

If you don't have any preexisting condition, but are still worried about getting sick away from home, it's a good idea to buy medical travel insurance (see the section "Travel Insurance: Better Safe Than Sorry?" in chapter 9). It will probably cover you more completely than your existing health insurance.

Pass the Sugar, Please

In an emergency, ordinary white table sugar can be put directly into a wound as a temporary antiseptic. Contrary to what you'd expect, bacteria don't like it and it helps prevent infection.

The Portable Medicine Cabinet

Pack all the medications you need—plus a copy of your prescriptions, in case you lose them or run out (see "Pharmacies," below). Also carry an extra pair of glasses and contacts with you. You can get contact lens solution in Mexico, but it's much more expensive than it is in the United States.

If you'll be trekking far from civilization, by all means bring a good first-aid kit that includes water purification tablets, bandages, and so forth. However, if your trekking will be limited to checking out the local silver factory and maybe strolling through the plaza, don't bother with anything but a little pocket or purse version containing chewable Pepto-Bismol tablets, Band-Aids, aspirin, and possibly a wide-spectrum antibiotic cream to treat the odd scrape or blister.

Bring along insect repellent, too—not because you're likely to contract malaria, but because you don't want to mar that perfect suntan with unsightly little bite marks. You're going to the tropics after all, and mosquitoes like it there, too.

Above all, don't forget your sunscreen, minimum SPF 15 strength and preferably water-repellent, although you'll want to slather on more every time you step out of the ocean or pool. Sunburn is not only unattractive; it can be uncomfortable and even dangerous to your health.

Staying Healthy After You've Arrived

Most health problems foreign tourists encounter in Mexico are self-induced. If you take in too much sun, too many margaritas, and too many enchiladas within 24 hours of your arrival, don't blame the water if you get sick. You'd be surprised how many people try to make up for all the fun they've missed in the past year on their first day in Mexico.

La Turista

Call it Montezuma's revenge (although that's the offensive term—kind of like someone getting sick in the United States and blaming it on Abraham Lincoln), *turista*, or traveler's diarrhea—it strikes many people when they visit a foreign country such as Mexico. Regardless of the name, the symptoms can be miserable and include the runs and, sometimes, fever, nausea, and vomiting.

To prevent *turista*:
➤ Get enough sleep.

➤ Don't overdo the sun.

➤ Drink only purified water. In addition to drinking bottled water, that means sticking with tea, coffee, and other beverages made with boiled water. Avoid ice, which might be made with nonpurified water; however, in most resort restaurants and hotels, both water and ice are perfectly safe.

➤ Drink plenty of bottled water to avoid dehydration.

➤ Choose your food carefully. Avoid street food (as in vendors with little carts), salads, uncooked vegetables, unpasteurized milk or milk products, and undercooked meat, fish, or shellfish.

➤ Wash your hands often.

If you get sick anyway:
➤ Try something gentle, such as Pepto-Bismol, first.

➤ Rest.

➤ Drink soothing liquids, like *manzanilla* (chamomile) tea.

➤ Replace electrolytes by drinking Pedialyte, a rehydration solution available at most Mexican pharmacies; Gatorade or fruit juice work, too.

If symptoms are severe and persistent, call a doctor.

Special Guidelines for Infants & Children

Be extra careful to avoid anything that isn't bottled if you're traveling with infants and toddlers in Mexico. Infant formulas, baby foods, canned milk, and other baby supplies can be readily purchased from local grocery stores. Your best bet is to carry extra baby eats whenever you go out. Most Mexican restaurants will cheerfully warm bottles and packaged food for your child.

Because children have so much surface area in relation to their size, severe sunburn can be extremely dangerous. *Protect your children from the sun*, preferably by dressing them in special SPF 100 bathing suits and cover-ups that screen out 100% of the burning rays without cramping their style (cotton T-shirts and regular clothing are not effective sunscreens; kids can get too much sun right through their clothes). In addition, make your little ones wear hats, and apply SPF 30 sunscreen on all their exposed flesh.

Dehydration, through either diarrhea or insufficient fluid intake, can also make a child seriously ill. Make sure your child drinks lots of water and juice; like adults, they don't always remember they're thirsty when they're having fun, so it's up to you to remind them. Sunburn also contributes to and complicates dehydration.

Dollars & Sense

Some minibars and stores play on American fears of drinking *any* local water. Mexican bottled water *is* just as good as the imports. Don't shell out twice the price for the fancy French stuff.

If your child has severe sunburn or diarrhea, is running a fever, is lethargic, or otherwise seems very ill, get him or her to a pediatric hospital (*clinica para ninos* or *hospital pediatrico*) immediately. Once the child is stabilized, make arrangements to return home.

What Should I Do if I Get Sick in Mexico?

Don't panic. Medical services are generally good in Mexico. Most major hotels have English-speaking doctors on 24-hour call, or know how to contact one for you. Even the smaller hotels should be able to find someone to treat you quickly. In addition, within each of the individual chapters, I've recommended reliable medical facilities—some extremely high-tech and up-to-date—and, in a few cases, individual physicians.

For extreme medical emergency, the U.S.–based **Air Evac** (☎ **800/854-2569** or 510/786-1592 in the U.S., or 3/616-9616 or 91-800/90345 in Guadalajara), a 24-hour air ambulance, can fly you back to a U.S. hospital.

Yo, Gringo!

Mexican pharmacists expect you to know what you want and ask for it by name. They'll sometimes lend you their copy of the *Physician's Desk Reference*, so you can look up the name.

Pharmacies

There's no shortage of pharmacies in most of the beach resorts, and even the smallest town is required to have a pharmacy that's open 24 hours. In places that have only a few *farmacias*, all-night duty is done on a rotation basis. The front-desk clerk at your hotel should be able to find out which drugstore is on call that night. In the individual resort chapters, I've also recommended a number of good pharmacies that are always open 24 hours.

Although you won't find the gigantic array of over-the-counter cold, headache, and indigestion remedies you'd find in the United States, you will find many items that would be prescription-only in the States—and at far lower prices.

Just because you can buy antibiotics and some pain relievers without a prescription, however, doesn't mean you can bring them back into the United States legally (although you're not likely to be hassled about that tube of Retin-A at Customs). More important, don't be deceived into thinking you can buy Schedule 3 drugs of any kind. Sleeping pills, amphetamines, and narcotics are illegal in Mexico, too, and are *not* available at drugstores without a prescription from a doctor. Not only will pharmacists not sell these drugs to you, but they'll look at you suspiciously for asking.

What's Up, Doc?

Just because you can buy some prescription medicines cheaply and easily in Mexico doesn't mean you suddenly sprouted a medical degree. Self-diagnosis is dangerous, and you can worsen any medical condition you might have if you take drugs that weren't prescribed for you.

Getting Around in Mexico: Trains, Planes & Buses, Oh My!

Once you've chosen a resort, you'll find little justification for visiting another one. Only Cancún and Cozumel are sufficiently close to—and different from—one another to warrant the trip. (Because they're practically on top of each other, I've treated Ixtapa and Zihuatanejo as a single resort). Remember, you had good reasons for selecting your particular beach town in the first place.

In the side trips sections for the individual destinations, however, I suggest some interesting excursions. Although in many cases it's easiest and cheapest to take a package tour, you might want to head out on your own—in which case you can expect to encounter the following types of internal transportation. (I've already warned you against renting a car; if you need a reminder, reread chapter 9.)

On the Wrong Track

If you're tempted to ride the rails, I've got one word of advice for you: Don't. In the past decade, Mexico's government-owned train system has become not only run-down, but actually dangerous; I've heard several reports of passengers being robbed. Although there's been talk for years of privatizing the trains, it hasn't happened yet. I suggest you wait until it does—and then allow 10 years or so for any improvements to take.

Magic Buses

As bad as Mexico's trains are, that's how good the country's buses are. Book a place via a sophisticated computer system on a first-class bus and you'll get air-conditioning (it's sometimes a bit too glacial, so take a sweater), comfort-

Extra! Extra!

More good news: Smoking is prohibited on most first-class Mexican buses.

able seats (they lean all the way back), and, usually, a carry-on snack (soda and cookies, and maybe even a sandwich). Many buses even show American movies on small-screen monitors, but they're often dubbed and the soundtrack tends to be played a few thousand decibels above comfort level.

First-class buses are inexpensive enough that it's not worth saving a few pesos to take the far inferior second- or third-class ones. They're crowded, hot, and often used by people to move their entire households, which might include live chickens.

Mexican bus stations, including the first-class ones, are not especially appealing, but they're no worse than Port Authority in New York or any typical Greyhound station around the country.

Yo, Gringo!

You'll rarely find English-speaking personnel at the bus stations, even the first-class ones. If you're not fluent in Spanish, have someone at your hotel phone and book a place for you (you can do this through a travel agent in some towns, too). Then write down your destination and time of departure to show the reservations agent when you go to pick up your ticket.

Bus stations can be busy and confusing: Double-, triple-, and quadruple-check to make sure you get in the correct line to board your bus on time.

Up, Up & Away!

Don't be alarmed if you've booked a flight for a day trip and find yourself boarding a 20-seat puddle jumper. Mexico's small carriers are generally reliable and safe. **AeroLitoral** (☎ **800/237-6639**), a subsidiary of AeroMéxico, is especially good. I've taken a dozen flights on the airline and all have been smooth and even enjoyably scenic.

Playing It Safe

For the most part, you needn't worry about bodily harm in the Mexican beach resorts. The crime rate in Mexico isn't nearly as high as it is in the United States, and it's only logical that towns where tourism is the cash cow are going to do everything possible to protect that resource, including ensuring the security of their visitors. Tourist police patrol the main drags in most of the resorts. *Note:* At press time, there had been a few instances of attacks on tourists, mainly in Mexico City. Check the **Department of State** Web site at **travel.state.gov/mexico.html** for up-to-date travel advisories and warnings.

Will I Get Mugged?

On the other hand, tourists are prime targets for pickpockets wherever they go, and this is no less true in Mexico. You're especially vulnerable when you're in crowded places like markets. Expensive jewelry (don't wear it!) and big cameras make you particularly attractive to thieves.

It's always a good idea to carry any credit cards and cash you need in a money bag strapped securely to your person. Use your hotel safe to stash your jewelry, passport, tourist card, extra credit cards, cash, and return plane tickets. Don't forget to lock the door to your patio when you leave your hotel room to go down to the beach; thieves can be very mobile.

Use common sense and don't do anything you wouldn't do at home—like wandering off into dark alleys or unpopulated streets late at night. Strolling along dark, deserted beaches, especially if you've been drinking, is not the smartest plan, either.

Extra! Extra!

"Foiling Pickpockets and Bagsnatchers and Other Travel-Related Crimes" is a useful 24-page pamphlet available for $3.95 ($6 for two copies) through **Travel Companion Exchange,** P.O. Box 833, Amityville, NY 11701 (☎ **800/392-1256** or 516/454-0880; fax 516/454-0170).

I've given you numbers to phone for the police in each of the resort chapters. Unless you're fluent in Spanish, however, you're not going to be able to make yourself understood; it's best to find someone bilingual in a hotel or restaurant to help you report a crime. You may need a police report for insurance purposes or for proof if your passport and tourist card are stolen, but don't expect to get your goods back. The wheels of justice turn slowly, if at all, in Mexico. Decide in advance whether it's worth your while to disrupt your vacation further by spending the day being shifted from office to office.

Some of the Sneakier Rip-Offs

You won't have a very good time if you think everyone's out to con you, and for the most part, they're not. Even paranoids have enemies, however, and there are certain things you want to be on the lookout for:

➤ Be sure to count your change, especially on taxi lines in major transportation centers where ticket sellers may assume—perhaps correctly—that you're not yet peso savvy. If you don't get the right amount back, insist on more change (*mas cambio*).

➤ When you get into a taxi, make sure you're talking the same currency for the price of your ride. The driver may claim that the "20" you agreed to was dollars, not pesos. Check in advance what a fair fare to your destination is; then, if you're being asked for something that sounds too good to be true, you can assume the cabbie is quoting you a dollar rather than peso price.

➤ Try not to get distracted—say, by someone dropping down in front of you to pick something up, or by someone who tells you that you have some substance on your clothing that needs to be brushed off. The distracter usually has an accomplice who will quickly separate you from your wallet.

No Time for Time-Shares

More and more hotels in the Mexican beach resorts are setting aside a portion of their rooms as time-share units. The way it generally works is you pay anywhere from $10,000 and up in return for a 2-week annual stay in any such available unit of the resort for the rest of your life.

Time-share come-ons, decked out in the form of offers for free breakfasts, detailed tourist information, or discounted tours and activities, are not exactly scams in that you're not being bilked out of money—yet. If you take the bait, however, you'll have to spend at least an hour, maybe more, listening to a high-pressure spiel. You may love the beach town you visit so much that you might actually want to buy a time-share by the time you leave, but far too many people succumb to these hard-sell pitches prematurely and live to regret it—perhaps because they can't really afford to spend the money or decide they would prefer to take their vacations elsewhere in the future.

You needn't be rude about refusing anything you suspect is connected to a time-share (you'll be right 99% of the time). In general, a polite but firm, "No, gracias," or "I already own a time-share, thank you" should suffice to head off even the most aggressive salespeople.

If you do end up getting stuck in a deal you want out of, consumer protection agencies in the beach towns may be able to help get you unstuck. Ask the tourist information office for the address; your hotel (assuming it's the one trying to sell you the time-share) isn't likely to be very helpful.

Chapter 11

When in Mexico . . .

In This Chapter

➤ Mexican History

➤ Habla-ing Español: Overcoming the language barrier

➤ The Do's and Don'ts of Mexican Culture

So, you've made it beyond the border. Now what? Maybe you're worried because the culture, language, and food are unfamiliar. This chapter gives you some background information that will help you feel more comfortable. Here's a brief overview of Mexican history, government, politics, people, and culture that'll help you get a grip. But don't worry, this isn't school and you won't have to take a test.

A Brief History of Mexico (in Less Than 10 Chapters)

Before the 16th century, when the Europeans arrived, some of the world's most impressive early civilizations thrived in Mexico. The Olmecs, who lived in the vicinity of the modern states of Veracruz and Tabasco from around 1500 B.C. to 100 B.C., carved huge heads weighing several tons each—although no one knows exactly why. From A.D. 300 to 900, the Maya built magnificent cities in the Yucatán and created a calendar more accurate, if wildly more complicated, than our own.

When Spaniard Hernán Cortés and his crew landed in Cozumel in 1519, the Aztecs—an advanced people with a few nasty habits, such as human sacrifice—were on the top of the heap; their capital, on the site of today's Mexico City, was about 300,000 people strong. It took the newcomer conquistadors about 2 years to decimate 3 millenia of early civilizations, not only through war, but also by introducing Christianity, incurable diseases, and a class system (with the Indians at the bottom) that remains in effect today. In return, they took vast quantities of gold and silver—as well as smaller amounts of chocolate—back to Spain.

A Real Eye-Opener

The Aztecs invented an obsidian knife sharper than the best modern steel scalpels. An updated version is used by ophthamologists today for delicate eye surgery.

The Spanish ruled for nearly 300 years until, on September 15, 1810—now celebrated as Independence Day— Father Miguel Hidalgo exhorted his congregation to "recover from the hated Spaniards the lands stolen from your forefathers." This eloquent piece of rhetoric got him hanged but fueled the rebellion that lasted until 1821, when Mexico won its freedom from Spain.

The French tried (unsuccessfully) to take over in the 1860s, but it's been mostly internal reform movements and revolutions that have rocked Mexico since the Spanish left the scene. The most famous, in the early 20th century, involved Pancho Villa, Emiliano Zapata, and Álvaro Obregón, who tried to return power to the peasants. Since 1934, when President Lázaro Cárdenas redistributed land, built rural schools, and took the oil companies out of foreign control, things have been relatively peaceful—if you don't count the recent Zapatista uprising in Chiapas and various political assassinations (see "Government & Politics," below).

In the past decade, the country's economy has been on a roller-coaster ride, with the signing of the North American Free Trade Agreement in 1993, a major recession and peso devaluation in 1994, and a successful $28 billion bailout by the United States in 1995. Growth is still slower than it was before the peso dip, but you'll see signs of recovery all around you.

Government & Politics

Mexico is a democracy in the form of a federal republic. The president, whose term of office is 6 years, appoints a cabinet of 18 secretaries plus 3 other cabinet-level ministers; a separate Senate and Chamber of Deputies are elected. Local governments are set up similarly to those in the United States: each of the 31 states has an elected governor, and cities have an elected mayor.

For decades, however, the PRI (Institutional Revolutionary Party) has had a near stranglehold on all local and presidential elections in Mexico. It wasn't until July 1997, when an upset victory saw the PRD (Democratic Revolutionary Party) and PAN (National Action Party) form a coalition with two smaller opposition parties, that the PRI lost control of Congress for the first time since 1929.

Lots of analysts attribute this change to the assassination of the much beloved PRI reformist candidate, Luis Donaldo Colosio Murrieta, in 1994, as well as to the corruption uncovered in the PRI following the presidency of Carlos Salinas de Gortari, who fled the country under a cloud of suspicion in 1995.

Although you may not notice any of this during your visit, you're likely to be aware of one aspect of the government: the widespread use of federal police throughout the country. Known as *Federales,* these militiamen generally walk around armed to the teeth with submachine guns, pistols, clubs, and highly polished boots. Many of them look no older than 18, and they are best treated with extreme respect in all circumstances.

The People

The population of Mexico as of 1997 was about 90 million, with the most density in the cities of the central highlands. Ethnically, the people are a peppery mix: Some Mexicans can trace their roots back 4 centuries to Castille, while others have never left the mountain villages of their pure Indian ancestors. All the rest, whether they'll admit it or not, are *criollos*—a combination of Spaniard and Indian—or *mestizos,* a mix of Indian, African, European, or about any cultural or racial combination you can name.

Perhaps because of early struggles with class distinctions and discrimination, Mexicans are very aware of where everyone fits into their society. Although the past few decades have sparked an emerging middle class, a huge chasm still exists between the rich and the poor, and visitors to Mexico are sized up at a practiced glance. Although the overriding label blinking from your forehead is "tourist" and you're treated accordingly, your dress and manner also elicit judgments about your socioeconomic class and subtly influence the way you are treated.

Culture

Arts & Crafts　Some *Norteamericanos* regard Mexico as one huge, colorful folk art market. You'll find everything from intricate beadwork, wood carving, and embroidered clothing to glazed pottery, ceremonial masks, and pigskin furniture in the beach resorts, although few crafts actually originate in these towns. It would be impossible to completely cover Mexican crafts in this space—although I've suggested a good book on the subject in "Getting in the Mood Before You Go," below—but among the things to be on the lookout for are the wonderfully whimsical Day of the Dead tableaux. You might come across a framed scene of little papier-mâché skeletons dressed as a bride and groom enjoying their wedding night, or drunk skeletons happily engaged in a bar fight. Other delightful slice-of-the-cultural-psyche examples of Mexican art include ceramic buses crammed with people, chickens, and pigs.

Music & Dance　Mexicans take their music seriously—and often loudly. After a few hours in the country, you might be tempted to think society would screech to a halt if power were cut to all the boom boxes, car radios, and jukeboxes. You would be half right. No gathering, no matter how small, is complete without music.

You won't come across too many musical theater productions or highbrow symphonies in the resorts, as you would in the big cities, but you'll find mariachi ensembles wherever you go. Along with *ranchero,* Mexico's version of country-and-western—like our kind, it also evolved on the range—mariachi is an extremely popular home-grown musical form. Bands, as small as three people or as large as 15, consist of guitars, violins, and trumpets. Songs can be celebratory and rousing, but most often lament lost love.

The Wedding Singers

The word *mariachi* is said to be derived from the French word for wedding: *mariage.* During the French occupation of Mexico under the Emperor Maximilian (1864–1867), the French community of Guadalajara used to hire these lively bands to play at their weddings.

Naturally, traditional music is disdained by many younger Mexicans, who tend to idolize pop singers, both male and female. Luis Miguel, Christian, Anna Gabriel, and Lucero are especially big.

Although the best *Baile Folklorico* (folkloric dance) ensembles don't always make it to the beach resorts, you'll be able to catch some version at the Mexican fiestas held at the hotels. Always a dazzling multicolor whirl of vivid dresses, big sombreros, beautiful women, and handsome men, this dance form blends elements of flamenco, indigenous dance and costume, storytelling, and music to great effect.

Getting in the Mood Before You Go

Page Turners   Eric Wolf's *Sons of the Shaking Earth* gives a good general survey of Mexico's history and culture. Dip into *Ancient Mexico: An Overview,* by Jaime Litvak, if you're especially interested in the country's pre-Hispanic past.

Arts and Crafts of Mexico by Chloe Sayer is indispensable to the collector of folk art. The illustrations in Patricia Quintana's *The Taste of Mexico* are as mouth-watering as the author's recipes. Children from 9 to 12 years should enjoy *Angela Weaves A Dream: The Story of a Young Maya Artist,* by Michele Sola; it's illustrated with photos of Angela and her family, and explains the steps involved in spinning, carding, dyeing, and weaving textiles.

Tops among the fictional takes on the country from the Mexican point of view is Laura Esquivel's *Like Water for Chocolate,* a delightful tale of food, love, and revolution in the magic realist mode. *The Old Gringo,* by Carlos Fuentes, also deals with love and revolution, but in far more serious fashion.

Literary outsiders looking in include D. H. Lawrence, whose *The Plumed Serpent* is gripping, although perhaps a bit over-romantic for some contemporary sensibilities. Austin Olson's *Corcho Bliss* is a comic recounting of an American's misadventures with Pancho Villa. *The Sea of Cortez* by John Steinbeck should put you in the mood for some serious sportsfishing. Although *Under the Volcano,* by Malcolm Lowry, is a classic, it's pretty depressing; still, reading about a gringo who does little in Mexico but consume large quantities of tequila may inspire you to cut back on your bar tab.

The Big Screen   Many American film companies like to take advantage of Mexican scenery and non-union wages. You've seen lots of Mexican real estate at your local cineplex, whether you knew it or not. *Night of the Iguana* and *Predator* were both shot in Puerto Vallarta; Manzanillo's Las Hadas resort was featured in *10; Against All Odds* uses both Cozumel and the Mayan ruins as a backdrop; and the swimming pool scenes from *When a Man Loves a Woman* were filmed at La Casa Que Canta in Zihuatenejo.

Some films that'll give you a flavor of Mexico—although not necessarily an accurate one—include *The Old Gringo, Like Water for Chocolate, Under the Volcano, Treasure of the Sierra Madre, Juárez, Villa Rides, Viva Zapata,* and *El Mariachi.*

In Mexico's own thriving movie industry, soap opera–ish romances, overblown adventures, tales of revenge, and professional wrestling are especially popular. You'll have no problem finding dubbed or subtitled American films, particularly those with muscular leading men and lots of violence and fast action (Sylvester Stallone is practically a cultural icon).

No Comprendo: Making Yourself Understood

Not to worry: You're not going to have to learn a new language, or spend months poring over your old Spanish 101 textbook, to visit Mexico's beach resorts. Waiters, hotel desk clerks, shop owners, tour operators—most everyone in the widespread tourist industry—are geared up to compensate for any lack of Spanish language skills they may observe on your part.

That said, you wouldn't expect visitors to America to be completely clueless about your language, so it's only polite to at least make an effort to communicate on your host country's terms. Moreover, and especially if you're going to budget hotels and restaurants, you're likely to come across a few people who haven't gotten with the everyone-knows-English program. Unlike the French, who can't bear to hear their mother tongue mangled, Mexicans are very appreciative of even the smallest efforts you make to *habla Español.* Want a crash course in Spanish without having to do more than turn a few pages? Check out the handy tear-out card in front of this book for some phrases you're likely to hear.

Accentuating the Positive

In Spanish, there are no hidden agendas: Every letter is pronounced. And unless there is an accent mark, you can assume that the stress falls on the second-to-last syllable. Naturally, there are exceptions to both rules: The letter *h,* for example, is always silent.

The Battle of the Sexes

Yes, even the nouns in Spanish are divided into gender, that is, masculine and feminine. Many feminine nouns end with 'a' and many masculine with 'o'—but don't count on it. You'll have to do more intensive training than I can give you here to get that part of the language down. Don't worry, though. If you use "le" instead of "la," you'll still get your point across, although no one will mistake you for a native speaker.

Sounds Like . . .

Here's a key to the most common sounds:

a like the *a* in far
e like the *e* in best
i like the *i* in machine
o like the *o* in go
u like the *oo* in hoot
b and **v** sound virtually the same—roughly like a *b* in English
g before *a, o,* or *u* sounds like g in go; before *e* or *i,* like h in hip
j is always pronounced like *h* in hip
ll like *y* in yes
ñ like the *ny* in canyon
rr is trilled, making the tongue flutter against the roof of the mouth
que like the *ke* in kept
qui like the *kee* in keep
y when alone, like the *ee* in need

The Customs of the Country

Behave yourself. It's illegal in Mexico to urinate, have sex, or sunbathe nude in public, but tourists get arrested for doing these things all the time.

Drive carefully and never drive drunk; the consequences are far worse in Mexico than they are in the United States. If you get into an accident on a federal road, you can get thrown in jail until it's decided who's at fault—which is one of the many reasons I suggest you don't drive in Mexico (for the others, see chapter 9, "Tying Up the Loose Ends").

All Wet in Español

Before you hop into a shower or bath, remember that the *C* on Mexican porcelain handles stands for *caliente* or hot—NOT cold. If you have a problem keeping that in your head, think *F* for "frigid" (it's actually *frío*).

It's not illegal to act like a boor, but being an "Ugly American" won't earn you any Mexican friends, either. Be as respectful of shopkeepers, desk clerks, waiters, cab drivers, and other service personnel as you would be if you were at home; patience and smiles get you a lot further than angry words do. Speaking loudly won't help you get your English understood—and remember, you're the one at fault for not speaking Spanish.

Don't Be a Dope

If anyone offers you any illegal drugs, just say no. Just because some sleazebags traffic the stuff up north, it doesn't mean there's any tolerance for visitors who use it on Mexican soil. Mexico operates by the Napoleonic code—guilty until proven innocent. Trust me. You don't want to spend even a single night in a Mexican jail, and conviction on drug charges could earn you residence for far longer: Possession carries a penalty of 25 years to life, without parole.

The Mexican beach towns are casual, and very few places have dress codes, but that doesn't mean there isn't an implicit one. The best attire for women in Mexico (except when you're swimming, of course) is a loose, comfortable skirt that hits anywhere below the knee, nice chinos or slacks, or walking shorts combined with a short-sleeved blouse. For men, khakis, chinos, nice jeans, walking shorts, and a decent shirt together with some kind of closed shoe (as opposed to, say, flip-flops) are always appropriate. Wearing tank tops, crop tops, spandex, short-shorts, miniskirts, ratty jeans, and cutoffs will all influence the way you're treated by your Mexican hosts—and not always for the better.

Mexican Time

Mexicans like to joke that they're always in a different time zone than Americans are, and it's true: Our predeliction for punctuality isn't shared by our southern neighbors, who consider human relations more important than schedules. They tend to prefer to spend a few extra minutes chatting with someone instead of rushing on to the next appointment.

So relax. Don't ruin your vacation by stressing every time something doesn't get done exactly when you think it should. So what if you miss a few minutes tanning by the pool, or don't get in that extra hour of shopping?

But also keep in mind that you can't depend on doing things here at the last minute. If you have a plane to catch—and flights, as well as buses, trains, and tours, do tend to depart on time—build in enough room in your schedule to allow for delays at checkout. In general, avoid aggravation by automatically assuming there will be a wait for everything.

Chapter 12

Eat, Drink & Be Merry (for Tomorrow We Diet)

In This Chapter

➤ Mexican food from the familiar to the foreign

➤ A guide to Mexican drinks

You may think that because you've eaten at Taco Bell and just can't resist a frozen margarita, you know what you're going to find on your plate and in your glass when you head south of the border. Well, sink your teeth into this: Most *Norteamericanos* have experienced only Tex-Mex, a variation on Northern Mexican cuisine that, after decades of intermarriage with American products and tastes, is no more than a distant cousin to genuine Mexican food.

As for tequila? Well, you might be surprized to find out that some are more equal than others. And that's not to mention mezcal, Mexican beer, and fresh-squeezed fruit juices.

Have I tickled your taste buds yet? Read on, and tuck in.

The Whole Enchilada

The names of many dishes may be the same, but their ingredients—especially the cheeses and vegetables in the sauces—vary quite a bit. So do portion sizes. In Los Angeles, a single burrito may be enough to feed an entire focus group, but in Mazatlán, you'll get three to an order and just feel happily full when you finish.

Breakfast (*Desayuno*)

Many resort hotels lay on huge breakfast buffets, where in addition to the usual suspects—cereals, pastries, fruits, and scrambled eggs—you're likely to find **chilaquiles,** a tortilla-and-cheese casserole baked in a mild red (*rojo*) or green (*verde*) tomato, chile, and onion sauce. Eggs or chicken are add-ons.

On any à la carte Mexican breakfast menu, you'll usually see the following:

➤ **Huevos Mexicanos** Eggs with onions, green peppers, and tomatoes.

➤ **Huevos rancheros** A fried egg on top of a fried corn tortilla covered in tomato sauce.

➤ **Huevos motuleños** Eggs on top of a tortilla, smothered with beans, peas, ham, sausage, and cheese.

➤ **Huevos con chorizo** Eggs scrambled with a spicy sausage meat.

Dollars & Sense

If your hotel has a buffet, eat breakfast as late as possible and stash a few *bolillos* (rolls) away. You won't have to worry about buying lunch.

If you want to go light, *panaderias* (bakeries) sell a nice array of **pan dulce**—bread-like pastries, sweet but rarely gooey.

Lunch (*Almuerzo*) & Dinner (*Cena*)

For traditional Mexicans, lunch is the big meal of the day, usually eaten between 2pm and 4pm—which is why many offices and some stores are closed during those hours. Dinner often consists only of cold sandwiches or leftovers. Most authentic Mexican restaurants feature a *comida corrida,* a mid-day special that generally includes soup, a main course, and dessert—similar to a French prix-fixe, but far less pricey.

In the chapters devoted to the beach towns, I'll be highlighting regional specialties. Throughout the coastal regions, however, you can expect to enjoy good seafood, including **ceviche,** raw fish marinated in lime juice, diced, and mixed with tomatoes, onions, garlic, and chiles. You'll be entering shellfish heaven, too; in addition to shrimp (*camerones*), oysters (*ostiones*), and clams (*almejas*), there's lots of *langosta* (lobster) and even more *langostina* (crayfish) around.

The following are dishes you're likely to encounter in all the resorts:

➤ **Antojitos** Your basic finger-food appetizers (sausages, cheese, little fried things); also called **botanes.**

➤ **Chiles rellenos** Batter-dipped poblano peppers stuffed with cheese; they're sometimes baked, sometimes deep-fried.

➤ **Enchiladas** Rolled tortillas filled with chicken or cheese and usually topped with a tomato-based sauce;

Bet You Didn't Know

Mexican seafood comes from warmer waters, which is why it often tastes different from what you may be used to.

111

enchiladas *suizas* come with a combination of a mild green tomatillo sauce and sour cream.

➤ **Frijoles refritos**   Refried beans, which are pintos mashed and usually cooked with—sorry—lard. They taste great. Try not to think about it.

➤ **Guacamole**   Just like at home—avocados mashed up with lime juice and onions, tomato, salsa—the variations are endless.

Dollars & Sense

Although lobster and crayfish are common, they often arrive at the table over-cooked. Before shelling out for these most expensive seafood dishes, you might want to ask one of your fellow diners who have empty carapaces on their table if you should invest the extra pesos.

➤ **Mole**   A complex sauce usually served on chicken or turkey. The most famous of them, *mole Poblana,* uses bittersweet chocolate as one of its main ingredients. Almost every region has its own version of the dish—some use pumpkin seeds or other types of nuts—but all use chiles to varying degrees of heat.

➤ **Quesadilla**   Flour tortillas stuffed with melted white cheese and lightly fried.

➤ **Sopa de tortilla**   Mexican chicken soup for the soul. In the broth base swim deep-fried strips of tortilla, avocado, cilantro, and melted cheese.

➤ **Taco**   A catchall for corn or flour tortillas wrapped around or topped by practically any combination of ingredients.

➤ **Tamale**   Corn dough (*masa*) mixed with meat, vegetables, and/or cheese and steamed in a corn husk.

Extra! Extra!

Although, with the abundance of seafood, it's easy enough to avoid red meat at the resorts, it's hard to be a strict vegetarian. Mexicans can't imagine why you wouldn't want to eat meat if you can afford it, and even beans are gener-ally cooked in lard or served with bits of bacon.

➤ **Torta** A Mexican sandwich, usually consisting of meat, tomato, and maybe avocado served on a *bolillo* (a French bread–style roll).

Sweet Stuff

For the most part, desserts are not a Mexican strong point. Spanish-style flan is your best bet if you've got a sweet tooth; the typical Western knock-off cakes and pies are usually not worth the calories. Most Mexican candies have enough sugar in them to make your dentist start revving up his drill, long-distance. A pleasant exception, if you like coconut, is a confection called *cocada,* which is basically like a macaroon without the flour, or a Mounds bar without the chocolate. Another sweet treat is *crema de leche,* caramel goop made with milk. If you're hard-core, or under 14 years of age, it can be eaten right from the jar with a spoon; otherwise, it's great on ice cream, stirred into milk, or melted over baked apples.

Yo, Gringo!

It's considered impolite in Mexico to bring the check before you request it; it implies you're not welcome to stay as long as you like. You need to signal for your check by using the international sign for "Bill, please"—scrawling in your palm—or by saying "*La cuenta, por favor.*"

Feeding Your Inner Gringo

If you're chile resistant, chill: Mickey D has made his mark on Mexico, as have other American fast food franchises (there's even a Hooters in Puerto Vallarta). Plenty of home-grown places cater to gringo tastes, too, especially the Carlos Anderson chain—Carlos 'n Charlie's, Señor Frog's, Guadalajara Grill, and El Shrimp Bucket are all part of the group—where great ribs, chicken, and other U.S.–style specialties are served up in a fun, frenetic atmosphere.

Bet You Didn't Know

Mexico's best-known brand of bread is called "Bimbo."

Moreover, it's a misconception that most Mexican food is fiery hot: Garlic (*ajo*), not chile, is the spice of choice as often as not. Also, much of the Mexican menu comes down from the European-based Spanish conquistadors, who were pretty much meat-and-potatoes guys. It was the Aztecs who turned them on to things like chiles and chocolate (and look at the thanks they got!).

If you're worried, ask the waiter if a dish you're interested in is *caliente* (hot); he'll be honest. In fact, it's hard for non-wussy gringos to get dishes as hot as they like, so accustomed are Mexicans to the American fear of salsifying. (Of course, there's always the option of spooning on the table-top salsa, which is often rich in *chiletepines* or other warp-factor peppers.)

Finding the Worm: A Guide to Drinking in Mexico

Mexico is the source of two of America's favorite yuppie drinks: tequila and Corona. Long gone are the days when tequila was depicted as the beverage of choice strictly for hairy-chested types who would kick back a few shots before shooting up a saloon. Now designer tequilas are in—there are nearly 200 varieties, including brands so smooth they could give the most expensive single malts a run for their money.

As for beer, Corona is just one of many excellent brews you'll find in Mexico. Others include Tecate, Carta Blanca, Bohemia, Pacifica, Dos Equis, Sol, Modelo, and, my personal favorite, Negro Modelo, a dark but not overly rich or yeasty beer. Don't expect to find every type of Mexican beer in every restaurant: Owners often make deals with distributors to carry their brands exclusively. Just as you won't find Coke and Pepsi served in the same place in America, you're unlikely to see both Corona (produced by the Modelo brewery) and Dos Equis (made by Moctezuma) on a single Mexican menu.

Don't like the taste of beer but want a refreshing drink with a slight kick? Order a *michelada,* beer mixed with lime juice and served with salt on the glass's rim.

Dollars & Sense

Mexico is not known for its wines, but Monte Xanic and Chateau Camou are two very respectable local vineyards. If you want to save money, give one of these bottles a shot instead of buying the import brands.

The Soft Stuff

Even though Cafe Combate, the unofficial national coffee brand of Mexico, makes a great, whole-bean coffee, including a presweetened variety (consider buying some in the grocery store to take home), regular morning coffee in Mexico is usually nothing to write home about (no, Starbucks hasn't made inroads this far south yet). Order *cafe de olla,* often listed on the menu as Mexican coffee, after dinner, though, and you're in for a treat: Made with cinnamon and sweetened with brown sugar, it's served nice and strong in small clay mugs. If you like your coffee with milk or cream, try *cafe con leche,* the Mexican version of latte—instant, powdered coffee added directly to hot, steamed milk (trust me, it tastes a lot better than it sounds).

Good luck finding brewed decaf. If you order the low-octane stuff, you're almost certain to get a cup of hot water and a package of the instant brand, "Decaf."

Tequila Coupla Misconceptions . . .

➤ The town of Tequila, where the liquor originated (as early as 1520) and where the largest distilleries still exist, is in the Mexican state of Jalisco. Certain sections of the states of Guanajuato, Michoacan, Nayarit, and Tampaulipas have also been designated by the government as official tequila-distilling areas. But just as people sometimes use the term *champagne* to refer to bubbly that doesn't come from the you-know-what region in France, they may also incorrectly dub the liquor that comes from other parts of Mexico "tequila."

➤ Confusing mezcal with tequila is like mixing up brandy and cognac. Both are derivatives of the cactus-like agave plant, but tequila is made from the rarer blue agave and goes through far more stages of refinement than mezcal. Tequila may be flavored with anything from hot peppers to lemons, but it never, ever, ever has a worm in it.

. . . And To Take You on Some Detours from Margaritaville

Salt, no salt, frozen, straight up—who hasn't gotten the margarita drill down? Here are some postcards, instead, from the tequila edge:

➤ Jello shooters, made by combining your favorite flavor of Jello with equal parts of tequila and water. When chilled, they slide down the throat with the greatest of ease. You won't find Bill Cosby hawking these on TV.

➤ Tequila poppers, a shot of tequila combined with Sprite or 7-Up, and kicked back in one quick gulp. Sometimes they're shaken with a napkin on top of the shot glass; other times, your waiter will shake your head instead. Remember to keep your mouth closed.

➤ Sex on the Beach, a mixture of tequila, rum, Cointreau, grenadine, and orange juice. Hey, I'm just passing along the recipe; don't blame me 9 months from now.

Don't despair if you want something good without caffeine, however; the most common brand of tea is *manzanilla*—technically chamomile, but slightly darker and tastier than the usual U.S. version. (If you want the Lipton's type, you'll have to order *te negre,* or black tea).

Mexico has an abundance of juice bars in most resort towns, and fresh-sqeezed fruit juices are usually very good and very inexpensive (it's easier and cheaper to buy real oranges and bananas than it is to keep a freezer-full of the imported frozen stuff). Also good are **licuados,** a slush of fruit juice plus milk or water and ice, buzzed in a blender. Just be sure to check the cleanliness of the establishment and make sure purified water is being used before ordering one.

Part 4

Cancún

Three decades ago, Cancún was just a gleam in the eye of a group of ambitious government planners, who decided to develop a high-tone resort on Mexico's Caribbean coast. They chose a slip of coastline with all the necessary ingredients—sparkling aquamarine sea, pristine white powder beaches, limpid blue lagoons.

And, ¡ay caramba!, Cancún has become the hottest number for south-of-the-border sunseekers, the most visited destination in all of Mexico. Sleek and modern, it dazzles with luxury lodging, sea-vista restaurants, all-night discos, miles of air-conditioned malls, and endless water sports.

It's easy to have the time of your life in Cancún if you plan carefully—which is what the following chapters are all about. Read on for some guidelines to getting the very best out of your stay at this nonstop island.

Chapter 13

Choosing the Place to Stay That's Right for You

In This Chapter

➤ Where the hotels are

➤ The best in the bunch

➤ Hotel indexes

So you've decided to take that dream trip to Cancún. Congratulations or, as the Mexicans would say, *felicidades*. Of course, after you've got your airfare down, there are still a few petty details to settle—like how to choose a hotel from among the 150-odd properties waiting to welcome you.

Be prepared for some trade-offs. Cancún is the most expensive of all the beach resorts in Mexico. You'll get a lot of bang for your buck—but that exploding sound you hear could also be your savings account going belly-up. Expect to pay through the nose if you want to be where the action is—or to travel a bit to get to it, if you need to keep your budget down.

Here's the story. First, I'll give you a rundown of the three areas where Cancún's hotels are concentrated, summing up their pros and cons at the end of each section. Then I'll list my favorite hotels, and follow up with a list of other options should those be unavailable. At the end of the chapter, you'll find handy, at-a-glance indexes listing the hotels by price and by location.

As far as prices go, I've noted rack rates (the maximum that a resort or hotel charges for a room) in the listings to give you some sense of what to expect, although I know you'll avoid paying rack by following the advice I gave you in chapter 6, "The Lowdown on Accommodations in Mexico." I've also put a dollar sign icon in front of each hotel listing so you can quickly see whether it's within your budget. The more $ signs, the more you pay. It runs like this:

$ = $85 and below

$$ = $85–$140

$$$ = $140–$225

$$$$ = $225–$335

$$$$$ = $335 and above

Unless otherwise specified, tariffs are for a standard double room and include the 12% room tax. What I list here are high-season rates, in effect from around April 18 to December 20. The rest of the year, prices plummet anywhere from 15% to as much as 45%, depending on each hotel's unique—sometimes arcane—discount tabulation.

A kid-friendly icon highlights hotels that are especially good for families. All hotels have air-conditioning unless otherwise indicated, and if the review doesn't say anything to the contrary, you can safely assume that you can walk directly out of your hotel and onto the beach.

Bet You Didn't Know

Cancún's tax is 5% lower than that in the rest of the country—a leftover from the days when it was a duty-free port. Everywhere else you have to pay a whopping 17% tariff on your room.

Hint: As you read through the reviews, you'll want to keep track of the ones that appeal to you. I've included a chart at the end of the book (see p. 542) where you can rank your preferences, but to make matters easier on yourself now, why don't you just put a little check mark next to the ones you like (you've got my permission to write in the book, scout's honor).

Dollars & Sense

Cover every possible angle you can think of when you phone to ask about special rates—length of stay, corporate affiliation, honeymoon (so maybe you're just renewing your vows in your head—that counts, too), birthday, retirement . . . it never hurts to ask. Give the reservation agent any excuse you can think of to plug in a discount for you.

Location, Location, Location

As you can see from the map, Cancún comprises an island shaped like the number 7 and Cancún City, set off inland to the west. Although there's really only one large *Zona Hoteleria,* or hotel zone, that extends the entire length of

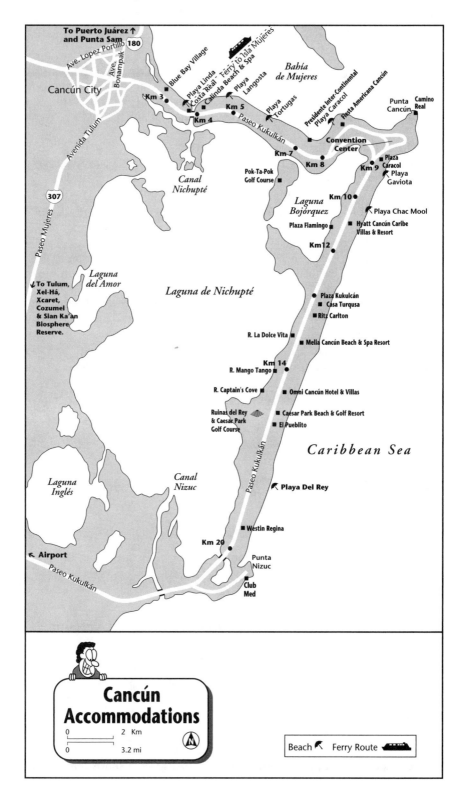

Cancún Accommodations

0   2 Km
0   3.2 mi

Beach   Ferry Route

Cancún Island, there's a distinct difference between staying on the north/south part of it and bedding down at the top of the 7, or the east/west section. I've divided the zone into two separate categories, described in the following sections.

The North/South Hotel Zone: Richie Rich Row

The longest stretch of luxury hotels in Cancún straddles a strip as skinny as a string bean on a map; two lagoons—little Laguna Bojórquez and the large Laguna Nichupte—sit serenely on one side of the strand, and the Caribbean Sea laps up against the other.

The upper tip of the north/south hotel zone, near Punta Cancún—the point that connects the two parts of the 7—is jam-packed with trendy discos, cafes, boutiques, marinas, malls, and movie houses. The farther south you go, the more isolated—and exclusive—you get. Many of the resorts here sit on huge spreads, and almost all are about as high-tone as they come. There are golf courses in this area, and several upscale restaurants (a number of them at the hotels themselves), but much less party or shopping action than you'll find in the upper part of the hotel zone.

Opulent hotels carry an opulent price tag, but if you want to live like a pasha, this is the place to be. Being removed from hoi polloi is part of what you're paying for, and you can always summon a taxi for $15 when you're ready to rejoin the sweating hordes.

In a nutshell . . .

> ➤ The newest, most luxurious hotels are here.

> ➤ There are beautiful golf courses and to-die-for restaurants.

> ➤ It's a short ride to the airport.

but . . .

> ➤ Room rates are steep.

> ➤ If you stay in the upper hotel zone, you may be isolated from the action.

> ➤ Some hotels have limited guest activities.

The East/West Hotel Zone: Cancún's High-Energy Playground

The slip of land that curves like a snake on the northern part of the hotel zone is flanked by the two lagoons to the south and the Bay of Mujeres to the north; on most of this stretch, you can walk down the middle and see two different bodies of water—in two distinct shades of blue. Face north and you can also see Isla Mujeres, a Robinson Crusoe–like getaway popular for day trips.

Because of its proximity to downtown, this was the first parcel of Cancún real estate to mushroom with high rises in the 1970s. It's where you'll find the greatest concentration of tourist services—malls, water sports rentals, fishing docks, the bus terminal to Xcaret, and the hottest restaurants and discos. The yacht cruises for Isla Mujeres, the ferry boat for Cozumel, and the submarine excursions all take off from this area's docks.

Because the beaches front the bay, they're among the best in Cancún, with calm and shallow water and no dangerous undertows. They're also among the most crowded—Playas Tortugas and Linda are especially popular with Cancún families on the weekends.

In a nutshell . . .

➤ The best variety in hotels

➤ The safest swimming beaches

➤ A quick cab ride from downtown

➤ Easy access to some of the best restaurants and discos as well as to shopping centers and excursions

but . . .

➤ Don't expect anything to be inexpensive.

➤ The trendy watering holes are crowded.

➤ Traffic is the heaviest here.

➤ You'll be farthest from the airport.

Cancún City: The Downtown Core

This part of town is sometimes called Old Cancún, a rather misleading moniker for a place that was born in 1974. But everything's relative, and this is the earliest section of the resort, the town that arose to house the workers hired to build—and work in—the glitzy hotels on the tourist strip.

As such, it's about as Mexican as Cancún gets. There's no history to this town, or only 3 decades' worth, but it's where you'll find people who are actually from the country you're visiting (and you thought you were in Miami Beach!). The city hall and municipal offices are all located here.

Which is not to suggest that Cancún City is without facilities for visitors. Far from it. Concentrated here are a modern bus terminal, the tourist information office, the most banks and currency exchanges—and all the inexpensive hotels. Moreover, soaking up local color can involve such tourist-friendly activities as taking in a bullfight, eating in an "authentic" Mexican restaurant, and shopping at the open-air handicrafts stalls lining the main street, Avenida Tulum. You're not on the beach here, but several hotels run free shuttles for guests to beach clubs in the hotel zone.

In a nutshell . . .

➤ The hotels are inexpensive.

➤ The restaurants and shops are cheap and unpretentious.

123

➤ It's closest of all to the airport.

➤ You can walk to many places you'll want to go.

but . . .

➤ Don't expect sumptuous living.

➤ Traffic is dense and noisy.

➤ There are no oceanview rooms.

➤ You'll have to take a cab or bus to where the glitzy tourist action is.

My Favorite Hotels from A to Z

Antillano
$. Cancún City.
This blocky white high-rise may not win any design awards, but it's cheap, centrally located, and has a friendly, accommodating staff. It also has some of the amenities of the luxury hotels, including a travel agency, a duty-free perfume shop, safety deposit boxes, and TVs with English-language channels. Rooms are brightened with pink floral bedspreads and drapes; the quietest ones face the pool.

Av. Tulum, corner of Claveles no. 1 SM-22. ☎ **98/84-1532.** *Fax 98/84-1878. E-mail: antillano@mpsnct.com.mx.* **Rack rate:** *$62 double. AE, DC, MC, V.*

Blue Bay Village
$$$. East/West Hotel Zone.
At this all-grownup all-inclusive—no kids under 16 allowed—you get a two-fer. You can eat and drink your way through the Blue Bay, where rooms are arranged in a red-tile-roofed low-rise, and then cross the bay to a marina resort and start all over again; there are six bars and seven restaurants in all, Chinese and Italian included. Choose from an activities menu of windsurfing, kayaking, snorkeling, tennis, and poolside scuba lessons. When it's time for a siesta, settle down in your colorful room, which somehow manages to make orange, red, green, blue, and salmon look harmonious (but pick one with an ocean view or you'll be staring at a wall). The "Crazy Bunch," as the staff call themselves, strut and sing on stage nightly. If you don't like the act, you can always duck out to one of the nearby bars.

Paseo Kukulkán, km 3.5. ☎ **800/BLUE-BAY** *or 98/83-0344. Fax 98/83-0904. www.bluebayresorts.com. E-mail: Cancun@bluebayresorts.com.* **Rack rate:** *$162 per person, double, including all meals, drinks, and activities. AE, MC, V. No children under 16 allowed.*

Caesar Park Beach & Golf Resort
$$$$$. North/South Hotel Zone.
Built with Japanese dinero, this sprawling resort attracts many Asian guests. You might not encounter the Royal Highnesses of Japan, Prince and Princess

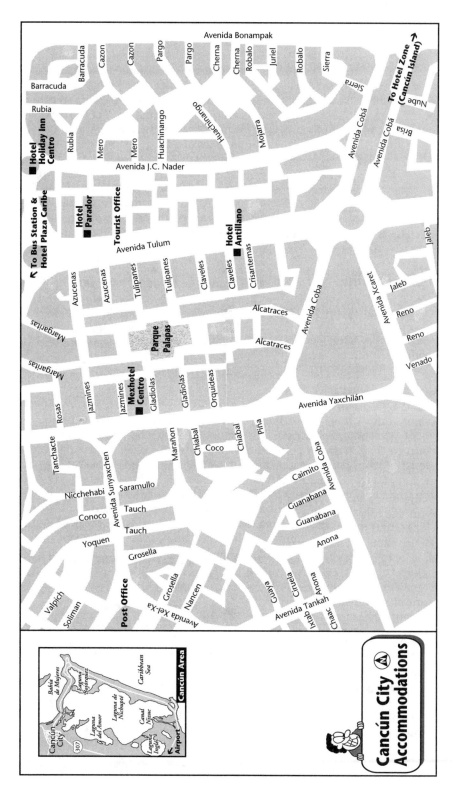

Cancún City Accommodations

Akishino, who made this their official residence on a state visit to Mexico, but you're likely to see Japanese lovebirds who've crossed several continents to have a mariachi wedding here. International business travelers also come for the state-of-the-art convention center. You can ramble along a 700-yard-long beach, plunge into any one of seven cascading swimming pools, play

18 holes of golf, get pampered in the fitness center, or graze your way through five restaurants; the best is Spices, which mixes Mexican, Argen-tinean, and Italian cuisine under one roof. Large, nicely proportioned rooms are done in earth tones, with contemporary wicker and hardwood furniture; all have terraces.

Best Bets for the Activity-Addicted

Club Med (North/South Hotel Zone, $$)

Caesar Park (North/South Hotel Zone, $$$$$)

Costa Real (East/West Hotel Zone, $$$)

Paseo Kukulkán, km 17, Retorno Lacandones. ☎ *800/228-3000 or 98/81-8000. Fax 98/81-8082.* **Rack rates:** *$370–$482 standard double; $482–$538 Royal Beach Club double (rates include continental breakfast and in-room coffee-makers). AE, DC, MC, V.*

Calinda Beach & Spa
$$$–$$$$. East/West Hotel Zone.
Rooms at this low-key, casual resort, part of a Mexican chain, are nothing to write home about, but the Calinda's tranquil bay-side beach is definitely worth an envy-inspiring postcard or 20. What with a deep-sea fishing fleet, two large pools, bars, and a pizza/steak/seafood restaurant at hand, you needn't part from this superb stretch of sand until nightfall (okay, you have to go indoors if you want to try the steam room or sauna at the spa). Of course, you might want to rent a bicycle and head to downtown, or take off for Isla Mujeres or Cozumel from the Playa Linda dock, just next door. Get back in time, and you'll catch a romantic trio and dancing at the lobby bar.

Paseo Kukulkán, lote C-1, km 4.5. ☎ *800/221-2222 or 98/83-1857. Fax 98/83-1857. www.hotelchoice.com.* **Rack rates:** *$218–$252 double. AE, MC, V.*

Dollars & Sense

With Camino Real's More Mexico for Less packages, the longer you stay, the more your room rates go down.

 Camino Real
$$$$. North/South Hotel Zone.
Here you can be as extroverted or as introverted as you wanna be. Step out the door and you're within walking distance of fancy shops, trendy restaurants, and happening nightlife. When you tire of hoi polloi, stroll the long, hacienda-like hallway to your marble-floored room, where you can lounge in a high-backed raffia chair or take a siesta

on your balcony's hammock. You can even retreat to a secluded beach (the hotel's also got a more social one). Ease your way back toward the human race by dipping into one of the hotel's nine bars and restaurants—Maria Bonita is the best (see chapter 16, "The Best of Cancún's Dining Scene"); by a fashionable hour, you should be ready for Azucar, the hotel's no-holds-barred Cuban dance club (see "What to Do When the Sun's Gone Down" in chapter 15). A great kids' program lets you decide how much time you want to spend with your offspring, too (or should I say how much time you can force them into spending with you).

Punta Cancún, between the Fiesta Americana Coral Beach and Hyatt Regency hotels. ☎ **800/7-CAMINO** *or 98/83-0100. Fax 98/83-1730. www.caminoreal. com/Cancun/. E-mail: cun@caminoreal.com.* **Rack rates:** *$325–$347 double. Two children 12 or under stay in the same room with parents for free. AE, DC, MC, V.*

Casa Turquesa
$$$$$. North/South Hotel Zone.
You may not be royalty or a super-celeb like many of the guests who hole up at this intimate, mansion-like hotel, but if you're willing to shell out for one of the 33 sumptuous suites, you can pretend to be. Each of the rooms is a self-contained pampering station, with a full bar; 24-hour maid and butler service; on-call massages, pedicures, and manicures; a video/CD library; and a balcony with a private Jacuzzi—ideal for stargazing. The best of the three restaurants is the subtly named Celebrity (see chapter 16), a gourmet dining room. The pool, surrounded by sun-shading pavilions, is a lot more inviting than the micro beach below it. If you get the urge to shop, the Plaza Kukulkán mall is a 5-minute walk away. Should you need anything else, just waggle your finger at the concierge.

Best Bets for a Romantic Retreat

Casa Turquesa (North/South Hotel Zone, $$$$$)

Fiesta Americana (East/West Hotel Zone, $$$$)

Hyatt Cancún Caribe (North/South Hotel Zone, $$$$$)

Paseo Kukulkán, km 13.5. ☎ **888/528-8300** *or 98/85-2924. Fax 98/85-2922. E-mail: Casaturquesa@sybcom.com.* **Rack rates:** *$381–$594 double. Honeymoon packages available. AE, MC, V.*

Club Med
$$. North/South Hotel Zone.
Mexico's first all-inclusive resort, Club Med is none the worse for wear, and still offers you the most for your hard-earned pesos. Set on a secluded peninsula at the far southern tip of the hotel zone, this country-clubbish property is far from the malls. You'll have more than enough to keep you busy here, however: tennis, waterskiing, windsurfing, and sailing, and, if you're willing to pay extra, scuba diving, deep-sea fishing, and horseback riding. Or check out one of the newest residents, Elvis, an alligator who likes snoozing in the

lagoon. Activities—well away from Elvis—are very spread out, so that even when the resort is booked solid, it never feels crowded. Average-sized guest rooms, which look onto the lagoon, gardens, or ocean, are in two- and three-story buildings; ask for one on the lowest floor if you don't like stairs.

Paseo Kukulkán, km 22 at Punta Nizac. ☎ ***800/258-2633*** *or 98/85-2900. Fax 98/85-2290.* **Rack rate:** *$111 per person, per night standard double (including all meals, drinks, and most activities). AE, DC, MC, V. No children under 12 accepted.*

Extra! Extra!

The Costa Real is a Spring Break fave. If you're over 25, you'll probably want to avoid it—and the rest of Cancún, for that matter—while the college kids on holiday wreak havoc on the island.

Costa Real
$$$. East/West Hotel Zone.

Not for the reclusive. At this hang-loose place, catering to a nonstop barrage of tour groups, you'll encounter a tutti-frutti blend of singles and Gen X couples—Brits, Canadians, South Americans, Oklahomans—who come for the great location and the best-priced rooms on this side of the hotel zone. A relentlessly upbeat staff programs games and contests around the pool all day long (fortunately, the nearby rooms are well insulated), and there's lots of beer swilling and mingling at the congenial lobby/sports bar. Free buses to different discos and bars move the party elsewhere at night. The cheerful, good-sized rooms get plenty of sunlight; the best ones are in the second tower, closest to the beach. If you want to bring the action inside, book a studio or suite with a full kitchen.

Paseo Kukulkán, km 4.5, across from La Boom disco. ☎ ***800/543-7556*** *or 98/83-2155. Fax 98/83-3974. E-mail: bestday@bestday.bestday.com.* **Rack rates:** *$189 standard double, $212 studio double. AE, MC, V.*

 ## El Pueblito
$$. North/South Hotel Zone.

One of Cancún's most Mexicano resorts, this moderately-priced all-inclusive has a low-key island ambience and an old-fashioned, gracious staff. During the day, most of the guests congregate in the long, meandering pool, which flows down to a thatched-roof restaurant on the shore. Come sunset, there's a mass exodus for the beach bar. Guest rooms are tucked away in clusters of three-story buildings (sans elevators) that face the Caribbean. They're nothing special, but do have oversized marble baths. If you want a balcony, request it at check-in. Kids activities aren't organized, but older children take to the toboggan water slide, while the littler ones splash around the nursery pool. Free fun is limited to tennis, kayaking, windsurfing, and nightly shows, but everyone here takes the maxim "Eat, drink, and be merry" seriously.

Paseo Kukulkán, km 17.5. ☎ *98/85-0422. Fax 98/85-0731. E-mail: pueblito@mail.interacces.com.mx.* **Rack rate:** *$134 per person, double (includes meals, drinks, activities except motorized water sports). AE, MC, V.*

Fiesta Americana
$$$$. East/West Hotel Zone.

This charming Mediterranean-style hotel, with its arches and sunny multihued facade, is more intimate than most of Cancún's luxury properties. It was originally designed for honeymooners, who still come and make goo-goo eyes at each other at the romantic lobby bar at night, but they're joined by families and less privacy-minded couples who like the proximity to the hottest shops, restaurants, and nightlife, not to mention the hotel's excellent beachside water sports concession. Dining options range from formal to casual to bathing suits at the swim-up bar. Spacious rooms have conventional modern furnishings; the best ones face Isla Mujeres.

Dollars & Sense

Check out the Fiesta Break packages. They can include such things as round-trip airfare from New York or L.A. and hotel transfers; free board and food for kids under 12 who stay in a room with their parents and Fiesta Kids Club (in season); and adult meal plans.

Paseo Kukulkán, km 7.5. ☎ *800/343-7821 or 98/83-1400. Fax 98/83-2502. www.fiestaweb.com.mex. E-mail: reser@fiestamericana.com.* **Rack rate:** *$273 double. AE, MC, V.*

Holiday Inn Centro
$$. Cancún City.

What distinguishes this Holiday Inn from, say, a Holiday Inn in New Jersey, is its low-slung Mexican colonial architecture, with loads of arches, massive pillars, and wrought-iron balconies. Once inside, however, your room's generic rattan furniture and flowery bedspreads won't give many clues to where you are. But the brand name says reliability, which is exactly what the business travelers and seniors who come here want. Sun worshippers take to the pool in the tropical garden, where a breakfast buffet is served, or hop the free shuttle to the hotel's beach. If you're taking an excursion from Cancún, it's convenient to have the ticket office of the first-class Elite bus company just outside the door.

Kids Best Bets for Families

Camino Real (North/South Hotel Zone, $$$$)

El Pueblito (North/South Hotel Zone, $$)

Ritz Carlton (North/South Hotel Zone, $$$$$)

Westin Regina (North/South Hotel Zone, $$$$)

Av. Nadar 1. ☎ *800/HOLIDAY or 98/87-4455. Fax 98/84-7954.* **Rack rate:** *$140 double. AE, DC, MC, V.*

129

Hyatt Cancún Caribe Villas & Resort
$$$$$. North/South Hotel Zone.
This tony boutique hotel reinvented itself after Hurricane Gilbert passed through in 1988. Completely redone from its beach garden to its dinnerware, it emerged as a chic hideaway for privacy seekers, particularly honeymooners and celebrities. All rooms in the crescent-shaped building have balconies facing the Caribbean and stylish decor in non-intrusive colors. The exclusive and more expensive Regency Club *casitas* (little houses) provide extra amenities—private concierge, pools, and jacuzzis. Of the three dining rooms, the finest is the Blue Bayou, which conjures up Cajun and Creole cuisine. Many folks compensate for any extra calories by taking to the jogging path, tennis courts, or 800-square-meter pool afterward. If you need to berth your yacht, there's a marina, too.

Paseo Kukulkán, km 10.5. ☎ ***800/233-1234*** *or 98/83-0044. Fax 98/831349.* ***Rack rates:*** *$364 standard double; Regency Club $437. AE, DC, MC, V.*

Yo, Gringo!
You may beat the prices in summer, but you won't necessarily beat the crowds. Come in July and August, and you'll have to compete with vacationing Mexican school kids for sailboats and jet skis.

Meliá Cancún Beach & Spa Resort
$$$$–$$$$$. North/South Hotel Zone.
Hotel in a jungle? No, jungle in a hotel—or at least it feels terribly tropical in the Meliá's atrium lobby, with its 8,500 square feet of lush gardens and streams. The waterfalls cascading down the entrance of this stunning pyramid-shaped property also add to the feeling you're in Mayan territory. You can sacrifice yourself to a snake-shaped pool (the second-largest in Cancún), laze on a sundeck, or play the executive golf course and then retreat to a luxurious, jumbo room, terrace streaming with tropical flowers. At Cancún's only spa with European-type services, you can get pampered from head-to-toe in a private cubicle lit with candles. Feeling truly sybaritic? Book a massage under the stars in a pavilion glowing with torches.

Paseo Kukulkán, km 16.5. ☎ ***800/33-MELIA*** *or 98/85-1160. Fax 98/85-1263. www.solmelia.es.* ***Rack rates:*** *$325–$364 double. AE, DC, MC, V. Spa and golf packages available.*

MexHotel
$. Cancún City.
European tour groups like this charming little lodge, part of a Mexican chain, and it wins my vote for best downtown value, too. It's got a quiet location on a residential street 2 blocks from Avenida Tulum, a nice staff, and attractive rooms, with carved wooden furniture, stucco walls, and bathrooms large enough to do a Mexican hat dance in. The pool is flanked by a pretty

flagstone patio, but most guests shuttle over to MexHotel's fancy oceanfront resort, where those who've opted for the meal program can eat and drink from 10am to 4pm. A cheerful Mexican restaurant, 24-hour medical service, money exchange, and an on-site travel agency are other perks.

Av. Yaxchilan 31. ☎ **888/594-6835** *or 98/84-3078. Fax 98/84-3478. E-mail: mexhotel@sybcom.com.mx.* **Rack rates:** *$78 double; meal plan $50 per person extra; children under 8 free, half-price for children 8–14. MC, V.*

Omni Cancún Hotel & Villas
$$$$–$$$$$. North/South Hotel Zone.
Perched on a bluff between the ocean and lagoon, this pretty, quiet resort hotel prides itself on personalized service—and the only Jacuzzi beach bar in Cancún. An Indiana Jones–style environment, replete with pseudo–rain forest, Mayan cave, and hammocks, this is where most of the 30- to 40-somethings mingle for some serious margarita sipping and nacho munching. Rooms are chockful of classy amenities—sun terraces, cushy robes, floor-to-ceiling mirrors, and cool marble floors. Start the day with a break-fast buffet at the colorful La Paloma coffee shop, catch a burger or fajitas later at the pool, and at night, dine by romantic candlelight at Da Vinci, the Italian/Mexican specialty restaurant. Let-it-all-hang-out beach barbecues and Mexican fiestas are also on the agenda. On-site activities are limited to pool splashing and beach volleyball, but there's a water sports center right down the road.

Paseo Kukulkán, L-48, km 16.5. ☎ **800/THE-OMNI** *or 98/85-0714. Fax 98/ 85-0059.* **Rack rates:** *$280–$381 double. AE, MC, V.*

Parador
$. Cancún City.
This nondescript hotel behind a noisy street bar has rock-bottom rates and proximity to good restaurants to recommend it. The clean, air-conditioned rooms face a narrow, grassy courtyard that leads to a postage-stamp-sized pool and an even tinier pool for tots.

Av. Tulum, no. 26. ☎ **98/84-0143.** *Fax 98/84-9712.* **Rack rate:** *$46 double; promotional rates available year-round. MC, V.*

Plaza Caribe
$. Cancún City.
Peacocks strut their stuff in the manicured gardens of this appealing Best Western, across the street from the bus station. Families mingle here with local politicians who appreciate the hotel's proximity to the business district and like to entertain in its old-style Mexican restaurant. It's usually only the pols who retire later to the somewhat garish, rowdy bar. Fortunately, the smallish rooms are far removed from the noise; all face the garden or the pool.

Av. Tulum and Uxmal. ☎ **800/528-1234** *or 98/84-1377. Fax 98/84-6352. E-mail: plazacbe@Cancun.rce.com.mx.* **Rack rate:** *$67 double. AE, DC, MC, V.*

131

Dollars & Sense

With the Presidente's Leisure Option package, book a minimum of 2 nights from December through April and you'll start racking up credits toward meals, drinks, airport transfers, and so on.

Presidente Inter-Continental

$$$$–$$$$$. East/West Hotel Zone.

You could initially mistake the Presidente, with its striking, contemporary lobby, for a modern art museum: A giant slab of marble is bisected by a reflecting pool, and walkways slope down to the reception area. Of course, art museums don't have swimming pools and hot tubs landscaped into lush gardens, a wonderfully tranquil beach, tennis courts, a health club, a full gamut of water toys, and bust-loose theme parties like Friday's "Caribbean Night." Enjoy seafood specialties at the thatched-roof palapa restaurant or light meals at an indoor coffee shop. Rooms are spacious, with attractive unfinished pine furniture; you'll pay more if you want a whirlpool tub or Club Floor privileges, which include free breakfast and snacks and drinks all day long.

Paseo Kukulkán, km 7. ☎ ***800/327-0200*** *or 98/83-0200. Fax 98/83-2515.*
Rack rates: *$302–$354 double. Children 13 and under stay free in parents' room. AE, DC, MC, V.*

Dollars & Sense

Don't forget—it'll cost you an arm and a leg to make a direct phone call to the United States from your room (see chapter 10, "Crossing the Border & What to Expect on the Other Side," for details). In Cancún, you can buy a calling card similar to the ones used in the United States; they're sold in denominations of $10 and $20. Use any Touch-Tone phone to make your call and you'll save from 40% to 70%.

 ## Ritz-Carlton

$$$$$. North/South Hotel Zone.

Probably the most prestigious hotel in Cancún, the peach-colored Ritz-Carlton might first appear to be a city slicker, what with its conservative drawing room–style lobby. One look at the powder-sand beach out back, though, and you'll quickly remember you're in the tropics. You're also in yuppie heaven: The Cigar Lounge sells every kind of serious smoke you can imagine, including Cubans, and a tequila tasting room next door has 120 ways for you to get snockered (don't worry—the staff has been trained to put you quietly to bed). In-room desks and computer outlets appeal to the expense-account business travelers, and leisure-minded couples revel in the

24-hour room service, poolside massages, and romantic Club Grill (see chapter 16, "The Best of Cancún's Dining Scene"). And parents love dropping off their children at the excellent Kids' Camp.

Retorno del Rey, off Paseo Kulkukán, km 13.5. ☎ *800/241-3333 or 98/85-0808. Fax 98/85-1015.* **Rack rates:** *$409–$554 double. Honeymoon packages available. AE, DC, MC, V.*

Westin Regina
$$$$. North/South Hotel Zone.

A striking minimalist structure by Mexico's leading architect, Ricardo Legorreta, the Westin is ultra-stylish through and through. A hand-picked collection of Mexican crafts lines the long, austere hallways, and rooms are oversized and fashionably underdecorated, with bold blue accents in rugs and chairs. The more expensive ones in the pink tower boast lavish Berber throw rugs, oak furnishings, and marble terraces with chaise longues. You're far from the hotel zone action if you stay here—it's 20 minutes by cab to the intense shopping and bar-hopping zone—but six watering holes and restaurants, as well as deep-sea fishing, snorkeling, windsurfing, and scuba-certification classes should keep you occupied. There's a good kids program, too, and beach lovers get double the pleasure with both a sandy lagoon and the Caribbean shore.

Paseo Kukulkán, km 20. ☎ *800/228-3000 or 98/85-0086. Fax 98/85-0779. www.westin.com. E-mail: westin@sybcom.com.* **Rack rates:** *$224–$280 double. AE, DC, MC, V.*

No Room at the Inn? Check Out One of These . . .

North/South Hotel Zone

➤ **Krystal.** At the tip-top of this stretch, it's where the action is and loaded with things to do. Paseo Kukulkán, km 7.5, lote 9. ☎ **800/231-9860.** $$$$

➤ **Fiesta Americana Condesa.** Midway down the strip, friendly and laid-back with a full menu of amenities and activities. Paseo Kukulkán, km 16.5. ☎ **800/343-7821.** $$$$

East/West Hotel Zone

➤ **Fiesta Americana Coral Beach.** A posh, plush giant of a place, with miles of embellished marble floors. Punta Cancún, Paseo Kukulkán, km 9.5. ☎ **800/343-7821.** $$$$

Cancún City

➤ **Howard Johnson Kokai.** A business hotel near the main action, with the scaled-down facilities of a luxury hostel—pool, restaurant, bars, car rental, and free transportation to the beach. Av. Uxmal 26, SM 2-A. ☎ **800/ 654-2000.** $$

Quick Picks: Cancún's Hotels at a Glance
Hotel Index by Price

$

Antillano (Cancún City)

MexHotel (Cancún City)

Parador (Cancún City)

Plaza Caribe (Cancún City)

$$

Club Med (North/South Hotel Zone)

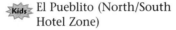 El Pueblito (North/South Hotel Zone)

Holiday Inn Centro (Cancún City)

$$$

Blue Bay Village (East/West Hotel Zone)

Costa Real (East/West Hotel Zone)

$$$–$$$$

Calinda Beach & Spa (East/West Hotel Zone)

$$$$

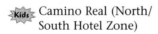 Camino Real (North/South Hotel Zone)

Fiesta Americana (East/West Hotel Zone)

Kids Westin Regina (North/South Hotel Zone)

$$$$–$$$$$

Meliá Cancún Beach & Spa Resort (North/South Hotel Zone)

Omni Cancún Hotel & Villas (North/South Hotel Zone)

Presidente Inter-Continental (East/West Hotel Zone)

$$$$$

Caesar Park Beach & Golf Resort (North/South Hotel Zone)

Casa Turquesa (North/South Hotel Zone)

Hyatt Cancún Caribe Villas & Resort (North/South Hotel Zone)

Kids Ritz-Carlton (North/South Hotel Zone)

Hotel Index by Location

Cancún City

Antillano $

Holiday Inn Centro $$

MexHotel $

Parador $

Plaza Caribe $

East/West Hotel Zone

Blue Bay Village $$$

Calinda Beach & Spa $$$–$$$$

Costa Real $$$

Fiesta Americana $$$$

Presidente Inter-Continental $$$$–$$$$$

North/South Hotel Zone

Caesar Park Beach & Golf Resort $$$$$

Kids Camino Real $$$$

Casa Turquesa $$$$$

Club Med $$

Kids El Pueblito $$

Hyatt Cancún Caribe Villas & Resort $$$$$

Meliá Cancún Beach & Spa Resort $$$$–$$$$$

Omni Cancún Hotel & Villas $$$$–$$$$$

Kids Ritz-Carlton $$$$$

Kids Westin Regina $$$$

135

Chapter 14

Finding Your Way Around Cancún

In This Chapter

➤ What to expect when you arrive

➤ The lay of the land

➤ Getting around

➤ Getting information

➤ Quick Facts: Cancún A to Z

Okay, so you needed a passport to get to Cancún, but of all the Mexican destinations you might have chosen, this is the one least likely to send you into culture shock. The greenback is almost as readily accepted as the peso, and if your Spanish is limited to *"una Corona, por favor,"* you won't be at a huge disadvantage.

That said, entering a foreign country compounds the unfamiliarity factor that kicks in whenever you visit a strange city. Not to worry—in this chapter, you'll find the lowdown on this tourist-friendly town.

You've Just Arrived— Now What?

Because of the growing number of flights into Cancún International

Yo, Gringo!

The portable storage lockers in Cancún's airport are like magician's rabbits—now you see them, now you don't. When they're available (and visible), they're in the departure terminal against the far right wall.

Airport, located 9 miles from the heart of downtown, facilities are constantly being expanded. That's good news—for the future. The bad news is that, for the time being, you may be herded into an arrivals area that looks more like a construction site than a terminal. Similarly, while the airport is still small and easy to get around, there's not much there: Such basics as a hotel reservations desk and visitor information kiosk are lacking.

Time-Savers

If there are three or more of you traveling together, you might want to shell out the extra dollars for a taxi. With so many hotels in Cancún for the collective van to stop at, it can easily take an hour to get to your room if you're at the end of the run. (Check the map in the previous chapter to see where your hotel is positioned in relation to the airport.)

The airport has different wings for arrivals and departures, but the international and national sections are under the same roof. The facility's sole ATM, in the departure area across the floor from the Mexicana check-in counter, accepts Cirrus, MasterCard, Visa, and PLUS network cards. (Another ATM is scheduled to be added to the international arrivals area.) There are also two *casas de cambio* (money exchange booths), open daily from 9am to 9pm.

After you've picked up your baggage, continue on to the exit, where a tiny desk sells tickets for *colectivos*—air-conditioned collective vans—and taxis. Collectives generally cost $7.50 per person, depending on how far away your hotel is, and private cabs are $27.50 a drop-off for up to four people.

Dollars & Sense

Don't be tempted to pick up souvenirs in the airport. With few exceptions, everything is as much as 50% higher here, and the selection is extremely limited. You'll have a far better choice of duty-free perfumes and cosmetics on the island, too.

Orientation: You Are Here

Cancún is divided into two parts, Isla Cancún (or Cancún Island) and, on the mainland, Cuidad Cancún (or Cancún City). Cancún City—also called downtown or *centro*—is where you'll find all the community services and many of the tourist facilities, as well as inexpensive hotels and restaurants. All are conveniently clustered within a 9-square-block area around Avenida Tulum, the town's main street. Avenida Tulum stretches south to the airport and continues on to join with the highway heading even farther south to Belize, hitting beach resorts such as Playa del Carmen along the way. Take Tulum north from town and you'll come to the intersection of the highway to Mérida and the road leading to Puerto Juárez and the ferry to Isla Mujeres.

You can easily walk anywhere you want downtown—if you can figure out how to get there. Streets aren't laid out in a grid pattern as they are in most Mexican towns, and addresses are defined by the number of the building lot (*lote*) and block (*manzana* or "m") or cluster of blocks (*supermanzana* or "sm"), an arcane vestige of Cancún's early years. You'll need a good map to help you out.

Avenida Cobá, which angles southwest off Avenida Tulum, leads from downtown via a short bridge to Isla Cancún, a 14-mile-long barrier island shaped like the number 7. Cobá turns into Paseo Kukulkán, the island's main drag. On the southern end of the island, just beyond Punta Nizac, Paseo Kukulkán bridges back to the mainland, joining up with Avenida Tulum right before the turnoff to the airport.

Both the top and bottom of Cancún Island make up the *zona hoteleria* or hotel zone; I've gone into detail about the differences between the two sections in chapter 13, "Choosing the Place to Stay That's Right For You." Following Paseo Kukulkán, the only road on the island, is far easier than pronouncing it (say: koo-cool-*CAN*). Most addresses refer to the distance in kilometers from a point on the mainland, near downtown, termed km 1; km 20, the end of the road, is Punta Nizac. You'll occasionally see a lot number address, too, but it's usually accompanied by a kilometer reference.

How to Get from Here to There (and How Not To)

You don't need to rent a car in Cancún. Taxis and buses are far better alternatives—especially since car break-ins are the only real crimes that occur in Cancún.

Yo, Gringo!

You'll see lots of signs for moped rentals around Cancún. I strongly suggest you ignore them. Traffic is congested, and there are lots of loco—sometimes drunk—drivers around. If you get hit, you'll be responsible for the cost of replacing the damaged vehicle, as you will if the moped gets stolen.

If you do decide to rent a moped despite my warnings, wear your crash helmet, and read the fine print in your contract regarding liability.

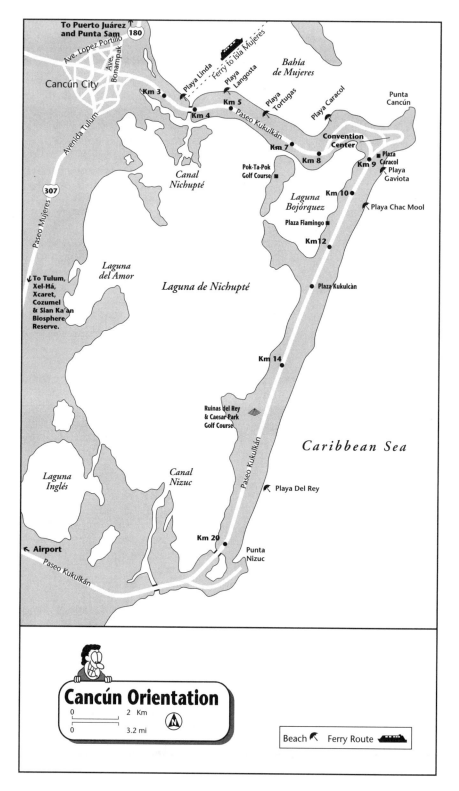

Traveling by Taxi

Taxis in Cancún are the most expensive in the country—there's been a lot of grumbling lately among residents, who can't afford to use them. But strong taxi union bosses set the fares, which are determined by zones that go from A (downtown) up to E (hotel zone). In the hotel zone, the fare is a minimum of $3 to $5 a pop, even if you go 1 block. There's no negotiating with cabs that you pick up at hotel taxi *sitios* (taxi stands); fares are usually posted near the hotel entrance. It'll run you about $15 to get from one end of the hotel zone to the other via hotel cab, and getting to the airport can cost as much as $19. Cabs that roam the hotel zone are about half as expensive—but remember to negotiate. Taxis downtown are a bit cheaper yet and charge about $2 minimum for a drop-off.

> ### Dollars & Sense
>
> Avoid the price-gouging taxi stand at the bus terminal, which banks on arriving tourists' not knowing cab fares. Walk half a block to Avenida Tulum and flag a street taxi down.

Traveling by Bus

Buses have become increasingly popular with Cancún tourists, who are tired of constant taxi use withering their wallets. These public vehicles are modern, air-conditioned, and rarely crowded, and they run a civilized 24 hours. For around 40¢ you can get from the southern outreaches of Punta Nizac to downtown. Exact fare (3 pesos) is appreciated by the drivers, although they will change bills up to 20 pesos or even a dollar bill if you've run out of local currency (change will be in pesos, though). You'll see bus stops—the sign with a picture of a bus is a dead giveaway—in front of practically every major hotel and mall along the hotel zone and every 3 blocks downtown. Take buses marked Ruta 1 or Ruta 2 ("Hoteles") for traveling back and forth between downtown and the hotel zone; take Ruta 8 from downtown to go to Puerto Juárez or Punta Sam for the Isla Mujeres ferries. It takes about an hour to get from Punta Nizac to downtown.

> ### Road Show
>
> Your bus can turn into a traveling road show when a freelance guitarist or two jump on board (feel free to join in when they get around to singing "La Bamba"). A hat is passed around afterward; pop in a coin if you liked the music.

Where to Get More Information & Guidance

The friendly bilingual staff at the **State of Quintana Roo Tourism Information Center** (Av. Tulum 26, next to the Inverlat bank; ☎ 98/ 84-8073) dispense maps, magazines, brochures, and other Cancún data as well as limited information on some of the state's other tourist spots, such as Isla Mujeres, Cozumel, and Playa del Carmen. It is open every day from

9am until 9pm. This office reports to the main **State of Quintana Roo Tourism Office** (Palacio Municipal or City Hall, Avenida Tulum, 1½ blocks east of the information center; ☎ **98/84-3238**), which does not have as much printed material; it's open 9am to 4pm Monday to Friday. The *Cancún Tips* (see below) folks set up informal tourist booths at the Plaza Caracol shopping center in the hotel zone and in Cancún City at the corner of Avenida Tulum and Chichén Itzá, but don't have materials on facilities or attractions that have neglected to advertise with them.

The Printed Page

You can pick up complimentary copies of the full-color, pocket-size *Cancún Tips,* published four times a year, at the tourist information center and, theoretically, at all the hotels in Cancún; it's also passed out when you arrive at the airport. It gives details on hotels, restaurants, and nightlife, as well as some useful general facts. Take what you read with a grain of salt, as it's hard to distinguish the text from the ads. A tabloid-sized *Cancún Tips* with good feature stories on the area is also free, but hard to find unless you drop into the tourism offices.

No Hablo Español?

If your Spanish is of the shaky, high school variety, carry a slip of paper with the name and address of your destination when you board a bus. Use it to show the driver (whose English may bear a strong resemblance to your Spanish) where you want to go.

Cancún A to Z: Facts at Your Fingertips

American Express: Av. Tulum 208 and Agua (☎ **98/84-5441**).

ATMs: Most of the banks downtown on Avenida Tulum have ATMs that are connected to the Cirrus, PLUS, MasterCard, and Visa networks; they include Banamex, Banca Serfin, Banco del Atlantico, Bancomer, and Inverlat. You'll find other cash machines in the east/west hotel zone at Plaza Terramar, Plaza El Parian, and Plaza Caracol.

No Time for Time-Shares

Although they've been banned from doing so, many time-share sellers set themselves up as tourist information booths. Only the places described above are legit; if you don't want to get sucked into an hour-long, high-pressure spiel, steer clear of the others.

Baby-Sitters: Most hotels offer baby-sitting services for approximately $8 per hour.

Business Hours: Offices are open 9am to 2pm and 4 to 7pm weekdays and sometimes 9am to 2pm on Saturday; shops generally open daily from 10am to 9pm, and malls from 10am to 10pm.

Currency Exchange: The banks noted in the ATM section, above, exchange dollars and travelers' checks, but only from 10am to noon or 1pm. Much more convenient are the *casas de cambio* (exchange booths), concentrated downtown along Avenida Tulum and in and around the shopping malls in the east/west hotel zone. They offer a similar exchange rate to the banks, but have longer hours (most are open until 5pm), and exchanges involve no paperwork or lines. Your hotel will also happily change dollars for you, but at rates way below those at exchange houses and banks. In fact, just about every business in Cancún, including taxi drivers and bus drivers, will trade dollars for pesos, but you'll get nowhere near market value.

Doctors: Most hotels have an English-speaking doctor either on staff or on 24-hour call; if yours doesn't, the reception desk should be able to find one for you. In a non-emergency, you can also contact the State Tourist Information Center (☎ 98/84-8073) or the U.S. Consul (see below) for a referral.

Dentists: The medical staff in your hotel or the State Tourist Information Center (☎ 98/84-8073) should be able to direct you to a good tooth doctor.

English-Language Newspapers/Magazines: The *Miami Herald,* International Edition, is often distributed free at hotel front desks; you can also expect to find *USA Today,* the *New York Times,* and the English-language *Mexico City News* at most hotel gift shops (you'll pay double what you'd pay at home, however). Hotel newsstands also carry the slicker U.S. magazines and paperbacks (mostly romances). The two branches of **Fama** (downtown on Av. Tulum 105 between Tulipanes and Claveles, ☎ 98/84-6586; and the east/west hotel zone at Plaza Kukulkán, no phone) offer the best selection of English-language books and newspapers.

Emergencies/Fire: Dial ☎ 06, Mexico's equivalent of 911 in the United States.

Hospitals: Total Assist (Claveles 5 at Avenida Tulum, downtown; ☎ 98/84-1092 or 98/84-8116), open 24 hours, treats emergencies and has bilingual doctors. **Hospital Americano** (Viento 15 SM 4, downtown DT; ☎ 98/84-6133) is also open 24 hours, but you may not find an English-speaking doctor on call.

Maps: The tourist office has maps, and you'll find more than adequate ones in the complimentary copies of *Cancún Tips.* The travel agency and concierge at most hotels can also supply you with workable maps.

Pharmacies: Downtown's **Farmacia El Canto** (Av. Yaxchilán 36, at Sunyaxchen, next to the Caribe Internacional Hotel; ☎ 98/84-4083) has a 24-hour prescription service. You'll also find plenty of drugstores, open until 10pm, at the major shopping malls in the hotel zone.

Police: Call ☎ 98/84-1913. The **Consumer Protection Agency** (Procuraduria del Proteccion del Consumidor, Av. Cobá 10, downtown; ☎ 98/84-2634 or 98/84-2701) also handles tourists' crime complaints.

Post Office: The main post office is downtown at Avenida Sunyaxchen and Avenida Xel-Há (☎ **98/84-1418**).

Safety: Cancún has a relatively low crime rate, but the occasional report of theft does surface. When visiting here, as when traveling anywhere else, don't leave your common sense at home. See chapter 10, "Crossing the Border & What to Expect on the Other Side," for additional advice.

Special Events: Cancún celebrates the traditional holidays outlined in chapter 2, "When Should I Go?" although not always with as much fanfare as you'll see in some of the older cities with larger churches. When it comes to contemporary entertainment, however, Cancún is on top of things. The city's Jazz Festival, held every May since 1991, has seen greats such as Wynston Marsalis, Stanley Clark, Gato Barbieri, and Glover Washington perform in the past. Contact the **Cancún Hotel Association** (☎ **98/ 84-2853**) for current information.

Telephone: The telephone area code for Cancún is 98. To call long distance within Mexico (abbreviated *lada*), dial 01, then the area code, and then the number. To call the United States, dial 001 and then the area code and number.

U.S. Consul: Marruecos Building 31, Av. Nadar 40, downtown (☎ **98/ 83-0272**), is open 9am to 1pm Monday to Friday.

Fun On & Off the Beach

The computer techies who put Cancún on the map were right on the money. The island's powdery white-sand beaches and blue-green Caribbean waters attract more tourists than any other resort in the republic. I'll give you a rundown of the best stretches of sand and ways to enjoy the water—with and without getting wet (should you feel your feline side emerging).

Cancún doesn't just sparkle with sun and sea, but also with those superficial pleasures that (just admit it) you came here for—great shopping and endless nightlife. But the icing on the cake? You can have it all because Cancún is just a day trip from some interesting archaeological sites.

Hitting the Beaches
Apart from some coves and sand dunes, beaches run in an almost unbroken line from one end of the hotel zone to the other. There are no bad beaches, as far as width and color and softness of the sand are concerned, but the ones in the east/west hotel zone that face the Bay of Mujeres are safest for swimming. The water is calm and shallow for quite a distance with no unexpected drop-offs. Beaches on the north/south side, washed by the Caribbean Ocean, often experience rough waves and strong riptides and undertows.

What Color Is Your Beach Towel?

Once you've booked your hotel, you've more or less assigned yourself a plot of sand. By law, all beaches are public property in Mexico, but in practice, alert hotel security guards are trained to spot outsiders; if you don't have a hotel-issue guest towel in tow, you will be politely asked to leave. Some hotels are less strict than others, but it's not worth the hassle and potential humiliation. If you want to stray from your own beach, keep as far as possible from hotel entrances.

Playa Tortuga, Playa Linda, and **Playa Chac-Mool** are considered public beaches; they're where locals and tourists staying at shoreless downtown hotels come to soak up the rays. As you've no doubt figured out, *playa* is Spanish for "beach."

Bet You Didn't Know

The unique composition of Cancún's sand—made up of porous limestone fossils millions of years old—keeps it cool even in midday.

Bay Beaches on the East/West Hotel Zone

You'll need to visit **Playa Linda,** the farthest west (just before the bridge at km 4) of the bay-side beaches, if you want to board a shuttle for Isla Mujeres; in addition to the dock, there are several dive shops and snack bars. **Playa Langosta** (km 5), a cove protected by a small jetty near the Hotel Casa Maya, has a tour boat pier, and you'll also find sports concessions, shops, and restaurants here. Next comes **Playa Tortuga** (km 7.5), named for the sea turtle that's long since left for less-touristed nesting grounds. The changing rooms, public rest rooms, and restaurants are overrun with local families come Sunday and holidays; on its quietest days, it's still pretty unappealing. The last beach before the island dips down towards the Caribbean, **Playa Caracol** stretches for about a mile west to Punta Cancún, fronting the Fiesta Americana Coral Beach and Camino Real hotels in the thickest of the thick tourist zones. It's got restaurants, but no public facilities.

Yo, Gringo!

If you don't want to be bothered while sunbathing, don't give the nod to any beach peddlers. Show the slightest interest, and you'll soon have dozens of new friends converging on your beach blanket.

145

Bet You Didn't Know

Chac-Mool was the most important deity to the ancient Maya, who depended on rain for their crops; they offered human sacrifices in the god's honor at Chichén Itzá. It's unlikely that modern installers of Chac-Mool figures have either this grisly background or an invocation to rain in mind; Chac is always in a reclining position, so he looks like the god of relaxation.

Caribbean Beaches on the North/South Hotel Zone

Playa Chac-Mool (km 13) is identifiable by the stone figure of the Mayan rain god perched on a dune at the entrance; its showers, rest rooms, and other bather-friendly facilities make it as popular as Playa Tortuga with locals on the weekends. **Playa del Rey,** the last beach on the island before you reach Punta Nizac, is still the most unspoiled; the water looks almost blindingly blue and the stretch of sand that ends at Club Med seems even whiter than the rest.

Yo, Gringo!

The Caribbean has lethal undertows in certain areas. If you don't want to be a statistic, heed the warning flags put out by hotels to advise guests of swimming conditions:

White	Excellent
Green	Normal (safe)
Yellow	Changeable (exercise caution)
Black or Red	Unsafe (head for the pool, instead)

Lots of hotels also have lifeguards. Don't ignore their warnings, either.

Water Fun for Everyone

Angling for the big one? Eager to get the jump on some jet skis? Always wondered what's going on underwater? Whatever your fantasy water pursuit, Cancún's got it sussed. I'll give you the scoop on where to play—and how much you can expect to pay—in Cancún's kingdom by the sea.

Hooked on Fishing

Mother Nature keeps the water even-temperatured enough in Cancún to make some kind of fish or other happy year-round. The sea abounds with blue and striped marlin in April and May, with sailfish and dolphinfish March through September, and bluefin tuna in May. During the summer months, you'll find red snapper, tarpon, swordfish, kingfish, and wahoo most often on the line.

Bet You Didn't Know

Cancún has dozens of docks, and more are popping up each year as the volume of tourists increases. Most line up along the east/west hotel zone, where five major piers and several minor ones face the Bay of Mujeres. The north/south area has few marinas on the ocean side, but new aquatic centers are popping up along the lagoon where the water is smooth as glass and never gets temperamental.

Just head for the travel agency at your hotel or any of Cancún's marinas—I recommend **AquaWorld** (Paseo Kukulkán, km 15.2; ☎ 98/85-2288), **Aqua Tours** (Paseo Kukulkán, km 6.2; ☎ 98/83-0400), and the **Royal Yacht Club** (Paseo Kukulkán, km 16.5; ☎ 98/85-2930)—and hire yourself a fishing yacht and captain. He'll provide the bait, fishing tackles, fishing license, beverages, and a first mate. The price for a full day (8 hours) of deep-sea fishing starts at $500 for up to six people; for a half day (4 hours), prices go up from $250. If you didn't come with a group of friends and can't make any quick to share costs with you, you'll end up paying full price for the boat, no matter if it's half empty.

You'll get similar rates if you book in advance from the United States through **Ixtapa Sportsfishing Charters** (19 Depue Lane, Stroudsburg, PA 18360; ☎ **717/688-9466,** fax 717/688-955). Their vessels range from a 26-foot panga ($215 for 4 hours) to a 37-foot pace ($640 for 8 hours). The 8-hour excursions include lunch, and if you want to combine fishing with diving or sightseeing, the company can arrange for a fresh-fish barbecue at one of the local beaches or islands.

Sportsfishing Tipping Tips

It's customary to tip 10% to 15% of the total price of your charter, depending on the quality of service received. Give the money to the captain, who will split it with the mate.

If you don't want to make a large investment in time and money, climb aboard the **Asterix Water Taxi** (☎ **98/86-4847** or 98/86-4270). For $50 a person, you can join a fishing party of 50. The price includes bait and tackle and an open bar (sho who caresh what you reel in, anyway?). If you do catch something, the cook will gladly prepare it for dinner. Departures are at the unorthodox fishing hours of between 6pm and midnight from the Carlos 'n Charlie's marina.

Getting Revved Up

Want to try your water wings? Many hotels on the island have first-class aquatic concessions (the Westin Regina, Presidente Inter-Continental, Camino Real, and Caesar Park, all open to the public, are among the best); if yours doesn't, they'll direct you to one nearby.

You can also check out one of several water sports companies operating from marinas such as **AquaWorld** (see "Hooked on Fishing," above), which has Waverunners ($39 a half hour), water skis ($39 a half hour), kayaks ($14 an hour), and paddleboats ($22 an hour); **Aqua Fun** (Paseo Kukulkán, km 16.2; ☎ 98/85-3260) offers speedboats ($35 a half hour for two people), jet skis ($25 a half hour), and Waverunners ($39 a half hour). Prices vary a little from place to place, so shop around.

On a Parasail Built for Two . . .

Why parasail off into the sunset alone? For $35 per person, you and a friend can book the **Skyrider**, get strapped into what looks like a double-seated beach chair, and soar above the crowds together. The view is magnificent, the ride is exhilarating, and you don't even have to get wet—when you're through pretending to be a seagull, you'll be landed back on the boat deck. Although it's brought to you by AquaWorld (☎ **98/85-2288**), the ride can be booked through most travel agencies in town.

Coral Revenge

It takes coral 10 years to grow less than an inch. Reefs are very fragile and can be damaged easily by your touch. If you get too close, they might take revenge by giving you a nasty cut or sting.

Exploring the Big Blue Sea

If you've decided that life without scuba is all wet, you've come to the right place. The coral reefs in this area—part of an ecosystem that's second in size only to the Great Barrier Reef in Australia— are teeming with sea life and are considered to be the best in Mexico.

A lot of the resorts have classes for beginners that start out in the hotel pool. If you want to go all the way and get certified, **AquaWorld** (☎ 98/ 85-2288) offers PADI certification courses, which take 4 or 5 days and cost $300 (advanced certification) or $350 (open water certification). One-tank dives run $50 and twilight dives, $55. A 4-hour resort course with a one-tank dive is $80. **Scuba Cancún** (☎ 98/83-1011) and **Aqua Tours** (☎ 98/83-0400) also specialize in certification, resort courses, and diving excursions, at similar prices.

All these companies, as well as the travel agencies, also offer snorkeling trips. Most popular are the jaunts to Isla Mujeres (see "Side Trips: Getting Out of Cancún," below), where colorful tropical fish like to show off, or the Jungle Tours through the mangrove canals of the Cancún lagoons (around $40 per person for a 2½-hour excursion). If you want to snor-kel on your own, you can rent gear on Playa Tortuga or Punta Cancún for $10.

Time-Savers

If you are already a qualified diver, don't forget to bring proof of certification.

Catching a Wave (or Two)

You can matriculate from **Windsurfer Sailing School** (Club International, next to the Calinda Beach Hotel, Paseo Kukulkán, km 4.5; ☎ 98/84-3212), or just rent equipment ($12 per hour, $25 for the day). Classes, which cost $50, are held in Bahía de Mujeres. **AquaWorld** (☎ 98/85-2288), which operates from the lagoon side of the hotel zone, also offers windsurfing with or without lessons ($22 per class or $16.50 an hour without instruction).

On Deck: How to Enjoy the Waves without Getting Your Hair Wet

When you're ready to spend some time on the water instead of in it, I've got some swell—only calm ones, of course—suggestions for you.

Getting Soaked at Sunset

The *Cancún Queen* (☎ 98/85-2288), an air-conditioned Mississippi pad-dlewheeler with waiters duded up to look like riverboat gamblers, lays on a three-option sunset cruise: For $22, you can confine yourself to the liquid pleasures of the open bar (domestic drinks only) and snacks; for $43, you can enjoy a chicken or fish dinner in your sloshed state; or for $65, you can go for the whole enchilada—limitless drinks plus a lobster and steak meal. One way or another, you'll be loose for the dancing and group warmer-uppers, such as a limbo contest (with prizes). The cruise leaves daily at 6pm from the AquaWorld pier and lasts 3 hours. Small fries under 11 are half price.

It's a similar deal on the *Columbus* (☎ 98/83-1488), a replica of a Spanish galleon with waiters dressed as (what else?) swashbucklers. On this 3-hour lagoon cruise—it's astonishing on full-moon nights—you'll enjoy an open bar on an open-air deck, a lobster or steak dinner, and live music (brush up on those macarena moves). The *Columbus* cruise departs at 7:30pm from the Royal Mayan marina (next to the Captain's Cove restaurant) and costs $61.

🛈Kids Splish Splash

The splashiest new family aquatic park in the Caribbean, **Wet 'n' Wild** (Paseo Kukulkán, km 23, past the Club Med; ☎ **98/81-3000**), opened in 1997 with a full contingent of water toys—the standard slides, chutes, and toboggans as well as the more exotic Twister, Bubble Up, and Space Bowl. This U.S. franchise has its own beach and beach club, several dry-dock restaurants and snack bars, as well as swim-up bars and endless kids' sections. Admission ($18.50 for adults, $15.50 for children 12 and under, 5 and under free) includes everything except food and drink, a $3 locker fee, and $3 rental rate for inner tubes. Hours are 10am to 6pm September 1 to December 19, 10am to 7pm the rest of the year. To get here, you can catch the inexpensive bus at any downtown bus stop marked "Wet 'n' Wild."

If you're into themed entertainment, the best deal might be the **Caribbean Carnaval Night Cruise** (☎ 98/84-3760). You get to de-board the boat at Isla Mujeres, where a beach has been set aside for the inevitable open bar, buffet supper, and live band that plays 3 hours of tropical dance tunes. Fun and loopy activities such as a limbo contest may have you eating the sand, but the Mexican folkoric dance show should give you time to recover your equilibrium. The price is $55 for the 5-hour cruise, which leaves at 6pm from Fat Tuesday's dock, in the east/west hotel zone, across from Farandula's restaurant.

Claustrophobe Alert

If you're not keen on spending extended periods of time underwater in an enclosed space with other people, these trips may not be for you.

Glass-Bottomed Subs

For an hour and 20 minutes, the glass-bottomed submarine *Nautibus* (☎ 98/83-3552) glides over and around a coral reef dense with tropical fish. From 9:30am to 2pm, it departs every hour and a half from the Playa Linda pier. The price is $22; children 6 to 11 pay half and kids under 5 ride for free.

AquaWorld (☎ 98/85-2288) will send you off in a slick glass-bottomed boat to tiny Paradise Island, a slip of land off Punta Nizac just large enough to hold a restaurant, rest rooms, showers, and lockers. You can pay for just the air-conditioned underwater sightseeing trip ($28), or the trip plus lunch on the island ($39), or—if you decide at the last minute to get wet after all—get snorkeling thrown in for a total of $50. Rates include guides, instruction, and equipment; children under 12 are half price. Boats leave every hour from 9am to 3pm from the AquaWorld pier.

The above tours can be be booked through most hotel travel agencies, too, with little variation in price.

Keeping Your Head Above Water: Cancún's Top Attractions

As a newcomer on the scene, Cancún doesn't have much in the way of cultural activities—hey, if you wanted history, you would have gone to Mexico City—but it abounds in guilty pleasures such as shopping and nightlife. Crave a culture fix after all that indulgence? A daylong side trip will take you deep into into Mexico's past.

Olé! Bullfighting

Introduced centuries ago by the Spanish viceroys, bullfighting is about as engrained in Mexican culture as a shot of tequila with lime and salt. Die-hard aficionados know the ranches where the best bulls are bred, the background of all the top bullfighters, and the names of all the passes executed by their capes. You're not going to see the best of the best in Cancún: That's reserved for places like Mexico City. But who knows? One of the dedicated *novilleros* (novices) on the program might someday be a star. Just remember, if you go to a bullfight, that's exactly what you're going to see. So stay away if you're an animal lover, or hate the sight of blood.

Lotsa Lizards

Can-cún, in the Mayan language, means "Bowl of Snakes." You won't see any of these reptiles on the island—maybe because of a Mayan version of St. Patrick or the influx of tourists chased them away—but you *are* likely to spot lots of iguanas darting among the Ruinas de Rey.

Corridas (bullfights) take place every Wednesday at 3:30pm year-round. Tickets are $31 and can be purchased through a travel agency for the same price or at the Plaza de Toros where the bullfights take place (Avenida Bonampak and Sayil, downtown; ☎ **98/84-8372**).

Ruin-ing an Afternoon

If you've scheduled a trip to Tulum or one of the other Mayan sites in the Yucatán, you can pass on these activities, but if you don't have time for a longer trip and want a quick peek into this area's rich past, read on.

For some background, start out at the modest **Museo Arquéologico de Cancún** (Cancún Archaeological Museum; Paseo Kukulkán, km 9.5, on the right side of the entrance to the Cancún Convention Center; no phone) where you can look at artifacts from various Mayan sites from around the state. The museum is open 9am to 7pm Tuesday through Saturday, 10am to

151

5pm Sunday; entry is $1.75 except Sundays and Mexican holidays, when there's no charge.

Take a Leap

If you're crazy enough to want to bounce (almost) to the ground on a giant rubber band, **Cancún Bungee** (no phone), Plaza Flamingo on Paseo Kukulkán between the Flamingo Cancún and Beach Palace hotels) is there for you Sunday through Friday, from 11am until dark. Affiliated with Free Fall Bungee of Arizona, the staff claims to have supervised over 10,000 jumps in the United States and Mexico. The first jump is free when you team up with five people or more, for moral support; the second is $20. If you go it alone the first time, you'll shell out the 20 bucks yourself. In either case, a Jump Master will ride the crane basket with you. If you're already expert, you can practice such moves as flips, ankle-wraps, and spiderman jumps; otherwise you can watch the staff go through the motions. Sorry—if you're not over 13, or under 250 pounds, you're grounded.

Then head over to the Caesar Park Hotel (Paseo Kukulkán, km 17; ☎ 98/81-8000) to see the **Ruinas del Rey** (Ruins of the King), a compact archaeological site surrounded by jungle—and a new golf course. Taking its name from a monumental sculpture discovered here (but long since gone), the site has two small roads and a central plaza around which are arranged platforms of small temples, some with traces of murals and glyphs. Admission is $2 (free on Sundays and Mexican holidays), and hours are 8am to 5pm daily.

Off with His Head?

Pok-Ta-Pok was an ancient Mayan ball game in which the captain of the winning team was either crowned with glory or decapitated—historians haven't yet been able to figure out which.

Hitting the Links

The newest and most exclusive place to tee off in Cancún is at the **Caesar Park Hotel** (Paseo Kukulkán, km 17; ☎ 98/81-8000), where the 18-hole championship, par 72 course is landscaped around the Ruinas del Rey archaeological site (see above). If you don't lose your ball in the Temple of Doom (okay, the jungly area behind the open-air court), there are 72 sand traps for you to shoot your way out of. The Japanese Aoki Corporation–designed course has clinics for all levels of play, rest stations with beverage service, a restaurant and bar, pro shop, and locker rooms. Facilities are open 6am to 6pm; you can get back to the hotel via shuttle or underground tunnel. Greens fees ($80 for hotel guests, $100 for outsiders) include electric carts; no caddies are available.

The older but no less magnificent 18-hole, par 72 **Pok-Ta-Pok** (Paseo Kukulkán, km 6.5; ☎ 98/83-0871) course, designed by Robert Trent Jones, overlooks the lagoon near the Holiday Inn Express hotel; two of the greens skirt the edge of the water. You've got all the up-to-date amenities here: clubhouse, electric carts, restaurant/bar, pro shop, and practice area. Greens fees run $100, including carts; caddies are another $20.

For a quick and easy game, play the **Meliá Cancún's** (Paseo Kukulkán, km 16.5; ☎ 98/85-1160) par 53, 18-hole executive course, across the road from the lagoon. Greens fees are $37 (including cart) for both guests and nonguests; equipment rental runs $17.

Cancún's Best Shopping

Cancún never developed its own handicrafts industry: All the locals who moved here were too busy building hotels to devote any time to traditions such as weaving and carving. The first shopping district, consisting of a few markets in the downtown area, sold goods from other parts of the Yucatán. Subsequently, retail moved to the hotel zone and went modern, with malls to match the 20th-century hotel architecture.

Yo, Gringo!

Before buying, cast a sharp eye over the merchandise for irregularities; there's no such thing as quality control in the little workshops where the goods are produced. Also, make sure anything that's supposed to be silver has the .925 government stamp on it. If it doesn't, it's anything but.

The shops in Cancún are more expensive than in any other place in Mexico—prices are about on par with those in the United States. Still, you can find some bargains. Brand-name sportswear outlets like Polo/Ralph Lauren, Benneton, Guess, and Dockers sell their goods at prices somewhat lower than those back home, and if you hit Cancún in the off-season, you'll usually come across some good sales.

To Market, To Market

Don't expect too much from the markets in Cancún. You'll spend lots of time there wading through T-shirts, baskets, blankets, pottery, and tacky souvenirs—most of which are sold in bulk by half the vendors in town. But the markets are as close as you'll come to local color in Cancún, and they're a good break from the over-slick malls.

The oldest market for crafts is downtown's **Ki-Huic,** Av. Tulum 17 between Banco Atlantico and Bancomer. If you don't find it, it'll find you—a few hustlers are always on the lookout for tourists to lure into their open-front stalls. In addition to the run-of-the-mill stuff you can buy anywhere in Mexico, you'll find a few regional items such as hand- or machine-embroidered *huipiles* (sack dresses worn by Yucatecan natives), *guayaberas* (loose shirts worn in the tropics), and hammocks. Bargain hard. Although Maya may be the first language of some of the vendors, they know enough English to drive a hard deal. *Note:* If you get dragged down by the heat and haggling, you can always retire to an air-conditioned mall where you'll find stylized, contemporary versions of many of the market's items—for far higher prices, of course.

Playing the Market

➤ Pretend you couldn't be less interested in the item, even if you'd rather take a slow boat to China than go home without it. The more you ooh and aah, the more the price goes up.

➤ Start by offering one-third the asking price and thrust and parry your way up from there.

➤ If the vendor doesn't come down enough, walk away. Just about everything you see in this market is being sold by the gross by a variety of different vendors.

Duty-Free Deals

Cancún's main claim to Mexican shopping fame is its duty-free status on such luxury goods as perfumes, cosmetics, and watches, established through a special government dispensation of the normal 10% value-added tax. The easiest places to stock up on discounted brand-name fragrance and beauty products from the United States are the **Ultra Femme** stores, found at the Plaza Caracol and Plaza Kukulkán malls. For untaxed timepieces, try **Chronos de Peyrelongue** at Forum By the Sea or **World of Watches** at Plaza Caracol.

Bet You Didn't Know

If you see a vendor discretely crossing himself in the Catholic tradition after selling you something, he's not warding off the evil eye. It's a time-honored way to express gratitude for the first sale of the day.

Getting Mall'd

Cancún's elegant, air-conditioned malls lie mainly between km 7 and km 12 on Paseo Kukulkán—from west to east, they are Plaza Lagunas, Costa Brava, La

Mansión, Mayfair, Plaza Terramar, Plaza Caracol, Plaza Flamingo, and Plaza Kukulkán. Here's where you come to shop for the really fine—and accordingly expensive—locally made crafts, such as Panama hats, leather goods, silver and gold jewelry, and wood carvings, as well as upscale Mexican lines of casual wear and hand-painted T-shirts. Most of the malls also have banks, money exchange booths, pharmacies, liquor stores, and travel agencies. Hours are generally 10am to 10pm daily. A roundup of the best follows.

Dollars & Sense

Although you can't really bargain at the malls, you *can* get cash discounts. If they can avoid paying high commissions to the credit card companies, merchants are happy to pass along some of their savings to you. Use the ATMs or money exchange booths at the malls to get pesos before you shop.

The chicest mall is the winding **Plaza Caracol** (no phone) on Paseo Kukulkán, km 8.5, next to the Cancún Convention Center. Among the 200 shops and boutiques you'll find Waterford, Samsonite, Gucci, Ralph Lauren, Benneton, and Cartier and Pelletier jewelers. When you get shopped out, you can take a leisurely refueling break at La Fisheria, Savio's, and Casa Rolandi (see chapter 16, "The Best of Cancún's Dining Scene") or a quick one at Baskin Robbins or McDonald's.

In addition to its 130-odd shops, the less crowded **Plaza Kukulkán** (Paseo Kukulkán, km 13; ☎ 98/85-2200) offers entertainment venues such as a movie complex showing U.S. films, a video and laser center for kids, and a bowling alley. There's a food court with 16 different ways to load up on quick calories plus such restaurants as Splash, Cenacolo's, and 100% Natural (see chapter 16, "The Best of Cancún's Dining Scene"). Shops include a Guatemalan store selling beautiful, if rather overpriced textiles; a boutique with hand-beaded wooden folk art made by the Huichol Indians of Mexico; leather sandal and shoe stores; a record and tape outlet; and lots of silver shops stocking pieces from Taxco.

The smaller **Plaza Flamingo** (Paseo Kukulkán, km 11.5, across from the Hotel Flamingo; ☎ 98/83-2855) draws crowds to Planet Hollywood—and to its logowear boutique. You'll also find duty-free stores, designer sportswear outlets, and a Cuban cigar boutique. The fast food options range from Mickey D's burgers to Checándole's mole enchiladas.

The double-story **Forum by the Sea** (across from Dady O disco, at about km 10; ☎ 98/87-5717) is the swankest shopping/entertainment center in town, boasting duty-free shops and upscale boutiques, such as Bulgari Berger jewelers, Chronos de Peyrelongue, and Tommy Hilfiger. This place moves to the beat of the Hard Rock and Rain Forest cafes (see "Eat 'n' Rumba: Restaurants with a Musical Menu," below, and chapter 16, respectively); stay in the marble lobby and you can shop to more soothing live classical guitar or flute. A great people-watching perch, this mall is open a bit later than the others, generally until midnight.

What to Do When the Sun's Gone Down

Cancún has more night moves than any other place on the Yucatán peninsula—and most places in Mexico, for that matter. At daybreak, don't be surprised to see as many night owls just departing from their favorite bars and discos as joggers heading for the beach. But never fear, Cancún won't let you down if you want to avoid megadecibel madness and just enjoy a quiet, intimate soiree.

Forbidden Fruit

You might come across tortoiseshell products in some shops—barrettes, cigarette cases, jewelry boxes, and so forth. They're pretty, but they cost members of an endangered species their lives, so they're not allowed into the United States. Cuban cigars, a different form of endangered species, are not permitted into our country for political reasons. Puff away on them in Cancún if you like, but don't try to sneak them through Customs.

Saturday Night Fever: Cancún's Discos

You'll get '70s flashbacks in Cancún, where dance clubs have the latest in sound-and-light effects and everyone dresses to impress. Be prepared for a long, slow line at the door. Cover charges range from $10 to $20, although there are free nights, especially for women. The music starts around 10pm and goes on 'til 4 or 5am or later.

Fashionably Late

When Mexicans do the town, they do it late. Don't even think about arriving at a bar before 10pm or at a disco before 11:30pm.

The name **La Boom** (Paseo Kukulkán, km 3.5; ☎ **98/83-1152**) should give you a hint of the decibel level you'll find here. You can choose between a video bar with live music, a split-level flashing-light section, and a special room above it for more mature couples (read: anyone over 25) who want to dance without the ear-splitting music. Most nights, there's a different "special": hot male body or bikini contests, free bar, ladies' night, or a waiter's show.

Christine's (Paseo Kukulkán, km 7.5 at the Krystal Hotel; ☎ **98/83-1133**) is Cancún's oldest disco and still going strong. The 30-something and older crowd come here to check out the latest rock videos on giant screens—not to mention the latest, hottest clothes. The laser show gets strobing after midnight.

At the top of the charts is **Dady O** (Paseo Kukulkán, km 9.5; ☎ **98/ 83-3333**), with lines so long you're reminded of clubbing in New York or Los Angeles. The nondescript facade—just some big stucco letters spelling out the name—gives no hint of the high-tech special effects, including a "third dimension" laser show. Don't dance? Sit at one of the five bars and ogle. If you do, there's a snack bar for when you need refueling. No one older than 40 churns up the dance floor here.

Dress to Impress

Most Cancún discos have a dress code: Men aren't allowed to wear tennis shoes, sandals, baseball caps, or tank tops, but women can pretty much get away with anything as long as they're not barefoot. Don't count on squeaking in, either; there's always a checker at the door eyeballing the waiting crowd.

Up & Down (Paseo Kukulkán, km 15.5, across the street from the Oasis Hotel; ☎ **98/85-2909**) isn't on the disco "A" list, but it'll do if all your favorites are full. When soap suds are released on dancers during the foam party, it's not always good clean fun: The Gen X crowd can get pretty raunchy. You can always retreat to the high-tone restaurant upstairs, where the music is more subdued, and the soap restricted to the rest room.

Dirty Dancing

At **Azucar** (Camino Real Hotel; ☎ **98/83-0441**), a bona fide Cuban dance club, you can swing your hips to merengue, Mexican boleros, and more, courtesy of sizzling bands from Cuba, Jamaica, and the Dominican Republic. Unlike the age-segregated discos, golden-agers and their grandchildren all feel comfortable here.

You'll have to order a meal before waltzing out on **Club Grill's** (Ritz-Carlton Hotel, Retorno del Rey, off Paseo Kukulkán, km 13.5; ☎ **98/85-0808**) small dance floor, where you can take a turn to the band's slow 'n' easy tunes. That's true, too, at **La Farandula** (Paseo Kukulkán and Calle Cenzontle, across from Fat Tuesday's; ☎ **98/83-0160**), which mixes mambo, cha-cha, danzón, and salsa with its cheek-to-cheek numbers.

Eat 'n' Rumba: Restaurants with a Musical Menu

Carlos 'n Charlie's (Paseo Kukulkán, km 5.5; ☎ **98/83-1304**) heats up around 9pm with a DJ or band spinning out jazz, blues, reggae, or rock while couples dance under the stars or on the tables. Downtown, **Périco's** (Calle Yaxchilán 71; ☎ **98/84-3152**) caters to a similarly raucous crowd with loud and mostly canned music (see chapter 16, "The Best of Cancún's Dining Scene"). Brought to you by Bruce Willis, Sly Stallone, et al, **Planet Hollywood** (Plaza Flamingo, Paseo Kukulkán, km 11.5; ☎ 98/85-3022) is the all-American contributor to the hearing-loss cause. In a similar vein, the **Hard Rock Cafe** (Forum by the Sea; ☎ 98/83-0915) and **Señor Frog's** (Paseo Kukulkán, km 9.5; ☎ 98/83-2198) lay on live music, sans cover, most nights.

Most of these places close at around 2am. If you think the night is still young—and that you are—you can always take in a disco afterwards

A Taste of Mexico: Dinner Shows & Fiestas

The **Ballet Folklorico de Cancún** puts on a bang-up performance nightly at the Cancún Convention Center (Paseo Kukulkán, km 9; ☎ 98/83-0199). You have the option of the show alone ($30) or show with buffet dinner ($48)—it's definitely worth paying for the pig-out. Dinner begins at 6:30pm and the show starts at 7:30pm. Tickets are sold through travel agencies or from 8am to 9pm daily at a booth inside the entrance to the center.

You can also take in dinner and a show at the red-awninged **El Mexicano** restaurant (☎ 98/83-2200) in the Costa Blanca shopping center, next to Plaza Caracol. The show, which starts at 8pm, is touristy, with neon-colored costumes and lots of leg, but people seem to love it; the place is always packed elbow-to-elbow and thick with cigarette smoke. The entertainment's free when you order from the Mexican/international menu (nothing to write home about, but okay); come before 7:30 if you want a seat.

For something completely different, **Mango Tango** (Paseo Kukulkán, km 14.2; ☎ 98/85-0303) puts on a lively Caribbean revue at 7 and 9:30pm; the show is included in the price of any dinner. If you like reggae and jerk chicken, you can't lose with this one.

Want a one-stop tour of the country's tastes and entertainment traditions? Buy a ticket to a Mexican fiesta, held at various hotels. You'll get a buffet dinner, open bar, folkloric show, mariachis, and often fireworks thrown in. Prices range from $25 to $50, depending on how much entertainment is provided. **The Hyatt Regency** (Paseo Kukulkán between km 9 and km 10; ☎ 98/83-1234) and the **Camino Real** (☎ 98/83-1200) both host fiestas Tuesday through Saturday nights in high season; the **Costa Real** (across from La Boom disco; ☎ 98/83-2155) holds one every Wednesday.

Side Trips: Getting Out of Cancún

Take a day away from Cancún and you can experience mysterious Mayan ruins, swim with dolphins, snorkel on island paradises, or view southeast Mexico's grandest wildlife preserve. The first time out, you may want to take a package tour through a travel agency to get a taste for the different attractions without the hassle; you can decide whether you want to spend more time in the area on your next trip. Whenever feasible, however, I've also noted on-your-own alternatives.

Yo, Gringo!

The sun is intense in these parts: Pack a water bottle, sunscreen, hat, and good walking shoes for these day trips. The mosquitoes can be pretty intense, too. Bring along a DEET-based insect repellent.

Tulum/Xel-Há

Tulum, a walled fortress some 80 miles south of Cancún that flourished around A.D. 1200, wasn't the most important of the Mayan settlements, but its location on a cliff overlooking the Caribbean makes it an extremely scenic ruin. The most impressive structure, a temple called the Castillo, is perched on the edge of a bluff that has a sheer 40-foot drop to the sea. In all, you can visit about a dozen structures, including the Temple of the Frescos, which has traces of murals, and the Temple of the Upside Down God, famous for a stone carving of a "diving" god.

Excursions to Tulum are usually combined with a visit to Xel-Há (say: Shell-*HAH*), a national park some 8 miles to the north. The big attraction here is swimming or snorkeling in the warm, calm waters of the lagoons and canals, but you can also amble down one of several walking paths or visit a small museum.

Trips booked through travel agencies depart at 8am and return at 4:30pm; the price ($58) includes lunch at Xel-Há (snorkeling equipment is extra). If you want to go to Tulum on your own, you can catch a bus from downtown's main bus terminal. I don't recommend this, however; you're left off on the highway and it's a long hike to the entrance to the ruins.

Cozumel

If you want a quick side trip to another Mexican resort town, check out Cozumel, a diving and snorkeling paradise. For more information, see part 5. Most travel agency tours leave at 8am, return at 8pm, and cost around $75. Continental breakfast on the boat and lunch on the beach is included, but snorkeling gear is extra.

Air-conditioned ferries make the 45-minute journey from Playa del Carmen to Cozumel and back every 1 or 2 hours; the first departs at 5am and the last at 11pm. Tickets, at $10 for a round-trip, can be purchased at a small open booth a half block from the pier. You can get to Playa del Carmen from Cancún by an inexpensive bus from the downtown terminal at Avenida Tulum and Avenida Uxmal; it leaves approximately every 20 minutes.

If you want to shave off an hour or more of travel time to Cozumel, Mexicana Airlines subsidiaries **Aerocaribe** and **Aerocozumel** (☎ **98/84-2000** for both airlines) have eight flights a day from Cancún, starting at 7am and finishing at 7:30pm. The cost is around $47, one-way, for the 20-minute trip.

Kids Xcaret

Xcaret (say *ISH*-car-et), 50 miles south of Cancún, isn't exactly nature at its purest: This 250-acre "ecological park" was built around natural grottoes and pools but is overdeveloped and often crowded. Still, the beaches are lovely and kids enjoy this place. Pseudo-Mayan ruins dot the park entryway, beyond which are several subterranean rivers for snorkeling, a series of fresh- and saltwater pools, an aquarium, an aviary, stables, a museum, and a few (expensive) restaurants. If that's not enough entertainment, you can swim with some dolphins for an additional $60. A Mayan-themed light-and-sound show, which starts at 6pm, ends with the flying Indians of Papantla swinging by their feet from a tall pole in an age-old ritual. Everything's been designed to keep adults and kids busy for a full day.

Travel agency tours, which cost approximately $67, include the evening show and, usually, lunch. Departure is at 8am with an 8pm return.

You can go on your own by taking the bus (marked "Xcaret," it's the only bus here) that leaves frequently from the Xcaret Terminal (Playa Caracol, across Paseo Kukulkán from Plaza Caracol) for a few dollars. The park entrance fee of $30 (children 5 and under are free) includes the evening show.

Isla Mujeres

The small "Isle of Women," less than an hour's boat ride from Cancún, is the quintessential laid-back fishing village. Book a tour and you'll spend the morning snorkeling at Garrafón National Park, an underwater paradise; have lunch at a beachfront restaurant; visit a turtle farm and wander the rest of the waterfront where the fishing boats come in; play beach basketball; or poke around the shops in the quaint town square. If you go on your own, you can rent a bike and swing around the entire island, stopping to visit a pirate's graveyard or a tiny Mayan ruin overlooking the ocean.

Bet You Didn't Know

No one's quite sure why Fernández de Córdoba and his crew dubbed this fish-shaped bit of land the Isle of Women when they landed here in 1517. Some say the men were out fishing, so the conquistadors were met by a female-only reception committee.

Travel agency tours run from 9am to 4:30pm and cost $44; rates include continental breakfast on the yacht en route and lunch on the beach.

If you want to go on your own, the best deal is the ferry from Puerto Juárez, north of Cancún; take the no. 8 bus from Avenida Tulum to get there. The air-conditioned *Caribbean Express* and *Caribbean Miss* depart every half hour from 7am to 7:30pm; it takes about a half hour to cross, and the cost is about $3 one-way.

Water taxis depart to Isla Mujeres from the Club Nautico at Playa Caracol (☎ **98/86-0777**) several times a day starting from 9am, with the last boat returning at 5pm; the cost is $10 each way. You can also take the Isla Mujeres shuttle over from Playa Tortuga (☎ **98/83-3448**) four times a day from 9:15am to 3:45pm and return from 10am to 5pm for approximately $15 each way. Call for exact schedules.

Sian Ka'an Biosphere Reserve

In 1986, 1.3 million acres of tropical forests, salt marshes, savannas, beaches, mangroves, and 70 miles of coral reef were set aside as the Sian Ka'an Biosphere Reserve. Among the animals protected here are jaguars, spider monkeys, manatees, and 366 species of birds (you might spot a toucan or a graceful white ibis). Some 22 archaeological sites have been charted within the reserve, too.

To get the full flavor of the place, take the 6-hour, biologist-guided tour sponsored by the nonprofit Amigos de Sian Ka'an. The **Ecologos Travel Agency** (☎ **98/84-9580**) is the only one authorized by the Amigos to conduct tours from Cancún. Visitors get an in-depth explanation of the reserve before setting off in motor launches that wind through the mangroves and channels; there's a stop along the way to float with the current. Tours, which start at 7am and end around 7:30pm with hotel pick-ups and drop-offs, cost $90.

Chapter 16

The Best of Cancún's Dining Scene

> ### In This Chapter
>
> ➤ Cancún dining: The big picture
>
> ➤ Keeping costs down
>
> ➤ The best restaurants from A to Z
>
> ➤ Restaurant indexes

You wouldn't confuse Cancún with a sophisticated restaurant town like San Francisco—or even Puerto Vallarta—but you won't have to worry about varying your menu or your mood here, either. You'll find intimate rendezvous, trendy spots, upscale places for bon vivants, and even some ethnic eateries. Cancún's dining rooms tend to avoid chile-hot dishes—or at least serve the chiles on the side. One pleasant surprise: Contrary to the common rule, some of Cancún's best restaurants are in malls and hotels; in the latter, gourmet fare is frequently whipped up by recipients of prestigious international food awards.

A Dining Overview: Where's the Burrito?

Cancún Island's extended hotel zone has by far the most dining choices—which is to be expected, as that's where most of the people who come to Cancún stay. The east/west section of the hotel strip tends toward trendy party places, although some sedate dining rooms are left over from earlier days. From there, you can literally go in two directions: If you want fancy gourmet food in a luxurious setting, head south for the lower section of the hotel zone, and if you're interested in more traditional fare in low-key surroundings, go inland to Old Cancún. (For a wrap-up of the character of each

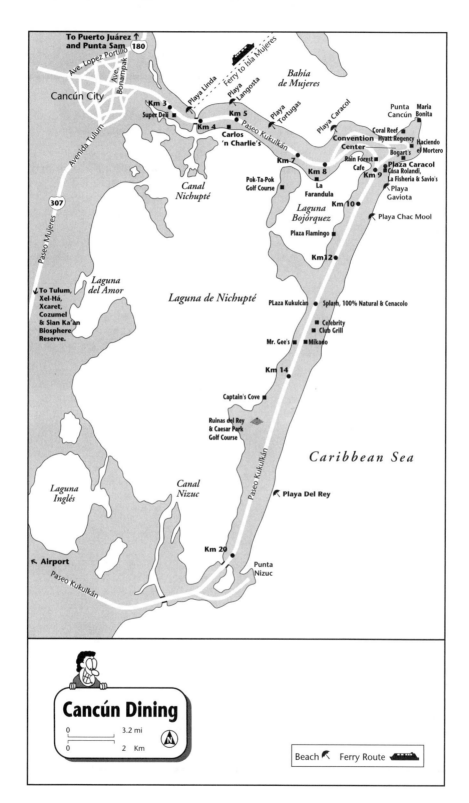

To Puerto Juárez ↑
and Punta Sam (180)

Ave. Lopez Portillo

Ave. Bonampak

Ferry to Isla Mujeres

Bahía de Mujeres

Cancún City

Playa Linda
Playa Langosta

Km 3
Super Deli

Km 5

Playa Tortugas

Playa Caracol

Punta Cancún

Maria Bonita

Km 4
Carlos 'n Charlie's

Paseo Kukulkán

Coral Reef
Hyatt Regency

Convention Center

Haciendo el Mortero

Bogart's

Km 7

Rain Forest Cafe

Plaza Caracol
Casa Rolandi,
La Fisheria & Savio's

Avenida Tulum

Canal Nichupté

Pok-Ta-Pok Golf Course

Km 8
La Farandula

Km 9

Playa Gaviota

307

Laguna Bojórquez

Km 10

Playa Chac Mool

Plaza Flamingo

Km 12

To Tulum,
Xel-Há,
Xcaret,
Cozumel
& Sian Ka'an
Biosphere
Reserve.

Laguna del Amor

Paseo Mujeres

Laguna de Nichupté

PLaza Kukulcán

Splash, 100% Natural & Cenacolo

Celebrity
Club Grill

Mr. Gee's

Mikado

Km 14

Captain's Cove

Caribbean Sea

Ruinas del Rey
& Caesar Park
Golf Course

Laguna Inglés

Canal Nizuc

Playa Del Rey

← Airport

Paseo Kukulkán

Km 20

Punta Nizuc

Paseo Kukulkán

Cancún Dining

0 — 3.2 mi
0 — 2 Km

N

Beach ↖   Ferry Route 🚂

163

neighborhood, see "Location, Location, Location" in chapter 13, "Choosing the Place to Stay That's Right For You").

Restaurants have been arranged alphabetically, and I've also supplied indexes at the end of this chapter that organize my favorite dining places by price and location.

The fast food chains jumped in as soon as word got out that Cancún catered to an American crowd, so if you're traveling with kids, you won't have to worry about McDonald's, Wendy's, Burger King, or Pizza Hut withdrawal. Your older offspring should take to the standard fare at Planet Hollywood, Carlos 'n Charlie's, Péricos, and Señor Frog's—as well as to the superloud music and thick throngs. See chapter 15, "Fun On & Off the Beach," for the addresses of the restaurants not reviewed below.

Check, Please

It's easy to dine too expensively too many times in Cancún if you're not careful. By following some simple strategies (see "Eating Well without Gobbling Up Your Dollars" in chapter 7), however, it's possible to eat economically and still eat well.

Cancún's 10% IVA, or value-added tax, has already been figured into your bill. (Remember, Cancún's tax is 5% lower than that in the rest of the country.) *Propina* or *servicio incluida* means the tip has also been included in the bill (this sometimes occurs at hotels). When it's not, the customary tip is 10% to 15%, depending on the quality of the service and how long you've been lingering.

Smoke Gets in My Eyes

Cancún is more Americanized than the rest of Mexico as far as public puffing goes. Upscale restaurants generally set aside nonsmoking areas, and several less expensive eateries do, too. Moreover, places that put no restriction on their customers' nicotine use are likely to have outdoor terraces. So, not to worry: You won't get smoked out in Cancún.

I've set up price categories with the worst-case scenario in mind: They're based on a per-person meal tab that includes appetizer, entree, dessert, one drink, and tip. To help you get even more focused, a price range for entrees is included in the individual reviews. In general, the more $ signs you see, the more money you'll be shelling out at the restaurant listed:

$ = Under $15

$$ = $15–$30

$$$ = $30–$50

$$$$ = Over $50

Unless otherwise noted, reservations are either unnecessary or not accepted.

My Favorite Restaurants from A to Z

Kids 100% Natural
$. North/South Hotel Zone. HEALTH FOOD.

Cancún's only card-carrying vegetarian eatery isn't for purists: You'll find no ovo-lacto or wheat-free selections, and chicken and fish also show their faces. It's not for gourmets, either: The chef could use a few more cooking classes. But the price is right, the food is fresh and abundant, and coffee refills are free. Sit in a white rattan chair on the pretty patio and enjoy a fruit shake, soy burger, veggie sandwich, or salad with yogurt dressing; it's all a nice, light change of pace. Besides this location, there are others at Terramar Plaza, Paseo Kukulkán behind Plaza Caracol (☎ **98/83-1180**), and Av. Sunyaxchen 6, downtown (☎ **98/84-3617**).

Kukulkán Plaza, Paseo Kukulkán, km 13. ☎ *98/85-2904.* **Main courses:** *$2.50–$7. AE, MC, V.* **Open:** *Daily Plaza Kukulkán and downtown locale 7am–11pm; Terramar Plaza open daily 24 hours.*

Bogart's
$$$–$$$$. North/South Hotel Zone. INTERNATIONAL.

No problema finding this place: Just look for something that resembles the Taj Mahal with bronze statues of Humphrey Bogart and Ingrid Bergman out front. You don't have to be a *Casablanca* buff to come here—anyone seeking a drop-dead romantic dining room will enjoy the place—but you'll get more of a kick out of the constant references to the film if you are. The interior, with its plush Persian carpets, potted palms, silk drapes, Mata Hari–style dining alcoves, and waiters dressed in fezzes is straight out of the *Arabian Nights.* The *Casablanca* theme

Yo, Gringo!

Remember, it's considered impolite in Mexico for the waiter to bring the check before you ask for it.

even pervades the essentially Continental menu, which lists corny-sounding dishes such as "onion soup with a turban," "sea conch Mustafa in Arab butter"—billed as an aphrodisiac—and "Humphrey's favorite," an extravagant mixture of lobster and chicken. The atmosphere is more exciting than the food; don't splurge on any of the big-ticket items.

Krystal Hotel, Paseo Kukulkán, km 7.5. ☎ *98/83-1133. Reservations suggested.* **Main courses:** *$17–$28. AE, MC, V.* **Open:** *Daily 6pm–1am.*

Kids **Captain's Cove**
$$$–$$$$. North/South Hotel Zone. SEAFOOD.

Heaping servings, reasonable breakfast buffets, good happy hours, and first-rate sunset views from the alfresco dining decks keep locals and tourists alike returning to this friendly restaurant. The day starts off with a bountiful breakfast buffet ($6.95) from 7 to 11am. Hearty seafood and USDA Angus steak are the mainstays of the lunch and dinner menu, and key lime pie and crêpes the most popular meal cappers, although some diners go for the drama of the flaming coffee. There's a special menu for small fry. *Note:* Beware the time-share friendlies at the front door who will try to talk you into signing up for a tour of the properties across the street.

Paseo Kukulkán, km 15, across from the Omni Hotel. ☎ **98/85-0016. Main courses:** *$17–$44. AE, MC, V.* **Open:** *Daily 7am–11pm.*

Carlos 'n Charlie's
$–$$. East/West Hotel Zone. MEXICAN/AMERICAN.

No stuffed shirts need show up at this link in the Carlos Anderson chain, a raging success that's the envy of other restaurateurs, who've tried unsuccessfully to copy its madcap formula. If gags such as the signs, "Exchange Rate: 1 husband = 2 waiters. I prefer husbands with dishwashing or cooking experience" don't get you, the moppets—shots of tequila taken straight while one of the staff blindfolds you and shakes you silly—will. Although more people come for the atmosphere than the food, the homemade sesame seed bread is good, and the entrees, which run the gamut from "moo-moo," "peep-peep," and "splash" (beef, chicken, and fish dishes) to "crunch" (boring mixed salad) and "Viva Mexico" (enchiladas stuffed with chicken or cheese) are decent. You can eat at a picnic table on an upper terrace or indoors at a comfy booth.

Paseo Kukulkán, km 5.5. ☎ **98/83-1304. Main courses:** *$7–$16. AE, MC, V.* **Open:** *Daily 11:59am–2:59am.*

Casa Rolandi
$$$. East/West Hotel Zone. NORTHERN ITALIAN/SWISS ITALIAN.

You may have the urge to yodel your approval when you enter this restaurant, fresh and airy as the Swiss Alps with its floor-to-ceiling windows. Although you won't find many Swiss in here, except for the owners, you'll encounter lots of foot-weary shoppers who've just retreated from the attached mall. They keep returning for award-winning dishes prepared in a wood-burning oven imported from Italy, as well as for the impeccable service. Try the fish fillet and squid baked in foil and seasoned with tomato, anise, lemon, and garlic, or one of the daily specials, such as venison. The cooked cream cheese bathed in wild berry sauce makes a great finale.

Plaza Caracol, Paseo Kukulkán, km 8.5. ☎ **98/83-1817. Main courses:** *$12–$24. AE, MC, V.* **Open:** *Daily 1–11:30pm.*

166

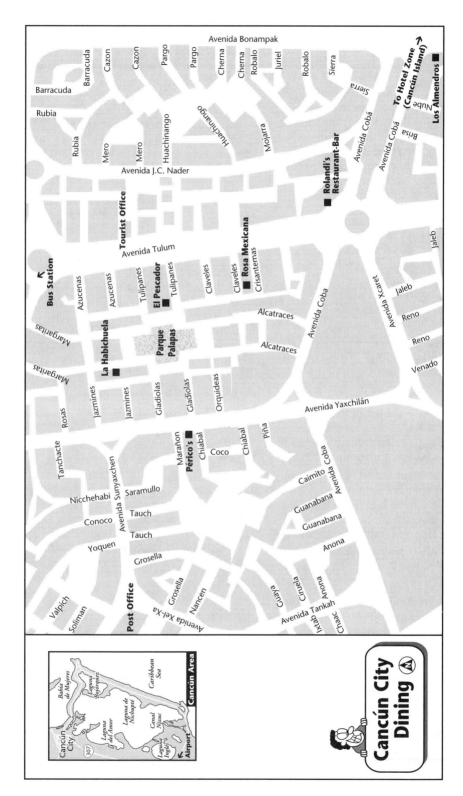

Best Bets for Romantic Dining

Bogart's (North/South Hotel Zone, $$$–$$$$)

Celebrity (North/South Hotel Zone, $$$$)

Club Grill (North/South Hotel Zone, $$$$)

La Habichuela (Cancún City, $$–$$$)

Celebrity
$$$$. North/South Hotel Zone. INTERNATIONAL.

This signature restaurant of the Casa Turquesa is so exclusive, you need a map to find it once you're inside the hotel— but it's worth the search. Gleaming tropical-wood floors, swirling overhead fans, a thatched-palm ceiling, plants galore—not to mention the elegantly attired clientele—make you feel as though you're in an Old Havana hideaway. Add the soft strains of a flute and the excellent but unobtrusive service, and the sophistication meter soars. For an exotic combination of denizens of the deep, try the shellfish mosaic spiced with ginger. If you want a switch from seafood, Swiss chef Iona Bocek's does an excellent pork tenderloin and morel mushrooms in puff pastry. The carmelized French apple tart is sublime. Celebrities? Wasn't that Steven Segal sitting in the corner?

Casa Turquesa Hotel, Paseo Kukulkán, km 13.5. ☎ **98/85-2924.** *Reservations required.* **Main courses:** *$19–$39. AE, MC, V.* **Open:** *Daily 6–11pm.*

Cenacolo
$. North/South Hotel Zone. ITALIAN.

For a quick meal at way-cheap prices, grab a counter stool and enjoy food that's passed through a slot from the pricier restaurant of the same name next door. You'll forgo the atmosphere and the flourishes, but enjoy the dishes on the spare. Spaghetti, fettuccine, or ravioli come with a choice of bolognese, puttanesca, pesto, or tomato sauces. The dessert list consists of flan, tiramisu (a wonderfully creamy version made with sherry and chocolate shavings), and Italian ice cream. Wash it all down with an espresso, beer, or wine.

Plaza Kukulkán, Paseo Kukulkán, km 13. ☎ **98/85-3706.** **Main courses:** *$4.25–$6.25. No credit cards.* **Open:** *Daily noon–9pm.*

Club Grill
$$$$. North/South Hotel Zone. INTERNATIONAL.

The classiest dining room on the island, and arguably the best, the Club Grill oozes Old World charm. Everything from the richly appointed surroundings—hardwood walls, bay windows enshrined in voluminous drapes, huge vases of flowers, and tables laden with a ton of crystal and silver—to the discreet European-style service, whispers elegance. The menu specializes in creative preparations of fresh fish, seafood, and prime meats. Favorites include the delicately peppered scallops, truffles, and potatoes in tequila sauce and the perfectly grilled lamb. Finish off with a cognac and a Cuban cigar or, after 8pm, take a turn on the dance floor.

Ritz-Carlton Hotel, Retorno del Rey, off Paseo Kukulkán, km 13.5. ☎ *98/ 85-0808. Reservations required.* **Main courses:** *$45–$55. AE, DC, MC, V.* **Open:** *Tues–Sun 7–11pm.*

Coral Reef
$$$–$$$$. East/West Hotel Zone. NORTHERN ITALIAN/ INTERNATIONAL.
If you haven't broken any—okay, more than 20—of your New Year's resolutions, treat yourself to this intimate eatery as a reward. You'll be dining on hand-painted china and wielding fine English silverware to a classical harp backdrop. Start with the carpaccio Toscani (thinly sliced raw marinated beef) and continue on to the pièce de résistance, filet mignon stuffed with watercress and pine nuts, topped with a light mustard sauce. You'll need a hearty appetite to take full advantage of the seafood plate, with five different "fruits of the sea" in garlic sauce. If this isn't your day for counting calories (and it shouldn't be), indulge in the three-chocolate cake for dessert. The wine cellar has bottles from Italy, Spain, France, and California. You'll need to dress a bit for the occasion: No shorts, T-shirts, jeans, or tennis shoes, please.

Fiesta Americana Coral Beach Hotel, Paseo Kukulkán, km 9.5. ☎ *98/83-2900. Reservations advised.* **Main courses:** *$26–$38. AE, MC, V.* **Open:** *Mon–Sat 6:30–11:30pm.*

El Pescador
$–$$. Cancún City. SEAFOOD/MEXICAN.
Relaxed and rustic, this is the best Cancún City spot for fresh seafood in all its incarnations: black conch cocktail—a speciality of the Mexican Caribbean—plates of shrimp, octopus, stone crabs, and lobster, charcoal-broiled or otherwise cooked to your taste. If you want to try a little of everything, order the *zarzuela* combination plate. The menu packs a list of good (and fish-free) Mexican specialties, too. Workers from nearby offices jam the second-floor terrace at lunchtime.

Calle Tulipanes 28, off Av. Tulum. ☎ *98/84-2673. Reservations advised for lunch.* **Main courses:** *$5–$20. AE, MC, V.* **Open:** *Daily 11am–10:30pm.*

Hacienda El Mortero
$$–$$$. North/South Hotel Zone. MEXICAN.
When you want to pull out all the stops, come to this replica of a 17th-century hacienda, with stucco walls, polished tile floors, and big-beamed ceilings. Waiters dress as classy charros (Mexican cowboys), and strolling mariachis sing their hearts out for you. If you're really hungry, order the prime rib with bone marrow and garlic; the lobster tail in drawn butter is no slouch in the portion department either. Want to dine light? Try one of the classic Mexican dishes such as *flor de calabaza* (squash flower) crêpes. Everything comes with hot, hand-patted tortillas—just like back on the

169

hacienda. Tequila turns up in desserts such as *copa de Colonel Zapata* (Colonel Zapata's cup), a "revolution" of sherbets, and in the Mayan coffee, which also includes *xtabetun* (a honey liqueur) and vanilla ice cream. Warning: If your appetite is affected by grisly tales, best read the story of the hacienda's first owner after you eat, rather than before.

Krystal Hotel, Paseo Kukulkán, km 7.5. ☎ *98/83-1133. Reservations suggested.* **Main courses:** *$11–$25. AE, DC, MC, V.* **Open:** *Daily 6–11pm.*

Most Mexicano Restaurants

El Pescador (Cancún City, $–$$)

La Farandula (East/West Hotel Zone, $$–$$$)

Rosa Mexicano (Cancún City, $–$$)

La Farandula
$$–$$$. East/West Hotel Zone. MEXICAN.

This nostalgic, romantic restaurant, illuminated by bulbs from movie marquees and chandeliers from various bordellos, pays tribute to Mexico's silver screen idols. Dining areas are dedicated to comics such as Cantinflas and sex goddesses such as Dolores Del Rio—their films and others play on video screens—and waiters wear the baggy suits and feathered hats of the "Pachucos" films of the 1950s. The memorabilia comes from the private collection of the Rebolledo family, who also own Périco's (see below). The menu—also 100% Mexican—includes pasta, meat, and seafood dishes. A favorite is the rib eye "Badu" with garlic sauce, serrano chiles, and shrimp. For dessert, try the *crepas de cajeta,* crepes with sweet Mexican caramel. You can just sit back and listen to the songstress or take your place on the dance floor.

Paseo Kukulkán and calle Cenzontle, across from Fat Tuesday's. ☎ *98/83-0160. Reservations advised Fri–Sun.* **Main courses:** *$8–$23. AE, MC, V.* **Open:** *Daily 1pm–2am.*

La Fisheria
$$–$$$. East/West Hotel Zone. SEAFOOD.

At this spacious, light-filled, and very unmall-like eatery, you can look out over the Paseo and enjoy seafood from around the world—New England clam chowder, Spanish seafood paella, Acapulco-style ceviche, and grilled *tik-n-xic* fish in a sour orange and achiote sauce from the Yucatán. (Sea creatures, it seems, swim long distances to spawn and to sacrifice themselves to tourists.) If you find fish too healthy (or fishy), you can resort to chicken and beef dishes as well as to decent vegetarian pizza.

Plaza Caracol, Paseo Kukulkán, km 8.5. ☎ *98/83-1395.* **Main courses:** *$7–$28. AE, MC, V.* **Open:** *Daily 11am–11:30pm.*

La Habichuela
$$–$$$. Cancún City. CARIBBEAN/MEXICAN.

Isn't it romantic? You can dine alfresco on the vine-draped patio of a classic Mayan mansion that flickers with candlelight. Portions are generous and the waiters are old-fashioned courtesy personified. The house special is *cocobichuela,* curried lobster and shrimp served in a coconut with tropical fruit. Other shrimp dishes come with exotic sauces such as ginger-and-mushroom or Jamaican tamarind. There are also old Mexican standbys— enchiladas *suizas* or *carne tampiqueña* (flank steak). The bar adjacent to the main dining area is always hopping. The protecting deity of the house is Ixchel, goddess of beauty; when the owner is around, he dispenses small statues of her.

Margaritas 25. ☎ *98/84-3158. **Main courses:** $9–$32. AE, MC, V. **Open:** Daily 1pm–midnight.*

Los Almendros
$. Cancún City. MEXICAN (YUCATECAN).

An authentic Yucatecan restaurant in a town awash in international cuisine, this large, colorful eatery takes you back to Cancún's ancestral roots. You can start with an order of *panuchos* (tortillas stuffed with beans and topped with shredded meat or chicken) or lime soup, then light into such traditional dishes as chicken or pork *píbil,* baked in banana leaves. Hearty eaters should go with the *combinado Yucateco*—a chicken, pork, and sausage glut-fest. For dessert, try the candied papaya or *caballero pobre* (Yucatecan bread pudding). There's live music from 7 to 10pm.

Av. Bonampak and calle Sayil, across the street from the bullring. ☎ *98/87-1332.* ***Main courses:*** *$4–$7. AE, MC, V. **Open:** Daily 11am–9:30pm.*

⭐Kids Maria Bonita
$$–$$$. North/South Hotel Zone. MEXICAN.

You can't get more Mexican than this restaurant. Three dining levels, decked out in typical pinks, yellows, and cobalt blues and decorated with handi-crafts, take you through the specialities of the states of Oaxaca, Michoacan, and Jalisco. The restaurant is named after a famous love song written to actress Maria Feliz, and mariachis, marimbas, and soulful duets take up the musical theme. You might start with an appetizer of cactus salad followed by fillet of grouper wrapped in banana and corn leaves, served with mild red chile adobo sauce. Nouvelle Mexican dishes include *chile poblano* stuffed with lobster bits and *huitlacoche,* a rare corn fungus that's the Mexican equivalent of truffles. As a concession to the chile novice, each dish on the menu is ranked on a heat scale of 0 to 2 chile peppers.

Camino Real Hotel, Punta Cancún, Paseo Kukulkán (between the Fiesta Americana Coral Beach and Hyatt Regency hotels). ☎ *98/83-1730.* ***Main courses:*** *$7–$28. AE, MC, V. **Open:** Daily 6–11pm.*

Mikado
$$–$$$. North/South Hotel Zone. THAI/JAPANESE.
The name may be strictly Japanese, but you can enjoy Thai spring rolls along with your sushi here. Order teppanyaki and you'll be reminded of those late-night Ginsu knife commercials as you watch the chef slice and dice your food like a whirling dervish. The dishes in the Thai division come curry-hot if that's how you like them, or toned down if you'd prefer to walk on the mild side. If you're not in the mood to visit the Orient at all, simple lobster and steak dishes are available. Except for the purple chairs and bold splotches of color over the grill, it's rather sober in-doors; sit on the patio, and you can gaze out at the ocean.

Marriott Hotel, Paseo Kukulkán, km 20. ☎ *98/81-2000, ext. 6325.* **Main courses:** *$11–$21. AE, DC, MC, V.* **Open:** *Daily 5–11pm.*

Can't Face Another Taco? Try . . .

Mr. Gee's (North/South Hotel Zone, $$$)

Rain Forest Cafe (North/South Hotel Zone, $$)

Rolandi's Restaurant-Bar (Cancún City, $–$$)

Super Deli (East/West Hotel Zone, $)

Mr. Gee's
$$$. North/South Hotel Zone. AMERICAN/STEAKHOUSE.
The Windy City meets Cancún at this clubby Chicago-style steakhouse, its handsome interior gleaming with hand-carved wood. It's the ideal setting for such carnivorous pursuits as imported roast prime rib served au jus—the house special—or the filet mignon with crêpes in béarnaise sauce. If your fancy steers you away from steers, try the roast duck in a light black-pepper sauce, or one of the pasta, chicken, shrimp, and salmon dishes. The flambéed mango dessert will remind you you're in the tropics—as will a table overlooking the lagoon.

Paseo Kukulkán, km 14.6, across from the Marriott Hotel. ☎ *98/85-1615.* **Main courses:** *$12–$20. AE, MC, V.* **Open:** *Daily 5pm–midnight.*

Périco's
$$. Cancún City. MEXICAN.
You'll recognize Périco's by the horse-and-buggy on the roof and the waiters out front dressed like bad boys from Pancho Villa's army. In this gigantic restaurant, so large it looks as though it could sub as a dance hall, revolution is the theme, and rowdy fun the means. At night, your table is likely to be surrounded by a waiter-led conga line; mock cockfights and bullfights are staged between mariachi and marimba sets. The food is somewhat beside the point, although it's pretty decent. The menu favors such traditional Mexican dishes as chiles rellenos, enchiladas, and quesadillas, but you can also order regular old spaghetti, steak, seafood, fish, and chicken dishes. This place fills up fast; arrive before 8pm if you want a sit-down dinner.

Calle Yaxchilán 71. ☎ *98/84-3152.* **Main courses:** *$7–$18. AE, MC, V.* **Open:** *Daily 1pm–2am.*

Rain Forest Cafe
$$. North/South Hotel Zone.
AMERICAN.
Here you can indulge both your inner child and your inner gringo under the canopy of a green plastic, air-conditioned rain forest, where a menagerie of mechanical animals hiss, slither, roar, and chitter-chatter. The burgers, pizza, spaghetti, and non-fussy chicken and meat dishes are what you'd expect—plain, decent food. A shop on the premises is stocked with the Minnesota franchiser's logo'd leather jackets, water bottles, and T-shirts, so you can dress to impress on your next trek through the rain forest.

Most Likely to Have to Be Carried Home From

Carlos 'n Charlie's (East/West Hotel Zone, $–$$)

Périco's (Cancún City, $$)

Forum by the Sea, Paseo Kukulkán across the street from Dady O's. ☎ *98/84-7038.* **Main courses:** *$8–$18. AE, MC, V.* **Open:** *Daily 11am–midnight.*

Rolandi's Restaurant-Bar
$–$$. Cancún City. NORTHERN ITALIAN/PIZZA.
Got a jones for pizza? Come to this casual downtown cousin to Plaza Caracol's Casa Rolandi (see above). The two dozen types, all baked in an authentic Italian oven, include the margherita, made with cheese and basil, and the *frutti de mare,* topped with seafood and olive oil. You can also get homemade pastas and entrees, such as lobster in white wine and fish fillet in parsley, accompanied by beer, wine, and mixed drinks from the bar. Tables are set out sidewalk cafe–style under a huge red awning.

Calle Cobá 12. ☎ *98/84-4047.* **Main courses:** *$4–$10. MC, V.* **Open:** *Daily noon–11pm.*

Rosa Mexicano
$–$$. Cancún City. MEXICAN.
If you want to make a night of it downtown, follow the townies to this low-key Mexican bistro with its colorful piñatas and *papel picado* (paper cutouts) streamers. The chef, who culls his specialties from all over the country, calls his cooking "refined Mexican." Translation: Instead of just plain old *pollo,* you'll get chicken smothered in a cream sauce and chopped almonds. There's not too much you can do to a traditional *carne tampiqueña* (flank steak), served with rice, guacamole, refried beans, and quesadillas, except make the portions bigger, which Rosa Mexicano does. The traditional Mexican rice pudding is a sweet success. Dine indoors or on the patio. A guitar trio spins out romantic ballads nightly.

Claveles 4. ☎ *98/84-6313. Reservations recommended on weekends and for groups of 6 or more.* **Main courses:** *$6–$20. AE, MC, V.* **Open:** *Daily 5–11pm.*

Savio's

$$. East/West Hotel Zone. NORTHERN ITALIAN.

Not only a stylish forum for the cuisine of owner George Savio's native Italy, this restaurant is also a comforting oasis for Plaza Caracol shoppers. The white-tile-floored dining room with its plants and wicker furniture quickly transports you from the world of clothing and handicrafts into a country of appetizers such as delicate quail liver pâté and entrées like chicken-cheese cannelloni smothered in creamy tomato sauce. The catch of the day char-broiled with cilantro consistently gets rave reviews. Finish off whatever you order with a rich espresso.

Plaza Caracol, Paseo Kukulkán, km 8.5. ☎ *98/83-2085.* **Main courses:** *$10–$19. AE, MC, V.* **Open:** *Daily 10am–midnight.*

Splash

$$. North/South Hotel Zone. SEAFOOD/INTERNATIONAL.

Splashy it ain't, but travelers looking to stretch their pesos couldn't care less. Breakfast ($4.99) and lunch ($6.99) are all you can eat; with the latter, you get soup, salad, and a choice of beef fajitas, enchiladas, burritos, nachos, tacos, and club sandwiches. The $11.99 dinner might include onion soup and shrimp with linguini in lobster sauce. You can also dine à la carte—but hardly anyone does. A terrace freshened by overhead ceiling fans overlooks Paseo Kukulkán; the inside dining room has neat, little round tables on a cool tile floor. There's also a low-lit bar with a TV that's always tuned into U.S. sporting events.

Plaza Kukulkán, Paseo Kukulkán. ☎ *98/85-3012.* **Main courses:** *$10–$18. MC, V.* **Open:** *Daily 6am–midnight.*

Super Deli

$. East/West Hotel Zone. DELICATESSAN.

If you crave plain old American meals, large or small, day or night, seek out this grocery store deli. It serves everything from pastries and baguette sand-wiches to pizzas, burgers, pastas, and even steaks, accompanied by coffees, wines, and beer. You can also stock up on Oreos and other U.S. staples to take back to your hotel room. You'll have to pay the price, however—literally double or triple what you'd spend back home. The downtown branch, (Calle Tulum at the crossroads of Calle Xcaret/Cobá; ☎ *98/841412*), is slightly cheaper than its hotel zone sibling, and also open round the clock.

Plaza Nautilus, Paseo Kukulkán, km 8.5. ☎ *98/83-2919.* **Main courses:** *$3–$9. No credit cards.* **Open:** *Daily 24 hours.*

Sound Bites: Cancún's Restaurants at a Glance
Restaurant Index by Price

$

Kids 100% Natural (North/South Hotel Zone, Health Food)

Cenacolo (North/South Hotel Zone, Italian)

Los Almendros (Cancún City, Mexican)

Super Deli (East/West Hotel Zone, Delicatessen)

$–$$

Carlos 'n Charlie's (East/West Hotel Zone, Mexican/American)

El Pescador (Cancún City, Seafood/Mexican)

Rolandi's Restaurant-Bar (Cancún City, Italian)

Rosa Mexicano (Cancún City, Mexican)

$$

Périco's (Cancún City, Mexican)

Rain Forest Cafe (North/South Hotel Zone, American)

Savio's (East/West Hotel Zone, Italian)

Splash (North/South Hotel Zone, Seafood/International)

$$–$$$

Hacienda El Mortero (North/South Hotel Zone, Mexican)

Kids Maria Bonita (North/South Hotel Zone, Mexican)

La Farandula (East/West Hotel Zone, Mexican)

La Fisheria (East/West Hotel Zone, Seafood)

La Habichuela (Cancún City, Caribbean/Mexican)

Mikado (North/South Hotel Zone, Thai/Japanese)

$$$

Casa Rolandi (East/West Hotel Zone, Italian)

Mr. Gee's (North/South Hotel Zone, American/Steakhouse)

$$$–$$$$

Bogart's (North/South Hotel Zone, International)

Kids Captain's Cove (North/South Hotel Zone, Seafood)

Coral Reef (East/West Hotel Zone, Italian/International)

$$$$

Celebrity (North/South Hotel Zone, International)

Club Grill (North/South Hotel Zone, International)

Restaurant Index by Location

North/South Hotel Zone

Kids 100% Natural $

Bogart's $$$–$$$$

Kids Captain's Cove
   $$$–$$$$

Celebrity $$$$

Cenacolo $

Club Grill $$$$

Hacienda El Mortero $$–$$$

Kids Maria Bonita $$–$$$

Mikado $$–$$$

Mr. Gee's $$$

Rain Forest Cafe $$

Splash $$

East/West Hotel Zone

Kids 100% Natural $

Carlos 'n Charlie's $–$$

Casa Rolandi $$$

Coral Reef $$$–$$$$

La Farandula $$–$$$

La Fisheria $$–$$$

Savio's $$

Super Deli $

Cancún City

Kids 100% Natural $

El Pescador $–$$

La Habichuela $$–$$$

Los Almendros $

Périco's $$

Rolandi's Restaurant-Bar
$–$$

Rosa Mexicano $–$$

Part 5

Cozumel

Balmy and carefree, Cozumel is a typical Caribbean port—except that many of its main attractions are under water. Jacques Cousteau first discovered Cozumel's stupendous reefs in the 1960s, and the island still lives up to its reputation as one of the world's premier diving and snorkeling destinations.

That's not to say diving is all that Cozumel's about. Miles of sugar-spun beaches, sportsfishing galore, mysterious Mayan ruins, appealing waterfront restaurants, and an unpretentious, friendly capital with Mayan roots are great lures, too.

It's easy to kick back in Cozumel, and I'm here to help you do it, according to the dictates of your budget and your travel spirit. I'll give you the lowdown on the best of Cozumel, both on land and down under.

Chapter 17

Choosing the Place to Stay That's Right for You

> ### In This Chapter
>
> ➤ Where the hotels are
>
> ➤ The best in the bunch
>
> ➤ Hotel indexes

Maybe you've been counting hotel lobbies instead of sheep lately, but don't let deciding where to stay in Cozumel cause you any sleepless nights. You couldn't have chosen a better destination for both good value and good locations. If you're willing to forgo a beachside perch, you can get great bargains, and if you're willing to spend some extra pesos, you can have all the luxury you like—and there's plenty in between, too. Just leave the details to me.

First, I'll outline the three areas where hotels are most plentiful in Cozumel and tell you the pros and cons of staying there. Then I'll give you an alphabetical list of my favorite places, followed by a few alternatives if these are already booked. At the end of the chapter, you'll find at-a-glance indexes listing the hotels by price and by location.

As far as prices go, I've noted rack rates (the maximum that a resort or hotel charges for a room) in the listings. This will give you some sense of what to expect, although I know you'll avoid

Bet You Didn't Know

Cozumel has around 3,500 hotel rooms, and that's the way it's going to stay. Development is very carefully monitored because dirt from construction sites could filter into the ocean and damage the world-famous reefs.

paying rack by following the advice I gave you in chapter 6, "The Lowdown on Accommodations in Mexico." I've also put a dollar sign icon in front of each hotel listing so you can quickly see whether it's within your budget. The more $ signs you see, the more money you'll be shelling out to stay there. It runs like this:

$$\begin{aligned} \$ &= \$85 \text{ and below} \\ \$\$ &= \$85\text{–}\$140 \\ \$\$\$ &= \$140\text{–}\$225 \\ \$\$\$\$ &= \$225 \text{ and above} \end{aligned}$$

Unless specified, rates are for a standard double room and include the 12% room tax. I've listed high-season rates, which are in effect from around December 19 to April 30. Prices run anywhere from 10% to 40% lower the rest of the year, although hotels are not consistent in their discounts. You can find the biggest markdowns at the luxury beach resorts, but many smaller, more modest lodgings in the town of San Miguel keep their prices the same year-round.

A kid-friendly icon **Kids** highlights hotels that are especially good for families. All hotels have air-conditioning unless otherwise indicated; if the review doesn't say anything to the contrary, you can safely assume that you can walk directly out of your hotel and onto the beach.

Bet You Didn't Know

At 28 miles long and 11 miles wide, Cozumel is Mexico's largest island.

Hint: As you scan the reviews, it's a good idea to keep tabs on the ones you like most. You don't even have to wait until you get to the chart at the end of the book (see p. 542) where you can rank your preferences; just put a check mark next to the ones that strike your fancy when you come to them (yes, official permission to write in this book—now don't you feel liberated?).

Location, Location, Location

Located some 12 miles off the coast of the Yucatán peninsula, Cozumel looks like an amoeba or a slightly crooked teardrop. All of the island's best hotels—in fact, almost all of them, period—are on the west side of the island because that's where the best beaches and most placid waters are. The hotel areas divide easily into three separate, if not quite equal, sections: the northern hotel zone, the town of San Miguel, and the southern hotel zone.

The Northern Hotel Zone: A Beachside Enclave

The smaller and lesser developed of Cozumel's two hotel zones, the area to the north of the Cozumel's only town, San Miguel, has some excellent

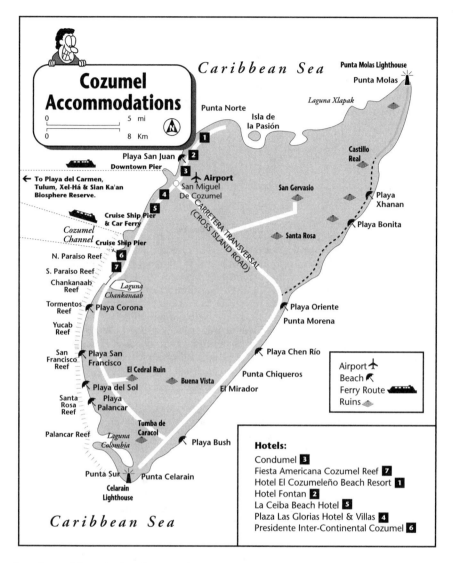

Cozumel Accommodations

0 — 5 mi
0 — 8 Km

Caribbean Sea

Punta Molas Lighthouse
Punta Molas

Laguna Xlapak

Punta Norte
Isla de la Pasión

1

Castillo Real

Playa San Juan **2**
Downtown Pier

3 Airport
San Miguel De Cozumel

San Gervasio

Playa Xhanan

4

5

Cruise Ship Pier & Car Ferry

Playa Bonita

Santa Rosa

Cozumel Channel Cruise Ship Pier

N. Paraiso Reef **6**

S. Paraiso Reef **7**

Chankanaab Reef

Laguna Chankanaab

Tormentos Reef — Playa Corona

Playa Oriente
Punta Morena

Yucab Reef

San Francisco Reef — Playa San Francisco

Playa Chen Río

El Cedral Ruin

Buena Vista

Punta Chiqueros

Playa del Sol

El Mirador

Santa Rosa Reef — Playa Palancar

Palancar Reef — *Laguna Colombia*

Tumba de Caracol

Playa Bush

Punta Sur — Punta Celarain

Celarain Lighthouse

Caribbean Sea

← To Playa del Carmen, Tulum, Xel-Há & Sian Ka'an Biosphere Reserve.

Airport ✈
Beach ☚
Ferry Route
Ruins

Hotels:
Condumel **3**
Fiesta Americana Cozumel Reef **7**
Hotel El Cozumeleño Beach Resort **1**
Hotel Fontan **2**
La Ceiba Beach Hotel **5**
Plaza Las Glorias Hotel & Villas **4**
Presidente Inter-Continental Cozumel **6**

beaches, although the shore isn't as consistently sandy as it is in the south, which is also where the best reefs are. As a result, there aren't as many hotels here as there are in the south, and those that have settled in tend to be a bit closer to one another. If you stay here, however, you have the benefit of being on the beach and close to town, and the hotels here offer a nice range of options, including some reasonably priced all-inclusives.

In a nutshell . . .

➤ Close to the activity of San Miguel

➤ Close to the airport

➤ Hotels in a lot of different price categories

181

but . . .

➤ Far away from the most popular reefs and dive spots

➤ Farther away from the must-see Chankanaab Park

➤ Not all the beaches are as spectacular as those farther south

Dollars & Sense

Most hotels tack on outrageous surcharges for phone calls, even collect calls. And using the long-distance public phones in San Miguel that advertise credit card use will cost you far above what it might cost in the United States. The good news is that you can buy Sprint Calling Cards here in denominations of $10 or $20 (10 or 20 minutes of use at $1 a minute), which work with any Touch-Tone phone; directions on how to use them are printed in English on the cards. You can purchase them at the Calling Station in San Miguel, Av. Rafael Melgar 27, at Calle 3 Sur, and you can also make operator-assisted long-distance calls from here at a flat $1.50 a minute. Hours are Monday to Saturday, 8am to 11pm, and Sunday 9am to 10pm.

San Miguel: Traditional Cozumel

San Miguel, the island's only town—referred to simply as *centro*—is a municipality of some 60,000. Although its roots go back to the ancient Maya and it has a traditional main square, it's also a hub of tourist activities, with a seaside boulevard lined with shops, bars, restaurants, and a museum. The island's banks, business offices, and most dive shops are here, as are the ferry pier and a handicrafts market. This is a compact walking town, and it's very easy to travel by foot to most places you have to go.

Bet You Didn't Know

The Mayan language is spoken by many natives in San Miguel and some women still wear the white, embroidered *huipil* dress and shawl that dates back to pre-conquest times.

Because it has no direct beach access, this is also where Cozumel's most inexpensive lodgings are. You'll have to take a cab every time you want to hit the sand—it shouldn't cost more than $4—but you'll be in the heart of the action and still save money in the long run.

In a nutshell . . .

➤ The least expensive lodgings

➤ A short walk to many tourist attractions, restaurants, and shops

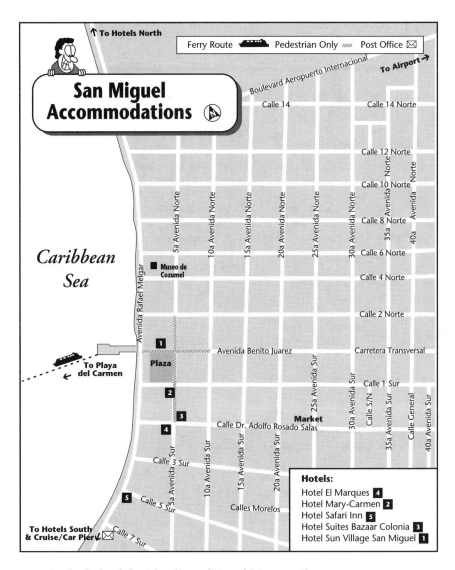

> In the hub of the island's traditional Mayan culture

> Closest to the airport

but . . .

> No luxury amenities in the hotels

> No beach

> It's often thronged with day trippers from the cruise ships

> Your room may be noisy

The Southern Hotel Zone: Luxury Row

The best reefs lie offshore in the area south of San Miguel, also home to some of the island's best beaches, including San Francisco, which is loaded

183

Bet You Didn't Know

Cozumel was discovered a year before Mexico City. Spanish captain Juan Grijalva first set foot on Cozumel in 1518; Hernán Cortés arrived in Mexico City in 1519.

with water sports concessions. The island's top visitor attraction, Chankanaab Park, is also here, as are the small ruins of El Cedral and Caracol.

It's no surprise, then, that this is where you'll find the largest number of resorts, including Cozumel's newest and most exclusive properties; many have private docks, and most offer diving courses and top-notch aquatic excursions. The hotels in this area also tend to be larger and farther apart than those in the other two hotel zones. Naturally, there's a price for all this, and staying here will disconnect you from San Miguel's pulsating action. Still, the top hotels have their own noisy nightspots and some decent restaurants, and a $10 or less cab ride will get you to town if you feel restless.

In a nutshell . . .

➤ Luxury hotels, services, and amenities

➤ Nearest the best diving sites and beaches on the island

➤ Excellent water sports facilities

but . . .

➤ It will take a bigger bite out of your pocketbook to stay here

➤ You'll be farthest from the airport

➤ You'll be away from the action of San Miguel

My Favorite Hotels from A to Z

Dollars & Sense

Use the kitchens at **Condumel** (☎ 987/ 2-0892), equipped with fridge, stove, coffeemaker, blender, and toaster for even a few meals and you'll be cutting down on expenses.

Condumel
$$. Northern Hotel Zone.
A condo in Cozumel is a Condumel—get it? Whatever you think of the pun, if you're in for the long haul, you'll like these Mayan-motif beachside lodgings. Thatched-roof buildings and limestone facades inscribed with Mayan carvings remind you that you're in the Yucatán. All eight units are large; the separate bedrooms have either a king-sized bed or two double beds plus hooks for hammocks; the baths offer both tub/showers and bidets. Snorkeling equipment can be

rented at owner Bill Horn's Aqua Safari store, a 15-minute walk out the front door. There's a grocery store 10 minutes away by foot, and the town square is a 20-minute stroll away.

Carretera San Juan, km 1.5 (right before the marina on the left). ☎ *987/2-0892. Fax 987/2-0661. E-mail: condumel@aquasafari.com.* **Rack rate:** *$140 per unit. No credit cards.*

Fiesta Americana Cozumel Reef

$$$. Southern Hotel Zone.

You won't be right on the beach if you bunk at this far southern hotel—the small-ish stretch of shore is just across the high-way, reachable by pedestrian bridge—but you'll get a lot of bang for your buck and you'll be near some of the best reefs in Cozumel. The lobby brims with marble, glass, polished brass, and high-priced bou-tiques. You can book a main-building room or one of the *casitas* suites, clusters of two-story thatched buildings land-scaped to look like they're in the middle of a jungle; all are extra spacious, with casual-elegant blond-wood furniture and bal-conies. Playing Jacques Cousteau is the main draw—this place has a super dive center—but when you're ready to come up for air, you can hit a few balls around the tennis court, sweat it out at the health club, or chow down at one of the three restaurants, ranging from casual to sophisticated.

> **Dollars & Sense**
>
> Fiesta Hotels offer discounts on meals with a minimum of 3 nights' stay. You might also check out the **Fiesta Break** packages (☎ **800/ 9BREAK9**), which include, among other things, deals on airfare if you're leaving from New York or Los Angeles.

Carretera Chankanaab, km 7.5. ☎ **800/FIESTA-1** *in the U.S., or 987/2-2622. Fax 987/2-2666. www.fiestamexico.com.* **Rack rates:** *$151 standard double; $177 casitas. AE, MC, V.*

Kids Hotel El Cozumeleño Beach Resort

$$$$. Northern Hotel Zone.

Situated on one of the best beaches in Cozumel, and only 5 minutes by cab from San Miguel and the airport, this moderately priced all-inclusive attracts families who are beholden to the great kids' program as well as couples who like their vacations tied up in tidy packages. Guest rooms, which all face the Caribbean, are extra roomy and nicely furnished in contemporary style. During the day, you can snorkel or sunbathe for free—windsurfing or diving cost extra. When you're waterlogged, it's tennis or minigolf time. Come sun-set, the social scene moves inside to the marble lobby, which has cozy pock-ets of chairs and couches. A spirited live show kicks off shortly after dinner.

Carretera Santa Pilar, km 4.5. ☎ **800/221-6509** *or 987/2-0050. Fax 987/ 2-0381.* **Rack Rate:** *$133 per person, standard double room (includes 3 meals,* *domestic drinks, room service, taxes and tips, all non-motorized water sports). AE, MC, V.*

Hotel El Marques

$. San Miguel.

Conveniently located a few blocks from the humming town plaza, this hotel is efficiency itself. Sun-filled rooms with cream-and-white decor have tile floors, a pair of double beds, and some pretty French provincial touches. If you want a panoramic view of the city and don't mind climbing stairs, get a room on the third floor. There are no in-room phones or TVs, but a pay phone in the lobby and a color TV with English channels in the big sitting area suffice for most guests. The friendly staff aim to please.

Av. 5 Sur no. 180 (almost at the corner of Salas next to Coco's restaurant). ☎ *987/ 2-0677. Fax 987/2-0537.* **Rack rate:** *$38 double. Discounts for 2 or more nights. MC, V.*

Hotel Fontan

$$. Northern Hotel Zone.

You're not likely to send home postcards of this hotel—it's a bland, tan, four-story job—but then, again, you might be too busy playing on the beach to do much scribbling: The Fontan has its own dock with water sports rentals. The pool is nice, there's a restaurant on site, and the rooms are sizable and well-maintained, with private balconies (most have ocean views). All in all, you get a lot of punch for your pesos here.

Carretera Santa Pilar, km 2.5. ☎ **800/221-6509** *or 987/2-0300. Fax 987/ 2-0105.* **Rack rate:** *$106 double. No credit cards (reservations must be prepaid in advance with check or money order).*

Hotel Mary-Carmen

$. San Miguel.

A favorite with Mexican couples, the Mary-Carmen's lengthy lobby is a bit Hallmark moment–ish, with red plush love seats and plastic flowers every-where. Beyond this kitschy enclave, however, is a lovely inner courtyard with a huge mamey tree—it bears fruit in August—surrounded by two floors of rooms. All units have standard motel-style furnishings, with either two or three double beds, but are carpeted and air-conditioned with screened win-dows; first-floor rooms also have overhead fans.

Av. 5 Sur no. 4 (a half-block south of the plaza and on the right). ☎ *and fax* **987/2-0581. Rack rate:** *$29 double. MC, V.*

Hotel Safari Inn

$. San Miguel.

One of the coolest budget hotels in town, the Safari is clean and simple, and gets right to the point: diving. The sea-themed rooms, with giant white stucco lobsters, angelfish, or other denizens of the deep sculpted above the beds, have little in the way of furniture but come equipped with red coolers for icing beer or other après-diving drinks. You have a choice of either a king-sized bed or two twin beds among the 12 units; some have additional bunk beds and sofa beds with space for five, total. At sunset, guests sit in the open-air hallways and watch the boats in the harbor below; then it's out to the plaza, only 4 blocks away, to play. The hotel is run by a local dive master, who also owns the Condumel (see above); he offers good dive packages through his adjacent Aqua Safari shop.

Extra! Extra!

Is an all-inclusive for me? Answer the questions in chapter 6, "The Lowdown on Accommodations in Mexico," to see.

Av. Rafael Melgar at Calle 5. ☎ **987/2-0101.** *Fax 987/2-0661. E-mail: dive@ aquasafari.com.* **Rack rate:** *$45 standard double. MC, V.*

Hotel Suites Bazaar Colonial
$. San Miguel.

You can't get a better price-to-size ratio than this snug three-story place off Av. 5 Sur, perfect if you're planning a long-term stay in the port. The larger-than-average studios and one-bedroom units are done in rattan with red-tile floors; all rooms on the second and third floors have kitchenettes. Guests like the easy 5-minute walk to the center of town and the way the hotel sits back from the avenue, making it noise-free and lending it an air of exclusivity. Guests gather around the TV and book exchange in the small lobby, which has dabs of Spanish colonial decor. When you don't feel like using your kitchenette, you can take advantage of the hotel's 10% discount

Kids Best Hotels for Families

Hotel El Cozumeleño Beach Resort (Northern Hotel Zone, $$$$)

Plaza Las Glorias Hotel & Villas (Southern Hotel Zone, $$$$)

Presidente Inter-Continental Cozumel (Southern Hotel Zone, $$$$)

at the Las Palmeras and Pepe's Grill restaurants (see chapter 20, "The Best of Cozumel's Dining Scene").

Av. 5 Sur no. 9 (across the street from the El Marques). ☎ **987/2-0506.** *Fax 987/ 2-1387.* **Rack rates:** *$61 1-bedroom apt; $72 apt with kitchenette. AE, MC, V.*

Hotel Sun Village San Miguel
$. San Miguel.

Formerly the Meson de San Miguel, this refurbished (and rechristened) hotel attracts U.S. and Canadian groups who prize the main plaza location. The best of the three floors of contemporary-designed units are the eight remodeled rooms with tiled balconies facing the town park; the new one-bedroom suites with sofa beds and two bathrooms are nice for families. Avoid the 17 rooms facing the hallways—you'll be stuck behind a vacuum-sealed window and have no privacy if you open the door for some fresh air—and those on the pier side of the hotel, which get blasts of noise from the downstairs bar. Fancy by downtown standards, all rooms have phones and color TVs with five channels in English. Other upscale amenities include a pool, video bar, coffee shop, and travel and car rental agencies. Guests also get discounts at various restaurants and tourist facilities.

Kids Best Hotels for Sports Addicts

Plaza Las Glorias Hotel & Villas (Southern Hotel Zone, $$$$)

Presidente Inter-Continental Cozumel (Southern Hotel Zone, $$$$)

Av. Juarez 2 Bis, on the main plaza. ☎ **800/783-8384** *or 987/2-0233. Fax 987/2-1820.* **Rack rate:** *$72 standard double. AE, MC, V.*

La Ceiba Beach Hotel
$$. Southern Hotel Zone.
One of Cozumel's first hotels, La Ceiba has had guests donning wet suits for years. They keep returning not only because of the great dive packages, but also for the fitness center and sauna—conveniently located near the freeform pool so you can dip into the cool water after toasting, Scandinavian style. The oversized palm trees shading the beach are also a rarity in Cozumel, and you need go no farther than the roped-off area next to the beach for snorkeling. The large rooms, while not the most stylish, compensate with extras such as minibars, satellite TV with VCR—movies can be rented at the reception desk—and balconies. Dining choices include the Galleon, with good seafood and an appealing old seafaring ambience, and the Chopaloca, where you dine close to the ocean.

Dollars & Sense

Dive packages are available year-round at La Ceiba (☎ **800/437-9609**). In high season, for $614 per person, based on double occupancy, you get 7 nights' and 8 days' stay at the hotel, plus 5 days of boat diving with two tanks a day and unlimited diving from the shore. It's $675 if you want to have breakfast thrown in.

Costera Sur, km 4.5. ☎ **800/437-9609** *or 987/2-0065. Fax 987/2-0844.* **Rack rate:** *$134 standard double. AE, MC, V.*

Kids Plaza Las Glorias Hotel & Villas
$$$$. Southern Hotel Zone.

This link in the Mexican Plaza Las Glorias chain is expensive, but you get the best of both worlds here: You'll luxuriate in a fancy suite on a great beach and you'll be only 5 blocks from the center of San Miguel. One of the few upscale resort hotels catering to scuba enthusiasts, the hotel boasts a full-service dive shop with PADI- and NAUI-accredited dive masters and certification courses. When you're tired of communing with fish, mingle with other guests at the pool's swim-up bar or root for the home team together in the lobby, where a giant satellite TV transmits live sports telecasts. Tiled guest rooms have sunken living rooms, terraces, and such deluxe amenities as safety deposit boxes and hair dryers. The hotel restaurants are decent, but you might as well go to town in town.

Rafael Melgar, km 1.5. ☎ **800/342-AMIGO** *in the U.S., or 987/2-2000. Fax 987/2-1937.* **Rack rate:** *$282 standard double suite. AE, MC, V.*

Kids Presidente Inter-Continental Cozumel
$$$$. Southern Hotel Zone.

One of the largest (253 rooms) and most elegant resort complexes on the island, the Presidente caters to a mix of families, couples, and groups. Veterans as well as novice scuba divers like to stay here for the professional diving classes, scuba excursions, and fine snorkeling, but others come to play tennis, sail, windsurf, or just laze the days away at the beach, perhaps the most beautiful landscape in all of Cozumel. All the rooms are attractive, with vivid textiles and light-toned furniture, but the deluxe

Dollars & Sense

The Presidente's Leisure Option packages, available December through April, offer credits toward meals, drinks, and airport transfers with a minimum 2 nights' stay.

units are far superior to the others; if your budget permits only a less expensive one, inspect your room first for moldy-smelling air-conditioning and other maintenance problems. Guests chow down at the dinner-only Arrecife with international cuisine or the more informal poolside Caribeño for breakfast and lunch. The children's program runs during Christmas and Easter vacations and July and August.

Carretera a Chankanaab, km 6.5. ☎ **800/327-0200** *or 987/2-0322. Fax 987/2-1360.* **Rack rates:** *$325–$370 standard double; $414–$504 deluxe double. Children under 13 stay in the same room with parents for free. AE, DC, MC, V.*

No Room at the Inn? Check Out One of These . . .

Northern Hotel Zone
➤ **Sol Cabaña del Caribe.** A friendly, low-key traditional Mexican hotel with real cabañas. Carretera Santa Pilar. ☎ **800/336-3542.** $$$.

San Miguel
➤ **Hotel Barracuda.** Cozy rooms with balconies and refrigerators on the waterfront with snorkeling area. Av. Rafael Melgar 628. ☎ **987/2-0002;** fax 987/2-0884. $.

Southern Hotel Zone
➤ **Fiesta Inn.** Mexico's answer to a standard Holiday Inn has carpeted rooms, its own beach, and a reliable water sports center. Carretera a Chankanaab, km 1.7. ☎ **800/343-7821.** $$$.

Quick Picks: Cozumel's Hotels at a Glance
Hotel Index by Price

$

Hotel El Marques (San Miguel)

Hotel Mary-Carmen (San Miguel)

Hotel Safari Inn (San Miguel)

Hotel Suites Bazaar Colonial (San Miguel)

Hotel Sun Village San Miguel (San Miguel)

$$

Condumel (Northern Hotel Zone)

Hotel Fontan (Northern Hotel Zone)

La Ceiba Beach Hotel (Southern Hotel Zone)

$$$

Fiesta Americana Cozumel Reef (Southern Hotel Zone)

$$$$

Kids Hotel El Cozumeleño Beach Resort (Northern Hotel Zone)

Kids Plaza Las Glorias Hotel & Villas (Southern Hotel Zone)

Kids Presidente Inter-Continental Cozumel (Southern Hotel Zone)

Hotel Index by Location

Northern Hotel Zone

Condumel $$

Kids Hotel El Cozumeleño
Beach Resort $$$$

Hotel Fontan $$

San Miguel

Hotel Mary-Carmen $

Hotel Safari Inn $

Hotel Suites Bazaar
Colonial $

Hotel Sun Village San
Miguel $

Hotel El Marques $

Southern Hotel Zone

Fiesta Americana Cozumel
Reef $$$

La Ceiba Beach Hotel $$

Kids Plaza Las Glorias Hotel
& Villas $$$$

Kids Presidente Inter-
Continental Cozumel
$$$$

Finding Your Way Around Cozumel

Okay, so maybe Cozumel doesn't look much like home—it's all those beaches and signs in a foreign language—but there's nothing to be concerned about. I'll have you changing money, getting information, and generally scooting around the island in no time.

You've Just Arrived—Now What?

The Cozumel International Airport, about 2 miles north of town, is small and easy to negotiate. Once you retrieve your luggage, you'll see a row of booths on the right as you exit the baggage claim area. One is a tourist information booth, where you'll be handed a free copy of the *Mexican Caribbean* guide (see "Where to Get More Information & Guidance," below) by a smiling volunteer. Next is a hotel reservations booth followed by car rental agencies, Budget and Hertz.

Both the international and national sections are in the same building. There's a *casa de cambio* (money exchange) in the international section, open 9am to 5pm, but no ATM.

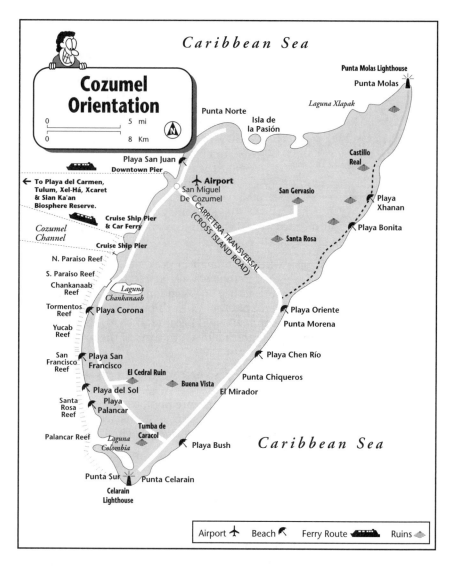

As you leave the airport building, you'll see the transportation desk. Because of a union agreement, there are no airport cabs; only eight-passenger collective vans called *colectivos* are permitted to take people from the airport into the island. (You can grab a cab from Cozumel to the airport, however.) It costs around $5 per person to go from the airport to the hotel zones; it's a bit cheaper to get to San Miguel. If you want to get where you're going more quickly, you can hire an entire van for yourself. Just ask for an *especial* and you'll be charged about $20 to the hotel zones, $8 to go into town.

Orientation: You Are Here

There's no mystery to getting around Cozumel. San Miguel, Cozumel's only town, lies roughly midpoint on the island's west coast; it's bordered by Avenida Rafael Melgar, or the *malecón* (seawalk), which skirts the Caribbean.

Bet You Didn't Know

Only 5% of Cozumel's land is developed.

Rafael Melgar transforms itself into Carretera Santa Pilar going north—it ends at the last hotel along this section of the coast—and into Costera Sur or Carretera a Chankanaab heading south; it loops in an unbroken line around the southern end of the island and continues up the east coast to the very top at Punta Molas—turning to dirt about halfway up, however. The only other road on Cozumel cuts across the midsection of the island, going past the airport and the San Gervasio ruins; it's usually just called the cross-island road, aptly enough.

San Miguel is the only place where you might need a map, although the grid pattern of the streets is fairly easy to follow. *Calles* (streets) run east-west, and *avenidas* (avenues) go north and south. The exception is Avenida Benito Juárez, which starts from the ferry pier, goes east through the main plaza (also called the *zócalo*) and beyond, where it becomes the cross-island road; it's the dividing line between the north and south parts of the town as well as of the entire island.

The street numbering can be confusing, so here's the rundown: Avenidas come in groups of five—Av. 5a, Av. 10a, Av. 15a, Av. 20a, and so forth. Calles run in sequences of twos. Those going north are numbered evenly—2a Norte, 4a Norte, and so on—while those heading south have odd numbers: 1a Sur, 3a Sur, and so on. For the sake of simplicity, I've eliminated the small *a* from the addresses in this chapter.

Bet You Didn't Know

The grid pattern of San Miguel's streets was laid out by the Spanish conquistadors who followed the same European pattern in all the Mexican cities they founded.

How to Get from Here to There (and How Not To)

I don't usually recommend that you rent wheels (see chapter 9, "Tying Up the Loose Ends") but Cozumel is an exception. There's no public transportation, and part of the fun of staying here is exploring the island by Jeep or moped. You don't have the traffic problems on most of Cozumel's roads that you have on the mainland, and many of the drivers are tourists—and thereby likely to observe the same customs of the road as you do. In town itself, you can hoof it or cab it (cheaply) to anywhere you need to go.

By Car

A car rental ranging from a Volkswagen Beetle to an open-top, Jeep-style vehicle costs about $40 to $55 a day, not including insurance, which is mandatory and runs you about another $20 a day. Although few of the vehicles are air-conditioned, the ocean breeze keeps things cool if you're riding along the coastal highways.

By Moped

Mopeds, like all-terrain vehicles, are a fun way to tool around the island; they're cheap—they cost around $25, including helmet, for 24 hours—and easy to operate. There are rental places in town and at many of the coastal hotels.

Yo, Gringo!

If you rent an all-terrain vehicle, use extreme caution when making sharp turns; most can roll over in the blink of an eye. Injuries and even deaths are not unheard of.

However, you should be very cautious when driving or riding a moped—the roads are often pitted and traffic around town can be heavy. If you get into an accident, injury isn't the only potential problem. If a Mexican is responsible, the case might languish in court for years without a conclusion. On the other hand, if the accident is your fault you may be forced to pay large bribes to "speed" up the legal process—and still end up in prison.

Yo, Gringo!

Let the renter beware. Check the terms and prices of moped lease agreements before you sign on the dotted line. Standard contracts state that the rentee is not insured (you can buy insurance, for about $2 extra), is obligated to ride on paved roads, and is responsible for all damage; if the vehicle is stolen, you pay for it. Look over the machine to see that everything's intact and working; if it's not, report this information on the rental agreement because otherwise you'll pay for damages you didn't cause. Wearing a helmet is also mandatory by law. You shell out $25 if you're caught without one.

By Taxi

You'll find taxis parked at several points on the *Malecón* in town as well as at all major hotels along the coast. They also roam the streets in San Miguel. They're unmetered and, in theory, have standard fares based on distance. Cabs are cheap in Cozumel and most drivers are courteous and bilingual, but it's still best to agree on a fare before getting in.

Taxis can carry up to five people; the fare goes up with the occupancy. It'll cost one person going from town to the north hotel zone up to $5, to the south zone, up to $10. It's approximately $5 to the airport from the hotel zones. A lot of hotels have rates posted in the lobby if they have their own taxi service; in that case, there's no negotiating. Unlike in other parts of Mexico, where tipping cabbies is rare, tips of 10% are commonly given to taxi drivers in Cozumel.

Playing Fare

If your cabbie is trying to charge you more than the going rate to a destination—ask at your hotel what's fair—offer an alternative price; if he doesn't go for it, walk away. Another cab will come along soon enough.

Where to Get More Information & Guidance

The **State Tourism Office,** on the second floor of the Plaza del Sol building, east side of the main plaza (☎ 987/2-0972), has limited hours of 8:30am to 3pm Monday to Friday. You'll have to fight your way through a bunch of handicrafts stalls to find the staircase leading to the second floor after you enter the Sol building. Brochures and maps are laid out on a long table; you're expected to help yourself. The staff are friendly once you summon them out of hiding, but they seem to get perplexed by specific questions. Better for data on lodging and other tourist information (but not for brochures) is the **Cozumel Island Hotel Association** (Calle 2 Norte and Av. 15 Sur; ☎ 987/2-3132), which serves the public Monday to Friday 9am to 2pm and 4 to 7pm. There are no branches of the tourist information offices in the north and south hotel zones, but concierges or front-desk staff should be able to help.

The Printed Page

The best of the free guides that you can pick up at hotels and businesses around town, and sometimes at the State Tourism Office, is the *Blue Guide.* Published quarterly, it's small—so's the print, unfortunately—and concise, with just about all the facts on Cozumel you need to know (and didn't know you needed to know). The text is less ad-driven than the rest of the guides, and the maps are good. Next best is the pocket-sized *Mexican Caribbean,* which devotes about a third of the book to Cozumel; it gives information on dive shops, restaurants, and shopping. The monthly *Cozumel Today: Cozumel Island's Restaurant Guide* and *Vacation Guide to Cozumel* are more difficult to find and not really worth trying to track down if you have one of the others.

Cozumel A to Z: Facts at Your Fingertips

American Express: Fiesta Cozumel, Calle 11 no. 598 (☎ **987/2-0725** or 987/2-0433).

ATMs: You'll find ATMs at the Bancomer and Banco Atlantico banks off the main plaza in San Miguel.

Baby-Sitters: Hotels charge a flat rate of $8 an hour.

Business Hours: Siesta is still observed in many shops on the island. Expect stores to open at 9 or 10am, close between 2 and 4pm, and reopen until 9pm weekdays and Saturdays. Government offices usually operate from 8am to 3pm weekdays.

> ### No Time for Time-Shares
>
> Watch out for the time-share sharks who disguise themselves behind "Tourist Information" booths on the main plaza.

Currency Exchange: In addition to the *casa de cambio* (exchange booth) at the airport, you'll find the **Promotora Cambiaria del Centro** at Av. 5 Sur between calles 1 Sur and Salas; it's open from 8am to 9pm Monday to Saturday. The exchange windows at banks along Avenida Rafael Melgar and the main plaza generally operate between 10am and noon. The bank offers slightly better rates, but often entails long waits on line; the currency exchange is not only open longer, but is far faster. Hotels will gladly change your dollars, but at a below-par rate.

Dentists: If your hotel can't find you a reliable dentist, check the **Cozumel Medical Specialities Clinic** or **Cozumel Walk-In Clinic** (see "Doctors," below).

Doctors: You'll find doctors on duty or on 24-hour call at most hotels. Alternatives include the new **Cozumel Walk-In Clinic,** Calle 6 Norte and Av. 15 (☎ **987/2-4070**); the **Cozumel Chiropractic Service,** Av. 5 Sur 24-A between calles 3 and 5 (☎ **987/2-5099**); the **Centro de Salud (Health Center)**, Av. 20 and Calle 11 (☎ **987/2-0140**), open 24 hours; and the **Cozumel Medical Specialities Clinic,** Av. 20 Norte no. 425 (☎ **987/ 2-1419**), which provides a 24-hour pharmacy and air-ambulance service. (See also "Recompression Chamber," below.)

English-Language Newspapers/Magazines: Publicaciones Gracia, on the east side of the main plaza (☎ **987/2-0031**), open Monday to Saturday 8am to 2pm and 4 to 10pm, and Sunday 9am to 1pm and 5 to 10pm, has a sparse supply of English-language books and magazines. Shops in the larger hotels carry the *Mexico City News,* about the only non-Spanish newspaper around.

Emergencies: For police, call ☎ **987/2-0409;** fire department, ☎ **987/ 2-0800;** and the Red Cross, ☎ **987/2-1058.**

Hospitals: Medica del Sur, Avenida Pedro Joaquin Coldwell between Calle 21 and Calle 23, in front of the CONALEP school (☎ **987/2-5787**), is a good, professionally staffed private hospital.

Maps: The American Express map is the best; if you can't find it anywhere else, drop into the American Express office (see above) and pick one up.

Pharmacies: The **Medical Specialities Clinic** has a 24-hour pharmacy. You'll also find lots of drugstores around the main plaza, most of them open until 9pm.

Police: See "Emergencies," above.

Post Office: The *correo*, or post office, is located on Avenida Rafael Melgar and Calle 7 Sur; it's open Monday to Friday 9am to 6pm and Saturday 9am to noon.

Recompression Chamber: Calle 5 Sur between Av. 5 Sur and Av. Rafael Melgar (☎ 987/2-2387), open daily 8am to 1pm and 4 to 8pm. Treats the two most common diving problems: the bends, and "rapture of the deep" or "diver's high."

Safety: Cozumel has a low crime rate, but take normal precautions with wallets and purses and don't take valuables to the beach (that's why hotels have safe-deposit boxes). See chapter 10, "Crossing the Border & What to Expect on the Other Side," for additional safety tips.

Special Events: Cozumel's whopper of a fishing contest is the 3-day International Sportsfishing Tournament, held at the beginning of May; check with the **State Tourist Office** (☎ **987/2-0972**) for details. The pre-Lenten Carnaval, celebrated the Thursday to Tuesday before Ash Wednesday, is very festive, with floats, dancing in the streets, competitions, and merry-making galore.

Telephone: The telephone area code for Cozumel is 987. To call long distance within Mexico (abbreviated *lada*), dial 01, then the area code, and then the number. To call the United States, dial 001 and then the area code and number.

U.S. Consul: Maruelos Building at Av. Nader 40 (☎ **98/84-2411**).

Fun On & Off the Beach

If you're looking for the perfect beach, you can't do better than Cozumel's stretches of white-as-confectioner's-sugar sand—each with its own personality. So you won't be spinning your wheels finding the one that's right for you, I'll give you the lowdown on your options. I'll also clue you in to what's happening underwater, explore various ways to play on the shore, and tell you how you can enjoy the water while giving your bathing suit a rest.

For those who like their fun dry, Cozumel's Mayan ruins won't make you swoon, but they're a nice introduction to the more magnificent structures on the mainland—which are covered, along with other touring options, in the side trips section. Besides poking around old buildings, there are several other things to do on the island during the day that won't put a hole in your pocketbook—and some that will—that is, shopping, also covered in this chapter. Don't worry about overdoing it; you won't be staying up until dawn at any discos, as you'll discover in the "What to Do When the Sun's Gone Down" section.

Beaches, Beaches, Everywhere

Although Cozumel gets hordes of tourists, many are day trippers who congregate on only certain beaches; many other shores remain little visited and pristine. You'll find miles of sparkling white beaches that are cool underfoot, even in the heat of the day, because of the large percentage of limestone that makes up the sand.

The beaches with the best "dispositions" are on the west coast, or leeward, side of the island, facing—and protected by—the mainland. Because the waters are calm and good for swimming, this is where the hotels are. Along this stretch, the southern beaches lay claim to being the best of the best. But the island's east, or windward, side is ruggedly beautiful, with higher winds, sand dunes, and lots of craggy limestone outcroppings dotting the shore; it's virtually undeveloped because of the less-than-benign ocean. About half of the east coast is accessible only by dirt road, so it's more of a hassle to traverse. If you can muster up a four-wheel-drive, however, you'll be rewarded by a mesmerizing landscape and a beach to call your very own.

Bet You Didn't Know

Cozumel's original name was *Ah–Cuzamil-Peten*, which means "land of the swallows" in the Mayan language.

As you can see on the map in chapter 18, "Finding Your Way Around Cozumel," there's only one road that goes around the island; it changes its name a few times, but you won't have any trouble sticking to it. The following beaches are clearly marked with signs. I'll profile the west coast beaches from north to south and the east coast beaches from south to north.

A West Coast (Leeward) Beach North of Town

Playa San Juan is the first beach you'll come to when heading north from San Miguel. It's popular for swimming, windsurfing, snorkeling, or just soaking up the rays. You'll find water sports equipment rentals, snack bars, and restaurants. Parents love the shady palapas on the beach for tucking in their broods.

Time-Savers

Get to Chankanaab early to stake out a beach chair and palapa before the cruise ships arrive.

West Coast (Leeward) Beaches South of Town

One of Cozumel's prime attractions and always included on a tour of the island, **Kids** **Chankanaab Park** was designated a state park in 1997. This long, wide beach—one of the most beautiful in Cozumel—boasts a lagoon created from a sinkhole, which makes it a natural aquarium (some 50 species of fish reside here); it's connected to the sea by a series of tunnels. Swimming is prohibited in the lagoon, both because it was deteriorating from too much suntan lotion and because it's undergoing research by a group of scientists.

But there are plenty of alternative activities, including snorkeling in the open sea and sitting under a thatched umbrella. The park has a seafood restaurant, a few snack huts, changing rooms and lockers, as well as several shops to rent diving and snorkeling gear. You'll find the park at Carretera Sur km 9. It's open daily from 8am to 5pm, and admission is about $1.25.

If you want the same exotic array of underwater marine life as Chankanaab without the crowds, **Playa Corona** is the place to come. There's a seafood restaurant, and you can rent snorkeling equipment on the beach and practically have the water to yourself.

Some consider the 3-mile-long **Playa San Francisco** to be the loveliest on the island; divers like it because it offers the best access to the Santa Rosa and San Francisco reefs. It's well stocked with facilities for the active, including water sports rentals and changing rooms, as well as for those who just want to loll on a beach chair and take a tanning break at a bar, restaurants, or gift shops. Head for the volleyball nets to work off some calories after lunch. Don't expect prices to be low here, however; this is a seller's rather than a buyer's market.

Extra! Extra!

To avoid crowds, don't come to **Playa San Francisco** on Sunday, when locals party to live music under the restaurant palapas. Check the cruise ship schedules, too; the beach is extremely popular with day trippers from the big boats.

Playa del Sol is another cruise ship hotspot with plenty to keep you busy for the day. There's horseback riding, water sports equipment rentals—including noisy jet skis—a beach club that sells food and drink at rather inflated prices, several gift shops, and even a diminutive zoo with small animals indigenous to Cozumel.

Named for the famous reef just offshore, **Playa Palancar** is a sandy oasis that gets relatively few visitors, but has the essentials: restaurant, bar, water sports rental hut, and dressing rooms. It's a low-key, relaxing spot.

For real solitude, **Punta Celerain,** the beach areas around the lighthouse at the southern tip of the island, fit the bill. Apart from some iguanas and a few Mexican soldiers trying to fight off boredom while guarding the coast, you'll be on your own. However, you'll have to tote supplies; there are no facilities of any kind here.

Yo, Gringo!

Be extremely careful about swimming on the east coast. The combination of open sea, dangerous undertows, and no lifeguards is potentially lethal.

East Coast (Windward) Beaches

Once you round the point at the lighthouse and head north along the eastern coastal road, the first beach you'll spot is **Playa Paradiso,** which has a snack shack. It's near the tiny ***Tumba del Caracol* (Caracol Tomb)** Mayan site, which isn't worth going out of your way for, although it's fun to imagine its builders taking to the same beach you're visiting when they got tired of working. **Playa Bonito,** the second beach on the way north, is similar, with the requisite restaurant/bar for wayfarers.

Regarded as the best beach along this shore, **Punta Chiqueros**—known by locals as Tortuga Desnuda or Playa San Juan—is set apart from the rest by a protected crescent-shaped inlet. You can swim here or windsurf, if you've got your own board. There's also a decent restaurant.

Playa Chen Río is often safe for swimming because of the wall of protective rocks shielding it from the open ocean. Locals like to picnic or camp over-night here, although there are no facilities of any kind.

Yo, Gringo!

Don't make the trip to Punta Molas unless you feel completely comfortable with your vehicle and are totally prepared for an emergency. There are absolutely no services along the road; if you break down, it could be a long, long time before someone comes by to help, especially in the late afternoon.

The only hotel on the east coast is on **Punta Morena;** it's a modest affair with a restaurant and bar, but no phone. This is sea turtle territory: On summer nights, the females make their way up from the sea to lay their eggs. It's protected by the government, which sends soldiers to patrol the beach so that poachers don't steal the future turtle offspring.

Playa Oriente marks the dividing line between the coast's paved and non-paved road. Beyond this point, it's four-wheel-drive terrain. The pleasant Mezcalito Café, overlooking the choppy ocean, serves light fare. The beach also marks the end of the cross-island road, or Avenida Juárez, which starts in San Miguel.

If you have an adventurous spirit, an all-terrain vehicle, and a good supply of water, food, and fuel, you can get to **Punta Molas,** the northernmost tip of eastern Cozumel. Once you near the point, which is marked by a lighthouse, there are virgin beaches for sunning, napping, or iguana-watching—but no swimming, please, because the waters are rough.

Underwater Exploration

Cozumel is rated as one of the top five dive spots in the world—with good reason. Sea currents that have been nourishing Cozumel's reefs since the beginning of time (well, as long as most scientists have been counting, anyway) have created amazingly colorful underwater scenery—and you can view it through crystal clear waters with a visibility of at least 100 feet, and sometimes as much as 200.

The Palancar Reef system is 3 miles off the west coast of Cozumel. The world's second largest reef colony, outranked only by Australia's Great Barrier Reef, it runs some 1,500 miles down the Caribbean coast to Central America. In the Cozumel area, there are more than 30 recorded reefs within this system, reaching depths of 50 to 80 feet.

In addition to coral, sponges are big here, literally as well as metaphorically: Of the 150 different kinds that flourish in the area, some, such as the elephant ear, can grow as large as 10 to 12 feet. There are

Reef PR

The Mexican Government recently renamed the Palancar Reef the Great Maya Reef to fit it into its Mundo Maya (Maya World) travel promotion.

also more than 230 types of fish, several of them unique to Cozumel. Among the more common ones that you're likely to come across are the electric blue-and-yellow queen angelfish, parrotfish, manta rays, sea fans, and anemones.

Warts and All

The Splendid Toadfish isn't found anywhere else in the world except Cozumel. It grows 12 to 16 inches and usually lurks in holes. If you're lucky, you can spy on one at mealtime—the guy's a fast eater and sucks in prey in a second flat.

Taking the Plunge

Luckily, you don't have to be an expert to dive near Cozumel. The best dive instructors in Mexico take to Cozumel like, well, fish to water, because this is where the dive business is. You also have access here to the latest safety procedures and emergency equipment.

Ocean Motion

The constant north-south ocean currents can carry divers along at between 1 and 1½ knots an hour. As a result, most of the underwater exploring around Cozumel is drift diving—which is exactly what its name sounds like.

The range of dive trips is exhaustive—and potentially exhausting. Day dives, night dives, wall dives, and open ocean dives all are options, and they branch off into subdivisions such as photo, sunken ship, or ecological dives. It'd be impossible to list all the prices, but here's a rough idea of what you can expect to pay for the basics:

➤ **Courses:** A 4-hour resort course for beginners costs about $60; a refresher course is $55; an advanced course, $250; open-water training dives, $165; 4- to 5-day PADI certification course, $350.

Dollars & Sense

Be sure to buy dive insurance, which you can get through any dive shop for about $1 a day. Its most important benefit is access to Cozumel's **Recompression Chamber** (Calle 5 Sur between Av. 5 Sur and Avenida Rafael Melgar; ☎ 987/2-2387), open daily 8am to 1pm and 4 to 8pm, which treats the two most common diving problems: bends, a painful bubbling that results when a diver comes to the surface too quickly and takes in toxic amounts of nitrogen, and "rapture of the deep" or "diver's high," again caused by too much nitrogen entering the bloodstream.

➤ **Dives:** Several shops can arrange half-day two-tank expeditions with lunch for $50. A two-tank morning dive (no lunch) also costs $50, but if you decide to tack on an afternoon dive, one tank runs $9 extra, and two tanks add $30 more. A one-tank night dive generally runs about $35.

➤ **Gear:** The going rate for scuba gear rental is $5 for a tank, $6 for a regulator, $7.50 for a buoyancy compensator, $5 for mask and fins, $5 for a wet suit, and $33 for a 35mm underwater camera.

Yo, Gringo!

Always check out credentials, safety standards, and equipment, and consult with diving pros. Avoid the *piratas* (pirates)—salesmen selling dive trips on the ferry pier or on the streets at cut-rate prices. They rarely represent reputable dive operations. Your safety is worth far more than the few pesos you might save.

Cozumel has about 100 dive shops that cater to more than 80,000 divers a year. Most are reputable; the following by no means excludes the others, but my favorites include **Aqua Safari** (Avenida Rafael Melgar at Calle 5, ☎ 987/2-0101, and at the Plaza Las Glorias hotel, ☎ 987/2-3362, e-mail dive@aquasafari.com); **Dive Cozumel** (Av. Salas 72 at Av. 5 Sur, ☎ 987/2-4110); **Dive House** (Avenida Juárez, on the main plaza, ☎ 987/2-1953); **Dive Paradise** (Av. Rafael Melgar 601, ☎ 987/2-1007); **Scuba Du** (Presidente Inter-Continental Hotel Cozumel, ☎ 987/2-0322); **Tico's Dive Center** (Av. 5 Norte 121, between Calle 2 and Calle 4, ☎ 987/2-0276); and **Zapata Divers** (Chankanaab Park, ☎ 987/2-0502).

Holy Cenotes!

In recent years, it's become the vogue to dive into underwater caverns and *cenotes*—deep sinkholes considered sacred by the Maya. **Yucatech Expeditions** (Avenida 15 between Avenida Salas and Calle 1 across the street from the Pepita Hotel; ☎ **987/2-5659**) offers 2-day introductory and advanced instruction in cave diving for $250 to $350; a weeklong course that'll move you from beginning to advanced status runs $1,100. Guided tours of the caves and cenotes south of Playa del Carmen run $130. Rates include ferry and land transportation, equipment, and lunch. Divers must be certified in open-water diving and/or cave diving before being accepted for the tours.

Reef Madness

Here are the reefs in brief:

The angelfish, tarpon, tiny minnows, and other fish that teem around **Chankanaab Reef** don't get much privacy because their home is near an extremely popular multi-activity park. The still beautiful coral formations are several hundred feet offshore, and the shallow cove has openings of several caves.

Colombia Reef is known for its deep (100-foot) dives and its elaborate towers, caves, and tunnels—similar to those at Palancar Reef (see below). Large marine specimens such as sea turtles, grouper, and eagle rays take shelter in the caves.

The **Maracaibo Reef** is for veteran divers only. This reef, which begins at about 120 feet underwater, is very challenging because of its fierce currents and enormous depth.

Palancar Reef boasts the most spectacular topography and landscapes of all the reefs; it's the one that starred in oceanographer Jacques Cousteau's 1961 film that put Cozumel on the diving map. Visibility is to 250 feet and a dazzling array of sponges and corals can be spotted at the bottom. Two of the most popular areas to explore are the **Caves site** with its intricate ravines and passageways, and the **Horseshoe site,** where you can swim through lofty columns of corals shaped like you-know-what. Nature not enough? There's also a 12-foot-high submerged bronze statue of Christ.

Yo, Gringo!

Reefs are protected marine property in Cozumel and spearing, touching, and taking coral or anything else from the bottom of the sea is prohibited. It has taken thousands of years for Cozumel's coral to grow to its current size. Don't mess with Mother Nature—or the Mexican government.

Paraíso Reef is good for beginners. It's only 30 feet deep and a couple of hundred feet from shore. Night-dive aficionados like the crabs, lobsters, octopus, and brain and star corals that are visible after dark. **La Ceiba** and **Villa Blanca** reef walls are within swimming distance.

The little-frequented **Paso del Cedral** is interesting for its caves and worth a visit if you want to look at marine turtles and green and spotted eels.

When the Mexican movie *Ciclon* (*Cyclone*) was shot at **Plane Wreck Reef,** a twin-engine plane was sunk as a prop—and never recovered. Only 300 feet from the La Ceiba hotel pier, this site is perfect for novices because they never have to go deeper than 30 feet. Enormous coral formations and colorful sponges are on the scene, too. This place is also popular for night dives.

Of all the wall reefs in Cozumel, **San Francisco Reef** is the tamest at depths of less than 50 feet. It measures half a mile and offers a bright array of eel fish.

Famous for its 3,000-foot drop-off, **Santa Rosa Wall** is for advanced divers who like to wander into and around its caves and look at the lettuce coral, tigerfish, angelfish, large groupers, and the occasional visiting shark.

Reaching depths of 70 feet, **Tormentos Reef's** coral city has become a favorite with underwater photographers who snap away at the vividly colored green eels, sea cucumbers, crabs, and other sea life.

Small by comparison with the rest of the reefs, **Yucab Reef** measures around 400 feet long and 55 feet deep, but has really strong currents that the resident lobsters and crabs don't seem to mind.

Snorkeling

If you don't like the feeling of having to rely on a tank attached to a hose to breathe—and many don't—snorkeling is a good alternative. You may not see the variety of fish you'd see if you plumbed the depths, but you won't be disappointed: Angelfish, parrotfish, sergeant majors, and a multitude of coral are all easily viewed from the surface.

Among the best snorkeling spots are the shallow waters of Chankanaab Park and Playa San Francisco; the docks at the Presidente Inter-Continental Cozumel, La Ceiba, and Club Cozumel Caribe hotels are also good. Snorkel rentals, available at most hotels and beaches along the west coast, run about $5 to $8 a day. Travel agencies can arrange 5-hour snorkeling trips, which include three separate reefs and lunch, for about $40. Many dive shops offer 2-hour afternoon excursions for around $25.

Time-Savers

Don't forget to pack your diving proof of certification. And bringing your own snorkeling gear is a good way to save a bit of money—and you'll know exactly where your equipment's been.

Hooked on Fishing

Before diving overshadowed all the island's other nautical activities, Cozumel was known as one of the country's premier sportsfishing resorts. Billfish—swordfish, marlin, and sailfish—are especially large and plentiful; several world records have been set here. The season is March through June.

Other favorites among anglers are wahoo, mackerel, mahi-mahi, bonito, barracuda, and amberjack, which are abundant all year. Bottom fishing for small sharks, snapper, tarpon, grouper, and yellowtail is also popular at the northern end of the island. Bonefishing is also done in the shallow flats.

Sportsfishing Tipping Tips

It's customary to tip 10% to 15% of the total price of your charter, depending on the quality of service received. Give the money to the captain, who will split it with the mate.

207

Charter boats vary in size and price from the small, modest *ballenera,* which goes for $100 for 4 hours (half day) for two people, to a super-luxury fishing yacht that runs $1,200 for 8 hours (full day) for six people. The going rate, though, for most charter boats is $300 a half day for up to six people, $350 for a full day. The price includes the captain, crew, fishing gear, bait, license, and lunch if you're on a full-day charter. At some deluxe hotels, such as the Presidente Inter-Continental Cozumel, you can arrange fishing through the on-site travel agency. Other reliable companies include **Aquarius Fishing and Tours** (Calle 3 Sur at Avenida Salas; ☎ 987/2-1092); **Club Nautico de Cozumel** (Puerto de Abrigo on Avenida Rafael Melgar; ☎ 987/2-1024), which will also arrange fishing trips from the United States for periods of several days; and **Dive Cozumel** (Avenida Salas at Avenida 5 Sur; ☎ 800/253-2701 in the U.S., or 987/2-1842).

Off the Hook

More and more anglers are taking part in the catch and release conservation program: You reel in your fish, tag it, and then send it back into the sea to create future fish (after it recovers from the temporary hook-in-the-mouth pain, of course).

An Assortment of Water Sports

Diving may be king on Cozumel, but there are plenty of other ways to enjoy the water, some more venerable than others. Among the most popular motorized sports are **jet skiing** ($45 for two for a half hour) and **parasailing** ($45 for the 10-minute ride). You don't have to rely on any power but your own if you go **kayaking** ($15 an hour in a two-person vehicle, $12 an hour in a one-person vehicle) or **pedal boating** ($15 an hour in two-person vehicles).

The best places to secure water toys, all on the activity-friendly western side of the island, include the following hotels: The **Presidente Inter-Continental Cozumel** (Carretera a Chankanaab, km 6.5; ☎ 987/2-0322), **Plaza Las Glorias** (Av. Rafael Melgar, km 1.5; ☎ 987/2-2000), the **Fiesta Americana** (Carretera a Chankanaab, km 7.5; ☎ 987/2-2622), and **Sol Cabañas del Caribe** (Carretera Santa Pilar, km 4.5; ☎ 987/2-6185) hotels. Concessions on Playa San Francisco (see above) also rent a full array of gear.

Windsurfing

You can sail the waves under the tutelage of a master: Raul de Lille and his partner Nilo Dzib, both Olympic champions, offer classes and equipment rental at the Sol Cabañas del Caribe hotel beach (Carretera Santa Pilar, km 4.5; ☎ 987/2-6185). Two hours of instruction cost $80. If you already know how to windsurf, you can rent a short board for $20 an hour or a long board for $30 an hour; additional hours get you a 30% to 50% discount.

On Deck: Enjoying the Waves Without Getting Your Hair Wet

The crowds have voted: Most visitors to Cozumel prefer fish-to-face contact. If you want a bit more distance between you and the denizens of the deep, however, you can book a ride on one of two glass-bottomed mini-subs, the **Nautilius IV** (☎ 987/2-0433) and the **Mermaid** (☎ 987/2-0588). You'll be observing marine life—and the occasional diver waving to you in passing—from the air-conditioned hull. Tours, which depart

Claustrophobe Alert

If you're not keen on spending extended periods of time underwater in an enclosed space with other people, these trips may not be for you.

from the downtown dock at 10am and noon, take less than 2 hours and cost about $30; the price includes a guide and soft drinks. Nautilius also offers a night tour departing about a half hour before sunset for the same price.

Keeping Your Head Above Water: Cozumel's Top Attractions

Most travel agencies in town offer a full-day tour of the island that typically includes Chankanaab Park, San Gervasio, the museum, and El Cedral and costs $40 per person. Taxi drivers who double as guides also provide island tours; depending on what you want to see, the price is around $30 to $50 for up to four people in the vehicle.

Dollars & Sense

If you do book a cabbie as a tour guide, you may not get the most accurate information—but then again, you might, because these guys have been around. If you have a comprehensive tour guide, such as *Frommer's*, with you anyway, this may be the way to go because the price is right. You'll know in advance how good your guide's English will be, which isn't always the case if you go the regular tour bus route.

Ruin-ing an Afternoon

The island is dotted with archaeological sites built by the Maya—more than 35 of them. Most are inaccessible, but the **San Gervasio ruins,** the oldest

Dollars & Sense

Guides on site charge $10 to take up to six people around the site. It's better, though, to get a copy of *San Gervasio*, a small booklet sold at San Miguel bookshops for about $2, and do the tour on your own.

and best preserved, can be visited. Built between 100 B.C. to A.D. 300, San Gervasio was the largest Mayan settlement on the island and reached the height of its splendor between A.D. 900 and 1200—a contemporary of the famed Chichén Itzá on the mainland. It served as an important trading center and a pilgrimage site for pregnant noblewomen who canoed over from the mainland to ask blessings from Ixchel, the Mayan goddess of childbirth, at her temple. The complex was made up of six groups of buildings, but little is left of them today except a central plaza surrounded by mounds, fractured columns, and lintels that may have been part of an observatory. Labels explaining the various structures are in English, Spanish, and Maya. There's a small snack bar at the entrance.

From town, you can reach San Gervasio by Avenida Benito Juárez, the cross-island road; the turnoff to the ruins is to the left a few miles past the airport. You'll pay a $1 road fee at the gate, and then drive about 4 miles to reach the ruins. Entrance to the site, open daily from 8am to 5pm, is $1.25. Alternatively, taxi drivers stationed along the waterfront in town can drive you there, wait while you tour, and drive you back to town. The going rate is $35 for up to four passengers for an hour and a half stint—which will give you plenty of time, as you can easily make the rounds in about half an hour.

Bet You Didn't Know

In the 16th century, Cozumel was used by the conquistadors as a supply depot for the Spanish armada. Two hundred years later, British pirates Jean Laffite and Henry Morgan used the coves of Cozumel to scout out their prey—the Spanish galleons.

Kids Touring Chankanaab Park

I know, I covered Chankanaab Park in the beaches section earlier in this chapter, but you can also have a great time here without getting wet. Stroll the botanical gardens, which have more than 300 different plant species from around the world; explore the archaeological park, where long pathways are lined with replicas of Mayan and Olmec artifacts, including giant Olmec heads and a Chac Mool figure from Chichén Itzá; or visit a small interactive museum for kids.

You can book a guided tour of Chankanaab Park through a travel agency; $45 will buy you a guided explanation of the botanical gardens, archaeological park, and museum, as well as lunch and snorkeling.

Exploring Cozumel's Past

The two-story Museum of Cozumel Island is great for a quick course on the island, past and present. The professionally executed displays, in four galleries, span the island's history from pre-Hispanic to modern times; they include Mayan relics as well as cannons and other ship memorabilia. Cozumel's geology and ecosystem is explained, and such pressing contemporary issues as threats to the coral reefs are addressed. A re-creation of a typical Mayan hut is on display. You can catch a free tour here and join various workshops on the Maya; check the schedule when you arrive. Located on Avenida Rafael Melgar, between calles 4 Norte and 6 Norte (☎ **987/2-1475**), the museum is open daily from 10am to 6pm; admission is $3. A rooftop restaurant with a terrific view of the waterfront serves pretty good food from 9am to 7pm.

Bet You Didn't Know

San Miguel (St. Michael) got its name after a perfectly intact ivory statue of the archangel, with a sword and crown of pure gold, was uncovered by a group of workmen digging near the village about 100 years ago—on September 29, San Miguel's holy day. Today, the statue can be viewed at the church of San Miguel on Avenida 10 and Benito Juárez. The mysterious artifact is believed to have been a present to the Maya from the Spanish conquistador Juan de Grijalva.

Climbing a Lighthouse

Located at the extreme southern point of the island and past El Cedral, the **Punta Celerain Lighthouse** is watched over by the Garcia family, who serve up fish and beer for visitors at midday. Sr. Garcia, the lighthouse keeper and host of this somewhat surreal gathering, will also guide you to the 127 steps leading to the top of the building if you want to gaze at the sea from the summit. Sand dunes, jungle, and mist—it's very atmospheric here.

To get to Punta Celerain, follow the southern coast road; it's a little less than 18 miles from town. You'll see the lighthouse in the distance before you turn off the highway onto the sandy road leading to it. A four-wheel-drive is best for negotiating the 2½ miles to the point; don't even think of trying it on a motorbike. There's no phone and no admission price; daylight hours are the recommended visiting times.

Horsing Around

For a swing through the Cozumel outback and visits to three Mayan ruins, saddle up with Rancho Buenavista (☎ **987/2-1537**). The 4-hour jaunt costs $60 and includes a guide, transportation to the ranch, and beer or soda.

211

Departures are from Acuario Restaurant (Avenida Rafael Melgar at Calle 11) Monday to Friday at noon and Saturday at 11am.

There's also horseback riding on Playa del Sol for about $15 an hour, but don't expect frisky, well-fed thoroughbreds. These are mixed breeds either already put out to pasture or that work a second shift on a farm.

A Ruined Ruin

Once the largest Mayan site on Cozumel and supposedly the site of the first Spanish mass celebrated in Mexico, now there's little left to see of El Cedral. What wasn't destroyed by the conquistadors was taken care of by the U.S. Army Corps of Engineers, who built an airstrip through the ruins during World War II, when Cozumel served as a strategic air base. In addition to a one-room temple, several other unimpressive artifacts lie in the underbrush; on-site guides will show you around for a small fee. An extremely modest church near El Cedral hosts a lively religious festival each May.

If you want to detour to this site, turn off the coastal road going south at km 17.5 and drive 2 miles inland. There's no admission fee.

Cozumel's Best Shopping

Shopping in Cozumel is driven by the cruise ships, which deposit over a million passengers a year into the port. Since the two piers used by the luxury liners are close to town, that's where you'll find the largest conglomeration of shops.

Dollars & Sense

Pay cash for your purchases; the credit card companies' hefty commissions are passed along to you when you use plastic. You can pay with U.S. greenbacks at most places—several shops even list their prices in dollars—but prices tend to be higher and exchange rates lower. You're likely to get a better deal by paying with pesos at a place that has prices listed in the local currency.

Many carry the same monotonous, mass-produced array of clay figurines, T-shirts, and tacky souvenirs, but some sell diamonds, gemstones, gold and silver jewelry, designer clothing (don't expect New York or even Dallas), and high-quality Mexican handicrafts. The stretch of Avenida Rafael Melgar along the waterfront has the chicest shops. The area surrounding the main plaza is another major shopping district, with more than a hundred small outlets; the merchandise is less upscale here.

Markets

At the **Mercado de Artesanias,** inside the Plaza del Sol building on the plaza, stalls selling regional Mexican handicrafts take up the entire ground floor. This is a good place to absorb the local market tradition, as venerable as the Mayan people who still tend many of the stalls; you'll often hear snatches of Maya being spoken among the vendors. It's never crowded or overwhelming, and thus well worth visiting even if you're not buying. To be sure, you'll have to pick through a lot of modernized, dowdy-looking stuff. Stick to the *tipica* (typical) handicrafts like the hand-embroidered Yucatecan *huipil* dresses and blouses—you'll see some Mayan vendors wearing them—sandals (*huaraches*), blankets, baskets, and oven-fired *barro* (clay) household items.

Market Tips

It's common—required, really—to bargain in Indian markets but a no-no in stores where items are price-tagged. If you don't see a tag, the price is open to negotiation.

As a reminder, here are some bargaining strategies:

➤ Before heading to the market, check established handicrafts stores to get an idea of the price of the items you're interested in.

➤ Keep a poker face. Gush and the vendor will automatically ask for more.

➤ Start by offering 30% of the asking price and work your way up from there; you've done well if you end paying half of what you were originally quoted.

➤ Walk away if the vendor refuses to come down in price. If that doesn't jolt him into calling after you with a better deal, pick another stall and start over.

➤ Wait until close to closing; some merchants will sell at any price if their day hasn't gone well. Of course, much of the good stuff will already have been grabbed up by then.

Arts & Crafts

Try **Na Balam** (Av. 5 Norte 14; no phone), another long-established store, for batik T-shirts with Mayan motifs and reproductions of Mayan art. **El Sombrero** (Av. Rafael Melgar 29; ☎ 987/2-0374) sells well-made leather clothing, and more. Locals send their friends to **Unicornio** (Av. 5 Sur 1; ☎ 987/2-0171) for wood and glazed folk art at good prices. **Bugambilias**

(Avenida 10 Sur between Calle Sala and Avenida 1; no phone) sells unusual and traditional handmade lace—everything from blouses to tablecloths—from all parts of Mexico, including Zacatecas, Guerrero, and Aguascalientes.

Galeria One (Calle 17 Sur between Avenida 20 Sur and Avenida 25 Sur, ☎ 987/2-2659) displays the works of the Scottish artists Gordon and Jennifer Gilchrist—lithographs of Mayan ruins, silkscreens, and watercolors.

Yo, Gringo!

When buying market handicrafts, look them over carefully for defects. Vendors aren't trying to pass off inferior products; it's just that the small village workshops where the goods are produced rarely practice quality control. When buying silver, always check for the tiny .925 government stamp, which means the product is 92.50% pure silver. Street vendors often try to sell nickel alloys (*alpaca*).

Jewelry

At **Roberto's Black Coral Studio** (Av. 5 Sur 199; ☎ 987/2-5383), local diver Roberto Ramos has been fashioning coral into beautiful jewelry for more than 20 years. Some of his creations have been presented to royal heads of state, such as Queen Sofia of Spain. Some days you can catch Roberto at work at a small table inside the entrance.

Designing women (and men) should drop into **Diamond Creations** (Av. Rafael Melgar Sur 131; ☎ 987/2-5330), where you can create your own jewelry by selecting the gemstone of your choice—ruby, emeralds, and sapphires are available, as well as diamonds—and the mounting. Your personalized necklace, bracelet, or earrings will be ready in an hour. **Rachet & Romero** (Av. Rafael Melgar 101; ☎ 987/2-0571) also features precious stones set in eye-catching designs.

Yo, Gringo!

Purchase black coral jewelry only from a dealer who has a government permit to extract it; they're issued year-to-year by the Mexican Fishing Ministry to prevent the coral's extinction. You should receive a certificate of authenticity. If you buy from a street vendor, you're likely to be getting black plastic—or the real thing, obtained illegally.

A Top Shop

If you have time for only one shop in Cozumel, make it **Los Cinco Soles,** Av. Rafael Melgar Norte 27 (☎ **987/2-0132**), where you can find high-quality, well-priced handicrafts from all over Mexico. There's a great selection of clothing, glassware, pottery, leather goods, hand-carved furniture, and jewelry (the gold and silver replicas of pre-Hispanic designs are a real find). There's almost always something on sale. When you need retail refueling, drop into the coffee shop.

What to Do When the Sun's Gone Down

Cozumel's dives aren't sleazy; the island has far more scuba shops than bars, and most visitors to Cozumel are early-to-rise, early-to-bed underwater types. But if you're hell-bent on raising hell, there are a few places to play after dark.

A favorite form of local diversion is hanging around the main plaza after sunset when the workday's done and the ocean breezes cool the air. The surrounding sidewalk cafes are great for people watching. If you're here on Sunday evening, check out the free concerts on the plaza.

Unless otherwise specified, all the nightlife listings are in San Miguel.

No-Holds-Barred Bars

Cozumel bars aren't age segregated; generations mingle at nearly all of these places (although if you already have hearing loss from too many rock concerts, you might want to avoid the louder ones).

Carlos 'n Charlie's (Av. Rafael Melgar 11; ☎ **987/2-0191**) follows the usual Carlos Anderson chain formula—silly slogans, crazy decor, fun-loving waiters, and full-blast music. **Fat Tuesday** (Av. Benito Juárez 2, on the main plaza; ☎ **987/2-5130**) has the best daiquiris in Cozumel—or so they claim. Doubtless, they dull the senses to the ear-shattering music that blasts the plaza. You've got your outer-limit-loud sounds at the **Hard Rock Cafe** (Av. Rafael Melgar 2A; ☎ **987/2-5271**), along with the requisite music memorabilia and souvenir store. **Joe's Lobster Pub** (Av. 10 Sur between Calle Salas and Calle 3; ☎ **987/2-3275**) looks

Dollars & Sense

You'll pay more for perfumes and cosmetics at Cozumel's so-called duty-free stores than you would in the United States, although the goods are low by European, Asian, and Mexican standards.

Oooh, Baby!

The Maya believed that Cozumel was sacred to Ixchel, goddess of fertility and childbirth. Think twice about that one–night stand—and double-check your protection.

like your standard hole-in-the-wall, with cracked tile floors and red-and-green lighting, but the locals and an imported baby boomer crowd love it. The night stays young 'til 3am with live salsa and reggae, and the management looks the other way if you decide to dance in the aisles. Tune up with a friend—or make a new one—at the lively **Laser Karaoke Bar** (Fiesta Inn hotel, south of town; ☎ **987/2-2811**), and be prepared for loud at the new **Planet Hollywood** (Av. Rafael Melgar 16; ☎ **987/2-5799**), brought to you by Schwarzenegger, Stallone, Willis, et al.

If a hangover keeps you from above-named bars, you can always head for **Video Bar Aladino** (Hotel Sun Village San Miguel; ☎ **987/2-0233**) for a quiet Bloody Mary and two aspirins while you watch the plaza life pass by.

Saturday Night Fever

Neptuno's (Avenida Rafael Melgar and Calle 11 Sur; ☎ **987/2-1537**), Cozumel's one and only surviving dance club, caters mostly to teeny boppers with techno rock and laser shows. If you like a dance floor to yourself, drop in during the week when—as opposed to the other places listed here—It's practically bare of bodies. Cover is under $10.

A Taste of Mexico: Fiesta Mexicana

The Fiesta Americana Cozumel Reef Hotel (Carretera a Chankanaab, km 7.5; ☎ **987/2-2622**) puts on a Fiesta Mexicana, which features a buffet dinner, drinks, regional Mexican folk dances, and music by mariachis and trios. Offered only during high season, the 3-hour shows go on at 6pm on Sunday and Thursday. The price is $33.

Side Trips: Getting Off the Island

The Caribbean coast across the channel from Cozumel offers so many great things to do, you may be hard-pressed to decide which to try first. You can take in a rustic fishing village with good shopping, go bananas over a bios-phere preserve, or visit a seaside Mayan ruin and make friends with a dol-phin on the same day. You can also journey deep into the Yucatán Peninsula to visit one of the most famous Mayan ceremonial centers.

Several of these sites were covered in the Cancún section (see chapter 15, "Fun On & Off the Beach"). So as not to repeat myself—and to avoid sacrific-ing any extra trees—I'll ask you nicely to flip back a few pages for the descriptions. I will, however, tell you in this section how you can get to these places from Cozumel, and how much it's likely to cost.

Playa del Carmen

Just a ferry ride across the channel from Cozumel, this once-humble fishing village has mushroomed into a town of 20,000—and the Caribbean coast's hottest spot.

You can easily spend the day lounging on the beaches—the best ones start at the ferry pier and work their way north along a line of hotels—or parked in one of the many sidewalk cafes along Avenida 5, the town's self-styled "boardwalk." The core of what used to be the village has managed to keep its rustic appeal in the face of development. Live bands knock out rock and roll and reggae in open-air restaurants from afternoon into the night, and sophisticated boutiques, mainly run by foreigners, carry unusual hand-crafted items, such as amber jewelry, wooden masks, batik clothing, and handmade sun hats.

Comfortable, air-conditioned waterjets make the 45-minute journey from Cozumel to Playa del Carmen from Cozumel's main pier from 4am until 10pm. Tickets, available at the entrance to the pier, cost $10, round-trip.

Chichén Itzá

This impressive Mayan site, a powerful city-state from A.D. 900 to 1200, is one of the most famous ruins in the Yucatán. The Castillo, Temple of the Warriors, and the Observatory are just a few of its magnificent reconstructed buildings. It's also the site of the sacred *cenote* (sinkhole), where human sacrifices took place and where priceless gold and jade ornaments were thrown as offerings to the gods.

If you have time for only a day visit, air is the best way to go. **Caribe Tours** (Avenida Rafael Melgar and Calle 5 Sur; ☎ **987/2-3100**) will fly you in and out and throw in a guide and lunch for $145. Tours leave early in the morning and return at about 8pm.

Tulum/Xel-Há

Travel agencies book trips that include a round-trip ticket on the Cozumel–Playa del Carmen ferry, an air-conditioned bus ride to Tulum and Xel-Há, entrance fees, and a box lunch (snorkeling equipment is extra). They depart at 9am, return at 5:30pm, and cost $75.

If you go on your own, after you leave the ferry in Playa del Carmen, you'll have to catch a taxi or one of the frequently running buses to the sites. Buses cost a few dollars and the **bus station** is on Avenida 5, 2 blocks due west and 2 blocks north of the ferry terminal. When you buy a ticket, they'll tell you which bus to catch. Taxis, which four people can share, should run about $25 to Tulum and $20 to Xel-Há. The entrance fee to Tulum is less than $3 and to Xel-Há, it's $10. See chapter 15 for more information on Tulum and Xel-Há.

Kids Xcaret

Travel agency tours, which cost approximately $50, include transportation via ferry to Playa del Carmen, an air-conditioned motor-coach ride from Playa to Xcaret, the entrance fee to Xcaret and a guide, but not the evening show. Lunch, snorkeling gear, and swimming with dolphins are on you. Departure is at 8am, with a 6pm return.

If you go on your own, the entrance fee is $30 (children under 6 are free), which includes the evening show. Swimming with dolphins costs $60. You'll have to grab a taxi (about $10) or cheap bus from Playa del Carmen; they run frequently. See "Tulum/Xel-Há," above, for information on getting to the bus station, and see chapter 15 for more information on Xcaret.

Sian Ka'an Biosphere Reserve

Some Cozumel travel agencies offer flight tours to Sian Ka'an, followed by the boat trip and lunch. They set out at 8am, return at around 5:30pm, and cost $160.

It's a little complicated to go on your own, but it can be done. You'll have to make a reservation with the Ecologos travel agency in Cancún (☎ 98/84-9580) in advance. Then take the ferry to Playa del Carmen, and from there grab a taxi to the Cabañas Ana y José hotel, a few miles south of Tulum—it'll run you about $25—where the Amigos de Sian Ka'an will pick you up and take you to the preserve. The tour costs $50. For more information, see the section on Sian Ka'an Biosphere Reserve in chapter 15, "Fun On & Off the Beach."

Chapter 20

The Best of Cozumel's Dining Scene

In This Chapter

➤ Cozumel dining: The big picture

➤ Keeping costs down

➤ The best restaurants from A to Z

➤ Restaurant indexes

For a low-key island, Cozumel has a surprisingly diverse dining scene. You've got a choice of divers' dives, hoity-toity places for the snob-inclined, candle-lit hideaways, and simple thatched huts oozing island atmosphere. Since Cozumel restaurants bank on the cruise ship trade for the lion's share of their clientele, they're poised to appeal to very cosmopolitan tastes (remember, cruise liners serve some fabulous food).

Cozumel restaurants are a lot more innovative than they were centuries ago when the main staple of the Mayan diet was fish . . . or fish tacos. You still have the fish, but Yucatecan specialties with chicken and pork, served *pibil* style (marinated in a sour orange sauce with annatto seed) or *escabeche* style (cooked in lots of sliced onions), started drifting over from the mainland long ago; as the island grew, the cuisine was influenced by sojourners from other lands, some of whom stayed on. Today you have knock-me-dead lobster, crab, and fish dishes, as well as prime Angus steaks and Italian, French, American, and Mexican specialties.

A Dining Overview: Where's the Burrito?

The town of San Miguel is the oldest part of the island and the one closest to the cruise piers, so it stands to reason it's got the most restaurants—more than 80, in fact. Not surprisingly, it's also where you'll find the best mix of prices, ambience, and local color. The hotels along the northern and southern hotel zones are excellent for peso-stretching breakfast and lunch buffets, but for dinner, I suggest you stay in—or take a cab to—San Miguel.

Although, they've been (blessedly, most people believe) slow in coming, a few fast food chains such as Subway and Dairy Queen have arrived in Cozumel, which is good news for parents of picky eaters. If you can stand the loud music—and hustle them quickly past the souvenir concessions—Planet Hollywood, Hard Rock Cafe, and Carlos 'n Charlie's are good places to take culinarily conservative teenagers. See chapter 19, "Fun On & Off the Beach," for the locations.

All restaurants are listed in alphabetical order, and then indexed by price.

Cheese-it

A traditional Mayan dish called *queso relleno* (stuffed cheese) is made from imported Dutch cheese, which has been around the Yucatán so long it's been adopted into local recipes. First, you remove—by eating, of course—the cheese inside the red waxed ball, leaving a thin layer sticking to the inside. The ball is then filled with ground beef, raisins, capers, and white sauce and baked. This special dish is served in Yucatecan restaurants on Sundays and various holidays.

Check, Please

It's easy to eat inexpensively in Cozumel, but you may find food costs creeping up on you if you're not careful (even bargains add up if you take advantage of too many of them). A few tips (see "Eating Well without Gobbling Up Your Dollars" in chapter 7) should help keep your budget—and maybe your waistline—from ballooning.

Cozumel's 12% tax—3% less than that on the mainland—has already been figured into your bill. However, unless a bill says *servicio incluido* at the bottom, the tip's your baby. The rule of thumb is 10% unless the service has been extraordinary or unless you've lingered until after closing hours; then it's appropriate to tip 15% or more.

The price categories below are set up with the piggiest-case scenario in mind: They're based on a per-person meal tab that includes appetizer, entree, dessert, one drink, and tip. You'll also see a price range for meal entrees in each of the reviews. The more $ signs, the more you'll be paying for the privilege of dining at the place listed:

$	=	Under $10	$$$	=	$25–$40
$$	=	$10–$25	$$$$	=	Over $40

Unless otherwise indicated, reservations are not necessary or accepted.

My Favorite Restaurants from A to Z

Café Caribe
$. San Miguel. COFFEE SHOP.

Although it calls itself Caribbean (*Caribe*), this cozy cafe looks more Austrian than tropical, what with its old-fashioned flouncy table coverings (but, hey, the Viennese are known for their coffeehouses). Enjoy a variety of java—Cuban, mocha, espresso, or cappuccino—with carrot cake, bagels, cheesecake, or quiches. When you can't take the island heat, duck in here for an ice cream or milk shake. You won't have any problem finding this place; just look for the large yellow sign.

Av. 10 Sur no. 215 (from the plaza, turn right on Av. 5 Sur for 1 block, then left on Salas and take another right on Av. 10). ☎ ***987/2-3621. Main courses:*** *Coffee and munchies $2–$4.50. No credit cards.* ***Open:*** *Mon–Sat 8am–1pm and 6–9:30pm.*

Most Romantic

Café del Puerto (San Miguel, $$$–$$$$)

La Cabaña del Pescador (North of Town, $$$)

Café del Puerto
$$$–$$$$. San Miguel. INTERNATIONAL.

The quintessential seaport restaurant, with its nautical embellishments and waterfront location, the Café del Puerto exudes romance. An old-fashioned spiral staircase leads to the elegant dining room where you can order a hearty helping of prime rib, flambéed mustard steak, or, if you're feeling like something less meaty, various well-prepared pastas. The soft music playing in the background is known to aid digestion. The Café opens about an hour before sunset so you have time to settle in before the sky puts on its light show; you can also linger here whispering sweet nothings over an after-dinner cordial.

Av. Rafael Melgar no. 3 (across the street and to the left of the pier). ☎ ***987/ 2-0316.*** *Reservations suggested.* ***Main courses:*** *$15–$26. AE, MC, V.* ***Open:*** *Daily 5–11pm.*

A Northern Notable

La Cabaña del Pescador *($$$. North of Town. SEAFOOD.)*
It's a one-trick pony—or should I say crustacean? Lobster, plucked from Cozumel's waters, is all that's served here—but that's what you came for, isn't it? The dining room, reached via a small bridge, is intimate and low-lit, and decked out with shells and hanging fish nets; it's super-romantic in a Gilligan's Island kind of way. You pay for your lobster (or prized lobster tails) by weight— about $25 for half a kilo, which is slightly more than a pound—and the rest of the meal (salad, rice, coffee, and dessert) is thrown in for free. Talk about rustic—there's not even a phone.

Carretera Pilar, km 4.5, across the street from the Plaza Azul hotel. No phone. ***Main courses:*** *Usually a minimum of $25. No credit cards.* ***Open:*** *Daily 6–10pm.*

Coco's
$. San Miguel. AMERICAN/MEXICAN.

The "in" breakfast place for locals and tourists in the know has a menu that straddles both sides of the border. People line up at ungodly—by vacation standards—hours for eggs and hash browns, fresh-made blueberry muffins and cinnamon rolls, or classic Mexican *rancheros* (eggs with tomato-and-onion sauce); if you don't mind the culture clash, you can order your *huevos mexicanos* (scrambled eggs with chile) with egg substitute. Coco's has a small book exchange and gift food items for sale, too.

Av. 5 Sur no. 180, corner of Salas. ☎ *987/2-0241.* **Breakfasts:** *$3–$6. No credit cards.* **Open:** *Tues–Sun 7am–noon. Closed from mid-Sept to second week of Oct.*

Comida Casera Toñita
$. San Miguel. MEXICAN (YUCATECAN).

Talk about homey: the Toñita serves delicious victuals in the converted living room of a family residence. A different Yucatecan dish is whipped up daily—perhaps *pollo en escabeche* (chicken baked in sliced onion sauce), *pollo a la naranja* (chicken in sour orange sauce), or *chuletas de puerco con achiote* (pork chops with annatto seed). There's also a regular menu of fried fish, chicken, and beef dishes. The family shops early in the morning at the local produce market for the ingredients. Classical music plays in the background, and you can browse the bookshelves after having breakfast, lunch, or early dinner here.

Av. Salas no. 256, between calles 10 and 15 North (catch Av. 5 Sur from the plaza and walk 1 block south, then take a left on Av. Salas and walk east for 1½ blocks). ☎ *987/2-0401. Reservations not necessary.* **Main courses:** *Lunch $4–$5.50; breakfast $2–$3.25. No credit cards.* **Open:** *Mon–Sat 8am–6pm.*

Hold the Chile!

Ask or sniff before you dig into typical *Ixnepech* sauce served at many restaurants. It's got the Yucatán's hottest chile pepper—the habeñero—slightly disguised with chopped onions, cilantro, tomatoes, lime juice, and vinegar. The name means "dog's nose" in Maya—not a very appealing term for something you put on, not under, the table.

El Moro
$–$$. San Miguel. YUCATECAN/INTERNATIONAL.

The hordes of diners—especially divers—who pack this Yucatecan restaurant don't seem to mind its fast-food tacky decor. There's 40 years' experience behind every dish, and a jumbo margarita will soon render you oblivious to the orange-on-orange color scheme. Try the house specialty, Yucatán *pollo Ticuleño*—fried chicken breast layered with a baked tortilla, mashed potatoes, and tomato sauce, topped with peas and cheese. You can get fresh seafood prepared to your taste or steaks and sandwiches, too. El Moro is a longish—13 block—walk from the plaza or a $2 cab ride.

75 Bis Norte 124, between calles 2 and 4 Norte. ☎ *987/2-3029.* **Main courses:** *$4.50–$13. MC, V.* **Open:** *Fri–Wed 1–11pm.*

La Choza
$$. San Miguel. MEXICAN.

Most Mexicano

Comida Casera Toñita (San Miguel, $)

El Moro (San Miguel, $–$$)

La Choza (San Miguel, $$)

Named after the simple thatched homes of the Maya, La Choza is modest-looking but roomy enough to fit the extended families of an entire village. It's always crammed with locals and tourists and buzzing with conversation. We're talking seriously authentic: Some dishes are so traditional, you'd be hard-pressed to find them in any other restaurants in Mexico. For a treat, try the beef smothered in poblano pepper sauce or chiles stuffed with shrimp; if you're lucky, the avocado pie will be in season. Folk art murals adorn the sloping ceilings, and marimba music fills the air most evenings.

Av. Salas 198 and Av. 10. ☎ *987/2-0958.* **Main courses:** *$6–$16. AE, MC, V.* **Open:** *Daily 7:30am–11pm.*

La Cuchina Italiano
$$. San Miguel. ITALIAN.

Yo, Gringo!

Remember, it's considered impolite in Mexico for your waiter to bring the check before you signal for it.

It's a family affair: The Tarronis manage, host, and cook at this popular Italian bistro, which looks more Caribbean than Mediterranean with its tropical thatching, wood-beamed ceiling, and rustic wooden tables. The products of the pasta rack in the dining room and of an herb garden planted with seeds brought over from Italy turn up in such dishes as the house specialty *fettuccine al frutti di mar* (shrimp, muscles, clams, squid, and fish in a white wine sauce); ravioli with ham and mushrooms in cream cognac; and the meat-stuffed lasagne, derived from a 200-year-old family recipe passed along by great-grandma Tarroni. There's only one dessert turned out daily—perhaps tiramisú—but count on it to be delicious. The wine cellar stocks Chianti and other Italian labels.

Av. 10 between Av. 1 and Salas (look for the white stucco facade). ☎ *987/2-5230.* **Main courses:** *$7.50–$12. AE, MC, V.* **Open:** *Mon–Fri 1pm–midnight; Sat–Sun 4pm–midnight.*

Palmeras
$$. San Miguel. AMERICAN.

This large, open-air eatery, an old Cozumel standby near the pier, is always bursting at the seams with day trippers from the cruise lines. They come for the all-day Yankee menu: eggs any way you want them for breakfast, and barbecued chicken, minute steak, or a cholesterol-plus combo of fried shrimp, smoked spare ribs, and French fries for lunch or dinner. The giant mango, banana, peach, or strawberry daiquiris and margaritas are renowned and make for a very vivacious crowd after sunset.

Av. Rafael Melgar, on the plaza. ☎ *987/2-0532.* **Main courses:** *$5–$16. AE, MC, V.* **Open:** *Daily 7am–10:30pm.*

Kids Pepe's Grill
$$$–$$$$. San Miguel. STEAK/SEAFOOD.

After long shopping sprees, tourists like to take a load off their feet at this bustling harborside restaurant. Sometimes it's a bit too popular; you may have to wait a long time for a table if you haven't reserved. It's quietest upstairs, and you'll have the best view of the Caribbean; stay downstairs if you like a livelier scene. This is old-style cooking, with various foods set on fire or served with heavy sauces. Stick with the simple preparations, such as the grilled lobster or cuts of steaks from Sonora, where Mexico's finest beef is produced. A children's menu includes broiled chicken and breaded shrimp.

Av. Rafael Melgar at Salas. ☎ *987/2-0213. Reservations recommended.* **Main courses:** *$13–$24. AE, MC, V.* **Open:** *Daily 5–11pm.*

Pizza Rolandi
$–$$. San Miguel. ITALIAN.

Just follow your nose: The delicious aroma should lead you to Pizza Rolandi's wood-burning oven. The creatively topped pizzas are primo, but the weekly specials—for example, a sea bass carpaccio appetizer with a choice of either fish, pizza, or pasta—are worth checking out. The minestrone gets consistently high marks. The patio out back is the prettiest area for dining, but the open-air dining room facing the street sees all the waterfront action.

Av. Rafael Melgar on the waterfront between calles 6 and 8 Norte. ☎ *987/2-0946.* **Main courses:** *$8–$10; pizza $9; daily specials $5–$13. MC, V.* **Open:** *Mon–Sat 11am–11pm; Sun 5–11pm.*

Prima
$–$$. San Miguel. ITALIAN.

Italian restaurants seem to thrive in Cozumel, but this one, on a covered second-floor terrace, is a standout. The small, daily-changing menu might turn up seafood ravioli in cream sauce, shrimp scampi, or fettuccine with pesto; there's always a catch-of-the-day as well as sourdough pizzas and calzones. All come with a house salad—the veggies are grown in the owner's garden—and puff pastry garlic bread. The small Prima Deli next door specializes in sandwiches served with great gourmet coffee. And—listen up Domino's—they deliver.

Av. Salas no. 109 (turn right on Av. Rafael Melgar from the plaza, walk 2 blocks to Av. Salas and turn left; walk another 1½ blocks). ☎ *987/2-4242.* **Main courses:** *$4–$15; pizzas $5–$13. MC, V.* **Open:** *Daily 3–11pm.*

The Waffle House
$–$$. San Miguel. AMERICAN.

Best Gringo Fix

Coco's (San Miguel, $)

Palmeras (San Miguel, $$)

The Waffle House (San Miguel, $-$$)

If you're jonesing for waffles at four in the afternoon, say, settle in at one of Jeanie De Lille's Formica-topped tables for a treat. Prepared by De Lille, a pastry chef who gave up a flourishing bakery business to dedicate herself to the boxy treats, the waffles are crisp and light and topped in nontraditional ways—with eggs and salsa (waffles ranchero), whipped cream and chocolate, or eggs and Hollandaise (waffles Benedict). Realizing that man (and woman) cannot live by waffles alone, De Lille has expanded her menu to include pepper steak, enchiladas, grilled fish, pastas, vegetarian dishes, and blended fruit drinks. There's a full bar too. Waffles and tequila? Hmm . . .

Av. Rafael Melgar between Av. 5 and Av. 7, next to the Vista del Mar hotel. ☎ *987/2-0545.* **Main courses:** *$5–$7; waffles $3.50–$6. MC, V.* **Open:** *Daily 6am–9pm.*

Sound Bites: Cozumel's Restaurants at a Glance
Restaurant Index by Price

$

Café Caribe (San Miguel, Coffee Shop)

Coco's (San Miguel, American/Mexican)

Comida Casera Toñita (San Miguel, Yucatecan)

$–$$

El Moro (San Miguel, Yucatecan/International)

Pizza Rolandi (San Miguel, Italian)

Prima (San Miguel, Italian)

The Waffle House (San Miguel, American)

$$

La Choza (San Miguel, Mexican)

La Cuchina Italiano (San Miguel, Italian)

Palmeras (San Miguel, American)

$$$

La Cabaña del Pescador (North of Town, Seafood)

$$$–$$$$

Café del Puerto (San Miguel, International)

Kids Pepe's Grill (San Miguel, Steak/Seafood)

Part 6

Acapulco

Acapulco. The name alone, a Latin beat between an "ah" and an "oh," has the sound of excitement. It may not have the cachet it had in the 1950s, when it was the darling of the jet set, but Acapulco is still a serious party town, with glittery all-night discos, dazzling bay-view restaurants, and miles of white-sand beaches on which you can worship the twin gods of sun and water sports.

Having a good time in Acapulco is a no-brainer—if you've planned your trip to suit your lifestyle and your budget. In the following chapters, I'll help you decide the best ways to spend your days—and nights—in this no-stop town.

Choosing the Place to Stay That's Right for You

Congratulations! You've decided to go to Acapulco. But now you realize the place is awash in hotel rooms (about 20,000 of them, in fact). How on earth are you going to decide which one to stay in?

Here's the story. First, I'll profile the three areas where Acapulco's hotels are concentrated, summing up their pros and cons at the end of each section. Then I'll list my favorite hotels alphabetically, and follow up with a list of alternatives if my A-list choices are filled. At the end of the chapter, you'll find at-a-glance indexes listing the hotels by price and by location.

As far as prices go, I've noted rack rates (the maximum that a resort or hotel charges for a room) in the listings. This information will give you some sense of what to expect, although I know you'll avoid paying rack by following the advice I gave you in chapter 6, "The Lowdown on Accommodations in Mexico." I've also put a dollar sign icon in front of each hotel listing so you can quickly see whether it's within your budget. The more $ signs under the name, the more you pay. It runs like this:

$ = \$90 \text{ and below}$

$\$\$ = \$90-\$145$

$\$\$\$ = \$145-\$235$

$\$\$\$\$ = \$235 \text{ and above}$

Extra! Extra!

In Acapulco, you can taxi over to the bus station, where a representative of the Acapulco Hotel Association can help you choose a place and make the phone call for you. In return, you'll pay for one night in advance and receive a voucher for the hotel.

The rates listed are for high season, which runs from around December 19 until the end of April. Low-season rates run anywhere from 20% to a whopping 60% less. Unless otherwise specified, rates are for a standard double room and include the 17% room tax.

A kid-friendly icon **Kids** highlights hotels that are especially good for families. All hotels have air-conditioning unless otherwise indicated, and if the review doesn't say anything to the contrary, you can safely assume that you can walk directly out of your hotel and onto the beach.

Hint: As you read through the reviews, you'll want to keep track of the ones that appeal to you. I've included a chart at the end of the book (see p. 542) where you can rank your preferences, but to make matters easier on yourself now, just put a little check mark next to the ones you like. Remember how your teachers used to tell you not to write in your books? Now's the time to rebel. Scrawl away!

Location, Location, Location

Acapulco has been entertaining visitors for a long time—but not always in the same part of town. The first hotels arose in the downtown area, on the western end of the bay. The action began moving east to the section called the Costera in the 1960s, and continues heading in an easterly direction to this day, as the lodgings in the Acapulco Diamante area begin to encroach on the airport. I've started the following survey of the hotel scene with the Costera, the section that has the greatest concentration of lodgings; after that, I explore the city's future, Acapulco Diamante, before returning downtown to Acapulco's past.

The Costera: Acapulco's Tourist Center

Most of Acapulco's high-rise hotels line up next to one another like dominos on the Costera Miguel Alemán—just call it the Costera—a super-long stretch of sidewalk that abuts and completely encircles Acapulco Bay. The Costera is also home to many of the city's restaurants, discos, shops, malls, banks, and a huge Convention Center, the largest in Latin America. It's Acapulco's main tourist drag, where at almost any time of day or night, you can find anything you want—including McDonald's and Wal-Mart (just look for the longest taxi queue). The adjacent beaches are some of the best in the area, and unquestionably the most popular.

If you want to be in the thick of things, this is the place to stay. The downside? The thick can get thick indeed: thick with traffic, thick with commission-hungry hustlers who try to draw you into their restaurants, thick with bronzed bodies vying for a place in the sun. Because the Costera is so long, however, it's not hard to find some less hectic spots. There are so many hotels that you're bound to find one to fit your budget, even if it means walking a block or so to the beach. Of course, no prime place on the sand comes cheap—you'll have to head for the downtown hills to get the rock-bottom rates—but compared to the ritzy Acapulco Diamante area to the east, the Costera is a bargain.

In a nutshell . . .

➤ Lots of lodging choices for all budgets

➤ Within walking—or busing—distance of major tourist facilities

➤ Lots of water sports concessions along the beaches

but . . .

➤ You can't turn down the volume when you're tired of it.

➤ In the most popular areas, you can't take a stroll without being hustled (harmless but annoying).

➤ It's more expensive, especially at the northern end, to get to the airport.

Honeymoon Central

Elizabeth Taylor and Michael Todd, Jack and Jackie Kennedy, and Bill and Hillary Clinton all honeymooned in Acapulco . . . but not all at the same time.

Acapulco Diamante: Posh, Exclusive & Luxurious

As sparkly as the diamond it's named after, Acapulco Diamante is what downtown used to be: the "in" place for rich people and celebrities. This vast luxury development east of the Costera—it runs along the Carretera Escénica (literally: "scenic drive") from the Westin Las Brisas resort to just behind the airport—already encompasses the city's three best golf courses and is slated to take in two marinas and more tony hotels by early next century. Sylvester Stallone, Luis Miguel, and Placido Domingo all have homes in the lush hills rising above the pristine shoreline, and Warner Brothers maintains deluxe digs here for its hardworking Hollywood artistes.

Exclusivity doesn't come cheap, nor do the hotels that bank on it. If you stay in this area, you'll be cut off from the throb of the Costera—but then, escaping the madding crowd is the whole idea. Some of Acapulco's best restaurants and even a few discos are nearby, and if you feel like slumming, you can always cab it into town for about $10.

In a nutshell . . .

➤ Luxury, luxury, luxury

➤ Great golf courses and scenic restaurants

➤ Closest of all to the airport

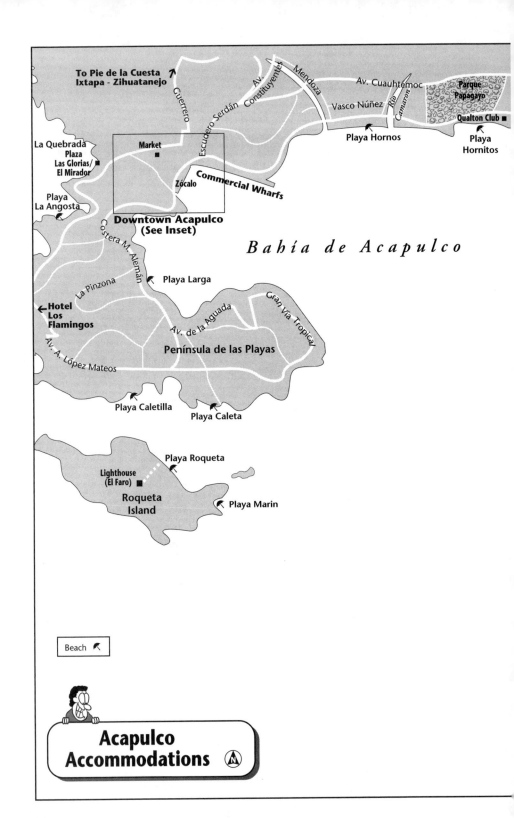

To Pie de la Cuesta
Ixtapa - Zihuatanejo

Av. Constituyentes

Mendoza

Av. Cuauhtémoc

Parque
Papagayo

Guerrero

Escudero Serdán

Vasco Núñez

Río Camarón

Qualton Club ■

La Quebrada
Plaza
Las Glorias/
El Mirador ■

Market ■

Playa Hornos

Playa
Hornitos

Zócalo

Commercial Wharfs

Playa
La Angosta

Downtown Acapulco
(See Inset)

Bahía de Acapulco

Costera M. Alemán

La Pinzona

Playa Larga

←Hotel
Los
Flamingos

Av. de la Aguada

Gran Vía Tropical

Av. A. López Mateos

Península de las Playas

Playa Caletilla

Playa Caleta

Playa Roqueta

Lighthouse
(El Faro) ■

Roqueta
Island

Playa Marin

Beach ⬉

Acapulco
Accommodations Ⓝ

234

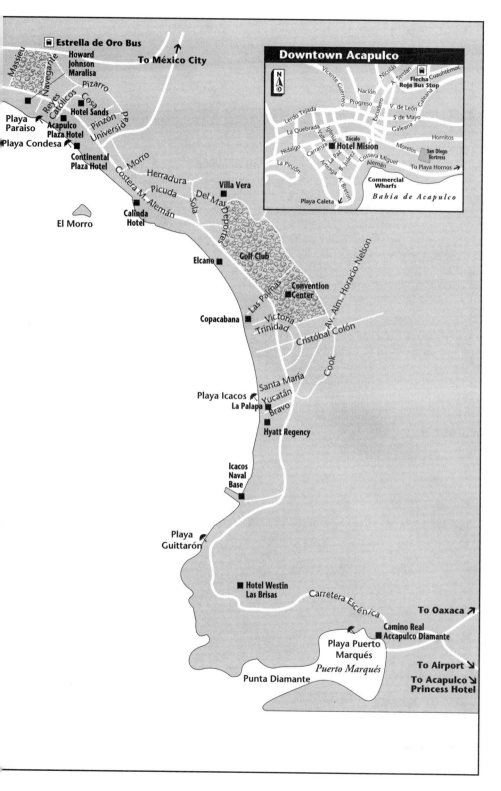

Estrella de Oro Bus

Howard
johnson
Maralisa

To México City

Pizarro

Reyes
Católicos
Cosa
Hotel Sands

Navegante
Massieu

Playa
Paraiso

Acapulco
Plaza Hotel

Pinzon
Universid

Playa Condesa

Continental
Plaza Hotel

Paz

Morro

Herradura

Costera M. Alemán

Picuda

Sola

Del Mar

Villa Vera

El Morro

Calinda
Hotel

Deportes

Golf Club

Elcano

Las Palmas

Convention
Center

Av. Alm. Horacio Nelson

Copacabana

Victoria

Trinidad

Cristóbal Colón

Cook

Santa María

Yucatán

Playa Icacos

La Palapa

Bravo

Hyatt Regency

Icacos
Naval
Base

Playa
Guittarón

Hotel Westin
Las Brisas

Carretera Escénica

To Oaxaca

Camino Real
Accapulco Diamante

Playa Puerto
Marqués

Puerto Marqués

Punta Diamante

To Airport

To Acapulco
Princess Hotel

Downtown Acapulco

Vicente Guerrero

Nicolás

A. Serdán

Flecha Cuauhtémoc
Roja Bus Stop

Nación

Progreso

V. de León

Galeana

Lerdo Tejada

La Quebrada

Valle

Iglesia

Escudero

5 de Mayo

Galeana

Hornitos

Hidalgo

Carranza

La Paz

Zócalo

Hotel Misión

Morelos

Costera Miguel
Alemán

San Diego
Fortress

La Pinzón

Arteaga

B. Juárez

A. Bretón

Commercial
Wharfs

To Playa Hornos

Playa Caleta

Bahía de Acapulco

235

but . . .

➤ It's expensive.

➤ It's far from the bustling party scene of the Costera.

➤ Not all the hotels are on the beach.

Downtown/Old Acapulco: Traditional Mexico

In the pre-air-conditioned era of Acapulco's Hollywood heyday, the town's prime hotel real estate sat on the cooler hills to the west of the Costera in the section known as Old Acapulco, or downtown. Although most of the sheen has worn off this area, an air of glamour still clings to some of the old hotels in this now-inexpensive part of the city. If you stay in this area, you'll be close to the heart of a more traditional Mexico. The *zócalo* (town square), the artisans' market, and the municipal market are all located here, as is the old Fort of San Diego and Acapulco's most famous attraction, the cliff divers at La Quebrada. Many of the tourist cruises take off from the nearby docks.

And it's not as though you won't be near any beaches: Caleta and Caletilla, separated from each other by an outcropping of land where the Magico Mundo Marino aquarium and water park sits, are extremely popular with locals. Which is also their drawback—if you've got no great fondness for kids, you won't want to come on the weekends, when the beaches are packed with *Acapulqueño* families. Still, it's only a short boat ride from Caleta Beach to Roqueta Island, where there's a small zoo and good snorkeling.

In a nutshell . . .

➤ The cheapest hotel rates in town

➤ Proximity to cheap restaurants

➤ At the heart of the city's traditional Mexican culture

➤ Easy access to three beaches: Caleta, Caletilla, and Roqueta

but . . .

➤ Don't expect much luxury.

➤ The beaches are crowded.

➤ Traffic can be loud.

➤ It's the farthest of all from the airport.

My Favorite Hotels from A to Z

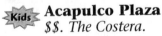 **Acapulco Plaza**
$$. The Costera.

Its many water sports concessions make the wide swath of sand fronting the Acapulco Plaza one of the most popular beaches on the Costera, but the hotel's no slouch, either, when it comes to attracting good-time Charlies (and Charlenes). Because the property has the biggest ballroom in town, its clientele tends to be business-oriented, but the Fiesta Kids Program attracts families, and young couples get a kick out of La Jaula, a tropical bar suspended from 28 floors above. Rooms in this soaring 28-story tower are pretty, with coral-and-cream marble floors and rattan headboards; all have balconies and ocean views. Three bars (one with live music and dancing) and three restaurants keep things hopping. Those who want a bit more privacy can retreat to the adults-only Oasis Club, with two pools, two Jacuzzis, a gym, sauna, massage, and steam bath.

Costera Miguel Alemán 123. ☎ *800-FIESTA-1 or 74/85-9050. Fax 74/85-5493.* **Rack rate:** *$140 double. AE, DC, MC, V.*

Acapulco Princess
$$$$. Acapulco Diamante.
Maybe it's pyramid power, emanating from the stunning triangular guest tower at the center of this resort; otherwise, it's hard to explain how this sprawling 480-acre property—arguably the largest in Mexico—manages to feel friendly and intimate. In the various niches of the lushly landscaped grounds, you'll spot everyone from honeymooners who want both exclusivity and activity to old-timers who devote their days to playing the combined 36 holes of the Princess's superb course and its sister property, Pierre Marques. You'll be far from the Costera action if you stay here, but seven high-quality restaurants (including the Hacienda for fine dining); an on-site disco; five freeform pools, a saltwater lagoon with a water slide; a beautiful, wide beach (although not ideal for swimming); 11 tennis courts; a fitness center; and a slew of tony boutiques should keep you more than satisfied. The spacious rooms are casually elegant; if the sight of a golf course, gorgeous as the Princess's is, doesn't thrill you, insist on one with an ocean view.

El Revolcadero Beach, just west of the airport, Box 1351. ☎ *800/223-1818 or 74/69-1000. Fax 74/69-1016.* **Rack rate:** *$357 double (rates include breakfast and dinner). AE, DC, DISC, MC, V.*

Dollars & Sense

At the **Camino Real Acapulco Diamante** (☎ 800/7-CAMINO) ask about the More Mexico for Less Packages, offering lower rates for longer stays. The **Acapulco Princess** (☎ 800/223-1818) and the **Westin Las Brisas** (☎ 800/223-6800) have golf, romance, and meal packages available. The Acapulco Princess also offers discounts for stays of 5 days or more.

Camino Real Acapulco Diamante
$$$$. Acapulco Diamante.

So exclusive that it sits on a separate bay, far from the Costera, Acapulco's newest property features tasteful contemporary rooms descending from a palm-decked hillside. Lots of Mexican and American conventioneers converge during the week, but this place is sufficiently pricey to stave off hoi polloi. A narrow beachfront is compensated for by water consistently calm enough to swim in, as well as scads of water sports. Other features include a free program for kids ages 4 to 12 on weekends, daily during high season, and the best spa and health center in Acapulco (which isn't saying all that much; the gym doesn't have many machines and it costs $5 a day for guests). You can start your day with a big Mexican breakfast buffet, laid on in the air-conditioned Cabo Diamante, and end it at the standout restaurant of the hotel's five, the beachside La Vela, where a live lobster will sacrifice its life for you, if you like.

Carretera Escénica, km 14, Calle Baja Catita 18, Fracc. Pichilingue Diamante. ☎ **800/7-CAMINO** *or 74/66-1010. Fax 74/66-1111. www.caminoreal.com/ acapulco/. E-mail: aca@caminoreal.com.* **Rack Rate:** *$304 double. AE, DC, MC, V.*

Continental Plaza
$$$. The Costera.

This is your quintessential tropical retreat, a lushly landscaped let-it-all-hang-out place where you can laze away the day playing in a huge meandering pool (a world in itself, with a kids' section, bridge, water slide, and swim-up bar) or move a few yards out to Condesa Beach, which has sports concessions out the wazoo. You've only to raise a suntanned hand from under your palapa and a waiter from the beachside restaurant will appear to take your piña colada order. There's a nice grassy playground for kids, but they're likely to ignore it in favor of watching the caged tropical birds. Rooms are nothing to write home about, but are comfortable enough for shaking off the sand and donning your dancing duds, as the hotel is in the heart of the Costera. There are plenty of places to eat at the hotel itself, including a Tony Roma ribs restaurant if you need a gringo fix.

Costera Miguel Alemán 1220, at Condesa Beach. ☎ **800/88-CONTI** *or 74/ 69-0505. Fax 74/84-2120. www.wotw.com/wow/situr/sidektur.html.* **Rack rate:** *$152 double. AE, MC, V.*

Best Hotels for the Active-Minded

Acapulco Princess (Acapulco Diamante, $$$$)

Acapulco Plaza (The Costera, $$)

The Qualton Club (The Costera, $$)

Copacabana
$$. The Costera.

A reasonably priced beach option, this slightly off-the-Costera hotel has unusually attractive rooms, done in vibrant colors with rattan furniture; all have small balconies with ocean views. The public areas are a restful, sea-foam green; even the building, with its dramatically curving wings, has more style than your typical high-rise. The hotel's beach is fairly small and crowded, but the pool is large and has a swim-up bar as well as an adjacent taco stand. Other features include a 24-hour doctor, a copious breakfast buffet, and two balcony-level Jacuzzis. All-inclusive packages are available through wholesalers such as Apple Vacations.

Tabachines 2, a block (toward the beach) from the Costera, across from the Convention Center. ☎ *800/562-0197 or 74/84-3260 and 84-3155 in Mexico. Fax 74/84-6268. E-mail: copacabana@infosel.net.mx.* **Rack rate:** *$109 double. AE, MC, V.*

Elcano Hotel
$$. The Costera.
If you've got a strong sense of style and nostalgia, you'll adore the 1950s-era (but completely refurbished) Elcano, in the thick of the Costera action, but with the feel of a Mediterranean retreat. Classical music wafts through the lobby (at night it comes live from the lobby bar), and rooms have uncluttered art deco lines. You'd probably be satisfied with even the smallest rooms (called studio suites), but it's tempting to shell out a bit extra for a gleaming wooden deck, overlooking the hotel's beach and huge pool; the latter has four Jacuzzis and piped-in underwater music. The beachside Bambuco restaurant (see chapter 24, "The Best of Acapulco's Dining Scene") is a perpetual favorite. In high season, it's complemented by the more formal Victoria, attached to an intimate bar where you can be serenaded by romantic guitar music. A video game room for kids is discreetly tucked away among these more sophisticated entertainment centers.

On Elcano Beach, Costera Miguel Alemán 75, just west of the Convention Center. ☎ *74/84-1950. Fax 74/84-2230. acapulco-travel.web.com.mx/hotels/elcano. E-mail: ika@delta.acabtu.com.mx.* **Rack rates:** *$135 (studio) to $176 (junior suite). AE, DC, MC V.*

Hotel Los Flamingos
$. Downtown/Old Acapulco.
You don't have to be a Hollywood nostalgia buff to want to stay here—a soaring cliffside perch and far-from-soaring room rates are other reasons—but it's hard to be blasé when you see the photo gallery of movie greats who hung out at this place, formerly run as a private club by John Wayne and Johnny Weissmuller, the big screen's most famous Tarzan. In fact, the lush grounds, awash with tropical trees and flowers, look like something out of one of Weissmuller's flicks. Rooms can be a little dizzying—pink walls, say, with blue-and-orange bedspreads—but some have balconies or decks with super views. Because you're looking out at the ocean rather than the bay from here, you'll have unobstructed sunset vistas from the bar and restaurant, which serves good, very reasonably priced food. Not all rooms have air-conditioning, but the hotel was built at 450 feet to take advantage of ocean breezes.

Av. Lopez Mateos s/n, P.O. Box 70. ☎ *74/82-0690. Fax 74/83-9806. **Rack Rates:** $76 double; $117 junior suite. AE, DC, MC, V.*

Hotel Mision

$. Downtown/Old Acapulco.

You'd be hard-pressed to find a more peaceful place—or a less expensive one—than this 19th-century hacienda, featuring a plant-filled courtyard shaded by an enormous mango tree. Wrought-iron bedsteads and hand-painted floor tiles lend colonial color to otherwise austere rooms (mattresses are good, though). Drawbacks include no air-conditioning—although there are plenty of fans and breezes—no pool, and erratic hot water. Hotel guests enjoy breakfast on the pretty patio; they're joined on Thursday afternoons by visitors converging for the traditional *pozole* pig out (see chapter 24, "The Best of Acapulco's Dining Scene").

Felipe Valle 112, between La Paz and Hidalgo, 2 blocks inland from the Costera and the zócalo. ☎ *74/82-3643. Fax 74/82-2076. **Rack rate:** $20 double. No credit cards.*

Hotel Sands

$. The Costera.

A block inland from fast-paced Condesa Beach, the Sands is a good choice for budget-conscious families and couples. Rooms in the hotel section have four beds (two singles and two cots) and look out on a lawn decked with a playground and kiddie rides (it's often rented out for local parties—but, hey, you'll probably be on the beach during the day). The child-free are better off in the pretty garden across the street, where you'll find a group of plainly furnished, red-tile-roof bungalows, all with refrigerators. Other pluses include a squash, volleyball, and badminton court. There's a restaurant on the premises, but signs let you know Domino's Pizza and KFC are just a phone call away.

Costera Miguel Alemán no. 178, across from the Acapulco Plaza, Box 256. ☎ *74/84-2260 or 84-1019. Fax 74/84-1053. www.sands.com.mx. E-mail: sands@ infosel.net.mx. **Rack rates:** $69 standard room (sleeps 4 people); $51 bungalow. AE, MC, V.*

Howard Johnson Maralisa Hotel

$. The Costera.

This low-rise hotel not far from Old Acapulco isn't glamorous, but then, neither are the budget-conscious families and mature couples who tend to stay here. And with its archways, bougainvillea-draped bowers, and Mexican-tile pathways, the place has plenty of laid-back charm. Rooms are underwhelming, but easy access to a good beach, especially from the less expensive ground-floor units, makes up for their generic quality. Three pools, two for adults, and one for kids, and an open-air bay-view restaurant are among the amenities that make it feel like a larger hotel; laundry service and a beauty parlor are others.

Calle Alemania s/n, just off the Costera (turn toward the beach when you see Baskin-Robbins). ☎ **800/I-GO-HOJO** *or 74/85-6677. Fax 74/85-9228. acapulco-travel.web.com.mx/hotels/maralisa.html. E-mail: maralisa@aca.novenet.com.mex. **Rack rate:** $82 double. AE, DISC, MC, V.*

Hyatt Regency Acapulco
$$$. The Costera.

A longtime Costera landmark—it marks the beginning of the hotel strip at its eastern end—the high-rise Hyatt has become competitive with pricier Acapulco Diamante properties since it completed a

Address Unknown

When you see "s/n" in an address, it stands for "*sin numero*" (without number). Don't worry—you won't have any trouble locating places in Acapulco.

multimillion-dollar face-lift in 1997. A gleaming marble lobby hosts a dimly lit piano lounge where older couples swirl to live marimba music at night and where, during the day, an arcade of tony boutiques wears a come-hither-with-your-plastic look. The attractive accommodations are done in rich turquoise and terra-cotta; suites offer two separate rooms, not just a little sitting area. Some of the seafood dishes at the excellent beachside El Pescador restaurant have an Asian influence; the indoor Zapata, Villa y Compania restaurant (see chapter 24, "The Best of Acapulco's Dining Scene") features the largest selection of tequila (114 kinds) in Acapulco. Also unique is the Glatt kosher restaurant that opens near the pool during high season. Acapulco's only synagogue is on the premises, too, and seders are held at the hotel every Passover.

Costera Miguel Alemán 1. ☎ **800/233-1234** *or 74/69-1234. Fax 74/84-3087. www.hyatt.com. **Rack rate:** $146 double. DC, DISC, MC, V.*

 ## La Palapa
$$. The Costera.

The Costera's only all-suites hotel is a good bet for families, offering nice-size condo units (but with the kitchens closed off; only the owners get to use them) that sleep four comfortably, five if you're all on very good terms. Decor is motel moderne, but the rooms, especially the redone ones, feel open and fresh; all offer oceanview balconies and two showers. Kids under 12 stay free, and they'll enjoy the property's ice cream parlor and video-game room. Lots of German and Canadian groups take advantage of the all-inclusive option available in winter. The beach is small but offers lots of water sports, and the swimming pool is big. A location slightly off the Costera means you're away from the street noise, even on the lower floors.

Fragata Yucatán 210, on Icacos Beach just off the Costera and 2 blocks east of the Convention Center. ☎ **74/84-5363.** *Fax 74/84-8399. acapulco-travel.web.com.mx/hotels/lapalapa. E-mail: lapalapa@aca.novenet.com.mx. **Rack rate:** $117 double. AE, DC, MC, V.*

Best Hotels for Families

Camino Real Acapulco Diamante (Acapulco Diamante, $$$$)

Continental Plaza (The Costera, $$$)

Hotel Sands (The Costera, $)

La Palapa (The Costera, $$)

Plaza Las Glorias/El Mirador

$. Downtown/Old Acapulco.

This hotel isn't what it was in its glory days, when its views of the La Quebrada divers made it a gathering spot for the stars, but the old-timers who have been coming here since the 1950s don't seem to mind. Rooms have lots of character, with Saltillo tile floors and other Mexican decorative touches; they've also got refrigerators. It's easy to ignore lapses in upkeep if you get one with a balcony and an ocean view. Even if you can't see the divers from your room, you can watch them from the attractive lobby or from La Perla Restaurant and Bar, where you can also check out the signatures of the many famous people who ate here (or at least held a pen in their hands). The hotel's hillside aerie is beautiful, but if the funicular railway is broken, as it often is, you may be huffing and puffing too much to enjoy it.

Quebrada 74. ☎ *800/342-AMIGO or 74/83-1221. Fax 74/82-4564.* **Rack rate:** *$124 double. AE, MC, V.*

Bet You Didn't Know

Swiss bandleader Teddy Stauffer, married to actress Hedy Lamarr, created the world's first swim-up bar at the Villa Vera Hotel & Racquet Club.

The Qualton Club

$$. The Costera.

The assorted couples, families, and groups of friends who frequent this all-inclusive resort have two common goals: Eat and drink as much as possible and take advantage of every activity (including non-motorized water sports, beach volleyball, poolside scuba lessons, aerobics, nightly shows, and an on-premises disco). As a result, you won't find much tranquillity except maybe in La Cava Restaurant, the Qualton Club's fine dining spot (reservations required), and in your room. All bedrooms are blandly attractive, but those in the taller tower are larger and have tubs as well as showers. If you snag a corner room with a wraparound balcony, you've hit the jackpot (a few units in the smaller tower have no balconies at all).

Should you somehow manage to get bored here, the Gran Plaza shopping mall is right across the Costera.

Costera Miguel Alemán no. 159, just east of Papagayo Park. ☎ *800/521-5200 or 74/86-8210. Fax 74/86-8324. www.qualton.com. Rack rates: $135 single; $117 per person double (includes all meals and activities). AE, MC, V.*

Villa Vera
$$$. The Costera.

Built in the 1950s as a deluxe residence, Villa Vera still feels like a private home, although probably not one owned by anyone you know. Its 15 garden-filled acres are perched on a hillside about 5 minutes from the Costera; if you don't mind walking to the beach, it's the perfect romantic retreat. Two lighted championship tennis courts and two paddleball courts are bonuses. Room layouts can be a bit odd—the private pool villas have gigantic closets that would better serve as sitting areas, for example—and the furnishings aren't always as subtly tasteful as the property,

> **Best Hotels for a Romantic Retreat**
>
> Elcano Hotel (The Costera, $$)
>
> Villa Vera Hotel & Racquet Club (The Costera, $$$)
>
> Westin Las Brisas (Acapulco Diamante, $$$$)

but those are quibbles. The stylish blue-and-white restaurant overlooking the bay is the see-and-be-seen spot for a late breakfast; visitors often join the well-toned yuppie guests afterward at the inviting pool. No children under 16 allowed.

Lomas del Mar 35 (from the Costera, take Av. de los Deportes inland, and go left on Av. Prado, which curves right and turns into Av. Lomas del Mar). ☎ *800/ 327-1847 or 74/84-0333. Fax 74/84-7479. E-mail: vipinc@cadvision.com. Rack rates: $175 double; $205 suite. AE, MC, V.*

Westin Las Brisas
$$$$. Acapulco Diamante.

Welcome to honeymoon central—jokingly called "the baby factory" by employees—a super-romantic retreat perched on a hillside in the posh Las Brisas neighborhood. Accommodations are all in separate bay-view *casitas* (little houses), many of which have their own private pools (but no TVs). Because the property is so spread out, you'll need to phone for a Jeep to take you to the front lobby; to the property's restaurants (which include Bella Vista, a fine dining room with a superb view); and to the La Concha Beach Club, about 10 minutes away. This last doesn't actually have a beach, but makes up for it with a freshwater pool and two fantastic saltwater pools, one deep enough for diving practice. If you're allergic to pink, Las Brisas is not for you: Everything bears that color (there's even a Pink Shop on the property). The place is showing its age a bit—it was 40 years old in 1997—but service is as top-notch as ever.

Carretera Escénica s/n, Las Brisas, Box 281. ☎ ***800/223-6800*** *or 74/84-1580. Fax 74/84-2269. E-mail: lasbrisas@infosel.net.mx.* **Rack rates:** *$257 shared-pool casita; $374 private pool casita (rates include continental breakfast delivered to your room). $16 daily service charge covers all tips. AE, DC, MC, V.*

No Room at the Inn? Check Out One of These . . .

The Costera
➤ **Fiesta Americana Condesa.** Completely in the thick of things, with lots of on-premises places to play. Costera Miguel Alemán 1220. ☎ **800/ 243-7821.** $$$.

➤ **Plazas Las Glorias (Paraiso).** On the western end of the Costera, somewhat low-key but not lacking for any amenities. Costera Miguel Alemán 163. ☎ **800/342-AMIGO.** $$$.

Acapulco Diamante
➤ **Vidafel Mayan Palace.** Huge, over-the-top opulent, with its own fish-stocked canal. Playa Revolcadero. ☎ **800/843-2335.** $$$$.

Downtown/Old Acapulco
➤ **Majestic.** Recently remodeled and thus more facility-laden than most downtown hotels, with TVs, A/C, and the like. Av. Pozo del Rey 73. ☎ **74/83-2713.** $$.

➤ **Hotel Lindavista.** Nice views, well-kept rooms, lots of character. Playa Caleta s/n. ☎ **74/82-5414.** $.

Quick Picks: Acapulco's Hotels at a Glance
Hotel Index by Price

$

Hotel Lindavista
(Downtown/Old Acapulco)

Hotel Los Flamingos
(Downtown/Old Acapulco)

Hotel Mision (Downtown/
Old Acapulco)

Kids Hotel Sands (The
Costera)

Howard Johnson Maralisa
Hotel (The Costera)

Plaza Las Glorias/El Mirador
(Downtown/Old Acapulco)

$$

Kids Acapulco Plaza (The
Costera)

Copacabana (The Costera)

Elcano Hotel (The Costera)

Kids La Palapa (The Costera)

Majestic (Downtown/Old
Acapulco)

The Qualton Club (The
Costera)

$$$

Kids Continental Plaza (The Costera)

Fiesta Americana Condesa (The Costera)

Hyatt Regency Acapulco (The Costera)

Plaza Las Glorias (Paraiso) (The Costera)

Villa Vera (The Costera)

$$$$

Acapulco Princess (Acapulco Diamante)

Kids Camino Real Acapulco Diamante (Acapulco Diamante)

Vidafel Mayan Palace (Acapulco Diamante)

Westin Las Brisas (Acapulco Diamante)

Hotel Index by Location

The Costera

Kids Acapulco Plaza $$

Kids Continental Plaza $$$

Copacabana $$

Elcano Hotel $$

Kids Hotel Sands $

Howard Johnson Maralisa Hotel $

Hyatt Regency Acapulco $$$

Kids La Palapa $$

The Qualton Club $$

Villa Vera $$$

Acapulco Diamante

Acapulco Princess $$$$

Kids Camino Real Acapulco Diamante $$$$

Westin Las Brisas $$$$

Downtown/Old Acapulco

Hotel Los Flamingos $

Hotel Mision $

Plaza Las Glorias/ El Mirador $

Chapter 22

Finding Your Way Around Acapulco

In This Chapter

➤ What to expect when you arrive

➤ The lay of the land

➤ Getting around

➤ Where to get information

➤ Quick Facts: Acapulco A to Z

Arriving in a foreign country can be intimidating, even when you know your destination is as tourist-friendly as Acapulco. Not to worry: I'll walk you through the basics, explaining everything from how to find a taxi at the airport to how to locate an English-language newspaper.

Yo, Gringo!

Don't expect to find an arrival/departure board at most of Mexico's airports, including Acapulco's. Mexicans have a hard time fathoming the American need for a constant flow of information. Your plane will take off when it takes off, whether you know when that is or not.

You've Just Arrived—Now What?

For a facility that serves a city of nearly a million and a half, Acapulco's Juan N. Alvarez International Airport, 15 miles east of the city center, is surprisingly small. On the plus side, it's super-easy to negotiate. The bad news is that there's precious little available in the way of information—no hotel booking service, not even a tourist booth.

Dollars & Sense

The day before you depart, get your hotel's front desk to book you a place on **Transportes Terrestres** (☎ **74/83-6500**), which runs the collective van service to the airport. It can cost a third less than taking a taxi.

The airport's two sections, international and domestic, occupy the same compact building. There's a *cambio* (money exchange) open daily from 9am to 7pm in high season, shorter hours in low season, as well as two ATMs, which sit side by side near the international airline counters. Only the one on the right takes international credit cards (Cirrus, MasterCard, and Visa), however.

Near the airport exit you'll also see price lists for the *colectivos*—collective vans that can take you to your hotel—and for taxis. Rates are determined by the distance from the airport. All the major hotels are on the lists; if yours isn't, the ticket seller will know which zone you're headed for. *Colectivos* start at around $3.50 for the zone nearest to the airport and run to about $10 for downtown destinations. Taxi rates range from about $15 to $27.

Time-Savers

Don't plan on spending much time in the duty-free shop in the Acapulco airport. It's just a counter with a pretty pathetic selection of cosmetics, liquor, and cigarettes.

Orientation: You Are Here

Acapulco stretches for more than 4 miles around a huge bay. The main boulevard, Costera Miguel Alemán, where most of the hotels are located, follows the outline of the bay on the west side from downtown, or Old Acapulco, to the Hyatt Regency hotel on the east side. Past Papagayo Park on the west, the Costera curves around Hornos and Hamacas beaches to the steamship dock; it becomes the *malecón* (seaside walkway) when it passes Old Acapulco's *zócalo* (town square). To the east, the Costera continues by the name Carretera Escénica past the ritzy section known as Acapulco Diamante all the way to the airport.

It's as easy as following your nose to get around on the Costera, but Old Acapulco is a bit more complicated, with lots of little, winding streets. *Hint:* If you're walking uphill, it's a good bet you're walking away from the water.

You'll need a good map (see "Maps," below in the "Acapulco A to Z: Facts at Your Fingertips" section) if you're planning to wander around downtown.

Yo Gringo!

Numbers don't always follow each other logically on the Costera, nor do people always recognize names of cross streets. Find your bearings, the way the locals do, via landmarks; you'll see them on the maps.

How to Get from Here to There (& How Not To)

Unless you're planning to leave town on an excursion, don't even think about renting a car. It's illegal to park anywhere on the Costera, which is the place you'll most likely to want to go.

Traveling by Taxi

Taxis don't have meters, but fares are relatively cheap: It shouldn't run you more than $2.50 to get from one end of the Costera to the other. It's about $5 or $6 to get to the Costera from Acapulco Diamante, maybe $4 to get to the central Costera from Old Acapulco. Many hotels have signs at the front desk listing prices of common destinations; if yours doesn't, ask the front desk clerk to give you a ballpark figure before you head out.

Dollars & Sense

The laws of supply and demand are on your side when it comes to Acapulco taxis. Be prepared to walk away—or pretend to—if you don't like the price. And never climb into a cab without first establishing what you're going to pay.

Traveling by Bus

If you don't mind going a bit slower, try the buses. They're old yellow school-type models that might give you fourth-grade flashbacks, but the fares are only about 25¢. Bus drivers will be happy to give you change, but not for anything more than a 10 peso note. Stops are marked by blue signs; some are covered and have color-coded maps on the walls showing routes to major sights and hotels. If you want to go downtown from the Costera, take the bus marked "Centro" or "Zócalo"; to get to the east side, approaching

Acapulco Diamante, take the one marked "Base" (pronounced *BAH*-say). Buses to the most popular destinations come along every 10 minutes or so.

Dollars & Sense

Taxi drivers jack up their prices if they see you coming out of a large hotel or fancy restaurant. If you walk a block or two away, you may still have to bargain, but you'll be starting from a lower base.

Where to Find More Information & Guidance

The **State of Guerrero Tourism Office** (Costera Miguel Alemán s/n, across from the Gigante supermarket; ☎ **74/86-9164** and 86-9167) is open Monday through Friday from 9am until 9pm; it's possible that someone will be there on Saturday morning, too, but don't bank on it. You can get maps, brochures, and other general information about the state of Guerrero, which includes Ixtapa/Zihuatanejo and Taxco as well as Acapulco. There's always at least one English-speaker on hand. As its name implies, the **Acapulco Convention and Visitors Bureau** (Costera Miguel Alemán 3111, in the Oceanic 2000 building; ☎ **74/84-7621** and 74/84-7630) is devoted strictly to Acapulco. It has a smaller staff, many of whom are bilingual. Hours are Monday through Friday 9am to 9pm, and Saturday 9am to 2pm.

The Printed Page

At your hotel's front desk, you might find the ad-driven *Acapulco Guide,* a glossy bilingual mag that comes out every 2 months and lists special events as well as some general around-town information. The more interesting *Acapulco Heat* is a good source of local gossip and includes apartment listings, but it's hard to get your hands on (theoretically it, too, is available at all the Costera hotels).

Acapulco A to Z: Facts at Your Fingertips

American Express: Gran Plaza shopping center, Costera Miguel Alemán 1628 (☎ **74/691-166**).

ATMs: All the large banks along the Costera—Banamex, Bancomer, Bital, and Serfin—have ATMs; other money machine locations include the airport, the downtown, and Oceanic 2000 branches of Sanborn's (see "English-Language Newspapers/Magazines," below) and the lobby of the Plaza Las Glorias/El Mirador, downtown. Some hotels carry Visa coupon booklets that give precise locations on a color-coded map of Acapulco's 46 Visa and PLUS ATMs. Also common are MasterCard and Cirrus.

To Pie de la Cuesta
Ixtapa - Zihuatanejo ↗

La Quebrada

Plaza
Las Glorias/
El Mirador

Playa
La Angosta

Guerrero

Escudero Serdán

Av. Constituyentes

Mendoza

Av. Cuauhtémoc

Vasco Núñez

Río Camarón

Parque
Papagayo

Playa Hornos ↖

Playa
Hornitos ↖

Market

Zócalo

Commercial Wharfs

Downtown Acapulco
(See Inset)

Bahía de Acapulco

Costera M. Alemán

La Pinzona

Playa Larga ↖

Av. de la Aguada

Gran Vía Tropical

Av. A. López Mateos

Bullfighting Ring

Península de las Playas

Playa Caletilla ↖

Playa Caleta ↖

Lighthouse
(El Faro) ■

Playa Roqueta ↖

Roqueta
Island

Playa Marin ↖

Acapulco Region

200

95

200

Río Coyuca

Laguna de
Coyuca

Pie de la Cuesta

Acapulco

Laguna de
Tres Palos

Barra Vieja ↖

Bahía de Acapulco

Acapulco Orientation Ⓐ

Beach ↖

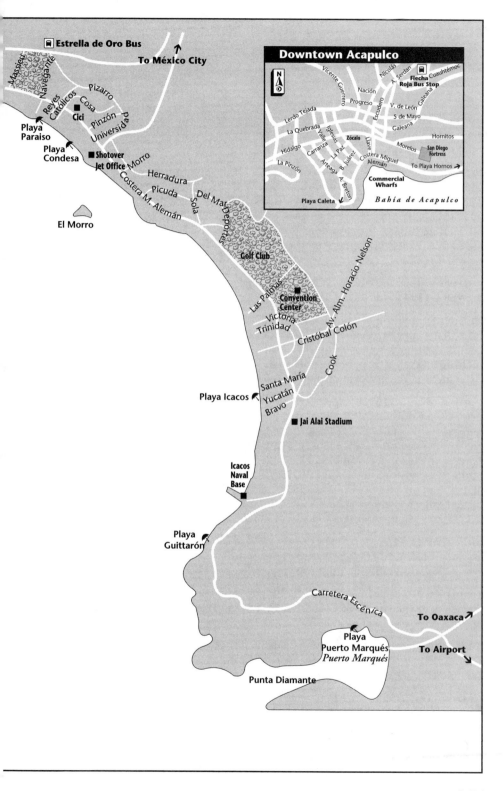

Estrella de Oro Bus

To México City

Downtown Acapulco

N

Vicente Guerrero
Nicolás
A. Serdán
Cuauhtémoc
Flecha Roja Bus Stop
Nación
Progreso
Escudero
V. de León
5 de Mayo
Galeana
Lerdo Tejada
Iglesias
Valle
La Quebrada
Llave
Zócalo
Galeana
Hornitos
Hidalgo
Carranza
La Paz
Costera Miguel
Morelos
San Diego
Fortress
La Pinzón
Arteaga
B. Juárez
Alemán
A. Bretón
To Playa Hornos
Commercial Wharfs
Playa Caleta
Bahía de Acapulco

Massieu
Navegante
Reyes Católicos
Pizarro
Cosa
Cici
Pinzón
Universidad
Playa Paraiso
Shotover Jet Office
Playa Condesa
Morro
Herradura
Picuda
Del Mar
Costera M. Alemán
Sola
Deportes
El Morro
Golf Club
Las Palmas
Convention Center
Victoria
Trinidad
Cristóbal Colón
Av. Alm. Horacio Nelson
Santa María
Yucatán
Playa Icacos
Bravo
Cook
Jai Alai Stadium
Icacos Naval Base
Playa Guittarón
Carretera Escénica
To Oaxaca
Playa Puerto Marqués
Puerto Marqués
To Airport
Punta Diamante

Baby-Sitters: Most hotels can arrange baby-sitting. Rates are approximately $4 per hour, with an additional charge of $3 for a taxi if you stay out past 10pm.

Business Hours: Offices are open 9am to 2pm and 4 to 7pm on weekdays and sometimes from 9am to 2pm on Saturday; shops generally are open 10am to 9pm daily.

Currency Exchange: Exchange windows at banks, found all along the Costera, generally have the best rates, but they're usually open only from 10am to noon or 1pm. *Casas de cambio* (exchange booths), found pretty much everywhere tourists congregate, have only slightly lower rates and much longer hours, and you don't have to fill out any forms or shuffle from line to line. Hotel front desks are the most convenient—and naturally offer the worst exchange rates.

Dentist: Call Dr. David Avila (Mateo F. Maury #1750, Col. Costa Azul; ☎ 74/84-4524).

Doctors: Many hotels have doctors on the premises or on 24-hour call; at those that don't, the desk clerk should be able to locate a physician for you. In addition, you can contact English-speaking members of the **International Association for Medical Assistance to Travelers** (**IAMAT**) at the medical department of the Acapulco Princess (☎ 74/691-000).

English-Language Newspapers/Magazines: The larger Costera hotels, such as the Continental Plaza, carry a good selection of U.S. magazines and newspapers (such as *USA Today* and the *L.A. Times*) in their tobacco shops, and you're likely to find the English-language *Mexico City News* at most news-stands. For the largest number of gringo-friendly paperbacks and magazines, head for one of the three Sanborn's department stores (downtown at Costera Miguel Alemán 209, across from the steamship dock, ☎ 74/84-4413; Costera Miguel Alemán 1226, in the Condo Estrella Tower, ☎ 74/84-4465; and Costera Miguel Alemán 163 at the Hotel Calinda, ☎ 74/81-2426).

Emergencies/Fire: Call ☎ 74/84-4122. You can find members of the English-speaking **tourist police** patrolling the Costera; they wear safari-style white-and-light blue uniforms, replete with shorts and helmet.

Hospitals: Hospital Magellanes (1 block from the Costera at Wilfredo Massieu 2, at the corner of Colon; ☎ 74/85-6544) is a good private hospital for office visits or emergencies.

Maps: The American Express map, usually available at the tourist offices and at the American Express office, is one of the best around. You might also be able to pick up a good map at Sanborn's.

Pharmacies: There's a 24-hour pharmacy at Hospital Magellanes (see "Hospitals," above; ☎ 74/85-6706), and lots of smaller pharmacies open until 9 or 10pm all along the Costera. The three branches of Sanborn's (see "English-Language Newspapers/Magazines," above) all have pharmacies that stay open until midnight in high season, and 11pm in low season.

Police: Call ☎ **74/85-0650.**

Post Office: The central post office is in the Palacio Federal, across the Costera from the steamship dock and 3 blocks west of the zócalo. There are also branches at the Estrella de Oro bus station, on Cuauhtemoc and Massieu, and on the Costera near Caleta Beach.

Safety: As in any large city, it's best to stick to the well-lit streets—which leaves you the entire Costera to stroll for most of the night. If you're worried about taking valuables to the beach, lots of street vendors sell a waterproof plastic tube—large enough for your room key and a little bit of money. See chapter 10, "Crossing the Border & What to Expect on the Other Side," for advice about walking around crowded markets.

Special Events: Aside from celebrating the traditional Mexican holidays (see chapter 2, "When Should I Go?"), Acapulco is trying to recapture its stellar celluloid past by running a series of film fests. For the past 2 years, a French Film Festival drew the likes of Catherine Deneuve to town. The first African-American festival, held in May 1997, was attended by Halle Berry, Robert Townsend, and Ceci Winans, among others. Call the **Convention and Visitors Center** (☎ **74/84-7621** or 84-7630) for more details.

Yo, Gringo!

If you're ambling along the beach in the early morning, keep an eye out for joggers coming from both directions. Some are very mobile thieves.

Telephone: The telephone area code for Acapulco is 74. To call long distance within Mexico (abbreviated *lada*), dial 01, then the area code, and then the number. To call the United States, dial 001 and then the area code and number.

U.S. Consul: Hotel Club del Sol, Costera Miguel Alemán at R. Católicos (☎ **74/85-6600**), across from the Hotel Acapulco Plaza.

Fun On & Off the Beach

Gorgeous white-sand beaches fringing a deep blue bay are what brought the beautiful people to Acapulco in the first place, and what continue to attract the reddening throngs (don't leave home without your high-octane sunscreen!) But because not all beaches are created equal, I'm devoting this chapter to helping you decide among them, although I won't tell if you decide just to veg out on the stretch of sand closest to your hotel. I'll also explore the various ways you can play in the water and the best places to do so.

Although I'm not going to try to pass Acapulco off as the cultural capital of Mexico—you'd find out the truth as soon as you got there, and it would destroy my credibility—that's not to suggest there aren't plenty of things to keep landlubbers occupied day and night, night, night. If you do feel the need for a cultural fix, the "Side Trips: Getting Out of Acapulco" section has that yen sussed.

Hitting the Beaches

Time was when Acapulco was a victim of its own success, and you wouldn't want to think about what came lapping up with the waves. Aware that its cash cow of pristine beaches was choking with garbage, however, the city has worked very hard to solve its pollution problem. These days, mystery debris rarely washes up on Acapulco's shores.

The city's attempt to solve its peddler problem has been a little less successful. To keep beach vendors from bothering people trying to sun themselves in peace, Acapulco supplied them with rent-free booths in newly created artisans' markets on the Costera (see the section "Acapulco's Best Shopping," below). Fewer people try to sell you trinkets than in the past—but some of the most tenacious remain. The first to spot the tourist fuzz sends a "Cheese it, it's the cops" signal to the rest, who miraculously disappear.

Yo, Gringo!

If you don't want to be bothered on the beach, don't bring any money down and just keep shaking your head no. Buy a single item, and you'll soon have dozens of new friends converging on your palapa.

It's said there are at least 50 names for all the little coves on Acapulco Bay, but I won't trouble you with them. What follows is a list of the best, and the most popular beaches, from west to east.

Pie de la Cuesta

A laid-back atmosphere, a long, wide stretch of sand, and spectacular sunsets draw visitors to Pie de la Cuesta, about 8 miles west of town (you can get a taxi from the Costera for about $12). The waves here are too powerful for swimming, but you can take a lagoon tour, go waterskiing or jet skiing, or kick back and enjoy a coco loco at one of the many little seafood restaurants. Don't go on Sunday, when you'll have to share the resort with the entire population of Acapulco.

Shady Deals

Little boys on the Pie de la Cuesta beach may try to charge you for sitting under a palapa. Don't fall for it; the shade is free.

Old Acapulco/Downtown Beaches

Little **Playa la Angosta** is an often-deserted cove just around the bend from La Quebrada, where the cliff divers perform. The water's usually too rough for swimming, but great sunsets—this is the only beach near Acapulco with an unobstructed horizon—compensate. Walk east up the cliffside boulevard from the beach to Sinofia del Sol Amphitheater to watch the spectacle from a ringside seat with the locals.

South of downtown, on the Peninsula de las Playas, the **Caleta** and **Caletilla** beaches are separated by a small outcropping of land that's home to the Magico Mundo Marino aquarium and water park. Once *the* exclusive spots to lay a towel on, these days the coarse-sand beaches are thronged with Mexican families enjoying the gentle waves, thatch-roofed restaurants, and water-toy concessions. Brightly painted boats ferry passengers to Roqueta Island (see below) all day, and in the late afternoon, when fisherman pull their boats up on the sand, you might be able to snag some fresh-caught oysters on the half shell.

Boozing Burros

Beer-drinking burros roam Playa Roqueta, descendants of sober ones that the lighthouse keeper brought over to haul goods decades ago. Their preferred brand seems to be Corona—strangely enough, also the one favored by the enabler humans.

Roqueta Island

Of the two small beaches on the shoreline of this hilly, forested island, **Playa Marin** is more deserted but has fewer facilities, and **Playa Roqueta** is the place to snorkel, swim, or chow down at a beachside restaurant. While you're here, you can check out the small zoo, which has a decent selection of exotic local animals (although in depressingly small cages), or climb to the top of the lighthouse, which has knockout views of Acapulco Bay. A small boat will take you over from Caletilla Beach for a round-trip fare of about $2.50 or $3. Boats leave approximately every 15 to 20 minutes from 10am to 6pm daily.

Extra! Extra!

The trek to the top of Roqueta Island's lighthouse is a rare opportunity for exercise—much needed if you've been overindulging in tequila and tacos—but go only in the morning or late afternoon, when the sun won't overwhelm you.

The Costera Beaches

As you approach Papagayo Park from downtown (west), the first beach you come to is **Hornos** (sometimes called Playa Papagayo), which soon turns into **Hornitos,** which then merges with **Condesa** and metamorphoses into **Icacos,** the closest to the Hyatt Hotel and the naval base. They're hard to distinguish from one another, as all are fairly wide with gentle surf. The lodgings along the Costera rope off sections for their guests, so many times the beaches are referred to by the names of the hotels they flank. Condesa Beach is probably the most popular, both as a pickup spot and a place to rent water sports equipment; Icacos is arguably the calmest. Hornos and the beach that fronts the Acapulco Plaza Hotel offer the widest stretches of sand.

Don't Be a Statistic

A few people get sucked into Acapulco's deadly riptides and undertows every year. Pay serious attention to the warning flags posted on the beaches. Red or black flags mean stay out of the water altogether, yellow suggests you use caution, and white or green says go ahead, have a good time. Don't even think about swimming on any of the beaches that front the open sea.

The Eastside Beaches

Past the hillside Las Brisas hotel and condo complex, the Carretera Escénica curves down to **Puerto Marques Bay,** which has a nice, sheltered beach for swimming—but not an undiscovered one. Come during the week, or you'll have to fight Mexican families for the palapas and chairs in the beach-side restaurants (you can take a bus, but they run only about once an hour). About a mile farther, but on the ocean, is **Playa Revolcadero,** which fronts the Acapulco Princess Hotel. The hotel posts lifeguards, but strong tides often discourage swimming. Still, this is a good place to hang with the rich—who knows, you might make friends with someone who owns a sailboat. Farthest of all (about 16 miles east of Acapulco) is **Barra Vieja,** a magnificent wide beach that offers beautiful sunset views because it's on the open ocean. Waves are strong, so swimmers are out of luck again, but joggers like the firm sand. You can hire a boat for about $12 to take you around the jungly Laguna Tres Palos wetlands at the east end of the fishing village that adjoins this beach.

Water Fun for Everyone

Daredevil or wuss, you can find a way to play in Acapulco's waters. This is one of the most water toy–laden resorts around, and there are plenty of places to help you try to hook the big one (although if diving's your thing, you'll probably be disappointed). What follows are suggestions for some of the best places to arrange your favorite splashy pursuit, along with the prices you can expect to pay.

Angling for a Good Time

Maybe fish are brain food, but they don't seem to have had the sense to stay away

Off the Hook

More and more anglers are taking part in the catch and release conservation program: You reel in your fish, tag it, and then send it back into the sea to create future fish (after it recovers from the temporary hook-in-the-mouth pain, of course).

from Acapulco, even when it was polluted. The city may not be as well known for angling as other Mexican resorts, but deep-sea fishing has always had a firm niche here. Excursions generally leave at 7am and return at 2pm. You'll typically travel from 3 to 8 miles away from the coast, depending on the current, and cast out for sailfish, tuna, or marlin.

Sportsfishing Tipping Tips

It's customary to tip 10% to 15% of the total price of your charter, depending on the quality of service received. Give the money to the captain, who will split it with the mate.

If you want to book your own boat, go to the pale-pink building of the cooperative **Pesca Deportiva** (☎ **74/82-1099**) on the dock opposite the zócalo. Charter fishing trips arranged here run from about $125 to $175 for four people. If you book through a travel agent, a beach concession off the Costera, or a hotel tour desk, the same trips start at around $200. The fishing license (about $5), food, and drink are extra. Tour operators will get you the license; if you're hiring your boat from the cooperative, you can pick it up from the Secretaria de Pesca at the same dock (but not between the hours of 2 to 4pm, when the office is closed).

If you're going with a group, consider booking in advance through one of two reliable American sportsfishing outfitters: **Ixtapa Sportsfishing Charters** (19 Depue Lane, Stroudsburg, PA 18360; ☎ **717/688-9466;** fax 717/688-9554 or 755/4-4426 in Zihuatanejo) and **Mexico Sportsman** (14542 Brook Hollow, no. 124, San Antonio, TX 78232; ☎ and fax **210/494-9916**). Their boats run from 40-foot custom cruisers that hold six and cost $275, to 48-foot Hatteras Twins, capacity eight people, for around $500. Prices include crew, tackle, and tax, but not fishing license.

Getting Revved Up

The beaches along the Costera, and especially the ones behind hotels such as the Qualton Club, the Acapulco Plaza, the Continental Plaza, La Palapa, and the Hyatt, have the most water sports concessions. You'll typically find banana boats ($3 per person for about 10 minutes); parasails ($15 for about 8 minutes); Waverunners ($35 for two people for a half hour); water skis (anywhere from $30 to $60 an hour—shop around for the best deals on this one); and jet skis ($50 per hour). Parasailing is especially big—at any given moment, look up and you're likely to see someone soaring in a parachute above Acapulco Bay.

You'll also find some concessions on Caletilla Beach, Puerto Marques Bay, and Coyuco Lagoon near Pie de la Cuesta, although they are not as well stocked as the ones along the Costera.

Exploring the Deep Blue Sea

If you've never gone diving and have always wanted lessons, Acapulco is as good a place as any to take the plunge. Experienced divers aren't going to be too happy here, however. Although Acapulco Bay's pollution problem has improved, visibility still isn't great most of the time.

Time-Savers

If you're already a qualified diver, don't forget to pack proof of certification.

If you want to take the plunge, try calling one of the following companies: **Nautilus** (Costera Miguel Alemán 450; ☎ **74/83-1108**) and **Arnold Brothers** (Costera Miguel Alemán 2005; ☎ **74/82-1877** or 82-0788) both charge $30; and **Divers de Mexico** (Costera Miguel Alemán 100; ☎ **74/82-1398** or 83-6020) charges $55. Prices at all three companies include equipment, an instructor, and a boat for 3 hours. It's about $45 to $55 for the same amount of time if you make arrangements through a hotel or travel agency.

The best snorkeling is off Roqueta Island. If you've brought your own gear, take a boat over on your own (see "Roqueta Island," above). If you haven't, you can book a snorkeling trip from one of the water sports concessionaires along the Costera beaches or on Caleta Beach. They usually cost about $20 per person for 2 hours, including equipment.

Yo, Gringo!

Always ask to see proof of an instructor's certification, and ask how many others will be in your class. Anyone can hang up a dive instructor's shingle, and you really need personal attention when doing something as potentially dangerous as diving. All the dive companies I've listed in this chapter come recommended by Acapulco's tourist board.

Getting Soaked on a Booze Cruise

If gazing out at the water in a state of complete sloshdom is what you're in the mood for, these excursions have your name on them.

The converted ***Bonanza*** (☎ **74/83-1550**) and ***Hawaiiano*** (☎ **74/82-0785**) yachts and the ***AkaTiki*** catamaran (☎ **74/84-6140** or 84-6786) all run cruises from their downtown docks. One or the other of them offer the following:

➤ A **breakfast buffet and open bar** outing in the morning (daily from 11am to 1pm), which takes you past downtown's houses of the rich and famous as well as the La Quebrada cliff divers and leaves you half an hour for swimming or snorkeling.

➤ **Sunset cruises** (daily from 4:30 to 7pm) have a similar food and drink setup, but they leave out the getting-wet part and turn up the volume with a disco and live tropical music or a dinner show.

➤ **Moonlight cruises** (nightly from 10:30pm to 1am) around Acapulco Bay also feature an open bar and live music or an international show with lots of scantily clad women.

Prices range from about $12 to $40 per person, depending on the meal and show. Book directly through the companies or go through a travel agent—there's no difference in price.

You'll likely find cruises of Puerto Marquez Bay and Coyuca Lagoon, too. Tour operators and itineraries come and go as quickly as fashionable places to eat in Los Angeles; check with your hotel desk for a recommendation.

Only in New Zealand, Fiji—and Acapulco

Brought to Acapulco by a New Zealand company in late 1996, the Shotover Jet boats have taken off like a flash. Literally. These spiffy 12-person crafts, propelled by 8-liter V-8 engines, skim the surface of the Papagayo River at 40 to 50 m.p.h., making 360-degree turns that leave everyone gasping (the skillful drivers also like to pretend they're about to crash into rocks). Book this thrill ride at the Shotover Jet office just outside the Hotel Continental Plaza (Costera Miguel Alemán no. 121; ☎ **74/84-1154** or 74/841-55). Tickets, which include the round-trip from the office to the river, run $44 for a half-hour ride for adults and $22 for children under 12; no children under 3 allowed. Plan to spend at least 4 hours, factoring in the driving time to the river. If you're thinking about going anyplace afterward, take along a change of clothes. You'll come off the boat looking like a drowned rat.

Keeping Your Head Above Water: The Five Best Things to Do on Dry Land

Note: The cliff divers and other downtown sights are usually covered on city tours, which can be booked at most hotels or travel agents for around $15.

Gaping at the Cliff Divers

You can't say you've been to Acapulco if you haven't seen the **cliff divers at La Quebrada**, daredevils who plunge into 15 feet of water from a spotlighted ledge on a cliff 134 feet above the pounding surf. The graceful

plunge is breathtaking, but the ritual surrounding the dive is as interesting as the
act. The divers mill around, looking as
though they're trying to steel their nerves,
and then cross themselves at a small
chapel on the top of the cliff. Since the
dive shows were formalized in the 1930s
by Swiss bandleader Teddy Stauffer, no one
has been killed or even seriously injured.

Bet You Didn't Know

The cliff divers at La
Quebrada are unionized
and have a health-care plan.

La Quebrada is uphill from Avenida Lopez,
which is 3 blocks west of the zócalo; the
best way to get there is by cab. Shows take place daily at 1, 7:30, 8:30, 9:30,
and 10:30pm; admission to the viewing platform is about $1.25, and you're
expected to tip—50¢ is fine—when the dripping divers file by afterward to
greet you. The best show is the last one of the day, when the divers carry
flaming torches.

Dollars & Sense

If you want to watch the cliff divers from the bar at the Plaza Las Glorias/
El Mirador hotel, you have to pay a steep cover ($9) that includes only one
drink. Come more than half an hour before the scheduled show, and there's a
good chance you can get by with nursing a less expensive drink without being
hit up for the cover.

Scaling the Fortress

The 18th-century **San Diego Fortress** on
the Costera Miguel Alemán, east of the
zócalo, is worth visiting not only for its
excellent Acapulco Historical Museum, but
also for the fantastic views it affords of the
entire bay (hey, surprise—that's what mili-
tary lookout points are for). There are no
English-speaking guides or English labels
on the exhibits, but you should be able to
get the gist of what you're seeing:
Cannonballs, model ships, and gilded car-
riages are pretty much self-explanatory.
The museum is open Monday through
Saturday from 9:30am to 6:30pm; admission is $2.

A Cool Time to Visit

Get to the museum at the
San Diego Fortress as early
as possible because it's not
quite air-conditioned
(although if you're lucky, a
little cool air occasionally
wafts through some of the
rooms).

Meditating at the Chapel of Peace

If you look to the east from anyplace in Acapulco at night, you'll see a large, lighted cross in the Las Brisas hills. It's also the location of the **Chapel of Peace (La Capilla de la Paz),** sometimes called the Trouyet Chapel after the wealthy family that constructed it and the cross. The chapel, open daily from 10am to 1pm and from 4 to 6pm, is a lovely, simple structure, surrounded by beautiful gardens. The views from the top of the hill are super, and on the way up, you can see how the other half live in Las Brisas (be sure to ask the cabbie to point out Sylvester Stallone's place). A taxi to the chapel costs about $10 round-trip.

Strolling the Zócalo

Acapulco's **town square** is its cultural heart, the place where locals gather on benches to gossip, listen to music at the bandstand, and celebrate religious holidays at the church of **Nuestra Señora de la Soledad,** a striking art deco structure with Moorish-looking blue and yellow domes. The Costera turns into the *malecón* (seaside promenade) here; it's fun to hang around and scope out the fishing boats and sightseeing yachts. When your feet start hurting, there are plenty of sidewalk cafes to repair to.

Kids Checking Out Cici

Cici (Centro Internacional de Convivencia Infantil) isn't exactly a dry-dock activity, but not every member of the family is required to get wet at this children's marine and water park, located on the east side of the Costera at Colon (☎ 74/84-1970). Kids can splash around wave pools, water slides, and toboggans, and giggle at the antics of dolphins and seals (shows at noon, 2:30, and 5pm). The park is open daily from 10am to 6pm; admission is $4. All the buses that run along the Costera stop right in front of CICI. Newer, air-conditioned buses cost 35¢; a regular bus is about 24¢. Taxi fare will run you approximately $15.

Let the Games Begin

➤ **Bullfights** are held at a ring near Caletilla Beach and start at 5:30pm on 14 Sundays during the winter season. Tickets bought through travel agencies cost around $40 and include transportation to and from your hotel. You won't see the best bullfights in the country here—you've got to go to Mexico City for that—but this is a respectable spectacle, played out by aspiring young matadors. Don't go if you have a weak stomach or want to stage a protest; the sport is taken very seriously here.

➤ **Jai alai** has no moral quandaries attached—just amazement that humans can move a ball around a court at such supersonic speeds. These games are held from January to April. The Basque sport is similar to handball but played with a *fronton,* which looks like a skinny, hollowed-out basket. Betting is a big part of the game, and you can wager on other sports as well at the downstairs sports book. A bingo hall just opened in the same stadium (on the Costera, across from the Hyatt Regency), so after jai alai, you can join the N-5, B-19 crowd.

Jai alai admission is around $10; check with your hotel for the current schedule.

Hitting the Links

The Costera doesn't have any great golf courses, but for a cheap and easy game, there's the public nine-hole **Club de Golf** (Avenida Costera Miguel Alemán s/n, near the Convention Center; ☎ 74/84-0781 or 84-0782) near the Convention Center. *Warning:* Upkeep isn't up to par. Greens fees are about $20 for one go around the course, or $35 if you want to play an 18-hole game. No carts, but caddies cost approximately $10, and club rentals are the same. The course is a par 36, with a 36.5 rating.

The top-notch greens lie to the east, at the sister hotels **Acapulco Princess** (El Revolcadero Beach, just west of the airport; ☎ 74/69-7000) and **Pierre Marques** (☎ 74/66-1000). Greens fees at either 18-hole course run $60 for hotel guests, including carts, and $80 for outsiders. There are no caddies. If you're not staying at the hotel, you'll need to phone on the same day to find out if you can play, as guests get the first crack at reserving tee times. The Princess's course, designed by golf architect Ted Robinson, is relatively flat and has narrow fairways with water on 12 of the 18 holes (par 72; rating 69.4). The one at the Pierre Marques, redesigned by Robert Trent Jones, Sr., for the World Cup Golf Tournament in 1972, is longer and more challenging, offering flat terrain with water on 13 holes (par 72, rating 69.8). The fairways and greens are extremely well bunkered.

Farther east and equally prestigious is the 18-hole course at the **Mayan Palace Golf Club** at the Vidafel Mayan Palace (Geranios 22, Fracc. Copacabana, Playa Revocadero; ☎ 74/66-1924); it's unrated, with a par 72. The $75 greens fee includes a cart; a caddie will run you another $15. Designed by respected Latin American golf guru Pedro Guerica, it was the site of the World Airlines tournament in 1998.

Acapulco's Best Shopping

Paint Acapulco's shopping scene without much local color: In spite of its location in the state of Guerrero, which has some excellent crafts—my favorites are the quirky, hand-carved ceremonial masks—Acapulco doesn't offer as much in the way of unique Mexican goods as you'd expect from a city of its size. You'll find the usual assortment of tacky serapes and onyx chess sets mixed in with high-quality dishes from Puebla, but few unique items.

In particular, Acapulco's proximity to the Silver City, Taxco (see the sidebar called "Silver Savvy," below, and the section "Side Trips: Getting Out of Acapulco"), should have ensured the existence of more designer silver shops, but that hasn't been the case. You can spot some stunning (and costly) pieces in the upscale arcades of hotels such as the Acapulco Princess, Westin Las Brisas, and Hyatt Regency; there's also a good silver shop in front of the Fiesta Americana Acapulco Plaza, and two large ones outside the Plaza Las Glorias/ El Mirador. Otherwise, you have to look hard to find any silver linings.

There are, however, plenty of stores selling good sportswear and resortwear on the Costera, including Polo/Ralph Lauren and Nautica, most of the times at prices lower than those you'd find in the United States. You can come across some killer sales here; if you do, be sure to stock up.

Silver Savvy

➤ Lots of Acapulco shops advertise goods "imported from Taxco," implying an automatic assurance of quality. The stuff they sell probably *is* from Taxco—much of Mexico's silver is—but Taxco is not without means of mass production.

➤ Cab drivers may try to take you to "silver factories," which conjure up images of craftspeople huddled over intricate work. Not so. Most of these places just sell lots of low-quality goods. The driver gets a kickback for bringing you—and you're likely to be socked with a round-trip cab fare, to boot.

➤ Always look for the ".925" mark on a piece of jewelry, which guarantees a silver content of 92.5%. You'll occasionally find ".950" or ".985," which means the percent of silver to alloy is even greater. Anything marked ".8" is low-quality, and no mark at all means you've probably got *alpaca* (pure imitation) on your hands.

To Market, To Market

As noted in the section on beaches, beach vendors have been set up in booths at makeshift **flea markets** strung along the Costera to compensate for the loss of their sandy sales turf. Quantity, not quality, is the hallmark here; the endless T-shirts, ceramic ashtrays, straw bags, and serapes are much of a muchness. Still, these places aren't bad for picking up last-minute trinkets, provided you bargain your heart out.

Dollars & Sense

Several shops in Acapulco offer browsers soft or hard drinks. If you don't want your resistance lowered or your bargaining skills impaired, pass on the margaritas and beer. Acquisition goes better with Coke.

The best market for crafts is **Mercado Parazal** (sometimes called Mercado de Artesanias), located on Calle Valazquez de Leon near 5 de Mayo in the downtown zócalo area. It's chockfull of stalls selling curios from around the country, including embroidered cotton dresses, papier-mâché dolls, leather sandals, and glazed pottery; I've even found some good Guerrero masks here. You'll also see lots of stuffed frogs wearing sombreros and holding miniature banjos. The market can get really hot and loud as vendors try to shout you into their stalls. If you start feeling claustrophobic, walk outside the perimeters for a minute and grab a cold drink. Your will to haggle should be quickly restored.

Some Market Strategies

Don't forget that for Mexicans bargaining is as normal as eating rice and beans. Follow their lead with the tips below:

➤ Before heading to the market, check established handicrafts stores to get an idea of the price of the items you're interested in.

➤ Keep a poker face. Gush, and the vendor will automatically ask for more.

➤ Start by offering 30% of the asking price and work your way up from there; you've done well if you end up paying half of what you were originally quoted.

➤ Walk away if the vendor refuses to come down in price. If that doesn't jolt him into calling after you with a better deal, pick another stall and start over.

➤ Wait until close to closing; some merchants will sell at any price if their day hasn't gone well. Of course, much of the good stuff has already been grabbed up by then.

Getting Mall'd

Of the two major malls on the Costera, both with air-conditioning and food courts, **Gran Plaza** (Costera Miguel Alemán 1628; ☎ 74/69-3000) is the more downmarket, with lots of mid-range sportswear stores and American chains such as Radio Shack and Foot Locker. A video arcade should keep the older kids fixated; the younger ones score a playground with crawling spaces and plastic slides. **Plaza Bahia** (Costera Miguel Alemán 125, just west of the Acapulco Plaza hotel; ☎ 74/86-2452) veers toward the upscale, with designer lines such as Calvin Klein, Izod, and Platinum featured prominently and prices escalated accordingly.

Department Stores

The three branches of **Sanborn's** (downtown at Costera Miguel Alemán 209, across from the steamship dock, ☎ 74/84-4413; Costera Miguel Alemán 1226, in the Condo Estrella Tower, ☎ 74/84-4465; and Costera Miguel Alemán 163 at the Hotel Calinda, ☎ 74/81-2426) carry a nice selection of handicrafts at reasonable rates; even if you don't buy anything, consider using the downtown branch for a price base before plunging into the fray of

El Parazal market. **Artesenias Finas de Acapulco** (Avenida Oracio Nelson at the corner of James Cook, off the Costera behind Baby O disco; ☎ 74/84-8039) is the darling of the tour bus trade, but if you're willing to sift through the schlock, you can score some decent Mexican clothing and silver jewelry.

What to Do When the Sun's Gone Down

Acapulco, like New York, never sleeps. If you're a night owl, you can really spread your wings: Between the discos, dance clubs, and bars, there's no reason for you to see your turndown chocolates until dawn. In search of more mellow evenings? *No problema.* This city has plenty of serene and soulful scenes, too.

Saturday Night Fever

Acapulco's discos may be the glitziest in Mexico, with all the latest in high-tech sound-and-light effects, and its patrons might possibly be the best dressed. With the exception of Discobeach, these shrines to the '70s don't allow entry to anyone wearing tank tops, shorts, or sandals. Covers change year-round, but can go as high as $20; they're often lower (or nonexistent) for women. Doors open at around 10:30pm, but don't bother going until almost midnight unless you're trying to advertise just how uncool you are. Closing hours? Whenever the last weary dancers straggle out, sometimes as late as 8am. Phone to make reservations in high season. Here are the current faves:

Andromeda (Costera Miguel Alemán, at the corner of Fragata Yucatán; ☎ 74/84-8815) attracts throngs of duded-up 20-somethings to its fortress-like building, complete with drawbridge. Inside, the place looks like a bathosphere; accordingly, a mermaid and merman perform in a giant fishtank after midnight.

Bet You Didn't Know

Acapulco was the site of North America's first disco, Tequila a Go-Go.

Baby O (Costera Miguel Alemán 22; ☎ 74/84-7474) is a singles jungle, with the decor to match. Maybe it's the huge screen with booming MTV, but young (18 to 25) Americans tend to favor this place. Baby O has been around for a while, but keeps hopping, even during the week.

Yep, as the name **Discobeach** (Condesa Beach; ☎ 74/84-7064) implies, it's on the beach, and you don't have to get dressed up to play in the sand. The waiters do, though—sometimes in togas or pajamas. The house drink? Sex on the Beach, of course. This place is seriously popular and seriously loud. Don't bother turning up if you're over 30.

Extravaganzza (Costera Miguel Alemán s/n, next to El Ranchero Restaurant and near the Naval Base; ☎ **74/84-7154** and 74/84-7156) pulls in an older crowd (Gen X and up) for the knockout views of Acapulco Bay from the floor-to-ceiling windows and for the latest in special effects. Suffering from rock-concert hearing loss? Retire to the new Sibony Bar for some champagne and caviar.

Fantasy (Carretera Escénica, at La Vista shopping center; ☎ **74/84-6764**) is still a class act, and a see-and-be-seen spot, although most of the celebrities pictured in the downstairs photo gallery have seen better days—O. J. Simpson, for example. Boomers won't feel out of place here, as long as they get really duded up. The bay views are killer.

Rating the Discos

Most Mexicano: **Salon Q**

Best Singles Scene: **Baby O**

Most Beloved by Teeny-Boppers: **Palladium**

Most "In" at This Very Second: **Andromeda**

Best Views of Acapulco Bay: **Extravaganzza**

Best for Boomers: **Fantasy**

Most Informal: **Discobeach**

The younger (both in crowd and opening date) version of Extravaganzza, **Palladium** (Carretera Escénica s/n, near Las Brisas; ☎ **74/81-0330**) was created by the same person. This huge dance palace (capacity: 1,200) features the ultimate in high-tech sound-and-light systems and amazing bay views to boot. You can't miss it from the road—just look for the giant waterfall.

More romantic than the others along the Costera, **Salon Q** (Costera Miguel Alemán no. 3111, near Oceanic 2000; ☎ **74/81-0114**) is popular with Mexican couples, who sit at intimate tables and listen to the sizzling salsa sounds or dance to slower "tropical" tunes. Different styles of music are represented on different nights, from Cuban and Caribbean to Mexican.

Isn't It Romantic?

Piano bars in the **Hyatt Regency, Elcano,** and the **Copacabana** hotels see older couples dancing cheek-to-cheek to a smooth Latin beat. **Pepe's Piano Bar** (☎ **74/84-8060**) on the Carretera Escénica at the La Vista shopping center is the same scene, sans hotel.

A Taste of Mexico: Dinner Shows & Fiestas

Every Monday, Wednesday, and Friday night at 8pm, you can catch the **Fiesta Mexicana** show at the Convention Center (Avenida Costera Miguel Alemán 4455). This rousing repertoire of footwork from around the country includes a spot by the famed flyers of Papantla, who leap with the greatest of ease from a flagpole. The show will run you $20 for admission and two drinks; add an open bar and dinner, and you've got the tab up to $35. There are no Monday shows off-season. Call ☎ **74/84-3218** for reservations or book through a travel agent.

Eat 'n' Rumba: Restaurants with a Musical Menu
Who does dinner and din best: Mexico, England, or the United States? You can decide for yourself on the Costera, where **Carlos 'n Charlie's** (Costera Miguel Alemán 112; ☎ **74/84-0039; Hard Rock Cafe** (Costera Miguel Alemán 37; ☎ **74/84-0047**), and **Planet Hollywood** (Costera Miguel Alemán 2917; ☎ **74/84-4284**) all compete for the party peoples' pesos. Think loud music and basic American food.

Side Trips: Getting Out of Acapulco
Those who want a culture fix—and super shopping, to boot—shouldn't miss the chance to get to Taxco. Oaxaca is costlier to reach, but if you can afford the plane fare, it's a must for the same reasons. You could spend days in both cities, especially Oaxaca, but a taste is better than nothing.

Time-Savers
Feeling overwhelmed by the "too many choices, too little time" dilemma? Turn to the Must-See Attractions worksheet in Appendix A for help with planning your days.

Taxco
The colonial-era "Silver City" absolutely oozes charm. Located in the mountains about 4 hours from Acapulco, Taxco is famous for its high-quality jewelry shops, as well as for its cobblestoned streets and gorgeous baroque Santa Priscia church, in the center of a traditional zócalo. Most travel agencies sell trips to Taxco that depart at 6:30am, return around 9pm, and cost approximately $60.

Oaxaca
Another beautiful colonial city, Oaxaca boasts a colorful central square where members of local Indian tribes come to sell their crafts, some of the most interesting in all of Mexico. The Monte Alban and Mitla archaeological sites are fascinating, too. Fifty-minute flights leave for Oaxaca Tuesday, Thursday, Friday, and Sunday at 7am via AeroCaribe (☎ **74/84-3242**) and return Monday, Wednesday, Thursday, and Saturday at 7:50pm. On Thursday, a 1-day Oaxaca package, which includes a city tour and round-trip airfare, will run you $146. Hotel packages are also available from the airlines, as well as from local travel agents.

Chapter 24

The Best of Acapulco's Dining Scene

In This Chapter

➤ Acapulco dining: The big picture

➤ Keeping costs down

➤ The best restaurants from A to Z

➤ Restaurant indexes

Whether you want a pull-out-the-stops romantic hideaway, a see-and-be-seen scene where the food is almost secondary, or a down-home dive, you'll be spoiled for choice in Acapulco. Because the resort relies on Mexico City residents for much of its business, it's accustomed to catering to some of the most sophisticated palates in the country (think New York or San Francisco foodies with Latino leanings).

If It's Thursday, It Must Be Pozole

A specialty in Guerrero state, *pozole verde* is a hominy-based soup that often includes pumpkin seeds and pork rinds among its ingredients, although chicken is more common these days. Extended pozole lunches on Thursday are a long-standing tradition in Acapulco. Here's the drill: A mildly spiced bowl of pozole arrives with chopped onions, radishes, avocado, and various types of ground spices on the side. You just keep adding ingredients to your taste, and schmooze your way through the afternoon.

A Dining Overview: Where's the Burrito?

It stands to reason that since the Costera has the most hotels, it also has the most restaurants. I've included plenty of places to suit your mood and budget on the main tourist strip. But you might want to splurge on one of the glitzy Acapulco Diamante dining rooms or head downtown for some local color, so I've reviewed options in those other areas, too. All are arranged alphabetically, and in the indexes at the end of the chapter, I've broken them down by location and by price for you, too. (For a wrap-up of the character of each neighborhood, see "Location, Location, Location" in chapter 21, "Choosing the Place to Stay That's Right for You.") Want to narrow down your decision? If you're planning to go out on the town after dinner, check the restaurant map against the nightlife map in chapter 23, "Fun On & Off the Beach."

There are plenty of American fast food chains in Acapulco if you're traveling with kids who aren't especially adventurous; you don't need me to describe McDonald's to you. If your kids are older—and you can stand the ear-splitting music for a while—Planet Hollywood, Carlos 'n Charlie's, or the Hard Rock Cafe are good options. See "What to Do When the Sun's Gone Down," in chapter 23, for the addresses.

Yo, Gringo!

Don't wander around the Costera at dinnertime, thinking you'll find a place that strikes your fancy. Always decide where to eat in advance. The restaurant touts come out like vampires when the sun goes down, and they can spot an indecisive diner a mile away.

Check, Please

You can blow your restaurant budget on a single meal in some of Acapulco's restaurants if you're not careful—or you can watch what you're doing and eat well, and well within your means. Flip back to "Eating Well without Gobbling Up Your Dollars" in chapter 7 for some money-saving tips.

Don't worry about taxes; the 15% surcharge is included in your bill. The tip isn't, however. The standard in nice restaurants is 15%. Mexicans rarely tip that well in less pricey places—10% is about average—but if the service was good, sticking with the 15% rule is an easy way to help the Mexican economy without breaking your budget.

I've arranged price categories with the worst-case scenario in mind: They're based on a per-person dinner tab that includes appetizer, entrée, dessert, one drink, and tip. In addition, a price range for dinner entrées is included in the individual reviews: The more $ signs you see, the more money you'll be shelling out at the restaurant listed.

$	=	Under $15
$$	=	$15–$30
$$$	=	$30–$50
$$$$	=	Over $50

Unless otherwise noted, reservations are either not accepted or needed.

My Favorite Restaurants from A to Z

100% Natural
$. The Costera. HEALTH FOOD.
You can get healthful versions of the Mexican standards at this family-run chain (there are six links in Acapulco), but most people come here to cure taco burnout. Freshly squeezed fruit drinks, yogurt shakes, steamed vegetables, or cheese sandwiches on wheat should restore that righteous feeling—if only temporarily. All the restaurants are comfy and casual. A centrally located one on the Costera looks like a two-tier beach shack, although it's on the inland side of the thoroughfare.

Costera Miguel Alemán 200, near the Acapulco Plaza hotel. ☎ **74/85-3982.** *Most food items $2–$5. No credit cards.* **Open:** *Daily 24 hours. Other locations: Miguel Alemán 34, corner of Andrea Doria,* ☎ *74/84-8440; and Miguel Alemán 112 (2nd floor, Club Deportivo),* ☎ *74/84-6447.*

Bambuco
$$–$$$. The Costera. SEAFOOD/ INTERNATIONAL.
Ahhhh. Palm trees swaying, a gentle breeze wafting from the water over to your beachfront table. Settle into a tapestry-back chair at Bambuco and raise a glass to the good life. A fork, too. If one of your culinary goals is to plumb the depths of Acapulco's seafood, you've come to the right place. You might start with crispy codfish croquettes or deep-fried squid, and then move on to giant shrimp in garlic or red snapper in parsley. If the ocean isn't your favorite source of protein, try the beef fillet with tarragon. Portions are more than generous. This is also a favorite breakfast spot for local businesspeople. Who knows how many deals have been closed over waffles stuffed with fruit and nuts?

Smoke Gets in My Eyes

Every restaurant I've listed offers an alfresco option or is open-fronted, with whirling fans to move the air around. So if you're a nonsmoker, you're not going to get stuck in any closed-off, smoke-filled rooms.

271

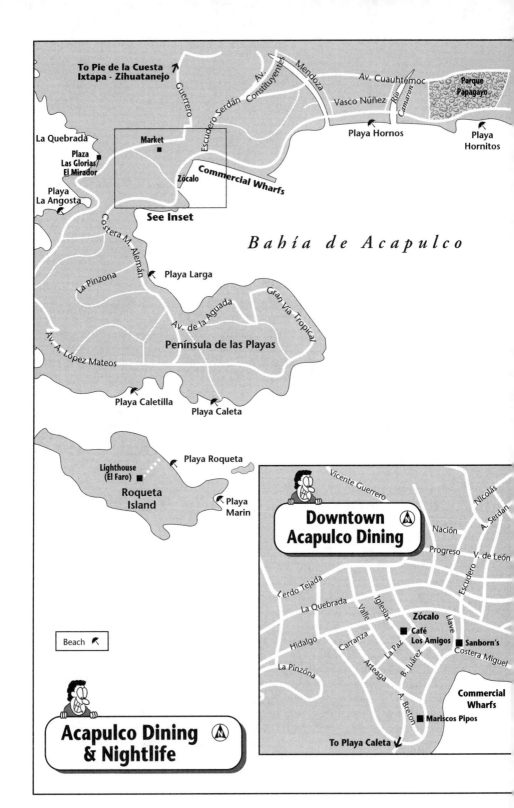

To Pie de la Cuesta
Ixtapa - Zihuatanejo

Guerrero

Escudero Serdán

Av. Constituyentes

Mendoza

Av. Cuauhtémoc

Vasco Núñez

Río Camarón

Parque Papagayo

La Quebrada

Market

Plaza
Las Glorias/
El Mirador

Zócalo

Commercial Wharfs

Playa
La Angosta

See Inset

Playa Hornos

Playa
Hornitos

Bahía de Acapulco

Costera M. Alemán

La Pinzona

Playa Larga

Av. de la Aguada

Gran Via Tropical

Av. A. López Mateos

Península de las Playas

Playa Caletilla

Playa Caleta

Lighthouse
(El Faro)

Playa Roqueta

Roqueta
Island

Playa
Marin

Beach

**Acapulco Dining
& Nightlife**

Vicente Guerrero

**Downtown
Acapulco Dining**

Nicolás

A. Serdán

Nación

Progreso

V. de León

Escudero

Lerdo Tejada

La Quebrada

Iglesias

Valle

Zócalo

Llave

Café
Los Amigos

La Paz

B. Juárez

Sanborn's

Costera Miguel

Hidalgo

Carranza

Arteaga

La Pinzóna

A. Bretón

Commercial
Wharfs

Mariscos Pipos

To Playa Caleta

272

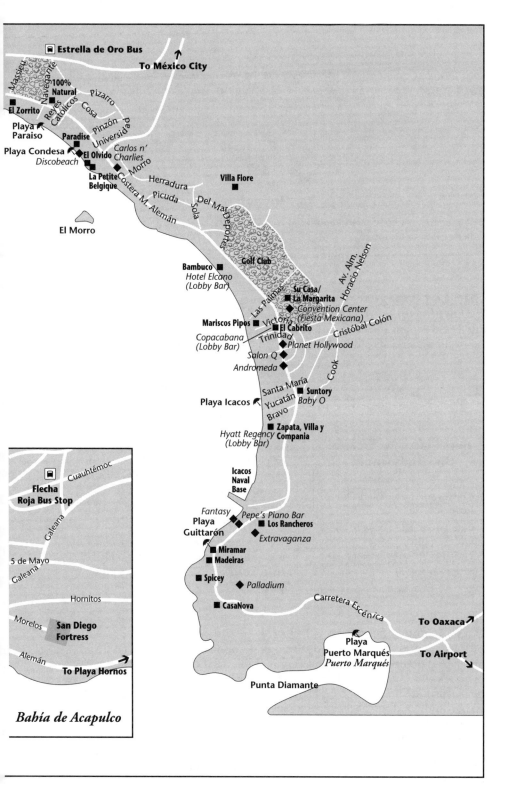

Estrella de Oro Bus

To México City

Massieu
Navegante
100% Natural
Reyes Católicos
El Zorrito
Pizarro
Cosa
Pinzón
Paz
Universid
Playa Paraiso
Paradise
El Olvido
Carlos n' Charlies
Playa Condesa
Discobeach
La Petite Belgique
Morro
Costera M. Alemán
Herradura
Del Mar
Villa Fiore
Picuda
Sola
El Morro
Deportes

Golf Club
Bambuco
Hotel Elcano (Lobby Bar)
Las Palmas
Av. Alm. Horacio Nelson
Su Casa/
La Margarita
Convention Center (Fiesta Mexicana)
Mariscos Pipos
Victoria
El Cabrito
Cristóbal Colón
Copacabana (Lobby Bar)
Trinidad
Planet Hollywood
Salon Q
Andromeda
Cook
Santa María
Suntory
Playa Icacos
Yucatán
Baby O
Bravo
Zapata, Villa y Compania
Hyatt Regency (Lobby Bar)

Icacos Naval Base

Fantasy
Playa Guittarón
Pepe's Piano Bar
Los Rancheros
Extravaganza
Miramar
Madeiras
Spicey
Palladium
CasaNova
Carretera Escénica

To Oaxaca

Playa Puerto Marqués
Puerto Marqués
To Airport

Punta Diamante

Cuauhtémoc
Flecha Roja Bus Stop
Galeana
5 de Mayo
Galeana
Hornitos
Morelos
San Diego Fortress
Alemán
To Playa Hornos

Bahía de Acapulco

273

Hotel Elcano, Costera Miguel Alemán 75. ☎ *74/84-1950. Reservations suggested.* **Main courses:** *$7.50–$17. AE, DC, MC, V.* **Open:** *Daily 7am–11pm.*

Yo, Gringo!

Remember, it's considered impolite in Mexico for the waiter to bring the check before you ask for it.

Cafe Los Amigos

$. Downtown/Old Acapulco. MEXICAN/AMERICAN.
You'll find Americans in the know at this friendly family-owned cafe, reading the paper under a spreading ficus tree. They've discovered you could come here and get a Tex-Mex breakfast—eggs, peppers, and onions rolled in two flour tortillas, baked with cheese, and served with fries—for less than $3, or a hefty charcoal-grilled ribeye steak, salad, and fries for about five bucks. Preparations have the *Norteamericano* palate in mind— hot peppers are served on the side, for example—and portions are BIG. Also in stateside style, breakfast is served all day. Wash down whatever you get with a big glass of fresh-squeezed fruit juice.

Best Places to Escape Burrito Burnout

100% Natural (The Costera and Downtown/Old Acapulco, $)

Cafe Los Amigos (Downtown/Old Acapulco, $)

Sanborn's (Downtown/Old Acapulco, $–$$)

Av. de la Paz 10 (at the southwest corner of the zócalo) at Ignacio Ramirez. No phone. **Main courses:** *$2.50–$6. No credit cards.* **Open:** *Daily 9am–10pm.*

Casa Nova

$$$$. Acapulco Diamante. ITALIAN.
With its dramatic bay views and stunning decor, including *trompe l'oeil* murals and oodles of marble, this is one of the most gorgeous restaurants in town. It's also, quite possibly, the most expensive. Presentations of dishes like the classic Caesar salad or such standards as seafood ravioli and veal piccata are beautiful, and service is impeccable. As for taste—well, my criterion for deciding whether a place so pricey is worth the money is whether I would die happy if someone were to shoot me afterward, and I'm not quite ready to give up the ghost in this dining room. On the other hand, if a man were to take me here to demonstrate his devotion, I would feel very kindly disposed toward him.

Carretera Escénica no. 5256, across from the Westin Las Brisas. ☎ *74/84-6815. Reservations required.* **Main courses:** *Pastas $22–$30; meat, poultry, or seafood $25–$60. AE, DC, MC, V.* **Open:** *Daily 7–11:30pm.*

El Cabrito
$. The Costera. MEXICAN.
Don't be put off by the sight of the little animal turning slowly on a spit in front of this colorful, open-front restaurant—unless you're vegetarian, you wouldn't pass up a Hawaiian luau because of the pig, right? In this case, the rotating creature is a small goat, the Northern Mexico specialty for which the restaurant is named, but you can choose from plenty of other dishes less reminiscent of a petting zoo—the rich, dark chicken mole from Oaxaca, for example (made with grapes, almonds, cocoa, and chiles, among other things), or shrimp cooked in tequila. The charro beans that come with most everything are terrific, as is the coconut flan desert.

Costera Miguel Alemán 1480, opposite the Hard Rock Cafe. ☎ *74/84-7711.* **Main courses:** *$4–$8. AE, MC, V.* **Open:** *Daily 1pm–1am.*

El Olvido
$$$. The Costera. NOUVELLE MEXICAN.
Probably the hippest dining room on the Costera, with all the cachet of the Las Brisas restaurants but without the long cab ride. A striking blue-and-white room overlooking the water prepares you for the gorgeous presentations of the food, which might be dubbed New American with a southwest twist, if El Olvido were in the States. Because it's in Acapulco, it's more accurately New Mexican, pun intended—the menu wouldn't be out of place in

Trendiest Restaurants

El Olvido (The Costera, $$$)

Madeiras (Acapulco Diamante, $$$)

Spicey (Acapulco Diamante, $$$)

Santa Fe. You might start with a chilled avocado cream soup, touched with cilantro, followed by a chicken breast in green mole with pistachios or fresh salmon with serrano chiles and *huitlacoche* (the Mexican version of truffles). The house-made sherbets and ice creams rely on equally exotic ingredients—the guanabana mousse in a rich black zapote sauce is a delicious specialty.

Costera Miguel Alemán, Plaza Marbella. ☎ *74/81-0214 or 81-0240. Reservations suggested.* **Main courses:** *$11–$23. AE, MC, V.* **Open:** *Daily 6pm–1:30am.*

El Zorrito
$. The Costera. MEXICAN.
A local favorite for a post-disco nosh, El Zorrito rarely closes—only from 6 to 9am and on Tuesdays does a retractable iron gate bar entry to this open-front eatery. It's a good place to try pozole or any number of standard Mexican dishes, such as *huevos rancheros* or Tampico-style beef steak (the most expensive item on the menu at about $6.50, it comes with massive numbers of side

**Most Romantic
Restaurants**

Bambuco (The Costera,
$$–$$$)

Casa Nova (Acapulco
Diamante, $$$$)

El Olvido (The Costera, $$$)

Madeiras (Acapulco
Diamante, $$$)

Miramar (Acapulco
Diamante, $$)

Su Casa/La Margarita (The
Costera, $$–$$$)

Villa Fiore (The Costera,
$$–$$$)

dishes). You can watch the simple but tasty food being prepared at an open kitchen. This is a real local place, drawing businesspeople for weekday breakfast and lunch and families for weekend brunch. There's live music every evening.

Costera Miguel Alemán at Anton de Alaminos, east of Gran Plaza Mall. ☎ *74/85-3735. Reservations not accepted.* **Main courses:** *$3–$6.50. AE, MC, V.* **Open:** *Wed–Mon 9am–6am.*

La Petite Belgique
$$$. The Costera. BELGIAN.
Wear loose-fitting clothing to this pretty European-style bistro—the food is seriously rich. (When I asked the chef what the difference was between French and Belgian food, he said "If the French put in one tablespoon of butter, we put in half a cup—just to make sure.") Share appetizers if you want to fully appreciate dinner. One slice of mega-dense goose-liver terrine, for example, might even be enough for three or four. Whether it's onion soup made with a subtle blend of cheeses, steak tournedos with a three-pepper sauce, or lobster flambéed with Armagnac, the painstaking attention to detail shows in the taste. You can see a bit of the bay from the front tables, but the view of the pastry case when you walk in is even more scenic.

Plaza Marbella. ☎ *74/84-7725 or 84-2017. Reservations required.* **Main courses:** *$12–$17. AE, MC, V.* **Open:** *Daily 1:30pm to 3 or 4am.*

Los Rancheros
$$. Acapulco Diamante. MEXICAN.
A cheerful bargain in the Las Brisas area. Colorful chairs and paper cutouts hanging from the ceiling, not to mention mariachis in the afternoon, help create a festive mood in this large, open-front dining room; a super view of Acapulco Bay does nothing to dampen it. The food moves all over the Mexican map, with specialties such as beef tenderloin from the state of Tampico and Yucatán-style charcoal-broiled pork. Tex-Mex chicken or shrimp fajitas even give a nod to *norteamericano* cooking. Monday afternoon, there's a buffet, and Thursday is pozole day.

Carretera Escénica s/n, Las Brisas, across from Fantasy disco. ☎ *74/84-1908. Reservations not necessary.* **Main courses:** *$6–$11. AE, DC, MC, V.* **Open:** *Daily noon or 1pm to midnight.*

Madeiras

$$$. Acapulco Diamante. INTERNATIONAL/NOUVELLE MEXICAN.

You might feel a sudden urge to shop when you walk into this gracious converted home, that's how beautiful its hand-crafted furnishings are. No problem—an adjoining boutique sells dishes and jewelry by one of Taxco's finest artists. In any case, you'll soon become absorbed by the watery vistas and by the superb food. Pace yourself. The prix-fixe menu requires that you choose from appetizers such as seafood *coquille* or duck salad, a total of 15 main courses such as beef tournedos or Yucatán-style red snapper, and a luscious array of house-made pastries and sherbets. The cooking is highly creative, complementing classics from Europe with updated versions of Mexican regional dishes. All the rooms are romantic, but the one with the Mayan decor is the most intimate.

Carretera Escénica 33. ☎ 74/84-4378. Reservations required in high season. **Prix-fixe** *$30 (includes appetizer, soup, entrée, dessert, and coffee). AE, DC, MC, V.* **Open:** *Mon–Fri 7–10:30pm; Sat–Sun 7–11:30pm. No shorts, and no children under 6.*

Mariscos Pipos

$$. Downtown/Old Acapulco. SEAFOOD.

This unassuming seafood restaurant is the first place many fish-savvy folks from Mexico City head for when they arrive in Acapulco; you may seem them lined up outside the door. The decor is duly nautical, with hanging nets and shell lanterns—a suitable setting for such specialties as the chunky mixed seafood soup and red snapper, crawfish, or octopus grilled in garlic butter. If you're walking from the zócalo, you'll find this place 5 blocks to the west on Breton, just off the Costera. Another branch across from the Hard Rock Cafe (Costera Miguel Alemán and Canada; ☎ 74/84-0165) is open daily from 1 to 9pm.

Almirante Breton 3. ☎ 74/82-2237. **Main courses:** *$5–$11. AE, MC, V.* **Open:** *Daily 11am–8pm.*

Miramar

$$. Acapulco Diamante. INTERNATIONAL.

Maybe it's the competition from the trendier restaurants in the area that made the somewhat old-fashioned Miramar drop its prices. No matter. Don't look a gift horse—or is that chateaubriand?—in the mouth. You'll have a dramatic view of Acapulco Bay on whichever of the three plant-decked tiers you choose to dine. The menu is tough to classify. You might start with ceviche, Greek salad, or onion soup, and move on to duck à l'orange, veal piccata, or Mexican-style red snapper. The desserts tend toward the Gallic—profiteroles, say, or white chocolate mousse. Everything is equally well prepared, so just let your mood dictate the country you feel like dining in. Dress up—this is one of the more formal places in town—but dress cool: The ceiling fans are a bit anemic.

Carretera Escénica s/n, Plaza la Vista. ☎ *74/84-7874. Reservations suggested.* **Main courses:** *$7.50–$12.50. AE, DC, MC, V.* **Open:** *Daily 6:30pm–12:30am.*

Paradise/Paradiso
$$. The Costera. SEAFOOD.

There's a price to pay for the good seafood at this super-popular beachfront restaurant: intact eardrums. But portions are large, the fish is fresh, and everyone's too sloshed to be saying anything worth listening to, anyway. The music and movement get cooking at lunchtime and pick up again after about 9pm. Plenty of hard-bodied hipsters under 30 make this their restaurant of choice.

Costera Miguel Alemán 107, at del Prado. ☎ *74/84-5988.* **Main courses:** *$6–$12.50. AE, DC, MC, V.* **Open:** *Daily noon–12:30am.*

⭐Kids Sanborn's
$–$$. Downtown/Old Acapulco. AMERICAN/MEXICAN.

A cross between a coffee shop and a 1970s suburban lounge, Sanborn's is the place to come for comfort food, whether it's burgers, bacon and eggs, spaghetti, or cheese-smothered enchiladas that ease your soul. Sink into one of the padded booths and people-watch. Everyone turns up here sooner or later, whether for a power breakfast, a girls' dish-the-dirt lunch, or a post-shopping treat for the kids (there's a good pastry shop). The menu is bilingual, the servers are friendly, and the bathrooms are spotless. There are two additional branches on the Costera: Costera Miguel Alemán 1226, in the Condo Estrella Tower, ☎ **74/84-4465**; and Costera Miguel Alemán 163 at the Hotel Calinda, ☎ **74/81-2426.**

Costera Miguel Alemán 209 at Escudero, across from the steamship dock. ☎ *74/84-4413.* **Main courses:** *$4–$10. AE, DC, MC, V.* **Open:** *Daily 7:30am–1am in high season, till 11pm in low season.*

Local Favorites

El Zorrito (The Costera, $)

Los Rancheros (Acapulco Diamante, $$)

Mariscos Pipos (Downtown/ Old Acapulco, $$)

Spicey
$$$. Acapulco Diamante. INTERNATIONAL.

If it weren't for the view of Acapulco Bay, Spicey's trendy menu might lead you to believe you were in New York or Los Angeles. You've got your requisite Asian influence and mix of dissonant flavors: The marinade on the house specialty shrimp appetizer, for example, combines coconut, marmalade, and wasabi, and the red snapper entrée has an anise, honey, and rosemary glaze. But what might be just plain weird in the wrong hands works very well here, so a hip, Eurotrash-looking crowd keeps coming back. All the ingredients are super-fresh, and there's an air-conditioned room downstairs to keep you from wilting.

Carretera Escénica s/n, Marina Las Brisas. ☎ *74/81-1380 or 74/81-0470. Reservations recommended on weekends.* **Main courses:** *$12.50–$22. AE, DC, MC, V.* **Open:** *Daily 7–11:30pm.*

Su Casa/La Margarita
$$–$$$. The Costera. MEXICAN/INTERNATIONAL.
Imagine being invited to someone's lovely hillside hacienda, with miles of colored tile and tropical plants, and having the choice of dining from either a creative Mexican or Continental menu. Gourmet chefs Shelley and Angel Herrara personally welcome visitors to their *casa, con mucho gusto.* Among the favorites are the Mexican combination—grilled steak, an enchilada, taco, and guacamole—and the mahi-mahi in garlic, which crosses the Continental taste divide. Whatever you try, it'll contain only fresh ingredients, bought in the market that morning and beautifully prepared. In high season, two dining rooms are used, one upstairs and one downstairs, both equally charming and with equally knockout bay views. Slightly out of the way, this place is definitely worth the detour from the Costera.

Av. Anahuac 110, Lomas de Costa Azul. ☎ *74/84-4350 or 84-1261. Reservations suggested.* **Main courses:** *$8–$18. AE, MC, V.* **Open:** *Daily 5:30pm–midnight.*

Suntory
$$–$$$. The Costera. JAPANESE.
Some people seek out this pretty pagoda for sushi standards such as salmon roll, California roll, or assorted sashimi. (There are also odd combos with chiles, onions, and mayonnaise, but you don't want to go there.) Others come for the teppanyaki—beef, chicken, fish, or seafood cooked tableside on a grill. The chef's slice 'n' dice pyrotechnics alone are worth the price of the meal. If you can't decide between the raw and the cooked, full-course combination dinners offer both. The two rooms with the grill tables can be a bit noisy, but they're cool, while an interior courtyard has a beautiful Japanese garden with a koi pond—but no air-conditioning. Never mind. You'll be well satisfied with the food and the ambience at this longtime favorite of locals and tourists alike.

Costera Miguel Alemán at Maury, just a little west of the Hyatt Regency. ☎ *74/84-8088 or 74/84-8766. Reservations recommended.* **Main courses:** *Teppanyaki $10–$17; sushi rolls $5–$9; assorted sashimi $20. AE, DC, MC, V.* **Open:** *Daily 2pm–midnight.*

Villa Fiore
$$–$$$. The Costera. NORTHERN ITALIAN.
A re-creation of a 17th-century Venetian villa by a renowned Acapulco architect, this restaurant is about as romantic as they get. You'll dine by candlelight on white-clothed tables in a gorgeous, lush garden (seating is inside by the bar during rainy season). Under the same ownership as Madeiras (see above), Villa Fiore has a similar all-inclusive menu, although in this case, the price varies with the entrée. Select a pasta dish such as fettuccine with

chicken, say, and your bill will be about $7 lower than if you opt for veal saltimbocca. Appetizers, such as an excellent spinach salad or squid stuffed with ham, capers, and olives, are part of the deal, as are soup, dessert and coffee.

Av. del Prado 6 (a few blocks inland from the Costera). ☎ *74/84-2040. Reservations required.* **Fixed-price menu:** *$18–$25. AE, DC, MC, V.* **Open:** *Thurs–Tues 7–11pm.*

Zapata, Villa y Compania
$$. The Costera. MEXICAN.

Sure, this place hauls out every Mexican cliché you can come up with—*banditos,* carbine-toting revolutionaries, mariachis, even a live burro wearing a sombrero—but it also serves nonstereotypically outstanding dishes from around the country. Appetizers include a great shrimp ceviche; if you're hungry, go for the *botanos* sampler platter. A gigantic cut of beef tenderloin with guacamole and beans for two, and Yucatán-style snapper cooked in banana leaves, are among the house specialties. And, corny as it is, this restaurant is entertaining. Having 114 types of tequila at the bar doesn't hurt, and the burro, Polita, is adorable.

Hyatt Regency Acapulco, Costera Miguel Alemán 1. ☎ *74/69-1234. Reservations not needed.* **Main courses:** *$5.50–$11 (higher for shrimp and lobster). DC, MC, V.* **Open:** *Daily restaurant 7–11:30pm; bar (serving appetizers) 7pm–2am.*

Sound Bites: Acapulco's Restaurants at a Glance
Restaurant Index by Price

$

Kids 100% Natural (Branches in the Costera and Downtown/Old Acapulco, Health Food)

Cafe Los Amigos (Downtown/Old Acapulco, American/Mexican)

El Cabrito (The Costera, Mexican)

El Zorrito (The Costera, Mexican)

$–$$

Kids Sanborn's (Downtown/Old Acapulco location and two Costera branches, American/Mexican)

$$

Los Rancheros (Acapulco Diamante, Mexican)

Mariscos Pipos (Branches Downtown/Old Acapulco & in the Costera, Seafood)

Miramar (Acapulco Diamante, International)

Paradise/Paradiso (The Costera, Seafood)

Kids Zapata, Villa y Compania (The Costera, Mexican)

$$–$$$

Bambuco (The Costera, Seafood/International)

Su Casa/La Margarita (The Costera, Mexican/International)

Suntory (The Costera, Japanese)

Villa Fiore (The Costera, Italian)

$$$

El Olvido (The Costera, Nouvelle Mexican)

La Petite Belgique (The Costera, Belgian)

Madeiras (Acapulco Diamante, Mexican/International)

Spicey (Acapulco Diamante, International)

$$$$

Casa Nova (Acapulco Diamante, Italian)

Restaurant Index by Location

Downtown/Old Acapulco

100% Natural $

Cafe Los Amigos $

Mariscos Pipos $$

Kids Sanborn's $–$$

The Costera

Kids 100% Natural $

Bambuco $$–$$$

El Cabrito $

El Olvido $$$

El Zorrito $

La Petite Belgique $$$

Mariscos Pipos $$

Paradise/Paradiso $$

Kids Sanborn's $–$$

Su Casa/La Margarita $$–$$$

Suntory $$–$$$

Villa Fiore $$–$$$

Kids Zapata, Villa y Compania $$

Acapulco Diamante

Casa Nova $$$$

Los Rancheros $$

Madeiras $$$

Miramar $$

Spicey $$$

Part 7

Ixtapa/Zihuatanejo

In The Shawshank Redemption, *Zihuatanejo's gorgeous beaches inspire Tim Robbins to make an elaborate jailbreak. Your trip to Zihuatanejo and neighboring Ixtapa is bound to be somewhat less complicated—especially if you follow the advice in these next few chapters.*

Conventional wisdom has it that Ixtapa, the newcomer on the resort scene, is all fast-paced action, while Zihuatanejo, an old-time fishing village, is the place to kick back. In fact, Ixtapa doesn't register very high on the go-go scale, especially compared to larger, more developed resorts like Acapulco or Cancún, and sleepy Zihuatanejo has had a wake-up call, resulting in several world-class hotels and restaurants.

What's indisputable is that both have plenty to offer sun-and-fun seekers and that it's simple to shuttle back and forth between them. You can have the best of both worlds—which is what I'm about to introduce you to.

Choosing the Place to Stay That's Right for You

There's nothing but good news if you've decided to book a room in Ixtapa/Zihuatanejo: You've got a terrific pick of places that are oozing with character or amenities—and sometimes both (okay, it'll cost you big in that case, but I said good news, not fantasy). And if you're willing to forgo a few creature comforts—but not the basics, like safety and cleanliness—you can snag some rock-bottom bargains, too.

It works this way: First, I'll describe the three areas where Ixtapa and Zihua-tanejo's hotels are concentrated, and sum up their pros and cons for you. Then I'll list my favorite hotels alphabetically, and follow up with a few alternatives should these A-list choices be filled. At the end of the chapter, you'll find at-a-glance indexes listing the hotels by price and by location.

As far as prices go, I've noted rack rates (the maximum that a resort or hotel charges for a room) in the listings. This information will give you some sense of what to expect, although I know you'll

Address Unknown

When you see "s/n" in an address, it stands for "*sin numero*" (without number). Don't worry—you won't have any trouble locating places in either Zihuatanejo or Ixtapa.

avoid paying rack by following the advice I gave you in chapter 6, "The Lowdown on Accommodations in Mexico." I've also put a dollar sign icon in front of each hotel listing so you can see quickly whether it's within your budget. The more $ signs under the name, the more you pay. It runs like this:

$$
\begin{aligned}
\$ &= \$80 \text{ and below} \\
\$\$ &= \$80\text{--}\$130 \\
\$\$\$ &= \$130\text{--}\$190 \\
\$\$\$\$ &= \$190\text{--}\$260 \\
\$\$\$\$\$ &= \$260 \text{ and above}
\end{aligned}
$$

Unless otherwise specified, rates are for a standard double room in high season, which runs from mid-December through after Easter; rates drop from 15% to 40% the rest of the year. Prices quoted here include the 17% room tax.

A kid-friendly icon **Kids** highlights hotels that are especially good for families. All hotels have air-conditioning unless otherwise indicated, and if the review doesn't say anything to the contrary, you can safely assume that you can walk directly out of your hotel and onto the beach.

Hint: As you read through the reviews, you'll want to keep track of the ones that appeal to you. I've included a chart at the end of the book (see p. 542) where you can rank your preferences, but to make matters easier on yourself now, why don't you just put a little check mark next to the ones you like? Remember how your teachers used to tell you not to write in your books? Now's the time to rebel, so scrawl away!

Location, Location, Location

The hotels in Ixtapa/Zihuatanejo fall fairly neatly into three distinct geographical areas. I'll start in the north with Ixtapa, move southeast into the town of Zihuatanejo, and then continue south along the coast to the Zihuatanejo beaches area.

Ixtapa: The Resort Center

It's new, it's glitzy, it's got its ducks all lined up in a row. Stay in Ixtapa, a child of the 1970s, and every amenity designed for today's pampered tourist will be at your disposal: Shopping centers, tony eateries, golf courses, and one high-rise hotel after another are strung along the main drag, Boulevard Ixtapa, which ends in a posh marina complex. Whatever's not within easy pedestrian range—and most things are—is a cheap cab ride away.

Not that you especially need to go anywhere: All the hotels are self-contained cities, with restaurants, boutiques, bars, pools, activity centers, and so on. The numbers might vary, but the comfort level is consistently high. And all (except the Westin Brisas Ixtapa) sit on the 3-mile-long Palmar Beach: wide, fine-grained, and chock-a-block with water sports concessions.

The downside? Not a whole lot of character—remember, the '70s weren't exactly renowned for their style or taste—and few surprises; most things are

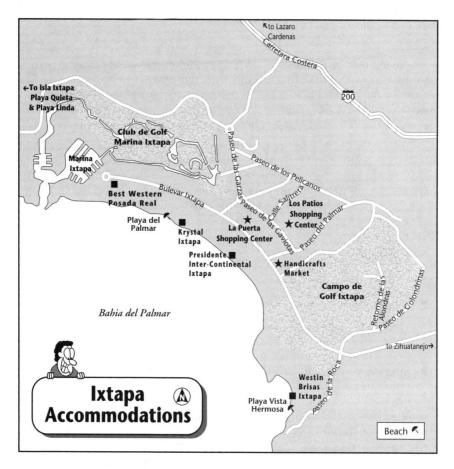

Ixtapa Accommodations

about as imaginative as the name of the main drag. You won't find many bargains, either, although prices are relatively modest in comparison with those in the larger, more Americanized beach towns.

In a nutshell . . .

> ➤ A nice beach

> ➤ All the modern comforts

> ➤ Convenient nightlife, restaurants, and shops

but . . .

> ➤ Not much character

> ➤ Little variation in the accommodations

> ➤ Relatively expensive

Downtown Zihuatanejo: Traditional Mexico

Fancier tourist enclaves have sprung up on the beaches to the east, but downtown, or *centro,* is still the heart and soul of Zihuatanejo. Fishermen display the catch of the morning on the Paseo de Pescador, the beachside promenade, and town meetings are held in the central square. Maybe there are more tourist shops and restaurants than there were before Ixtapa arrived, but locals still greet each another by name as they pass along narrow, brick-lined streets. If you like leisurely after-dinner strolls and glimpses of old Mexico, it's hard to beat this location.

With the exception of Puerto Mio (which isn't really downtown), lodgings in this area are modest and priced accordingly. Not all have air-conditioning and few go beyond the basics; none of the hotels sits directly on the beach, and only Puerto Mio and the Hotel Avila look out on the water. You'll have to put up with a bit of street noise if you stay here, but things settle down fairly early, and you won't be kept up by disco noise or wild partying in the streets.

In a nutshell . . .

> ➤ The cheapest hotel rates in town

> ➤ Lots of restaurants and shops within walking distance

> ➤ Plenty of local color

but . . .

> ➤ Don't expect much luxury.

> ➤ Rooms can be noisy.

> ➤ You have to travel to get to a good beach.

Zihuatanejo/Beaches: Rooms for Every Budget

Not only are the beaches lovely in the area just east of downtown—Playa la Ropa is one of the dreamiest stretches of sand imaginable—but they host two of the most exclusive small hotels in all of Mexico. Nor are most of the less expensive lodgings in this area anything to sneeze at. You get lots of character for your pesos in this part of town, along with—for the most part—easy access to the surf.

Although most of the hotels have their own restaurants and there are some places to eat on the beaches, if you want to vary your menu, you'll have to cab over to central Zihuatanejo or Ixtapa. Ditto for doing any shopping or enjoying much nightlife; those who want to drop a few retail dollars or a few inhibitions on the dance floor are going to have to go the distance (but, then, nothing is very far from anything else in these two towns).

In a nutshell . . .

> ➤ You can enjoy great beaches.

> ➤ Rooms have character to spare.

> ➤ You can get some real bargains.

Zihuatanejo Accommodations

↑ To Ixtapa ↗

Main Bus Terminal

Tres Estrellas Bus Terminal

Morelos

Avenida

Paseo Zihuatanejo

Paseo del Palmar

I. Altamirano

Cuáuhtémoc

Avenida Nava

Municipal Market

Cinco de Mayo

Benito

C. González

Kioto ○ Plaza

Vicente Guerrero

Ejido

Juárez

Camino a la playa la Ropa

Galeana

Paseo de la Boquita

Canal

Calle Adelita

Artisan's Market

Las Salinas

N. Bravo

Avenida Ramírez

3

Pedro Ascencio

Museo de Arqueología

Calle Mateos

4

5

Juan N. Álvarez

2

Playa La Madera

Calle de la Noria

Paseo del Pescador

Playa Municipal

Muelle Pier

Andador Contramar

↑ Playa el Almacén

Bahía de Zihuatanejo

Playa La Ropa

6

7

1

8

9

Bungalows Pacifico **4**
Hotel Avila **2**
Hotel Catalina
  & Sotavento **7**
Hotel Citali **3**
Hotel Paraiso **9**
Hotel Puerto Mio **1**
La Casa Que Canta **6**
Villa del Sol **8**
Villas Miramar **5**

Beach ↑ Post Office ⊠

but . . .

➤ You have to cab it to the restaurants and nightspots.

➤ Rooms in the more exclusive hotels can be quite pricey.

➤ There are few shops and no markets in the area.

My Favorite Hotels from A to Z

Best Western Posada Real
$$$. Ixtapa.
Less expensive and impersonal than most of the properties along Ixtapa's hotel drag, the Posada Real is set back from the road a bit, making it less exposed. Done in bold yellows and blues, the rooms go beyond generic,

though the TVs are bigger than the baths, relatively speaking, and there are no ocean views. The lobby is too small for much socializing, but two pools, two restaurants, a bar, and a dance club take up the slack. A big, grassy area sees plenty of amateur soccer action.

Blvd. Ixtapa s/n, Hotel Zone. ☎ ***800/528-1234*** *or 755/3-1805.* **Rack rates:** *$129 double. Discounts for extended stays. AE, MC, V.*

Bungalows Pacifico
$. Zihuatanejo/Beaches.
Basic, but with nice artsy touches, these Madera Beach digs are among the most popular of the area's furnished bungalows, in part because the owner enjoys sharing her considerable knowledge of the area—she's had this place almost 30 years. Although all seven units are large (they can comfortably sleep four) and have kitchenettes, they're not ideal for families because it's a short hike down to the beach and there are no facilities on the premises. The hotel is close to town, though, and good for economy-minded couples or groups of friends. No air-conditioning.

Calle Eva S. de Lopez Mateos, Playa Madera. ☎ *and fax* ***755/4-2112.*** **Rack rates:** *$59 two people, $12 more per person. No credit cards. Travelers' checks accepted.*

Hotel Avila
$. Downtown Zihuatanejo.
The rooms here won't knock your socks off, but if you get one that faces the water, the views will. You can sit and watch the boats go by on plant-filled patios shared by every three of these nine units; score one on an upper floor where you won't hear the street noise and you've hit the jackpot. All have TVs as well as fans and air-conditioning; tile floors and marble sinks lend a touch of class. The upkeep isn't overly fastidious, however.

Juan N. Álvarez 8, off Paseo de Pescador. ☎ *and fax* ***755/4-2010.*** **Rack rates:** *$67 city view; $82 sea view. AE, MC, V.*

Hotel Catalina & Sotavento
$. Zihuatanejo/Beaches.
Boomers and Gen-Xers who used to come with their parents now bring their kids to this Playa la Ropa institution, a pair of adjacent cliff-side hotels under single management. Once the only luxury properties in this area, they grabbed prime spots on a prime beach. They're budget-quality now, but they're clean and well-maintained. Wooden headboards and furniture crafted in a carpenter shop on the premises lend character to the otherwise plain rooms. The standard-size but comfortable accommodations in the five-story Sotovento share large terraces, while Catalina has individual red-tile roof cabanas, some of them huge. You'll have a beach-view hammock to laze in, no matter which hotel you select. You'll also have some stairs to climb, either to the beach if you're near the top of the cliff, or to the restaurants or swell sunset bar if you're closer to the bottom.

Playa la Ropa s/n. ☎ *755/4-2032, 4-2033, 4-2034, or 4-2037. Fax 755/4-2975 or 4-6870. giga.com/_sotavent/. E-mail: sotavent@mail.giga.com.* **Rack rates:** *$53 double (small oceanview room) to $111 (oceanview bungalow). Meal plans available. AE, DC, MC, V.*

Hotel Citali
$. Downtown Zihuatanejo.
You might be awakened by the sounds of kids rushing into a nearby school in the morning, and you'll have minimal space for moving around, but otherwise this is a major bargain. Everything is spotless, the shady central courtyard is charming (it's even got a hammock hanging from a spreading ficus tree), and the location avoids the worst of the evening traffic noise. Rooms have nice tiled showers but no air-conditioning.

Vincente Guerrero 3, corner of Álvarez. ☎ *755/4-2043.* **Rack rate:** *$29 double. No credit cards.*

Hotel Paraiso
$$. Zihuatanejo/Beaches.
Opened in 1997 at the far end of Playa la Ropa, this casual hotel is perfect for divers—one of its owners also has a share in the Zihuatanejo Scuba Center—as well as for anyone wanting an escape from loud music. Things are kept quiet here so as not to disturb the residents of an adjacent nature preserve, including three alligators (one of the reasons kids under 12 are discouraged from coming). Twenty simple, tile-floor rooms, all freshly redone with furniture from Guadalajara, have fans but no air-conditioning. The half that sit on the beach have hammocks on their decks; the rest, surrounding a garden, feature terraces for sitting out and listening to the birds. An unassuming bar/restaurant serves breakfast and snacks such as hot dogs, burgers, and ceviche.

Playa la Ropa s/n. ☎ *and fax 755/4-3873. E-mail divemexico@mail.com.* **Rack rate:** *$94 double. AE, MC, V.*

Dollars & Sense

At the **Hotel Paraiso** (☎ **755/4–3873**), dive packages in high season range from 2 nights and one double dive for $154 per person, double occupancy ($84 for a non–diving companion), to $473 per person for 7 nights and four double dives ($262 for a non–diving companion). Honeymoon packages start at $228 in high season for 3 nights, including a bottle of wine, fruit basket, and continental breakfast.

Best Places to "Dive" In

Hotel Paraiso (Zihuatanejo/
Beaches, $$)

Hotel Puerto Mio
(Downtown Zihuatanejo,
$$$–$$$$)

Hotel Puerto Mio

$$$–$$$$. Downtown Zihuatanejo.
Neither in town proper nor on one of
Zihuatanejo's eastern beaches, this
little-known gem has its own domain on
the Puerto Mio marina, from which most
of the area's sports and pleasure boats
depart. The more casual of its two sec-
tions, adjoining the marina, has a great
bar, a pool with super-cool mosaic bar
stools, a romantic restaurant, and a
Cuban-style nightclub—all with dramatic
bay views. Rooms in its red-roof cabanas
have tile floors, gauze-draped beds, and
cushy banquettes. "The Mansion" section on the hill takes that casual-chic
style to new heights, with suites that could come straight off the pages of
House Beautiful (make that *Casa Bonita*). Room service and an on-site pool
make the Mansion ideal for a romantic getaway, but the cabanas below are
where the action is. Neither section has a beach, but at press time direct ser-
vice from the dock to Los Gatos was scheduled to start.

Playa del Almacen 5. ☎ **888/633-3295** *in the U.S.;* ☎ *and fax 755/4-3344
or 4-3745 in Mexico. E-mail puertomio@cdnet.com.mx.* **Rack rates:** *$176
cabana; $169 standard mansion room; $293 deluxe junior suite. Dive, sportsfish-
ing, and honeymoon packages available. AE, MC, V.*

Kids Best for Families

Hotel Catalina & Sotavento (Zihuatanejo/Beaches, $)

Krystal Ixtapa (Ixtapa, $$$)

Presidente Inter-Continental Ixtapa (Ixtapa, $$$)

Villas Miramar (Zihuatanejo/Beaches, $)

Krystal Ixtapa

$$$. Ixtapa.
You'd have to work hard to get bored at the Krystal. This link in the
Mexican-owned chain (the seven classical columns found in each one represent the members of the de la Parra family) is huge, with plenty of room for
racquetball and tennis courts, a pool with a waterfall and water slide, and
more. The large convention halls attract a business trade, but families like
the three playgrounds and great kids' program ($7 a day buys a breakfast

buffet, lunch, T-shirt, and all sorts of supervised fun and games). The hotel's top two restaurants are Il Mortero, serving gourmet Mexican food, and Bogart's (see chapter 28, "The Best of Ixtapa/Zihuatanejo's Dining Scene"). Christine is the best disco in town. Don't dance? Catch a film in the open-air movie theater or listen to live Latin music in the lobby. Rooms—but who's ever in them?—are pleasant and light.

Blvd. Ixtapa s/n. ☎ ***800/231-9860*** *or 755/3-0333. Fax 755/3-0216. www.wotw. com/krystal. E-mail: kixtapa@krystal.com.mx.* ***Rack rate:*** *$220 double. Honeymoon and other packages available. AE, DC, MC, V.*

Extra! Extra!

Don't forget to ask for specials. A high-season "commercial" rate of $145 per night was available at **Krystal Ixtapa** (☎ **800/231-9860**) in 1998—all you had to do was guarantee your reservation with a credit card (which many hotels require anyway).

La Casa Que Canta
$$$$$. Zihuatanejo/Beaches.

Architects from around the world come to pay homage to Casa Que Canta, which looks as though it was organically grown from its cliffside perch and decorated by Frida Kahlo (when she wasn't having nightmares). The Mexican design details are pseudo-rustic—thatched roofs, cobblestone paths, colored tiles, folk art furnishings—but come together to create a totally elegant picture. With only 24 suites and no children under 16 allowed, this is the ultimate romantic getaway. You won't be directly on the beach—Playa la Ropa is a short walk away—but two gorgeous pools more than compensate. And wherever you are—lazing on your private terrace, dining at the excellent restaurant or tapas bar— you'll have picture-postcard views of Zihuatanejo Bay. You needn't fear your minibar here: In-room refrigerators are generously stocked with free soft drinks and beer.

Bet You Didn't Know

The swimming pool scenes from a *When a Man Loves a Woman*, starring Meg Ryan and Andy Garcia, were shot at La Casa Que Canta's dramatic infinity pool, which looks as though it plunges over the side of a cliff.

Camino Escenico, Playa la Ropa s/n. ☎ ***800/ 525-4800*** *or 755/4-7030. Fax 755/ 4-7040.* ***Rack rates:*** *$328 terrace room; $573 master private pool suite. AE, DC, MC, V.*

Presidente Inter-Continental Ixtapa
$$$. Ixtapa.

The only all-inclusive hotel in Ixtapa's hotel zone, the Presidente has it all. Bicycle tours to Playa Linda, tennis, diving clinics, snorkeling, language and cooking classes, a kids' program (with free video games), even the greens fees for the Marina Ixtapa Golf Club are part of the deal. With its legion of restaurants and menus, including 24-hour room service, and unlimited name-brand drinks (ordinarily you get only the domestic stuff), it's hard to figure how this reasonably priced place breaks even. Rooms in the high-rise building, which cost only slightly more, are farther away from the sound of day- and nighttime activities than those arrayed, pueblo-style, around the gardens. Feeling guilty about your self-indulgence? The hotel even runs a program to save and release baby sea turtles.

Best for Activity Addicts

Krystal Ixtapa (Ixtapa, $$$)

Presidente Inter-Continental Ixtapa (Ixtapa, $$$)

Blvd. Ixtapa s/n. ☎ ***800/327-0200*** *or 755/ 3-0018. Fax 755/3-2312.* **Rack rates:** *$281 (rate covers all meals and drinks, including imports, and activities for 2 people). AE, MC, V.*

Villa del Sol
$$$$$. Zihuatanejo/Beaches.

This intimate beachside hotel offers dozens of different ways to relax. Hammocks and hot tubs on the decks of folk art–filled guest suites, magnificent buffets in the palapa restaurant, two pools, tennis courts, coconut palms, meandering pathways, and bar-to-lounge-chair margarita delivery service are among the best. Well-heeled couples, many from Europe, gather at this posh property, the only member in Mexico of both the Relais & Chateaux and Small Luxury Hotels of the World. Amenities increase with the room rates, from just phones in the standard minisuites to minibars, TVs, stereo CD players, and fax machines in the new oceanside suites. No matter where you stay, you'll get a tray with croissants and coffee outside your door each morning. The bartender, Orlando, for whom the hotel's friendly watering hole is named, will have your drink order down by your third bar visit.

Camino Escenico, Playa la Ropa s/n. ☎ ***888/389-2645,*** *755/4-2239, or 755/ 4-3239. Fax 755/4-2758 or 755/4-4066. E-mail: villasol@iwm.com.mx.* **Rack rates:** *$246 standard mini-suite to $761 beach suite with ocean view. Manda-tory MAP (breakfast and dinner plan) $50 per person per day. Low season $187 to $585, meal plan optional. No children under 14 in winter; small pets welcome year-round. AE, MC, V.*

Villas Miramar
$. Zihuatanejo/Beaches.

Sure, the grounds are beautifully landscaped and the hacienda-style low-rises (two buildings, across the road from each other) look lovely from the outside, but you still don't expect rooms so reasonably priced to be this attractive and well-equipped, too. All are craft-filled and colorful, with small separate sitting areas. Book a two-bedroom kitchenette and bring the entire family (you can afford it here). Some units look out on the garden; from others you can see Madera beach, just outside the gate. Perks include two pools, two decorative bars, and a casual seafood restaurant, open for breakfast and lunch.

Playa Madera s/n, Zihuatanejo. ☎ *755/4-2106 or 4-2616. Fax 755/4-2149.* **Rack rates:** *$76 garden view; $82 beach view; $129 two-bedroom suite. AE, MC, V.*

Best Romantic Love Nests

Hotel Puerto Mio (Downtown Zihuatanejo, $$$–$$$$)

La Casa Que Canta (Zihuatanejo/Beaches, $$$$$)

Villa del Sol (Zihuatanejo/Beaches, $$$$$)

Westin Brisas Ixtapa (Ixtapa, $$$$–$$$$$)

Westin Brisas Ixtapa
$$$$–$$$$$. Ixtapa.

Created by one of Mexico's leading architects, the Westin Brisas Ixtapa is a dazzler, spilling down a lush green cliff to the secluded Vista Hermosa beach below (this is the only major hotel that's not on Boulevard Ixtapa). Designed to contrast with the surrounding jungle, the lobby is super austere; only a pile of giant round boulders breaks the severe lines. Each level of the flower-decked resort reveals another pleasure center—say, one of the four swimming pools, connected to each other by waterfalls, or the night-lit tennis courts. The stylish rooms are a bit cramped, but you can always hang out in a hammock on your spacious bay-view terrace. Business and leisure guests line up for the lavish breakfast buffet at the Bellavista restaurant. For an ultra-romantic Italian dinner, Portofino is the place.

Playa Vista Hermosa. ☎ *800/WESTIN-1. Fax 755/3-0751 or 755/3-1038. www.westin.com.* **Rack rates:** *$219–$257 deluxe (all oceanview). AE, MC, V.*

No Room at the Inn? Try One of These . . .

Ixtapa
➤ **Hotel Aristos.** A bit run-down, but a major Ixtapa bargain, with all the amenities of the bigger hotels at less than half the price—and breakfast thrown in. Boulevard Ixtapa. ☎ **800/527-4786.** $–$$.

Downtown Zihuatanejo
➤ **Hotel Susy.** The rooms are small but consistently clean, the plants are cheerful, and the prices are as low as they go. Juan Álvarez 3. ☎ **755/4-2339.** $.

Zihuatanejo/Beaches
➤ **Hotel Irma.** Perched above Madera beach, this hotel has lots of Mexican character, although rooms are fairly basic. Cousteau-wannabes take diving lessons in the deep pool. Avenida Adelita. ☎ and fax **755/4-3738.** $.

Quick Picks: Ixtapa/Zihuatanejo's Hotels at a Glance
Hotel Index by Price

$

Bungalows Pacifico
(Zihuatanejo/Beaches)

Hotel Avila (Downtown
Zihuatanejo)

Hotel Catalina &
Sotavento (Zihua-
tanejo/Beaches)

Hotel Citali (Downtown
Zihuatanejo)

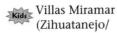Villas Miramar
(Zihuatanejo/
Beaches)

$$

Hotel Paraiso
(Zihuatanejo/Beaches)

$$$

Best Western Posada Real
(Ixtapa)

Krystal Ixtapa (Ixtapa)

Presidente Inter-
Continental Ixtapa
(Ixtapa)

$$$–$$$$

Hotel Puerto Mio (Downtown
Zihuatanejo)

$$$$–$$$$$

Westin Brisas Ixtapa (Ixtapa)

$$$$$

La Casa Que Canta
(Zihuatanejo/Beaches)

Villa del Sol
(Zihuatanejo/Beaches)

Hotel Index by Location

Ixtapa

Best Western Posada Real $$$

Kids Krystal Ixtapa $$$

Kids Presidente Inter-
Continental Ixtapa $$$

Westin Brisas Ixtapa
$$$$–$$$$$

Downtown Zihuatanejo

Hotel Avila $

Hotel Citali $

Hotel Puerto Mio $$$–$$$$

Zihuatanejo/Beaches

Bungalows Pacifico $

Kids Hotel Catalina &
Sotavento $

Hotel Paraiso $$

La Casa Que Canta $$$$$

Villa del Sol $$$$$

Kids Villas Miramar $

Chapter 26

Finding Your Way Around Ixtapa/ Zihuatanejo

In This Chapter

➤ What to expect when you arrive

➤ The lay of the land

➤ Getting around

➤ Where to get information

➤ Quick Facts: Ixtapa/Zihuatanejo A to Z

So you've made it to Ixtapa/Zihuatanejo and you're collecting your luggage at the airport. That should take about 3 seconds—we're talking one baggage carousel—after which you have to face negotiating the resort. *No problema.*

Read on and I'll guide you over the speed bumps, including some literal ones between the two towns.

Bet You Didn't Know

Called *topes* and ubiquitous in Mexico, speed bumps not only destroy any meager vestige of traffic flow but also chew up a car's suspension system—one of the reasons you see so many junkers on the roads.

You've Just Arrived—Now What?

I'd like to report that this pair of reasonably sophisticated beach resorts rolls out the red carpet for its visitors the second they arrive, but the fact is you're on your own at the tiny Ixtapa-Zihuatanejo airport, which has zip when it comes to tourist support: no information booth, no ATM, not even a *cambio* (money exchange booth). *Nada.*

Fortunately, it's simple enough to leave here. Right near the aforementioned lone baggage carousel, you'll see booths selling tickets for both *colectivos* (collective vans) and taxis, with prices set according to the distance you're going. A taxi to Zihuatanejo costs about $12.50, a *colectivo* $3.50; to Ixtapa, it's $16.50 versus $4.50. Taxis are always around; *colectivos* gather only for the larger flights.

Orientation: You Are Here

Zihuatanejo spreads out around the beautiful Bay of Zihuatanejo, framed by downtown to the north and a series of lovely long beaches and the wooded Sierra Madre foothills to the east. Its heart is the waterfront walkway, Paseo del Pescador (also called the *malecón*), bordering the Municipal Beach. To the right of the town square, Plaza de Armas, which faces the beach, is the *muelle,* or dock. Go left and you'll eventually get to Madera, La Ropa, and Las Gatas beaches, described in more detail in the next chapter. The main thoroughfare for cars in downtown is Juan Álvarez, parallel to the Paseo del Pescador. It's intersected by Cuauhtemoc and Guerrero, the busiest pedestrian streets, comparatively speaking—they're in perpetual Sunday stroll mode by most urban standards.

Yo, Gringo!

Because there's no money exchange at the airport, you can't get any pesos, and the taxi/*colectivo* ticket sellers offer a lousy rate for your dollars. Try not to dwell on this. It's no reflection on the rest of the resort—scout's honor.

The recently repaved Highway 200 leads northwest from Zihuatanejo to **Ixtapa,** about 4 miles away. The beginning of its main drag, called either Paseo or Boulevard Ixtapa, is marked by the Ixtapa Golf Club. High-rise hotels and low-slung shopping centers face off on opposite sides of this straightforward, 3-mile-long road; it ends just before the Marina Ixtapa complex, which contains another posh golf course. Playa del Palmar, behind Boulevard Ixtapa, is the only beach in this area. You'd really have to make an effort to get lost in Ixtapa (although people have been known to disappear into its shopping centers for hours).

Chump Change

You don't have to have exact change to ride the bus, but bus drivers don't like to take anything larger than a 10-peso note. Hoard small bills and coins whenever possible—they're crucial for tips, too.

Getting Around by Bus

Minibuses depart frequently for Ixtapa from the corner of Moreles and Juárez streets in Zihuatanejo. You can also use these small buses, most of which terminate at the Marina Ixtapa, to go up and down the main drag of Ixtapa.

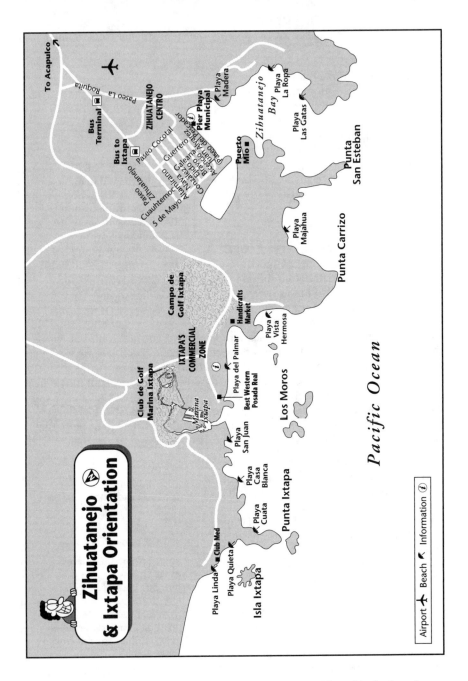

More infrequent vans leave from the Marina Ixtapa to Playa Linda (see the next chapter) and from downtown Zihuatanejo to Playa la Ropa. All cost about 25¢.

Getting Around by Taxi

Taxis are also inexpensive. It'll run you about $4 to get from central Zihuatanejo to Ixtapa, about $2 to get from Playa la Ropa to downtown Zihuatanejo, and approximately $1.25 to get from one end of the Ixtapa hotel zone to the other.

Where to Get More Information & Guidance

You won't suffer from information overload in Ixtapa and Zihuatanejo. There's no local English newspaper or even an ad-driven tourist publication, although the excellent American Express map does plot out its contributors' hotels, restaurants, and shops. You can usually find this map and a few brochures at the **State Tourism Office** in Ixtapa (La Puerta mall, across from the Hotel Presidente; ☎ **755/3-1967;** fax 755/3-1968), open 9am to 7pm Monday through Friday, and 10am to 2pm on Saturday. However, you can't always count on finding someone who speaks English here. You'll get a bit more information at the smaller **Zihuatanejo Tourist Office** (Juan N. Álvarez, next to city hall; ☎ **755/4-2207,** ext. 120 or 755/4-2285), open Monday through Friday 9am to 3pm and 6 to 8pm, Saturday 9am to 2pm and Sunday 9am to 3pm; however, your best resource may be the concierge or front desk of your hotel.

Ixtapa/Zihuatanejo from A to Z: Facts at Your Fingertips

American Express: Hotel Krystal Ixtapa, Boulevard Ixtapa (☎ **755/3-0853;** fax 755/3-1206).

ATMs: You'll find ATMs in Ixtapa at Bancomer, in the La Puerta shopping center, and at Bital, in front of the Hotel Riviera. In downtown Zihuatanejo, across from each other at the corners of Avenida Benito Juárez and N. Bravo, are a Bancomer and Banco Serfin with ATMs; the Banamex on Cuauhtemoc, just north of the central plaza, also has a money dispenser.

Baby-sitters: Most of the hotels in the Ixtapa hotel zone can arrange for baby-sitting; however, don't count on it if you're staying in Zihuatanejo (some of the more upscale places discourage children, and the more modest ones may not have the resources).

Business hours: Shop hours are from 10am to 2pm and 4 to 8pm, daily; offices keep similar hours, but close Saturday afternoon and all day Sunday.

Currency Exchange: In addition to the banks noted in the ATM section, above, which exchange money in the morning, there's a *casa de cambio* in downtown Zihuatanejo at Galeano and Bravo streets. The exchange rates here or at the hotel desks—the only other off-hour alternatives—are not great.

Dollars & Sense

Most of the beach towns have *casas de cambio* that give you rates close enough to those at the bank to compensate for the time saved avoiding lines. Not Ixtapa and Zihuatanejo. If you don't have an ATM card, it's worth heading inside a bank one morning. (You may have little choice if you're staying in a small hotel in Zihuatanejo, where the front desks often have a limited amount of pesos.)

Dentists/Doctors: Most of the large hotels in Ixtapa have doctors either on the premises or on 24-hour call. The **IAMAT** (International Association for Medical Assistance to Travelers) representative can be reached at the Presidente Inter-Continental Ixtapa (☎ **755/3-0914**). In Zihuatanejo, try the **Clinica Maciel** (Calle de la Palma 12; ☎ **755/4-2380**), whose staff includes a reliable dentist.

English-Language Newspapers/Magazines: It's out of the way if you're not staying there, but the **Westin Brisas Ixtapa** probably has the best selection of English-language reading material around. In Zihuatanejo, there's a **newsstand on the main plaza** that carries some popular U.S. newspapers and magazines. You can find a few English books at **Byblos** (Galeana 2 between Ejido and Bravo).

Emergencies: For police, call ☎ **755/420 40;** fire department, ☎ **755/ 473-51;** and the Red Cross, ☎ **755/420 09.**

Hospitals: There are no really modern medical centers in Ixtapa/Zihuatanejo; Acapulco has the closest good facilities. The **Naval Hospital** (Avenida El Palmar s/n, behind the tourist market; ☎ **755/3-0499**) is your best bet in Ixtapa. In Zihuatanejo, try **Hospital General** (Avenida Moreles, corner of Mar Egeo; ☎ **755/4-3858** or 4-3965).

Maps: You can usually pick up the good American Express map at the tourist information offices in Ixtapa and Zihuatanejo (see "Where to Get More Information & Guidance," above); many hotels in Ixtapa have them, too.

Pharmacies: There are plenty of pharmacies in downtown Zihuatanejo, all pretty much equal (a rotation system always keeps one of them open 24 hours). In Ixtapa, try **Farmacia Coyuca** on Gustavo Alarcón Boulevard.

Police: Call ☎ **755/4-3837.**

Post Office: There's only one post office for the two towns, in Zihuatanejo on Avenida Jose M. Moreles, next to the Oficina de Autos; it's a long walk from the town center.

Safety: You can walk along the main drag in Ixtapa at all hours without a problem. Downtown Zihuatanejo is equally safe, although you wouldn't want to wander down any small, unpopulated streets—more because you're likely to get lost than because you're going to be harmed. However, see chapter 10, "Crossing the Border & What to Expect on the Other Side," for advice about keeping your money safe and for walking around crowded markets.

Special Events: The **Ixtapa/Zihuatanejo Billfish Classic** is held in January and the **International Sailfish Tournament** takes place in May. Both involve serious prizes; call the Fondo Mixto tourism trust at ☎ **755/ 3-1270** or 3-1570 for details.

Telephone: The telephone area code for Ixtapa/Zihuatanejo is 755. To call long distance within Mexico (abbreviated *lada*), dial 01, then the area code, and then the number. To call the United States, dial 001, and then the area code and number.

Fun On & Off the Beach

There's not a whole lot to do in Ixtapa and Zihuatanejo besides staking out the stretch of sand and sea that suits you. The waves are gentle, the coral is healthy, and the fish are hungry, so you'll find plenty of ways to play in, on, or about the deep blue sea. The pickings are slimmer when it comes to cruising, but hey, you can ride only one boat at a time, anyway.

You've done the bulk of your hard-core cultural touring if you've visited Zihuatanejo's beaches. What to do when you're waterlogged, then? I've got a few tempting suggestions, such as shopping and maybe even a bit of nightlife. When you're ready to hit the road, I've got some ideas on that subject, too.

Sunshine, Almost Always . . .

The sun shines an average of 340 days a year in Ixtapa/Zihuatanejo.

Hitting the Beaches

Whether you're rooming in Ixtapa or Zihuatanejo, you won't be disappointed in the nearby beaches. A few Playa la Ropa exceptions aside, it's easiest to hit the sand running (or lounging) in Ixtapa: You walk out the back of your hotel, and there you be. But it's worth doing a bit of beach hopping wherever you stay—you won't wear an indentation in your hotel's lounge chairs that way.

Zihuatanejo Beaches

Playa Municipal, Zihuatanejo's town beach, is fronted by the Paseo de Pescador, or Fisherman's Walkway—the name's a dead giveaway to the main activity here. The smell of fish and the sound of motorized launches makes it a less-than-serene spot to sunbathe, but it's ideal for photo-ops, especially if you come at the crack of dawn, when the local housewives and restaurateurs compete for the catch of the day. Sections of Playa Municipal are fine for wading and splashing around if you don't mind a little noise, as the beach is protected from the main surge of the Pacific.

History's a Beach in Zihuatanejo

The Spanish brought the first date palms in the Americas from the Philippines into the Bay of Zihuatanejo.

Bet You Didn't Know

The Spanish used to ship the trees they chopped down from the surrounding foothills of the Sierra Madre Sur out of Playa Madera, which means "wood beach."

Just east of Playa Municipal, **Playa Madera** is accessible by a lighted concrete-and-sand walkway that cuts through the rocks for about 100 yards from the Paseo de Pescador. The generally pacific Pacific that laps up to the flat grayish-white shore renders it an ideal spot for swimming. A number of budget lodgings overlook this area from the wooded hillside, and beachside restaurants are there to help you keep up your strength so you can roll over and maintain an even tan.

Lots of people consider **Playa la Ropa** to be Zihuatanejo's most beautiful beach; it's unquestionably the bay's largest (about half a mile) and most popular, with water sports concessions aplenty and terrific

All Washed Up

Playa la Ropa, or "clothing" beach, got its name from the silk garments that washed ashore here when a Spanish galleon returning from the Orient was shipwrecked.

305

The Princess & the Playa

Legend has it that the mysterious breakwater just offshore of Playa Las Gatas was built by a Tarascan king to render the beach private and safe for his daughter.

sunset views from the low-slung hotels and restaurants flanking its golden shores. Across a rocky point from Playa Madera, it's also open to the ocean, but waves are usually gentle here, too. Access to Playa la Ropa from downtown Zihuatanejo is via the main road, Camino a Playa la Ropa; a taxi from town costs about $2.

The other contender for Zihuatanejo's "most beautiful beach" award, **Playa Las Gatas** is the ribbon of sand you see when you look out across the bay from downtown or Playa la Ropa. Its name, "gatas," refers not to cats but to the harmless nurse shark that used to swim here. Protected by the Punta El Faro (Lighthouse Point) on its seaward side, the beach's waters are swimming-pool calm. Accessible only by boat, the beach is relatively secluded, although you won't suffer from any lack of water sports concessions and open-air restaurants (Arnoldo's is the best). Pangas (motorized skiffs) run from about 8am to 4:30pm from the downtown pier to Playa Las Gatas and cost approximately $2.50, round-trip. Check to make sure when the last boat is going back.

Dollars & Sense

Hang on to your return boat tickets when you're going to Playa Las Gatas and Isla Ixtapa. Lose them—and it's easy to do, what with the sun and the sand and the surf and the Corona—and you'll have to pay again.

Ixtapa Beaches

Although all of Mexico's beaches are public, to all intents and purposes many of Ixtapa's best sections of shore have been closed off to tourists because of private real estate developments. In addition, Playa Vista Hermosa, a beautiful, cliff-bordered cove—and the first of Ixtapa's beaches if you're coming from Zihuatanejo—sits at the foot of the Westin Brisas Ixtapa. Non-guests are welcome, but you'll have to cab it in and out of this slightly out-of-the-way cove.

Playa del Palmar, a curving arc of sand that buttresses the hotel zone, was chosen by Ixtapa's creators to be the centerpiece of a new resort for good reasons: It's wide, it's almost 3 miles long, and it looks out on a number of *morros* (rocky islands) jutting dramatically from the ocean. These and other breakwaters help keep the waters swimmable most of the time, even though you're facing the open Pacific here. But don't kid yourself—the surf can be seriously rough sometimes. Always be careful, and *never* swim when a red flag is posted.

Although lots of people use **Playa Linda** as just a jumping-off point for Isla Ixtapa (see below), there are plenty of reasons to linger. About 8 miles north of Ixtapa (a 10-minute trip by cab, maybe 15 minutes by bus), it's a long, flat stretch of sand that's ideal for horseback riding as well as water sports. It faces open ocean but also abuts a freshwater estuary that hosts birds, iguanas, alligators (you can see a couple at a safe remove if you press up against the chain link fence in the arrival area), and a type of morning glory, similar to ice plant, that grows along the beach. A cluster of shops sells trinkets and crafts at the entry point, and the nearby La Palapa restaurant has good, fresh seafood. Minibuses leave regularly from Marina Ixtapa to Playa Linda from 7:30 to 9:30am and from 4 to 8pm.

While **Isla Ixtapa** isn't the nature preserve it's sometimes billed to be— daily mass landings of *Homo sapiens* tend to drive other species away—it still has great beaches, clear offshore waters, lush vegetation, plenty of places to eat and play, and even some wildlife. Of the four small beaches, the busiest is **Playa Cuachalatate,** named for a local tree used to treat liver problems. This is where the boats arrive, and it's lined with thatched-roof restaurants. Take the paved walkway to your right and you'll come to **Playa Varadero,** whose calm, clear waters make it ideal for snorkeling. Group tours usually include lunch at El Marlin restaurant—good, but not appreciably better than any of the others in this area. North of Varadero and reachable via the same footpath lies **Playa Coral,** which, as its name suggests, also offers plenty of underwater-viewing possibilities. The most isolated of the four beaches, **Playa Carey** is on the other side of the Playa Cuachalatate dock; it doesn't have any facilities, so bring your own picnic and snorkel gear.

Boats leave frequently from the Playa Linda jetty to Isla Ixtapa, about 10 minutes away. A round-trip ticket costs about $2.50 and the last boat back usually leaves the island about 4:30 or 5pm (be sure to check). You can also book this outing through a local travel agent; it's convenient (no waiting for buses) and not necessarily much more expensive (taking into account cab fare if you don't want to bus it and lunch, which is included), but you'll be locked into a schedule (generally 10am to 3pm) and a specific restaurant.

Water Fun for Everyone

Development may have blocked access to some good beaches, but Ixtapa and Zihuatanejo are still free of pollution and overfishing, so there are plenty of great places to snorkel, dive, or cast a couple of lines. There's no shortage, either, of the other water sports that have become a staple of Mexico's shrines to splash.

Hook, Line & Sinker

Billfish such as blue and black marlin and Pacific sailfish have drawn in-the-know anglers to Zihuatanejo for decades, although these days, instead of

307

doing that old taxidermy thing, successful fishers are likely to participate in catch-and-release programs.

If you want to try your luck at hooking these and other, more edible species—yellowfin tuna and dorado are big, and outfitters can direct you to restaurants that'll cook your catch—you can hire a boat, captain, and crew through one of the local fishing cooperatives, based at the dock in downtown Zihuatanejo. For a full day, the largest (36-foot) boats, which seat six and have four or five lines, cost about $200 to $250. Four-seaters with three lines can run anywhere from about $100 to $125, also for a full day. Booking through a travel agent will raise the price a bit.

Off the Hook

More and more anglers are taking part in the catch-and-release conservation program. You reel in your fish, tag it, and then send it back into the sea to create future fish (after it recovers from the temporary hook-in-mouth pain, of course).

You can also make arrangements in advance through **Ixtapa Sportsfishing Charters** (19 Depue Lane, Stroudsburg, PA 18360; ☎ **717/688-9466;** fax 717/688-9554, or 755/4-44-26 in Zihuatanejo). Custom cruisers ranging from 28 to 36 feet all cost $309; two-person "super pangas" are $190 a day. Rates include 8 hours of fishing, a fishing license, lures, dead bait, ice, and tag-and-release equipment. **Mexico Sportsman** (14542 Brook Hollow, no. 124, San Antonio, TX 78232; ☎ and fax **210/494-9916**) is another reliable U.S. outfitter; its prices are exactly the same.

If you just want to piddle around close to shore, a small boat with tackle and bait will cost about $15 to $20 an hour. Hire one from the fisherman on the docks in Zihuatanejo or from the aquatics shops on Playa la Ropa or Playa del Palmar.

Sportsfishing Tipping Tips

It's customary to tip the captain 10% to 15% of the total price of your charter, depending on the quality of the service. Give the money to the captain, who will split it with the mate.

Exploring the Depths

Ixtapa/Zihuatanejo is a diver's dream. Water visibility often reaches more than 100 feet, especially from December through May, and the temperature is always comfortably warm. Moreover, the convergence of the Humboldt Current and the Equatorial Counter Current in this area has resulted in an incredibly rich sea life. You never know what you're going to see—huge schools of Mexican yellow goatfish, giant manta rays, sea horses, maybe even a humpback whale. You're unlikely to recover any lost Spanish treasure, but you might spot a 400-year-old anchor or other artifacts from the conquistador days.

Expert at helping people take the plunge is the **Zihuatanejo Scuba Center** (Cuauhtemoc 3; ☎ and fax **755/4-2147;** www.divemexico.com; e-mail: divemexico@mail.com), co-owned by marine biologist and NAUI-certified instructor Juan Bernard. For $70, beginners can learn the basics in a hotel pool and then take an afternoon dive at one of 30-odd deep-sea sites (the location depends on the time of day and season as well as the level of expertise). Certified divers pay the same amount for two deep-sea dives; it's $10 less if you've brought your own equipment.

Time-Savers

If you're already a qualified diver and you want to participate in advanced dives, don't forget to pack proof of certification.

Certification courses are available, too. This is a class operation, with only one diver master for every three people, and gloves provided so you can pick up prickly fish.

Want to see what's in the sea but don't want to go so low? Zihuatanejo's Playa Las Gatas, Isla Ixtapa's Playa Varadero, and Playa Hermosa in front of the Westin Brisas Ixtapa are excellent spots for **snorkeling.** All offer equipment rentals at anywhere from $5 to $15 a day.

Diving in the Dark

For $55, you can surprise some fish at night: You wear a headlight to illuminate a honeycomb of caverns teeming with coral and psychedelically luminescent sea life. Another forty bucks will buy you a video of your dive and ensure your 15 minutes of underwater fame.

Sailing, Skiing, Kayaking & More

Walk along Playa la Ropa in Zihuatanejo and Playa del Palmar in Ixtapa for the best water sports pickings; Playa Las Gatas in Zihuatanejo is a runner-up, and Ixtapa Island also has a few concessionaires. You'll find parasailing (about $20 for a 15-minute ride), waterskiing and Waverunners (about $30 per half hour), jet skis ($25 per half hour), and banana boat rides ($5 for a 20-minute trip). You can also hire small sailboats, sailboards, and sea kayaks at these aquatics booths.

Dollars & Sense

Invest in your own mask, snorkel, and fins. It'll be cheaper than using the inexpensive gear even four or five times—and you'll know exactly where the equipment has been.

On Deck: Enjoying the Waves without Getting Your Hair Wet

The only show in town is the one run by **Yate del Sol,** moored at the Puerto Mio marina in Zihuatanejo. In high season on Thursdays, the company's 67-foot *Tristar* trimaran takes off on a sunshine cruise to Isla Ixtapa (10:15am to 4:30pm). Monday, Tuesday, Wednesday, and Friday from 10am to 2:30pm, the ship sets sail for the beach and coral reef of Playa Manzanillo, where you'll have time for swimming, snorkeling, and shell collecting. On the return trip, the *Tristar* anchors in front of Playa la Ropa; if you like, you can take a flying (parachute) leap from the company's 2400-square-foot spinnaker. The $49 cost for the Isla Ixtapa cruise and $59 for the Playa Manzanillo cruise includes transportation to and from your hotel, lunch, and an open bar with domestic drinks; snorkeling gear is $5 extra. Nightly (except Saturday) sunset cruises around the bay of Zihuatanejo cover the same bases, but include snacks instead of lunch and no water sports. They depart at 5:15pm, return at 7:30pm, and cost $39. You can reserve all directly through the company (☎ **755/4-2694** or 4-8270) or with a travel agent for no extra charge.

Keeping Your Head Above Water: The Top Attractions

For a **walk into the past,** amble along the beachside Paseo del Pescador. The small fishing boats may have outboard motors now, but the economy of the sea that sustains Zihuatanejo has continued uninterrupted for centuries. And the ceremonial ball court has been replaced by a basketball court (which always seems to have a pickup game going, no matter when you come), but a sense of traditional community prevails.

Near Guerrero, at the east end of the Paseo del Pescador, the **Museo de Arqueologia de la Costa Grande** gives you a brief look at the cultures that occupied the coastal stretch from Acapulco to Ixtapa/Zihuatanejo before the Spanish arrived. Pottery and stone sculpture from the Toltecs, based near Mexico City, and the Olmecs, who settled on the Gulf Coast, show just how far the ancient trade routes extended. Displays are modest and marked only in Spanish; it shouldn't take you more than half an hour to cover the museum, open Tuesday through Sunday from 10am to 5pm. Admission is $1.

What's in a Name?

Zihuatanejo is said to have gotten its name from a captain who sailed with conquistador Hernán Cortés. Sent out to explore the settlement, he reported back to his boss that it was called *Cihuatlan,* or "place of women" in the Nahuatl language. The suffix *nejo,* Spanish for "insignificant," was his editorial comment.

Ixtapa, another Nahuatl word, means "White Place." The reference is to the area's long, sandy beach, not to the pasty Anglo tourists who started converging on it after Ixtapa became an international resort.

Teeing Off in Ixtapa

The two excellent golf courses that sandwich Ixtapa's hotel zone should keep duffers happy for days.

The 18-hole **Ixtapa Golf Club,** designed by Robert Trent Jones, Jr., in 1977, was part of the Ixtapa master plan, which included protecting much of the area as a wildlife preserve. You might spot flamingos on the 5th hole, bordered by a large lake, or cranes at the 15th, where you have to aim your ball 200 yards over a lagoon.

Greens fees for this par 72 course are $45 ($30 after 3pm). Club rentals are $12, and carts cost $20 for one or two people. Call ☎ **755/3-1062** for reservations.

The 18-hole **Marina Ixtapa Golf Club** (☎ **755/3-1410** for reservations) is a Robert Von Hagge creation, completed in 1994. At the far end of the hotel zone, it's known for its meandering canals—more than a mile of them—and its rolling dunes-style topography, as well as for its proximity to the restaurants and shops of the tony Marina complex. (And, yes, there are crocs in this course's waters, too.) The par 72 course, considered one of the most challenging in Mexico, costs $55 to play

A Water Trap with Teeth

Don't even think about trying to recover a ball from water traps at Ixtapa Golf Course. Zoologists from Mexico City are regularly called out to the club to relocate oversized crocodiles.

311

The Buzz on Bugs

What's wrong with this picture? You're riding along a beautiful beach, watching the sun descend over an azure sea . . . and being devoured by mosquitoes. Don't forget your insect repellent if you're going out in the late afternoon.

($30 after 4pm); a cart is included in the price, but a caddie will run you an additional $20, as will club rentals.

Riding into the Sunset

If you want to hit the beach trails on horseback, try the guided rides at **Rancho Playa Linda** (☎ 755/4-3085). The first one, at 8:30am, is nice and cool; take the last one, at 5pm, if you want to catch the sunset. You can trot along the beach to the mouth of the river, returning through thick coconut plantations, or hug the shore for the entire ride, which usually lasts an hour or an hour and a half. It costs about $20 if you book directly with the outfitter, but considerably more (as much as $33) if you go through a travel agent (higher transportation costs, it's called). Whatever you decide, be sure to make reservations if you're traveling in high season.

Hitting Some Balls Around

Tennis, anyone? The answer is yes in Ixtapa, where both of the golf courses (see above) also have night-lit public courts; it's $7.50 an hour at the Marina Ixtapa Golf Club, $4 during the day, and $5 at night at the Ixtapa Golf Club. You can play at most of the major hotels on Boulevard Ixtapa, too, even if you're not staying there, but guests naturally have priority. It can get a bit toasty for tennis at midday, but the courts are usually comfortable in the morning and late afternoon.

Ixtapa/Zihuatanejo's Best Shopping

Like all the other activities in Ixtapa/Zihuatanejo, shopping is relatively low-impact. A really dedicated retail hound could sniff out the best boutiques in Zihuatanejo in a single morning. It might take an entire day to scour Ixtapa completely, but I'm talking comprehensive coverage, as in actually eyeballing every establishment. For concentrated crafts shopping, you're best off in Zihuatanejo. If it's resort wear you're after, Ixtapa's the place.

Markets

Both Ixtapa and Zihuatanejo have a **Mercado de Artesenia Turistico,** or tourist crafts market, comprising warrens of covered stalls set up by the government when beach vending was outlawed in the state of Guerrero in 1990. The one in Ixtapa, with 150 stalls, is at the beginning of the hotel zone, across from the Sheraton Hotel; the larger one in Zihuatanejo (255 stalls) is west of the central square, on Cinco de Mayo from Catalina Gonzales to Pedro Ascencio. You can pick up some good Guerrero crafts at both, but be prepared to wade through some onyx chess sets and tacky

T-shirts. The markets are fairly similar, but the one in Zihuatanejo has slightly lower prices, perhaps because the vendors assume you can afford to pay a bit more if you're bunking in Ixtapa.

Guerrero Crafts

The state of Guerrero produces a variety of interesting crafts, including brightly painted, whimsical ceramics, carved wooden fish, bark paintings, and wooden ceremonial masks. The masks can be grotesque, depicting a woman with an iguana instead of a nose, say, or amusing—you'll see lots of angels with Elvis hair. The small masks should run anywhere from $7 to $12; large, very elaborate ones can cost $50 or more.

Only in Ixtapa

Across the wide road from Ixtapa's hotels are a series of *centros commercials*, frequently called malls but actually low-slung collections of shops built to resemble Spanish villages. The first, starting from the part of the tourist zone closest to Zihuatanejo, as well as the best, is **Los Patios.** Its highlights include La Fuente, which carries great folk art—Talavera pottery, jaguar-shaped wicker tables, and tinwork mirrors. In the wrought-iron gated **Plaza Ixpamar,** just behind Los Patios, Armando's sells nicely designed Mexican clothes. Back on Bulevar Ixtapa is **Plaza Las Fuentes,** followed by **La Puerta,** home to the Ferrioni collection, Mexican sportswear recognizable by its cute Scottie logo.

Only in Zihuatanejo

In addition to its more touristy artisans' market, Zihuatanejo also has a **municipal market,** located about 5 blocks inland from the waterfront on Avenida Benito Juárez. You won't find much here in the way of conventional souvenirs, but you can get good deals on the huaraches, hammocks, and baskets in the dry goods section.

Specialty shops line all the blocks radiating off Paseo del Pescador; a stroll up and down Cuauhtemoc is particularly productive. Some favorites on the block include **Galeria Ixchel Maya** (no. 1), which sells intriguing wood-carvings of women and goddesses of Mexico; **Alberto's** (no. 15),

How Low Do You Go?

In a Mexican market, you need remember only three words: bargain, bargain, bargain. If you end up paying about 50% of the original asking price, you've done well. Start out by offering 30% of the asking price and move up from there.

featuring high-quality silver jewelry, with many original designs; and **Boutique D'Xochitl** (corner Ejido), which specializes in gauzy resortwear and colorful appliquéd jackets. Also worth checking out is **Casa Marina** (Paseo del Pescador 9), a complex of four shops that focus on different wares from Mexico and Guatemala, including rugs, textiles, clothing, jewelry, and masks. (Note, however, that the selection of masks is better at the nearby artisans' market and prices are lower.) You'll also find unique crafts at **Coco Cabana Collectibles** (Guerrero and Álvarez) and at **Calli-Diseno** (Elido 7), which has some very unusual lamps.

What to Do When the Sun's Gone Down

Everyone will tell you to head for Ixtapa if you want after-dark action. Of the two resort towns, Ixtapa definitely has the livelier nightlife—but that's not saying much. You can play lounge lizard at the hotels or get loose at a Mexican fiesta, but there are only a few places where you can really kick up your heels.

Zihuatanejo doesn't really have any let-loose spots. Still, for a town that pretty much folds up after sunset, it's got a few aces up its sleeve, including some lively local music venues.

Ixtapa After Dark

The best spots to **watch the sunset** are at opposite ends of Ixtapa: the **lobby bar at the Westin Brisas Ixtapa** and the **Bar El Faro,** at the top of the pseudo-lighthouse in the Marina Ixtapa complex.

Want to do the nighttime circuit? Start out at **Carlos 'n Charlie's,** the frenetic bar/restaurant next door to the Hotel Posada Real, where you can boogie on a platform by the beach. Move on to the other link in the Carlos Anderson chain, **Señor Frog's,** at La Puerta shopping center (the dancing's strictly indoors here). Then turn up at the witching hour at the Krystal Ixtapa hotel's **Christine,** Ixtapa's tony disco, to hear classical music blasting from a megasound system during the light show (cover: about $7.50). The visuals and acoustics are also fine at Ixtapa's other disco, **La Valentina**—it's right near Carlos 'n Charlie's—but the crowd is younger and less sophisticated than at Christine. Because the hefty cover charge—$12.50 for women and $17.50 for men—includes an open bar, patrons tend to dedicate their time to drinking their money's worth.

Time-Savers

If you want to do the nightlife circuit without having to backtrack to your hotel room, don't go out dressed like a beach bum. Christine doesn't allow shorts or sandals or (for men) tank tops.

If you feel like lounging around, try the lobby lounges at the **Westin, Sheraton, Dorado Pacifico,** and **Krystal** hotels, where you'll usually catch live sounds of the tropical persuasion. No cover—just keep ordering those piña coladas.

The best of the **Mexican fiestas** is at the **Sheraton** (Blvd. Ixtapa s/n; ☎ 755/3-1858) on Wednesday night, where $33 will buy you entry into a market, buffet, folkloric show, contests, and more. It's the only one that operates year-round. The **Dorado Pacifico's** (Blvd. Ixtapa s/n; ☎ 755/3-2025) Tuesday night fiesta is also good; check around to see if there are any others going on at the hotel strip at the time you visit.

Zihuatanejo After Dark

Because of the curve of the bay, sunset views are blocked in many parts of Zihuatanejo. Not affected are the **Sunset Bar,** at the Catalina & Soto vento hotels (see chapter 25) on Playa la Ropa, and **Restaurant Gaviota** (☎ 755/4-3816), at the end of the same beach.

After dark, head back into town, where live Mexican bolero or salsa sizzle at **El Canto de la Sirena,** a friendly local club near the main bus terminal, just south of the road to Ixtapa and the airport (you'll have to cab it here— a cab is only about $1 or $2 from downtown Zihuatanejo, maybe $4 from Ixtapa and Zihuatanejo beaches). Closer to the center of town, at Pedro Ascencío and Agustín Ramírez, is **El Rincon de Agustín Ramírez,** a cozy guitar bar dedicated to a musician who wrote in, and about, the state of Guerrero. A Peruvian trio with a mean flute player often performs at **El Patio** restaurant, and mariachis mix it up at **Tamales y Atoles Any** on Thursday nights (see chapter 28, "The Best of Ixtapa/Zihuatanejo's Dining Scene," for both). There's no cover charge at any of these places, although you're expected to buy a few drinks.

Side Trips: Getting Out of Town

If, somehow, you should find even Zihuatanejo overstimulating, I've got a couple of outings for you—to get more mellow than Troncones or Barra de Potosí, you'd have to consume large quantities of Valium. If, on the other hand, you need a quick adrenaline hit, consider spending the day in Acapulco.

Troncones

You want quiet? This tiny fishing hamlet, 20 miles northwest of Ixtapa, is so remote it doesn't even have direct phone lines (there are cell phones for basics, such as booking hotels). It does have Anglos, however, a number of whom operate guest houses and restaurants. When you get tired of strolling the long, empty beach, hiking into the jungle, or splashing around in the ocean, stop in at **El Burro Borracho** (on Troncones beach), where a chef from San Francisco does amazing things with shrimp.

You can get to Troncones by taking a third-class bus from Zihuatanejo's main bus station to the highway outside the town and then boarding a shuttle to the beach; it shouldn't cost you much more than $1, total, but it's a somewhat complicated, uncomfortable trip. Another option is to hire a taxi to take you there and back at a designated time for about $30. Some travel agencies also book day trips for about $25, which usually include lunch; it's cheaper but less flexible.

Visiting Acapulco

If you just want a taste of Acapulco without committing yourself to its more frenetic lifestyle, book a day tour through one of the travel agencies for $120. The 150-mile drive down the coast is scenic, with the ocean on one side and lush vegetation on the other (the ride past Acapulco's slums as you enter town is less so); you'll stop en route for a continental breakfast. In Acapulco, the tour includes the cliff divers' show, time out for shopping, and lunch at one of the hotels. Tours leave at about 7am and return at approximately 8pm.

Barra de Potosí

Lazing in a hammock at a lagoon-front restaurant is a major activity at Barra de Potosí, 14 miles south of Zihuatanejo. Bird watching and swimming—the south end of the beach is especially calm—are big, too, as are kayak rides through the mangroves. The journey through a lush, tropical landscape to get to Barra is itself worth the price of the 4-hour tour via a travel agency—generally about $33, which includes lunch. Taxis from Ixtapa or Zihuatanejo alone run around $50, round-trip. Alternatively, you can take a second-class bus, which costs less than a $1, from the main bus station. You're likely to be sweaty and crowded for the journey, but it's only about half an hour, and you'll save a bundle. The *Central de Autobuses* (central bus station) is about a mile from the center of town on Paseo Zihuatanejo at Paseo la Boquita, opposite the Pemex station and the IMSS hospital.

Yo, Gringo!

Paradise is lost at Barra de Potosí on the weekends, when teenagers with major radios descend. Come during the week if you want to preserve the peace.

Chapter 28

The Best of Ixtapa/ Zihuatanejo's Dining Scene

In This Chapter

➤ Dining in Ixtapa and Zihuatanejo: The big picture

➤ Keeping costs down

➤ The best restaurants from A to Z

➤ Restaurant indexes

What Ixtapa/Zihuatanejo lack in sightseeing options, they make up for in restaurant-hopping possibilities. On any average-length vacation, you can easily change scene and cuisine every night (although seafood is a common denominator, preparations vary wildly).

You want water views? They've got 'em. In Ixtapa they tend to be clean and serene, whether from a table side at the Marina Ixtapa or from the cliffs above Vista Hermosa. In downtown Zihuatanejo, more people come into the picture: Dine along Paseo del Pescador, and you'll get a great snapshot of village and tourist life at no extra charge. The restaurants on Zihuatanejo's Playa Madera and Playa la Ropa run the gamut from places that deliver lunch to your lounge chair to upscale, romantic hideaways.

On the opposite end of the spectrum are a couple of Zihuatanejo bakeries: **El Buen Gusto** (Guerrero 4, half a block inland from the museum; ☎ 755/ 4-3231) and **Panaderia Francesca** (Gonzales 14, between Cuauhtemoc and Geurrero; ☎ 755/4-4520). Both will more than satisfy your need for a carbo fix or the call of a sweet tooth.

The Hotel Restaurant Hop

In addition to the places reviewed below, consider the restaurants at the Westin Brisas Ixtapa (either Bellavista or Portofino), Puerto Mio, La Casa Que Canta, and Villa del Sol, all listed in chapter 25, "Choosing the Place to Stay That's Right for You." None is a bargain, but the food's consistently good and the settings are beautiful. And who knows? You might fall in love—if not with your companion, then with one of the hotels. Coming for dinner is a good way to decide if you want to try different digs next time.

A Dining Overview: Where's the Burrito?

Except for the restaurants on the marina and those above Vista Hermosa, Ixtapa's eateries aren't especially scenic. Still, the Spanish-style patios of the *centro commerciales* are pleasant enough, and there are even a few surprises once you get inside. Zihuatanejo's restaurants have a lot more character, whether they're located along the narrow downtown streets or set out on the sand of one of the eastern beaches.

All restaurants are listed in alphabetical order, and then indexed by price and location.

Although some of the most expensive restaurants are in Ixtapa, you can, in fact, easily eat economically there—you'll find branches of two of Zihuatanejo's least pricey places. And you can blow a bundle on food in Zihuatanejo, too, without half putting your mind to it.

A Bite of Regional Flavor

For a light lunch, try *tiritas,* a Guerrero favorite: Strips of fish are "cooked," like ceviche, by being marinated in lemon or lime juice mixed with red onion and chile, and served with fried tortillas.

Check, Please

I've reviewed plenty of places where you can eat well—and well within your budget. Still, if you want to treat yourself to some of the more upscale dining rooms, check out "Eating Well without Gobbling Up Your Dollars" in chapter 7 for some wallet-saving tips.

Don't worry about taxes; the 15% surcharge has already been included in your bill. The tip isn't, however. The standard in nice restaurants is 15%. Mexicans rarely tip that well in less pricey places—10% is about average—but if the service was good, stick with the 15% rule. You can afford to be a bit more generous.

As part of the effort to help you stay within budget, I've arranged price categories with the worst-case scenario in mind: They're based on a per-person dinner tab that includes appetizer, entrée, dessert, one drink, and tip. In addition, a price range for dinner entrées is included in the individual reviews. It's simple: The more $ signs, the more you'll be shelling out.

$	=	Under $12
$$	=	$12–$25
$$$	=	$25–$40
$$$$	=	Over $40

Note: Because shrimp and lobster run so much higher than the other entrées, unless they're a major part of the menu, the price ranges noted below are exclusive of those dishes.

Unless otherwise specified, reservations are not accepted or not necessary.

My Favorite Restaurants from A to Z

Beccofino

$$$. Ixtapa. NORTHERN ITALIAN.

A bit of northern Italy in southern Mexico—and why not? Spanish and Italian are both romance languages, and it's no stretch to imagine this place being in the Mediterranean, especially if you sit out on the covered deck that extends over the sparkling Marina Ixtapa slip. The innovative menu created by owner/chef Angelo Rolly Pavia, who hails from the Old Country, focuses on seafood and pasta; in season, the house special ravioli might be stuffed with swordfish or shrimp. The garlic bread is terrific and the menu is complemented by a good wine list, with lots of interesting imported bottles.

Marina Ixtapa, near the lighthouse. ☎ *755/3-1770. Reservations suggested.* **Main courses:** *$8–$18 (pastas $8–$15). AE, MC, V.* **Open:** *Daily 9:30am–midnight.*

Bogart's

$$$$. Ixtapa. CONTINENTAL.

Casablanca never looked so good. Dedicated to the film classic—posters of Ingrid, Bogie, and all the usual suspects line the entryway—Bogart's does an ultra-romantic spin on the Moroccan hideaway idea, with arches, plush Oriental rugs, white draperies, and, of course, a piano player. How retro is this place? If a couple comes in, only the man gets a menu with prices (the woman gets a pillow to place under her feet). The fantasy's more exciting than the food, which is somewhat overpriced. The pumpkin cream soup is soothing, and entrées like the Shrimp Krystal, breaded and baked to a crisp turn, are fine, but don't blow your life savings on the overcooked, oversauced lobster.

Krystal Ixtapa hotel (to the right on the main entryway, on Blvd. Ixtapa). ☎ *755/3-0303. Reservations required.* **Main courses:** *$15–$27 (lobster $38). AE, MC, V.* **Open:** *Daily 6:30pm–12:30am.*

Most Romantic (Without Water Views)

Bogart's (Ixtapa, $$$$)

Coconuts (Downtown Zihuatanejo, $$$)

El Patio (Downtown Zihuatanejo, $$–$$$)

Bucanero's

$$–$$$. Ixtapa. SEAFOOD/CONTI-NENTAL.

Gazing at the boats bobbing in Marina Ixtapa while savoring fresh ceviche or red snapper with almonds—when you're dining on Bucanero's terrace, you know you've found the good life. The oysters Florentine are rich and delicious, and you can't go wrong with the catch-of-the-day stuffed with shrimp. There's not nearly as much turf as there is surf at this nautically themed restaurant, but those with an aversion to things that have

Zihuatanejo Dining

↑ To Ixtapa ↗

Main Bus Terminal

Tres Estrellas Bus Terminal

Morelos

Avenida

Paseo Zihuatanejo

Paseo del Palmar

C. I. Altamirano

Cuáuhtémoc

Avenida Nava

Benito

Municipal Market

Cinco de Mayo

Vicente Guerrero

C. González

Kioto ◯ Plaza

Juárez

Ejido

8

9

Galeana

Artisan's Market

5

6

Paseo de la Boquita

Calle Adelita

N. Bravo

Avenida Ramírez

7

Canal

Calle Mateos

Las Salinas

Pedro Ascencio

Museo de Arqueología

10

3 4

Juan.N. Álvarez

2

Playa La Madera

Calle de la Noria

Paseo del Pescador

1

Playa Municipal

Muelle Pier

Andador Contramar

Playa el Almacén

Bahía de Zihuatanejo

Playa La Ropa

11

12

Casa Elvira	②
Coconuts	⑦
The Deli	④
El Patio	⑤
Garrabos	③
Kau-Kan	⑩
La Perla	⑫
La Sirena Gorda	①
Nueva Zelanda	⑥
Restaurant Paul	⑨
Rossy	⑪
Tamales Any y Atoles	⑧

Beach ↑ Post Office ✉

spent their lives underwater have a few Continental-style chicken, beef, and lamb entrées to choose from. For more casual fare—fish empanadas or *tiritas* (see sidebar, above)—try the same family's La Marea restaurant next door.

Plaza Marina Ixtapa. ☎ *755/3-0916. Reservations suggested in high season.* **Main courses:** *$8–$16. AE, MC, V.* **Open:** *Daily 8am–11pm.*

Casa Elvira
$–$$. Downtown Zihuatanejo. MEXICAN/SEAFOOD.
Elvira, both restaurant and owner, have been around forever— to be exact, Señora Campos, who is in her 80s, opened her place in 1956. It's not nostalgia that draws the crowds, however; thank a prime seafront location and well-prepared, reasonably priced lunches and dinners. Red snapper and lobster are always worth trying, when available, and the chicken mole is

consistently good. *Note:* As opposed to the way you'd pronounce the name of the deep-cleavaged horror film queen, in Mexico you say "El-*VEE*-rah."

Paseo del Pescador (west end, near the town pier). ☎ *755/4-2061.* **Main courses:** *$3.50–$10. MC, V.* **Open:** *Daily noon–10:30pm.*

Coconuts
$$$. Downtown Zihuatanejo. INTERNATIONAL.
In a historic building that served as a coconut weigh-in station in the 19th century, the expat-run Coconuts has a romantic garden, lively bar, and great food. Small wonder that many longtime returnees to Zihuatanejo make this

Yo, Gringo!

Remember, it's considered impolite in Mexico for the waiter to bring the check before you ask for it.

their first (sometimes only) dinner stop. Not that the menu here is all-American—far from it. But dishes such as lobster tacos are prepared in gringo-friendly fashion; they're made with imported cheeses, for example, and use less fat. Large "safe" salads reassure many visitors' health concerns; large, unsafe margaritas address their fun concerns. Menu highlights include shrimp breaded with coconut and topped with a tangy orange sauce, and scampi with tomatoes, garlic, and basil.

Augustín Ramírez 1 (at Vincente Guerrero). ☎ *755/4-2518. Reservations advised in high season.* **Main courses:** *$11–$20. DISC, MC, V.* **Open:** *Daily noon–4pm and 6pm–midnight. Closed late summer–early fall.*

The Deli
$–$$. Downtown Zihuatanejo. INTERNATIONAL.
A cross between a railroad waiting room and a 1950s diner—don't ask me to try to fit the pretty back garden into the picture—The Deli has a menu that can't be easily typecast either. Breakfast does an American/Mexican split (you can have hotcakes or chilaquiles to start your day), lunch veers heavily toward the north with sandwiches like Philly cheese-steaks, and dinner throws Italian specialties, such as spaghetti carbonara, into the mix. The food's fine, but more than anything this is a daily check-in station for foreign residents and long-term visitors.

Cuauhtemoc 12. ☎ *755/4-3850.* **Main courses:** *$5–$10. MC, V.* **Open:** *Daily 8am to 11pm or midnight.*

El Infierno y La Gloria
$$. Ixtapa. MEXICAN.
A bit of surrealism in Ixtapa, this restaurant has a name that means "Hell and Glory," decor resembling a Mexican cantina on acid, and a location in a strip mall. The ensemble of grinning Day of the Dead skeletons might

explain the hell part of the moniker; the glory's clearly in the food, which includes a tempting array of regional specialties at reasonable prices. Try an assortment of corn tortillas filled with cactus, cheese, avocado, or sausage for starters, and then move on to the Veracruz-style fish or the Mayan chicken. Daily specials range from shrimp with garlic or pork with adobo sauce to grilled ribeye steak.

La Puerta shopping center. ☎ *755/3-0272.* **Main courses:** *$6–$9 (shrimp and steak specials may be higher). AE, DC, MC, V.* **Open:** *Daily 8am–midnight.*

El Patio
$$–$$$. Downtown Zihuatanejo. MEXICAN/SEAFOOD.
Come here for a slightly elegant but not overly formal evening out. The blue-and-white pottery that lines the brick walls of El Patio's outdoor garden is lovely in the candleglow, but rounded archways and rich Mexican colors make the open-front dining room appealing, too. You'll find everything from burgers and enchiladas to tuna steak and lobster on the eclectic menu, as well as a number of pasta dishes. The mixed seafood tacos and chicken breast *pibil*—a tasty Yucatán dish that uses a sauce of tomato, onion, mild red pepper, cilantro, and vinegar—are high on the hit parade.

Cinco de Mayo 3 (next to downtown Zihuatanejo's only church). ☎ *755/4-3019.* **Main courses:** *$6.50–$12.50. AE, MC, V.* **Open:** *Daily noon–midnight (from 8am in high season).*

Garrabos
$$. Downtown Zihuatanejo. MEXICAN/SEAFOOD.
From the pier to your plate could be the logo at this casual, nautical-decor restaurant, where you can also enjoy dishes that don't involve fish (but not iguana, which is what *garrabos* means; it was an affectionate nickname for the owner's grandfather). For starters, try the *camaronillas*—similar to quesadillas, only stuffed with shrimp instead of cheese—and then consider the paella or the Veracruz-style snapper, with olives, bell peppers, onions, and tomatoes. The filet mignon with mushrooms is a good ocean-free option. Many entrées come with vegetables, which is unusual, and the presentations are always pleasing.

Álvarez 52 (off Cinco de Mayo). ☎ *755/4-2977 or 4-2191.* **Main courses:** *$5.50–$11.50. AE, MC, V.* **Open:** *Daily 2–11pm.*

The Golden Cookie Shop
Kids
$. Ixtapa. CAFE/GERMAN/INTERNATIONAL.
Great coffee (including frozen cappuccino in tall iced-tea glasses), fresh-baked breads, and pastries inspire locals and tourists alike to find their way to this *gemütlich* German bakery and cafe, on the second floor, rear, of the Los Patios center. Others come for the overstuffed deli sandwiches—the smoked ham is excellent—and such hot entrées as chicken curry (one of the owners is German, and the other hails from Singapore). Wear loose clothing for the

hearty German buffet, laid on every Friday night at 7pm, or be prepared to open your belt a few notches.

Los Patios, Blvd. Ixtapa. ☎ *755/3-0310.* **Main courses:** *$3–$8 (sandwiches $3–$5). MC, V.* **Open:** *Mon–Sat 8am–3pm and 6–10pm.*

Kau-kan
$$–$$$. Zihuatanejo/Beaches. SEAFOOD.
This place defines casual elegance. In 1995, gourmet chef Ricardo Rodriguez, formerly of nearby Casa Que Canta and the Champs-Elysées in Mexico City, opened his own restaurant on a small rise just above Madera Beach. Although easy-going during the day, evenings see the three-tier dining room—there's rooftop, indoor, and outdoor deck seating—basking in the glow of candles and fairy lights. Soft guitar music plays in the background. The combination of amorous atmosphere and superb seafood has put Kau-kan on the top of every local's most-recommended list. Preparations of whatever's fresh—mahi-mahi, shrimp, even manta ray—are simple but imaginative. If the baked potato stuffed with shrimp and baby lobster in a basil garlic sauce is on the menu, don't pass it up.

Playa Madera, below the Hotel Brisas del Mar. ☎ *755/4-8446. Reservations essential in high season.* **Main courses:** *$9–$15. MC, V.* **Open:** *Daily noon–4pm and 6pm–midnight.*

La Perla
$$. Zihuatanejo/Beaches. SEAFOOD.
A family affair—it was established by Don Francisco Ibarrez and his wife, Doña Raquel, in 1977, and now is managed by their sons. In the mornings, Americans, Canadians, and Europeans gather for gringo-style breakfasts, such as scrambled eggs with bacon or toast and jam (you can order a side of coconut). During prime sunbathing time, lounge-chair lizards staked out in front of the open-air dining room ask the waiters to bring over something light—say ceviche or a clam cocktail—to accompany their Tecates. At night, it's back under the palapa roof, this time to sample one of the hot seafood dishes; Doña Raquel's special fish fillet, wrapped in tinfoil and steamed in spices, is especially popular. There's a sports bar with three satellite dishes and a humidor with Cuban cigars out back.

Local Favorites

Casa Elvira (Downtown Zihuatanejo, $–$$)

El Infierno y La Gloria (Ixtapa, $$)

Tamales Any y Atoles (Downtown Zihuatanejo, $)

Playa la Ropa. ☎ *755/4-2700.* **Main courses:** *$6–$10. AE, MC, V.* **Open:** *Daily 9am–10pm.*

La Sirena Gorda
$. Downtown Zihuatanejo. MEXICAN.

The fact that a couple of years back, this seaside restaurant and the chubby mermaids for which it was named got a huge spread in *Bon Appetit* didn't hurt business any. Then again, Zihuatanejo residents who had never even heard of *Bon Appetit* had always been fans. What has both foodies and locals raving are the seafood tacos, which come in unusual combinations such as conch with cactus, fish *machaca* (a barbecuing process usually reserved for beef), and fish mole. Service is friendly, and the people-watching from the outdoor tables on Paseo del Pescador is unbeatable.

Paseo del Pescador 20-A (next to the pier). ☎ *755/4-2687. **Main courses:** $3.50–$7. MC, V. **Open:** Daily 7am to 10 or 11pm.*

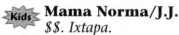 ## Mama Norma/J.J.
$$. Ixtapa.
ITALIAN/SEAFOOD.

There are a few indoor tables, but most of this restaurant's action is outside on a cheery La Puerta center patio. Mama Norma recently hooked up with J.J., a local seafood/Mexican chain, and as a result pizzas, pastas, and seafood dinners are delivered to the red-cloth-covered tables in about equal quantities. The pizza here is probably the best in Ixtapa, and the thick tuna steaks are prepared just right. North of the border–style grinders, burgers, and salads are available, too. Draft beer for $1, beach-resort-hearty service, and live ranchero music during high season all make this a fun spot.

> **Best Bay Views**
>
> Beccofino (Ixtapa, $$$)
> Kau-kan (Zihuatanejo/Beaches, $$–$$$)
> Villa de la Selva (Ixtapa, $$$$)

La Puerta shopping center. ☎ *755/3-0274. **Main courses:** $8–$20; pizzas $7–$10 (large). AE, MC, V. **Open:** Daily 3pm–midnight.*

Nueva Zelanda
$. Downtown Zihuatanejo. MEXICAN.

Here's the drill: You walk in, peruse the menu on the wall—don't let the weird food pictures put you off—then check off what you like on a printed form and wait for the waiter to bring your order. Get it down in advance, and you'll fit right in with the faithful who gather here for breakfasts of eggs Mexican style, huge fruit salads with yogurt and granola, or rolls with beans and cheese. There's seating indoors, where you can watch your meal being prepared in a spotless open kitchen, or on a pleasant street-side patio. Enchiladas, *sincronizadas* (quesadillas with ham), and other light meals are served all day, and the fresh juice drinks always hit the spot. There's another Nueva Zelanda in Ixtapa (Los Patios shopping center, back section; ☎ **755/3-0838**).

Cuauhtemoc 23 at Ejido. ☎ *755/4-2340.* **Main courses:** *(tortas, enchiladas, and so on) $2–$4. No credit cards.* **Open:** *Daily 7am–10pm.*

Restaurant Paul

$$–$$$. Downtown Zihuatanejo. INTERNATIONAL/SEAFOOD.
Swiss chef-owner Paul Carrer has acquired a fanatical following for his creative international cuisine; if you want to eat after 7pm, expect to wait (no reservations are accepted). It's well worth any delay. You're not going to find anywhere else in town that serves both fresh artichoke and escargots as appetizers, or entrées such as quail, sashimi, pork chops, and duck breast. Even old Zihuatanejo standards, such as fish fillet, achieve transcendence through Paul's delicate shrimp-and-dill sauce. The cozy open-front room is pretty enough, but you can't say the same for the view, mostly of passing cars. Never mind. You'll be too busy concentrating on the food to notice.

Benito Juárez s/n, near N. Bravo. ☎ *755/4-2188.* **Main courses:** *$7–$12. No credit cards.* **Open:** *Daily 6–10pm.*

Rossy

$$. Zihuatanejo/Beaches. SEAFOOD/STEAK.
Some locals claim that this casual beachside dining room has the best seafood on Playa la Ropa. You won't break the bank trying to find out if that's true: Octopus, fried or in garlic sauce, will run you only $5, and the breaded fish fillet of the day costs even less. Steak lovers can wallow in big meat: T-bone steaks, prime rib, top sirloin, or New York cut (okay, it ain't The Palm— but neither are the prices). Those who want sand-free feet can head up to the slightly more formal upper deck; beach lounge service is available off the lower level. One caveat: During the day, the canned music here is LOUD. Weekend nights, the live sounds are far more mellow.

Playa la Ropa, south end. ☎ *755/4-4004.* **Main courses:** *$4.50–$9. MC, V.* **Open:** *Daily 9am–11pm.*

Best North-of-the-Border Cuisine

The Deli (Downtown Zihuatanejo, $–$$)

The Golden Cookie Shop (Ixtapa, $)

Nueva Zelanda (Downtown Zihuatanejo, $)

Tamales Any y Atoles

$. Downtown Zihuatanejo. MEXICAN.
Ask anyone. Any's (say: "Annie's") has the best down-home Mexican food in town. It's worth coming in just to look at the wildly colorful murals, but you'll definitely want to stay for the tamales—pork with green sauce, poblano chiles and chicken, even squash blossoms and cheese. Other options are white or green pozole, the hominy soup that's a staple of Guerrero

cuisine, maybe washed down with mezcal distilled in the Vallecitos mountains. Dress lightly: Sometimes it's not only the food that's hot. The open-front restaurant has large fans, but if the weather's too intense, they just don't cut it. A branch of Any's recently opened in Ixtapa (Paseo de las Garzas s/n; ☎ **755/3-0041**).

Calle Ejido at the corner of Vincente Guerrero. ☎ *755/4-7373.* **Main courses:** *Tamales 75¢–$2 each. No credit cards.* **Open:** *Daily 8am–11:30pm.*

Villa de la Selva
$$$$. Ixtapa. CONTINENTAL.

Talk about political perks. Mexicans who dine at this stunning cliff-side restaurant, the converted summer home of one-time president Luis Echevarria, can see first-hand that their tax dollars were well—make that tastefully—spent. There's water, water everywhere: A flowing Spanish-tile fountain greets you at the entryway, and from any of the three tiers of white-clothed tables, you can watch the sea beat against the rocks of Vista Hermosa beach (this restaurant sits just above the Westin Brisas Ixtapa). Don't expect to diet here. Any healthful qualities red snapper might

Foodies' Choice

Beccofino (Ixtapa, $$$)

La Sirena Gorda (Downtown Zihuatanejo, $)

Restaurant Paul (Downtown Zihuatanejo, $$–$$$)

have had are lost in the melted cheese and hollandaise, for example, and the New York–cut steak comes topped with béarnaise sauce. Diners clearly couldn't care less. In spring and summer, lots of people save something on their plate for the *coatimundi* (relatives of the raccoon), who come calling from the adjacent lush hillside.

Paseo de la Roca. ☎ *755/3-0362 and 3-0462. Reservations essential.* **Main courses:** *$10–$23. AE, MC, V.* **Open:** *Daily 6pm–1am.*

Sound Bites: Ixtapa/Zihuatanejo Restaurants at a Glance
Restaurant Index by Price

$

 The Golden Cookie Shop (Ixtapa, Cafe/German/International)

La Sirena Gorda (Downtown Zihuatanejo, Mexican)

Nueva Zelanda (Downtown Zihuatanejo, Mexican)

Tamales Any y Atoles (Downtown Zihuatanejo, Mexican)

$–$$

Casa Elvira (Downtown Zihuatanejo, Mexican/Seafood)

The Deli (Downtown Zihuatanejo, International)

$$

El Infierno y La Gloria (Ixtapa, Mexican)

Garrabos (Downtown Zihuatanejo, Mexican/ Seafood)

La Perla (Zihuatanejo/Beaches, Seafood)

Kids Mama Norma/J.J. (Ixtapa, Italian/Seafood)

Rossy (Zihuatanejo/Beaches, Seafood/Steak)

$$–$$$

Bucanero's (Ixtapa, Seafood/Continental)

El Patio (Downtown Zihuatanejo, Mexican/Seafood)

Restaurant Paul (Downtown Zihuatanejo, International/Seafood)

Kau-kan (Zihuatanejo/Beaches, Seafood)

$$$

Beccofino (Ixtapa, Northern Italian)

Coconuts (Downtown Zihuatanejo, International)

$$$$

Bogart's (Ixtapa, Continental)

Villa de la Selva (Ixtapa, Continental)

Restaurant Index By Location

Part 8

Manzanillo

Unlike Bo Derek, whose 15 minutes of fame came from a film shot in this city, Manzanillo is hard to typecast. It's in part the hedonist heaven of that babefest, 10, but also Mexico's busiest industrial port, and a town still so unjaded by tourists that it welcomes them warmly as friends.

Most of Manzanillo's attractions lie somewhere in between the extremes—and widely scattered around town. I've gathered the best of them for you in the following chapters, the better to help you arrange your visit, whether you're desparately seeking somewhere to sleep, swim, tee off, or eat.

Chapter 29

Choosing the Place to Stay That's Right for You

In This Chapter

➤ Where the hotels are

➤ The best in the bunch

➤ Hotel indexes

Manzanillo's hotels are all over the map—literally as well as figuratively. A few isolated little lodging enclaves exist, but the city has no hotel zone per se, no shop-and-restaurant-strewn strip where tourists gather. Moreover, accommodations vary from low-key beachside apartments to over-the-top pleasure palaces. Because there's no abundance of off-property places for visitors to play, however, you'll find more all-inclusive resorts here than usual. (See chapter 6, "The Lowdown on Accommodations in Mexico," for a definition of these all-in-one resorts and for information that'll help you decide if they're right for you.)

It works this way: First, I'll give you an overview of the areas where Manzanillo's hotels are concentrated, including their pros and cons. Then I'll list my favorite hotels alphabetically, noting where they fall within those areas, and follow up with a few alternatives should my A-list choices be filled. At the end of the chapter, you'll find at-a-glance indexes listing the hotels by price and by location.

Hot Legs

Turnabout's fair play at a number of Manzanillo's all-inclusive resorts, where guys' gams come under scrutiny in "good legs" contests. On other nights, natch, gals' limbs get their turn in the limelight, too.

As far as prices go, I've noted rack rates (the maximum that a resort or hotel charges for a room) in the listings. This will give you some sense of what to expect, although I know you'll avoid paying rack by following the advice I gave you in chapter 6. I've also put a dollar sign icon in front of each hotel listing so you can quickly see whether it's within your budget. The more $ signs under the name, the more you pay. It runs like this:

$	=	$70 and below
$$	=	$70–$140
$$$	=	$140–$235
$$$$	=	$235 and above

Unless specified, rates are for a standard double room in high season, which runs roughly from December 19 to April 21. Expect to pay anywhere from 20% to 50% less the rest of the year. The prices listed include the 17% room tax.

A kid-friendly icon ⭐Kids⭐ highlights hotels that are especially good for families. All hotels have air-conditioning unless otherwise indicated, and if the review doesn't say anything to the contrary, you can safely assume that you can walk directly out of your hotel and onto the beach.

Hint: As you read through the reviews, you'll want to keep track of the ones that appeal to you. I've included a chart at the end of the book (see p. 542) where you can rank your preferences, but to make matters easier on yourself now, just put a little check mark next to the ones you like. Remember how your teachers used to tell you not to write in your books? Now's the time to rebel—scrawl away!

Location, Location, Location

Location is less key in Manzanillo than it is in the other resort towns covered in this book. More important are budget and comfort considerations. You won't need to get away from it all because there's no "all" to escape, nor will you have a burning need for access to downtown (a nice place to visit once or twice, but you wouldn't want to live there). Still, a few of the distinguishing features of the tourist areas in greater Manzanillo are noted below, as are those of Barra de Navidad to the north.

Greater Manzanillo

➤ **Las Brisas.** About 4 miles north of downtown (which lies at the southern end of Manzanillo), the main Highway 200 branches off to the Las Brisas highway and leads to a quiet residential area also called Las Brisas, home to a number of low-key hotels, bungalows, and condos. Stay here and you can walk straight out the door to a nice, wide beach, one of the best for swimming; there's good diving and snorkeling off a southern jetty, too. A few hotels have restaurants, but you'll have to cab it or bus it whenever you want a bit of variety in your diet. This is also the tourist area farthest from the airport. Still, it's a straight

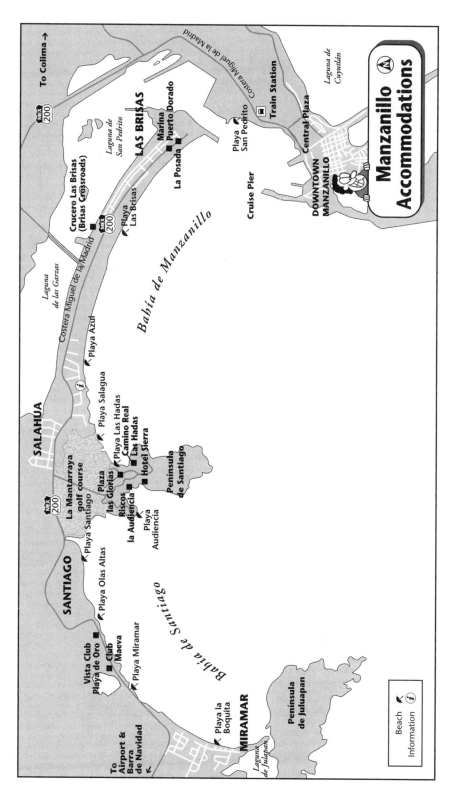

Manzanillo
Accommodations

Laguna de Cuyutlán

To Colima →

Costera Miguel de la Madrid

LAS BRISAS

Train Station

Central Plaza

Crucero Las Brisas
(Brisas Crossroads)

Marina
Puerto Dorado

Playa
San Pedrito

DOWNTOWN
MANZANILLO

Laguna de
San Pedrito

La Posada

Playa
Las Brisas

Cruise Pier

Laguna
de las Garzas

Bahía de Manzanillo

Playa Azul

Costera Miguel de la Madrid

SALAHUA

Playa Salagua

Playa Las Hadas
Camino Real

Las Hadas

Hotel Sierra

La Mantarraya
golf course

Plaza
las Glorias

Península
de Santiago

Playa Santiago

Riscos
la Audiencia

Playa
Audiencia

SANTIAGO

Playa Olas Altas

Vista Club
Playa de Oro

Club
Maeva

Playa Miramar

Bahía de Santiago

To
Airport &
Barra
de Navidad

Playa la Boquita

MIRAMAR

Península
de Juluapan

Laguna
de Juluapan

Beach
Information

333

shot north to some good restaurants and even a few nightspots; there's no need to be on the road for more than 10 minutes.

➤ **Santiago Peninsula.** Three miles north of Las Brisas, the wide Santiago Peninsula marks the divide between Manzanillo's two bays: Santiago and Manzanillo. The peninsula is best known as the home to Las Hadas, the hotel immortalized—or at least seriously advertised—in the film *10*, but it also hosts a variety of other properties, some modest, one a high-rise all-inclusive. Not all the hotels here have direct access to the beach, but when you do get to the shore, you'll be where the best sports toys are. Hotels in this area are also close to Las Hadas's excellent La Mantarraya golf course. Although the hotel restaurants here are more varied than those in Las Brisas, they're not within walking distance from one another, and bus service on the peninsula is spotty. Plaza Manzanillo, the city's only real mall, is close to the southern entrance to the peninsula.

➤ **Santiago Bay.** Stay on Santiago Bay, just north of Santiago Peninsula, and you'll be closest to the airport (which isn't saying much; the terminal is still a good 25 minutes away). A vacation home complex and assorted beachfront condos aside, this area is too spread out to really be considered a tourist community, but two all-inclusive properties that I like are located here. Restaurants are no more concentrated on this stretch than they are farther to the south, but bus service is good and you'll have little need to leave your hotel's premises.

Barra de Navidad

The little beach town of **Barra de Navidad** is about as far north of the Manzanillo airport as Santiago Bay is south, approximately 25 to 30 minutes by taxi. Until the 1997 arrival of the gigantic Grand Bay Resort golf, marina, and condo complex, this was a laid-back budget destination, but the times they are, well, already changed. The pace here is still much slower than that of Manzanillo, however, and Barra is still cobblestoned and charming (more so, in fact, after the spiff-up that followed a 1996 earthquake). The arrival of a few more restaurants and nightspots is no drawback, and the town hasn't yet bit the hand that fed it its modest tourist dollars by raising prices.

My Favorite Hotels from A to Z

Camino Real Las Hadas

$$$$. Santiago Peninsula, Greater Manzanillo.

Rising like a fairy-tale city from a sparkling blue bay, Las Hadas is as breathtaking as it was when the movie *10* was filmed here in 1979. An army of gardeners tends the sprawling complex, where towers, spires, and domes gleam white against the lush foliage. You'll happen on a delightful detail—say, a kissing corner or a bust of the owner's mother—at every niche (good luck not getting lost while you're exploring!). The classically elegant rooms, all arches and cool marble, are in low-slung *casitas* (little houses). Honeymooners and still-in-love couples compete with business travelers for front-row tents on

El Conchero

Marina

C. Veleros

Av. Andres de Urdaneta

C. Puerto de La Nav.

Canal 1

C. Armada

Canal 2

C. Astilleros

Canal 3

Punta
Vela

Isla de
Los Puercos

Isla de
Navidad

C. Tampico

C. Manzanillo

Hotel Sands

Hotel Delfin

Laguna Barra de Navidad

Golf
Course

C. Puerto Cebu

C. 21 De Noviembre

C. Filip Nas

C. Mazatlan

Morelos

Fishing
Co-op

Grand
Bay
Hotel

C. Michoacan

C. Veracruz

de Legazpi

C. Sinaloa

C. Jalisco

C. Yucatán

C. Veracruz

Water
Taxi

C. Miguel

C. Guanajuato

Hotel Barra
de Navidad

Malecon

Bahia de la Navidad

BARRA DE NAVIDAD AREA

To Hwy 200

MELAQUE (SAN PATRICIO)

Playa
Mayorca

*Bahia
Navidad*

Playa
del Sol

**BARRA
DE NAVIDAD**

Pacific Ocean

Barra de Navidad Accommodations

the resort's sheltered beach, for tee times on the excellent La Mantarraya golf course, for places on the 10 tennis courts, and for reservations at Legazpi, the hotel's renowned fine-dining room (see chapter 32, "The Best of Manzanillo's Dining Scene"). Maybe the marble's a little chipped and the service isn't as flawless as it once was, but this is still one of Mexico's great hotels.

Peninsula de Santiago. ☎ *800/7-CAMINO or 333/4-0000. Fax 333/4-1950. www. caminoreal.com. E-mail: zlo@caminoreal. com.* **Rack rate:** *$295 standard double (price includes continental breakfast). AE, DC, MC, V.*

Dollars & Sense

Camino Real's **More Mexico for Less** program discounts Las Hadas's deluxe rooms ($337 rack); the longer you stay, the lower the rates. Six nights or more will get you a tariff of $243, including breakfast and 1 hour of free daytime tennis during your visit.

Kids **Club Maeva**

$$$. Santiago Bay, Greater Manzanillo.

All-inclusive resort? With 90 acres of pleasure centers geared to all ages, this is

Bet You Didn't Know

The movie *10* caused both a surge in tourism to Manzanillo and a spate of copycat architecture in town—lots of buildings in town sport Las Hadas–style domes and Moorish towers.

practically an all-inclusive city. There's a separate suburb for small kids, replete with puppet theater, crawl-through railroad cars, and water slides. If you don't enjoy the pitter-patter of adolescent feet, you can retreat to a pool restricted to ages 18 and over. All ages get together at the 12 tennis courts, the soccer field, poolside scuba lessons, a gym, the beach club (a bridge takes you across the highway to the shore), and five restaurants. At night, the family-oriented Tropical Hut features karaoke and arm-wrestling contests, while the Boom Boom disco organizes a variety of theme nights, including some for singles. Rooms in the pueblo-style complex are immaculate and cool, with white stucco walls, blue-and-white marble floors, and glacial air-conditioning.

Costera Miguel de la Madrid, km 16.5. ☎ *800/GO-MAEVA or 333/4-0431. Fax 333/5-0395.* **Rack rates:** *$152 per person (double occupancy); singles $249 (rates include all meals, drinks, and activities). AE, DC, MC, V.*

Grand Bay Hotel
$$$$. Barra de Navidad.
Since the 1997 opening of this 1200-acre hotel/golf/marina complex across the yacht channel, Barra de Navidad has probably seen more wealthy couples and businesspeople than in its entire previous history. And they're likely to keep on coming, because the Grand Bay is gorgeous, combining cool classical elegance and Mexican warmth to anything but tepid effect. Your room won't look exactly like anyone else's, but you can expect lots of marble and tasteful tapestry fabrics in colors like mint or coral; book a suite and you'll get your own steam room or Jacuzzi. All the accommodations are lovely, but those in the La Punta section aren't quite as light and open as the others. If golf isn't your game, you can hit some balls around the tennis court or work up a sweat in the state-of-the-art fitness center while training for the real endurance event: sampling the 146 types of tequila poured at Antonio's, the fine dining room.

P.O. Box 20, Jalisco, Barra de Navidad. ☎ *888/80-GRAND or 335/5-5050. Fax 335/5-6071. www.grandbay.com.* **Rack rate:** *$527 standard double; tennis, golf, honeymoon, fishing, and scuba packages available. AE, DC, MC, V.*

Hotel Barra de Navidad
$. Barra de Navidad.
At the northern end of Legazpi, Barra's main beachfront street, this white stucco low-rise is popular for its friendly management, shaded courtyard, and comfortable rooms, some of which have oceanview balconies. The least

expensive ones look out on the street, but both have access to a pretty pool and a decent restaurant—and, of course, to the sand. No A/C.

Legazpi 250, Barra de Navidad. ☎ ***335/5-5122.*** *Fax 335/5-5303.* ***Rack Rates:*** *$54–$64 double. MC, V.*

Dollars & Sense

Unless you have a sugar daddy or mommy or your company is sending you, rates are prohibitive at the **Grand Bay Hotel** (☎ **888/80-GRAND**) from December 21 through February, when there's a 7-day minimum stay and all discounts are on hold. The rest of the year, tennis, golf, honeymoon, fishing, and scuba packages reduce your rates considerably.

Hotel Delfin
$. Barra de Navidad.
One of Barra's better-maintained hotels, the four-story Delfin is on the landward side of the lagoon, which is not necessarily a disadvantage; the ocean can sound surprisingly loud at night. Red-tile-floor rooms are plain, but well cared for and well lighted; those on the top floor afford magnificent views of the lagoon (the price is having to walk up four flights of stairs). A tiny courtyard with a pool is shaded by a huge rubber tree. Even those not staying at the hotel stop by for the terrific breakfast buffet—try the banana pancakes—and for the large, reasonably priced dinners, both served on a lovely second-floor terrace. All the in-and-out action doesn't always make for a serene atmosphere.

Av. Moreles 23, Barra de Navidad. ☎ ***335/5-5068.*** *Fax 335/5-6020.* ***Rack rate:*** *$29 double high season. AE, MC, V.*

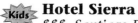 Hotel Sierra
$$$. Santiago Peninsula, Greater Manzanillo.
Staying at this friendly all-inclusive is like taking a cruise without ever getting seasick. An international assortment of baby boomers works hard to keep up with the frenetic round of organized activities—diving classes, pool volleyball, all kinds of games and contests. Others just ship their offspring to the kids club, and throw back the unlimited free drinks that are part of the package. Unlike many of the hotels in Manzanillo, this is a high-rise with elevators, so you can devote your energies to activities other than stair-trekking or grounds-wandering. You can also zip down directly to the wide beach, where lots of water sports concessionaires converge. Shows and fiestas keep things moving at night, and the El Tibores restaurant (see chapter 32) is

Best Hotels for Families

Club Maeva (Santiago Bay, $$$)

Hotel Sierra (Santiago Peninsula, $$$)

Marina Puerto Dorado (Las Brisas, $$)

Vista Club Playa de Oro (Santiago Bay, Greater Manzanillo, $$)

excellent. Many of the attractive, contemporary-style rooms have patios overlooking the sea, and some are handicapped-accessible—a rarity in Mexico.

Av. de la Audiencia no. 1, Peninsula de Santiago. ☎ ***800/342-AMIGO** or 333/ 3-2000. Fax 333/3-2272. E-mail: sierra@ bay.net.mx. **Rack rate:** $260 double, including all meals, alcoholic and nonalcoholic beverages, and activities (children 7 to 12 are $25 extra per day; children 6 and under free). AE, DC, MC, V.*

La Posada

$$. Las Brisas, Greater Manzanillo. Owned by an American expat and former pilot, this Pepto Bismol–pink hotel complex draws a cadre of hippies (aging and next generation) and seasoned travelers who wouldn't dream of staying anywhere else. They come for the laid-back atmosphere (you can help yourself to soft drinks or beer on an honor system, for example); for the pretty cobblestone courtyard, fountain, and brick archways; for the out-your-door access to a good beach; and for the American-style breakfasts and lunches served in the *sala*, a funky combination library, lounge, and dining room. Guest units are simple, but beamed ceilings and other rustic Mexican details add character.

Extra! Extra!

La Posada wins my vote for the most Americana hotel in Manzanillo.

Las Brisas, main road near the dock. ☎ *and fax **333/3-1899. Rack rate:** $84 double (rate includes full breakfast); long-term rates available. AE, MC, V.*

Marina Puerto Dorado

$$. Las Brisas, Greater Manzanillo.
If you've got the entire brat pack in tow, or are coming down with a group of friends, you'll like this low-rise, where you can book a two-bedroom suite that sleeps four or five comfortably, or a penthouse for up to eight people; both types of units have oceanview balconies. The nautical blue-and-white decor is a bit 1970s, but not hard on the eyes, and the kitchens are up to date. You can hang out by the good beach in the hotel's backyard, soak in the hot tub, or swim in the adult pool (there's a separate one for kids). The food at the pleasant thatched-roof restaurant is decent, but, for a change, you can also eat next door at La Posada (see above). A unique perk is a vending machine that sells Modelo beer for about 75¢.

Av. Lázaro Cárdenas 101, Las Brisas Playa Azul. ☎ *and fax* **333/4-1480. Rack rates:** *$152 2-bedroom suite; $211 penthouse suite. AE, MC, V.*

Plaza Las Glorias
$$. Santiago Peninsula, Greater Manzanillo.
You get lots of character for your pesos at this ochre and terra-cotta hotel, arranged like a Mediterranean village on the slopes of a lush hillside. You also get lots of exercise negotiating the steep brick steps that lead to the romantic palapa-roof restaurant and pretty blue-trimmed pool; hit that StairMaster to prepare. One- to three-bedroom villas are designed to accommodate from three to eight people; all have separate sitting rooms and full kitchens stocked with Talavera ceramic dishes. You can rent just a bedroom, but be prepared for cramped quarters if you do. An additional $40 per person will buy you the use of the sports facilities and restaurants at the all-inclusive Hotel Sierra (see above) from 9am to 6pm. It's no extra charge just to shuttle down to the Sierra's beach (this hotel doesn't have one of its own).

Av. de Tesoro s/n. ☎ **800/342-AMIGO,** *333/4-1098 or 333/4-1054. Fax 333/ 3-1395.* **Rack rates:** *$82 bedroom alone (sleeps two); $117 1-bedroom villa. AE, MC, V.*

Riscos la Audiencia
$$. Santiago Peninsula, Greater Manzanillo.
You won't mistake this place for Las Hadas, which is right next door, but, then, you won't mistake your bill for a down payment on a sports utility vehicle, either. And with each simple but perfectly serviceable one- or two-bedroom suite in this five-story (non-elevator) hotel, you get a balcony with incredible bay views. There's Las Hadas beach access via a series of rough stone steps—take it slow—as well as a pool on the premises. The larger units have kitchens, and all share the barbecue pit on the sundeck. If you like to read at night, bring along a flashlight; there are no bedside lamps.

Best to Book with Friends
Marina Puerto Dorado (Las Brisas, $$)

Riscos la Audiencia (Santiago Peninsula, $$)

Best for Romance
Camino Real Las Hadas (Santiago Peninsula, $$$$)
Grand Bay Hotel (Barra de Navidad, $$$$)

Calle de los Riscos 27, Peninsula de Santiago. ☎ ***333/4-1236*** *or 333/3-0632. Fax 333/3-0631.* **Rack rates:** *$99 1-bedroom unit; $152 2-bedroom unit. AE, MC, V.*

Vista Club Playa de Oro
$$. Santiago Bay, Greater Manzanillo.

For a no-fuss budget vacation, it's hard to beat the low-end, all-inclusive Vista Club. Canadian snowbirds and Mexican families mingle at the pools, tennis courts, game room, putting green, language classes, and nightly dinner shows. There's a separate kids' club with a small pool and playground, too. Breakfast and lunch are served buffet style, and you can start hitting one of the three no-holds-barred bars as early as 10am. Rooms aren't glitzy but have attractive hand-carved headboards and red-tile floors. The village-style complex is hilly, spread out, and not all that smoothly paved; to avoid major schlepping, try to get a room close to the main pool and restaurants. Miramar beach lies across the main highway from the hotel; it's not far, but it may take a while before you can safely drop your beach towel on the other side.

Carretera a Cihuatlan, km 15.5. ☎ ***800/882-8215,*** *333/3-1870, or 333/ 3-2540. Fax 333/3-2840.* **Rack rate:** *$73 per person based on double occupancy (includes all meals, drinks, and activities). AE, DC, MC, V.*

No Room at the Inn? Check Out One of These . . .

Greater Manzanillo

➤ **Fiesta Mexicana.** A full service high-rise on the highway, with a nice central courtyard and pool. Some of the smallish rooms have ocean views. Santiago–Manzanillo Road, km 8.5, Playa Azul, Santiago Bay. ☎ **333/ 3-2180.** Fax 333/3-2180. **$$.**

➤ **Hotel Star.** Modest but tidy and well managed, a sunny two-story complex facing a courtyard and beachside pool. Av. Lázaro Cárdenas 1313, Las Brisas. ☎ **333/3-2560** or 333/3-1980. **$.**

➤ **Villas la Audiencia.** A pretty red-tile-roof complex, with simple but attractive villas and rooms and a beach shuttle. Av. de la Audiencia and Las Palmas, Santiago Peninsula. ☎ **333/3-0861.** Fax 333/3-3653. **$.**

Barra de Navidad

➤ **Hotel Sands.** Colonial style and pleasant, with small but homey rooms and a beautiful pool by the lagoon. Av. Moreles 24. ☎ **335/5-5018.** **$.**

Quick Picks: Manzanillo's Hotels at a Glance
Hotel Index by Price

$

Hotel Barra de Navidad (Barra de Navidad)

Hotel Delfin (Barra de Navidad)

$$

La Posada (Las Brisas, Greater Manzanillo)

Kids Marina Puerto Dorado (Las Brisas, Greater Manzanillo)

Plaza Las Glorias (Santiago Peninsula, Greater Manzanillo)

Riscos la Audiencia (Santiago Peninsula, Greater Manzanillo)

Kids Vista Club Playa de Oro (Santiago Bay, Greater Manzanillo)

$$$

Kids Club Maeva (Santiago Bay, Greater Manzanillo)

Kids Hotel Sierra (Santiago Peninsula, Greater Manzanillo)

$$$$

Camino Real Las Hadas (Santiago Peninsula, Greater Manzanillo)

Grand Bay Hotel (Barra de Navidad)

Hotel Index by Location

Santiago Peninsula, Greater Manzanillo

Camino Real Las Hadas $$$$

Kids Hotel Sierra $$$

Plaza Las Glorias $$

Riscos la Audiencia $$

Santiago Bay, Greater Manzanillo

Kids Club Maeva $$$

Kids Vista Club Playa de Oro $$

Las Brisas, Greater Manzanillo

La Posada $$

Kids Marina Puerto Dorado $$

Barra de Navidad

Grand Bay Hotel $$$$

Hotel Barra de Navidad $

Hotel Delfin $

341

Finding Your Way Around Manzanillo

Manzanillo isn't small, but it's easy to manage—which is lucky, because there's not exactly a glut of information waiting for you when you get there. This chapter will walk (well, mostly ride) you through arriving at the airport, reaching your hotel, getting what additional information there is to be got, dealing with emergencies, and more.

Yo, Gringo!

Mexican Customs are generally *problema* free, but don't forget to push the button on the pseudo-traffic signal to get the official green light to walk on through with your luggage.

You've Just Arrived—Now What?

You can eat, shop, and go to the bathroom at Manzanillo's diminutive international airport. You can't, however, exchange money, book a hotel room, or get any sort of tourist information.

So, aside from engaging in the third-mentioned of the available activities (a good idea, as it's a long ride into town), you have no reason to linger here. After you collect your luggage—the location of the single carousel will be abundantly obvious—head over to the booth just outside the arrival gate that sells both *colectivo* ($6 to most Manzanillo hotels) and taxi ($15) tickets. Don't panic if you don't have any pesos; dollars are accepted, although at a fairly unfavorable exchange rate. *Colectivos* (collective vans) only go to Barra de Navidad (see chapter 29, "Choosing the Place to Stay That's Right For You") in high season, but it won't cost you much more to get there by taxi than it will to reach greater Manzanillo, approximately the same distance (about 20 miles) away.

Dollars & Sense

The day before you depart, get your hotel's front desk to book you a place on **Transportes Terrestres** (☎ 333/4-1555), which runs the collective van service to the airport. It can cost a third less than taking a taxi.

Time-Savers

If there are two or more of you, consider shelling out the few extra bucks for a taxi rather than a collective van. Manzanillo is so spread out that if you're staying in the south, you might be totally done in by the time the other passengers are dropped off.

Orientation: You Are Here

Greater Manzanillo encompasses two gorgeous, sparkling blue bays: the one to the north named Santiago and the one to the south called Manzanillo. Dividing them is the hilly Santiago Peninsula.

Downtown Manzanillo, the bustling business district, lies at the southern end of Manzanillo Bay. Social activity revolves around a central plaza, Jardín Álvaro Obregón, separated from the waterfront by a railroad and shipyard. Most offices and shops are on the streets that parallel Avenida México, which begins just behind the plaza's gazebo.

At downtown's Pemex station, the bay-front Avenida Moreles turns into Avenida Niños Héroes, which in turn merges into the main Barra de Navidad–Puerto Vallarta road or Highway 200 (as it passes north through greater Manzanillo, this thoroughfare goes through as many incarnations as Shirley MacLaine). Locations on this main road, no matter what its name, are indicated by their distance from the Pemex station, designated km 0. The northern ETN bus station, for example, is at km 13.8.

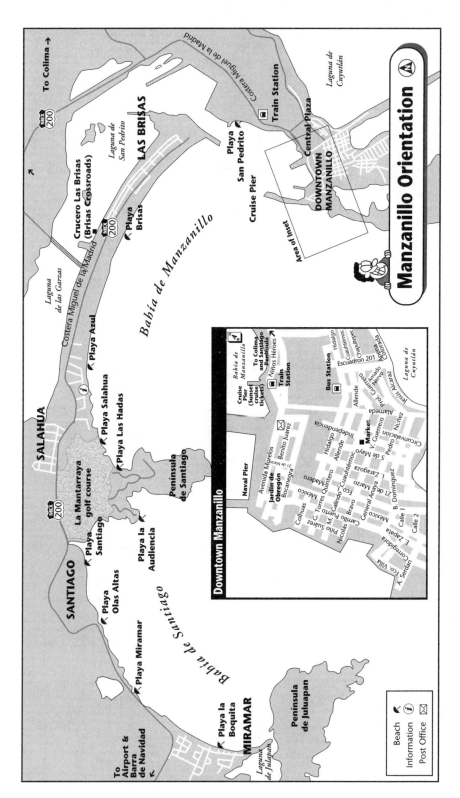

Manzanillo Orientation

Beach
Information
Post Office

Downtown Manzanillo

344

As you head north, you'll pass a number of small townships, each with their own central square. The first is Las Brisas, which tails off to the south at an intersection not far from downtown. Next comes Salagua, located just before the turnoff into the Santiago Peninsula. Soon after the road passes the peninsula, you'll come to Santiago. Continue north and eventually you'll reach the airport.

Getting from Here to There

If I were to recommend renting a car at any of the beach towns, far-flung Manzanillo would be at the top of my list. But even if you take taxis everywhere—and there's no reason that you should—it'll still come out cheaper than getting your own wheels.

Cabs & Buses

Taxis are relatively pricey because of the distances between many Manzanillo destinations, but they come in mighty handy at night when you may not feel comfortable riding the buses—not because of safety, but because it's harder to tell if you're nearing your stop when it's dark. During the day, however, taking the bus is a piece of cake. Those marked "Las Brisas," "Salagua," and "Santiago" make frequent runs back and forth along the main highway to downtown; bus stops are marked with (surprise!) signs with little buses on them. Service to the Santiago Peninsula isn't so swift; buses theoretically run every 20 minutes, but don't bet the farm on it. The fare should be no more than 50¢, no matter how far you go.

Dollars & Sense

If you do decide to cab it, be sure to agree on a price before you step into the taxi. Check at the front desk of your hotel to find out what's a fair fare for your destination.

Where to Get More Information & Guidance

The federal, city, and state **tourism office** (Costera Miguel de la Madrid 4960, km 8.5; ☎ 333/3-2277 or 333/3-2264), open Monday through Friday from 9am to 3pm and 6 to 8pm, can provide you with a fairly sketchy map of Manzanillo and the town of Colima—good luck trying to find a better one!—and answer your basic questions.

There are no English-language tourist publications, but don't feel left out—there's not much around in the way of Spanish tourist info, either.

Manzanillo A to Z: Facts at Your Fingertips

American Express: The American Express representative is Bahías Gemelas Travel Agency, with branches at Costera Miguel de la Madrid, km 10 (☎ 333/3-1000 or 333/3-1053), and at the Hotel Sierra (Av. de la Audiencia no. 1, Peninsula de Santiago; ☎ 333/3-0204 or 333/3-2000, ext. 451).

ATMs: Downtown, there are ATMs at the Bancomer (Av. México 122) and Banamex (Av. México 136) banks. In greater Manzanillo, you'll find ATMs at the Banpais bank in the Plaza Pacifico strip mall on Avenida Audiencia (at the beginning of Santiago Peninsula); at the Banamex in Salagua's Plaza Manzanillo or the Bancomer across the main road and a block north; and in Santiago Bay at the Bital bank on Highway 200 outside the ETN bus station at km 13.8.

Baby-sitters: Most hotels can arrange for a baby-sitter, although not necessarily a bilingual one. Rates run from around $3 to $6 per hour.

Business Hours: Stores are open daily from 10am to 2pm and from 4:30 or 5 to 9pm; office hours are generally 10am to 2pm and 4pm to 6 or 7pm Monday through Friday. Some offices are also open 10am to 2pm on Saturday.

Currency Exchange: You can exchange money from 9am to noon at the banks listed in "ATMs," above. There are also two money exchange booths in Plaza Manzanillo.

Doctors: Larger hotels such as the Sierra and Las Hadas have physicians on 24-hour call, and smaller ones should be able to find a good (and often English-speaking) doctor or dentist for you. See also "Hospitals" and "Pharmacies," below.

Emergencies/Fire: To report a fire, call ☎ **333/2-5238.** For the Red Cross, call ☎ **333/2-5169.**

English-Language Newspapers/Magazines: Revistas Saifer, with branches downtown (across from the Hotel Colonial) and in Plaza Manzanillo, carries the *Mexico City News* and a few English-language magazines. The shopping arcades in the Las Hadas and the Sierra hotels stock a decent supply of reading material for their Spanish language–deficient customers.

Hospitals: Centro Médico Quirúrgico Echuari (Costera Miguel de la Madrid, km 9.7; ☎ **333/4-0001)** and **Médica Pacífico Cruz Azul** (Av. Palma Real 10, km 13; ☎ **333/4-0385)** are Manzanillo's most reliable private hospitals. Both have English-speaking staff and 24-hour service.

Maps: See "Where to Get More Information & Guidance," above.

Pharmacies: The best-stocked and least expensive pharmacy is the one in the **Comercial Mexicana supermarket (☎ 333/3-0005)** in Plaza Manzanillo; you get a 25% to 30% discount on most items and orders for things not in stock arrive the next day. The **Farmacia Continental** in Santiago (Highway 200, km 14.5, next to Juanito's; ☎ **333/3-8286)** is run by the English-speaking Dr. Joseph Cadet, Jr., who has an office next door.

Police: Call ☎ **333/2-1004.**

Post Office: There is a post office in Santiago at Venustiano Carranza 2, and one in central Manzanillo on Avenida Júrez and 21 de Marzo, 2 blocks east of the Jardín.

Safety: Manzanillo does not have a significant crime rate, but that doesn't mean you should throw your common sense to the sea breezes. Don't go wandering unlit streets or unpopulated beaches at night—especially if you've been drinking—and guard your possessions when you're strolling around downtown's congested streets. See chapter 10, "Crossing the Border & What to Expect on the Other Side," for additional safety tips.

Special Events: Manzanillo celebrates all the national holidays (see chapter 2, "When Should I Go?") in traditional high fashion. In addition, the Las Hadas marina hosts the annual international billfish tournament in February and the national billfishing competition in November; call ☎ **333/3-2770** for information on exact dates.

Telephone: The telephone area code for Manzanillo is 333. To call long distance within Mexico (abbreviated *lada*), dial 01, then the area code, and then the number. To call the United States, dial 001, and then the area code and number.

Fun On & Off the Beach

Whether you want to do the beach towel shuffle or stay put on your personal plot of sand, plumb the depths or keep your body dry while fathoming the deep blue sea, Manzanillo will take care of you.

Extra! Extra!

If you're trying to entertain the kids, keep in mind that activity-packed all-inclusive hotels and the beach are your best bets. Other than horseback riding, there's not much in the way of dry-land activities that will interest them.

Although you won't wear yourself out trying to see everything there is to see in Manzanillo—you didn't really want to go back home exhausted, did you?—there's still enough going on in and around town to keep you out of trouble for a few days. And I'll even suggest a number of ways for you to get back into trouble—only the good kind, of course—come nightfall.

Beaches, Beaches, Everywhere

Manzanillo's distinctive sand, ranging from golden to brown and black, is the result of lots of ancient volcanic action. In general, the farther south you get, the darker the shoreline.

Because distances in Manzanillo are so great, many of the visiting carless prefer to stick close to their rooms and showers. Why drag beach gear on a bus or sit, sand-bottomed, in a hot taxi, when your hotel has staked out a swell bit of shore or will shuttle you to one for free? Of course, you wouldn't want to eat the same thing every night, even your favorite food. So here are some options for the restless—young and otherwise.

How Ya Like Them Apples?

Some say Manzanillo got its name from the great stands of manzanillo trees that were used for wood during the Spanish ship-building era; they bear a red-yellow fruit that looks like an apple but is poisonous. Others insist the town's moniker derives from the yellow manzanilla bushes that once proliferated in the surrounding fields, and whose flowers are still used to make chamomile tea.

Downtown
Playa San Pedrito has gentle waves and is shallow for a long way out, but unfortunately the water is often polluted by debris from the nearby port. Seafood stands and shady palms are pluses. Because it's so close to downtown, this beach can get crowded, especially on the weekends. Best come here when the locals are working if you value your personal space.

Manzanillo Bay
Playa Las Brisas, not far north of Playa San Pedrito—although you'll have a tough time going between the two unless you regularly swim the English Channel—is clean and lovely and safe for swimming. Because it's not backed up against the highway, as many of the other bay beaches are, it's one of the most peaceful strands of sand around. You'll have no problem finding an isolated spot here, but if you want to socialize, park yourself in front of one of the beachside hotels; the best for snacking are La Posada and Marina Puerto Dorado, both at the south end of the beach. Also near the two hotels is a jetty, popular with divers and snorkelers.

Yo, Gringo!

Heed the red or black warning flags that go up when swimming conditions are dangerous. They mean business. Be careful about going in if the flag is yellow, and have fun in the water if a white or green signal gives you the go-ahead.

As you continue north, the same stretch of sand turns into **Playa Azul,** not generally great for much besides toe-dipping because of strong waves. It's followed by **Playa Salahua,** which doesn't offer anything safer in the way of recreational immersion, but does provide great photo ops at sunset, when locals throw out their nets or lines at the north end of the beach. Hotel restaurants and seafood palapas dot the 5-mile bay shore, easily accessible via city buses marked "Salagua."

The Santiago Peninsula

The Manzanillo Bay side of the peninsula is home to **Las Hadas** beach, an extremely tranquil inlet that's perfect for swimming and enjoying the many available water sports. If you're not staying at the swank hotel that this beach fronts, paste on your best "I-belong-here" expression—or take along enough money to buy a meal at one of the restaurants. Technically, the entire Mexican shoreline is public, but you're at a disadvantage arguing politics with hotel personnel if your Spanish is high school vintage.

Bet You Didn't Know

Playa la Audiencia is said to have gotten its name because the local Indians granted conquistador Hernán Cortés an audience here.

Cross over to the Santiago Bay side of the peninsula if you want to play on **Playa La Audiencia,** not quite as calm as Las Hadas but equally well-equipped with water toys. Much of the beach is the domain of guests at the all-inclusive Sierra Hotel, but locals frequent the north end, where a pleasant seafood restaurant does beach-lounge delivery— even providing the lounges.

Both Santiago Peninsula beaches are (blissfully) away from the main highway, but both can be reached by public buses marked "Península de Santiago"— eventually.

Santiago Bay

Just beyond the Santiago Peninsula and the town of Santiago, the first beach you'll see on Santiago Bay is named, surprisingly enough, **Playa Santiago.** This popular local spot is the beginning of a 5-mile arc of sand, called **Playa Olas Altas** when it meets the Rio Colorado creek; the surfing here is excellent. Next comes **Playa Miramar,** site of the Maeva Club's beach (private), some sports concessionaires (public), and lots of beach vendors (very public). For bathtub-gentle water and an offshore wreck that's a magnet for divers and snorkelers, continue on to **La Boquita,** idyllic during the week but best avoided on Saturday and Sunday when the seafood palapas struggle to keep up with local demand. The Julúapan Lagoon on the other side of this point is a bird-watcher's haven.

Water Fun for Everyone

Manzanillo may not have an overabundance of splashy sports such as parasailing, but when it comes to standards like fishing and diving, this town can hook 'em and sink 'em with the best of the lot. You won't have any trouble trolling for snorkeling gear, kayaks, and other low-tech water-engagement equipment, either.

A Bucket Full of Water Sports

Sports concessions at Playa La Audiencia and Las Hadas can get you on Waverunners (about $30 per half hour), kayaks ($15 per hour for a one-person boat, $23 for a kayak built for two), windsurfers ($20 per hour), and water skis ($30 per half hour). It's about $4 per person to hop on a banana boat and about $5 to hit the surf with a boogie board. Playa Miramar has some of the same equipment, at similar prices.

For a Reel Good Time

As the huge hauls at annual sportsfishing tournaments held here since 1954 attest, Manzanillo is a great place for bringing in the big ones. Marlin and sailfish hang around all year; winter is a winner for dorado (mahi-mahi), while wahoo and roosterfish tend to take the bait in summer.

You can arrange a fishing trip through a hotel travel agent for about $40 per person, or hire a boat and crew directly through the **fishermen's cooperative** (☎ **333/2-1031**), located about 1 block north of the Pemex station in downtown Manzanillo (you'll see their yellow Flota Amarilla ships moored at the dock). Five-person boats with three lines run about $110. If you go this route, you won't have to book in advance, but on the other hand, because of the queuing system (kind of like a taxi line), you won't be able to choose the boat and captain you like.

Off the Hook

More and more anglers are taking part in the catch and release conservation program: You reel in your fish, tag it, and then send it back into the sea to create future fish (after it recovers from the temporary hook-in-the-mouth pain, of course).

Another option is to lease the 28-foot *Rosa Elena*, owned by Americans Sam and Marilyn Short (☎ **333/4-0784**). It'll cost you a bit more than the fisherman's cooperative ($140 for the five-passenger, three-line boat), but you'll be assured captains who are proven trophy winners. Additionally, the Shorts have an arrangement with the Guadalajara Grill to cook whatever their clients bring in (only drinks and side dishes are extra). The couple's 38-foot S.S. *Marlin* is also available.

Yo, Gringo!

If you book a fishing trip with a tour operator, you won't have to pay for boat space you're not using, but your trip can get canceled at the last minute if your boat isn't filled. Hire a boat through the fisherman's cooperative and you know that the person who's actually doing the work is the one getting the pesos for it—but you might not be able to communicate with him as well as you would with a captain hired through a hotel tour rep.

Sportsfishing Tipping Tips

It's customary to tip the captain 10% to 15% of the total price of your charter, depending on the quality of the service. Give the money to the captain, who will split it with the mate.

Exploring the Deep Blue

Decent visibility (about 30 to 90 feet), warm water (averaging 78°F and up), and a relative scarcity of visitors make for good diving and snorkeling around Manzanillo. Add a sunken ship (see La Boquita beach in "Santiago Bay," above), lots of live coral, and sea life ranging from angelfish to moray eels, and you've got a pretty interesting underwater picture.

The best-known and most reliable dive operation is **Underworld Scuba** (Plaza Pacifico, Avenida Audiencia, ☎ and fax **333/3-0642**; or Hotel Sierra, ☎ **333/ 3-2000,** e-mail scubamex@bay.net.nx), owned by Susan Dearing and Carlos Cuellar. Novices get a free qualifying lesson in the Hotel Sierra's pool, and then pay $50 for an offshore dive. It costs those already certified $50 for one tank, and $85 for two for the deeper boat dives. The instructor-to-instructee ratio is impressively high. A variety of intensive certification courses are available, with dive discounts for those who complete them.

Time-Savers

If you want to go on some advanced dives and you're already a qualified diver, don't forget to pack proof of certification.

For about $13 per day, concessions at Las Hadas and La Audiencia beaches on the Santiago Peninsula rent **snorkeling** gear. Equipment is also available at La Posada hotel at Playa Las Brisas. Playa La Audiencia and Playa Las Brisas are especially marine-life rich, so you won't be deprived if you stay put, but consider spending a second day snorkeling at the lagoon behind Playa Ventanas, south of downtown. It's a bit of a long haul by taxi or public transportation (you'd have to switch at downtown Manzanillo for a bus marked "Campos" and then take a taxi from the end of the line), but this **seahorse sanctuary** hosts some very rare specimens, including the Giant Pacific, which can grow to a foot long.

Getting Sloshed on Deck

The trimaran *Aguamundo* takes off from the Las Hadas marina at 5pm for Manzanillo's only booze cruise. While you're trying to slosh down your money's worth of domestic drinks, you'll tool around Manzanillo Bay, returning at 7pm. In addition to an open bar, your $23 buys you snacks and live guitar music—more romantic than the loud disco sounds that often blast from speakers on this type of excursion. Book through any travel agent, or buy a ticket when you get to Las Hadas—same difference.

Keeping Your Head Above Water: Exploring Manzanillo

Heading downtown from the north (if you're going by bus, take the one marked "Jardín") you'll pass what seems like miles of unloading containers, including humongous oil tankers arriving to store crude. Watching Mexico's largest commercial port in action may not be everyone's idea of a prime tourist activity, but if you're even mildly drawn to things industrial or nautical, you're bound to find it interesting (probably not enough to get out of the bus or cab, however).

You'll eventually come to the central Jardín (pronounced Har-*DEEN*) Alvaro Obregón, the city's prime people-watching spot; bands play in the ornate gazebo on cooler nights. The 1950s-style Bar Social on the northwest corner is where all the politicos hang out during their siestas, while the nearby Colonial, Manzanillo's first hotel, is somewhat faded but still worth peering into. Stroll down the main Avenida México and turn left at Cuauhtémoc to see the produce, meat, and fish (some of them live) at the central market— shopping in its primal state.

Dollars & Sense

Invest in your own mask, snorkel, and fins. You'll come out ahead if you use the inexpensive gear even four or five times—and you won't have to wonder who got up close and personal with the equipment before you did.

Stepping into the Past

Opened in late 1996, the free **Museo Universitario de Arqueologia** (Glorieta San Pedrito s/n, near the entrance to downtown; ☎ 333/3-3356) gathers pre-Hispanic artifacts from the state of Colima, including some found in the hills around the Las Hadas resort. The museum's five exhibit areas include the usual archaeological suspects—clay figurines, pottery shards, grinding stones, ax heads—as well as a rotating exhibit of Mexican art. The displays are perhaps less impressive than the gallery itself, modeled after the famed museum of anthropology in Mexico City. Well-designed, well-signed (in Spanish and English), and well air-conditioned (hey, don't knock it), this is a pleasant place to spend an hour. It's open 10am to 1pm and 5 to 8pm Tuesday through Saturday, and 10am to 1pm on Sunday. You can get here via any downtown bus.

The Sporting Life

If you really want to get moving, you can hit some tennis balls around at the **Hotel Sierra** (☎ 333/3-2000), which rents its four courts to non-guests for about $7 per hour in day, $10 at night (hey, electricity's expensive). Private lessons from the hotel's pro cost approximately $17 per hour. Not feeling quite so energetic? How 'bout hitting the links? Or better yet, let a horse do all the work.

Getting Tee'd Off

Manzanillo's **golf courses** are even more far-flung than most of the city's other attractions, but you won't be disappointed if you take the time to play the more remote ones. You may, however, have to pay royally for the privilege.

Best in greater Manzanillo is Las Hadas' spectacular **La Mantarraya** golf course, designed by Pete and Roy Dye. There are water traps on a total of 11 holes, including those created by the Salahua river, which weaves through the fairways. Flamingos, gulls, orange trees, and royal palms are all part of the lush landscape of this course, which costs $40 to play. In addition, a caddie will run you $8, a cart $28, and club rentals $20. Call ☎ 333/4-0000 to make reservations. Las Hadas guests have priority, of course, but you may luck out with a decent tee-time.

Bet You Didn't Know

Mantarraya means "sting ray." That's one of the sea creatures likely to eat your ball if it doesn't make it onto the green on the last hole, which overlooks the pounding surf.

It'll cost you $25 to play the more modest nine-hole course at the **Club Santiago** (Hwy. 200, km 19; ☎ 333/5-0370), plus $28 for a golf cart and $14 for equipment.

The Robert Von Hagge–designed **Isla Navidad Golf Course** (☎ 335/5-5050) near Barra de Navidad (see

"Getting Out of Manzanillo," below) is one of Mexico's newest, but it's already among the country's most popular places to tee off. Combining rugged dunes, a lagoon, and tropical terrain—not to mention the Pacific Ocean—this stunning 27-hole course is challenging on a lot of levels. Guests of the Grand Bay hotel, part of the new marina/golf complex, pay $65 to play; it's $100 (including cart) for day trippers.

About 1½ hours north of Manzanillo, the 18-hole, par 72 **El Tamarindo** course (Careyes, Jalisco; ☎ **335/1-5031**) was designed by golf architect David Fleming as part of a very exclusive lodging and residential complex that's not yet completed. Minimizing ecological impact was a prime directive, so as you hit the balls around, you'll come across large swatches of jungle treetops, brilliant flowers, and towering cactus counterpointed against the rolling greens, brilliant blue ocean, and black cliffs below. It'll cost you a whopping $110 for greens fees (including cart) and another $20 if you want a caddie—and of course there's the added expense of getting up here. Still, you'll be hard-pressed to find vistas more impressive than El Tamarindo's.

Riding Off into the Sunset

Cantering along the beach and trotting through the jungle—a cooler, if sometimes buggier, option—are both possibilities in Manzanillo. You can find your own steed at Playa Miramar near the Vista Playa de Oro hotel or book a ride through a travel agent for about $15 per hour. If you just want an animal gentle enough for kids, you can usually hire docile horses and ponies at La Boquita beach.

Better Shops Around

Sorry to report, much of Manzanillo has been declared a shopping-free zone. The gift shops of the more expensive hotels carry some Mexican crafts (Las Hadas's

Bug Off!

What's wrong with this picture? You're riding along a beautiful beach, watching the sun descend over an azure sea . . . and being devoured by mosquitoes. Don't forget your insect repellent if you're going out in the late afternoon.

Indigeno has a good, but pricey, selection), but for the most part you won't have to worry about breaking the bank at any of them. Ditto for the warren of shops downtown, where you'll find far more T-shirts and onyx chess sets than interesting folk art. You'll do as well for only slightly higher prices in Salagua's Plaza Manzanillo, which has the advantage of being air-conditioned (El Sol carries a nice selection of silver jewelry).

Centro Artesana Las Primeraveras (Av. Júrez 40 at Reforma in Santiago; ☎ **333/3-1699**) is your best bet for one-stop crafts shopping, with two disarrayed floors of paper flowers, pre-Hispanic style pottery, clay masks, furniture, and more. Don't be put off by the dust. Poke around and you'll be sure to find something.

It's a Dog's Life

The pot-bellied pottery canines you'll spot in some trinket shops are reproductions of the "Colima Dog," an ancient clay artifact discovered in many parts of the Mexican state where Manzanillo is located. The pups on which they're modeled are believed to have been kept as pets until they were plump enough to eat—or to be sacrificed in religious ceremonies. Rrruff stuff.

What to Do When the Sun's Gone Down

You're not likely to mistake the nightlife scene in Manzanillo for that in New York or L.A., but there are a few good places to let loose (or get tight) after the sun goes down.

At **Carlos 'n Charlie's** (Avenida Audiencia, at the beginning of Santiago Peninsula; ☎ 333/4-0555), adjoining the Guadalajara Grill, you can expect the typical raucous Carlos Anderson–chain fun. The same can be said for **Colima Bay,** Hwy. 200, km 8, Playa Azul (see chapter 32, "The Best of Manzanillo's Dining Scene"), which gave up its Carlos Anderson affiliation, but not its wacky sense of humor. **Ollas,** Blvd. Costera Miguel de la Madrid km 7.5 (see chapter 32), a beachside sports bar with pool tables and video games, is somewhat more laid back.

If you contract Saturday night fever, you might head for **Vog** (Hwy. 200, km 9 on Playa Azul; ☎ 333/4-1660) or the smaller **Baby Rock** in Santiago (Hwy. 200, km 14; ☎ 333/3-2839), although they're mainly magnets for Mexican teens. **Boom Boom** at Club Maeva attracts a somewhat older international crowd, but it's not always open to non-guests in high season. All have cover charges, and none get hopping until well after 11.

For live salsa or merengue, it's **Tropigala** (Hwy. 200, km 14, right next to Baby Rock; ☎ 333/3-2837); the $4 cover charge includes some snacks. Club Maeva's **Tropical Hut** at Club Maeva (see chapter 29) usually has live bands, too, but like Boom Boom lets outsiders in only if things are slow. Want to turn down the volume? There's a good bar and live music nightly at **Jalapeños** (see chapter 32) and a piano player tickles the ivories every night in **Las Hadas's lobby lounge** (see chapter 29).

Las Hadas also throws a great poolside **Mexican fiesta** on Saturday nights during high season; $23 buys you an open bar, buffet, mariachi music, and brightly clad dancers. True to its name, the **Fiesta Mexicana Hotel** (Santiago–Manzanillo Road, Playa Azul; ☎ 333/3-2180) lays on a food and music bash year-round on Friday nights. The price ($7.50) doesn't include drinks.

Getting Out of Manzanillo

If you're not staying in Barra de Navidad (see chapter 29, "Choosing the Place to Stay That's Right for You"), it's worth exploring on a day trip—especially while it's still quieter than Manzanillo. Culture vultures should set out for the state capital, Colima.

Barra de Navidad

Located on a gorgeous crescent-shaped beach with striking rock outcroppings, Barra de Navidad is about 65 miles north of Manzanillo. A continuous stretch of sand connects Barra with Melaque, another small beach town. Although the sand is softer near Melaque, Barra is by far the more charming of the two villages, with some brick and cobblestone streets and an increasing number of restaurants, bars, and shops. While in town, you can go sportsfishing in a panga, take a lagoon tour, hop on some water skis, or board a water taxi across the inlet to the Grand Bay Hotel to see how the other half lives.

No Boat to China

The Spanish sailed out from Barra de Navidad in 1564 in an attempt to locate China (they didn't find it). In the 17th century, the bay was a popular harbor and ship-building port.

Buses leave frequently from Manzanillo to Barra de Navidad and cost only about $1 for the 1½ hour trip. You can get buses from the *Central Camionera* (central bus terminal) downtown at Hidalgo and Aldama. The Elite, Transporte de Norte de Sonora, and Autotransportes del Pacifico bus lines all head north, so you should be able to catch a bus every half hour or so—but wait until you can get a first-class ride, which costs only a few pesos more than the far more uncomfortable second class.

Bet You Didn't Know

The recent movie *McHale's Navy* was filmed in Barra de Navidad.

If you go with a travel agency, it'll run you about $40, but you'll get air-conditioning, a stop at a banana and coconut plantation, and a seafood lunch. Tours leave at 9am and return at around 3pm.

Colima

Two good archaeological museums, lots of well-preserved colonial buildings, and crafts shops that sell reproductions of the Colima Dog are all reasons to trip out to the state capital, Colima, some 60 miles northeast of Manzanillo. Sitting at about 1,400 feet, the city also enjoys cooler temperatures. As backdrop, Colima has two ice-peaked volcanoes, both higher than 13,000 feet and one of them not quite dormant.

Less than 1½ hours away via a good toll road that continues on to Guadalajara, Colima can be reached by a number of Manzanillo bus lines. Tickets run anywhere from $3 on the kind of bus that carries live chickens to $5 on a first-class Mercedes-Benz bus. You can catch the first-class bus at the ETN bus station (Hwy. 200, km 17; ☎ **333/4-1060**); it runs about six times a day. Tour agencies will take you there for about $42 per person, including lunch; tours leave at 8am and return at 5pm.

Chapter 32

The Best of Manzanillo's Dining Scene

In This Chapter

➤ Dining in Manzanillo: The big picture

➤ Keeping costs down

➤ The best restaurants from A to Z

➤ Restaurant indexes

Leave those Chanel gowns and Armani suits at home: Manzanillo isn't a dress-up kind of town, although a couple of places can satisfy any preening instincts that might overtake you. Nor, with a few exceptions, does the city provide much fertile ground for foodies. But you can get wonderful seafood at great prices here, and you can always use the money you save to put on the ritz when you return.

A Dining Overview: Where's the Burrito?

There's a good chance you'll be eating where you're sleeping in Manzanillo, not only because of the abundance of all-inclusives and rooms with kitchens, but also because Manzanillo's restaurants are even more spread out than its hotels. In addition to the locations outlined in chapter 29, "Choosing the Place to Stay That's Right For You," I've also included a couple of new areas—Manzanillo Bay, Santiago Bay's sibling on the southern side of the Santiago peninsula, and Julúapan Peninsula, a largely residential area jutting out to the north of Santiago Bay.

Those who do venture out to explore Manzanillo's restaurants will be rewarded by extremely friendly service, more-than-reasonable prices, and good, fresh cooking. You won't find much in the way of upscale, trendy fare—although I've recommended a few places where you can get that, too—but if you've chosen to come to Manzanillo, that's probably not your priority.

If you're traveling with kids who require regular fast-food fixes, you'll have to break it to them gently that this is one of those outposts of the universe that McDonald's hasn't yet reached. The Guadalajara Grill, part of the Carlos Anderson chain, should have something to satisfy most children's need for the familiar, and this chapter lists other places they're likely to enjoy—look for the kids icon . No matter where you go, though, you're bound to find something for even the pickiest eater, whether it be a *hamburguesa* or a *quesadilla* (cheese crisp).

Not all the indoor restaurants here are air-conditioned—Mexicans have taken to this amenity slowly, and Manzanillo is a conservative town. If you're especially susceptible to the heat, check ahead on the warmest days or pick a place that has open-front dining rather than one with an outdoor terrace only. Mother Nature isn't always forthcoming with those cooling sea breezes, and overhead ceiling fans often give her a boost.

All restaurants are listed in alphabetical order, and then indexed by price and location.

Botanas, Booze, & Babes

Unique to the state of Colima is the **botanero,** a cantina where drinks come with free snacks or *botanas* (everything from pickled pigs' feet and fried pork rinds to ceviche, chicken wings, and tacos) and a Las Vegas–style show. Most botaneros open at about 2pm and close at around 8. You get a seat, order a round, and then eat and drink away the afternoon; you don't pay until you're ready to leave, at which time the empties at your table are toted up. Women are allowed in, and Mexican families even come here for special occasions, but shows tend to include lots of women wearing tight dresses, and things can get rowdy after 5 or 6pm, when everyone's had more than a few snootfulls. One of the most tourist-friendly botaneros is **El Caporal** (Costera Miguel de la Madrid, km 6; ☎ **333/3-0450**), set in a large, tented yard with a raised stage.

Check, Please

It's easy to eat within your means in Manzanillo, even taking into account the occasional splurge. Still, if you're not careful, you can find yourself spending more than you intended—or needed—to. For some help in this area, check "Eating Well without Gobbling Up Your Budget" in chapter 7.

Don't worry about taxes; the 15% surcharge has already been included in your bill. The tip isn't, however. The standard in nice restaurants is 15%.

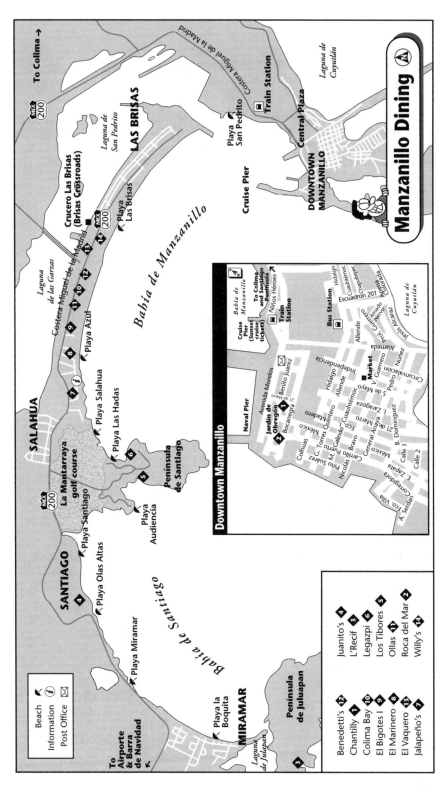

Manzanillo Dining Ⓝ

To Colima →

MEX 200

LAS BRISAS

Costera Miguel de la Madrid

Laguna de San Pedro

Playa San Pedrito

Crucero Las Brisas (Brisas Crossroads)

MEX 200

Playa Las Brisas

Train Station

Central Plaza

Cruise Pier

DOWNTOWN MANZANILLO

Laguna de Cuyutlán

Laguna de las Garzas

Costera Miguel de la Madrid

Laguna de las Garzas

Playa Azul

Playa Salahua

Bahía de Manzanillo

SALAHUA

MEX 200

Playa Las Hadas

La Mantarraya golf course

Playa Santiago

Península de Santiago

Playa Audiencia

SANTIAGO

Playa Olas Altas

Playa Miramar

Bahía de Santiago

MIRAMAR

Playa la Boquita

Península de Juluapan

Laguna de Juluapan

To Airporte & Barra de Navidad

Downtown Manzanillo

Ⓝ

To Colima and Santiago Península ↗

Niños Héroes

Bahía de Manzanillo

Cruise Pier (Sunset cruise tickets)

Naval Pier

Avenida Morelos

Jardín de Obregón

Benito Juárez

Bocanegra

21 de Marzo

Train Station

Escuadron 201

Hidalgo

Cuauhtémoc

Colorada

Arena

Arnulfo Colorada

Bus Station

Allende

Alameda

Jesús Cuautémoc

Independencia

Circunvalación

Hidalgo

Allende

5 de Mayo

Market

V. Guerrero

Pedro Núñez

Laguna de Cuyutlán

Colnuas

G. Torres Quintero

Pino Suárez

Nicolás

Camillo Puerto

Galindo

Cuauhtémoc

Bravo

Madero

Zaragoza

General Anaya

I. Zaragoza

México

B. Domínguez

21 de Marzo

México

Fco Villa

Corregidora

Calle 1

Calle 2

E. Zapata

A. Serdán

Legend

- Beach ⚓
- Information ⓘ
- Post Office ✉

- Benedetti's ⑫
- Chantilly ①
- Colima Bay ⑩
- El Bigotes I ⑨
- El Marinero ⑧
- El Vaquero ⑬
- Jalapeño's ⑦
- Juanito's ④
- L'Recif ③
- Legazpi ⑥
- Los Tibores ⑪
- Ollas ⑪
- Roca del Mar ②
- Willy's ⑫

Mexicans rarely tip that well in less pricey places—10% is about average—but if the service was good, stick with the 15% rule. You can afford to be a bit more generous.

As part of the effort to help you stay within budget, I've arranged my price categories with the worst-case scenario in mind. They're based on a per-person dinner tab that includes appetizer, entrée, dessert, one drink, and tip. In addition, a price range for dinner entrées is included in the individual reviews. It's simple: The more $ signs, the more you'll be shelling at each restaurant.

$	=	Under $10
$$	=	$10–$20
$$$	=	$20–$35
$$$$	=	Over $35

Note: Because lobster runs so much higher than the other entrées, unless it's a major part of the menu, the price ranges noted below are exclusive of the costly crustacean.

Unless otherwise specified, reservations are not accepted or not necessary.

My Favorite Restaurants from A to Z

Benedetti's
$. Las Brisas. PIZZA.

A pizza joint is a pizza joint, and this one doesn't transcend the genre. But you'll get decent, thick-crust (only occasionally soggy) pies with good, fresh-tasting toppings—ham, mushrooms, chorizo, jalapeños, onions, or just plain cheese. Burgers, sandwiches, calzones, pastas, and even a reasonable salad are offered, too. You can get your pizza delivered to your hotel room, but don't expect Domino's-style swiftness.

Calle del Mar no. 1 (on the left just after the Las Brisas crossroad turnoff). ☎ *333/3-1592 or 4-0141.* **Main courses:** *Pizza $3.50 (small, plain) to $19 (mega, with everything); everything else $4–$6.50. AE, MC, V.* **Open:** *Daily 10am–6pm.*

Local Favorites

Chantilly (Downtown, $)

El Vaquero (Las Brisas, $$)

Chantilly
$. Downtown. MEXICAN/ ECLECTIC.

Come to this modest, open-front restaurant for the huge *comida corrida* (set-price meal) priced at $4.50 and served from 1pm to 4pm. As you make your way through a meal that might start with fresh fruit cocktail and proceed through soup, a meat course, dessert, and coffee, you can watch practically everyone in

Manzanillo pass through the central town square. For breakfast, you can get everything from hotcakes to *huevos rancheros* with fresh-squeezed orange juice; if you need a banana split, that's on Chantilly's huge menu, too.

Av. Juárez and Madero (just across from the plaza). ☎ **333/2-0194. Main courses:** *$2–$4.50.* AE, MC, V. **Open:** *Daily Sun–Fri 8am–10pm.*

 Kids **Colima Bay**
$$–$$$. Manzanillo Bay.
MEXICAN/SEAFOOD.

The name may have changed, but Colima Bay still has the same madcap decor and haywire attitude of its former incarnation as a Carlos 'n Charlie's. Come early and you can enjoy a quiet, romantic dinner at one of the tables looking out on the sea; come later and you'll be greeted with a free tequila slammer and may end up literally swinging from the rafters in the front room. The cocolima appetizer, a coconut filled with mixed seafood, is delicious, as are the *molcajete* entrées—shrimp, chicken, and beef served on a stone platter with salsa, onions, and fresh cheese. Ribs, burgers, and chicken fingers are definite kid-pleasers. If your Spanish is sketchy—although it might seem perfect to you by the end of an evening here—ask your waiter to translate the home-remedy hangover cure on the back of the menu.

> **Yo, Gringo!**
>
> Remember, it's considered impolite in Mexico for the waiter to bring the check before you ask for it.

Hwy. 200, km 8, Playa Azul. ☎ **333/3-1150. Main courses:** *$5–$14.* AE, MC, V. **Open:** *Mon–Sat 2pm–midnight (bar open later) high season; Mon–Sat 5pm–midnight low season.*

El Bigotes I
$$. Manzanillo Bay. SEAFOOD.

Don't leave Manzanillo without at least one seafood pigout at this beachside, open-air restaurant, a local favorite replete with strolling mariachis. You might start off with the Colima style–ceviche (fish marinated in lime and then chopped up with cilantro, tomato, and carrots) or with the seafood salad, more like standard ceviche but combining conch, squid, shrimp, and scallops. Mahi-mahi *serreando,* grilled with onions and chiles, is a great-tasting, healthy entrée. You can order almost every type of fish in a variety of

> **Best Seafood**
>
> El Bigotes I (Manzanillo Bay, $$)
>
> **Best Gringo Fix**
>
> Juanito's (Santiago Bay, $)

styles—with garlic butter, hot sauce, or "drunken" (cooked in tequila). Lunch is for fish-lovers only, but steak and poultry pop up the dinner menu. There's

a second Bigotes restaurant on Carretera Manzanillo-Santiago, km 4.5
(☎ **333/6-5043**).

Costera Miguel de la Madrid 3517, on Playa Azul. ☎ ***333/4-0831*** *or 333/
4-0341.* **Main courses:** *$5.50–$12.50. DC, MC, V.* **Open:** *Daily 1pm–1am.*

El Marinero
$$$. Manzanillo Bay. SPANISH.
Owned by a native of Spain, this restaurant is popular for its authentic
Iberian cuisine, its casual but upscale nautical atmosphere, its ocean view—
and its air-conditioning. El Marinero may be considered expensive by locals,
but portions of entrées such as the excellent baked leg of lamb are huge, and
the seafood-packed paella, intended for two, could easily feed three or four.
Start out sharing; in the unlikely event you're still hungry, you can always
order more. The $6.50 lunch buffet, featuring some of the same dishes, is a
favorite with successful business types, who no doubt got that way because
they could spot a good deal.

Marbella Hotel, Costero Miguel de la Madrid, km 9.5. ☎ ***333/3-1105*** *or 3-1103.*
Reservations suggested in high season. **Main courses:** *$9–$15. AE, DC, MC, V.*
Open: *Daily 8am–11pm.*

El Vaquero
$$. Las Brisas. STEAKHOUSE.
This here's big meat heaven—exactly what you might figure to find at a place
named for the Mexican cowboy. Whichever cut of beef or sausage you
choose will be grilled tableside and served with soupy beans. Sweet grilled
onions, guacamole, baked potatoes, and melted cheese are extra. Try the
arrachera especial, a thick flank steak marinated until it's butter-soft.
Everything is priced by the kilo (2.2 pounds); unless you've been fasting for
days, two of you should easily get by with a half kilo. The decor is as stereo-
typically western as you might expect, air-conditioning aside.

Crucero Las Brisas 19. ☎ ***333/3-1654.*** **Main courses:** *Steak about $16 per kilo;*
sausage about $12 per kilo. MC, V. **Open:** *Daily 2–11pm.*

Jalapeño's
$$. Manzanillo Bay. MEXICAN/SEAFOOD.
Far more romantic than its peppery name and outdoor neon sign would sug-
gest, Jalapeño's seats its devoted customers in a pretty, coral-colored room,
with brick walls, beamed ceilings, and cushy booths. No matter what you
order—the chicken, beef, and shrimp fajitas, or a combo plate of chile rel-
lenos, enchiladas, steak tips, and quesadillas—you can expect huge quantities
of food to arrive at your table. The bar has 100 different kinds of tequila, and
the owner recommends Sexy Coffee (flaming brandy and kahlua with coffee,
ice cream, and sugar) for dessert, although he disclaims all responsibility if
you order it. A branch of this restaurant just opened in Barra de Navidad.

Costera Miguel de la Madrid, km 10. ☎ *333/
3-2075. **Main courses:** $4.50–$8.50
(lobster $15). AE, MC, V. **Open:** Daily 5pm–
midnight.*

Juanito's
Kids *$. Santiago Bay.*
AMERICAN/MEXICAN.
American expats and long-term visitors
eventually turn up at one of Juanito's colorful red-and-green checked tables,
whether they have a yen for a milkshake,
ribs, a burger, or fried chicken, or want to
catch the Green Bay game on satellite TV.
The friendly diner is owned by an
American/Mexican couple, which means
you'll find an equal—and equally good—representation of the local cuisine.
Have breakfast here if you want to start your day off right.

**As American as . . .
Refried Beans?**

Historians say the cowboy is
an offshoot of the Mexican
vaquero, who rode the
range far earlier than our
Wild West icons. (It was the
Spanish who introduced
horses into the New World.)

Costera Miguel de la Madrid, km 14. ☎ *333/3-1388. **Main courses:** $1.50–$4.
AE, MC, V. **Open:** Daily 8am–11pm.*

Legazpi
$$$–$$$$. Santiago Peninsula.
INTERNATIONAL.
Las Hadas's premier restaurant is pull-out-
the-stops romantic, replete with glittering
chandeliers, intimate dining nooks, and
impeccable but not hoity-toity service.
Whether you eat indoors or on the adjoin-
ing terrace, you'll enjoy gorgeous bay
views. The food and presentation are duly
impressive—how many places still serve
palate-cleansing sorbets between courses?
You might start with a classic Caesar salad
or lobster bisque and then move on to
raviolis stuffed with foie gras, duck breast
with lemon sauce, or Chateaubriand for two. Be sure to save room for the
warm raspberry tart or the chocolate Charlotte.

**Most Romantic
Restaurants**

Legazpi (Santiago Peninsula,
$$$–$$$$)

L'Recif (Julúapan Peninsula,
$$–$$$)

Willy's (Las Brisas, $$$)

Camino Real Las Hadas Hotel, Peninsula de Santiago. ☎ *333/4-0000.
Reservations required. **Main courses:** $9–$18. AE, DC, MC, V. **Open:** Daily
6pm–midnight, high season only.*

Los Tibores
$$–$$$. Santiago Peninsula. CONTINENTAL.
You might not expect an all-inclusive hotel, even one as upscale as the Sierra,
to have a gourmet fine-dining room, but Los Tibores falls outside many

norms. The menu is not only adventurous—you'll find zucchini flower, corn, and mushroom crêpes among the appetizers, and fettuccine with clams in a smoked tomato and chipotle pepper sauce among the entrées—but it also has heart-healthy listings, extremely rare in Mexico. Even classic dishes such as veal medaillons in basil have a light touch—and so do most of the prices. The room is lovely in an understatedly elegant way, but because there's no terrace, it can get smoky.

Hotel Sierra, Av. de la Audiencia no. 1, Peninsula de Santiago. ☎ **333/3-2000.** *Reservations required.* **Main courses:** *$6.50–$12.50 (lobster extra). AE, DC, MC, V.* **Open:** *Mon–Sat 7am–11pm.*

L'Recif
$$–$$$. Julúapan Peninsula. CONTINENTAL.
En route to this restaurant, perched on the tip of Santiago Bay's northern peninsula, you may begin to wonder if your cabbie took a wrong turnoff to Central America. Relax. It takes forever to get here, but it's worth it when you do. Not so much for the food, which is fine if rather retro—they're overly fond of setting dishes on fire—but rather for the astounding surf and cliff views. The Continental menu focuses on seafood, including oyster soup and the signature L'Recif shrimp in garlic butter and white wine. End your meal with crêpe suzettes if you don't mind the attention. The white-clothed tables are arranged in an open-front palapa and on a terrace nearer to the cliff's edge. Prices are quite reasonable by U.S. standards, but you've got to factor in a $15 round-trip cab ride.

Cerro del Cenicero s/n, at Vida del Mar, Julúapan Peninsula. ☎ **333/5-0900.** *Reservations suggested.* **Main courses** *$6–$11.50. AE, MC, V.* **Open:** *Daily 2pm–midnight.*

Ollas
Kids
$$. Manzanillo Bay. MEXICAN/SEAFOOD.
You can easily spend the day hanging around this colorful, thatched-roof restaurant. Have some *huevos rancheros* for breakfast, and then go directly out to the beach or to a pool filled with miniature bumper cars—kid paradise. Later, you can order from the casual lunch/dinner menu—say, the catch-of-the-day Ollas style, stuffed with seafood and smothered with melted cheese (but I don't advise going swimming directly afterward). Steak, pasta, and tacos are also available. Stick around until 4pm and a guitar player starts tuning up. There's even a good sports bar downstairs (see chapter 31, "Fun On & Off the Beach") that you can retire to after dinner.

Costera Miguel de la Madrid, km 7.5. ☎ **333/4-0383.** **Main courses:** *$4–$9.50 (lobster extra). AE, MC, V.* **Open:** *Tues–Sun 7am–1am.*

Roca del Mar
$. Downtown. MEXICAN.
A bit more open to the breeze and more cheerful than Chantilly (see above), which is just across the main plaza, Roca del Mar has a similar menu,

although it's in Spanish only. You can tuck into seafood cocktails, sandwiches, enchiladas, or grilled steaks, or just linger over espresso while watching the constant parade of passersby through the main square.

21 de Marzo 204 (between Av. Moreles and Av. Juárez). ☎ *333/3-0302.* **Main courses:** *$1.75–$6. MC, V.* **Open:** *Daily 7:30am–10:30pm.*

Willy's
$$$. Las Brisas. FRENCH/SEAFOOD.

This barefoot elegant restaurant, with a terrace directly on the beach, is a favorite of locals and tourists alike; some visitors have been known to eat here every night of their stay. The views across Manzanillo Bay are killer—you can see the harbor and Las Hadas—and so is the food, French with a contemporary twist. Starters include a luscious lobster terrine and robalo salad with chiles; for a main course, you might choose jumbo shrimp wrapped in bacon and cheese or mahi-mahi with mango. Finish off with the fabulous chocolate-rich profiteroles.

Carretera Las Brisas, just off Hwy. 200. ☎ *333/3-1794.* *Reservations required.* **Main courses:** *$8–$15. AE, MC, V.* **Open:** *Daily 7pm–midnight.*

Sound Bites: Manzanillo's Restaurants at a Glance
Restaurant Index by Price

$

Benedetti's (Las Brisas, Pizza)

Chantilly (Downtown, Mexican/Eclectic)

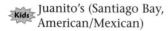 Juanito's (Santiago Bay, American/Mexican)

Roca del Mar (Downtown, Mexican)

$$

El Bigotes I (Manzanillo Bay, Seafood)

El Vaquero (Las Brisas, Steakhouse)

Jalapeño's (Manzanillo Bay, Mexican/Seafood)

Ollas (Manzanillo Bay, Mexican/Seafood)

$$–$$$

Colima Bay (Manzanillo Bay, Mexican/Seafood)

Los Tibores (Santiago Peninsula, Continental)

L'Recif (Julúapan Peninsula, Continental)

$$$

El Marinero (Manzanillo Bay, Spanish)

Willy's (Las Brisas, French/Seafood)

$$$–$$$$

Legazpi (Santiago Peninsula, International)

Restaurant Index by Location

Downtown

Chantilly $

Roca del Mar $

Las Brisas

Benedetti's $

El Vaquero $$

Willy's $$$

Santiago Bay

Kids Juanito's $

Manzanillo Bay

Colima Bay $$–$$$

El Bigotes I $$

El Marinero $$$

Jalapeño's $$

Kids Ollas $$

Santiago Peninsula

Legazpi $$$–$$$$

Los Tibores $$–$$$

Julúapan Peninsula

L'Recif $$–$$$

Part 9

Puerto Vallarta

Puerto Vallarta is no longer the sleepy fishing village of 1963, when Liz and Dick's doings on the set of Night of the Iguana *(known locally as "The Movie") drew the international press corps here, but it still has the world's attention as a prime place to vacation, both for its cobblestoned past and its glitzy present.*

If you're here on a weeklong vacation, your biggest problem might be fitting in a host of dry-dock activities while setting aside sufficient stretches of kick-back beach time. Oh, and there's also the which-great-restaurant-should-I-go-to-tonight dilemma. But that's what I'm here for. The next few chapters will help you streamline your choices so that whatever you decide to do, from budget to deluxe, will be top of the line.

Chapter 33

Choosing the Place to Stay That's Right for You

In This Chapter

➤ Where the hotels are

➤ The best in the bunch

➤ Hotel indexes

You'd be hard-pressed to find a beach resort that offers a wider range of places to lay your weary head than Puerto Vallarta. You can sequester yourself in luxury lodgings far from the hubbub, stay downtown in charming Mexican digs, opt for an all-inclusive resort in the hotel zone—and more.

Getting from one section of town to another is no great problem for the most part, but where you decide to bed down will still have a big impact on your vacation. So in this chapter, I'll give you an overview of the areas where Puerto Vallarta's hotels are concentrated, summing up their pros and cons. Then I'll list my favorite hotels alphabetically and follow up with a few alternatives should my A-list choices be filled. At the end of the chapter, you'll find at-a-glance indexes listing the hotels by price and by location.

As far as prices go, I've noted rack rates (the maximum that a resort or hotel charges for a room) in the listings. This information will give you some sense of what to expect, although I know you'll avoid paying rack by following the advice I gave you in chapter 6, "The Lowdown on Accommodations in Mexico." I've also put a dollar sign icon in front of each hotel listing so you can quickly see whether it's within your budget. The more $ signs under the name, the more you pay. It runs like this:

$	=	$90 and below
$$	=	$90–$145
$$$	=	$145–$235
$$$$	=	$235 and above

Unless specified, rates are for a standard double room in high season (around December 20 through April 19th). The rest of the year, prices plummet from 20% to 50%. During Christmas and Easter weeks, you can expect to pay as much as 25% above the usual high-season rates—if you can get a room. The prices listed below include the 17% room tax.

A kid-friendly icon [Kids] highlights hotels that are especially good for families. All hotels have air-conditioning unless otherwise indicated, and if the review doesn't say anything to the contrary, you can safely assume that you can walk directly out of your hotel and onto the beach.

Hint: As you read through the reviews, you'll want to keep track of the ones that appeal to you. I've included a chart at the end of the book (see p. 542) where you can rank your preferences, but to make matters easier on yourself now, why don't you just put a little check mark next to the ones you like? Remember how your teachers used to tell you not to write in your books? Now's the time to rebel, so scrawl away!

Location, Location, Location

In hotel real-estate terms, the catchall name "Puerto Vallarta" covers a major geographical spread, crossing over Mexican state lines and encompassing miles of coast curving around Mexico's largest natural bay, the Bay of Banderas. My summaries of the various hotel enclaves start in the north in the state of Nayarit and continue south into Jalisco beyond Puerto Vallarta's downtown.

Nuevo Vallarta: Northern (Under)Exposure

Carved out of a mangrove swamp some $3\frac{1}{2}$ miles north of the Puerto Vallarta airport in the early 1980s, the Nuevo Vallarta complex was designed for the high life, with luxury homes, condos, and a marina. It still hasn't quite taken off; so far, there are less than a dozen lodgings, running the gamut from low-key bungalows to high-rise resorts. Which is not a bad thing, if you enjoy quiet. You've got all the modern amenities—and the surrounding jungle, where you can spot creatures such as iguanas, deer, and even crocodiles. Miles of flat roads meandering through the complex are ideal for walking, running, biking, and bird watching (keep an eye out for great white herons), and the beaches are superb and fairly vendor free. After a few days here, a trip into Puerto Vallarta feels like culture shock.

Of course, swamps mean mosquitoes—and if they're not around, it's because of major pesticide action. Although there are enough shops and restaurants to keep you souvenired and fed, you'll be far from the really good food and retail shops. It takes at least 45 minutes to get into town by taxi and it'll run you between $15 to $20. Buses cost less than a dollar, but you'll double your travel time and discomfort level.

In a nutshell . . .

➤ Remote and quiet

➤ Great, hassle-free beaches

➤ Lots of natural attractions and outdoor activities

➤ Fairly close to the airport

but . . .

➤ You're far from the center of things.

➤ Public transportation into town takes forever, and cabs are pricey.

➤ Many places have hard-sell timeshares.

➤ Mosquitoes like it here, too.

Marina Vallarta: The Yacht Set Suburb

One of Puerto Vallarta's newest developments, the Marina Vallarta complex has caught on more quickly than a trendy L.A. restaurant—although it's clearly here to stay. Storefronts are filling with restaurants, boutiques, and minimarts, and expensive apartments are getting snapped up by the wealthy and powerful—as are guest rooms in the rows of deluxe hotels that line the boulevards. The marina itself, sister to Marina del Rey in California, is considered by the cognoscenti to be the best on Mexico's Pacific Coast. Stay here and you'll have great fishing charters at your doorstep, as well as a world-class golf course and even a bowling alley. The complex is sparklingly pretty, clean, and well serviced by public transportation.

Of course, none of this comes cheap. You'll find few hotel bargains here, nor will you experience much local color. Moreover, because the marina was created out of landfill, the beaches are nothing to write home about: They are narrow and rough, and the waterfront is pebbly. And you won't starve or go shopless here by any means, but the best restaurants and galleries are downtown, which is about half an hour away.

In a nutshell . . .

➤ It's clean, pristine, and pretty.

➤ Hotels are exclusive and luxurious.

➤ You're near lots of sports facilities, restaurants, and shops.

➤ You're 5 minutes from the airport.

but . . .

➤ The beaches are not very good.

➤ It's expensive.

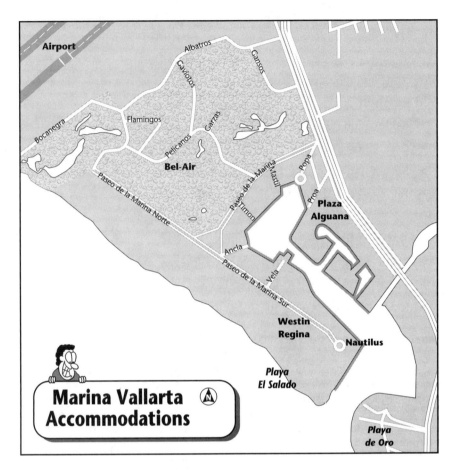

Marina Vallarta Accommodations (A)

(Map labels: Airport, Albatros, Gaviotas, Cansos, Bocanegra, Flamingos, Garzas, Pelicanos, Bel-Air, Paseo de la Marina, Mastil, Popa, Proa, Plaza Alguana, Paseo de la Marina Norte, Patrimon, Ancla, Vela, Paseo de la Marina Sur, Westin Regina, Nautilus, Playa El Salado, Playa de Oro)

➤ There's little authentic Mexican character.

➤ It's a trip to downtown, where the shopping and restaurants are better.

The Hotel Zone: The Middle Road

When tourists began their big-time descent on Puerto Vallarta in the 1970s, savvy international hotel chains began staking out oceanside lots north of downtown. The stretch of high-rises that sprouted beyond Old Puerto Vallarta quickly became known as the Hotel Zone. If you wanted both modern amenities and easy access to the city center, this was the place to stay. The arrival of the high-glitz Marina Vallarta complex to the north in the mid-1980s stripped many of the more modest hotel-zone properties of their cachet, but it also added to their visitors' options; stay here, and on any given day you can decide whether you feel like going down or up on the social scale—or just happily straddle the middle ground.

The long beach fronting the hotel zone is far nicer than those in either Marina Vallarta or downtown, with smoother sand and more water sports concessions than the former and fewer crowds than the latter. You won't be in the cultural heart of town, but neither will you be cut off from everyday Mexican life; beyond the rows of hotels, this is largely a middle-class residential area. However, there's not much in the way here of scenic strolling, along

374

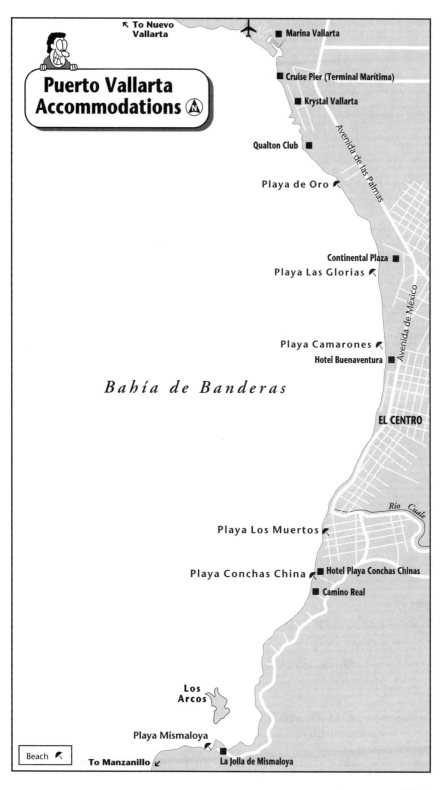

Puerto Vallarta Accommodations

To Nuevo Vallarta

Marina Vallarta

Cruise Pier (Terminal Marítima)

Krystal Vallarta

Qualton Club

Playa de Oro

Avenida de las palmas

Continental Plaza

Playa Las Glorias

Avenida de México

Playa Camarones

Hotel Buenaventura

Bahía de Banderas

EL CENTRO

Río Cuale

Playa Los Muertos

Playa Conchas China

Hotel Playa Conchas Chinas

Camino Real

Los Arcos

Playa Mismaloya

Beach

To Manzanillo

La Jolla de Mismaloya

either a pretty dock or cobblestone streets, nor are there many gourmet restaurants or interesting nightspots. You'll have to bus it or cab it back to your room if you want to amble around after a great meal.

In a nutshell . . .

➤ There's a good range of hotels.

➤ It's convenient to both downtown and Marina Vallarta.

➤ It's less formal—and less expensive—than Marina Vallarta, with far better beaches.

but . . .

➤ There are fewer great restaurants and nightspots than there are downtown.

➤ There's nowhere to take a nice after-dinner stroll.

➤ You'll have to bus it or cab it to both Marina Vallarta and downtown.

South of Town: A Luxurious Stretch

Unlike downtown or the hotel areas to the north, the stretch of town south of the center doesn't really have a distinct character—in part because it's so spread out. As you wind your way down Highway 200 towards Mismaloya Beach, considered the southern limit of Puerto Vallarta, you'll pass capacious private homes, expensive condo complexes—and a few luxury hotels.

Stay at one of these and you'll be away from it all—but perhaps a bit too far. Your hotel will probably have a fine beach and all the material comforts, but leave it and you'll find little to keep you occupied. Buses to the center are slow, and it'll cost you about five bucks every time you want to cab it downtown.

In a nutshell . . .

➤ It's a good escape route.

➤ The beaches are nice and, in some cases, uncrowded.

➤ Hotels are generally luxurious.

but . . .

➤ You'll be cut off from the center of town, with no shops or restaurants around.

➤ Transportation is either slow or costly.

➤ Most of the hotels are expensive.

Downtown: Old Puerto Vallarta

If you want the charm of a traditional Mexican village with all the perks of contemporary city life, this is the place to park yourself. You can catch a baptism at Our Lady of Guadalupe church, listen to mariachis at the open-air

Los Arcos theater, join young Mexican lovers strolling the *malecón* (seaside promenade)—or shop at tony art galleries, dine at some of the most sophisticated restaurants in Mexico, and check out a cabaret at a gay disco. For better or worse, even McDonald's, KFC, and Hooters are here.

Most of the hotels in this area are south of the Río Cuale, where you'll also find the popular Los Muertos beach—good if you like action, but bad if you're trying to stake out a secluded spot in the sand or avoid beach peddlers. You can expect downtown's digs to be small and family-run. Few are expensive, but they're rarely quiet or luxurious, either.

In a nutshell . . .

➤ There's a great Mexican village atmosphere.

➤ You can walk to the best shops and restaurants in town.

➤ The hotels are inexpensive.

but . . .

➤ You'll have to travel to find a secluded beach.

➤ It can get pretty noisy at night.

➤ You won't find many luxury amenities.

My Favorite Hotels from A to Z

Bahia del Sol Resort
$$. Nuevo Vallarta.

A hidden gem in Nuevo Vallarta, this intimate all-suites hotel is for those seeking low-key relaxation at a low-key price. The ample rooms—basic with cheerful Mexican touches—all have kitchenettes, but no TVs or telephones; sliding glass doors open onto either balconies or patios. Lounge under a palapa at the beach, rousing yourself only to order some good grilled shrimp from the hotel restaurant, or surround yourself with flowers by the shaded pool. If you wander over to the south boundary of the property, one of the biologists at the Federal Marine Studies Center turtle hatchery might invite you to take part in its turtle-release program.

Best Bets for Lovers

Bahia del Sol Resort (Nuevo Vallarta, $$)

Krystal Vallarta (Hotel Zone, $$$)

Sierra Plaza Golf and Spa Hotel (Marina Vallarta, $$$$)

Paseo Cocteros and Cozumel s/n, Nuevo Vallarta Nayarit. ☎ *and fax* **329/ 7-0527,** *7-0526, or 7-0527.* **Rack rate:** *$111 double. MC, V.*

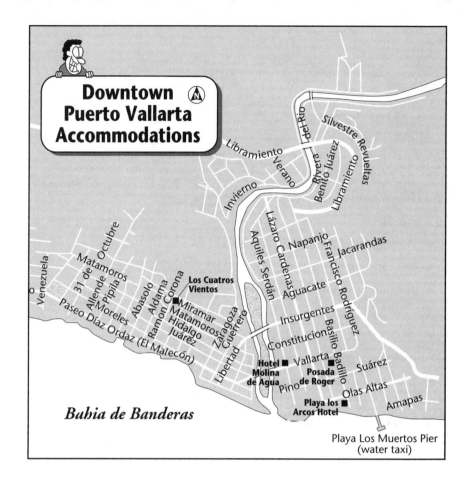

Downtown Puerto Vallarta Accommodations

Camino Real

$$$$. South of Town.

Dazzling Mexican design makes a stay at the Camino Real memorable, from the whitewashed stucco walls and extra-large *matromonial* hammocks on your room's terrace, to the blue-glass chandelier of the beachside buffet restaurant and the domed ceiling of La Perla, the hotel's terrific fine-dining room (try the margarita scallops with mild poblano chiles if they're on the menu). This early Puerto Vallarta hotel pioneer snagged one of the best beaches in town, a long white stretch of sand with a dramatic mountain backdrop. The shopping arcade has a good art gallery, and if you're both aesthete and athlete, you'll enjoy looking at the mural by Puerto Vallarta's famed naif painter, Manuel Lepe, while sweating it out at the health club.

*Playa Las Estacas s/n, at km 3.2 of Hwy. 200. ☎ 800/722-6466 or 322/ 1-5000. Fax 322/1-6000. www.caminoreal.com/puertovallarta/. E-mail: pvr@caminoreal.com. **Rack rates:** $205–$246 double; suites start at $263. Discounted rates for stays of 6 nights and more. AE, DC, MC, V.*

Continental Plaza

$$$. Hotel Zone.

Part of a bustling hotel complex in the busy Villas Vallarta shopping center, the Continental Plaza appeals to extroverts. Happy-faced activity directors keep up the pace around the pool where singles and roving-eye business travelers mingle at water volleyball and group exercise—often to a heavy metal beat. The property sits on a great beach, it's got a good health club, and it has the best tennis facilities in town (lots of Mexican tournaments are held here, but Wimbledon has no cause for concern). Bas-relief seashell headboards and beamed ceilings lend a bit of character to the ample rooms. If you enjoy sleeping, avoid those on the lower floors, which look out on the pool; upper-level units with ocean views are quieter. The on-site restaurants, including the oceanfront Los Pesces for seafood and Cantaros for international and Mexican cuisine are decent, and you only need to step out the door to find sushi, Italian, and German food.

Yo, Gringo!

Be sure to check that your vacation dates don't coincide with spring break—unless you like falling asleep (or trying to) to the sound of crashing furniture.

Blvd. Francisco Medina Ascencío s/n, on Playa de Las Glorias. ☎ **800/88-CONTI** *or 322/4-0123. Fax 322/4-4437.* **Rack rate:** *$181 double. AE, MC, V.*

Hotel Buenaventura

$$. Hotel Zone.

This friendly beachside hotel has a great location at the southern end of the hotel zone, 5 minutes from Old Vallarta, and a price that'll appeal to peso pinchers. It's got character, too, with a blue-domed, Moorish-style exterior, open lobby, and beamed-ceiling rooms. Rooms on the ground floors smell musty and are viewless; try to get an upper interior one with a balcony. You can breathe in fresh salt air while exercising at an oceanside gym and soak in invigorating negative ions at the outdoor Jacuzzi afterward. This is a cutoffs and tank-top kind of place and both restaurants are accordingly casual, but the food is surprisingly good.

Av. México 1301. ☎ **322/2-3737.** *Fax 322/2-3546. www.puerto-vallarta.com/ buenaventura. E-mail: buenaven@pvnet.com.mx.* **Rack rate:** *$123 double. AE, MC, V.*

Hotel Molina de Agua

$$. Downtown.

A hidden treasure in the heart of the south-of-the-river tourist zone, this sprawling red-tile-roof complex hugged by both the ocean and the Río Cuale has been in the same family since the 1950s; Mexicans and Europeans in the know have been returning here year after year. After enjoying a great $4.50

Most Mexicana

If you want a taste of traditional Mexico in Puerto Vallarta, check out **Hotel Molina de Agua.**

breakfast buffet at the Lion's Court, you can stroll through the tropical gardens, watch the antics of the caged parrots, soak in a Jacuzzi in a rock grotto, or hang out in a hammock under a huge rubber tree. All the rooms ooze Old Mexico charm, but lack TVs and telephones. The step-up platforms on the beds in the oceanfront units can be bad news in the middle of the night—especially if you've been hitting the local bars—and units closest to the front get some street noise. Best are the partial oceanview doubles that flank the beachside pool.

Ignacio L. Vallarta 130. ☎ **322/2-1957** *or 322/2-1907. Fax 322/2-6056. www.go2vallarta.com. E-mail molina@acnet.net.mx.* **Rack rates:** *$88–$111 Garden area cabin; $135 junior suite. AE, MC, V.*

Hotel Playa Conchas Chinas
$$. South of Town.
Many painters and writers enjoy the seclusion, Old Mexico charm, and reasonable rates of Playa Conchas Chinas, which clings to the rocks above the beach for which it's named. A rabbit warren of halls and stairways lead to rooms quaintly decorated with Talavera tiles and leaded glass lamps (but with newly redone kitchens); each has a balcony overlooking the beach. You can relax around the pool or enjoy the sunset or a summer storm at the palapa restaurant/bar at the water's edge. It's a beautiful, if longish, stroll north along the beach into town. Now if only you didn't have to climb all those stairs to your room when you returned . . .

Mismaloya Hwy. 200, km 2.5. ☎ **322/1-5770** *or 322/1-5230. Fax 322/ 1-5763.* **Rack rate:** *$105 double. MC, V.*

Hotel Sierra
$$$. Nuevo Vallarta.
No fuss, no muss. Book a room at this large, luxurious all-inclusive and you'll have your day arranged, from the morning buffet breakfast to the nonstop poolside activities, beach parties, excursions, and cabarets or karaoke fests after dark. There are tons of water toys to play with, and a nice, wide beach to snooze on. Cocktails flow freely and the food is fine, if not exactly gourmet; basics like shrimp, chicken, and steak are well prepared. Aside from the accents of the staff and a few of your fellow guests, it won't feel much like Mexico, however. The dominant hotel color is beige and the rooms are pastel-generic. Still, they're airy and comfortable, with updated amenities such as hair dryers and HBO; some have ocean views.

Paseo de los Cocoteros 19. ☎ *800/882-6684 or 329/7-1300. Fax 329/7-0800.* **Rack rates:** *$293 for 2, including all meals and drinks; children under 7 free; ages 7–12 additional $25 charge per day. AE, DC, MC, V.*

Dollars & Sense

Don't forget to ask for specials. If you're willing to guarantee your reservation with a credit card—the actual charges aren't added until you depart your room—the Krystal might book you at a high-season rate of $145, buffet breakfast included, for a standard room.

Krystal Vallarta
$$$. Hotel Zone.

This hotel has it all: A great beach, amenities galore, and personality to spare. It's built to resemble a Mexican village, with a series of low-slung Spanish-style buildings and individual villas connected by little streets, surrounded by lush vegetation, and dotted with waterfalls, bridges, and fountains. The grounds are huge. If—say, after a night at Christine, the hotel's superhot disco—you don't feel like walking back to your room, there are carts to scoot you around. All the units are different, but you can depend on lovely Old World details, such as brick walls, beamed ceilings, or a rough-hewn Spanish Colonial–style armoire (which hides a cable TV, of course). There's a good pool scene, and the tennis courts are top-notch. The world-class restaurants include Kamakura, featuring exquisitely presented Japanese food; Tango, an Argentinian steakhouse; and Bogart's, a super-romantic Casablanca-themed restaurant with a Continental menu.

Av. de la Garza s/n. ☎ *800/231-9860 or 322/4-0202. Fax 322/4-0222. www.wotw.com/krystal. E-mail: krystalmex@iserve.net.mx.* **Rack rates:** *$220 double; $240 1-bedroom villa with shared terrace and pool; $290 1-bedroom villa with private pool, terrace, and dining room. Rates include buffet breakfast for two. AE, DC, MC, V.*

⭐Kids La Jolla de Mismaloya
$$$$. South of Town.

Dominating the once-secluded bay where *Night of the Iguana* was filmed— you can see the movie set from some of the rooms—this sprawling luxury resort is at once romantic and family-friendly. Use the kitchen in your airy, colorful suite to prepare meals for hungry kids—or to keep you from having to live on love alone if you want to hole up for a while. Of course, with a Kids' Club to occupy the offspring with piñatas, treasure hunts, and tons of beach activities, the room can serve both purposes. You'll be far from town,

381

Bet You Didn't Know

Elizabeth Taylor wasn't in *Night of the Iguana*. It was Liz's nighttime activities with Richard Burton that brought the world's attention to Puerto Vallarta, but during the day, Dick was paid to play against Ava Gardner.

but three pools with waterfalls and Jacuzzis, a fitness center, tony shops, and several good dining rooms should keep you occupied. Or just walk down the beach a few yards, where the small boats and thatched-roof restaurants will make you think you're visiting a remote fishing village.

Zona Hotelera Sur, km 11.5, Mismaloya Beach. ☎ *800/322-2343 or 322/8-0660. Fax 322/8-0500. www.puerto-vallarta.com/ jolla. E-mail: lajolla@pvnet.com.mx.* **Rack rate:** *$293 1-bedroom suite. Romance packages available. AE, DC, MC, V.*

Dollars & Sense

Los Cuatro Vientos offers Women's Getaway Week packages in June which include cultural discussions, exercise classes, hikes, and some meals. **Camino Real** has discounted rates for stays of 6 nights or more.

Los Cuatro Vientos
$. Downtown.
It's a bit of an uphill walk from downtown to this quiet, vine-draped hotel, but worth every single huff and puff. Thirteen delightful guest rooms—all with domed brick ceilings, hand-decorated walls, and folk art knickknacks—are arranged around a lush patio with a pool. The Mexican/international food at Chez Elena is excellent, and the rooftop bar has a panoramic view of the city and the bay; it's one of the best seats in town at sunset. Rates include continental breakfast, served on the terrace. Massages and facials are available. Book as far in advance as you can; even though there's no air-conditioning, word's out that this one's a winner.

Matamoros 520, between Josefa Ortiz de Dominguez and Corona. ☎ *322/2-0161. Fax 322/2-2831.* **Rack rate:** *$53. Women's Getaway Week packages including cultural discussions, exercise classes, hikes, and some meals are available. MC, V.*

Nautilus Hotel and Yacht Club
$$. Marina Vallarta.
Okay, so you don't have your own yacht—yet. Stay at this marina-front hotel and you'll feel like a member of the seafaring set without paying an arm and

a leg for the privilege. The comfortable rooms, arranged in a U-shape around an Olympic-size pool, all have kitchenettes. Try to get one on an upper floor; they have balconies and good marina views. Pleasures here are understated: You can play shuffleboard, shoot a few rounds of pool, rent a bike—the marina is a perfect place to ride—or just kick back with a cold one in a separate hammock area. A friendly, open-air restaurant features a moderately priced international menu. Yachts and sailboats can dock here for a small fee and use the hotel's facilities, so you can mingle with the old salts and find out which way the wind is blowing.

Paseo de la Marina Sur no. 210. ☎ ***322/1-1015.*** *Fax 322/1-1017.* **Rack rates:** *$123 double; $222 American Plan (meals included). AE, MC, V.*

Buddy, Can You Spare Some Time?

It's safe to assume that anyone offering you free meals or activity discounts is trying to sell you a piece of Puerto Vallarta. Steer clear. At best, you'll suffer through an hour of hard-sell stress; at worst, you'll sign on for something you could regret forever. See chapter 10, "Crossing the Border & What to Expect on the Other Side," for more dire details.

 ## Paradise Village Resort
$$$. Nuevo Vallarta.

Arrive here with the clothes on your back, a bathing suit—and lots of cash or a credit card—and you won't have to think about another thing. Deep-sea fishing, snorkeling, and scuba trips, as well as guided bike, horseback riding, and adventure tours all depart from here. Stay on the premises and you can climb a Mayan temple and exit through the mouth of a crocodile into one of the swimming pools; visit a small zoo near the tennis courts; or get evaluated, exercised, wrapped, massaged, and scrubbed at a full-service spa. All rooms, from the junior to the three-bedroom suites, have balconies and kitchens; some offer Jacuzzis, too. Decor is Miami Beach pastel, with a Latin dash. *Warning:* This is a time-share property. Try to avoid the hard-sell reps.

Paseo de los Cocoteros 1, Nuevo Vallarta, Nayarit C.P. 63730. ☎ ***800/995-5714*** *or 329/7-0770. Fax 329/7-0551. www.paradisevillage.com.* **Rack rates:** *Junior suite $150 (marina view); $185 (oceanview). Children under 12 no charge with adults. AE, MC, V.*

Best Bets for Singles

Continental Plaza (Hotel Zone, $$$)

Playa Los Arcos Hotel (Downtown, $)

Playa Los Arcos Hotel

$. Downtown.

This Spanish-style low-rise is where the action is. Los Muertos, the beach directly in back, is pick-up heaven, while the street in front sees some of the rowdiest nightlife in town. You don't even have to leave the premises to party: Poolside games go on all day, and the bar pulses with live dance music after dark. Rooms are smallish and fairly plain, but have nice carved headboards and balconies—the better to check what you're missing downstairs when you stop in for a quick shower and change. Breakfast is included in the room rates, and dinner at Cafe Maximillian (see chapter 36, "The Best of Puerto Vallarta's Dining Scene") is a surprisingly sedate Old World experience. But then again, this south-of-the-river section of town gets lots of European visitors (single women can expect come-ons in a variety of Continental languages).

*Olas Altas 380. ☎ **800/468-2403** or 322/2-1583. Fax 322/2-2418. www.* *playalosarcos.com.* ***Rack rate:*** *$76 double, includes breakfast buffet. AE, DC, MC, V.*

Posada de Roger

$. Downtown.

Sit around the pancake house attached to this appealing budget hotel long enough, and you'll get the inside scoop about what's happening in town from a savvy international crowd. Rooms are fairly basic, but they're comfortable, clean, and connected to the outside world by telephone. Try to get one that opens out onto the lovely bougainvillea-decked courtyard, which has a small pool. Those facing the street—which happens to be Puerto Vallarta's restaurant row—can be a bit noisy.

*Basilio Badillo 237, between Piño Suarez and Ignacio Vallarta. ☎ **322/2-0639** or* *322/2-0836. Fax 322/3-0482.* ***Rack rate:*** *$45 double. AE, MC, V.*

Best Bets for Activity Addicts

Hotel Sierra (Nuevo Vallarta, $$$)

Qualton Club (Hotel Zone, $$$)

Qualton Club

$$$. Hotel Zone.

It's exhilarating just sitting around the lobby of the Qualton Club, watching the young international crowd buzzing around this activity hive. Although it's a pretty typical all-inclusive, it's got far better health facilities than most. You could even lose weight if you took advantage of the good tennis courts, top-of-the-line cardio machines, and relentless aerobics, step, and yoga classes—and ignored the unlimited quantities of food and drink. There's nightly entertainment on the premises as well as outings to discos, which waive the cover charge for hotel guests. Rooms are bright and cheerful, with light-wood furnishings; their most outstanding feature is a sweeping bay view from the balconies.

Av. Francisco Ascencío, km 2.5. ☎ ***322/4-4446.*** *Fax 322/4-4447. www.qualton. com. E-mail: qualton@pvnet.com.mx.* **Rack rate:** *$140 per person based on double occupancy, including all meals and activities. AE, MC, V.*

Sierra Plaza Golf and Spa Hotel
$$$$. Marina Vallarta.
Fulfill your Roman villa fantasies at the Sierra, where oversized rooms feature hand-painted armoires, stepped marble floors, and, in many cases, Jacuzzis. A freeform pool overlooks one of Puerto Vallarta's best golf courses (greens fees are included in the room rate), and the fitness center is excellent. An award-winning chef presides over El Candil's sophisticated international menu; the harp music at the sumptuous Sunday brunch may convince you that you've ascended to heaven. The only thing missing is a beach—which would be more of a disadvantage if Marina Vallarta's shoreline were better.

Pelicanos 331. ☎ ***800/362-9170*** *(Sierra Hotels), 800/525-4800 (Small Luxury Hotels), or 322/1-0800. Fax 322/1-0801.* **Rack rates:** *Suites start from $234. AE, MC, V.*

Westin Regina
$$$$. Marina Vallarta.
This dramatically designed high-rise may have the most amenities in the Marina Vallarta complex—and if you don't find what you want, chances are one of the helpful staff will be able to get it for you. Excellent convention facilities mean lots of business travelers, but plenty of families take advantage of the Kids' Club, and yuppie couples like the high-toned but relaxed atmosphere. Rooms are stylish and colorful; if the stippled concrete faux rug seems strange at first, you'll soon discover how cool it feels to hot, tired feet.

All units have terraces facing a series of meandering pools and the ocean beyond it; in those on the lower floors, you can't see the water for the lush gardens, but you'll have easier access to it. Dining possibilities ranges from poolside to haute, and the Cascade lobby bar has live piano music nightly. *Note:* If you don't want to deal with even a soft-sell time-share pitch, avoid the Club Regina desk.

Paseo de la Marina Sur 205. ☎ ***800/ WESTIN-1*** *or 322/1-1100. Fax 322/1-1131. www.westin.com. E-mail: westinpv@ pvnet.com.mx.* **Rack rate:** *$216 double; romance packages available. AE, DC, DISC, MC, V.*

Best Bets for Families

La Jolla de Mismaloya (South of Town, $$$$)

Paradise Village Resort (Nuevo Vallarta, $$$)

Westin Regina (Marina Vallarta, $$$$)

No Room at the Inn? Check Out One of These . . .

Marina Vallarta
➤ **Marriott CasaMagna.** A sprawling luxury retreat with every play area imaginable, including an artificial lake. Paseo de la Marina 5. ☎ **800/228-9290.** $$$$.

Hotel Zone
➤ **Fiesta Americana.** The giant palapa at the entryway says it all: Relax and have a good time on a grand scale. Carretera al Aueropuerto. ☎ **800/FIESTA1.** $$$$.

➤ **Hacienda Buenaventura.** It doesn't have its own beach (the Krystal's is a short walk away), but it's got personality and a good price. Paseo de la Palma. ☎ **800/307-1847.** $$.

Downtown
➤ **Posada Río Cuale.** One block from the beach, and with lots of local color. Serdán 242. ☎ **322/2-0450.** Fax 322/2-0914. $.

Quick Picks: Puerto Vallarta's Hotels at a Glance
Hotel Index by Price

$

Los Cuatro Vientos (Downtown)

Playa Los Arcos Hotel (Downtown)

Posada de Roger (Downtown)

$$

Bahia del Sol Resort (Nuevo Vallarta)

Hotel Buenaventura (Hotel Zone)

Hotel Molina de Agua (Downtown)

Hotel Playa Conchas Chinas (South of Town)

Nautilus Hotel and Yacht Club (Marina Vallarta)

$$$

Continental Plaza (Hotel Zone)

Hotel Sierra (Nuevo Vallarta)

Krystal Vallarta (Hotel Zone)

Kids Paradise Village Resort (Nuevo Vallarta)

Qualton Club (Hotel Zone)

$$$$

Camino Real (South of Town)

Kids La Jolla de Mismaloya (South of Town)

Sierra Plaza Golf and Spa Hotel (Marina Vallarta)

Kids Westin Regina (Marina Vallarta)

Hotel Index by Location

Nuevo Vallarta

Bahia del Sol Resort $$

Hotel Sierra $$$

Kids Paradise Village Resort
$$$

Marina Vallarta

Nautilus Hotel and Yacht
Club $$

Sierra Plaza Golf and Spa Hotel
$$$$

Kids Westin Regina $$$$

Hotel Zone

Continental Plaza $$$

Hotel Buenaventura $$

Krystal Vallarta $$$

Qualton Club $$$

Downtown

Hotel Molina de Agua $$

Los Cuatro Vientos $

Playa Los Arcos Hotel $

Posada de Roger $

South of Town

Camino Real $$$$

Hotel Playa Conchas Chinas
$$

Kids La Jolla de Mismaloya
$$$$

Chapter 34

Finding Your Way Around Puerto Vallarta

In This Chapter

➤ What to expect when you arrive

➤ The lay of the land

➤ Getting around

➤ Where to get information

➤ Quick Facts: Puerto Vallarta A to Z

Smoked Out

Surprise! Puerto Vallarta's airport is nonsmoking—sort of. Smoking is banned in all the public areas, but nicotine clouds still seep out of the open-front restaurants and bars where it's permitted.

Not to worry. You won't have to wander, clueless, in Puerto Vallarta. As soon as you step off the plane, you'll be thrown an information safety net. Okay, it'll have some holes—this town is extremely tourist-friendly, but it's still in Mexico—but never ones large enough to fall through.

You've Just Arrived—Now What?

Puerto Vallarta's Gustavo Díaz Ordaz International Airport may be relatively sophisticated when it comes to welcoming visitors, but it's still a small-town transit center. You won't have any problem locating your luggage at the single carousel, or finding your way beyond the cursory Customs line to the arrival room, where there's an information booth (usually with a human

being attending it), an ATM (frequently
functional), and a money-exchange
counter (don't expect great rates). There
are also some travel agencies, mostly there
to meet tours. If you spot a copy of
Vallarta Today—more about that, below—
grab it. You may never see one again.

Yo, Gringo!

Puerto Vallarta's departure
area is far more North of
the Border than most. There
are two well-stocked duty-
free shops and a chalkboard
that lists flight departures—a
rare bird at the Mexican
resort airports.

Step outside on the curb and you'll see a
booth selling tickets for *colectivos* (collective vans) and taxis. Prices for both forms
of transport are determined by distances.
For a colectivo, you'll pay about $3 per
person to both Marina Vallarta and the
hotel zone, around $5 to downtown, and
approximately $7 to Mismaloya, in the far
south. Oddly, the price of a cab to Marina
Vallarta, the hotel zone, and downtown is the same—roughly, $6—although
when you return to the airport from Marina Vallarta (about 2 seconds away),
it'll run you only $2. Expect to pay about $11 to cab it as far as Mismaloya.

Orientation: You Are Here

Puerto Vallarta hugs the Bay of Banderas, a body of water so huge that it
crosses two states and is fed by 18 rivers—including the Río Cuale, which
runs through the heart of downtown. In the hotel chapter, I discussed the
northern Nuevo Vallarta complex, and in the following one I'll cover the
beaches at the far reaches of the bay, but here I'll just stick to the central
tourist route—from the airport to Mismaloya.

Taking the airport highway, Carretera Aeropuerto (a.k.a Avenida de las
Palmas or Bulevar Francisco Medina Ascenicío), south from its source, you'll
soon come to the Marina Vallarta complex, with its hotels and condos, cruise
ship pier, and yacht dock. Hard upon its heels is the hotel zone, a long
stretch of high-rise lodgings, restaurants, and shopping centers. Past the
Sheraton hotel, the airport highway turns into Avenida México and, soon,
Paseo Díaz Ordaz. A half-mile later and it's the *malecón* (mah-leh-*CONE*), or
seafront promenade, sometimes referred to as the boardwalk.

Now you're in the original town, *centro* or *Viejo* (old) Vallarta. This is Puerto
Vallarta's cultural and civic heart, home to City Hall, the open-air Los Arcos
theater, and the church of Our Lady of Guadalupe, as well as loads of restaurants, shops, and art galleries. It's also the site of Gringo Gulch, which,
though it sounds like a place where badly-behaved tourists get thrown to the
vultures, is actually named for the thousands of U.S. expats who arrived in
the late 1950s.

Continue south on Avenida Moreles, behind the malecón, and you'll reach
one of the two bridges across the Río Cuale. Bypass the island in the middle
of the river, Isla Río Cuale, and you'll be in the southern part of downtown,
which has no official name. Here you'll find two of the city's most popular

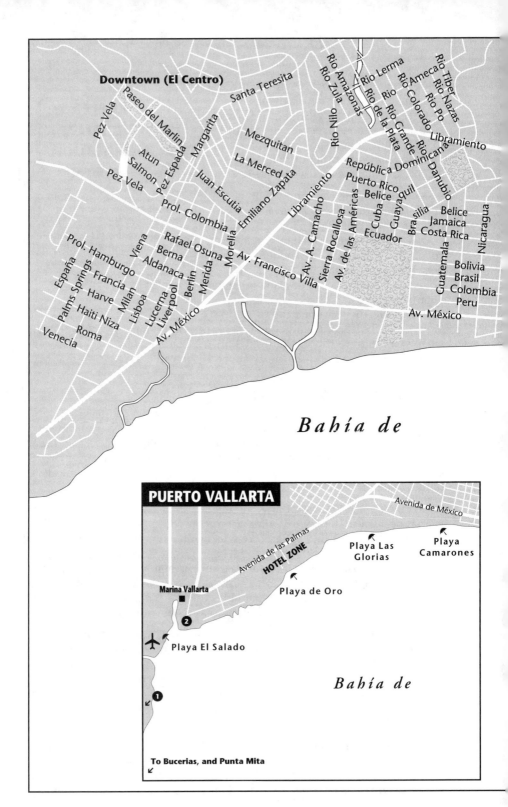

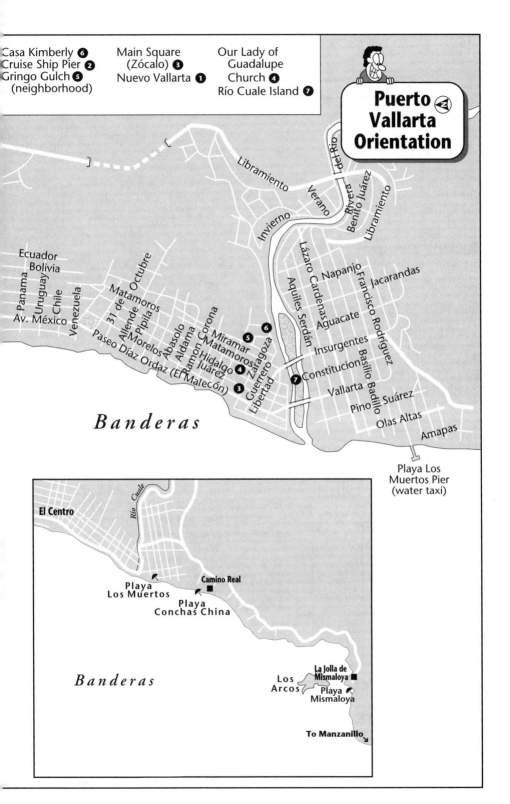

Casa Kimberly **6**
Cruise Ship Pier **2**
Gringo Gulch **5**
  (neighborhood)

Main Square
  (Zócalo) **3**
Nuevo Vallarta **1**

Our Lady of
  Guadalupe
  Church **4**
Río Cuale Island **7**

Puerto Vallarta Orientation

Libramiento

del Río

Verano

Invierno

Rivera Benito Juárez

Libramiento

Ecuador
Bolivia

Octubre

Lázaro Cardenas

Napanjo

Francisco Rodríguez

Jacarandas

Panama
Uruguay
Chile
Venezuela
Av. México

Matamoros

31 de

Allende

Pipila

Aquiles Serdán

Aguacate

Morelos

Abasolo

Aldama

Ramon Corona

Miramar

Matamoros

5

6

Insurgentes

Basilio Badillo

Paseo Díaz Ordaz (El Malecón)

Ramon Hidalgo
Juárez

4

Zaragoza

Constitucion

7

Vallarta

Guerrero

Libertad

3

Pino Suárez

Olas Altas

Amapas

Banderas

Playa Los
Muertos Pier
(water taxi)

El Centro

Río Cuale

Playa
Los Muertos

Camino Real

Playa
Conchas China

La Jolla de Mismaloya

Los
Arcos

Playa
Mismaloya

Banderas

To Manzanillo

391

beaches—Playa Olas Altas and Playa Los Muertos—as well as Basilio Badillo (Restaurant Row). You'd never guess that this section, as charming and cute shop-laden as Viejo Vallarta, was built in the past couple of decades.

Go beyond the ultra-walkable downtown and you're on the road again. Avenida Insurgentes turns into Highway 200, which winds past the ritzy Concho Chinas residential area and a couple of luxury hotels to Playa Mismaloya. Out of the way, but no longer as wildly remote as it was when "The Movie" (*Night of the Iguana*) was filmed here, the beach is considered the southern boundary of Puerto Vallarta.

Getting Around by Bus . . .
Puerto Vallarta's buses ain't pretty, but they're cheap (about 25¢) and easy to use. From 6am to 11pm, buses marked "Centro" run frequently from the airport and Marina Vallarta through downtown to Plaza Lázaro Cárdenas, just south of the Río Cuale on Olas Altas beach.

To return north, just wait at one of the blue bus stops for a vehicle marked Zona Hoteleria or, if you're going farther, Marina Vallarta. You'll have to switch buses at the downtown terminus (Plaza Lázaro Cárdenas) if you want to go as far south as Mismaloya, and the runs are less frequent, but eventually you'll get where you want to go.

Dollars & Sense

Colectivos stop running when there are no more passengers in the arrival hall to fill them. Be quick about your airport business or you might miss the last one.

. . . and by Taxi
If you want to hurry things along, splurge on a cab. They're easy to find and easy to bargain for along the busy downtown and hotel zone streets. Cabs don't cruise by the front of the Marina Vallarta resorts, however, so you'll have to depend on cab queues, which pretty much leave you stuck with what you get (if the quoted price is out of line with what the hotel transportation desk suggests, however, you can argue). On the way back from downtown to Marina Vallarta, you may be able to get away with a third less than what you paid on the way south—say $4 instead of $6.

Where to Get More Information & Guidance
The small **tourist information** office on the ground floor of the white Presidencia Municipal building in downtown's main square (Juárez and Independencia; ☎ **322/2-0242** or 2-0243) supplements its rather meager assortment of brochures with (sometimes) copies of *Puerto Vallarta Lifestyles* and (rumor has it) issues of *Vallarta Today*. If you come before they run out, you can also get an excellent foldout map of downtown here. Open Monday

through Friday from 9am to 2pm and 4 to 8pm, Saturday from 9am to 1pm, the office is understaffed but tries to be helpful.

Yo, Gringo!

Always settle the fare before you step into a cab. Many taxi drivers in Puerto Vallarta will quote you the correct price for your ride right off, so you won't have to bargain. If you have a different figure in mind, however—ask the front desk at your hotel what's fair for your journey—make a counteroffer. If the driver doesn't agree, look for another cab.

The Printed Page

Vallarta Today, a free tabloid-style English-language daily, publishes interesting local stories, as well as restaurant, nightlife, and events listings. Theoretically, it's available at tourist hotels and restaurants, but the last time I was in Puerto Vallarta, I picked up a copy at the airport and never saw another again.

You won't have that problem with the slicker and ubiquitous **Puerto Vallarta Lifestyles,** published quarterly. The cover price is $2.50, but many of the magazine's advertisers distribute copies for free. The publication may be ad-driven, but it's very professional, with lots of useful tips and information on everything from how to convert dress sizes to where to find the nearest AA meeting. It also has good color maps of all the major tourist areas.

Puerto Vallarta A to Z: Facts at Your Fingertips

American Express: Downtown at Av. Moreles 660, corner of Avenida Abasolo (☎ **322/3-2995**).

ATMs: In addition to the magic money dispenser at the airport, ATMs at several downtown banks are hooked into the major U.S. networks: Bancomer (Juárez and J. Mina), Banamex (Juárez and Zaragosa), Bital (Libertad and Miramar), and Serfin (Juárez 419). In Marina Vallarta, there's a branch of Bancomer at Plaza Marina, at the entrance to the complex.

Baby-sitters: The concierge can arrange baby-sitting for you at the large hotels; prices usually run about $10 per hour. Expect to pay a lot less for sitters hired through the reception desk at the small hotels; typical rates are about $3.50 an hour.

Business Hours: *Shops:* Monday through Saturday 10am to 2pm, and 4pm to 8 or 9pm; some are also open on Sunday. *Offices:* Monday through Friday 10am to 2pm and 5 to 8pm, and Saturday 10am to 2pm.

Currency Exchange: You can change money Monday through Friday at the banks noted in "ATMs," above; hours vary, but you're safe if you come from 10am to noon. The various *casas de cambio* (exchange booths) that line the streets of downtown (look along the malecón and Avenida Olas Altas south of the river) have less favorable rates but much longer hours. And, yes, there's always your hotel front desk, if you're desperate for cash at any cost.

Dentist: If you're in dental distress, try the English-speaking Dr. Fernando Peñalva (Plaza Marina, Marina Vallarta; ☎ **322/1-0165**).

Doctors: The large hotels all have doctors on call or can recommend a good one. Reliable English-speaking doctors in town include Dr. Guadalupe Lewgot (Manuel M. Dieguez 360; ☎ **322/3-0444**); Dr. Rodolfo Ruiz Nieves, at CMQ Clinic, and Dr. Alberto Sola, at Ameri-Med Hospital (see "Hospitals," below, for both).

Emergencies: For the police, call ☎ **06;** for the **Red Cross,** call ☎ **322/ 2-1533** or 322/2-4973.

English-Language Newspapers/Magazines: The lobbies of practically every high-rise hotel in Marina Vallarta and the hotel zone have tobacco shops with a decent selections of U.S. magazines and, often, *U.S. News and World Report,* along with the English-language *Mexico City News.* Many of the minimarts that line the marina also have magazine racks catering to the print-starved.

Hospitals: The U.S.–run **Ameri-Med Hospital** (Plaza Neptuno, at the entrance to Marina Vallarta; ☎ **322/1-0023**) has excellent diagnostic and emergency facilities; it also has helicopters to air-evacuate patients to the United States. Other good local hospitals include downtown's **CMQ clinic** (364 Basilio Badillo; ☎ **322/3-1919**) and **Hospital Medaist** (Manuel M. Dieguez 360; ☎ **322/3-0444**).

Maps: See "Where to Get More Information & Guidance," above.

Pharmacies: All the following pharmacies are open 24 hours. *Downtown:* The **CMQ Clinic pharmacy** (see "Hospitals," above) and **Farmacia Guadalajara** (Insurgentes, corner of Lázaro Cárdenas; ☎ **322/2-5678**). *Hotel Zone:* **Farmacia CMQ** (Plaza Caracol, Francisco Medina Ascensío s/n, Edificio Andrea Mar; ☎ **322/4-8700**). *Marina Vallarta:* **Farmacia Expres** (Plaza Neptuno; ☎ **322/1-2223**).

Police: The police headquarters is at the Presidencia Municipal Building in the central plaza (Juárez and Independencia; ☎ **322/2-0123**). In an emergency, call ☎ **06.**

Post Office: You can do your mailing downtown on Mina, between Juárez and Moreles; at the Maritime building, near the cruise ship dock; or at the airport. There's also a Mail Boxes Etc. in the hotel zone (Blvd. Francisco Medina Ascencío, Edificio Andrea Mar; ☎ **322/4-9434**)—a more expensive but more efficient way to send packages home.

Safety: If you stick to the tourist areas and use common sense, you shouldn't have any safety problems in Puerto Vallarta. Avoid dark, untraveled streets; don't go wandering the beach at night; leave your good jewelry at home; and don't flash wads of money (see chapter 10 for additional general tips). The Zoo, a bar on the Malecón, is sufficiently rowdy to have been deemed off-limits to the U.S. and Canadian Navy, so I don't suggest you go there; there have also been reports of robberies on the road to El Eden, off Mismaloya Beach.

Special Events: In addition to celebrating the traditional Mexican holidays (see chapter 2, "When Should I Go?"), Puerto Vallarta packs several additional festivals into the month of November, when the 2-week-long Fiesta del Mar comes to town. Events include an excellent boat show—the only one in Latin America—a sailfishing tournament (the 40th one took place in 1997), a gastronomic festival, and an arts festival. Call ☎ **322/4-2939** for more information.

Holy Mariachi!

On November 22, the state of Jalisco pays tribute to Santa Cecilia, patron saint of mariachis. In Puerto Vallarta, a special mass is held at Our Lady of Guadalupe church and some of the best bands in the country give a free concert at the open-air Aquiles Serdán theater.

Telephone: The telephone area code for Puerto Vallarta is 322 (329 for Nuevo Vallarta and other locations to the south). To call long distance within Mexico (abbreviated *lada*), dial 01, then the area code, and then the number. To call the United States, dial 001, and then the area code and number.

U.S. Consul: U.S. Consul is at Zaragoza 160, Edificio Vallarta Plaza, 2nd floor (☎ **322/2-0069**).

Chapter 35

Fun On & Off the Beach

***

In This Chapter

➤ Puerto Vallarta's top beaches

➤ Fun in the water

➤ Sightseeing, shopping and nightlife

➤ Some super side trips

***

Given Puerto Vallarta's many great beaches and fun ways to play in the water, you can expect to spend a lot of time with sand between your toes and wrinkly fingertips. And when you're ready to just look at some waves, rather than pitch yourself into them, Puerto Vallarta is happy to let you do that, too.

And when you're waterlogged and sun-soaked and want to spend time on dry land, never fear: Puerto Vallarta's many dry-dock options will pose a challenge to your schedule—and your stamina.

Sunshine on Your Shoulders, Sand Between Your Toes

You may not find Puerto Vallarta's creamy stretches of sand quite as isolated as they once were, but if you make an effort, you can still find some genuine getaways. And if seclusion is secondary, you'll have no problem finding places to enter the fray of frying—don't forget your sunscreen!—and water-logged bods.

The following wrap-up of Puerto Vallarta area beaches starts in the north with the state of Nayarit's shores and works southward into Jalisco.

The Northern Beaches

The Bay of Banderas tips out about 28 miles north of Puerto Vallarta's airport at **Punta Mita,** a rocky promontory that appears rather stark after the lush, jungly coastline leading up to it. But the views of the bay and the Sierra Madres from here are awesome, the white coral beaches are inviting, and the gentle water is ideal for swimming. You'll share the area around the water sports concessions and casual restaurants, but walk along the coast in either direction and you'll soon have a piece of shoreline to yourself.

The first beach you'll come to as you head south is **Playa Anclote (Anchor Beach),** a wide stretch of fine sand that curves around a turquoise cove. The water is gentle and shallow for a long way out, and it's a good spot for beginning surfers and boogie boarders. You've got your pick of seafood places here—El Dorado is especially good—and you can rent a *panga* (motorized skiff) from one of the fisherman south of the restaurants for about $15 an hour.

You can also hire someone from the fisherman's cooperative on Playa Anclote to take you to the **Marietas Islands,** a bird-watcher's, diver's, and snorkeler's dream. On shore, you'll see every kind of tropical marine bird imaginable, including blue-footed boobies. Below water, manta rays, sea turtles, and dolphins cavort around pristine coral cliffs with schools of brightly colored fish. The islands are honeycombed with caves and hidden beaches, too (you'll need a local or tour guide to direct you to some of the best ones). Trips cost around $20 per person an hour; it's usually a better deal to go from town on a snorkeling tour or on an excursion on the *Marigalante.* See the section "Pick A Peck of Playful Water Sports," below, for details.

Yo, Gringo!

Using a restaurant's palapa is a reciprocal arrangement. In return for some shade and a comfortable chair, you buy your drinks, snacks, and lunch there.

Next comes **Playa Pontoque,** a small strand of white sand leading to crystalline waters good for snorkeling. The beach is equally famous for Las Ampas restaurant, where you never know what might land on your table—everything from iguana to rattlesnake (but only if you order it). To the south, past Punta del Burro, a headland popular with local surfers, the beautiful **Playa las Destiladeras** has talc-smooth sand and a backdrop of sandstone cliffs. Two thatched-roof restaurants complete the idyllic picture.

Playa Piedra Blanca (White Stone Beach) is named for the limestone outcropping that separates it from **Playa Manzanillo** to the south. Both are lovely and quiet, but Piedra Blanca has no shade or services. Unless you want to drag along a beach umbrella, you're better off parking yourself under a palapa (a pittance to rent) or at the table of a rustic restaurant on Playa Manzanillo.

Bet You Didn't Know

Destiladera, which means "still," refers to the fresh water that trickles down to the shore from Punta del Burro. You can pick out the tranquil pools right beside the ocean.

The fishing village of **Bucerías,** 11 miles north of the airport, doesn't look like much from the road, but its relaxed pace and cobblestoned streets are a throwback to pre-media-hype Puerto Vallarta. (Transplanted Americans have already discovered it, however, and luxury villas hide behind the high walls.) The palm-dotted beach that abuts the town is uncrowded and seemingly endless. Sunday is street-market day; come for the local color but be prepared to mingle with more people at the shore. Most of the restaurants in town are good but modest; gringos gravitate to Mark's (at Lázaro Cárdenas 56; ☎ 329/8-0303), featuring gourmet pastas and whole wheat–crust pizzas, open evenings only, and Pie-in-the-Sky, an excellent bakery just south of town.

Dynamite gold-sand beaches top the list of reasons why many people stay in **Nuevo Vallarta,** discussed in more detail in chapter 33, "Choosing the Place to Stay That's Right For You." They're great for swimming and, sometimes, surfing and they're practically flat, so joggers and bikers like them too. Best of all, they're rarely crowded.

Yo, Gringo!

Red or black warning flags go up when swimming conditions are risky. Don't be a macho (or macha) fool and ignore them. Use caution if you see a yellow flag, and have fun if a white or green signal gives you the go-ahead.

Reaching the Beaches   To get to Nuevo Vallarta and Bucerías by public transportation, go to the bus stop opposite the entrance to the airport and board a minivan marked "Bucerías"; it runs from 6am to midnight. Several second-class bus lines go as far north as Punta Mita, with stops at Bucerías, Playa Piedra Blanca, Playa las Destiladeras, and Playa Anclote. Best to check at your hotel for current information on schedules and rates. You can ask the driver to let you off at any beach along the way that's not a formal stop, but make sure to check the schedule so you can flag a bus down on the return route.

Town Beaches

The 3-mile-long stretch of sand that starts just beyond Marina Vallarta and reaches south to the Malecón shifts names from Playa de Oro to Playa Las Glorias to Playa Camarones, but most people just identify these hotel zone beaches by the name of the property they front. This virtually indistinguishable series of beaches is wide, soft, clean—and surprisingly uncrowded between hotels. The waves are generally gentle, but be careful—the shore drops off rather suddenly. Beach peddlers are on patrol, but they're not usually a huge annoyance.

The most popular beach is downtown's **Playa de los Muertos,** just below the Río Cuale. A victim of its own success, it's been cleaned up since the 1980s, but I still wouldn't recommend swimming here. Never mind—that microbikini is far less striking when it's entirely submerged. Between the cafes, bronzed bodies, and beach vendors, the stimulation level is off the scale. Eating fried fish on a stick is de rigeur.

Bet You Didn't Know

A battle between the Spanish and Indians gave Playa de los Muertos, or Beach of the Dead, its grisly name. Sporadic attempts to rename it Playa del Sol (Beach of the Sun) have never taken, but it's sometimes called Playa Oltas Altas (Beach of the High Waves)—although there really aren't that many.

Playa Mismaloya, a sheltered cove some 6 miles south of downtown, is no longer the idyllic enclave it was when *Night of the Iguana* was filmed here— the construction of the sprawling La Jolla de Mismaloya hotel took care of that—but it's still a mighty pleasant place to drop a beach towel. The water is clear and beautiful; fishing boats bob, postcard pretty, in the bay; and you've got a primo view of Los Arcos, a set of striking rock formations set aside as a federal marine preserve.

Iguana Heroin Chic

If a guy on the beach offers to take your picture with his pet iguana, he's going to hit you up for at least $1, sometimes more, after the shutter clicks. Rip-off price aside, you'll be contributing to animal cruelty if you pay. The iguanas are drugged; they'd never be so docile otherwise.

Past the partially roped-off section that "belongs" to the hotel—remember, all the beaches in Mexico are public—a flotilla of fishing boats are waiting to ferry you to Yelapa (see "The Southern Beaches," below). Beyond them, a fairly indistinguishable row of palapa restaurants compete for your pesos; I recommend Ramada Miramar. If you don't think you want to move a muscle

399

for the rest of the day, order some *raicilla*, the local moonshine—a country cousin to tequila but with a far greater kick.

Reaching the Beaches   You can get to all the hotel zone beaches via the bus marked "Zona Hotelera"; to get to Playa de Los Muertos, stay on the bus marked "Centro" until the end of the line, which is also the place where you can pick up the bus to Playa Mismaloya (appropriately marked "Mismaloya").

Extra! Extra!

If you've never seen "The Movie," or want to see it again at its source, climb the stairs at the south end of the beach to the newly restored film set. At the Night of the Iguana restaurant—the seafood's overpriced, but the views of Los Arcos are great—ask the bartender to screen the video for you.

The Southern Beaches

Three miles south of Mismaloya, picturesque little **Boca de Tomatlán** is the last town accessible by the highway before it turns inland towards Barra de Navidad and Manzanillo. The Tomatlán River empties into the sea here, and the fish practically jump out of the water; much of the seafood in the region comes from this spot. This is another spot where you choose your palapa restaurant and settle in for the afternoon, watching the Canadian ducks, white pelicans, and other seabirds cruise by. It's also a jumping-off point for the three southern beaches that are unreachable except by boat—Las Animas, Quimixto, and Yelapa, described below.

Just past the town, overlooking a freshwater swimming hole, you'll find the best of the "jungle" restaurants, Chico's Paradise; see chapter 36, "The Best of Puerto Vallarta's Dining Scene," for details.

The bus to Boca de Tomatlán leaves from Lázaro Cárdenas Park, on Playa de los Muertos in front of Daiquiri Dick's restaurant; it takes around half an hour to get there and costs about 50¢.

The first of the secluded beaches beyond Boca de Tomatlán—at least until the tour boats descend—**Playa Las Animas** is a lovely white-sand cove protected by two rocky headlands. A small community, including several expatriate Americans, occupies the lush hills behind the shore. The gentle waves are good for swimming, and you'll find sports concessions along with the requisite seafood shacks.

Next comes **Quimixto,** another rock-sheltered, palm-fringed crescent of sand. The snorkeling and swimming are good, but often take a back seat to hiking or horseback riding to a waterfall; if you come at the end of the dry season (February to April), however, you'll be underwhelmed.

The most remote of the southern beach towns, **Yelapa** was once hippie central, the quintessential escape from society's restraints. The mellow attitude has changed with the influx of tourists, but 1960s icons such as Bob Dylan and Dennis Hopper still turn up occasionally to visit the Hollywood bigwigs who have maintained houses here (Barbra Streisand's been spotted, too). At night, Wavy Gravy and other groups still do their thing at the Hippie Disco, but for about 3 hours each day, this tiny (500-person) community shares its sparkling beach with large groups of sometimes inconsiderate diving, snorkeling, swimming, seafood-consuming, and waterfall-hiking day trippers.

Serenity Now!

Las Animas, Quimixto, and Yelapa are lovely, but visit them on a booze cruise and you'll be far more in touch with your fellow tourists than with nature. If you want a more serene experience, get to Mismaloya or Boca de Tomatlán early and hire a *panga* to take you over before the crowds arrive (around 11:30am or noon). Trips from Mismaloya to any of the three beaches cost about $3 to $6 per person each way, depending on how full the ten-person boat is; departure times are based on demand. At Boca de Tomatlán, water taxis go every hour from 10am to 1pm (returning 2:30, 3:30, and 4:30pm) for about $3. Unscheduled boats that fit up to eight people can be hired for $32 (round-trip) to Las Animas, $38 to Quimixto, and $50 to Yelapa. They leave after 8am and return no later than 6pm.

In the "Serenity Now!" box I've noted ways you can get to Las Animas, Quimixto, and Yelapa on your own; later in this chapter, I'll tell you a bit about the guided cruises you can take. Another option is the water taxis that leave from the New Pier at Playa de los Muertos (on Francisco Rodriguez, near the Hotel Marsol); you won't miss the crowds, but you'll save some money—and avoid excess alcohol content. Boats depart at 10:30 and 11am and return at 3:30pm; the fare is about $12 round-trip.

Water Fun for Everyone

Whether you want to put some wind in your sails, tip the (fish) scales, or flounder around underwater, you've come to the right place. In Puerto Vallarta, you can enjoy the amenities of a modern marina or the satisfaction of interacting with local seafolk.

Pick A Peck of Playful Water Sports

Scope out the hotel zone beaches if you want to amuse yourself with water toys like jet skis (about $30 per half hour), water skis ($35 per half hour), parasails ($25 for a 10-minute ride), or banana boats ($5 per person for a

15-minute ride). Concessions come and go, but you'll be sure to find some in front of the Sheraton, Fiesta Americana, and Krystal hotels. You can also locate outfitters on Playa de los Muertos, especially around the Playa Los Arcos Hotel, but you'll be sharing the waves with far more people.

⭐Kids⭐ A Water Park

Your kids will love swooshing down water slides, splashing under waterfalls, or floating along a lazy river at the **Oasis Water Park** in front of the Vidafel Hotel in Marina Vallarta (☎ **322/1-1500**). There's a separate shallow zone for the littler ones and a nursery for toddlers who need a nap. The park is open every day from 11am to 7pm; admission is $6 per body, large or small, if you're not a hotel guest.

Deep-Sea Fishing

Puerto Vallarta isn't one of the great fishing destinations in Mexico—in part because the bay is so large that it takes forever (okay, about 2 hours) to get out to where the water is deep enough for the big ones—but that doesn't stop lots of anglers from happily casting off anyway. It's worth it for the scenic trip alone, and you might be surprised. Sailfish and blue marlin hang around the Bay of Banderas for a good part of the year, and January and February are prime for hungry yellowtail, tuna, and snapper.

Off the Hook

Mounting your catch is one tradition that's dying out. More and more sports-fishers are taking part in catch-and-release programs. You tag any big one you reel in so the next guy knows you were there first (or second or third . . .) and then let it back into the water—no doubt to tell its friends about a painful, but not fatal, free lunch.

Stroll around the docks at Marina Vallarta and dozens of tour operators will try to sell you a place on their fishing vessels by showing you pictures of the ships, written testimonials from satisfied passengers, and so forth. The experience can be interesting or overwhelming, depending on how much you know about things nautical. If the only knots you're familiar with are the ones in your shoelaces, you'll be out of your depth. You can avoid all this by booking a boat through your hotel, or put aside your pride and just have fun walking around, asking questions and collecting information. Prices are competitive—about $65 per person, including ice, fishing license, and bait—so go with your gut instinct. There are no guarantees.

Chartering Through a Tour Operator: Fish or Foul?

It's smart to book your fishing trip with a tour operator for these reasons:

➤ If you're alone or with one other person, you won't have to pay for boat space you're not using.

➤ Tour reps can get your needs across to boat captains who may not be fluent in English.

But . . .

➤ The trip could be canceled at the last minute if your boat isn't filled.

➤ The boat might be overcrowded.

➤ The rep gets the commission while the captain and crew do all the work.

Another option is to go through the **Cooperativo de Pescadores** (fishing cooperative; ☎ **322/2-1202**) on the Malecón, north of the Río Cuale, next door to the Rosita Hotel and across from McDonald's. Fishing charters cost $200 to $300 a day for four to eight people, the price varying with the size of the boat. Although the posted price at the fishing cooperative is likely to be the same as the one you'll get through the travel agencies, you may be able to bargain because there's no middleman—and you'll know exactly who the captain is going to be.

You can also arrange fishing trips in advance with **Mexico Sportsman** (14542 Brook Hollow, no. 124, San Antonio, TX 78232; ☎ and fax **210/494-9916**), a reliable U.S. outfitter. It'll run you $350 per day for a 40-foot vessel that fits six anglers, and $400 a day for a 50-footer that seats eight. Prices don't include fishing licenses (an extra $8 per person), food, or tips.

It's customary to tip 10% to 15% of the total price of your charter, depending on the quality of service received. Give the money to the captain, who will split it with the mate.

If you just want to fiddle around in the water a bit, you can hire a *panga* (a small, motorized skiff) from skippers all along the hotel zone, at Playa Mismaloya, at Boca de Tomatlán, and at several of the more remote beaches to the north and south. It'll cost you anywhere from $15 to $25 an hour for a boat that can fit about three people comfortably.

Time-Savers

If you're already a qualified diver, don't forget to pack proof of certification—it's unlikely that anyone's going to take your word for it if you forget.

Sailing Away

The folks at **Sail Vallarta** (Club de Tenis Puesta del Sol, Local 7-B, Marina Vallarta; ☎ **322/1-0096** or 322/1-0097; e-mail: sail@puerto.net.mx) will set you on course with a skipper and crew. Prices for a day charter range from $50 to $65 per person, or $400 to $600 for the boat.

Also at Marina Vallarta, **Island Sailing International** (Isla Iguana, Hotel Plaza Iguana; ☎ **322/1-0880**) offers lessons as well as rentals. For $200, you can get American Sailing Association certification after completing a 12-hour course.

A Fish-Eye View: Diving & Snorkeling

Good visibility—up to 130 feet in summer—plus lots of underwater action makes Puerto Vallarta an ideal place to take the plunge. Great spots for diving and snorkeling include the Marietas Islands (described in the section "The Northern Beaches," above), Los Morros Islands, south of the Marietas, and Los Arcos, an underwater preserve just north of Mismaloya beach.

Dollars & Sense

Invest in your own mask, snorkel, and fins. It'll be cheaper than using the inexpensive gear even four or five times—and you'll know exactly where the equipment has been.

Reliable dive operators include **Chico's** (downtown, 772 Díaz Ordaz, near Carlos O' Brien's; ☎ **322/2-1895;** www.chicos-diveshop.com; e-mail: chicoss@tag.acnet.net), with branches at the Marriott, Vidafel, Vila del Palmar, Camino Real, and Continental Plaza hotels; and **Vallarta Adventure** (Marina Vallarta, Edificio Marina Golf, Local 13-B; ☎ **322/1-0657** or 322/1-0658; www.vallarta-adventures.com; e-mail: adventure@tag01. acnet.net). Two-tank dives run around $80 to $120, depending on the destination; rates include lunch. Both Chico's and Vallarta Adventure offer night dives and 3-day PADI certification courses.

Snorkeling trips with the same companies and with **Open Air Expeditions** (downtown at Guerrero 339; ☎ **322/2-3110;** www.vivamexico.com; e-mail: openair@vivamexico.com) can run anywhere from $30 for a 3-hour trip to $60 for an all-day excursion that adds on bird watching or sea kayaking. If you just want a quick peek below the surface, you can hire a small boat at Mismaloya Beach to take you to Los Arcos; the cost is about $8 per person for an hour, including snorkeling equipment.

Surf's Up

Want to learn how to hang ten or ride some of the best tubes and beach breaks on mainland Mexico? Take a surfing tour with **SurfMex** (downtown at Guerrero 361; ☎ **322/3-1680;** www.vivamexico.com; e-mail: bikemex@ zonavirtual.com.mx). The cost for all-day tours is $55 ($45 if you bring your own board), including transport.

On Deck

About a dozen ships depart the maritime terminal every morning at 9:30 or 10am for trips to Las Animas, Yelapa, and Quimixto (see "The Southern Beaches," above). Most make a 45-minute stop at Los Arcos for snorkeling and return by 4pm. Continental breakfast and open bar are usually included in the price, approximately $35; lunch is on your own at whichever beach you land on. The excursions run by *Princesa* (☎ 322/4-4777) and *Bora Bora* (☎ 322/4-3680) are among the most popular, but any travel agent should be able to steer you in the right direction.

More unusual is a tour on the *Marigalante,* a replica of Christopher Columbus's *Santa Maria.* Built in Veracruz, the pseudo-Spanish galleon took part in the worldwide 400-year anniversary celebration of Columbus's historic journey; a museum on board displays gifts from the many foreign ports the ship visited. These days, the *Marigalante* goes only as far as the Marieta Islands, where you get off to snorkel and kayak; on the way back, you can hop on a banana boat at Playa Piedra Blanca. All the activities, as well as breakfast, lunch, and an open bar, are included in the $50 price tag, and even the corny pirate stuff is loads of fun. Trips, which depart every day except Saturday at 9am and return at 5pm, can be booked through any travel agent or hotel tour desk.

While there's a chance you may spot some whales in January and February on the *Marigalante,* the excursions run by **Open Air Expeditions** (see "A Fish-Eye View: Diving & Snorkeling," above) from November to May focus entirely on observing the humpbacks that return to Banderas Bay to breed and raise their young. You can listen to the whales sing through special hydro phone sound equipment and take part in the photo-identification research program. Your $62 buys you a marine biologist guide as well as lunch and snacks.

After-Dark Cruises

Lots of the vessels that set out to the remote beaches during the day spiff up and take off again on sunset cruises. Departing at 5:30pm and returning at 7:30pm, they usually stay fairly close to shore in the main tourist areas—the better to see the shore lights begin to twinkle along with the stars. The price of $20 usually includes an open bar, an hors d'oeuvre buffet, and dance music. Ask any travel agent for details.

The ***Marigalante*** (see "On Deck," above) is among the ships that do double duty as a sunset cruiser, departing at 5:30pm, going as far as Los Arcos, and returning at 9pm. The fireworks set off from the ship are spectacular. On this open-bar ride, it's $30 if you just want snacks, or $48 if you need something more substantial to anchor all that booze.

An evening standout, the ultra-romantic **Rhythms of the Night** cruise transports you to Caleta Beach, where director John Huston built a home. There's no electricity here, so you'll dine by candlelight on the terrace of his lushly landscaped estate, overlooking the bay, and then watch pre-Hispanic dances performed by torchlight in a natural amphitheater. Trips depart daily at 6pm from the Maritime terminal, returning at 11pm, and cost $50 per person. Book directly through **Vallarta Adventure** (see "A Fish-Eye View: Diving & Snorkeling," above) or through a travel agent.

Keeping Your Head Above Water: Puerto Vallarta's Top Dry-Land Attractions

You can walk your feet off exploring downtown's sights and shops, or do the same thing in the jungle, where it's called hiking. And you can't count on having nothing but quiet nights to recover from your days' adventures; there's so much to do after dark that, if you don't watch it, you can come home needing a vacation.

Bet You Didn't Know

A new word has entered the Puerto Vallarta vocabulary: *maleconear,* meaning to stroll the malecón.

Strolling the Malecón

Mexicans tend to be traditionally religious, but the most faithfully observed ritual in Puerto Vallarta is a secular one: strolling up and down the *malecón*. You'll see young lovers, grandparents, teens, and entire families slowly patrolling this seaside promenade, which extends about 16 blocks from just north of the Cuale river to 31 de Octubre street.

Along with great people-watching, you'll get a culture fix when you come here. At the open-air **Aquiles Serdan Amphitheater** (better known as Los Arcos) on the southern end, artists labor over seascapes they're hoping you'll buy; you might catch anything from a folk-dancing performance or Hai Kwan Do demonstration to a classical piano concert here. Farther to the north, at the main **Plaza de Armas** (also called the *zócalo*), the municipal band entertains in the kiosk on Thursday and Saturday evenings at 6pm.

The malecón is also an outdoor gallery of **sculptures,** including the Friendship Fountain, in which three dolphins cavort; an image of Triton with a friendly sea nymph; Puerto Vallarta's signature seahorse; and two lovers gazing out to sea. A group of huge bronze chairs by Guadalajara artist Alejandro Colunga, installed December 30, 1997, has become a photo op favorite; everyone wants to be snapped on the bench that has two giant ears as a backrest.

Bet You Didn't Know

Elizabeth Taylor and Richard Burton were married for the first time in the Virgin of Guadalupe church—she in a Mexican wedding dress, he in a Mexican *charro* outfit.

More conventional benches are strung all along the malecón as well; when you get tired of strolling, you can sit and watch the sunset, enjoy a Baskin-Robbins cone, or listen to the music emanating from the nightspots across the street.

From the Malecón, it's just a short detour to the **Virgin of Guadalupe church,** behind the Plaza de Armas on Calle Hidalgo. You'll recognize the structure by its lacy crown, said to be a replica of the one worn by Carlota, empress of Mexico in the late 1860s. Much to many traditionalists' dismay, it was recast in fiberglass after the original concrete one collapsed during an earthquake in October, 1995.

On the north side of the Plaza de Armas, the **Palacio Municipal** (City Hall) is worth peering into for its mural by naif artist Manual Lepe (see "A Gallery of Galleries," below) on the second floor.

Checking Out Liz & Dick's Digs

Go ahead. Even if you're not the groupie type, there's so much hype in Puerto Vallarta about Elizabeth Taylor and Richard Burton's love match that it's hard not to get caught up in the story. Besides, it's for a good cause. The $5 you spend to tour Casa Kimberly (Zaragoza 445; ☎ 322/2-1336) goes toward providing cleft-palate operations for local kids. Movie posters, furniture, and personal photographs are displayed in the couple's surprisingly low-key pair of houses, connected by an arching pink bridge. Tours are given 9am to 6pm daily during high season, and Monday through Saturday from 10am to 2pm the rest of the year. To get here, take Zaragoza Street, on the south side of Virgin of Guadalupe church, and climb the steep set of stairs until you come to Miramar.

Prurient interest in celebrity affairs aside, you'll have a great view over the red-tiled rooftops down to the sea from this hilly vantage point. This section

Yo, Gringo!

Wear comfortable shoes when you're walking around downtown Puerto Vallarta, preferably something well insulated. Those cobblestones can do a number on your feet.

of town was dubbed Gringo Gulch after thousands of U.S. expats descended on it in the late 1950s, but you'll still see donkeys ambling along the cobblestoned streets.

Visiting Río Cuale Island

An artsy enclave flanked on both sides by lovely tree-lined river banks, Río Cuale Island is a great place to while away an afternoon. At the western tip (closest to the sea), the tiny **Museo Río Cuale** (no phone) exhibits pre-Columbian ceramics and works by local artists; it's free and theoretically open Monday through Saturday from 10am to 4pm, but that depends on whether the volunteers turn up. Farther upstream, you'll come to a **municipal market** (see "Puerto Vallarta's Best Shopping," below, for details); a **community art center** where you can often encounter local painters; and a **music school** that shares space with the prestigious **Instituto de Allende** language school. A wonderfully naturalistic **bronze statue** of John Huston, seated in his director's chair, presides over the main square, which is named after him. If you continue beyond all the boutiques and cafes, you'll hit on a slice of traditional Puerto Vallarta life—women doing laundry on the river rocks as they have for centuries.

From the north, you can get to Río Cuale Island by crossing over the concrete bridge at Encino and Juárez or the one at Liberatad and Miramar; from the south, you'll find rickety suspended footbridges (scary-looking, but safe) at Ignacio Vallarta and Aquiles Serdán, or the one at Aquiles Serdán and Insurgentes.

Chilling Out at a New Age Spa

Want to get into a sweat in a pre-Hispanic hut, contact your inner child by playing with clay, or cleanse your lymphatic system with a neurosedative drain? (It probably feels better than it sounds.) **Terra Noble** (276 Miramar; ☎ **322/3-0308;** fax 322/2-4058; www.vivamexico.com/terra; e-mail: terra@vallarta.zonavirtual.com.mx) is the place. The hilltop view and the hand-sculpted adobe architecture of the central building are stunning. If you're not up for anything New Age-y, you can just get a European facial or a Swedish massage. The various treatments, which last from 60 to 90 minutes, cost $55 each. *Warning:* Stay away from the tourist markets after a visit. You'll feel far too mellow to bargain.

Chatting Up Some Artists

If you want to peek behind the scenes of a thriving art scene, consider taking a studio tour. Mondays at 10am from December through April, art lovers gather at the **Galería Pacifico** (Insurgentes 109; ☎ **322/2-1982**) and head out for four studios, where they look at works in progress and learn about participating artists' techniques. The cost is $22 per person. On Saturday at 10am, December through March, **Galería Uno** (Moreles 561; ☎ **322/ 2-0908**) is the place to meet for a similar art trek at $20 a head.

The Sporting Life

Actively inclined and tired of sightseeing? Whether you want to use your own leg power to bike to nearby jungles, blaze a trail along a river, or leave the work to someone else and soar through the air with the greatest of ease, Puerto Vallarta won't let you down.

Biking

Bike Mex (downtown at Guerrero 361; ☎ **322/3-1680;** www.vivamexico. com; e-mail: bikemex@zonavirtual.com.mx) runs a series of full- and half-day bike trips for all levels of cyclers. The terrain covered ranges from jungle to small town and beaches; swimming is often involved. Prices, which include top-quality equipment, snacks, and experienced English-speaking guides, begin at $44 for a 4-hour trip.

If you just want to tool around on your own, you can rent all types of two-wheelers at **B-B-Bobby's Bikes** (downtown, Miramar 399 at Iturbide; ☎ **322/2-3848** or 322/3-0008; e-mail: bbikespv@acnet.net); $35 nets you a bike, a helmet, gloves, and a water bottle for the day. Tours are available, too.

To see more scenery with less sweat in Nuevo Vallarta, check out the easy-ride vehicles available from **Electric Bikes** (Club de Playa, Paseo de los Cocos s/n, southern entrance to Nuevo Vallarta; ☎ **329/7-0144**). The price depends on the weight of the rider, but the average person can expect to pay $32 for a 4-hour rental ($60 if two people rent at the same time).

Hiking

Bike Mex (see above) transforms itself into **Hike Mex** for a series of all-terrain trekking tours that generally require a bit of bush-whacking. The cost—beginning at $30 for a 4-hour hike—includes transportation to the hiking area, and lunch (or snacks) and bottled water. **Open Air Expeditions** (Guerrero 339, downtown; ☎ **322/2-3110;** www.vivamexico.com; e-mail: openair@zonavirtual.com.mx) offers a similar menu of hiking adventures; a 3-hour river-trail walk goes for about $35, for example.

Golfing

If you're staying in one of the major luxury hotels in Puerto Vallarta, chances are you'll be able to tee off at the 18-hole, Joe Finger–designed **Marina Vallarta Golf Course** (Marina Vallarta; ☎ **322/1-0701** or 322/1-0171). It's private, but playing privileges are a common perk. The $80 greens fees at this excellent par 71 course include a cart.

Located just north of Nuevo Vallarta, the 18-hole **Los Flamingos Golf Course** (☎ **329/8-0606**), designed by Percy Clifford, is somewhat less challenging, but it's also less exclusive; everyone who can shell out $35 for

409

greens fees can play. Carts cost $25, and a caddie will run you another $14. A shuttle bus makes regular runs from the Sheraton hotel (Blvd. Francisco Medina Asceníon) to the course; ask about the current schedule when you phone to reserve a tee time.

Saddling Up

Want to temporarily turn centaur? You can trot along the beach for about $6 to $8 an hour; just go to end of Basilio Badillo, south of the Río Cuale by the Restaurant Corral (you can tell you've come to the right place when you see the horses) and book a ride. For a rumble in the jungle, go a short way up the dirt road that veers off from the main highway toward the mountains at Mismaloya Beach. You'll soon see a stand selling horseback tours into the lush hills. These guided rides include a stop for a swim near a waterfall and for lunch at El Eden restaurant, where *Predator* was filmed (Arnold Schwarzenegger is another name you'll hear a lot in this town). The price is $10 an hour or $20 for 3 hours.

Don't Bug Me!

What's wrong with this picture? You're riding along a beautiful beach, watching the sun descend over an azure sea . . . and being devoured by mosquitoes. Don't forget your insect repellent if you're going out in the late afternoon.

Most popular are the various "rancho" trips sold through travel agents. About $35 will buy you a 3-hour (10am to 1pm or 3 to 6pm) excursion, including hotel pickup and drop-off. Tours are geared for beginning to experienced riders. After trotting around some flat ranchland for a while, you'll ride up into the mountains, where you can look out over huge spreads of town and ocean. Reliable outfits include **Rancho Ojo de Agua** (☎ 322/4-0607), **Rancho El Charro** (☎ 322/4-0114), and **Rancho Las Mexicanas** (☎ 322/4-7222)—worth booking for its come-on logo alone: "Why pay more when you can peso little?"

Flying

You'll have a bird's-eye view of the coastline, jungle, and farmland if you sign on with **Hot Air Balloon Tours** (Av. Moreles 36 at Corona, downtown; ☎ 322/3-2002). In high season, there are two daily ascents, weather permitting, one at 7am, the other at 5pm. The price ($120 to $140 per person) includes celebratory champagne at the end of the flight.

Puerto Vallarta's Best Shopping

No contest. Puerto Vallarta wins the "Beach Town Where You're Mostly Likely to Max Out Your Credit Card" award, hands down. Blame it on the American and European influence, and an influx of Mexican artists; Puerto Vallarta knows what foreigners with good taste want and is happy to provide it. You'll find folk art from all over Mexico—not necessarily at the best prices, but it would cost you a lot more to go on a countrywide shopping spree—as well as sophisticated contemporary artwork. Jewelry, clothing, practically anything you can think of to adorn your person or your home, abound.

Not only is the selection good, but shopping here is surprisingly low-stress. Aside from the market, where bargaining is essential, you can expect the kind of treatment you'd get in nice U.S. stores—welcoming, but not pesky. Salespeople rarely pounce on you when you enter, and sometimes you even have to ask for help.

A series of shopping centers dot the hotel zone—the best is Villa Vallarta, outside the Plaza las Glorias hotel—and Marina Vallarta has some nice upscale boutiques and galleries, but downtown rules the shopping scene. I'll recommend some specific stores below, but if you just want to wander around, you might start in *centro* on **Avenida Moreles Street,** which runs parallel to the *Malecón* and 1 block inland from it; there's a good concentration of folk art and furniture shops between Alvaro Rodriguez and Abasolo streets. Within those same perimeters, **Juárez,** an additional block away from the sea, is particularly rich in art galleries. South of the river, try **Basilio Badillo** from Olas Altas to Insurgentes, lined with crafts and clothing boutiques. This street also happens to be restaurant row, so while the stores are shuttered for lunch, you can fortify yourself for the afternoon round of acquisition.

Unless otherwise indicated, all the stores listed below are downtown.

A Gallery of Galleries

Want to spend a few hours checking out the greatest hits? The following galleries are must-sees:

➤ **Galería Olinala** (Lázaro Cárdenas 274; ☎ **322/2-4995**) specializes in Mexican tribal art, including an impressive collection of masks and Huichol beadwork.

➤ **Galería Pacifico** (Insurgentes 109; ☎ **322/2-0908**) has helped foster the careers of many up-and-coming artists from around the country. Interesting local talent is represented, too. If you're in town the first and third Wednesdays of the month, don't miss the openings held here.

➤ **Galería Indígina** (Juárez 270; ☎ **322/2-3007**) features a wide array of high-end crafts, including silver, Oaxaca pottery and wood carvings, and lacquer chests. There's a room of contemporary painting upstairs.

➤ **Galería Parroquia** (Independencía 231; ☎ **322/2-6222**), with a prime location in front of Our Lady of Guadalupe church, is the showcase for three well-known Puerto Vallarta artists who work in watercolor, collage, and acrylic.

➤ **Galería Rosas Blancas** (Juárez 523; ☎ **322/2-1168**) has a small cafe and art bookstore waiting for you when you finish exploring its excellent collection of Mexican and Latin American art.

411

➤ **Galería Uno** (Moreles 561; ☎ 322/2-0908) is one of Puerto Vallarta's oldest (1971) and most respected showcases of contemporary art. The work comes from all over Mexico, but the main focus is on Puerto Vallarta talent.

➤ **Galería Vallarta** (Juárez 263; ☎ 322/2-0290) represents the over-flow from the huge folk-art collection of its owners. Paintings, sculp-tures, ceremonial masks, and clothing are among its many treasures.

➤ **Mañuel Lepe Museo-Galería** (Juárez 533; ☎ 322/2-5515) is devoted to Puerto Vallarta's best-known artist, who died in 1984. Lepe's naif landscapes, often featuring angels, children, and birds, have been col-lected by everyone from Queen Elizabeth II to John Travolta. The paint-ings here aren't for sale, but you can buy Lepe prints and T-shirts and check out the artist's former workspace—which still contains his brim-ming ashtray.

➤ **Sergio Bustamante Gallery** (Juárez 275; ☎ 322/2-1120) features jewelry and sculptures by Mexico's renowned and wonderfully whimsi-cal surrealist artist. You'll probably recognize his trademark sun and moon faces.

Folk Art

In addition to the galleries mentioned above, **Querubines** (Juárez 501-A; ☎ 322/2-1168 or 2-2988) has room after room of wonderful hand-crafted furniture, housewares, jewelry, and clothing. **Lucy's Cucú Cabaña** (Basilio Badillo 295; no phone) claims the largest variety of hand-crafted cats in the world—hard to prove, but she's definitely got a swell collection of artsy felines and much more. **Mundo de Azulejos** (Carranza 374; ☎ 322/2-2675) is the place to go for tiles, **La Rosa de Cristal** (Insurgentes 272; ☎ 322/2-5698) specializes in blown glass, **Talavera, Etc.** (I. Vallarta 266; ☎ 322/2-41000) carries colorful ceramics, and **La Tienda de Maria** (Juárez 182; no phone) concentrates on miniatures and Day of the Dead art.

Clothing

At **Tabu** (Río Cuale 28, behind the John Huston statue; ☎ 322/2-3528), owner Patti Callardo creates unique-to-you hand-painted clothing. You'll need to phone **Barbara Eager** (☎ 322/3-0132) if you want her to whip up a custom bathing suit for you; she's often busy flattering the figures of film crews who come to town. **Maria's of Guadalajara** (Moreles 550, ☎ 322/2-2387; and Puesta del Sol condominiums in Marina Vallarta, ☎ 322/1-0262, ext. 1015) carries the gauzy, loose-fitting clothes that Mexican resorts seem to cry out for.

Markets

The **Mercado Municipal,** at the Río Cuale bridge near Avenida Miramar and Libertad, is a two-story indoor market chock-a-block with stalls selling jewelry, tinwork mirrors, ceramics, leather, stuffed armadillos, and all manner of tourist-friendly items. It's open daily 8am to 8pm, but lots of shopkeepers don't turn up on Sunday. The selection is large and you'll have everything concentrated in one area, but it can get hot and crowded in here. If you're looking for inexpensive trinkets to take home as gifts, this is a good place to come. Otherwise, you're probably better off at the downtown shops where the quality is higher, the owners are accountable, the prices are fair, and you won't feel compelled to haggle over every peso.

An Art Apart

In a remote region high in the Sierra Madres where the states of Jalisco and Nayarit meet, an Indian tribe called the Huichol create some of the most beautiful, intricate crafts you'll ever see. Using needles, the artists embed tiny glass beads into the waxed bottom of a hollowed-out gourd in elaborate, wildly colorful patterns. They also use yarn to "paint" similar designs on waxed wooden boards.

Huichol art was once used only in religious ceremonies, but now it's often created for public consumption. The work is as painstaking as before, however, the designs still draw on ancient myths and rituals, and the proceeds from the sales help keep the members of the tribe alive. You can buy Huichol art in several Puerto Vallarta galleries but **Arte Mágico Huichol** (Corona 178; ☎ **322/2-0377**) has the largest selection, filling several rooms. If you think the work is expensive, keep in mind the amount of time it took to create.

What to Do When the Sun's Gone Down

No matter what your nocturnal style, you won't be wanting for someplace to prowl after dark, nor will you have to spend much time getting there. Although much of Puerto Vallarta's nighttime action is concentrated around the *malecón* and south of the Río Cuale on Vallarta, Lázaro Cárdenas, Carranza, and Basilio Badillo streets, the hotel zone has its fair share of hot spots and even Marina Vallarta can keep you amused for a while.

How Low Should You Go?

Start out with a price about 70% below the one you've been quoted, and be happy if you end up with about 50% off the original asking price.

Bar None: Puerto Vallarta's Best Drinking Spots

Andale (Olas Altas 425, across from Los Arcos hotel; ☎ **322/2-1054**), a cantina-style dive, is big with both tourists and locals. It can get pretty rowdy, but the fun's usually harmless. You don't have to be gay to frequent

Paco Paco's (I. Vallarta, between Basilio Badillo and Carranza; ☎ 322/2-1900), a straight-friendly gay bar with fabulous floorshows, including blowout Broadway cabarets (the cover ranges from $6 to $12.50, depending on the night and the show). **Yukon Jack's** (Marina Vallarta, Marina Las Palmas, Bldg. no. 2; ☎ 322/1-0510) is the watering hole of choice for the yachting crowd. Down a bargain Corona or Bud (75¢) and find out who caught the big one.

Fiestas: A Taste of Mexico

For a somewhat artificial, but enjoyable, take on the country's cultural traditions, book a Mexican fiesta. You can expect an open bar, huge quantities of food, mariachis, folkloric dancers, and more. The best of these blasts are thrown at **La Iguana** (downtown south, Lázaro Cárdenas 311, between Insurgentes and Constitucíon; ☎ 322/2-0105), which has been hosting them for 3 decades (Thursday and Sunday, $25); **Hotel Krystal** (hotel zone, Avenida de la Garza s/n; ☎ 322/4-0202), where they're held at an open-air plaza (Tuesday and Saturday, $30); and the **Sheraton Buganvilias** (hotel zone, Av. de las Palmas 999; ☎ 322/3-0404), with a grand finale including fireworks (Thursday, $30). On Saturday nights at the **Hotel Playa Los Arcos** (downtown south, Olas Altas 380; ☎ 322/2-1583), there are two seatings for a more low-key—because the alcohol flow isn't free—fiesta (7 and 10:30pm, $10). You can book all these shows directly or through a travel agent. *Note:* Fiestas are not always held in low season, or at least not as frequently.

Eat 'n' Rumba: Restaurants with a Musical Menu

The burgers, ribs, and other hearty American fare are good but incidental at **Carlos O Brian's** (Díaz Ordáz 786 at Pipila; ☎ 322/2-1444), **Hard Rock Cafe** (Díaz Ordáz 652 at Absolo; ☎ 322/2-2230), and **Planet Hollywood** (Moreles and Galeana; ☎ 322/3-2710), all on or about the malecón. These members of the Mexican, British, and American chains, renowned for their raucous atmosphere, wacky memorabilia, and loud rock 'n' roll, draw crowds young enough not to be concerned about hearing loss—yet. The action starts at about 11pm. Arrive before 10pm if you want a downstairs table.

Bet You Didn't Know

Mariachis and tequila both originated in Puerto Vallarta's state of Jalisco.

Don't come to **Tequila's** (Galeana 104–101; ☎ 322/2-5725) for the Mexican seafood, but for a sampler of the potent potable for which it's named—five types for $10—and the mariachis who serenade you from 8:30 to 10:30pm each night. If you're lucky enough to get a balcony table, you've got ringside seats on the malecón.

Another musical malecón eatery, **Mogambo** (Paseo Díaz Ordáz 644; ☎ 322/2-3476) has a wild African theme—lions and tigers and crocodiles, oh my—and a comparatively tame jazz ensemble.

For other good live dinner sounds in the downtown area, try **Le Bistro, La Dolce Vita,** and **Café des Artistes,** all covered in chapter 36, "The Best of Puerto Vallarta's Dining Scene."

Saturday Night Fever

If you're a dancing fool, head for the north side of town. The undisputed queen of Puerto Vallarta discos, **Christine** (hotel zone, Hotel Krystal; ☎ 322/4-0202, ext. 878) takes the usual 1970s paraphernalia—fog machines, pulsating lights, mega sound system—into the '90s. The place draws a well-heeled (the cover is $15), well-dressed (no shorts, sandals, or tank tops for men allowed) 20-something crowd. When your feet get weary at **Friday López** (hotel zone, Hotel Fiesta Americana, off Avenida De las Palmas; ☎ 322/4-2010), you might be able to exercise your voice if it's karaoke night; the cover ranges from $5 to $10. At **Collage** (on the highway in front of the Marina Vallarta complex; ☎ 322/1-0505), video games, billiards, shuffleboard, and even a bowling alley compete with the disco (cover $6.50) for the revelers' attentions. There's something here to satisfy all ages.

Isn't It Romantic?

For an elevating experience, ascend to the top of the landmark **El Faro Lighthouse** (Marina Vallarta; ☎ 322/1-0541 or 322/ 1-0542), where a glass-encased cocktail lounge chases its superb views of the marina with tender-hearted songs. You'll also be soothed by the sounds emanating from the piano at the **Westin Regina** (Marina Vallarta, Paseo de la Marina Sur 205; ☎ 322/1-1100) lobby bar. Downtown, **Chez Elena** (Matamoros 520, between Corona and Aldama; ☎ 322/2-0161)

Bet You Didn't Know

More photographs of Puerto Vallarta are taken from El Faro than from anywhere else.

boasts a panoramic view of the city—and a juicy history. It's said to have been built by a retired Acapulco madame with funds from satisfied customers. On the open-air terrace at **Stars** (Zaragoza 160, 3rd level, on the main Plaza de Armas; ☎ 322/2-6061), you sit above the hubbub of the city, with the mountains and bay spread before you. Although the name of the hilltop **El Set** (south, Carretera a Barra de Navidad, km 2.5; ☎ 322/2-0302) refers to a film, not a sunset, it's still a lovely spot to have a drink and watch the old fiery orb descend.

Mariachi Madness & More

After 10pm, they let the R & B roll at **Roxy** (downtown south, Vallarta 217 between Madero and Lázaro Cárdenas; ☎ 322/3-0240); there's no cover. For something more Mexicano, backtrack to **Mariachis Locos** (Cárdenas at Vallarta; ☎ 322/3-2205), where a ranchero band warms you up for the main attraction, the 11pm mariachi show. The cover is nominal, but if you don't want to pay anything beyond that and the price of your drinks, shake your head no when the mariachis come to your table.

Yo, Gringo!

It's customary to tip mariachis about $1 per band member per song. Be careful: If you let an eight-person ensemble croon a couple of heartbreak ballads directly to you, you'll really have something to cry about.

Side Trips: Getting Out of Puerto Vallarta

Visiting some of the more far-flung northern and southern beaches, detailed in the beaches section of this chapter, is one way to get away from town for a day. In addition, nature lovers who prefer jungle to shore might consider setting out for San Blas. If, on the other hand, you need an even heavier dose of shopping and culture than Puerto Vallarta can provide, a day trip to Guadalajara might be just the thing.

San Blas

Serious birders may want to stay overnight at San Blas, a not-so-scenic fishing town (population: about 10,000) some 150 miles north of Puerto Vallarta. Approximately 300 avian species—one of the highest counts in the western hemisphere—have been spotted in this area. Surfers who want to test their mettle against the mile-long, 20-foot-high waves at nearby Las Islitas beach might also want to settle into this town for a while. Otherwise, however, there's little to recommend sleeping in San Blas; I suggest you take a day trip, which you can book at any travel agent for about $55.

You'll take an inland highway toward Tepic, looking at small villages and tropical plantations along the way; mangos, papayas, pineapple, and tobacco all thrive in this area. San Blas sits at the edge of a mangrove swamp—bring your bug spray!—and the highlight of the day is a foray into its watery mazes by boat. As you wind along the dense canals toward Tovara Springs, a lovely spot for swimming, the guide will point out birds, sea turtles, and maybe even a crocodile or two (keep those hands inside the boat).

Most San Blas tours depart at 8am, return at 7:30pm, and include continental breakfast, lunch, and the Tovara Springs boat tour. You can go on your own by bus, but you'll spend a far longer time in transit without the benefit of anyone to point out the sights. You'll also have to pay to hire a boat (about $10 per person) when you get there and shell out for your own food; all in all, you come out ahead by going through a travel agent.

Guadalajara

I'd love to tell you all about Guadalajara, a wonderful, culture-filled city, but that's another book. I'm going to assume that you want to spend most of your time near the beach, and just take a brief guided foray into the big city. If you do want to devote more of your vacation to Guadalajara, about 6 hours by bus from Puerto Vallarta, *Frommer's Mexico* is a good source of information.

Day tours to Guadalajara, which usually depart at 9:30am and return at 8:45pm, don't come cheap. Expect to pay a travel agent about $230 per person, which includes a round-trip flight on a small chartered aircraft. A typical excursion starts in the suburbs of Tonala, renowned for its pottery, and Tlaquepaque, a crafts center that's also notable for its cobblestone streets and 16th-century buildings. After lunch (on your own) in Tlaquepaque, you'll be guided around downtown Guadalajara, taking in its opera house, museums, and immense cathedral. A visit to the flea market or Mariachi Square are other options.

Chapter 36

The Best of Puerto Vallarta's Dining Scene

In This Chapter

➤ Dining in Puerto Vallarta: The big picture

➤ Keeping costs down

➤ The best restaurants from A to Z

➤ Restaurant indexes

Puerto Vallarta is one of the most cosmopolitan restaurant towns in Mexico, thanks in part to an influx of American and European visitors, some of whom stayed on to become chefs. You can get everything from schnitzel to sushi here—and expect it to be top quality. Along with a dazzling variety of international eateries, you'll also find a wide range of Mexican restaurants. In Puerto Vallarta, you can be as conservative or as adventurous in your eating as you want, and as down-home or as dressed up.

A Dining Overview: Where's the Burrito?

You can find decent places to eat in most Puerto Vallarta neighborhoods, but the greatest concentration of good restaurants by far is downtown. With some notable exceptions in both cases, the area around the malecón tends to have the rowdier and more touristy eateries, while the section south of the Río Cuale, and especially Basilio Badillo, known as Restaurant Row, is a gourmet mecca. It's easy enough to walk from one side of the river to the other, but for convenience's sake, I've divided listed restaurants into "Downtown/North" and "Downtown/South" categories to reflect this division.

In addition, the increasingly successful Marina Vallarta complex has begun to come into its own, culinarily speaking. Time was when you had no choice but to go south if you wanted to eat well. Now, with lots of branches of *centro* eateries opening in the marina, you can have downtown food without the trip. Accordingly, I've included a few restaurants in the marina. All listings are arranged alphabetically, and at the end of the chapter I've also indexed them by price and by location.

Kids If you're traveling with young children who aren't especially adventurous, not to worry: Mickey D's is right there on the *malecón,* and KFC and Burger King are on the main plaza. If you've got teenagers in tow, Planet Hollywood, Carlos O Brian's, and the Hard Rock Cafe are good bets (if you don't want to spend a fortune, though, you might have to hustle them quickly past the logowear concessions). See chapter 35, "Fun On & Off the Beach," for the addresses.

Check, Please

You can blow your restaurant budget on a single meal in some of Puerto Vallarta's restaurants, if you're not careful—or you can watch what you're doing and eat well, and well within your means. Page back to "Eating Well without Gobbling Up Your Dollars" in chapter 7 for some wallet-friendly tips.

Don't worry about taxes; the 15% surcharge has already been included in your bill. The tip isn't, however. The standard in nice restaurants is 15%. Mexicans rarely tip that well in the less expensive places—10% is about average—but if the service was good, sticking with the 15% rule is an easy way to help the Mexican economy without breaking your budget.

As part of the effort to help you stay within budget, I've arranged the price categories with a worst-case scenario in mind: They're based on a per-person dinner tab that includes appetizer, entrée, dessert, one drink, and tip. In addition, a price range for dinner entrées is included in the individual reviews. It's simple: The more $ signs you see, the more you'll be shelling out at each restaurant:

Yo, Gringo!

Don't take restaurant tips from taxi drivers—they're likely to be getting their own tips (otherwise known as kickbacks) from the owners of the restaurants they recommend.

$	=	Under $10
$$	=	$10–$25
$$$	=	$25–$45
$$$$	=	Over $45

Unless otherwise specified, reservations are not accepted or not necessary.

My Favorite Restaurants from A to Z

Café de la Olla

$. Downtown/South. MEXICAN.

Although this homey Mexican cafe keeps on expanding, it's still not large enough to accommodate everyone who wants in; come high season, scores of hungry people line up outside from about 7 to 9pm. They're waiting for the likes of chicken tamales steamed in a banana leaf, Yucatán style, or sizzling *carne asada* (barbecued beef), all served with fresh-made tortillas. The perfectly charbroiled ribs and chicken have their die-hard defenders, too, and the margaritas are killer.

Yo, Gringo!

Remember, it's considered impolite in Mexico for the waiter to bring the check before you ask for it.

Basilio Badillo 168, between Olas Altas and Pino Suárez. ☎ *322/2-1626. **Main courses:** $2.50–$6.50. No credit cards. **Open:** Daily 9am–11pm.*

Café des Artistes

$$$$. Downtown/North. INTERNATIONAL.

At this Puerto Vallarta institution, owner-chef Thierry Blouet set a standard for stunning presentations and creative cooking that other serious chefs have had to contend with. His fans claim this restaurant has changed the cooking scene for the better; others argue it's brought pretentiousness to town. Serious gastronomes will love Blouet's adventurous pairings of local Mexican ingredients with nouvelle French recipes. You might find cream of prawn and pumpkin soup, or a salad of smoked provolone, cactus, and tomato as starters. Main courses could include sea bass with vermicelli or roast duck with honey and soy sauce. The place looks like a castle from outside, and the main dining room is gorgeous but a bit formal; if you want to relax, get a table on the terrace (birdsongs are a trade-off for missing the nightly piano/flute duo).

Quickest Tickets to Europe

Café Maximilian (Downtown/South, $$$–$$$$)

Little Switzerland (Marina Vallarta, $)

Guadalupe Sánchez 740. ☎ *322/2-3228. Reservations essential. **Main courses:** $16–$25. AE, DC, MC, V. **Open:** Daily 8am–3pm and 6–11:30pm.*

Café Maximilian

$$$–$$$$. Downtown/South. INTERNATIONAL/TYROLEAN.

Sigmund Freud wouldn't have felt out of place at this Old World Viennese-style bistro (although he might have been taken aback by the unrepressed displays

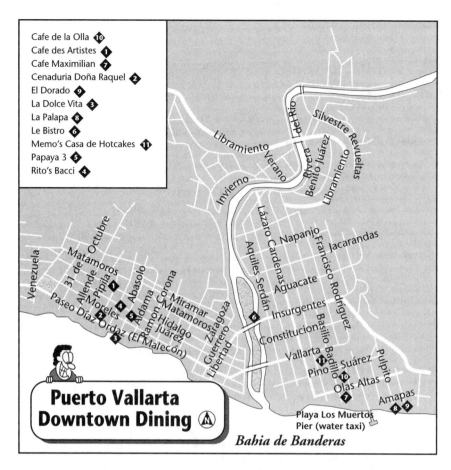

Cafe de la Olla ⑩
Cafe des Artistes ①
Cafe Maximilian ⑦
Cenaduria Doña Raquel ②
El Dorado ⑨
La Dolce Vita ③
La Palapa ⑧
Le Bistro ⑥
Memo's Casa de Hotcakes ⑪
Papaya 3 ⑤
Rito's Bacci ④

Puerto Vallarta Downtown Dining Ⓝ

Bahia de Banderas

of libido at the Playa Los Arcos Hotel, to which it's attached). Fresh flowers, mirrored columns, and white tablecloths create an elegant atmosphere in which to enjoy *gemütlich* dishes like Wiener schnitzel with sautéed potatoes, or pan-fried fish with paprika and white cabbage. Desserts such as *rumwuchtelm,* a brioche filled with plums and apricots and doused with vanilla sauce, should hammer the last nail into the coffin of your diet. You can also enjoy these decadent sweets at the charming little cafe next door.

Olas Altas 380-B, Playa de los Muertos. ☎ *322/3-0760. Reservations recommended.* **Main courses:** *$10.50–$19. AE, MC, V.* **Open:** *Mon–Sat 6–11pm.*

Cenaduria Doña Raquel
$. Downtown/North. MEXICAN.
When the waiters from Carlos O Brian's and the Hard Rock Cafe get through with their shifts, they make a beeline for nearby Doña Raquel's for some good home cooking. The specialty here is *pozole,* a hearty hominy and pork stew; it used to be served only on Thursdays—the traditional day for that dish throughout much of Mexico—but by popular demand it's become a menu staple. You can also fill up on a four-taco plate for about $2.50. This is a bare-bones place with absolutely no atmosphere, but in the touristy

421

Bet You Didn't Know

A *cenaduria* (*cena* = dinner) is an evening cafe that specializes in traditional dishes.

malecón area, it's the genuine item. An accommodating staff will help you navigate the Spanish-only menu.

L. Vicario 131, between Morelos and Díaz Ordáz. ☎ *322/2-0618. Main courses: $2–$5. No credit cards. Open: Tues–Sun 6:30–11:30pm.*

El Dorado
$$. Downtown/South.
MEXICAN/SEAFOOD.

Countless business deals have been struck at this beachside palapa-roof restaurant since it opened in the early 1960s; maybe *huevos motuleños,* spicy Yucatán-style eggs with tortillas, ham, and peas, is the perfect power breakfast. American and Canadian expatriates also gather here, enjoying great Mexican seafood—ceviche tacos, say, or shrimp crêpes, or red snapper with garlic—or just sitting around over cocktails at sunset and checking out the waning Los Muertos beach action.

Pulpito 102, Playa de los Muertos. ☎ *322/2-1511. Main courses: $3–$12. AE, MC, V. Open: Daily 8am–9:30pm.*

Inoky Sushi & Bar
$–$$. Marina Vallarta. JAPANESE.

Where better to enjoy fresh sushi than at a table looking out on a marina? True, the yachts moored outside aren't the source of the tasty tuna, salmon, eel, or shrimp used in the various raw fish combinations, but it still feels right, somehow. A number of the maki rolls include cream cheese, for some reason; don't go there. You can also get teppanyaki, teriyaki, tempura, and other cooked food. If you don't want to eat in this small, modest restaurant, you can have your order delivered to your hotel room, but by the time it gets there anything that started out hot probably won't be anymore.

Marina del Rey, local 10. ☎ *322/1-2304. Main courses: Sushi $1–$3 per piece; maki rolls $2.50–$9; hot entrées $4–$7.50. AE, MC, V. Open: Tues–Sun 2–11pm.*

La Dolce Vita
$$. Downtown/North. ITALIAN.

Thank Stefano Santini's impulsive nature for some of Puerto Vallarta's best pizza. The young chef of this friendly Italian restaurant came here on vacation from northern Italy and never left. He still imports many of his ingredients—olive oil, cheese, certain spices—from home, and it shows. In addition to the great brick-oven-baked pies, there's a nice selection of fresh-made pastas and seafood, served in generous portions. This place is always bustling and the decibel level increases after 9pm Tuesday through Saturday, when a rock band takes the stage. Come early and grab an upstairs table overlooking the *malecón* if your mood is romantic rather than rowdy.

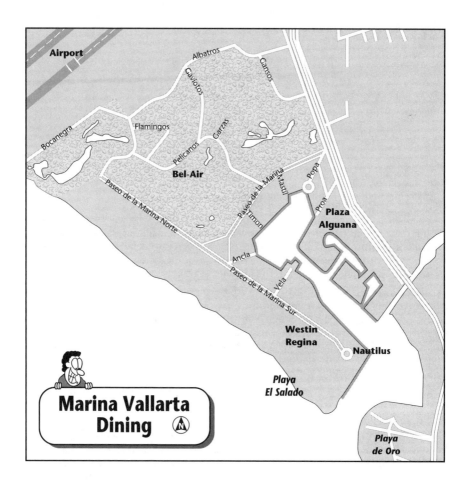

Marina Vallarta
Dining

Díaz Ordáz 674 (north end of the Malecón). ☎ 322/2-3852. **Main courses:**
pizza $5–$8; other dishes $5–$11. AE, MC, V. **Open:** *Daily noon–2am.*

La Palapa
*$$–$$$. Downtown/South. NOU-
VELLE MEXICAN/SEAFOOD.*
You can wiggle your toes in the sand of
Playa de los Muertos while downing delicious nouvelle-style Mexican specialties
such as smoked marlin enchiladas or *chiles
en nogada* (spicy poblano peppers stuffed
with beef and raisins and topped with a
creamy almond sauce). If you want to
avoid the vendors, settle into a colorful,

Extra! Extra!
My favorite seafood place in
Puerto Vallarta? **La Palapa**
(Downtown/South, $$–$$$).

hand-carved chair farther back from the sea and just survey the scene. Lunch
tends to be totally casual; come dinner, some serious fashion slaves strut
their stuff. This place has been in the same family since 1957; the soft guitar
serenades of current owner Alberto Perez enhance an already romantic
evening atmosphere.

423

Pulpito 103, Playa de los Muertos. ☎ **322/2-5225. Main courses:** *$6.50–$17.*
AE, MC, V. **Open:** *Daily 8am–11pm.*

Café Olé

As might be expected from a town popular with people who worship at the
shrine of a good cup of coffee, Puerto Vallarta has a small but thriving cafe
culture. South of the Cuale river, Olas Altas street is particularly big in the caffeine distribution business, but coffeehouses are scattered all around downtown. Some of the most interesting include:

➤ **Café Oro Verde** (Juárez 64, north downtown, next door to the post
office; no phone) is famous for its namesake brand of coffee, grown in the
Sierra Madre foothills above Nuevo Vallarta; the beans are so prized that
they're sold wholesale in Seattle. Coffeehouses in that city have nothing
over this place, where you can get latte, cappuccino, or espresso (although
not great decaf) in a friendly, genial setting.

➤ **Page in the Sun** (Olas Atlas and Manuel M. Dieguez, south downtown,
across from Los Arcos; no phone) has the largest collection of used English,
German, and French paperbacks for sale in town. The coffee, freshly roasted
and ground, is great and the outdoor patio is fine for people watching.

➤ **Si Señor's Books and Expresso** (Olas Altas at Rodolfo Gomez, south
downtown; no phone) carries a smaller selection of used reads, but has a
good choice of new books on Mexico. There's always a chess or cribbage
game going on. If you're not in the mood for a caffeine buzz, you can
linger here over a beer.

➤ **Café Superior** (corner of Encino and Juárez at Río Cuale in the Hotel
Encino Building; no phone) is a cool, quiet hangout under the Río Cuale
bridge. Locals like to gather for the economical lunches and breakfasts.

➤ **Café Estes** (Libertad 336, across from Color Vallarta, south downtown; no
phone), a recent addition to the scene, has something that the others
don't: air-conditioning. If you can't stand the heat, retreat here for an
espresso or cappuccino.

La Paz
$–$$. Marina Vallarta. MEXICAN.
Turn left at the whale sculpture at the entrance to Marina Vallarta to find
this open-front Mexican *fonda* (a small, economical restaurant). Local businesspeople gather at plastic cloth–covered tables for a variety of daily specials. The lunchtime *comida corrida* (set-price menu) might include pasta soup
and chicken mole for $3; the main course for the dinner special ($5) could
be filet mignon or shrimp thermidor. This is a rare slice of authentic Mexican
life in the generally touristy Marina.

Condominiums Marina Rey, local l 01A, entrance to Marina Vallarta. ☎ *322/ 1-0313.* **Main courses:** *$3.50–$8.50; set-price menus: $2.50 breakfast, $3.50 lunch, $5 dinner. No credit cards.* **Open:** *Daily 7:30am–10:30pm.*

Le Bistro
$$$. Downtown/South. INTERNATIONAL.

The menu is as stylish as the decor at Le Bistro, and a prime location on the Río Cuale adds to this restaurant's cachet. Ceiling fans swirl overhead and palm fronds sway on the water while you enjoy globe-trotting starters such as hummus, crab sashimi, or escargots in herbed garlic butter. Entrées include shrimp Portuguese, Caribbean-style Belafonte fish fillet, and filet mignon wrapped in bacon. There's

> **Most Romantic Restaurants**
>
> Café des Artistes (Downtown/North, $$$$)
>
> Le Bistro (Downtown/ South, $$$)

also that rarity in Mexico (or in the United States, for that matter)—a selection of gourmet vegetarian dishes. If you steer clear of the shrimp selections—although it's tough, given some of the tempting possibilities—you can get away with an outrageous meal for a far from outrageous price. On Monday, Wednesday, and Friday from 10pm to 1am, a piano players tickles the ivories in the super-chic cocktail lounge.

Río Cuale Island 161. ☎ *322/2-0283. Reservations suggested.* **Main courses:** *$6–$16. AE, MC, V.* **Open:** *Mon–Sat 9am–midnight.*

Little Switzerland
$. Marina Vallarta. BAKERY/DELI.

Come to this charming European-style cafe when you wake up to fortify yourself with fresh-baked pastries and good coffee for a hard morning of tanning; when it's time for a break, return for a great deli sandwich and an imported beer. If you want to pick up some fixings for a picnic, keep in mind that this place is a favorite with the yacht-owners who tie up nearby; the hot-from-the-oven bread—sunflower and oatmeal are among the choices— sells out fast. The pistachio sausage, smoked ham, and the quiche Lorraine are delicious, and the apple strudel is to die for.

Paseo de la Marina 245, local 117. ☎ *322/1-2070.* **Main courses:** *Sandwiches $3–$7; pastries $1.50–$3. No credit cards.* **Open:** *Mon–Sat 7am–8:30pm.*

Los Pibes
$$$. Marina Vallarta. ARGENTINIAN/STEAKHOUSE.

At this carnivore's carnival, you can watch your dinner being prepared Argentinian style—roasted oh-so-slowly in an open pit barbecue over mesquite. New Zealand lamb and a mixed grill with spicy sausage are among the menu's offerings, but what most people come for is the 1.8-pound rib eye (unless you're from Texas, you'll probably want to share). The meat is

425

delicious and comes with Argentinian salad—lettuce, tomato, and onion—but nothing else; it's annoying to have to pay extra for such sides as fries, baked potatoes, steamed vegetables, and even mustard sauce. You can enjoy your meal on the terrace, gazing out at at the marina, or in a dark, steak-house-style dining room. The original downtown Los Pibes (Basilio Badillo 261; ☎ **322/3-1557** or 322/3-2044) has the same menu but no outdoor seating.

Paseo de la Marina no. 245 (near the El Faro lighthouse). ☎ ***322/1-0609. Main courses:** Grilled meat $7–$15; pasta $6–$7. AE, MC, V.* ***Open:** Daily noon–midnight.*

Chez George of the Jungle

Don't leave Puerto Vallarta without lunching on Mexican seafood at one of the "jungle" restaurants south of town, around or beyond Mismaloya Beach. These casual, open-air eateries, surrounded by tropical foliage, are as touristy as all get-out, but loads of fun. The best way to reach all of them is by cab, but if you want to cut down on the fare, take the bus down to Mismaloya and catch your taxi there. Don't forget your bathing suit; in all cases, you'll be able to take a dip in a river or waterhole.

Chino's Paradise (off Hwy. 200, km 6.5; ☎ **322/3-3012**) has five open-air terraces that look out on huge boulders, a swift-flowing river, and a waterfall; a marimba band usually plays from 1 to 3pm. At **El Eden** (off Hwy. 200, km 6.5; no phone), the former film set of the Arnold Schwarzenegger machofest, *Predator*, you can look out on folks dropping from a rope swing into the river below—or try it yourself (but not after drinking too many margaritas, please).

My favorite, however, is **Chico's Paradise** (km 20, just beyond Boca de Tomatlán; ☎ **322/2-0747**). The food is a cut above the rest and the setting is especially spectacular. After the rainy season, the Tomatlán River rushes over the huge boulders that the local kids love to dive from. Settle in under the huge palapa roof and enjoy shrimp smothered in garlic butter, served with fresh, hot tortillas—you can watch them being made—or just order some nachos and a potent Coco Loco. Gorda, a friendly parrot, likes to table-hop.

Memo's Casa de Hotcakes
Kids *$. Downtown/South. AMERICAN/MEXICAN.*

If you haven't been to Memo's, you've been looking for pancakes in all the wrong places. This is *the* gringo gathering spot; any Anglo who's been in town any length of time—say more than 2 days—turns up here sooner or later. But although most customers are *Norteamericano*, the menu divides pretty evenly down NAFTA lines. In addition to the great pancakes and waffles, topped with anything you can think of—even peanut butter, which you can also order as a side—Memo's has huge breakfast burritos, *chilaquiles* (tortillas scrambled with cheese and eggs or chicken), or *huevos rancheros*. The food may be classic diner, but the room is open and airy; you'll have to get up early in the morning if you want a seat on the plant-filled patio.

Basilio Badillo 289. ☎ *322/2-6272.* **Main courses:** *$2.50–$5. No credit cards.* **Open:** *Daily 8am–2pm.*

A Recipe for Fun

If you want to take back more than memories of some of the delicious Mexican dishes you tasted in Puerto Vallarta, check out the cooking classes conducted by Memo Barroso in his Casa de Hotcakes. You eat and drink while Memo, with great humor, demonstrates everything from the proper way to prepare a margarita to how to seed chiles without burning your fingers, and gives fascinating histories of the various dishes. Classes, which cost $35, including food and booze, are held Wednesday, Thursday, and Friday in high season. Call ☎ **322/2-6272** to reserve a spot; classes fill up fast.

Papaya 3

$. Downtown/North. HEALTH FOOD.

Sick of fried, heavy food? Grab a stool at the wooden counter of this small, plant-filled restaurant (there are a few tables, too) and scale the health pyramid. You can get your greens with the Shanghai salad, a large plate of steamed vegetables; fill your fruit quota with a shake (the Cancún blends guayaba, coconut, melon, and milk); and put some protein on your bones with a fresh tuna entrée. Soft jazz plays in the background.

Absolo 169, between Juárez and Moreles.
☎ *322/2-0303.* **Main courses:** *$2.75–$6. No credit cards.* **Open:** *Mon–Sat 8am–10pm; Sun 9am–5pm.*

Rito's Bacci

$–$$. Downtown/North. ITALIAN.

If you care more about from-the-heart Italian cooking than atmosphere, head over to this no-frills restaurant, about 6 blocks north of the main plaza. Recipes for pizzas such as the Horacio, topped with tomato, oregano, and basil, or for the classic southern Italian lasagna were handed down to chef Rito Calzado by his grandfather, who emigrated from Italy. All the

Local Favorites

Café de la Olla (Downtown/South, $)

Cenaduria Doña Raquel (Downtown/North, $)

La Paz (Marina Vallarta, $–$$)

427

pastas are made on the premises. The sandwiches are super, too; grab lots of napkins if you plan to eat the spicy Italian sausage hero with your hands. If you want to attack it or anything else in the privacy of your hotel room, you can have your order delivered.

Dominguez 181, corner of Juárez. ☎ *322/2-6448. Pasta $3.50–$5.50; salads and sandwiches $3–$4; pizza $7–$10.50. MC, V.* **Open:** *Daily 1–11pm.*

If My Favorites Are Full

Many people rave about **Chef Roger,** a dinner-only place that features an innovative European-, Southwest-, and Mexican-influenced cuisine; I know someone who ate there every night of his Puerto Vallarta visit. Well, maybe I was there on an off night . . . You might want to give it a shot (and let me know what you think if you do). Downtown/North. A. Rodriguez 267. ☎ **322/2-5900.** $$$$.

Sound Bites: Puerto Vallarta's Restaurants at a Glance
Restaurant Index by Price

$

Café de la Olla (Downtown/South, Mexican)

Cenaduria Doña Raquel (Downtown/North, Mexican)

Little Switzerland (Marina Vallarta, Bakery/Deli)

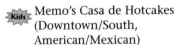 Memo's Casa de Hotcakes (Downtown/South, American/Mexican)

Papaya 3 (Downtown/North, Health Food)

$–$$

Inoky Sushi & Bar (Marina Vallarta, Japanese)

La Paz (Marina Vallarta, Mexican)

Rito's Bacci (Downtown/North, Italian)

$$

El Dorado (Downtown/South, Mexican/Seafood)

La Dolce Vita (Downtown/North, Italian)

$$–$$$

La Palapa (Downtown/South, Nouvelle Mexican/Seafood)

$$$

Le Bistro (Downtown/South, International)

Los Pibes (Marina Vallarta and Downtown/South, Argentinian/Steakhouse)

Restaurant Index by Location

Part 10

Mazatlán

The closest of the major beach resorts to the United States, Mazatlán has been making American tourists happy for around half a century—just about as long as Acapulco has. Unlike its more southern Pacific Coast rival, however, this town never caught on with the Hollywood crowd. Which is just fine with Mazatlán's loyal cadre of visitors, who come precisely because of the low-key atmosphere—and the low-impact prices. It doesn't hurt, either, that Mazatlán has some of the best billfishing in Mexico, as well as an eminently strollable downtown and lots of still-deserted stretches of seaside.

A long history of hospitality means lots of tourist facilities—and lots of choices for you to make. Grab a cold Pacifico—it's important to get into the swing of local customs—and let me guide you through the Mazatlán decision maze.

Choosing the Place to Stay That's Right for You

In This Chapter

➤ Where the hotels are

➤ The best in the bunch

➤ Hotel indexes

If you're looking to unpack your suitcase at an ultra-luxurious resort or a party-hearty all-inclusive, best choose another city to visit. Mazatlán's lodgings, for the most part, keep a low profile. If, on the other hand, you want a comfortable room on a nice stretch of sand without paying an arm and a leg for the privilege, you've come to the right place.

Here's how it works. First, I'll give you a thumbnail sketch of the areas where Mazatlán's hotels are concentrated, summing up their pros and cons at the end of each section. Then I'll list my favorite hotels alphabetically, and follow up with a list of alternatives if my A-list choices are filled. I've also included a couple of choices that fall outside the main hotel zones. At the end of the chapter, you'll find at-a-glance indexes listing the hotels by price and by location.

As far as prices go, I've noted rack rates (the maximum that a resort or hotel charges for a room) in the listings. This information will give you some sense of what to expect, although I know you'll avoid paying rack by following the advice I gave you in chapter 6, "The Lowdown on Accommodations in Mexico." I've also put a dollar sign icon in front of each hotel listing so you can quickly see whether it's within your budget. The more $ signs under the name, the more you pay. It runs like this:

$ = $70 and below

$$ = $70–$117

$$$ = $117–$175

$$$$ = $175 and above

Unless specified, rates are for a standard double room in high season (around December 20 through April 19th). The rest of the year, prices are reduced anywhere from 20% to 50%. During Christmas and Easter weeks, you might sometimes have to pay as much as 25% above the usual high-season rates—if you can get a room. If you want to come for Carnaval, Mazatlán's giant Mardi Gras, you'll have to book downtown hotels at least 6 months in advance (it's held a week before Lent, usually in late February or early March). The prices listed include the 17% room tax.

A kid-friendly icon **Kids** highlights hotels that are especially good for families. All hotels have air-conditioning unless otherwise indicated, and if the review doesn't say anything to the contrary, you can safely assume that you can walk directly out of your hotel and onto the beach.

Hint: As you read through the reviews, you'll want to keep track of the ones that appeal to you. I've included a chart at the end of the book (see p. 000) where you can rank your preferences, but to make matters easier on yourself now, just put a little check mark next to the ones you like. Remember how your teachers used to tell you not to write in your books? Now's the time to rebel—scrawl away!

Extra! Extra!

The ocean water near Mazatlán, the northernmost of the Pacific Coast resorts, can be a bit cool to swim in from mid-December to mid-February. Since this is also high season, you might want to come earlier, or wait until things heat up a bit.

Location, Location, Location

Mazatlán's tourist topography has gradually been shifting north. In the 1940s, most visitors stayed on Olas Altas beach, near the downtown city center. The subsequent decade saw hotels begin to rise up along Playa Norte, the adjacent stretch of sand. Two of the city's best beaches were developed next: Playa Gaviotas which buttresses what's now known as the Golden Zone, and Playa Sábalo, the sandbox for the most recent tourist enclave, the Platinum Zone (see chapter 39, "Fun On & Off the Beach," for details about the beaches). The imminent opening of a gigantic new marina—slated to be the largest in Mexico— just beyond the Platinum Zone virtually guarantees that this northward lodging drift will continue.

The older hotels to the south remain, but have mostly fallen into disrepair. They're usually booked only by rock-bottom budget travelers—and, once a

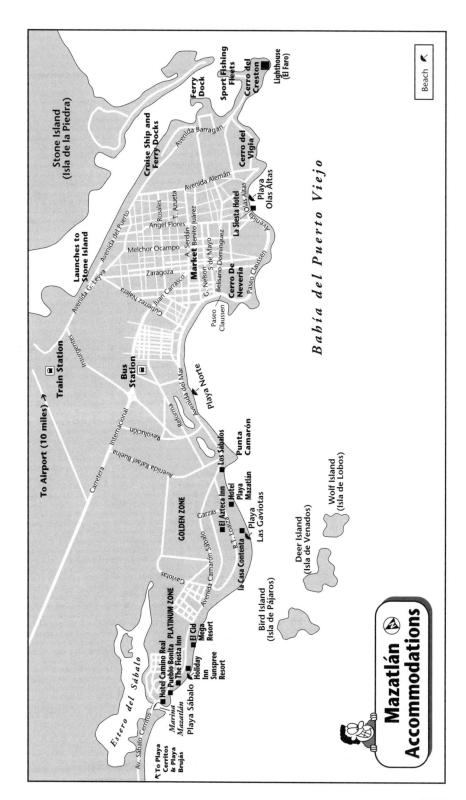

Mazatlán
Accommodations

Stone Island (Isla de la Piedra)

Cruise Ship and Ferry Docks

Ferry Dock

Sport Fishing Fleets

Cerro del Creston

Lighthouse (El Faro)

Avenida Barragan

Cerro del Vigía

Avenida Alemán

Rosales

T. Azueta

Angel Flores

A. Serdán

Benito Juárez

Melchor Ocampo

Market

Playa Olas Altas

La Siesta Hotel

5 de Mayo

Zaragoza

C. Nelson

Belisario Domínguez

Cerro De Nevería

Paseo Claussen

Paseo Claussen

Launches to Stone Island

Avenida del Puerto

Avenida G. Leyva

Gutierrez Nájera

Juan Carrasco

Insurgentes

To Airport (10 miles) →

Train Station

Bus Station

Playa Norte

Avenida del Mar

Reforma

Revolución

Internacional

Carretera

Avenida Rafael Buelna

Punta Camarón

Los Sábalos

Hotel Mazatlán

Playa Mazatlán

Garzas

El Azteca Inn

Playa Las Gaviotas

La Casa Contenta

R.T. Loaiza

GOLDEN ZONE

Avenida Carnarón Sábalo

Gaviotas

Bird Island (Isla de Pájaros)

Deer Island (Isla de Venados)

Wolf Island (Isla de Lobos)

Bahía del Puerto Viejo

Estero del Sábalo

Av. Sábalo Cerritos

To Playa Cerritos & Playa Brujas ↖

Hotel Camino Real

Pueblo Bonita

The Fiesta Inn

PLATINUM ZONE

El Cid Mega Resort

Holiday Inn

Sunspree Resort

Marina Mazatlán

Playa Sábalo

Beach ⌐

435

year, by the vast number of visitors who descend on downtown during Carnaval, when sleep isn't high on the list of major activities. I've listed the one Olas Altas area hotel (La Siesta Hotel, see below) that's up to snuff, but have otherwise concentrated choices in the two newest hotel zones.

The Golden Zone: Where the Action Is

Although its northern boundary isn't clearly defined, most locals would agree that the Golden Zone extends from Punta Camarón to the El Cid Mega Resort along Camarón Sábalo and Loaiza avenues. Mazatlán's tourist-friendly facilities are concentrated here—discos, beach bars, sportswear shops, trinket outlets, romantic lounges, trendy restaurants, as well as shoulder-to-shoulder hotels.

Stay here and you'll pay the lowest rates to the airport, which lies to the east, about equidistant from the Golden Zone and downtown. You can't hoof it through the entire elongated zone, but the southern beachside strip is good for wandering. When you tire, no matter where you are in this area, all types of transport are ready to whisk you away—or at least crawl through traffic with you.

In a nutshell . . .

➤ All the tourist action is here.

➤ You're nicely situated between downtown, the heart of Mazatlán's traditional culture, and Marina El Cid, the departure point for the fishing and tour boats.

➤ You've got a good choice of hotels in all price categories.

but . . .

➤ You can't turn down the volume when you've had enough.

➤ The beaches are crowded.

➤ Some of the hotels are a tad tired.

The Platinum Zone: Heading North to the Marina

The tourist stretch directly to the north of the Golden Zone doesn't really have an established name, but the hotels in the area like Platinum Zone, for obvious reasons (Blue Zone is another moniker you might hear, although for less obvious reasons, as there are no dubious movie houses in the area and the ocean is the same color here as it is everywhere else). A couple of the hotels have been around for a long time—the Camino Real opened in the late 1960s, when this was really the sticks, and El Cid got its start in 1972—but most were built in the past decade. The Marina El Cid at the far end of the zone was completed in 1995, and an even larger marina is slated to open soon.

As a result, you can expect things here to be pretty spiffy—and a bit less crowded than in the section to the south. You won't find any super-cheap hotels, but you'll get good value for your money. However, there are fewer shops, nightspots, and restaurants in this part of town than there are in other areas—although that's slowly changing—and it takes a longer time to bus downtown (or about $6 for a cab).

In a nutshell . . .

➤ It's less crowded than the Golden Zone.

➤ You're near Marina El Cid, the El Cid Golf Course, and the terrific tourism office.

➤ Many of the newer, more modern hotels are here.

but . . .

➤ It's more expensive to get to the airport.

➤ You're far from downtown's cultural attractions.

➤ You have to bus it or cab it to the best nightlife and restaurants.

Time-Savers

You can probably get a room in the Golden or Platinum zones as little as three months in advance for Carnaval week, but if you want to be where the action is, you'll need to book North Beach or downtown area hotels half a year ahead of time. Prices double during Carnaval, which isn't saying much, as these modest hotels don't usually run much more than $20.

My Favorite Hotels from A to Z

Camino Real

$$$. Platinum Zone.
Far from hoi polloi but still near tourist facilities, this northernmost hotel in the Platinum Zone sits right next to the El Cid Marina and close to the El Cid Golf Course. Although built on a prime cliff-side decades ago, it's not one of the poshest members of the Camino Real chain—neither standard rooms nor suites have the usual stylistic flair, although they're comfortable enough—but it's the least expensive of the group. The grounds

Dollars & Sense

With the Camino Real's **More Mexico for Less Program,** the rates go down the longer you stay. Book 4 nights, say, and you'll get a marina view room for $128 per night, plus breakfast (including tip) and 1 hour of free tennis.

are beautifully landscaped and though the beach directly in front of the hotel is a bit narrow, it's an easy walk to a much wider stretch of sand. If you want something fancier than the hotel's casual beachfront restaurant and bar, you've got Señor Pepper's, one of Mazatlán's nicest steakhouses, right across the street. Lizard alert: The Camino Real protects iguanas, so you're bound to see a few of these prehistoric-looking critters sunning themselves on the lawn or the seawall.

Punta del Camarón Sábalo s/n (just south of Marina El Cid). ☎ *800/7-CAMINO or 69/13-1111. Fax 69/14-0311.* **Rack rates:** *$152 (marina view); $175 (ocean view). AE, DC, MC, V.*

El Azteca Inn
$. Golden Zone.
Watching your pesos but don't want to miss any action? This is the nicest discount hotel in the heart of the Golden Zone. All the rooms face an inner courtyard, so they're fairly quiet, despite the outside hubbub. Most units have two double beds, but those in the corners offer kings; request one on an upper floor if you want to sleep supported by a cement base rather than a squishy box spring. You'll be across the street from the beach, but lots of guests hang around the small pool and Jacuzzi or sip margaritas in the wonderfully retro bar that overlooks them.

Av. Rodolfo T. Loaiza 307, on Playa Gaviotas. ☎ *69/13-4655 or 69/13-4425. Fax 69/13-7476.* **Rack rate:** *$53 double. AE, DC, MC, V.*

No Time for Time-Shares

It's safe to assume anyone at your hotel who offers you a free meal or discounted activities is trying to sell you a time-share. Just say no. At best, you'll suffer through an hour of hard-sell stress; at worst, you'll sign on for something you could regret forever. See Chapter 10, "Crossing the Border & What to Expect on the Other Side," for more dire details.

⭐Kids El Cid Mega Resort
$$$. Platinum Zone.
This gigantic 1,320-room resort, which has eaten up large chunks of the northern hotel zone since 1972, is hard to love—and impossible to ignore. If you're coming to town with a tour group or a convention, chances are you'll be booked into one of its four related properties, the low-lying Granada, the Castilla and El Moro high-rises, or, up the road a stretch from the others, the Marina El Cid Hotel & Yacht Club. It's worth paying a few extra dollars for the rooms in the latter, a Mediterranean-style complex looking out on the

marina. Those in the other properties fall into a Motel 6 mold, but then, you're not likely to be spending much time in them. Along with the marina, you've got a 27-hole golf course, 14 tennis courts, eight swimming pools, an aqua sports center, kids' club, sailing school, spa, disco, exercise room, shopping arcade, 15 restaurants and lounges (of these, the romantic beachside La Concha is the best), and—should you need to repent for some of your indulgences—Sunday mass service.

Av. Camarón Sábalo s/n. ☎ *800/525-1925 or 888/733-7308 (direct to property) or 69/13-3333. Fax 69/14-1311. www.elcid.com. E-mail: sales@elcid.com.* **Rack rates:** *$140 (El Castilla) to $158 (the Marina El Cid). Golf, fishing, honeymoon, meal plans, and family packages available. AE, DC, MC, V.*

 ### The Fiesta Inn
$$. Platinum Zone.

At this super-friendly, intimate resort, you get the amenities of the larger hotels without the hustle and bustle. Begin your day with an impressive breakfast buffet, then laze away the hours at the excellent beach—a breakwater makes it ideal for swimming—or book a jet ski ride from the water sports concession next door. If you prefer your water unsalted, make the lap-length pool your base of operations. Got children in tow? You'll appreciate the kids' program and spacious junior suites; snag one in the corner (they begin with the number 1) and you've got a sweeping view of both the beach and the bay to the south. The coffeemakers with free java in all the attractive, contemporary-style rooms are a nice, um, perk.

Best Bets for Families

El Cid Mega Resort (Platinum Zone, $$$)

The Fiesta Inn (Platinum Zone, $$)

Holiday Inn Sunspree Resort (Platinum Zone, $$)

La Casa Contenta (Golden Zone, $)

Av. Camarón Sábalo 1927. ☎ *800/FIESTA-1 or 69/89-0100. Fax 69/89-0130. www.fiestamexico.com.* **Rack rate:** *$88 double. AE, DC, MC, V.*

Dollars & Sense

Check out the Fiesta Break packages by phoning ☎ **800/9BREAK9.** They can include such things as round-trip airfare from New York or L.A. and hotel transfers; free board and food for kids under 12 who stay in a room with their parents and Fiesta Kids Club (in season); and adult meal plans.

Holiday Inn Sunspree Resort
$$. Platinum Zone.

Long a reliable retreat, this little Holiday Inn became smart, too, after a major revamp in the mid-1990s. Relatively speaking. It's still part of the plain-vanilla chain, but rooms are light and bright and have hair dryers and refrigerators as standard amenities (you'll have to shell out for the caffeine if you want to use your Mr. Coffee clone, though). Standard, too, are great ocean views. Most of your fellow guests will be conventioneers or tour groupies who like to gather in the exercise room or by the infinity pool, which, at certain angles, looks as though it falls off into the deep blue sea; it's more impressive than the small beach. A playground keeps kids happily swinging and teeter-tottering.

Av. Camarón Sábalo 696. ☎ **800/465-4329** *or 69/13-2222. Fax 69/14-1287. E-mail: hisunspree@red2000.com.mx.* **Rack rate:** *$94 double. AE, DC, MC, V.*

Best Hotels for Sports Addicts

El Cid Mega Resort (Platinum Zone, $$$)

Los Sábalos (Golden Zone, $$$)

Playa Mazatlán (Golden Zone, $$)

La Casa Contenta
$. Golden Zone.

Organize a group of friends or pack up the kids, and you can share a charming brick cottage on the beach for a loco low price. The red-tile-roofed units in this Spanish village–style complex can sleep from 4 to 10; all have decks or terraces with Mexican *equipale* furniture and full kitchens with gas stoves. Cottages 2, 4, and 6 offer ocean views, but those in the back are a bit cooler, so you don't always have to rely on the air-conditioning. Furnishings are simple, but more than sufficient for the time you're likely to spend in your room. You may sometimes feel as though you're in a remote tropical retreat, but you're in the thick of the tourist zone.

Av. Rodolfo T. Loaiza 224, on Playa Gaviotas. ☎ **69/13-4976.** *Fax 69/13-9986.* **Rack rates:** *$62 (1-bedroom unit) to $146 (3 bedrooms). MC, V.*

Dollars & Sense

Settle in for a month in winter at **La Casa Contenta** (☎ **69/13-4976**) and you'll get 10% to 15% off the already low price; in summer, your tab might be reduced by as much as 50% (nightly rates here in low season are about 30% lower than those in high season).

440

Los Sábalos

$$$. Golden Zone.

You'll see more buffed young bods at this 1970-ish high-rise than you will at many other hotels in Mazatlán. Having acquired glowing tans at the beach or large pool, and worked off any extra nachos at the health club or tennis courts, they gather after dark at Los Sábalos's happening nightspots, including a country-and-western grill and Joe's Oyster Bar. When it gets late enough, they move on to Valentino's disco, a short walk away. Guest rooms are a slight cut above many in town because of their splashes of vibrant color, but not all have windows that open (you'll have to get a suite if you want a sliding-door balcony).

Av. Rodolfo T. Loaiza 100. ☎ ***800/528-8760*** *or 69/83-5333. Fax 69/83-8156.* ***Rack rates:*** *$129 double; $152–$351 suite. AE, DC, MC, V.*

Playa Mazatlán

$$. Golden Zone.

It's not just nostalgia that's kept many of this hotel's guests coming back for more than 4 decades. This low-slung property, all archways, tiles, and brick columns, has lots of lush little niches where you can retreat if you're feeling romantic, as well as activities like Spanish lessons and aqua-aerobics for when you're in social mode. Beware: The arcade of super high-quality shops—not easy to find in Mazatlán—is likely to call out your name on a regular basis. The beachside Playa Terraza restaurant (see chapter 40, "The Best of Mazatlán's Dining Scene") is excellent, and three times a week you can indulge in the town's primo Mexican fiesta (see chapter 39, "Fun On & Off the Beach"). Rooms are large with elegant Mexican furnishings; many have ocean views, but the quietest ones look out on the interior lawn. Local hotel managers and restaurateurs often start their careers at this Golden Zone institution so they can learn from the masters of the trade.

Av. Rodolfo T. Loaiza 202. ☎ ***800/762-5816*** *or 69/13-4444. Fax 69/14-0366.* ***Rack rates:*** *$100 double (garden view) to $117 double (ocean view). AE, MC, V.*

Pueblo Bonita

$$$. Platinum Zone.

At Mazatlán's prettiest hotel, you can wake up and smell the coffee—and then drink it from a colorful Mexican ceramic cup. The stunning suites (the only kind of room available) all have hand-painted headboards, carved wood furnishings, and vibrantly tiled kitchens. From your vine-draped balcony or terrace, watch the flamingos roam the lush grounds at sunset. After spending the day bronzing by the pool or near a palapa on the beach, don your nicest duds and dine at Angelo's (see chapter 40), arguably the best Italian restaurant in town. The only snakes in this Eden are the aggressive time-share peddlers.

Camarón Sábalo 2121. ☎ ***800/937-9567*** *or 69/14-3700. Fax 69/14-1723. www.pueblobonito.com. E-mail: reserva@pueblobonito.com.* ***Rack rates:*** *$164 junior suite; $199 1-bedroom suite. AE, MC, V.*

Best Bets for a Romantic Retreat

Pueblo Bonita (Platinum Zone, $$$)

Rancho Las Moras (Las Moras, outside Mazatlán, $$$$)

A Couple of Choices Outside the Zones

La Siesta Hotel
$. Olas Altas.

Your room in this downtown hotel will be pretty basic—an extra $3 will net you a Spanish-speaking TV—but the ocean view from your window will be anything but. Accommodations are arranged around a nice, shady courtyard; it's quiet during the day, but turns into the live music venue for El Shrimp Bucket, the original link in the Carlos Anderson chain (see chapter 40), until about 11pm every night. Stay here and you'll be in walking distance of many historical buildings and wonderful old-time cafes. The hotel is on the Carnaval parade route, so reserve 6 months in advance if you plan to attend the town's all-out bash.

Olas Altas no. 11, Playa Olas Altas. ☎ **69/81-2640** *or 69/81-2334. Fax 69/ 13-7476.* **Rack rate:** *$35 double. AE, DC, MC, V.*

No Room at the Inn? Check Out One of These . . .

Golden Zone
➤ **Costo de Oro.** The best rooms at this high-rise terra-cotta complex are by the beach; suites have a bit of character. Av. Camarón Sábalo s/n. ☎ **800/ 351-1612.** $$.

Platinum Zone
➤ **El Quijote Inn.** A small hotel on the beach offering attractively furnished suites with kitchenettes. Av. Camarón Sábalo s/n. ☎ **69/14-1134.** Fax 69/ 14-3344. $–$$.

Rancho Las Moras
$$$$. Las Moras, outside Mazatlán.

A treasure in the Sierra Madres, this restored tequila ranch some 30 minutes northeast of Mazatlán is a cross between a nature preserve and a hacienda. Separate *casitas* (little houses) and villas all have beamed ceilings and furnishings that would have suited the elite families who lived here 150 years ago (in the spirit of that era, they have neither TVs nor phones). Hike or ride around the 3,000-acre property and you might get up close and personal with a goat or an emu; some 200 species of exotic and domestic creatures roam the grounds. When you're tired of wandering off on your own, shoot some pool in the game room, belly up to the bar in the Olympic-size pool, or take in the dazzling 360-views in the formal dining room. Three excellent meals are part of the deal; room service will let you enjoy any or all of them on the privacy of your terrace. The exact location of the ranch is revealed only to guests to discourage drop-ins.

For reservations, write Av. Camarón Sábalo 204–6, Mazatlán 82110 or ☎ or fax **69/16-5045. Rack rates:** *$410 double, villa, or casita; rates include meals, domestic drinks, and all activities. AE, DC, MC, V.*

Quick Picks: Mazatlán's Hotels at a Glance
Hotel Index by Price

$

El Azteca Inn (Golden Zone)

La Casa Contenta (Golden Zone)

La Siesta Hotel (Olas Altas)

$$

Kids The Fiesta Inn (Platinum Zone)

Kids Holiday Inn Sunspree Resort (Platinum Zone)

Playa Mazatlán (Golden Zone)

$$$

Camino Real (Platinum Zone)

Kids El Cid Mega Resort (Platinum Zone)

Los Sábalos (Golden Zone)

Pueblo Bonita (Platinum Zone)

$$$$

Rancho Las Moras (Las Moras, outside Mazatlán)

Hotel Index by Location

The Platinum Zone

Camino Real $$$

Kids El Cid Mega Resort $$$

Kids The Fiesta Inn $$

Kids Holiday Inn Sunspree Resort $$

Pueblo Bonita $$$

The Golden Zone

El Azteca Inn $

La Casa Contenta $

Los Sábalos $$$

Playa Mazatlán $$

Olas Altas

La Siesta Hotel $

Las Moras, outside Mazatlán

Rancho Las Moras $$$$

443

Chapter 38

Finding Your Way Around Mazatlán

In This Chapter

➤ What to expect when you arrive

➤ The lay of the land

➤ Getting around

➤ Getting information

➤ Quick Facts: Mazatlán A to Z

For a city of more than half a million, Mazatlán is surprisingly easy to negotiate—and fun, if you like zipping around in open-air electronic carts. It's also extremely user-friendly, with lots of English-language resources, including one of the most helpful tourist offices in all of Mexico.

You've Just Arrived—Now What?

Don't be misled by the rather long walk you'll take from your plane to the luggage collection area at Mazatlán's Rafael Buelna International Airport—at least it's long in comparison with many other Mexican airports, where you can practically pick up your belongings on the hangar. The facility is small and simple to get around.

Not that there's much here you'll need to locate, except the money exchange counter and—if you've ignored all my advice about renting a car—the car rental booths (Hertz, National, and Budget are the major chains represented). There's no tourist information booth, hotel booking service, or ATM.

At the airport exit, you'll see a counter selling tickets for taxis and *colectivos* (collective vans) into town, which is some 11 miles to the south. It's $4 to the Golden Zone or downtown, and $6 to the Platinum Zone by *colectivo*. Taxis to downtown or the Golden Zone cost $17; to the Platinum Zone, $18.50.

Orientation: You Are Here

You have to work really hard to get lost in Mazatlán. Except to go to the docks or explore downtown—I'll tell you more about that in the next chapter—you'll have little reason to stray from the 16-mile-long thoroughfare that hugs the sea for almost the entire length of the city.

Yo, Gringo!

There's no such thing as a free ride. Timeshare sellers will offer to take you to your hotel from the airport if you sign on to hear their hard-sell presentation. Give it a miss.

At its beginning on the far southern cape guarded by El Faro (the lighthouse), the road is called Joel Montes Camerena. Heading north through the old part of the city, it becomes, in quick succession, Paseo del Centenario, Avenida Olas Altas, and Paseo Classen. For an extended stretch along Playa Norte, it answers to the name Avenida del Mar; then, just beyond Punta Camarón, it metamorphoses into Calzado Camarón-Sábalo (for a few blocks, the hotel-lined Avenida Rodolfo T. Loaiza loops in closer to the sea). It sticks with that moniker as it leads north through both the Gold and Platinum zones all the way to the Marina El Cid. When it veers inland around the marina, the road is called Avenida Camarón Sábalo-Cerritos, the name it retains until it reaches the far northern tip of the city, hilly Punta Cerritos.

Because the main drag is so long and name-shifty, most people use landmarks when giving directions. The Fisherman's Monument is impossible to miss at the beginning of the Playa Norte area, and everyone recognizes Punta Camarón by Valentino's disco, a castle-like structure rising from the sea. The high-rise tower of the El Cid Mega Resort, which straddles the Golden and Platinum zones, is another favorite reference point, as is the Dairy Queen at the traffic circle where Avenida Rodolfo T. Loaiza feeds back into Calzado Camarón-Sábalo (the cross street is Avenida de las Gaviotas).

Bet You Didn't Know

Mazatlán's malecón (promenade) is the longest in Mexico—it stretches almost the entire 16-mile length of the city.

How to Get Around (and How Not To)

Unless you're planning to leave town on an excursion, don't even think about renting a car. There are far better ways to get around on the main beachside road, and it's hard to find parking downtown, which is fun to stroll, anyway.

By Bus

Mazatlán has seven main bus routes. Unless you're going somewhere off the beaten track, you can't go wrong if you hop on a bus marked "Camarón Sábalo-Centro," which goes south along the shore from beyond the Platinum Zone all the way to Olas Altas beach. "Camarón Sábalos-Cocos" is a similarly extended route, but veers inland for a bit instead of going along North Beach. If you're traveling within the Golden and Platinum zones, you can take any bus you see on the street; just be sure you don't go past Punta Camarón if you're heading south.

In theory, the city switched over to modern air-conditioned buses a few years back. You'll see some of them around, but plenty of the old, stuffy models are still in commission. There are regular bus stops, but drivers are very accommodating; stand on a corner and wave your arms—everyone does it— and you'll stop traffic (or at least one bus). Buses run from around 5:30am to 11pm. Fares are about 25¢, slightly higher after 8pm; you don't need exact change, but drivers aren't happy if you give them anything larger than a 10-peso bill.

Yo, Gringo!

Check with the front desk at your hotel for a fair price to your destination. Then, *before* you get into the taxi, ask the driver how much he wants to go there. If his quote is out of line, just walk away. He'll either come down in price—or you'll soon find another, more reasonable ride.

By Taxi

You'll have no trouble finding a taxi in any of the tourist areas. In fact, they'll find you—cabbies often slow down if you look tired, indecisive, or otherwise ready for a ride. The red-and-white or green-and-white Eco taxis have fixed rates—it's about $2 to $4 to go anywhere in town—but don't always observe them. You'll have to negotiate the fares.

Where to Get More Information & Guidance

Although the **State Tourism Office** (Camarón Sábalo, corner of Tiburón, in the Banrural Building, 4th floor; ☎ **69/19-5160**; e-mail: turismo@ red2000.com.mx) is outside the center of town, in the Platinum Zone, it's worth going out of your way if you need information. The office has detailed, up-to-date city maps and a helpful, bilingual staff who can answer all your questions. It's open Monday through Friday from 9am to 3:30pm. There's also an information booth on Rodolfo T. Loaiza, across from the

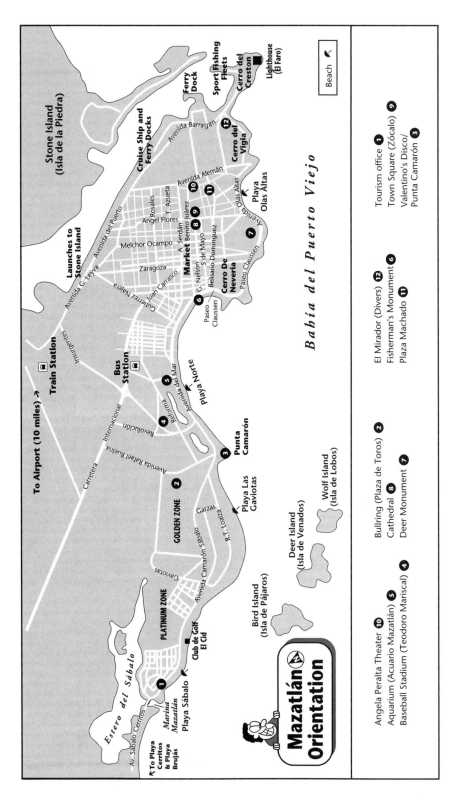

Mazatlán Orientation

To Airport (10 miles) →

Stone Island (Isla de la Piedra)

Launches to Stone Island

Cruise Ship and Ferry Docks

Ferry Dock

Sport Fishing Fleets

Cerro del Creston

Lighthouse (El Faro)

Cerro del Vigia

Avenida Barragan

Avenida Alemán

Playa Olas Altas

Olas Altas

Avenida del Puerto

Avenida G. Leyva

Gutierrez Najera

Gutierrez Juan Carrasco

Insurgentes

Train Station

Bus Station

Rosales

T. Azueta

Angel Flores

Melchor Ocampo

Zaragoza

C. Nelson

A. Serdan

Benito Juárez

Market

5 de Mayo

Belisario Dominguez

Paseo Claussen

Paseo Claussen

Cerro De Neveria

Playa Norte

Avenida del Mar

Reforma

Revolución

Internacional

Avenida Rafael Buelna

Carretera

GOLDEN ZONE

Playa Las Gaviotas

Punta Camarón

Garzas

R.T. Loaiza

Avenida Camarón Sábalo

Caviotas

PLATINUM ZONE

Club de Golf El Cid

Playa Sábalo

Marina Mazatlán

Estero del Sábalo

To Playa Cerritos & Playa Brujás

Av. Sábalo Cerritos

Estero del Sábalo

Bahía del Puerto Viejo

Deer Island (Isla de Venados)

Wolf Island (Isla de Lobos)

Bird Island (Isla de Pájaros)

Beach ↖

Tourism office ❶
Town Square (Zócalo) ❾
Valentino's Disco/
Punta Camarón ❸

El Mirador (Divers) ⓬
Fisherman's Monument ❻
Plaza Machado ⓫

Bullring (Plaza de Toros) ❷
Cathedral ❽
Deer Monument ❼

Angela Peralta Theater ❿
Aquarium (Acuario Mazatlán) ❺
Baseball Stadium (Teodoro Mariscal) ❹

447

Hotel Mazatlán (no phone), open December through April and July and August from 9am to noon Monday through Friday.

Bet You Didn't Know

The golf carts on steroids you'll see tooling around Mazatlán are called *pulmonías*—literally "pneumonias." The sickly name derives from the rumor that, long ago, a woman died after riding one of these open-air vehicles in winter. Those who subscribe to the germ theory of illness and other defenders of the pulmonía's reputation contend she was already ill when she took her fatal journey.

Pulmonías, which hold two or three people, are fun to ride and breezy, but don't offer any barriers between you and the traffic exhaust fumes. They cost roughly the same as, or slightly more than, taxis. Don't forget to bargain before you get in.

The Printed Page

The Pacific Pearl, a monthly English-language tabloid, is ad-driven but informative, publishing schedules of special events, emergency numbers, tourist maps, activity features, and more. It's widely distributed; you should be able to find a copy in your hotel lobby.

Mazatlán A to Z: Facts at Your Fingertips

American Express: Camarón Sábalo, Centro Comercial Shopping Center, Loc. 4/16 (☎ **69/13-0600**).

ATMs: You'll come across several banks with ATMs if you stroll around the Golden Zone. The Banamex on Camarón Sábalo, across the street from the Dairy Queen, and the one just outside Valentino's disco are the most convenient. (The map that the tourism office gives out thoughtfully marks off the city's banks; Bancomer, Banamex, and Serfin all have ATMs that connect with the U.S. networks Cirrus, PLUS, Visa, and MasterCard.)

Time-Savers

Make sure to arrange for baby-sitters at least 24 hours in advance.

Baby-sitters: Almost all the hotels can arrange for baby-sitters. The cost is about $4 per hour.

Business Hours: Most shops are open daily from 9am to 9pm; few close for siesta and some of the large grocery stores are open 24 hours. Businesses tend to operate from 9am to 2pm and from 4 to 6pm Monday through Friday. Some are open Saturday from 9am to 2pm.

Currency Exchange: The banks along the Golden Zone give the best exchange rates, but they conduct this type of transaction only from around 9 or 10am to 11am or noon Monday through Friday. The *casas de cambio* (exchange houses) that line the Golden Zone and Avenida del Mar to the south have slightly lower rates (they fluctuate all day long), but are open far longer every day (usually from 9am to 7 or 8pm Monday through Saturday, and Sunday from 10am to 4pm). Most convenient is your hotel front desk—which naturally offers the worst exchange rates.

Dentist: Dr. Hector Jorge Morelos Chong, an English-speaking dentist, is located in the Golden Zone above Domino's Pizza (Av. Camarón Sábalo 204–30, Lomas Shopping Center; ☎ **69/13-6068**). Ask your hotel or the tourism office for other suggestions.

Doctors: Your hotel should be able to recommend a reliable English-speaking doctor if they don't have one on 24-hour call. Dr. Jorge Luis Olalde Echeagaray (Plaza Riviera, Loc. 11, across from the Riviera Hotel and next to Blockbuster; ☎ **69/86-2050,** or 69/19-3950, emergency cell phone) is geared to tourist problems and makes hotel calls.

English-Language Newspapers/Magazines: Most hotels in the Golden and Platinum zones have gift shops with magazine/newspaper racks. You'll usually come across copies of the English-language *Mexico City News;* of the stateside papers, *U.S.A. Today* turns up most often, with the *L.A. Times* a fairly distant second. For the best selection of paperbacks, check out the book-store at **VIPs restaurant** (Camarón Sábalo s/n, about 4 blocks south of the Dairy Queen and across from the Albatros movie theater; ☎ **69/16-5501**). If you need a New Age fix, **Evolucíon** (Rodolfo T. Loaiza 204, Loc. 27; ☎ **69/16-0839**) is the place.

Emergencies/Fire: Call ☎ **06.**

Hospitals: Part of a San Diego chain, **Sharp Hospital** (Av. Rafael Buelna and Calzado Jesús Kumate s/n; ☎ **69/86-5676** or 69/86-5677) is not only one of the best medical facilities in western Mexico, but also accepts most insurance policies from the United States and Canada.

Maps: The tourism office (see "Where to Get More Information & Guidance," above) hands out excellent city maps.

Pharmacies: What with all the retirees who come to town, it's hard to find a block in Mazatlán that doesn't have a drugstore. **Farmacia Belmar** (Av. Camarón Sábalo 1504, across from the Balboa Club; ☎ **69/14-3199**) and **Farmacia Moderna** (Plaza Puebolito L-12, in front of the Costa de Oro; ☎ **69/14-0044**), both in the Golden Zone, advertise discounted rates. The chain of **Cruz Verde** pharmacies are open 24 hours; the Golden Zone branch is at Av. Camarón Sábalo 306 (☎ **69/16-5066**).

Police: Turn to the English-speaking **tourist police** (☎ **69/14-8444**), who patrol the Golden Zone, if you have any problems.

Post Office: The main post office is downtown, on the east side of the main plaza (Avenida Juárez, just off Angel Flores). More convenient to most is the

Yo, Gringo!

If you gotten yourself into a time-share fix, the **Consumer Protection Agency** (21 de Marzo 808, downtown; ☎ **69/82-2054**) may be able to help you get out of it.

Mail Boxes Etc. in the Golden Zone, Av. Camarón Sábalo 310 (☎ **69/16-4009** or 69/16-4010).

Safety: Mazatlán is a safe city. You can promenade up and down the Golden Zone all night without a problem; there's always someone—including the tourist police—around. But don't do things you wouldn't consider back in the United States, such as walking down dark alleys, wandering the beach alone at night, flashing around wads of money, and so forth. For other resort-specific safety and scam tips, see chapter 10, "Crossing the Border & What to Expect on the Other Side"; for swimming advice, see the section on beaches in the next chapter.

Special Events: Mazatlán celebrates all the traditional Mexican holidays in high style (see chapter 2, "When Should I Go?," for details), but really pulls out the stops when it comes to its pre-Lenten Carnaval. Anglers are in their glory at the city's huge annual Billfish Classic, usually held in November at the Marina El Cid—the purse in 1997 was $250,000—and at the smaller international billfish tournament, hosted by the Club Nautico, near the lighthouse, in early June. Call or e-mail the tourism office (☎ **69/19-5160** to 5165; e-mail: turismo@red2000.com.mx) for additional information on these events.

Telephones: The telephone area code for Mazatlán is 69. To call long distance within Mexico (abbreviated *lada*), dial 01, then the area code, and then the number. To call the United States, dial 001, and then the area code and number.

U.S. Consul: Av. Rodolfo T. Loaiza 202, across from the Hotel Playa Mazatlán (☎ **69/16-5889**), open 9:30am to 1pm Monday to Friday.

Fun On & Off the Beach

Despite Mazatlán's longstanding popularity with tourists, the resort still has untouched beaches, as well as plenty of places to play in the sand with others if you're feeling sociable. Deep-sea aficionados can enjoy some of the best sportsfishing in Mexico, and an array of cruises will keep your head above water when you're tired of taking the plunge.

There's good news for the waterlogged and the sand-sated, too. Unlike many of the other beach resorts, Mazatlán has an interesting history, and much of it can be explored by strolling around outdoors. Shoppers have a bit less to crow about than culture vultures—but then again, since peso pinching probably brought you to Mazatlán in the first place, no doubt the absence of major temptation is a good thing. Although the city isn't notorious for its wild nightlife, it might surprise you after dark. And when you've exhausted the in-town possibilities, you've got some interesting excursions in the wings.

Hitting the Beaches

Mazatlán has some of the most visitor-friendly beaches in the country. All, from the most crowded to the most secluded, are easily accessible by bus. If

Bet You Didn't Know

The Tropic of Cancer begins 12½ miles north of Mazatlán.

you want a bit more privacy, just stay on the line a bit longer. And if, after a day on the shore, you're sunstruck and gritty, you can catch a pulmonía or taxi back to your hotel.

I've arranged the beach listings from south to north, which is the way that the tourist trade moved, and followed them by descriptions of Mazatlán's offshore islands.

Playa Olas Altas

The 1950s were the tourist heyday of this stretch of sand just north of downtown; it's where the paved seaside walkway, or malecón, begins. A fairly narrow and sometimes rocky strand, it's been returned to the locals, who converge here on the weekends. The waves can be a bit rough for swimming and the water-toy rental concessions are limited, but it's a great place to come during the week and go back in time—the malecón is lined with small cafes that have been there for decades. Soak in some sun, dip into the ocean, and then spend a lazy afternoon munching on shrimp, sipping a Pacifico, and watching Mazatlán's street life pass by.

Surf's Up

Olas Altas means "high waves." Although the beach is no longer as popular with surfers as it was in the 1960s, older (over 35) high-wave riders still come here. The younger ones head for Punta Camarón, near Valentino's (especially if they like to show off), or Playa Bruja, a more remote beach for serious surfer dudes.

Playa Norte

Stretching some 4 miles from Punta Tiburón to Punta Camarón, this is the longest developed beach in Mazatlán. Older hotels, cafes, and markets line up across the road. The first section of beach gets lots of detritus from the fishing boats that pull up here in the early morning, but beyond the Fisherman's Monument, the sand is fairly clean. The swimming's usually fine, too, but don't take any chances if the waves look rowdy—the undertow can be evil. This is another beach that's big with the locals on the weekends; if you want to catch a baseball game, come on Sunday and grab a spot on the seawall near the Fisherman's Monument. You can get to this beach via the Sábalo-Centro bus.

Dollars & Sense

Whether you've got a room with a cooker or just want some local color, drag yourself out of bed at the crack of dawn one morning to visit the open-air fisherman's market at Playa los Piños, the southern end of Playa Norte. By 6am, the fisherman are back with their catch, and have they got a deal on seafood for you. By 7am, the haul's already been picked over by local restaurateurs and housewives.

Playa Gaviotas & Playa Sábalo

Get a glimpse of the wide swaths of creamy sand that run along the Golden and Platinum zones, and you may wonder why these weren't the beaches the tourists flocked to from the get-go. But then, the past few decades have more than compensated for any initial neglect. High-rise hotels, condos, bars, restaurants, and water sports rental outlets stretch from Punta Camarón, at the Valentino's complex, to Punta Roja, just south of the Camino Real hotel. Facilities are especially concentrated along **Playa Gaviotas,** the southernmost beach; **Playa Sábalo,** beyond the El Cid Mega Resort, is somewhat less hectic.

Aside from the area near Punta Camarón, which surfers like precisely because of its wave action, the rest of the beaches are good for swimming, largely because the Tres Islas, three offshore islands (see below), serve as breakwaters.

Yo, Gringo!

Gaviotas and Sábalo beaches are huge outdoor flea markets, with persistent vendors trying to press their pottery, blankets, and sombreros on you. If you'd rather sunbathe than shop, don't give any of them an initial nod; otherwise, your beach blanket will soon be besieged by strolling retailers.

Playa Cerritos & Playa Brujas

Encompassing almost 4 miles of coast from the north side of the Marina Mazatlán development to Punta Cerritos, **Playa Cerritos** is the last beach accessible by public transportation. (From the Golden and Platinum zones, take the Cerritos-Juárez bus.) It's largely undeveloped, however. Condos are beginning to crop up and locals head here on the weekends, but for most of the week, it's pretty much you and the pelicans. If you need sustenance during your hard day of tanning, you'll have to either pack a picnic or get off the bus at **Playa Brujas,** the subsection of beach just south of the rise by which you'll recognize Punta Cerritos; here food stalls and thatched-roof palapas sell fresh-from-the-sea food. The surf's up at Playa Brujas, which makes it less than ideal for swimming, but you can poke around the tide pools in the area or look for seashells. Most of the rest of Playa Sábalo-Cerritos is fine for splashing around.

Bet You Didn't Know

The *brujas* for which Playa Brujas is named are literally witches, but they're not the evil kind; rather, they're traditional herbal healers. Perhaps they set up their shingles on this beach once upon a time, but there hasn't been any white magic practiced here for a while.

Stone Island (Isla de Piedra)

Not actually an island but a large peninsula on the southeast side of town, Stone Island has huge coconut groves and miles of pale-sand beaches that are mostly untouched. Mostly. The 18-hole Estrella del Mar golf course recently opened, and an associated hotel/condo complex is in the works. Get here soon if you want to see this place in its relatively pristine state.

Not that people haven't been coming here for a long time, at least on Sunday, when there's music and dancing under the palms fronting the palapa restaurants (try Carmelitas, where you can get *lisachmo,* a delicious whitefish, served grilled and slightly blackened with fresh tortillas).

Don't Be a Statistic

Heed the posted flags alerting you to swimming conditions: Red means danger, yellow suggests you use caution, and blue or green signify the water's safe. A white flag is a jellyfish alert, something you'll rarely see except in July. If you do get stung, it's annoying, but by no means dangerous; local remedies include vinegar or lime juice.

To reach Stone Island, go downtown to the north side of the *zócalo* and take one of the many buses (marked "Circunvalacion," "Castillo," "Zapata," "San Joaquin," or "20 de Noviembre") to the boat landing (called Embarcadero Isla de la Piedra); if you want to save time, it shouldn't run you more than $4 to catch a cab or pulmonía from the hotel zone. From the dock, small motorized launches make the 5-minute trip to the island every 15 minutes or so around the clock; the cost is less than $1. When you land, you'll have a choice of walking past the small village to the beach (about three-fourths of a mile) or grabbing a seat on a tractor-pulled wagon for less than 50¢.

Three Islands (Tres Islas)

Of the three uninhabited islands that lie off Gaviotas and Sábalo beaches—Isla de los Pájaros (Bird Island), Isla de los Venados (Deer Island), and Isla de Los Lobos (Wolf Island)—Deer Island is the most accessible. Its beach is lovely and white, and you can easily spend the day shell hunting, hiking, and snorkeling; there's a restaurant, too, so you won't starve if you've forgotten to pack some burritos.

Reach Deer Island by taking an amphibious boat from the El Cid marina for $9, round-trip (don't lose your return ticket); snorkeling gear can be rented at the marina for another $5. Or hop aboard one of the catamarans that leave from Gaviotas and Sábalo beaches; the charge should be about $5 each way.

No one is permitted to land on Wolf Island, but snorkeling is allowed around it and Bird Island. You'll have to rent snorkeling gear on the mainland before you go and head out on your own via Hobie Cat (see "Assorted Water Sports," below).

Water Fun for Everyone

Although Mazatlán is especially outstanding in the billfishing department, it's no slouch when it comes to other splashy pursuits. Even better, you'll often be able to play in the water at prices below those in the other beach resorts.

Assorted Water Sports

You'll fly through the air with the greatest of ease—if you're the type who likes **parasailing.** Your daredevil trip on a parachute attached to a speedboat can be arranged near Playa Mazatlán, Los Sábalos, and Costa de Oro resorts in the Golden Zone and the El Cid, Pueblo Bonita, and Camino Real resorts in the Platinum Zone. Ten minutes of excitement will set you back around $25.

Jet skis are also big on Playa Gaviotas and Playa Sábalo, where the hotels noted above and other concessionaires along the beaches rent them for about $30 per half hour ($45 if you want to go tandem with a friend).

For a cheap thrill, hop on a **boogie board;** everybody and his brother has one to rent along the tourist beaches. It shouldn't run you more than $5 an hour; be sure to bargain.

455

If you want to sail to one of the offshore islands, consider arranging for a **Hobie Cat** (three-person, catamaran-style sailboat) from the El Cid resort or one of the other hotel water-toy shops. Rates are about $25 an hour, so don't lose track of time when you reach your tropical retreat of choice.

You won't see much if you don a **snorkeling** mask near Mazatlán's 16-mile lineup of beaches, and **diving** visibility isn't optimum in the area, either. Your best bet is to book an excursion to Isla de los Venados through the sports center at the Los Sábalos, Camino Real, or El Cid hotels. It'll run you about $50 to $70 per person for a 3-hour dive trip, including instruction. If you want to stick near the surface, a mask, fin, and flipper outfit plus transportation runs about $16 a day.

Kids Splish Splash

You'll find everything from mild-mannered wading pools to the 100-foot-long kamikaze water slide in the 4-acre **Mazagua Water Park** (Av. Sábalo Cerritos and Entronque Habal Cerritos, on Playa Cerritos; ☎ **69/88-0041**), open daily from 10am to 6pm. No age discrimination here: The admission is the same (about $10) for everyone over 3.

Hooked on Fishing

The Sea of Cortez and the Pacific Ocean converge near Mazatlán, which means that denizens of both deeps hang out here. From March through December, the fish practically leap out of the water at you; they play a bit harder to get in winter, but you should be able to coax several into your boat, anyway. Large billfish—sailfish and black, blue, and striped marlin—are the trophies everyone aims for, but you'll also get satisfaction out of consuming your catches of grouper, sea bass, dorado (dolphin fish, but no relation to Flipper), and grouper.

Please Release Me

Don't be a sea hog. When you get your hooks into the big one, have your friends make it a Kodak moment and then send the fishy fella back home. Lots of fleets in Mazatlán take part in tag-and-release programs, which involve marking your catch so the next guy or gal can see that you got there first.

Fishing trips leave from either the El Cid Marina (if you've booked the Aries fleet) or the downtown sportsfishing dock near Cerro Creston (the hill topped by the lighthouse). Rates are around $180 a day for a 24-foot panga for up to three people; $275 for a 28-foot cruiser that accommodates four; and $325 for a 36-foot cruiser that comfortably fits six. Costs don't include a Mexican fishing license ($7), food, beverage, live bait, or the tip (give the captain about 10% to 15% of the total price of the charter). Reliable local outfitters include **Star Fleet** (☎ **69/82-2665** or 800/CAUGHT-1 in the U.S.; fax 69/82-5155), **Mike Mexemins' Faro Fleet** (☎ **69/81-2824** or 69/82-4977), and **Aries Fleet** (☎ **69/163468** or 800/633-3085 in the U.S.). You can also reserve a boat in the states through **Ixtapa Sports-fishing Charters** (19 Depue Lane, Stroudsburg, PA 18360; ☎ **717/688-9466;** fax 717/688-9554, or 755/4-4426 in Zihuatenejo) and **Mexico Sportsman** (14542 Brook Hollow, no. 124, San Antonio, TX 78232; ☎ and fax 210/494-9916). The latter provides a complete breakdown of extra services, including packing you a boxed lunch and filleting, freezing, smoking, and cooking your catch.

Time-Savers

If you're planning to visit from November through April, it's a good idea to book a vessel a month in advance or—barring that—the second you get to town.

Dollars & Sense

Haven't arrived with your own personal fishing party? Not to worry. Most of the fleets listed above can hook you up with other interested anglers so you won't have to shell out for more boat than you need. Rates run from $60 to $85 per person. You might even make some new friends.

Cruise Control

In addition to calling the numbers listed for reservations, you can also book all the following trips through your hotel travel agent.

The **Fiesta,** a large double-decker yacht, departs from the dock near Cerro Creston every morning at 11am. During the 3-hour cruise around the harbor and bay, you'll see the shrimp fleet, the three offshore islands, pirate caves, the Pacifico Brewery towers, and more. To the background of a marimba band, a bilingual guide gives an interesting running narrative. Tickets cost around $20; they are half price for children 5 to 8, and free for those under 5. Phone ☎ **69/85-2237** for reservations.

From Tuesday through Sunday at 9:30am, the trimaran **Kolonahe** departs from the Marina El Cid at the northern end of the Platinum Zone (just beyond the Camino Real hotel and at the end of Playa Sábalo) for a 5-hour trip to Deer Island. The price of $30 includes snorkeling, boogie boards

Bet You Didn't Know

Mazatlán has the largest
shrimp fleet in the world,
hauling in nearly 400 million
tons of shrimp each year.

volleyball, and an all-you-can-eat buffet
lunch on the beach, with soft drinks.
Make arrangements by calling ☎ 69/
16-3468.

David Perez's **Mazatlán Jungle Tour**
combines a 1½-hour harbor tour and
foray into mangrove swamps with a 3-
hour stopover at Stone Island. There, if
you want to keep out of the water, you
can trot along the beach (it's $6 for a
half-hour horseback ride) and just kick
back and enjoy a grilled seafood lunch.
Tours, which cost $30, depart at 9:30am and return at 3:30pm. Days vary;
phone ☎ **69/14-2400** for exact dates and reservations.

On Tuesday, Thursday, and Saturday, the **Kolonahe** gears up again for a sunset cruise around the bay, departing at 4:30pm. For $25, you get 2½ hours of
music, snacks, and open bar (domestic) drinks.

Kids Carnaval: Super Fiesta

Only Rio de Janeiro and New Orleans throw bigger bashes than Mazatlán's
pre-Lenten celebration, which is held in late February or early March.

The weeklong celebration features major parades, concerts, the coronation of
a carnaval queen, fireworks, food booths, and open-air parties, most of which
take place downtown on Olas Atlas Boulevard and Plaza Machado. It can get
raucous, but this isn't the kind of decadent, drunken brawl you'll find in New
Orleans, say—lots of kids take part, and it's more of a family celebration.
Culture is key here, too: The Mexico City philharmonic or another important
orchestra performs every year and the winners of prestigious poetry and literature prizes are announced.

Keeping Your Head Above Water: Mazatlán's Top Activities

Many of the sights discussed below are covered on the city tours, offered
twice daily in high season, and are a good way to get oriented before heading
out on your own. You can book them through your hotel or a travel agent
for about $15.

Strolling the Olas Altas Malecón

Take a walk down the seaside promenade in the Olas Altas area and you can
absorb some history while breathing in the fresh salt air.

If you're up for a long walk, start north of downtown at the **Fisherman's Monument** (the Sábalo-Centro bus from the hotel zones will leave you off here, but continues inland soon after that, so you'll have to take a cab or pulmonía if you want to start your stroll farther south). This is Mazatlán's most famous—some might say notorious—sculpture (you'll see it where Avenida Del Mar turns into Paseo Claussen, at Blvd. Gutierrez). Bizarre in both subject and its oversized proportions, it depicts a nude man with a net trying to snare a nude woman. In 1956, when it was erected, it sat at the outskirts of the city.

Bet You Didn't Know

France occupied Mexico for 7 years and left behind a legacy of blond, blue-eyed people in the *sierras* (mountain regions).

Continue south along Paseo Claussen and you'll pass the **31st of March Fort,** constructed to repel the invading French in 1868 (it did). Next comes the **Continuity of Life Monument,** a fountain installed in 1993 and lovely when lit at night. Here another naked man and woman are poised on a snail shell, which stands for continuity in the Aztec culture; the 13 frolicking dolphins represent intelligence. Just past the diving tower, you'll see **Icebox Hill (Cerro de Neveria)** rising off to the left. At its base is a cave where, in the late 19th century, ice that was shipped in from San Francisco kept much of the city's fish fresh. The red wrought-iron gate is marked "Cueva Diablo," or Devil's Cave, alluding to the grotto's more recent function—storing dynamite during the Mexican Revolution.

Keep going along Paseo Claussen, and you'll encounter the **Women of Mazatlán** monument—the state of Sinaloa is supposed to be renowned for its pretty women—and finally the **Deer Monument,** a tribute to the city's pre-conquistador ancient history. You'll be at Flores Street here, a good spot from which to head inland and do a downtown tour—especially if you've rested for a while at one of the waterside cafes along the way.

Exploring Downtown Mazatlán

A Sábalo-Centro or Sábalo-Cocos bus will get you from the Platinum or Golden zones to the zócalo, or town square—formally, **Plaza Revolution.** The quintessential people-watching forum, it's centered by a gazebo that has, in its base, a restaurant with a CD jukebox and posters of American movie stars, including Marilyn Monroe—not what you'd expect in Mazatlán's oldest plaza and the heart of the city. Just across the street to the north (corner of Calle 21 de Marzo and Nelson), the **cathedral** is architecturally eclectic;

Bet You Didn't Know

The name "Mazatlán" comes from the Nahuatl (Aztec) word *Mazatl,* meaning "land of the deer"; large herds used to roam wild here.

Bet You Didn't Know

Neoclassical architecture was popular in many tropical cities because the high ceilings are ideal for air circulation.

started in 1875, it incorporates elements of baroque, neoclassical, and art deco styles. Its distinctive yellow-tiled twin steeples were added in 1935. **City Hall (Palacio Municipal)** is on the west side of the square; the main **post office** is on the east.

Go east half a block to Benito Juárez and north for another 2 blocks if you want to explore the Mercado Piño Suárez, or **central market.** Even if you don't want to shop for souvenirs, it's worth coming here to soak up some local color (see "Mazatlán's Best Shopping," below, for details). If you want your color more high-toned, go 2 blocks west from the central square to Avenida Carnaval; it soon leads you south to Avenida Constitución, just beyond which is the **Angela Peralta Theater.** Built in 1878, and reopened after a massive restoration in 1992, it's become the town's cultural heart again (see "What to Do When the Sun's Gone Down," below). During the day, you can visit a small art gallery and a museum that details the restoration (check out the photos of the theater with trees growing out of the middle). Admission (less than 50¢) helps maintain the lovely neoclassical structure.

The Angela Peralta theater isn't the only spiffed-up structure in this section of town, called **Viejo Mazatlán (Old Mazatlán).** About 20 blocks of neo-classical buildings dating back to the mid– and late 19th century have been restored. The town houses on Libertad between Domínguez and Carnaval and the mansions on Ocampo at Domínguez and Carnaval are especially notable. Wander around this pretty residential area just soaking in the atmosphere, and then rest your feet at **Machado Plaza,** a lovely leafy triangle. It's serene most of the time—except during Carnaval, when it's the center of activities.

Those Daring Young Men

Mazatlán's cliff divers are not as famous as those in Acapulco, but they're defi-nitely contenders in the high-drama department. If their perch isn't as lofty (45 feet compared to 134 feet) as that of their more southern counterparts, the water they leap into is shallower: 10 to 12 feet in high tide, but only 6 feet in low tide (in Acapulco, it's always at least 15 feet deep). You can see the divers take a leap from El Mirador, off Paseo Claussen (between the Women of Mazatlán and Continuity of Life monuments) at 11am and 1pm, which is, not coincidentally, when the tour groups turn up. They perform for tips; about $1 is appropriate.

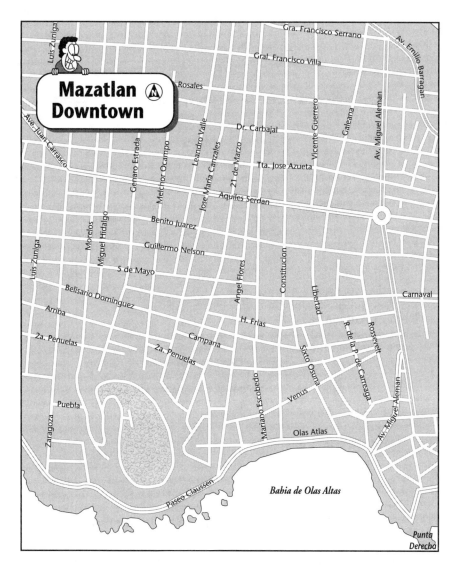

Mazatlan Downtown

Taking a Hike

For a knockout view of the city, hike to **El Faro,** Mazatlán's famous light-house; it's at the summit of Creston Hill (Cerro del Creston), the highest of Mazatlán's three lookout points and the only one you can't ascend by car. The winding, sometimes rocky, route to the top takes about 30 to 45 minutes—worth it for the fantastic vista of the harbor and coastline. You can't climb the lighthouse itself—like you'd want to at this point!—but the lighthouse keeper might open the gate for you and let you look around the base.

To reach the foot of Creston Hill, head over to the end of Paseo Centenario, near the sportsfishing docks. You can get here by taking the Playa Sur bus from the Aquiles Serdán Street side of the central market.

Plagued by Mystery

Angela Peralta (1845–83) was one of the world's most famous divas. Dubbed "the Mexican Nightingale," she performed at Milan's La Scala and sang *Aida* with Giuseppe Verdi conducting in Mexico City.

Facts get a bit murky when it comes to her death. Unquestionably, she was supposed to perform at Mazatlán's new opera house in 1883. She got sick and died, along with several members of her company, before she could sing a note, however. Some sources say she brought and spread the illness—variously described as yellow fever, cholera, and bubonic plague—to Mazatlán from Chile, killing off thousands, which made her rather unpopular in the city for a while; others have her coming in from San Francisco and tragically succumbing to an epidemic already in progress. The townspeople either forgave or paid retribution to Angela Peralta by naming their opera house after her in 1943.

Bet You Didn't Know

Mazatlán's El Faro is the highest functioning lighthouse in the world, rising 505 feet above the harbor. Others are taller, but don't sit so high from the ground—except for the one at Gibraltar, which no longer works.

Horsing Around

If you want to play Mexican *charro* (cowboy), the place for you is Playa Brujas, home of **Ginger's Bilingual Horses.** Run by an American expat and her Mexican husband, the concession has very well-kept animals. From 10am to 4pm every day except Sunday, you can trot along the beach and through a coconut plantation (bring along the bug spray); the price is about $7 for half an hour. To reach Playa Brujas, take any Cerritos bus north to the end of the line.

You can also go riding on **Rancho Las Moras,** the converted tequila ranch described in chapter 37, "Choosing the Place to Stay That's Right for You."

Contact the office in Mazatlán (Av. Camarón Sábalo 204, Suite 6; ☎ 69/16-5044) for more information.

Hitting the Links

The most convenient golf course to the tourist zones is the 27-hole course at **El Cid Mega Resort** (☎ 69/13-3333), currently being redesigned by Lee Trevino (the first 9 holes were completed in 1997). It's open to the public only from May through October, when greens fees are $60, with $10 extra for a caddie, and $20 for a cart. Guests at El Cid pay $50 greens fees, and the same price for cart and caddie. If you want to improve your game, consider enrolling in the **John Jacobs golf school,** recently opened on the property; call ☎ **888/733-7308** from the United States for details.

Since it opened in 1997, the 18-hole **Estrella del Mar Golf Course** (☎ **69/82-3300**) on Stone Island has become a big hit with duffers. The par 72 championship course, designed by Robert Trent Jones, Jr., has superb ocean views. Greens fees are $86; there are no caddies, but golf carts are included in the price.

Kids Doing Something Fishy

Although the **Acuario (Aquarium) Mazatlán** (Av. de los Deportes 111, one-half block off Avenida del Mar; ☎ **69/81-7815** or 69/81-7817) is billed as one of the largest and best in Mexico, it's probably not a good idea to take your kids here if they've just been to Sea World. If their expectations aren't high, however, it's a pleasant place to spend an hour or two; the sea lion shows are especially entertaining. Skip the adjoining zoo, where the animals pace in depressingly small cages. Open 9am to 6pm daily; admission is $4 for adults, and $2 for kids 12 and under.

Olé! Bullfighting

Although not for animal lovers or the weak of stomach, bullfights are a revered Mexican tradition; it's hard not to get caught up in the excitement if you go. You won't witness the best fights on regular basis here, but Mazatlán is a sufficiently large city that it occasionally draws big-time matadors; on those occasions, you can best appreciate the artistry in the gory proceedings.

Take Me Out to the Beisbol Game

Dodger star Fernando Valenzuela got his start playing for Mexico's Pacific Coast League, to which Mazatlán's professional baseball team belongs. You can see Los Venados (The Deers) go to bat October through December at Teodoro Mariscal stadium, off Avenida del Mar near Playa Norte (no phone); ask at your hotel about schedules and tickets.

Mazatlán's bullring (☎ 69/84-1666), located on Rafael Buelna about a mile from the Golden Zone (take the Sábalo-Cocos bus), is open from Christmas through Easter on Sunday at 4pm. Tickets range from $7 for open admission (ask for the shady side—*la sombrera*) to $25 for the front of the shaded section. Come by around 3pm if you want a good general admission seat. You can also buy tickets from a travel agency or tour desk, but they're a bit more expensive.

Mazatlán's Best Shopping

For a city of its size and volume of tourism, Mazatlán has a disappointing shopping scene. There's a great market, with lots of local color, and you won't have a problem finding trinkets and sportswear, but there are surprisingly few outlets for fine crafts or jewelry.

The Golden Zone

The good news is that you can concentrate your retail energy on a fairly small area in the Golden Zone; the section bounded by Avenida Rodolfo T. Loaiza, which loops off from the main thoroughfare, Avenida Camarón-Sábalo, to hug the sea for about half a mile, is by far the most productive for acquisition.

If you're pressed for time, make your one stop the Playa Mazatlán hotel (Av. Rodolfo T. Loaiza 202; ☎ 69/13-4444), where three shops have everything you might want (at a price—but a not-too-outrageous one): **Mexico, Mexico** carries colorful women's clothing and decorative household items; **Playa** has a good selection of well-crafted silver jewelry; and **La Carreta** gathers high-quality folk art from several regions in Mexico.

Just to the north, the large open-front **Mercado Viejo Mazatlán** (Av. Rodolfo T. Loaiza 315; ☎ 69/13-2120) is onyx ashtray heaven; it's a good place to pick up gifts for all those people in the office you don't want to spend much on, but don't want to have glaring at you, either.

Don't (or Do?) Bargain on It

If an item bears a printed price tag—as, say, in a department store—you won't be able to bargain for it. Hand-written prices in smaller shops tend to be negotiable; it never hurts to ask for a better price, especially if you buy more than one item (the shopkeeper might offer, too). No price tag = no-holds-barred bargaining.

Although shell art is one of Mazatlán's claims to fame, the much-touted **Sea Shell City** (Av. Rodolfo T. Loaiza 407; ☎ 69/13-1301) is, frankly, pretty tacky. Unless you're looking for a room divider or light fixture made of sea creature casings, you're unlikely to find much you'll want to, um, shell out for (okay, those little shell cars *are* kind of cute). The large fountain covered with seashells on the second floor is weirdly fascinating, though, and the display cases of hundreds of specimens is interesting, too.

A little farther down the road, **Madonna** (Las Garzas 1, at Laguna; ☎ 69/14-2389) offers a nice selection of jewelry and contemporary Mexican crafts; the blown-glassware is especially impressive. (There's another branch in the Platinum Zone at Av. Camarón Sábalo 2601 [☎ 69/13-0730], next to El Patio restaurant.) Across the street, **Pardo** (Rodolfo Loaiza 411; ☎ 69/14-3354) sells beautifully designed gold jewelry inset with unusual Mexican fire opals, among other gems.

Downtown Deals

Don't miss the huge, covered (but open-sided) **Mercado Piño Suárez**, also known as Mercado Centro, or central market; it's bounded by Melchor Ocampo, Aquiles Serdán, Leandro Valle, and Benito Juárez streets. This is the real people's market, where half the town goes to buy their necessities, everything from an entire side of beef to a pair of pliers, good luck charms, and tennis shoes. You have to poke around to find crafts—*huaraches* (sandals), say, or embroidered blouses and inexpensive silver jewelry—but if you've got time, patience, and good bargaining skills, you're bound to come away with something you like, as well as a sense of accomplishment.

How Low Should You Go?

➤ When the vendor states a price, counter with one about 75% lower, and then come up in increments of 5% and 10%. If you end up paying half the asking price, pat yourself on the back (in the privacy of your hotel room, please).

➤ Don't act terribly interested in the item you covet; just behave as though you're vaguely curious, in a scientific way, about what it might cost. The price goes up proportionately to your enthusiasm.

➤ Be prepared to walk away if you don't get the price you want. You can always come back if you don't find the same thing elsewhere for less.

The restored section around Plaza Machado known as Old Mazatlán (see above) has started to blossom with art galleries. One that's particularly interesting is **NidArt** (Av. Libertad 45, at Carnaval; ☎ 69/81-0002), which features leather masks in the Italian carnival style, as well as other contemporary crafts and paintings.

What to Do When the Sun's Gone Down

Although Mazatlán doesn't glow in the dark like some of the other resort towns, it more than holds its own come nightfall, with everything from raucous dance clubs to jazzy piano bars. Much of the rowdier action takes place in the southern end of the Golden Zone, especially around the Valentino's complex (technically, Fiesta Land) and Los Sábalos hotel, but stray in either direction and you'll find other places to get down—or get picked up.

Bar None: Mazatlán's Best Watering Holes

You might have to grab your drink through the legs of a bartop dancer at **Bora Bora** (Fiesta Land complex, Camarón Sábalo s/n; ☎ **69/84-1006** or 69/84-1722); beach volleyball is also big at this jungle-theme nightspot. Another eat-sand meat market—hey, it's not easy to keep your balance after all those Pacificos—**Joe's Oyster Bar** (Av. Rodolfo T. Loaiza 100, beachfront at Los Sábalos Hotel; ☎ **69/83-6212**) attracts the same eclectic (18 to 40ish) crowd. Across the street from Los Sábalos hotel, but on dry land, **Cowtown** (☎ **69/83-5333**) spins country-and-western sounds for its pool-playing clientele. **Tony's** (Av. Rodolfo T. Loaiza and Camarón Sábalo; ☎ **69/83-5700**) is big on '60s and '70s oldies, even though most of the people who hang out here weren't around for the originals.

Eat 'n' Rumba: Restaurants with a Musical Menu

If you want to combine dinner and an evening's entertainment, and like the former dependable but the latter anything goes, consider the following. At **Señor Frog's** (Av. Del Mar, North Beach Malecón; ☎ **69/85-1110** or 69/85-1925), your tequila is likely to be brought to you by a "bandito" who carries shot glasses in an ammunition belt. Its older and slightly more sedate sibling in the Carlos Anderson family, **El Shrimp Bucket** (Olas Altas 11 at Escobedo, downtown; ☎ **69/81-6350**), serves up live music nightly. TV sporting events and two happy hours a day keep the customers happy at the **No Name Cafe** (Av. Rodolfo T. Loaiza 417, Golden Zone; ☎ **69/13-2031**). Don't be surprised to find both waiters and diners joining in the congo line at **El Patio** (Av. Camarón Sábalo 2601, Platinum Zone; ☎ **69/16-5196**), which brings in the bands on Friday and Saturday nights. (See chapter 40, "The Best of Mazatlán's Dining Scene," for reviews of El Shrimp Bucket, No Name Cafe, and El Patio.)

Saturday Night Fever

Everyone turns up sooner or later at the castle-like **Valentino's** (Fiesta Land complex, Camarón Sábalo s/n; ☎ **69/84-1006** or 69/84-1722), a Mazatlán landmark and the town's most popular disco. It's later, rather than sooner, on nights other than Thursday and Sunday, when women drink free from 9 to 11pm. Although its center is a classic strobe-lit dance floor, this place also has several hideaways, including a romantic music nook and a karaoke bar. There's usually a $4 cover, and drinks range from $2 to $5 a pop. Clean up your act when you come here: No tennies or shorts allowed.

Fiestas: A Taste of Mexico

Eat, drink, and let the entertainment begin at the Fiesta Mexicana held Tuesday, Thursday, and Saturday nights from 7 to 11:30pm at the **Playa Mazatlán** hotel (Rodolfo T. Loaiza 202, Golden Zone; ☎ **69/13-4444**). While you're scarfing down the unlimited margaritas and burritos, you'll be entertained by mariachis and dancers from various regions of Mexico— including some that no longer exist, such as the Aztec empire. Bilingual magicians and comedians may be part of the show, too. The evening's fun will run you about $23. The fiesta at the **El Cid Mega Resort** (Av. Camarón Sábalo, Platinum Zone; ☎ **69/13-3333**) on Wednesday night has a Carnaval theme and gives you lots of bang for your 25 bucks.

Across a Crowded Room

If you want to light up an old flame, dine at the Playa Mazatlán's **La Terraza** (see chapter 40) and be serenaded by a trio. Or make the fireworks literal Sunday night at 8pm, when the restaurant's terrace affords ringside seats to beachside pyrotechnics (you'll need to come at least an hour earlier if you want a table). You'll enjoy a water view, too, at the palapa-roof **La Concha** (El Cid Mega Resort; see chapter 37), and when you're tired of watching the waves, you can make your own on the dance floor. The mellowest nightspot in the Valentino's complex, the piano bar at **Mikonos** (Camarón Sábalo s/n; ☎ **69/84-1006** or 69/84-1722) features Frank Sinatra–style crooning and another stellar ocean vista. When the piano man tickles the ivories at **Señor Pepper's** (Av. Camarón Sábalo 2121, Platinum Zone; ☎ **69/14-3700**), he turns out all that jazz. Downtown's **Café Pacifico** (Frías and Constitucíon; ☎ **69/81-3972**), an 1864 building with high-beamed ceilings, is as retro as they come. Swirling overhead fans, stained glass, and lots of rich wood complete the atmospheric picture.

Culture Fix

The program at the **Angela Peralta Theater** (Calle Carnival s/n; ☎ **69/82-4447**) runs the gamut from traditional deer dances to contemporary ballet, and retrospectives of John Lennon's music to a mainly Mozart trio—to give some examples from a single 3-month season. There are films, lectures, readings, and plays, too, although those may be harder for non-Spanish speakers to follow. Ticket prices range from less than $3 to about $9. Just sitting in the beautifully restored theater is worth the price of admission.

Side Trips: Getting Out of Mazatlán

Mazatlán beginning to feel familiar? I've got a few alternative universes for you. For a reasonable fee, you can be transported to places that seem fixed in amber, including a couple of Spanish mining towns, a furniture-making center, and a sleepy fishing village.

Bet You Didn't Know

There are about 43 miles of underground tunnels in Rosario—outnumbering the aboveground streets, according to locals.

Teacapán & Rosario

Some 2 hours (92 miles) south of Mazatlán, the shrimper's village of Teacapán sits at the tip of an isolated peninsula bordered by mangrove swamps and thick with native coconut palms. The area, which may become a formal ecological preserve, is a birder's paradise, too—at least 90 species have been spotted here. You can tour the lagoons on a catamaran and then kick back on one of the peninsula's pristine beaches.

It's hard to get here on your own unless you've rented a car. You'll spend the same amount of money (less, if there's only one of you) and avoid the hassle by going on a tour—which gives you the added advantage of a guided walk around Rosario, a silver- and gold-mining town founded by the Spanish in 1655. It's famous for its baroque cathedral with an ornate, gold-leaf-covered altar—and the fact that the structure had to be moved brick-by-brick to its present location to preserve it from caving in on the town's honeycomb of underground tunnels. You can also visit the house/museum of Lola Beltrán, a world-renowned Mexican singer.

Eight-hour tours to Rosario and Teacapán, which depart around 7am, generally include continental breakfast on the bus and a seafood lunch. Bookable through hotel tour desks or travel agents, these excursions generally run around $40.

Concordia & Copala

Concordia, some 40 minutes east of Mazatlán, was founded by the Spanish in 1571. Today it's best known for its pre-Columbian-style pottery and solid Colonial-design furniture, as the huge chair in the town square attests. San Sebastian, a baroque church with an ornate stone facade, is the town's other main attraction.

About 10 miles east, Copala is postcard picturesque, with its cobblestone streets and white houses perched on rolling hillsides. Dating back to 1565, the town produced tons of silver in the late 19th century, when it became the center of the region's vast mining wealth. Today, it's a National Historic Landmark with a population of about 600, including some Canadian and American retirees. The American presence is definitely felt at Daniel's, a restaurant renowned for its luscious banana-coconut cream pie.

Again, unless you've rented a car, it's difficult to get to these towns, which are ill-served by public transportation. Tours of the two towns, offered by most travel agencies, run around $30 and include lunch in Copala. They typically leave at 9:45am and return at 3:45pm.

The Best of Mazatlán's Dining Scene

Mazatlán isn't exactly a gourmand's dream, or a town where you'll need to dress to impress, but if you want to eat well at a reasonable price, you've come to the right place. And although Mazatlán has its share of chains, many restaurants here ooze local atmosphere; you rarely feel as though you've landed in Generic-ville.

A Dining Overview: Where's the Burrito?

Mazatlán's tourist zones are chock-a-block with restaurants, ranging from casual beachside palapas to ambitious international dining rooms that don't welcome sandy feet. The Golden Zone has the greatest concentration of eateries, but more and more restaurants are starting to pop up in the Platinum Zone (they tend to be the tonier ones). In general, I don't recommend that you lodge downtown, but I do urge you to eat there, at least a few times, so you can get a feel for the traditional life of the city—not to mention a good meal. All restaurants are listed in alphabetical order, and then indexed by price and location.

 Traveling with kids? Nearly any restaurant can whip up a burger or chicken sandwich for your picky eaters, but if they're brand-name dependent, KFC, McDonald's, and Dairy Queen are there for you. Older kids will get a kick out of such Mexican franchise favorites as Señor Frog's, Guadalajara Grill, and The Shrimp Factory, where the music is loud and the food caters to gringo tastes.

A Bit of Local Flavor

Surprise: The local specialties in Mazatlán involve shrimp. If you're among the some who like it hot, check out the *aguachile* shrimp, splayed butterfly style, marinated in lime, and then grilled with onions and chiles—very low-cal and very spicy. Those who walk on the mild (and high-caloric) side might prefer *camarones Mazatlán*, jumbo shrimp stuffed with yellow cheese and wrapped in bacon.

Check, Please

It's easy to stick to a budget in Mazatlán—if you're careful. Otherwise, you might find yourself so excited by the reasonable entrée prices that you get carried away and end up facing a far larger tab than you would if you were planning on peso-pinching in the first place.

If you're holed up in a room with a kitchen, you might want to make a supermarket run. Stocking up on a few favorite snacks can save you from having to go out every time you (or the kids) get hungry, and you'll save both money and time. You can get to the Gigante—as large is its name implies—by taking the Camarón Sábalo-Cocos bus; the store is right near the bullring. The Comercial Mexicana isn't far from the modern Gran Plaza shopping mall; you can reach it via the Cerritos-Juárez bus line.

Another budget buster? Shrimp *every* single night. Prices for the tasty crustaceans are surprisingly steep, considering the city is the world's major supplier (it's the old "we-just-export-'em" story). For other wallet-friendly dining tips see "Eating Well without Gobbling Up Your Dollars" in chapter 7.

Dollars & Sense

A nice, light lager, Pacifico has been produced in Mazatlán since the turn of the century, when it was developed by German brewers. Try it; drinking local brews is one fun way to keep costs down.

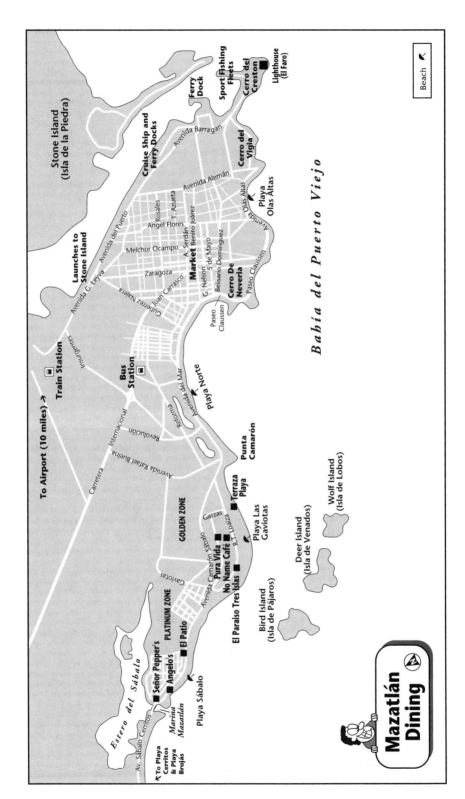

Mazatlán Dining

Don't worry about taxes; the 15% surcharge has already been included in your bill. The tip isn't, however. The standard in nice restaurants is 15%. Mexicans rarely tip that well in less pricey places—10% is about average—but if the service was good, sticking with the 15% rule is an easy way to help the Mexican economy without going broke.

Just in case, I've arranged price categories with the worst-case scenario in mind: They're based on a per-person dinner tab that includes appetizer, entrée, dessert, one drink, and tip. In addition, a price range for dinner entrées is included in the individual reviews; the more $ signs you see, the more money you'll be shelling out at the restaurant listed, as shown in this chart:

$	=	Under $10
$$	=	$10–$25
$$$	=	$25–$40
$$$$	=	Over $40

Unless otherwise noted, reservations are either not accepted or not needed.

My Favorite Restaurants from A to Z

Angelo's
$$$–$$$$. Platinum Zone. ITALIAN.
With its cushy tapestry chairs, sparkling chandeliers, candlelit tables, piano player crooning romantic ballads, and attentive servers, Angelo's is seriously high-tone; it's one of the few restaurants in Mazatlán where you'd feel out of place if you arrived in your sightseeing clothes (in fact, no T-shirts and shorts are allowed). The food doesn't always rise to the occasion, but when it does, it soars. You'll start your meal with crusty, hot-from-the-oven rolls—the pat of butter baked inside is a nice surprise—and then go on to one of freshly made pasta dishes. The shrimp entrées rarely disappoint, and the wine list is excellent.

Pueblo Bonito Hotel, Camarón Sábalo 2121.
☎ ***69/14-3700.*** *Reservations essential in high season.* **Main courses:** *$8–$28. AE, MC, V.* **Open:** *Daily 6pm–midnight.*

Smoke Gets in My Eyes

Every restaurant I've listed offers an alfresco option or is open-fronted, with whirling fans to move the air around, so you're not going to get stuck in any closed-off, smoke-filled rooms.

Copa de Leche
$–$$. Downtown. MEXICAN.
Time seems to have stopped at this open-front cafe overlooking Olas Altas beach. Come here for a breakfast of *huevos malaguena* (eggs with shrimp, peas, and melted cheese) or a dinner of *alambre* barbecue (beef cooked with onion, peppers, mushroom, ham, and bacon), and you'll

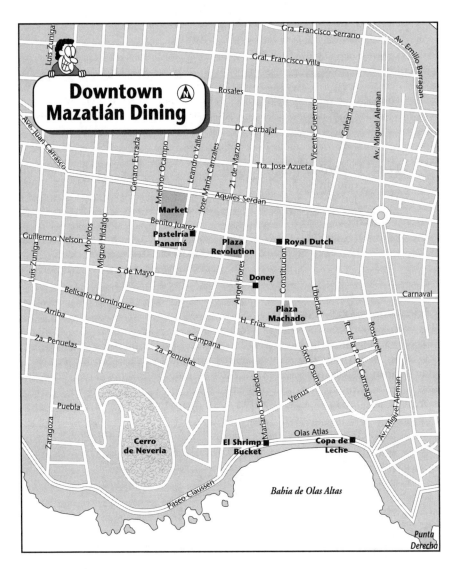

Downtown Mazatlán Dining

enter a kinder, gentler—and pre–cholesterol conscious—era. (You can always watch your waistline with delicious seafood dishes, such as shrimp with chipotle sauce.) You don't even have to eat—just join the regulars for a drink at the bar, made out of an old wooden boat, or while away a couple of hours over a coffee, watching the waves. It's an instant mini-retreat.

Olas Altas 33 Sur (between Miguel Alemán and Sexto Osuna). ☎ **69/82-5753.** ***Main courses:*** *$4–$10. MC, V.* ***Open:*** *Daily 7am–11pm.*

Doney
$–$$. Downtown. MEXICAN.
For traditional Mexican food in a traditional Mexican setting at traditional Mexican prices, Doney is the place. Local families and winter visitors have

been coming for years for such dishes as *asada a la plaza-Mazatlán*, a hearty beef stew, or the *camarones al mojo de ajo*, shrimp in butter and garlic sauce. The *comida corrida* (set-price meal) served from noon to 4pm is a great deal at $3 to $6. This converted 19th-century home with a domed brick ceiling and skylights is close to the Angela Peralta Theater, making it ideal for a pre- or post-show meal.

Local Favorites

Copa de Leche (Downtown, $–$$)

Doney (Downtown, $–$$)

Mariano Escobedo 610 (at 5 de Mayo). ☎ *69/81-2651. Main courses: $3.50–$9; set-price meal $3–$6. AE, MC, V. Open: Daily 8am–10pm.*

El Paraiso Tres Islas

$$. Golden Zone. SEAFOOD/MEXICAN.

You've got to strain your neck a bit to see the third of the three islands that this casual beachside restaurant is named for, but it's no stretch to declare that Paraiso Tres Islas serves some of the best seafood in Mazatlán. While you watch the parasailers play on Playa Gaviotas, you can chow down on great marlin or crabmeat tacos, wrapped in fresh-made tortillas (the charcoal grill gives them a wonderful, slightly smoky taste). The *aguachile* shrimp, spicy hot and marinated in lime, is also excellent. There's a selection of vegetarian dishes— very rare in Mexico—as well as pastas and steaks. If you want to kick-start your day, do as the locals do and come for a seafood *ranchero* breakfast—squid, marlin, and shrimp cooked with tomatoes, onions, and chiles.

Yo, Gringo!

Remember, it's considered impolite in Mexico for the waiter to bring the check before you ask for it.

Av. Rodolfo T. Loaiza 404. ☎ *69/14-2812. Main courses: $8.50–$15. MC, V. Open: Daily 7am–11pm.*

El Patio

$$. Platinum Zone. MEXICAN.

Once a downtown institution, El Patio has moved its zany act north to the Platinum Zone, and the area's fun-seekers are grateful. The menu is eclectic, with lots of familiar fare, such as the dynamite mesquite-grilled chicken and ribs, but interesting traditional dishes are on offer, too—the catch-of-the-day *zarandeado* style, baked in aluminum foil, or the sizzling beef served on a *molcajete* (hot stone dish). At the beginning of the meal, you'll be handed a maraca made from the pod of a tabachin tree so you can shake your stuff to the upbeat music. Constructed out of a variety of local wood to resemble an old-style hacienda—a very hip one, mind you—El Patio is constantly expanding by popular demand.

Av. Camarón Sábalo 2601 (between, but across the road from, the Oceano Palace and Pueblo Bonita hotels). ☎ **69/16-5196.** **Main courses:** *$4–$13. MC, V.* **Open:** *Daily 11am–3am (dinner served until 2am; bar open until 3am).*

Most Likely To Have to Be Carried Home From

El Patio (Platinum Zone, $$)

El Shrimp Bucket (Downtown, $$–$$$)

El Shrimp Bucket
$$–$$$. Downtown. SEAFOOD/MEXICAN.

How do they love shrimp? Let me count the ways. In soup, mixed with oysters and other seafood; in tacos, topped with sour cream, peppers, and guacamole; in fajitas; battered in beer; fried with coconut; grilled with garlic . . . and still counting. Shrimped out? You can order several other types of seafood, or dishes for "land rovers," which include barbecued ribs and chicken *tarasco,* stuffed with mango, onion, and green pepper. Although the food's great, many people also come for the fun atmosphere, with live music nightly and servers trained to keep you in stitches—unless you're terminally humorless.

Hotel La Siesta, Av. Olas Altas 11 at Escodebo. ☎ **69/81-6350** *or 69/82-8019. Reservations recommended during high season and major holidays.* **Main courses:** *$6–$16.* **Open:** *Daily 6am–11pm.*

Bet You Didn't Know

El Shrimp Bucket is where the Carlos Anderson chain started in 1963. It's since gone international, and includes Carlos 'n Charlie's, Guadalajara Grill, and several other successful franchises. Coming here is kind of like visiting the first McDonald's—except that the food's better and you can get tequila poppers.

No Name Cafe
$$. Golden Zone. AMERICAN/MEXICAN.

Barbecued ribs with a side of ESPN has proved to be a winning combo at this open-air sports bar in the heart of the Golden Zone. Along with the typical American jock fare—roast beef sandwiches, Buffalo wings, and half-pound burgers—you can get south-of-the-border food that goes great with beer: beef

Best North-of-the-Border Fix

No Name Cafe (Golden Zone, $$)

burritos, say, or chicken fajitas and, of course, nachos. The long, bilingual drinks list is extremely educational: Once you've learned that "screwdriver" is translated literally as *"desarmador,"* you can use that information in a hardware store. *Warning:* Crucial play-by-play voice-overs are sometimes drowned out by the resident parrots, who seem to get excited by certain teams (I won't reveal which ones).

Av. Rodolfo T. Loaiza 417. ☎ *69/13-2031.* **Main courses:** *$4–$12. MC, V.* **Open:** *Daily 8am "'til the party's over."*

Pastelría Panamá
$. Downtown. PASTRY SHOP/ECLECTIC.

When you need to refuel after some serious sightseeing or a hard round of bargaining at the market, join the throngs at this brightly lit corner restaurant that's part pastry shop, part diner. The sandwiches, burgers, and Mexican plates are okay, but the sweets—ice cream sundaes, malts, pastries, chocolate cake—are better. This is the oldest of the five branches; the one in the Golden Zone (Camarón Sábalo at Las Garzas; ☎ **69/136-977**) is the largest. Both are constantly packed.

Av. Juárez, corner Canizales. ☎ *69/85-1853.* **Main courses:** *$2–$3.50 breakfast; $2–$5 sandwiches and hot dishes. No credit cards.* **Open:** *Daily 7am–11pm.*

Pura Vida
$. Golden Zone. HEALTH FOOD.

Eating at this typical beach shack—which doesn't happen to be on the shore—won't guarantee you "the pure life" but it'll give you a quick taste of it. Grab a stool at the central counter or a bench at a wooden picnic table in the garden and enjoy a yogurt/fruit smoothie with a veggie omelet or a whole wheat–crust pizza. The sandwiches made with actual chicken are fine, but skip the pseudo-meat stuff, like the soyburgers.

Calle Laguna s/n, corner of Las Garzas. ☎ *69/16-5815.* **Main courses:** *$2.50–$6 (sandwiches, salads, and pizzas). No credit cards.* **Open:** *Mon–Sat 8am–10pm.*

Royal Dutch
$–$$. Downtown. PASTRY SHOP/CONTINENTAL.

The Dutch owner of this converted historic house used to be the chef on a cruise ship, where he perfected the formula for pleasing lots of people. Sit out on the leafy patio and enjoy French toast in the morning, a deli sandwich on fresh-baked bread for lunch, and hearty pork roast, bratwurst and sauerkraut for dinner—or the superb carrot cake and cappuccino any time of the day. If you just want to come by for a cookie to go, that's okay, too.

Av. Juárez 137, corner of Constitucíon. ☎ *69/81-2007. Main courses: $4–$9. AE. Open: Mon–Sat 8am–10pm.*

Señor Pepper's

$$–$$$. Platinum Zone. STEAK-HOUSE/INTERNATIONAL.

Its casual name is deceptive: This is Mazatlán's swankiest steakhouse, with tuxedoed waiters, lots of gleaming wood and brass, and atmospherically dimmed lights. You enter past a patio where a large mesquite grill brings the house specialty—first-class cuts of meat from the state of Sonora, Mexico's Marlboro country—to sizzling perfection. Pork, lobster, and shrimp are the other options on the brief, get-to-the-point menu. The nightly specials, which include appetizer, entrée, and soup or salad, are a good deal.

Av. Camarón Sábalo s/n, across from the Camino Real hotel. ☎ *69/14-0101 or 69/14-0120. Reservations suggested. Main courses: $8–$22; specials $8–$12. AE, MC, V. Open: Daily 6pm–midnight; bar open until 2am.*

Terraza Playa

$$–$$$. Golden Zone. MEXICAN/CONTINENTAL/SEAFOOD.

This popular beachfront eatery turns elegant after dark, when the white tablecloths, candles, and musicians come out, and the surf looks luminescent. You won't have any trouble finding what you like on this menu—and liking what you find. Entrées range from Mexican (the smoked marlin burritos are super) to Continental—say, the tenderloin tips Stroganoff—to such favorites as surf and turf (a tony combo of lobster thermidor and filet mignon). There's even a low-cholesterol, low-fat section, which most diners no doubt vow to take advantage of "next time." It gets a bit toasty here at lunchtime; breakfast and dinner are your best bets. If you want a front-row seat for the Sunday night fireworks, book early.

Hotel Playa Mazatlán, Av. Rodolfo T. Loaiza 202. ☎ *69/13-4455. Reservations suggested during high season. Main courses: $5–$17. AE, MC, V. Open: Daily 6am–midnight.*

Most Romantic Restaurants

Angelo's (Platinum Zone, $$$–$$$$)

Señor Pepper's (Platinum Zone, $$–$$$)

Terraza Playa (Golden Zone, $$–$$$)

Sound Bites: Mazatlán's Restaurants at a Glance
Restaurant Index by Price

$

Pura Vida (Golden Zone, Health Food)

 Pastelría Panamá (Downtown, Pastry Shop/Eclectic)

$–$$

Copa de Leche (Downtown, Mexican)

Doney (Downtown, Mexican)

 Royal Dutch (Downtown, Pastry Shop/Continental

$$

El Paraiso Tres Islas (Golden Zone, Seafood/Mexican)

El Patio (Platinum Zone, Mexican)

No Name Cafe (Golden Zone, American/Mexican)

$$–$$$

Señor Pepper's (Platinum Zone, Steakhouse/International)

Terraza Playa (Golden Zone, Mexican/Continental/Seafood)

El Shrimp Bucket (Downtown, Seafood/Mexican)

$$$–$$$$

Angelo's (Platinum Zone, Italian)

Restaurant Index by Location

The Platinum Zone

Angelo's $$$–$$$$

El Patio $$

Señor Pepper's $$–$$$

The Golden Zone

El Paraiso Tres Islas $$

No Name Cafe $$

Pura Vida $

Terraza Playa $$–$$$

Downtown

Copa de Leche $–$$

Doney $–$$

El Shrimp Bucket $$–$$$

Pastelría Panamá $

Royal Dutch $–$$

Part 11

Los Cabos

A singular destination but also a triple threat, Los Cabos boasts unique desert-meets-sea scenery and three distinct areas in which to revel in it—sometimes literally. There's the low-key town of San José del Cabo, party-hearty Cabo San Lucas, and the glitzy row of hotels and golf courses called the Corridor that connects the two.

Because Los Cabos is so diverse, where you want to spend most of your time—and how you want to spend it—are major considerations. The next four chapters are devoted to helping you out with those vacation make-or-break decisions.

Choosing the Place to Stay That's Right for You

In This Chapter

➤ Where the hotels are

➤ The best ones in the bunch

➤ Hotel indexes

Luxury, low-rent, relaxation, action—Los Cabos has them all, but rarely in the same area, so it's important to get your priorities straight before booking a room at this beach resort. You wouldn't want to have a nonrefundable reservation in the heart of Cabo San Lucas, only to realize that you're basically antisocial—or settle on a getaway in the Corridor and discover that you and your companion would really be much happier lost in a crowd.

Now that I've made you nervous, take a deep breath and read on. If you stay focused on your interests, needs, and budget, you shouldn't have any problem figuring out where you want to bed down.

Here's how it works. First, I'll give you a thumbnail sketch of the areas where Los Cabos's hotels are concentrated, summing up their pros and cons at the end of each section. Then I'll list my favorite lodgings alphabetically, and follow up with a list of alternatives should the A-list choices be filled. At the end of the chapter, you'll find handy, at-a-glance indexes listing the hotels by price and by location.

As far as prices go, I've noted rack rates (the maximum that a resort or hotel charges for a room) in the listings. This information will give you some sense of what to expect, although I know you'll avoid paying rack by following the advice I gave you in chapter 6, "The Lowdown on Accommodations in Mexico." I've also put a dollar sign icon in front of each hotel listing so you can quickly see whether it's within your budget. The more $ signs under the name, the more you pay. It runs like this:

$	=	Under $85
$$	=	$85–$140
$$$	=	$140–$195
$$$$	=	$195–$310
$$$$$	=	$310 and above

Unless specified, rates are for a standard double room in high season, which extends somewhat longer than most of the resorts, from November through May. The rest of the year, prices are reduced anywhere from a quarter to a third. During Christmas and Easter weeks, you might sometimes have to pay as much as 25% above the usual high-season rates—if you can get a room. The prices listed include the 12% room tax.

A Matter of Degrees

Weatherwise, the best months to visit are November to May, although it can be unpredictably cool in Los Cabos from January through March (but that's compensated for by it being whale-watching season). From June through September, the heat can be seriously uncomfortable. On the other hand, if you're a diver, summer is ideal—water temperatures are at their most comfortable, visibility is at its greatest, and room rates are at their lowest.

A kid-friendly icon **Kids** highlights hotels that are especially good for families. Unless otherwise noted, all hotels are air-conditioned, and if the review doesn't say anything to the contrary, you can safely assume that you can walk out of your hotel directly onto the beach.

Taxing News

The good news: The hotel taxes in Los Cabos, which was once a duty-free zone, are 5% less than those on most of the mainland. The bad news: Lots of hotels tack on a 10% service charge (I've noted this and added it to the rack rates in the relevant hotel listings).

Hint: As you read through the reviews, you'll want to keep track of the ones that appeal to you. There's a chart at end of the book (see p. 542) for that purpose, but to make matters easier on yourself now, why don't you just put a little check mark next to the ones you like as you go along?

Location, Location, Location

The Los Cabos airport is closest to San José del Cabo, so that's the town I'll cover first. It's westward ho, via the Corridor—where another group of hotels is strung out—to Cabo San Lucas, 22 miles from San José and the area with the greatest concentration of lodgings.

San José del Cabo: Remembering You're in Mexico

It's not exactly the town that time forgot—the ceaseless construction you'll glimpse as you ride in from the airport will quickly disabuse you of that notion—but San José del Cabo is as close to traditional Mexico as you'll come in Los Cabos. A pretty little park adjoining a town square and lots of inexpensive *panaderias* (bakeries) and taco shops remind you that this is where most of the people who work in the Corridor and Cabo San Lucas hang their hats.

Bet You Didn't Know

There's currently only one traffic light in San José, although four or five others are scheduled to be installed.

San José is a magnet for visiting retirees, tour groupies, families, and couples who can't afford to stay on the Corridor but want some solitude. There are a smattering of good restaurants and a few nightspots here, but for the most part, the town shuts down after dark. If you want some action, you'll have to cab it over to Cabo and pay about $30 or more each way or depend on a less expensive hotel shuttle to take you there. Shuttles don't often let you stay out as late as you might like, however, so if you've just met your prince (or princess), you might have to abandon him, Cinderella-like, at midnight—or shell out for a taxi in the hopes he doesn't turn into a frog.

Along with a low-key atmosphere, the great advantage of staying in San José is access to several comfortable, reasonably priced hotels. The least expensive of them, not surprisingly, don't sit directly on the sand, but in the down-town, or *centro*, area. Lack of beach access isn't as great a disadvantage as it might be in other places, however, because a strong undertow renders the town beach, lined with relatively pricier lodgings, unsuitable for swimming. With one notable exception, wherever you stay in San José, you'll be doing your dog paddling in a pool.

In a nutshell . . .

➤ Closest to the airport

➤ The least expensive and quietest accommodations

➤ A sense of (more) traditional Mexico here

but . . .

> ➤ You'll be farthest from the Cabo San Lucas action.

> ➤ There's not much in the way of luxury.

> ➤ You can't swim on the town beach.

The Corridor: All That Glitters—Plus Golf

Once upon a time, only a few decades ago, the area now termed the Corridor was a long dirt road flanked by a series of untouched beaches and coves. But that was then, before the transpeninsular road was built in 1973—and this is now. First slowly, and then at a rapidly accelerating pace, exclusive hotels and designer golf courses began cropping up along this stretch, all grabbing a piece of the shore.

We're talking a 20-mile span here, though, so the accommodations are hardly on top of one another (yet). Stay in this section of Los Cabos, and you'll have all the solitude you want and all the luxury—and all the credit card bills that accompany those privileges. Most of these resorts feature great beaches and provide more than enough activities to keep you happy all day—a good thing, because it's hard to get around in this area without a car. You can't even go out the door and hail a cab on your own because it's a long haul to the road, and taxis don't really cruise the Corridor; you'll have to depend on the front desk to summon one for you. It costs anywhere from $8 to $18 a pop (depending on which end of the Corridor you're staying) to get into the Cabo San Lucas groove if you don't want your nightlife limited by the schedule of the hotel shuttle.

Time-Savers

Because of the great distances and the high prices of taxis, the Corridor is one of the few places in Mexico where it's not a bad idea to rent a car (but see chapter 9, "Tying Up the Loose Ends," and chapter 42, "Finding Your Way Around Los Cabos," for some caveats).

In a nutshell . . .

> ➤ It's got the most exclusive accommodations, all on the beach.

> ➤ The best golf is here.

> ➤ The beaches are gorgeous—and often safe for swimming.

but . . .

➤ Rooms are expensive.

➤ You'll have to cab it to Cabo San Lucas if you want to party.

➤ There's no "there" there: It's very spread out, without a town to walk around.

Cabo San Lucas: Where the Boys (& Girls) Are

Just call it Cabo—all the Baja rats do—and refer to it as though it's the only place that exists in Los Cabos. For hordes of spring-breakers and cold-weather escapees of all ages, that's precisely the case. The revelry starts on Medano beach around noon, when up-'til-dawners drag themselves out of bed for a hair of the dog; after dark, the action spreads around town until well past the witching hour.

But it was sportsfishers who originally started the party that, some say, got out of hand. They came because the big ones were biting at Land's End, where the Sea of Cortez and Pacific Ocean embrace each other at Playa de Amor (Lover's Beach). The fish still like the scenery—and so will you. In Cabo, you've got a good choice of hotels in a variety of price ranges (although, again, the least expensive ones are sans beachfront), as well as easy access to water sports concessions, excursions, restaurants, and shops. In short, pretty much anything you might like is at your doorstep (as well as a few things you might not, including hard-sell timeshare peddlers).

In a nutshell . . .

➤ Nonstop nightlife, endless activities, plenty of restaurants

➤ Accommodations to suit lots of different budgets

➤ Closest to scenic Land's End

but . . .

➤ There's nowhere to run, nowhere to hide.

➤ The most accessible beaches are crowded.

➤ You're farthest from the airport.

My Favorite Hotels from A to Z

Casa del Mar Golf Resort & Spa
$$$$. The Corridor.
The ultimate sybaritic retreat. At this boutique hotel, you can sit in your room's Jacuzzi tub and look out beyond the balcony to the deep blue sea—or if you're feeling really decadent, let the warm jets of water wash over you while you're watching cable TV. Not that there's anything here you need to de-stress from, unless you consider playing golf at the adjacent Cabo Real golf course a high-anxiety activity. The state-of-the-art spa has a huge hot tub

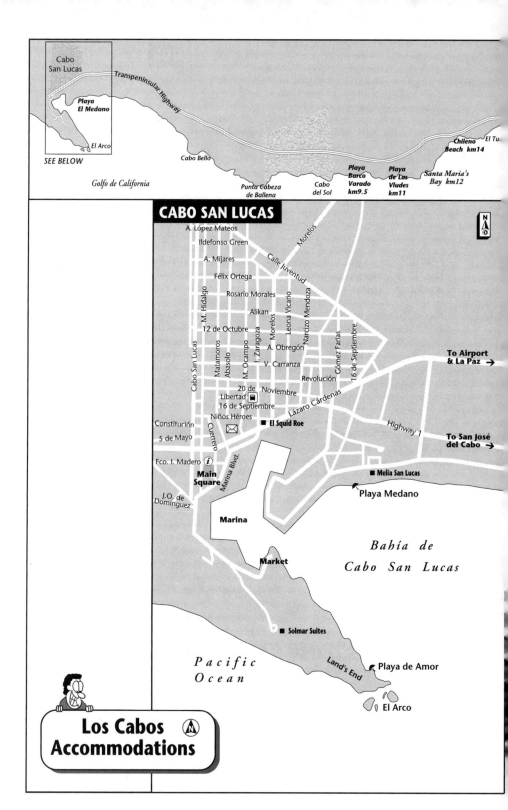

Los Cabos
Accommodations

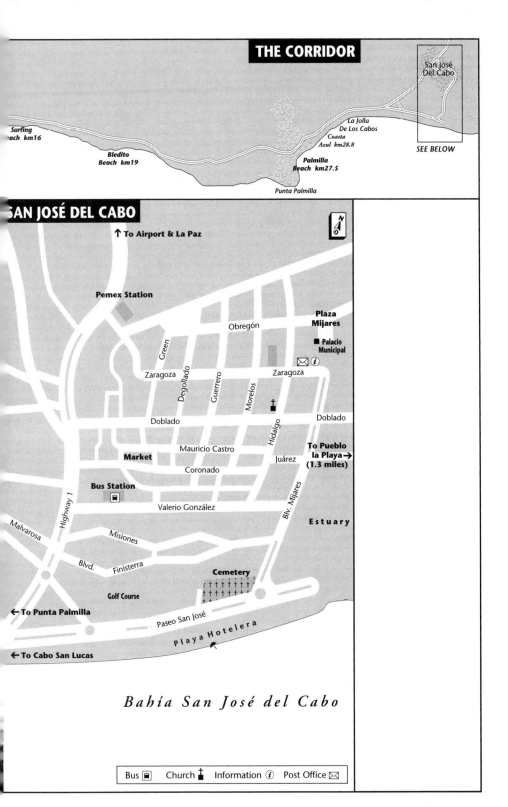

THE CORRIDOR

San José Del Cabo

SEE BELOW

Surfing
Beach km16

Bledito
Beach km19

Palmilla
Beach km27.5

Punta Palmilla

La Jolla
De Los Cabos
Coasta
Azul km28.8

SAN JOSÉ DEL CABO

↑ To Airport & La Paz

Pemex Station

Obregón

Plaza
Mijares

■ Palacio
Municipal

⊠ ⓘ

Green

Zaragoza

Degollado

Guerrero

Morelos

Zaragoza

✝
■

Doblado

Doblado

Hidalgo

Mauricio Castro

Market

Juárez

To Pueblo
la Playa →
(1.3 miles)

Coronado

Bus Station
🚏

Blv. Mijares

Estuary

Valerio González

Malvarosa

Highway 1

Mísiones

Blvd.

Finisterra

Cemetery
✝ ✝ ✝ ✝ ✝ ✝ ✝ ✝ ✝
✝ ✝ ✝ ✝ ✝ ✝ ✝

Golf Course

← To Punta Palmilla

Paseo San José

Playa Hotelera

← To Cabo San Lucas

Bahía San José del Cabo

Bus 🚏   Church ✝   Information ⓘ   Post Office ⊠

Dollars & Sense

It's often worth calling Mexican hotels directly instead of just booking through the U.S. reservation service. The Casa del Mar sometimes runs spa or golf packages that don't always get relayed to the United States.

with a waterfall; sign on here for nearly every form of pampering you can think of—how 'bout a massage for two under the stars? The fine dining room is ultra-romantic, and the food's good, too. The mutedly elegant rooms are arranged, hacienda style, around a central court-yard; fresh-cut flowers deck the halls and high-quality Mexican art graces the walls. Luxury like this doesn't come cheap—but compared to the rest of the resorts on the Corridor, this is a good deal.

Transpeninsular Hwy., km 19.5. ☎ *800/221-8808 or 114/4-0030 to 114/4-0033. (*☎ *800/393-0400 for golf reservations from the U.S.) Fax 114/4-0034. www. mexico.online.com/casamar.html. E-mail: casamar@cabonet.mex. **Rack rate:** $252 double. AE, MC, V.*

Hotel Finisterra
$$$–$$$$. Cabo San Lucas.

Old Cabo hands and new inductees alike flock to the Finisterra for its daz-zling views of the harbor and Land's End (which is what Finisterra means); its convenience to, but distance from, town; and its beach club, where two 6,000-square-foot freshwater pools are flanked by waterfalls, Jacuzzis, and lots of tropical foliage. When you need a pick-me-up (or a put-me-down under a beach umbrella for the rest of the day), swim over to the huge palapa bar, where the secret ingredient in the margaritas is Grand Marnier. The hotel has been around for decades, but a major refurbishing in 1997, which also saw the construction of a posh new tower, gave all the rooms a fresh, attractive

Best for Sports Addicts

Meliá San Lucas (Cabo San Lucas, $$$$)

Presidente Inter-Continental (San José del Cabo, $$$$)

look. The oldest units, in natural stone buildings near the lobby, are the least expensive, but their views are obstructed by the newer buildings and it's harder to reach the beach from them. This place is renowned for its service and for its Whale Watcher bar, which lives up to its cetacean-spying name.

Blvd. Marina s/n (almost at the end). ☎ *800/347-2252 or 114/3-3333. Fax 114/3-0590. **Rack rates:** $174 standard double (older building); $224 (newer buildings); includes 10% service charge. AE, DISC, MC, V.*

Hotel Mar de Cortez
$. Cabo San Lucas.

A real bargain and a pretty oasis in the (almost) thick of town, this Spanish-style hotel has its rooms arranged around a courtyard, where a large pool shaded by palms and banana trees is a guest magnet. On cooler evenings, everyone gathers near the fireplace in the semi-outdoor bar and swaps stories about the action at the various nightspots—or about the Big One that got away. The older rooms have dark wood furniture, tiny porches facing the courtyard, and either one double or two single beds; if you need to spread out a bit, book one in the newer section, which has rooms with two double beds. For more than two people, the best bet is a suite, which offers a king or two doubles plus a sleeper couch. There's an on-site restaurant and a freezer for your catch. Reserve early; word's out that this is a good deal.

Lázaro Cárdenas s/n, at Guerrero. ☎ *800/347-8821 or 114/3-0032. Fax (in the U.S.) 408/663-1904.* **Rack rates:** *$50–$76 double; $74–$87 suite; includes 10% service charge. DISC, MC, V.*

Kids Best for Families

Hotel Mar de Cortez (Cabo San Lucas, $)

Presidente Inter-Continental (San José del Cabo, $$$$)

Westin Regina (The Corridor, $$$$)

Howard Johnson Plaza
$$. San José del Cabo.

Forget the familiar orange roofs; this Howard Johnson is architecturally striking, appearing from the side of the road like a futuristic Mediterranean city. The sprawling complex, consisting of 12 low-rises, is connected by cobblestone thoroughfares, replete with street signs. Rooms are far from generic, either—all are light, with Mexican detail, although they look slightly worn and the baths smell a bit musty. It's worth shelling out the extra bucks for one of the suites—they're huge, with well-equipped kitchens and one or two bedrooms (share with another couple and you've got a real deal). Try to get one on the first floor, so you can walk out of your room to the large pool, surrounded by gardens. The hotel doesn't have its own beach, but there are frequent shuttles to its beach club, and it's right across the road from the Los Cabos Golf and Tennis Club. Hotel guests, who tend to be the retiring type, get discounts on greens fees.

Dollars & Sense

The Howard Johnson chain gives members of AARP (American Association of Retired Persons) a price break; if you belong, don't forget to ask about the discount when you make your reservation.

Paseo Finisterra s/n (about 5 blocks east of town, just off Hwy. 1). ☎ *800/*
654-2000 or 114/2-0990. Fax 114/2-0806. E-mail: hojocabo@cabonet.net.mx.
Rack rates: *$103 standard double; $148 1-bedroom suite; $215 2-bedroom suite.*
AE, DC, MC, V.

La Playita Resort
$$. San José del Cabo.
If you're seeking solititude—or are on the lam—La Playita is the place. To get
here, you have to travel two miles from the town of San José on a rutted dirt
road; unless you have rented wheels or call for a taxi to fetch you, you're
pretty much out of reach. But the guests at this small hotel like that arrange-
ment just fine. The rooms are spacious and comfortable (if not luxurious),
the restaurant is good, and you're on the only swimming beach in the San
José area. You can book a small fishing boat for an angling excursion—or just
lie by the pool and read something you've always intended to.

Pueblo La Playa. ☎ *114/2-4166.* **Rack rate:** *$67 double. AE, MC, V.*

On a Package Deal Billed for Two

The Meliá runs a series of low-season (April 13 to December 20) specials; all
include 3 nights in an oceanview room and a daily buffet breakfast. The
Escape to Los Cabos deal ($990 for two) adds on one dinner for two, an
ATV tour of the old lighthouse, and 1 hour each of horseback riding. The **fish-
ing** package ($1,176 for two) throws in 1 day of fishing on a 28-foot cabin
cruiser, and fish preparation with salad bar and a bottle of wine. A **diving** deal
($990 for two) also includes two tanks per person with a departure from the
hotel, dinner for two, and a car rental for 24 hours. All packages are subject to
22% tax and service charges.

Meliá San Lucas
$$$$. Cabo San Lucas.
If you don't want to miss even a minute of the party, you've come to the
right place. But although the Meliá sits smack on Medano Beach, Cabos's
most happening stretch of sand, it's no dash-in, shower, and split kind of
hotel. You'll want to linger over a cold drink in the tiled lobby, which has
smashing vistas of El Arco, Cabos's famous rock arch, and live entertainment
at night, or just relax by the poolside palapa bar. Three restaurants let you
decide whether you're feeling haute-y or casual. All the public areas are set
far enough back from the beach so that you hardly have to be aware of the
water sports–mad hoi polloi—until you're ready to join them. The building
itself is soothing, with its sand-colored stucco and red-tile roof, and rooms

are a rhapsody in blue. Get one with a seaview terrace, and you're made in the shade.

Playa Medano. ☎ *800/336-3542 or 114/3-1000. Fax 114/3-0418.* **Rack rates:** *$222 double; $297 suite; includes 10% service charge. AE, MC, V.*

Palmilla
$$$$$. The Corridor.
Don't let the relentless condo construction you'll pass on the long drive in put you off. This lovely Spanish-style hotel occupies a cliff top on a private point, Punta Palmilla, which boasts some of the most dazzling scenery in Los Cabos, as well as one of its best swimming beaches. Built in 1956 by the son of a Mexican president as a sportsfishing retreat—which would explain the private airstrip—the Palmilla has expanded its activity roster to include golf on a Jack Nicklaus signature course, volleyball, horseback riding, tennis, snorkeling, and diving; there's also a life-size chess game for the more cerebral. Rooms are done in the height of Mexican folk chic, with hand-painted tiles, wrought-iron curtain rods, and hand-carved furniture. Fresh juice, croissants, and coffee are delivered to your room every morning, and the hotel's La Paloma restaurant is excellent.

Transpeninsular Hwy., km 24.5. ☎ *800/637-2226 or 114/2-0582. Fax 114/ 2-0583.* **Rack rates:** *Doubles start at $426 (including 15% service charge automatically added to the bill); 3-night minimum on weekends, no Saturday arrivals or departures. From December 18 to January 3, 7-night minimum and higher rates are in effect. AE, MC, V.*

Dollars & Sense

If you can take the heat, get out on the links: The Palmilla has some great golf deals in summer. From July 5 to September 30, you can get accommodations in a junior suite with unlimited golf on the Palmilla course for $174 per person per night, with a minimum 3-night stay. Also available: more expensive golf packages in spring, and romance packages in spring and summer that include 1 night's dinner on your terrace.

Posada Terranova
$. San José del Cabo.
Come here for an authentic Mexican experience as well as bargain rates. Owner Rosario Aramburo, a member of an old San José family, was born in the large house that she now runs as a hotel. Nice touches in the clean, simple rooms include the cool tile floors and hand-painted designs over the bed;

Address Unknown

If you see "s/n" in an address, it stands for *sin numero*—without number.

baths are small, with showers only. You're not on the beach here, but you're on a quiet street near the center of town and have a cozy Mexican restaurant on the premises. Sit out on the patio and nurse a beer, and you can hear tales of Cabo past from the fishing aficionados who have frequented this place forever.

Degollado s/n, between Zaragoza and Dobaldo. ☎ *114/2-0534. Fax 114/2-0902.* ***Rack rates:*** *$50 double; weekly and monthly rates available. AE, DC, MC, V.*

Presidente Inter-Continental
$$$$. San José del Cabo.

The nicest of the properties on San José's town beach, the Presidente is also pricier, but you'll get your money's worth if you take advantage of even half the relentless activities that are part of the all-inclusive plan—tennis, snorkeling, dive classes in the huge pool, Spanish lessons, volleyball, shopping tours, free golf at the nearby Los Cabos Golf and Tennis Club, and more. You can also find several quiet areas to escape to, including the estuary/bird sanctuary next door (but get a room at this end of the hotel and you'll literally be up with the birds). A kids' club keeps youngsters 5 to 12 occupied all day, and you can get a sitter if you want to enjoy the hotel's good Mexican fiesta or Bones disco on your own. The accommodations are attractive, with vibrant pink and turquoise touches; even the standard ones are roomy.

Paseo San José, next to the San José estuary. ☎ *800/327-0200 or 114/2-0038. Fax 113/2-0232. www.interconti.com.* ***Rack rates:*** *$347 standard gardenview double to $582 oceanfront suite; rates include all meals, soft and alcoholic drinks, and nonmotorized sports for 2 people; up to 2 children under age 12 stay free in parents' room. AE, DC, MC, V.*

Siesta Suites
$. Cabo San Lucas.

Ideal for a long-term stay—there are weekly and monthly discounts on the already low rates, and the rooms have kitchenettes with refrigerators and sinks. This three-story inn opened in the mid-1990s and everything still looks new and sparkling. Perks include free movies in the lobby and a convenient location on a quiet side street that's only 1½ blocks from the marina and a 10-minute walk from Medano beach.

Zapata at Hidalgo. ☎ *and fax* ***114/3-2773. Rack rate:*** *$62 double. A/C. No credit cards.*

Solmar Suites

$$$. Cabo San Lucas.

Away from the Cabo fray, but just a long stroll (or cheap cab ride) from the action, this friendly, low-glitz property is ideal if you want to hedge your bets. It's also great if angling is your angle; the Solmar fishing fleet is first-rate, and the kitchen will freeze or prepare your catch for you. You're at the very tip of the Baja peninsula and the hotel is set against dark cliffs, so the scenery is spectacular, but the ocean is too rough for swimming. No matter—when you get your fill of the sand, you can always jump into the pool, which is where everyone gathers anyway. You can't go wrong with one of the standard rooms (termed "junior suites"). They're comfortably furnished and roomy, have coffeemakers with free coffee, and sit directly on the sand. The more expensive studio or deluxe units are set back on a hillside; there's another pool in this area, but you're farther from the beach.

Dollars & Sense

Solmar's "Fishing Rodeo" packages for $347 a person in high season include 3 nights in a junior suite, two dinners per person at two nearby restaurants, a welcome margarita, and 1 day of fishing on a shared (four-person) boat.

Av. Solmar 1 (at the end of Blvd. Marina). ☎ **800/344-3349** *or 114/3-3535. Fax 114/3-04-10. www.solmar.com.* **Rack rate:** *$185 junior suite. AE, MC, V.*

Tropicana Inn

$. San José del Cabo.

Stay at this delightful inn and you'll be in the center of town and the center of San José action (such as it is), but you'll feel as though you're a world apart. Rooms, which have nice folk art details, surround a bougainvillea-decked courtyard with a pool, swim-up palapa bar, and Spanish-style fountain; this enclave is so pretty that you won't miss not being on the beach. You can wake up and smell the coffee, courtesy of your in-room percolator, and then enjoy a complimentary continental breakfast by the pool. The restaurant and bar (both reviewed in later chapters) are the places to be at night. This place is popular with California anglers, who can store their catch in the restaurant freezer until they're ready to drive it home. Although the hotel is American-owned and you get a strong gringo contingent of all ages, lots of Mexicans also come to enjoy this *Norteamericano* interpretation of their country.

Blvd. Mijares 30, 1 block south of Mijares Plaza. ☎ **114/2-1580** *or 114/2-0907. Fax 114/2-1590 or 510/939-2725 in the U.S.* **Rack rate:** *$73 double, including tax; stay a week and you'll get a day free. AE, MC, V.*

Twin Dolphin
$$$$$. The Corridor.

The epitome of understated tastefulness, this low-slung hotel complex attracts an older, affluent crowd, who don't mind the lack of phones and TVs—as well as celebrities who want complete privacy. The use of native stone helps the guest units blend unobtrusively into a landscape that's hard to outdo, anyway; how often do you see cactus poised dramatically against the sea? The theme is marine: Two brass dolphins cavort in a fountain at the entryway, and a series of telescopes are poised on the beach to peer at the whales that pass this way during their winter migrations. You'll have plenty of opportunity to grow your own fins; the hotel is a short walk from Santa Maria beach, which has some of the best snorkeling in Los Cabos. Rooms are attractive, with lots of carved light wood and Mexican textiles, but a tad too rustic for the price. If you want to hole up here, you can opt for the full meal plan and never have to leave the premises.

Hotels with the Best Beaches

Meliá San Lucas (Cabo San Lucas, $$$$)

Palmilla (The Corridor, $$$$$)

Twin Dolphin (The Corridor, $$$$$)

Transpeninsular Hwy., km 10. ☎ *800/421-8925 or 114/3-2056. Fax 114/ 3-0496.* **Rack rates:** *$305 double, without meals (including the 15% service charge automatically added to the bill); $410 with breakfast and dinner; $465 with three meals. MC, V.*

Best for Romance

Casa Del Mar (The Corridor, $$$$)

Hotel Finisterra (Cabo San Lucas, $$$–$$$$)

Palmilla (The Corridor, $$$$$)

Kids Westin Regina
$$$$. The Corridor.

Unlike the other Corridor resorts, which tend to keep a low architectural profile, the huge Westin resort shouts "Look at me." The design is stunning, with its use of desert tones, open space, and freeforms, but it's not entirely people-friendly—wherever you're going, it's hard to get there from here. Still, there are plenty of swell places to settle into, including a series of meandering pools; a spa and fitness center where you can gaze at the ocean while climbing the StairMaster; and an array of restaurants, the best of which is the elegant Arrecife. With its kids' club and its lively atmosphere, the Westin is one of the few Corridor resorts where children will feel welcome. Businesspeople who convene here like the mingling action by the pool. Rooms are contemporary attractive, with both fans and air-conditioning as well as separate shower stalls and baths—the better to control your environment.

Transpeninsular Hwy., km 22.5. ☎ *800/228-3000 or 114/2-9000. Fax 114-29040. www.westin.com.* **Rack rates:** *$302 double (partial ocean view) to $342 (full ocean view). AE, DC, MC, V.*

No Room at the Inn? Check Out One of These . . .

San José del Cabo
➤ **Fiesta Inn.** Modest, but on the town beach, and with a good activities desk. Km 11.5 on Hwy. 1. ☎ **800/FIESTA-1.** $$.

The Corridor
➤ **Las Ventanas al Paraíso.** It's a huge splurge, but it's gorgeous and you get your own private telescope. Km 19.5 on Hwy. 1. ☎ **888/525-0483.** $$$$$.

Cabo San Lucas
➤ **Las Margaritas Inn.** One- and two-bedroom apartments right across from the marina. Not overly quiet, but not overly expensive, either. Cárdenas at Zaragoza. ☎ **114/3-0450.** Fax 114/3-1696. $.

Quick Picks: Los Cabos's Hotels at a Glance
Hotel Index by Price

$

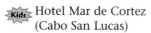 Hotel Mar de Cortez (Cabo San Lucas)

Posada Terranova (San José del Cabo)

Siesta Suites (Cabo San Lucas)

Tropicana Inn (San José del Cabo)

$$

Howard Johnson Plaza (San José del Cabo)

La Playita Resort (San José del Cabo)

$$$

Solmar Suites (Cabo San Lucas)

$$$–$$$$

Hotel Finisterra (Cabo San Lucas)

$$$$

Casa del Mar Golf Resort & Spa (The Corridor)

Meliá San Lucas (Cabo San Lucas)

Kids Presidente Inter-Continental (San José del Cabo)

Kids Westin Regina (The Corridor)

$$$$$

Palmilla (The Corridor)

Twin Dolphin (The Corridor)

Hotel Index by Location

Cabo San Lucas

Hotel Finisterra $$$–$$$$

Kids Hotel Mar de Cortez $

Meliá San Lucas $$$$

Siesta Suites $

Solmar Suites $$$

The Corridor

Casa del Mar Golf Resort & Spa $$$$

Palmilla $$$$$

Twin Dolphin $$$$$

Kids Westin Regina $$$$

San José del Cabo

Howard Johnson Plaza $$

La Playita Resort $$

Posada Terranova $

Kids Presidente Inter-Continental $$$$

Tropicana Inn $

Finding Your Way Around Los Cabos

Los Cabos may have a strong gringo accent, but it's still foreign territory if you've never been here before. And, more than in many other places, you need to be sharp from the second you step off the plane. Not to worry. I'll guide you through the airport, tell you how to get around, and then direct you to some additional sources of information.

You've Just Arrived—Now What?

It's possible that your flight to Los Cabos was a bit of a zoo, what with various species of party animals warming up for the serious drinkfest in Cabo by ordering mega beers and hooting at the flight attendants (I sometimes ask the most obnoxious ones where they hang out—and avoid those places like the plague). Maybe you're tired, since you couldn't nap, and a bit cranky, but I'm going to ask you to stay attentive for a few more minutes.

Here's why. It's not that the little Los Cabos International Airport is hard to negotiate; you step off the tarmac and walk directly into the luggage collection area and, if you're like most people, breeze through Customs (don't forget to push the button on the "traffic light," though, and wait for the signal to turn green). But when you enter the small arrivals area, you'll be faced with a throng of booths marked with the names of various hotels or labeled "information." Their reps will shout offers at you of rides to your hotel—or theirs. But unless you want the first activity on your vacation to be sitting, captive, and listening to a time-share spiel—because that's what all the come-ons are about—just walk on by. As soon as you clear the room, you'll come to a place where you can buy tickets for harangue-free transport.

Dollars & Sense

You'll save money by changing your dollars for pesos at the airport. The peso price for the *colectivos* and cabs is much lower than the equivalent dollar price (which the ticket booth is likely to quote gringos). There's a *casa de cambio* (money exchange) beyond the transport counter, but no ATM.

Nearby, you'll also see a row of rental car agents: Avis, Thrifty, Dollar, National, Hertz, Budget. As I'll explain below, in the case of Los Cabos, I've relaxed my usually strict rule against renting a car in Mexico, so you might want to make a stop here.

If you're not driving, you have a choice of taking a *colectivo* (a collective van) or a taxi. A *colectivo* to San José del Cabo, which is about 10 miles from the airport, costs $7 per person, to the Corridor $10, and to Cabo San Lucas, $12. If you opt for a private taxi, you'll pay $45 to San José (for up to four people), $50 to $55 to the Corridor, and $60 to Cabo San Lucas.

Dollars & Sense

Cabbies have to pay very high taxes for the privilege of securing a spot at the airport, and they're required to have nice, spiffy cabs. But most taxi drivers don't operate under those restrictions; as a result, it's much cheaper to get back to the airport than to get out of it. Cabs typically run $20 from San José, $45 from Cabo San Lucas, and somewhere in between from the Corridor, depending on which end you're located at. Hotels often have sign-up lists for guests wanting to share rides to the airport.

Orientation: You Are Here

When you depart south from the airport via Mexican Highway 1, also known as the Transpeninsular Highway, the first town you'll come to is San José del Cabo. The highway hugs the outskirts of town and continues southwest, becoming what's called **the Corridor,** until, after about 20 miles, it reaches Cabo San Lucas. In the center of Cabo, Highway 1 turns into the main street of Lázaro Cárdenas; then, under the name of Moreles, it zigzags briefly northwest before it transforms itself into Mexico Highway 19 (which loops north to merge with Highway 1 again just before La Paz).

If you're staying in **San José del Cabo,** you'll turn off Highway 1 on Zaragoza, the main thoroughfare leading into town. Zaragoza, in turn, runs east into Bulevar Mijares, San José's primary downtown tourist drag. The town's less expensive hotels, as well as most of its gringo-oriented shops and restaurants, are in this area. Take Bulevar Mijares south and you'll evenually come to Paseo San José, which abuts the town beach and is home to the town's pricier lodgings.

Cabo San Lucas grew up around the harbor of Cabo San Lucas Bay. Lázaro Cárdenas, the main street leading in to Cabo on Highway 1 from the Corridor, loops south around a shady plaza and turns into Marina Boulevard, which runs along the waterfront. Most of the town's shops and restaurants, and some of its less expensive hotels, are located on and within this loop. The more expensive accommodations and, in some cases, eateries, are on the beaches to the east and south.

How to Get from Here to There (and How Not To)

Because distances in Los Cabos are so great—and because there's virtually no public transportation system—getting around the resort poses some challenges. You often have to choose between spending lots of time or spending lots of money.

Traveling by Bus

Neither San José del Cabo nor Cabo San Lucas has a city transport system; both towns are fairly small, however, and you can usually get where you want to go by foot or by inexpensive cab ride. From the bus station in San José on Valerio Gonzalez, at Bulevar Mijares (☎ 114/2-1100), you can pick up a first- or second-class bus to Cabo San Lucas; they're cheap (about $6), but run only once an hour (between 7am and 7pm). The bus station in Cabo (☎ 114/2-1100) is on Héroes at Moreles. Call to check the current schedules.

If you're staying in the Corridor, though, you're out of luck as far as buses are concerned. They won't stop in the Corridor unless someone on the bus has requested it or unless they see you standing on the road and waving your arms—which you're not likely to want to do. Even if you could figure out when the bus is likely to pass you (fat chance!), it's a long haul between the entrance of many of the Corridor hotels and the highway.

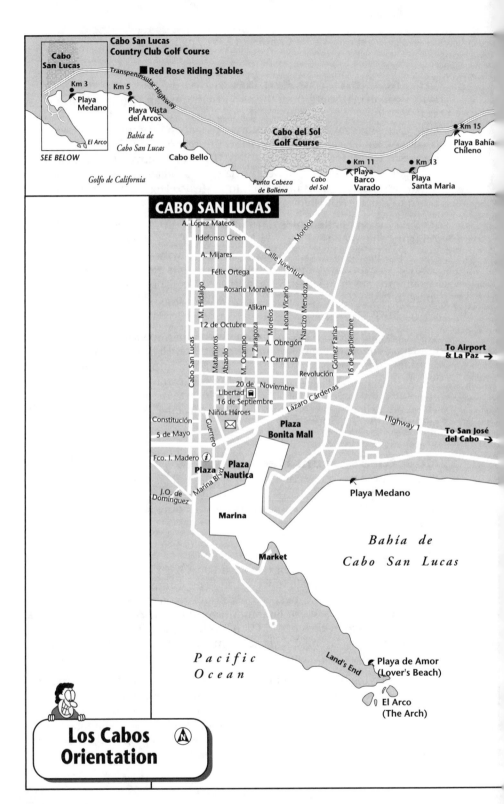

Cabo San Lucas
Country Club Golf Course

Cabo
San Lucas

■ Red Rose Riding Stables

Transpeninsular Highway

Km 3
● Playa
Medano

Km 5
●
Playa Vista
del Arcos

El Arco

SEE BELOW

Bahía de
Cabo San Lucas

Golfo de California

Cabo Bello

Punta Cabeza
de Ballena

Cabo del Sol
Golf Course

Cabo
del Sol

Km 11
● Playa
Barco
Varado

Km 13
● Playa
Santa Maria

Km 15
● Playa Bahía
Chileno

CABO SAN LUCAS

A. López Mateos

Ildefonso Green

A. Mijares

Félix Ortega

Rosario Morales

Alikan

12 de Octubre

Morelos

Calle Juventud

Leona Vicario

Narcizo Mendoza

A. Obregón

V. Carranza

Revolución

Gómez Farías

16 de Septiembre

M. Hidalgo

Matamoros

Abasolo

M. Ocampo

I. Zaragoza

20 de Noviembre

Libertad

16 de Septiembre

Niños Héroes

Constitución

5 de Mayo

Fco. I. Madero ⓘ

Plaza
Nautica

Cabo San Lucas

Guerrero

Plaza

J.O. de
Domínguez

Marina Blvd.

Lázaro Cárdenas

Highway 1

To Airport
& La Paz →

To San José
del Cabo →

Plaza
Bonita Mall

Playa Medano

Marina

Bahía de
Cabo San Lucas

Market

Pacific
Ocean

Land's End

Playa de Amor
(Lover's Beach)

El Arco
(The Arch)

Los Cabos
Orientation

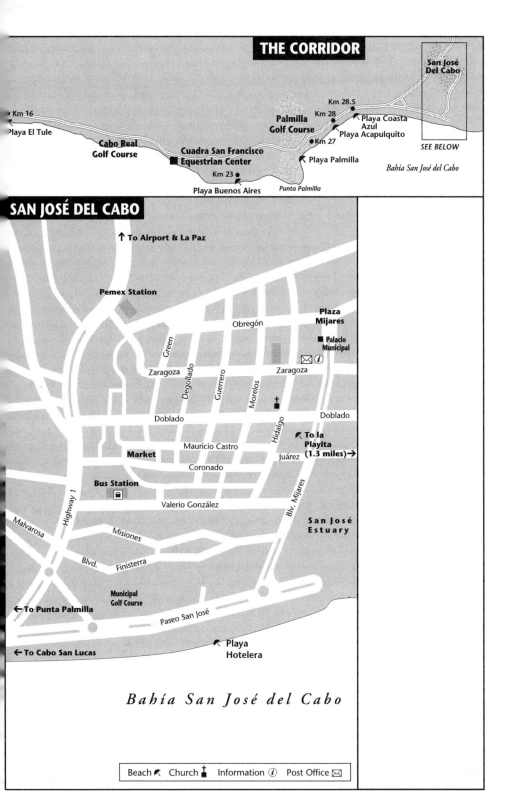

THE CORRIDOR

San José
Del Cabo

Km 16
Playa El Tule

Km 28.5

Km 28

Palmilla
Golf Course

Playa Coasta
Azul

Playa Acapulquito

Km 27

Cabo Real
Golf Course

Cuadra San Francisco
Equestrian Center

Playa Palmilla

SEE BELOW

Km 23

Playa Buenos Aires

Punta Palmilla

Bahía San José del Cabo

SAN JOSÉ DEL CABO

↑ To Airport & La Paz

Pemex Station

Obregón

Plaza
Mijares

Palacio
Municipal

Green

Zaragoza

Degollado

Guerrero

Morelos

Zaragoza

Doblado

Hidalgo

Doblado

Mauricio Castro

↖ To la
Playita

Market

Juárez

(1.3 miles) →

Coronado

Bus Station

Blv. Mijares

San José
Estuary

Highway 1

Valerio González

Malvarosa

Misiones

Blvd.

Finisterra

Municipal
Golf Course

← To Punta Palmilla

Paseo San José

← To Cabo San Lucas

↖ Playa
Hotelera

Bahía San José del Cabo

Beach ↖ Church † Information ⓘ Post Office ✉

501

Shuttling Around

To make up for the general lack of public transportation around Los Cabos, many hotels run shuttles between the tourist areas. They're sometimes free during the day but have limited schedules—perhaps one each way in the morning and one in the afternoon. In the evening, you're likely to have to pay; they generally cost about $10 round-trip between San José and Cabo and, from the Corridor, depending on where you're staying, anywhere from $5 to $8, round-trip, to either Cabo or San José.

Taxi Tips

In San José del Cabo or Cabo San Lucas, check with the front desk at your hotel for a fair price to your destination. Then, *before* you get into the taxi, ask the driver how much he wants. If his quote is out of line, just walk away. He'll either come down in price, or you'll soon find another, more reasonable ride.

If you're staying in the Corridor, your hotel will have to phone for a cab for you since you won't be able to hail one from the side of the road. Check the price with the front-desk clerk or bellhop who's making the call—and then confirm it with the cabbie *before* you climb into the back seat. If the taxi driver tries to pull a fast one on you by upping the price, just turn around and go back into your hotel (the cabbie is likely to reconsider and call after you).

Traveling by Taxi

Within Cabo San Lucas and San José del Cabo, taxis are reasonable; you should be able to get to wherever you're going in town for no more than $3. Rides to the Corridor or between the two towns are far more pricey. It can cost $30 or more to get from San José to Cabo, and as much as $15 from one part of the Corridor to another (or more than $20 if you're going almost the entire length).

Dollars & Sense

If you do decide to rent a car, you might want to arrange in advance to pick one up at the airport; this way, you'll save on cab fare. You don't have to drive back to the airport to return it; you can have it picked up at your hotel, in many cases, or return it to an office nearby.

Your Own Wheels: Driving

I know, I spoke sharply to you in chapter 9, "Tying Up the Loose Ends," about the hazards of renting a car in Mexico, and I'm about to give you some more warnings. Because of the difficulty and/or expense of getting from one place to another without wheels, however, it's not a bad idea to book a car in Los Cabos for a day or two.

Buggy Bartering

Believe it or not, you can bargain over the price of a rental car in Los Cabos. Sometimes you can get a good deal—when the lots are full in the off-season, rental car companies may be willing to let their autos go at a lower price—but mostly the rates are inflated. If you haven't booked in advance in the United States, ask at your hotel for the current going price.

If you want to settle in for a few days and decide where you want to drive before renting a car, you'll have no problem arranging for a rental at your hotel; again, most companies will deliver and pick up their vehicles, especially if you're staying in the Corridor.

Cars usually cost about $60 a day, including mandatory Mexican insurance, for a Volkswagen Beetle, which is the cheapest ride around. If you want an automatic, the least expensive will run you about $75 with insurance. Don't expect power steering, power windows—or even a brand name you'll recognize.

Yo, Gringo!

Always check for and point out any damages on the car before you (or the rental car rep) drive off. If you don't, you stand a chance of being charged for a ding, dent, or missing gas cap that you weren't responsible for.

Where to Get More Information & Guidance

For a destination that gets as many visitors as Los Cabos, there's surprisingly little in the way of official guidance for the Cabo clueless. On the other hand, you'll be awash in ad-driven print information sources.

Daylife Savings Time

Avoid driving at night. The Corridor is poorly lit, the roads are rutted, and lots of Cabo revelers get behind the wheel when they're drunk. If you drive in the dark, you might also run into an animal. Not only is that dangerous to your health as well as the animal's, but if the poor creature belongs to a local farmer, you'll have to pay property damages, which are likely to be exorbitant.

Empty Corridor

There are no services—tourism offices, banks, hospitals, and so forth—or anything else besides hotels and restaurants in the Corridor.

The **city tourist information office** in San José del Cabo is in the old post office building on Zaragoza at Mijares (☎ **114/2-2960,** ext. 150). You can get maps, advertising flyers, and some of the local publications listed below, but not a whole lot more.

In Cabo San Lucas, the **tourist office** is on Hidalgo, just off Guerrero (☎ **114/3-4180**); it's not really equipped to deal with visitors, however, as it has minimal staff and only a few brochures.

The Printed Page

Of the various publications that flood tourist gathering spots, the most comprehensive and professional is the slick biannual ***Los Cabos Guide.***

Time Out

Avoid the "tourist information" kiosks you'll see all around Cabo. Like those at the airport, they're fronts for timeshare touts.

The magazine's price is listed as $4.95, but many advertisers give it away to their customers, gratis. The others—newspaper-style, free, and published more frequently—include ***Los Cabos News, Baja Sun, Gringo Gazette,*** and ***Cabo Life.*** They all run articles on local restaurants and activities; *Cabo Life* has a useful map with a locator of all its advertisers. They're fun as a window on Los Cabos expatriate life—articles in one paper often comment on, or argue with, articles written in another—but take what's written with a grain of salt, as advertisers often determine the content.

Los Cabos A to Z: Facts at Your Fingertips

American Express: The representative in San José is **TourCabos,** Paseo San José and Blvd. Las Palmas (☎ **114/2-4040**); in Cabo, the office is at the **Hotel Pueblo Bonito** (Medano Beach; ☎ **114/3-2787**).

ATMs: In Cabo San Lucas, there's an ATM at the Serfin bank in Super Mercado Plaza, at Lázaro Cárdenas and Zaragoza. There's also one right behind Planet Hollywood in Plaza Bonita. Locals recommend it as being reliable, but as it doesn't have any signs on it of being affiliated with a particular bank, using it is a little scary.

Baby-sitters: Can be arranged at all major hotels.

Business Hours: Most offices are open Monday through Friday 9am to 1pm and 3 to 6pm, and Saturday from 9am to noon or 1pm. Shops operate from about 10am to 6pm daily, although some shopkeepers close for a midday siesta.

Currency Exchange: You'll get the best exchange rate at a bank, most of which exchange currency Monday through Friday from 8:30 to 11am. In San José, there are two banks, **Serfin** and **Bancomer,** on Zaragoza between Morelos and Degollado; in Cabo, there's a **Banamex** on Cárdenas, a block past the Pemex gas station as you drive into town, and a **Bancomer** on Cárdenas, at Guerrero, as well as the **Serfin** bank noted in "ATMs," above. You can also get pesos from a *casa de cambio* (money exchange house); the rates are slightly lower, but they're open far longer than banks, and you don't have to wait in line. In San José, you'll find them on Bulevar Mijares; in Cabo, you'll see at least a dozen of them along Lázaro Cárdenas.

Dentists: Ask at your hotel for a recommendation. In San José, additional possibilities include Dr. J. Mauricio Araiza, Colli Commercial Center, corner of Manuel Doblado and Hidalgo, upper floor (☎ **114/2-0525**), or Dr. Rosa Peña, Madero, Zaragoza s/n at Hidalgo (☎ **114/2-0955**). In Cabo, try Dr. Jorge Arciga, Avenida Cabo San Lucas, between Constitucíon and Libertad (☎ **114/3-0520**).

Doctors: Most hotels, especially the resorts, have doctors on 24-hour call; if yours doesn't, the front desk should be able to recommend a physician to you. In addition, if you're staying in San José, you might try Dr. José Cerda and Dr. José P. Arriago, who have a practice together on Zaragoza s/n, almost at the corner of Ildefonso Green street (☎ **114/3-1510**); in Cabo, try Dr. Alfonso Nájar Castañeda, Verustiano Caranza 11, Int. 3 (☎ **114/3-1216** or 114/3-2686).

Emergency Air Evacuation: Call ☎ **91/800-00-432** (toll-free in Mexico); in case of **fire,** call ☎ **114/3-3577.**

English-Language Newspapers/Magazines: The large resort hotels along the Corridor all have decent selections of English-language magazines and newspapers. In Cabo San Lucas, the bookstore with no name on it except **Libros** (books), Plaza Bonita Mall at Lázaro Cárdenas and Moreles, Loc. 17a (☎ **114/3-3171**), has a large array of English-language reading material, including a good supply of travel books on Baja and the rest of Mexico.

Hospitals: In Cabo, **Baja Médica,** Camino de la Plaza s/n, at Pedregal (☎ **114/3-0127** or 114/3-0175), is a 24-hour walk-in clinic.

Maps: *The Los Cabos Guide* contains accurate maps of San José, the Corridor, and Cabo; the one of Cabo in *Cabo Life* is useful because it's keyed to help you locate its many advertisers. You'll also find good maps in Libros (see "English-Language Newspapers/Magazines," above).

Pharmacies: In both San José and Cabo San Lucas, there's always one pharmacy on 24-hour call; the schedule rotates, but your hotel will know which one is on duty. There's no shortage of pharmacies in either San José or Cabo;

most are open until 11pm. In Cabo, **Farmacía del Rosaria,** Morelos at Lázaro Cárdenas, ☎ **114/3-49-59,** has good prices for medicines.

Yo, Gringo!

In Cabo, some drugstores advertise "muscle relaxers" or "strong antibiotics" in their windows as a come-on. Don't think you're going to get anything illegal over the counter. You need a prescription here, as everywhere in Mexico, for sleeping pills, pain killers, and other restricted drugs. You *can* get strong—or weak—antibiotics over the counter without a prescription, but make sure you know what you're buying; it's always dangerous to self-medicate.

Police: In San José, call ☎ **114/2-0361;** in Cabo, call ☎ **114/3-3977.**

Post Office: In San José, on Mijares at Valerio Gonzáles on the south side of town; in Cabo, Lázaro Cárdenas and Francisco Villa, on the highway to San José del Cabo, east of El Squid Row bar.

Safety: In Los Cabos, most of your safety concerns will have to do with driving (addressed above) and swimming (discussed in the next chapter). Both San José and Cabo are safe towns, and you're not likely to go wandering along the Corridor at night, but behave sensibly, as you would anywhere else. Don't walk down any dark, empty streets or beaches, don't flash money around, and don't invite strangers into your hotel room. See chapter 10, "Crossing the Border & What to Expect on the Other Side," for additional safety tips.

Special Events: In San José, the town's patron saint, St. Joseph, is celebrated during the week of March 15 with live music, folk dancing, and lots of special masses. During the third week of October, there's a lesser festival in Cabo San Lucas for its patron saint, St. Luke. The tourist offices, listed above, should be able to give you more details. Gringos in Los Cabos, on the other hand, tend to worship at the shrine of fishing. Several minor sportsfishing festivals are held in the fall, but the big event is the Bisbee Blue & Black Marlin Jackpot Tournament, which occurs in late October and offers huge purses (the location shifts every year, so call ☎ **714/650-8006** in the United States for current information). During spring break, the Cuervo Gold Volleyball Tournament takes place on Medano Beach; bikini contests and similar excuses for hard-bod displays naturally follow. For more information call the **tourist office** in San Jose (☎ **114/2-2960,** ext. 150).

Telephone: The telephone area code for both San José and Cabo is 114, but it's a toll call from one town to the other, so you've got to use the area code before dialing your number. In the Corridor, whether you need to dial the area code depends on how close your hotel is to one town or another. To call long distance within Mexico (abbreviated *lada*), dial 01, then the area code, and then the number. To call the United States, dial 001, and then the area code and number.

U.S. Consul: Consular representative David Greenberg, Blvd. Marina, at the entrance to the Pedregal mall (☎ **114/3-3566**); the hours are Monday to Friday from 10am to 1pm.

Fun On & Off the Beach

Its reputation as a sportsfishing mecca may have first drawn visitors to Los Cabos, but this splashy resort has more fish to fry than, well, fish. Among other things, there are gorgeous beaches to bronze on (speaking of frying—don't forget your sunblock!), underwater delights to dive to, and, in winter, migrating whales to ogle.

Although most of Los Cabos's attractions are of the wild 'n' wet persuasion, there are a few dry dock standouts—premier among them golf. You won't have any trouble unloading your pesos on souvenirs, either, and, as the hordes who come to Cabo solely to party know, there's plenty of nighttime action. Being based at the tip of a skinny peninsula kind of limits the choices (or at least the directions) of your day trips, but there are a couple of good exploring options nevertheless.

Beaches, Beaches Everywhere

With their dramatic dark outcroppings of rock, startling growth of cactus along the shore, and astonishing palate of blues as the Pacific merges with the Sea of Cortez, Los Cabos's beaches are among the most spectacular in Mexico. Some of the stretches of sand lure swimmers because they're protected by inlets and coves; others draw surfers or snorkelers.

Unfortunately, however, because of the lack of public transportation and the impossibility of hailing cabs along the Corridor, the only way to visit some of the best ones is by automobile—which is why, unless you're satisfied with the bit of beach in front of your hotel (and you may very well be in some cases), I've suggested renting a car.

No Turning Back

When you're driving along the Corridor, you've got about 3 seconds (literally) to make your turn when you see the sign for the beach you want. If you miss it, you'll have a tough time getting back because there are no turn lanes along the 20-mile stretch of road. You'll have to wait until the oncoming traffic thins (not always easy to determine because of the rises and curves in the road) and then make a quick U-turn.

The following shore survey moves from San José del Cabo in the west to the end of the earth (okay, of the Baja Peninsula) in the east.

San José del Cabo Beaches

The lodgings in San José's hotel zone line up along **Playa Hotelera,** a wide and lovely stretch of sand lapped by water that's, sadly, subject to a strong undertow, rendering it unsafe for swimming. There are not too many vendors here, however, so you can lie back and relax without being bothered. The beach begins just before the Presidente Inter-Continental hotel with the freshwater **San José Estuary,** an ecological preserve where some 270 species of birds have been spotted. You can enter it by foot for a short distance or explore it on a guided kayak tour (see "A Bucketful of Water Sports," below).

You'll often hear that the closest safe swimming beach to San José is **La Playita**, about 2 miles east of town. It's true, but access is along a rutted dirt road. For ease of travel as well as aesthetics, you're better off going the extra few miles to the more scenic Playa Palmilla (see below), some 5 miles from town. If you want local color, however, you can't beat La Playita. Come early in the morning and you can watch members of the local sportsfishing cooperative haul in their catch.

Don't Bug Me

Whichever way you enter the lagoon, don't forget your insect spray. Still waters run buggy.

Bet You Didn't Know

The original Spanish settlement of San José del Cabo was at La Playita beach. The Jesuits who built the church there were kicked out in 1730, and when they returned, they constructed their new church in town.

The Corridor Beaches

Every surfer knows how to find **Playa Costa Azul,** the first beach you come to as you go west from San José; the Costa Azul break is world renowned. Some campgrounds, casual restaurants, a surf shop, and a convenience store sit on the beachfront. To get here, exit the highway at km 28.5 and turn right at the bridge.

Much of the surfing action has migrated to **Playa Acapulquito** (a.k.a. Old Man's Beach), just west (km 28) of Playa Azul. You can swim here, but remember how territorial surfers are; if you get in the way of someone's wave, you might get cursed—or "accidentally" hit in the head with a board.

If doing the breast stroke is your thing, best to continue on to km 27 and **Playa Palmilla** (get off at the Hotel Palmilla sign). Protected by a rocky cove, it's one of the Corridor's best swimming beaches, and also one of the most scenic. You can rent snorkeling and diving equipment at a shop just before the hotel.

Off-Road Beaches

Real isolation requires an off-road vehicle. Beaches accessible only by four-wheel-drive roadsters include **Playa Buenos Aires** (exit km 22 or 24 and follow the old highway), a long, beautiful shore that's not good for swimming; **Playa El Tule** (exit km 16.2 at the Los Tules Bridge), which sometimes has good surf breaks; and **Playa Vista del Arcos** (exit km 5, across from Los Arcos restaurant), a rocky stretch of sand with a knockout vista of Land's End and El Arco (see "Cabo San Lucas Beaches," below)—and a mean undertow.

Among Los Cabos's most popular beaches, **Playa Bahia Chileno** has it all—swimming, diving, snorkeling, and surfing (there's another famous break here). Unlike Santa María (see below), the water gets deep nice and gradually. You can rent a beach umbrella and water sports equipment, and vendors come around with beer and soft drinks (as well as souvenirs), but you won't find any food, so tote your own picnic. To reach this beach, exit at km 15, by the Hotel Cabo San Lucas.

Privacy, Please

Lots of tour operators run snorkeling trips to Bahia Chileno and Santa María beaches. If you don't want to compete with the tour groupies for underwater space, check the excursion schedules (the masses usually descend midday) and plan to arrive at another time.

There's more great diving and snorkeling at **Playa Santa María,** a protected cove at km 13, next to the Twin Dolphin Hotel (park in the hotel lot and walk east down the service road to the shore). The water is gentle, and the crescent-shaped stretch of soft sand is lovely, but there are no shade trees (nor any umbrella rentals) and the water drops off suddenly.

The wreckage of an illegal Japanese freighter sunk in the mid-1960s provides both the name and the interest of **Playa Barco Varado (Shipwreck Beach),** which you can reach by taking the Cabo del Sol exit at km 11. The rusty remains of the boat jut out of a jetty that divides the beach in two. Swimming is iffy; don't go in if the water gives you any cause to pause. There are no facilities here now, but the completion of a new hotel on the beach should change that.

Yo, Gringo!

The beaches that are not fronted by hotels don't fly water safety flags and don't have lifeguards. Swim only at the ones that are considered safe—otherwise you're risking your life.

Cabo San Lucas Beaches

When it comes to playing in the water, watching well-toned bodies edge around each other, or just generally making the Cabo scene, **Playa Medano** rules. A soft span of white sand stretching almost 2 miles to the east of town, it's obviously not the place to go if you want to be alone, but the swimming is great (when you can avoid the water toys) and so is the jogging, if you come early in the morning when everyone's sleeping off their hangovers. This is prime beach-vendor territory, and several hotels rope off sections of sands for their guests that the peddlers are not allowed to cross. From town, you can get to Playa Medano most easily from the harbor entrance to the Plaza Las Glorias Beach Club; on the road, exit at km 1 or at any of the hotels (such as the Fiesta Americana, the Hacienda, or the Meliá San Lucas) that abut the beach.

Yo, Gringo!

If you don't want to be hassled by beach vendors, don't appear interested in their wares. Buy a single item, and you'll soon have dozens of new friends converging on your deck chair.

Although it's much more remote than Medano Beach, **Playa de Amor (Lover's Beach)** won't give you the quiet isolation that its name suggests—

Extra! Extra!

Snorkeling at Playa de Amor is strictly BYOF (Bring Your Own Fins); there are no rental facilities on the beach.

and that it once had. It is, nevertheless, a must-see because it's the beach that straddles both the Pacific Ocean and the Sea of Cortez. The wind-and-water-blasted rock formations are stunning and, on the Sea of Cortez side, the swimming and snorkeling are superb. There's no land access; to get here, take a glass-bottomed boat from the marina (see "Glass-Bottomed Boats," below). En route, you'll get a close-up look at **El Arco (the Arch),** the famous granite span that juts out into the sea.

You needn't take to the sea to reach **Playa Solmar,** shared by Solmar Suites, TerraSol Beach Resort, and Hotel Finisterra, but unless you're looking for a long uphill walk, you'll have to drive or cab it to any of these entry ports from town. It's too dangerous to swim here, but the sand is wide and soft and the tableau of cliffs poised against the deep azure Pacific is the stuff of picture postcards. This is also one of the best beaches for whale-watching in winter.

Row, Row, Row Your Kayak

If you're up for some steady rowing action, consider a **guided kayak trip** from San José. Prices range from about $50 for a 3-hour trip around the estuary to $105 for a full-day excursion to Cabo Pulmo, one of the best snorkeling sites in the Los Cabos area (see "Exploring the Depths," below). Most travel agents or hotel tour desks in San José offer one or more of these excursions or can direct you to someone who does. If you book these trips in Cabo, tour operators may or may not provide transportation to San José for an extra charge.

Water Fun for Everyone

You don't have to be in a Cabo San Lucas bar to sink to whatever depths you like in Los Cabos. Whether you just want to skim the surface of the water, extract some of its fishier contents, or get in over your head, this resort's got your number.

A Bucketful of Water Sports

For one-stop water sports shopping, Medano Beach can't be beat. If it floats, bobs, or zips around on the sea, you can rent it here. **Waverunners** and **jet skis** cost about $35 per half hour to $60 per hour, **waterskiing** starts at roughly $40 a half hour, **Hobie Cats** run around $30 an hour, a **Windsurfer** is some $15 an hour, and you'll pay approximately $30 for a 10-minute **parasailing** experience. You can hop on a **banana boat** for about $6 per person.

Time-Savers

The busiest (though not necessarily the best) diving months are from October to mid-January. Book in advance if you're planning to dive then.

Don't need to get your motor running? You can rent a **canoe** or **kayak** on Playa Medano for approximately $10 to $15 and row over to Land's End and Lover's Beach.

No other stretch of sand in Los Cabos is quite as stocked with water toys as Medano Beach, but in the Corridor, you can rent equipment at both Bahia Chileno (including kayaks and canoes) and Palmilla beaches. The town beach in San José del Cabo also has several sports concessionaires. Prices at other Los Cabos beaches are comparable to those on Medano.

Hands Off

The Pulmo Reef, off Cabo Pulmo, is the only living coral reef in the Sea of Cortez and the only one on the west coast of North America. Look, but don't touch. Not only is coral delicate and extremely slow-growing, it just might try to enact a stinging revenge.

Exploring the Depths

Marine flora and fauna from both the Sea of Cortez and the Pacific Ocean proliferate off the coast of Los Cabos, resulting in a unique underwater show. Visibility, which ranges from about 30 to 50 feet in the winter months, reaches over 100 feet from April to October. The water gets warmed up to an average of 80°F by the end of the summer and stays warm through December and into January.

Time-Savers

If you want to go on advanced dives, don't forget to bring along proof of certification.

Cabo San Lucas Bay, abundant with tropical fish, sea fans, manta rays, turtles, and more, hosts the most popular dive sites, most of them near El Arco. Among them (but for advanced divers only) is the **Sandfalls,** a mysterious cascade of sand created by a shift in currents and first discovered by Jacques Cousteau. The Corridor also has some interesting dive sites, including **the Blowhole** off Bahia Chileno beach. The water off Santa María beach doesn't have any special features, but is seething with sea life.

Farther away, beyond San José del Cabo on what's called the East Cape, are two major dive sites. **Gorda Banks,** an underwater mountain with a black coral bottom lies in water of up to 130 feet about 8 miles off the coast of Punta Gorda (it's about 45 minutes north of San José by land, but far quicker to reach by sea). The coral outcroppings are even more impressive off **Cabo Pulmo,** around 2 hours north of San José via the road.

The Depths of Luxury

If you want to spend more time under the Sea of Cortez, consider a trip aboard the 112-foot *Solmar V,* a state-of-the-art dive ship offering 12 staterooms with private baths as well as color TVs and VCRs. Eight-day explorations take in Gorda Banks and Cabo Pulmo as well as more remote sites; there are also 9-day excursions to the volcanic Socorro Island group, some 250 miles southwest of Cabo San Lucas and known as "Mexico's Galapagos." Rates, which run from $1,600 for a standard room on an 8-day trip to $2,400 for deluxe accommodations for 9 days, include three gourmet meals plus drinks and snacks. For additional details and the latest information on schedules and prices, contact Cabo Resort Reservations, Inc., P.O. Box 383, Pacific Palisades, CA 90272 (☎ **800/344-3349** or 310/459-9861; fax 310/454-1686; www.solmar.com; e-mail: CaboResort@aol.com).

One-tank dive tours in the Los Cabos area start at $35 ($45 at night); two tanks will run you about $65. Two-tank dives to Gorda Banks cost $100, and to Cabo Pulmo, $110. It's an additional $20 to rent equipment in all cases. Resort dive courses run about $90, and a full certification course sells for $400.

Two of the most reliable dive operators in Cabo are **Amigos del Mar** (Cabo San Lucas marina; ☎ **800/344-3349** in the U.S., or 114/3-0505), and **Cabo Acuadeportes** (Medano Beach, near the Hacienda Hotel, and Bahia Chileno Beach at the Hotel Cabo San Lucas; ☎ **114/3-0117**). In San José, contact **Tourcabos** (Plaza Garuffi, Local 10, Paseo San José and Blvd. Las Palmas; ☎ **114/2-4040**; e-mail: tourcabos@ 1cabonet.com.mx).

Snorkeling

The companies mentioned in the previous section, as well as several others in both towns and along the Corridor, also offer snorkeling tours to Playa de Amor, Playa Santa María, Playa Bahia Chileno, and Playa Barco Vardaro. A 2-hour cruise to sites around El Arco typically runs around $30, and a 4-hour trip to Playa Santa María costs $55; both rates include gear. Snorkeling equipment alone, available on Palmilla, Chileno Bay, and Medano beaches, rents for around $15.

Dollars & Sense

If you plan to do a lot of snorkeling, why not invest in your own mask, snorkel, and fins? You'll come out ahead if you use the inexpensive gear even four or five times—and you won't have to think about just where that mask and snorkel have been.

Hooked on Fishing

Once known as "Marlin Alley," Los Cabos was an exclusive fishing ground for the wealthy in the 1940s and '50s. Although those strictly seeking seclusion have moved to the more low-key East Cape, Los Cabos is still one of the hottest angling destinations in the world, hosting annual competitions with some of the largest purses around. You'll find something to take your bait year-round, including sharks such as mako, hammerhead, and lemon,

Bet You Didn't Know

There are more marlin caught in Cabo San Lucas than anywhere else on earth.

515

Bet You Didn't Know

A world-record 1,078-pound blue marlin was hooked in Cabo San Lucas in 1992. It was snared on the *Juanita X* from Juanita's Fleet (Plaza Karina, Local 1, Blvd. Marina; ☎ **800/421-8925** or 114/3-0522).

and peak seasons vary annually, but in general, July through November are the best months for billfish.

You don't have to be an expert to catch fish in Los Cabos, and you don't have to spend a ton of money. Angling excursions run the gamut from 3-hour trips in a two-person panga (motorized skiff) to all-day trips in a deluxe cabin cruiser that holds eight plus the captain and mate. If you haven't booked in advance and want to check out what feels right for you, you might go down to the main dock in Cabo San Lucas, which has the largest selection of boats. Arrive around 3pm, when everyone's returning from a hard day of fishing, and ask around about the companies and the crews (you'll be hard-pressed to find people who *won't* be thrilled to tell you all about their day . . . maybe more than you want to know). You can also talk to the captains to see if they seem compatible and are fluent in English and check out the boats for comfort and cleanliness (keeping in mind they've just been out for the day).

Sportsfishing Tipping Tips

It's customary to tip 10% to 15% of the total price of your charter, depending on the quality of service received. Give the money to the captain, who will split it with the mate.

Typical prices for a full day trip range from $150 for a "super panga" for two people and $340 for a 28-foot single-engine cruiser for four to $430 for a 33-foot twin-engine cruiser for six. Rates usually include 10% tax, a captain and mate, fishing equipment, license, passenger insurance, and ice; live bait, food, and drinks are extra, but you can generally arrange for the outfitter to lay in the bait (about $2) and provisions for you if you don't want to go to the trouble (it's cheaper if you get your own stuff, of course). Panga excursions depart at 5:30 or 6:30am and return 6 hours later; most larger cruisers leave at 7am and come back at 3pm.

There are lots of reliable companies in Los Cabos; my recommendations don't come close to covering the range of possibilities. That said, near San José del Cabo, I suggest **Victor's Sportsfishing** (Palmilla Beach, the Corridor; ☎ **800/521-2281** or 114/2-1092 or 114/2-0155); in Cabo San Lucas, **Pisces Fleet** (Blvd. Marina and Madero; ☎ **114/3-1288**; e-mail: pisces@1cabonet.com) and **Solmar** (Solmar Hotel, Blvd. Marina and Av. Solmar; ☎ **800/344-3340** or 114/3-0646 or 114/3-4542; www.solmar.com; e-mail: CaboResort@aol.com) are both large and dependable companies. You can also make arrangements in advance from the United States through **Ixtapa Sportsfishing Charters** (19 Depue Lane, Stroudsburg, PA 18360; ☎ **717/688-9466;** fax 717/688-9554).

Dollars & Sense

In some beach towns, you can buy a place on a larger fishing excursion; in Los Cabos, however, you pay for the entire boat, no matter how few of you there are. If you're outgoing and can find some people to share a cruiser with you, you can cut costs, although you'll need a group of six, rather than four, to make it worth your while to rub shoulders all day with virtual strangers (see prices, above).

On Board

The best surfing spots are noted in the "Beaches, Beaches Everywhere" section, above. For everything from equipment rentals to custom boards and up-to-the-minute surf reports, head over to the **Costa Azul Surf Shop** (Costa Azul Beach; ☎ **114/7-0071**).

Please Release Me

Most fleets in Los Cabos practice catch-and-release—you reel your fish in, tag it, and toss it back into the sea. But no one will think you had a bad fish day if you return to the dock in an empty boat: To compensate for the lack of any scaly corpus delicti—but not corpus delectable, because you don't have to send back anything you plan to eat—the captain hoists an array of flags that indicate exactly what came on board and what size it was.

Cruise Control

Whether you want to (literally) see the sea beneath your feet, cruise off into the sunset, or have a whale of a time in winter, Los Cabos can deliver. You'll find most of the action—as usual—in Cabo San Lucas.

Glass-Bottomed Boats

You can get the effect of snorkeling without putting your face in the water by hopping aboard one of the many small glass-bottomed boats that leave from the Cabo San Lucas marina daily between 9am and 4pm. A typical

517

hour-long tour takes you past the sea lions and pelicans to El Arco, at Land's End. The price is usually about $15 per person, but if things are slow, you might be able to bargain that down a bit—or get the captain to take you out for a longer trip for the same price. Most boats make a brief stop at Playa de Amor or will drop you off there if you ask. Your original ticket will get you back on a later boat, but be sure to check when the last one departs.

Boozing into the Sunset

There are almost as many sunset cruises as there are big boats. Most of them serve up pretty much the same thing—loud music and large quantities of booze—and take the same route around the El Arco and Land's End, so if your hotel tour desk has coupons for one rather than another, there's little reason not to take advantage of any bargains you can get.

Bet You Didn't Know

Stretching about 1,000 miles from Tijuana to Los Cabos, the Baja Peninsula is the longest peninsula in the world.

One exception, however, is the tour on *Kids* the **Sunderland,** a 110-foot-long sailing vessel dating back to the 1880s that's decked out to look like a pirate ship. The crew are dressed like pirates and the narrator relates the history of high-seas plunder in this region while the boat cruises around the tip of the Baja Peninsula. It's educational as well as fun; passengers are permitted to help raise and trim the sails and even take the wheel temporarily. Cruises depart daily at 4:30 or 5:30pm from boarding slip 19 of the Cabo Marina (behind the Plaza Las Glorias hotel) and return at 7 or 8pm, depending on the time of year. The $35 per person price—kids under 12 are free—includes beer, soda, and rum punch. You can book through most hotels, or call ☎ 114/3-4050 to make a reservation.

More typical cruises include the ones offered by the 42-foot catamaran **Pez Gato** (☎ 114/3-3797), which departs daily from the Hacienda Hotel dock on Medano Beach at 5pm; the 100-foot catamaran **Kaleidoscope** (☎ 114/8-7318), which leaves Monday through Saturday at 5pm from in front of the Office restaurant on Medano beach; and the **Encore** (☎ 114/3-4050), a 60-foot ocean-racing yacht that sets sail at 4pm daily from dock H-1 of the town marina. All cost around $35, last approximately 2 hours, and include unlimited soda, beer, and domestic brand liquor. You can book directly or through a travel agent or hotel tour desk.

A Whale of a Time

There are few marine experiences more thrilling than seeing a group of the sea's largest creatures swimming past you. When the gray whales migrate south between January and March, many come close enough to the Los Cabos shore to be spotted through binoculars—the Corridor has some of the best vantage points—but you can increase your odds of spotting them by booking a whale-watching tour. In San José, if you go over to Pueblo La Playa (La Playita), you can find a local fisherman to take you out; a 4-hour trip for a small group of three or four runs about $45 per person. Most of the boats mentioned under "Boozing into the Sunset," above, do whale-watching duty in winter; typical prices are about $35 per person for a 2-hour tour. You can also arrange these trips with any travel agent or hotel tour desk; there's never a shortage of vessels willing to take to the sea come cetacean migration time.

Bet You Didn't Know

The gray whale swims some 6,000 miles, one-way, from the Arctic to the Sea of Cortez.

Los Cabos's Top Dry-Land Diversions

Golf may be one of the biggest draws in Los Cabos, but there's more to the dry-land scene than plaid pants and small white balls. View the scenery from the back of a horse or an ATV, or check out a pick-up volleyball game and you'll see that Los Cabos has got it goin' on in more ways than one.

Hitting the Links

Los Cabos is Mexico's top golf destination and it's easy to see why. In the past decade, large swaths of the Corridor have been put in the hand of some of the game's prime designers—and of course, nature took its course on these courses, too. Club rentals are $15 at San José's municipal golf course, and around $40 at all the courses along the Corridor.

Time-Savers

In summer, you won't have a problem getting a prime tee time, but in winter, it's always best to phone ahead to reserve, especially if you're not staying at one of the hotels that has privileges at the course you want to play; the best slots are often reserved for the guests.

For a quick and easy practice game, you can start out in San José at the 9-hole, par 35 Municipal Campo de Golf (Blvd. Mijares, next to the Howard Johnson Plaza Suites; ☎ 114/2-0905). This is Los Cabos's oldest course and its least expensive: Greens fees are $18 for the 9 holes (double that if you want to do the course twice), and it's $15 for a cart.

Heading west, you'll come to the 18-hole, par 72 **Palmilla Golf Club** (Palmilla Hotel, Hwy. 100, km 27.5; ☎ **800/386-2465** or 114/4-5250), a

Bet You Didn't Know

The family that owns the Cabo del Sol course also owns the brewery that produces Corona.

gorgeous desert-meets-sea course designed by Jack Nicklaus in the early 1990s. The back "Mountain" nine holes play around small lakes, while the front "Arroyo" are a bit more prickly, having 400-year-old Cordon cactus as hazards. All holes have views of the Sea of Cortez. Greens fees—in high season, rates are $180 from Thursday to Saturday, and $165 the rest of the week—include a cart, practice balls, and bottled water.

Just a long-shot away (well, practically), Jack Nicklaus's par 72 **Cabo Real** (Playa Barco Vardaro; ☎ **800/386-2465** or 114/3-3990) has been described as Mexico's answer to Pebble Beach and is rated among the world's top 100 courses by *Golf Digest* magazine. Nicklaus himself said (somewhat immodestly) that it has "the three best ocean finishing holes in the world." There's about a mile of oceanfront property to play on, and from the seventh hole you get an especially good view of the wreck of the Japanese freighter that Barco Vardaro beach is known for. To play the course in high season, you'll shell out $175 Sunday to Wednesday and $190 from Thursday to Saturday. Carts, practice balls, and bottled water are, again, part of the package. A second 18-hole golf course is being designed by Tom Weiskopf as part of this gigantic condo/hotel complex.

The 18-hole **Cabo Real** course (Hwy. 100, km 19.5; ☎ **114/4-0040**; e-mail: caborealgolf@cabonet.net.mx) was designed by Robert Trent Jones, Jr., to challenge expert golfers and also be fun for your average Joe (or Joanna) duffer. The course is part of another huge mixed residential and hotel community; measuring 2,500 acres, it's flanked at one end by the Westin Regina and at the other by the Meliá Cabo Real Resort, and envelops the Casa del Mar hotel. Every hole looks out on the Sea of Cortez, and the 14th, which sits on a mesa, is especially impressive. More golf is slated to come on the scene here, too. It costs $165 to play the par 72 course in high season; rates include carts, driving range use, and water.

Just outside the town of Cabo, the 18-hole **Cabo San Lucas Country Club** (Hwy. 100, km 3.5; ☎ **800/854-2314** or 114/3-4653) is par for a Corridor course. It was designed by a top golf architect—in this case, Roy Dye; it's got stunning views (you can see Land's End as well as the Sea of Cortez from here); and it's part of a large community (a gated residential one). There are more golf layouts to come, too. These greens are comfortable for even older golfers to walk, but, in Dye's words, the course "has enough hazards, obstacles, and bunkers to make it interesting." The 7th hole is notorious for the latter, with a large lake that challenges even the pros. Greens fees during the winter are $121, with cart. If you need a little skill polishing, check out the country club's Golf Academy.

Sandy Net-scapades

Why hide that new bikini under water, when you can strut your stuff playing volleyball on Medano Beach? Just stroll along this popular stretch of sand and you'll find some net action sooner or later. It's a good way to get some exercise and make new friends—and who knows? You might be good enough to get invited back for the Cuervo Gold Tournament (see "Los Cabos A to Z: Facts at Your Fingertips" in chapter 42, "Finding Your Way Around Los Cabos.")

Horsing Around

If you want to giddee-yup along the beach or take a leisurely trot toward the mountains of the Baja backcountry, consider booking a ride with either the **Red Rose Riding Stables,** outside Cabo San Lucas at Hwy. 1, km 4 (☎ **114/7-5907**), or with the **Cuadra San Francisco Equestrian Center,** Cabo Real Resort, Hwy. 1, km 19.5 (☎ **114/4-0160**). Both outfitters have healthy, well-fed horses and accommodate all levels and types of experience, including either English or Western saddle; lessons are available, too. Rates for trail rides, which generally last either 1 or 2 hours and take place either in the morning (8 to 10am) or in the late afternoon (4 or 5pm), start at approximately $30 per hour. Reservations are advised; you can book directly through the stables or with your hotel tour desk.

Tooling Around on an ATV

ATVs—all-terrain vehicles—are big in Los Cabos, and especially in Cabo San Lucas, where companies specializing in these three- or four-wheel wonders line the main drag. You can rent your own ATV for 3 hours (cost: about $35 for a single rider, or $50 for two on one vehicle) or take a guided tour, which usually includes soft drinks, but no food. Whatever you decide to do, it's best to book through your hotel tour desk, or with a company they recommend. Make sure the price of your ride includes goggles and a helmet.

From Cabo, a popular excursion is to the southern tip of the peninsula, where an 1890 lighthouse used to guide ships en route from California to Panama. Prices for the 3-hour trip, which involves riding over 500-foot sand dunes and looking at a shipwreck, are around $50 per person or $65 for two on one ATV. Some companies also offer daylong tours (departing at 9am and returning in the early evening) to La Candelariá, an Indian village in the mountains some 25 miles north of Cabo; it's known both for its lush surroundings—the result of an underground river—and its alleged practice of witchcraft. These tours, which allow time for swimming and for exploring sea turtle nesting grounds, cost $95 per person or $110 for two.

One's Comfortable, Two's Allowed

If you're considering riding tandem on an ATV, keep in mind that the weight limit is 220 pounds *per vehicle,* not per person.

In San José, excursions generally go to a 1915 lighthouse on La Playita and then to a local *ranchito,* or cattle ranch, where you may be encouraged to buy the cheese made on the premises. You'll likely take in some sand dunes along the way. Prices run around $45 single, and $60 double.

Yo, Gringo!

The beach around the old lighthouse is littered and not especially scenic, but the dunes are fun to ride around and you can't beat the views of the Pacific at sunset.

Los Cabos's Best Shopping

The isolated Baja Peninsula isn't known for its indigenous crafts and, because it's cut off from the mainland, hasn't had a natural flow of imported crafts from other parts of Mexico in the past. Recent decades, however, have seen a huge increase in Los Cabos tourism—and a slower but steady increase in the appearance of items that tourists like to buy. There are no large department stores in Los Cabos as there are in many of the other resort towns, nor is there much in the way of "real people's" markets. The best retail pickings are concentrated in Cabo San Lucas; there are some nice boutiques in San José, but in the Corridor, it's pretty much just resort hotel gift shops.

The shopping scene in **San José del Cabo** is largely limited to Bulevar Mijares near the main plaza and a few surrounding streets, including Zaragoza. **Copal** (Plaza Mijares 10; ☎ **114/2-3070**) carries a high-quality selection of crafts from all over Mexico, some unavailable elsewhere in Los Cabos, as well as work by local artists. The focus is on interior design at both

Dollars & Sense

Don't expect any bargains in Los Cabos. Because nearly everything is imported, in many cases from the United States, prices are high—in some cases higher than those at home.

ADD (Art, Design, Decoration) (Zaragoza s/n at Hidalgo; ☎ **114/2-2727**) and **Casa Paulina** (Zaragoza s/n across from Bancomer; ☎ **114/2-2199**). De rigueur for San José surfers, **Killer Hook** (Av. Hidalgo s/n, next to Clio's; ☎ **114/2-2430**) carries boards and other sporting gear as well as funky men's beachwear.

If shopping in **Cabo San Lucas** is not limited as it is in San José, the problem here is sorting the wheat (high-quality crafts) from the chaff (made-in-Korea sombreros). Starting from the northernmost part of town, **Plaza Bonita,** an upscale shopping complex, sits next to the Hard Rock Cafe at the major intersection of Lázaro Cárdenas and Boulevard Marina. Continue south along Boulevard Marina and you'll encounter a series of modern strip shopping centers on the east side of the road; the best among them are **Plaza del Sol**—you'll recognize it by the strange fake-rock formations in the center—which has several shops selling good Mexican sportswear, and **Plaza Nautica** (this one's got a Domino's Pizza as a landmark). The side streets that angle off the west side of Boulevard Marina are home to the more traditional crafts and clothing shops, including some open-air stalls. I suggest you wander in and out of the shops in this area before hitting the **handicrafts market** on the marina, near the glass-bottomed boat dock (opposite the entrance to Pueblo Bonito); that way you'll have some idea of prices—and quality—before you commence the bargaining ritual. Don't expect much from the handicrafts market, however; it's strictly for tourists.

To Bargain or Not to Bargain

In theory, a price tag on an item indicates a fixed price, but rates in small shops tend to be negotiable; it never hurts to ask for a better deal, especially in slow season and particularly if you're thinking about buying more than one item. (Stand around looking very indecisive and the shopkeeper might be the one to lower the price.) No price tag = no-holds-barred bargaining.

If you're not in high-shopping gear, but want to hit a few good stores, you don't have to go farther than Plaza Bonita mall. Standouts among the shops there include **Joyeria Plaza del Sol** (☎ 114/3-1809), with nicely designed gold and silver jewelry; **Cartes** (☎ 114/3-1770), selling excellent folk art from all over the country; **Dos Luna** (☎ 114/3-1969), where some of the colorful women's sportswear lines hail from California and Hawaii; and **Aca Joe** (☎ 114/3-1033), Mexico's version of The Gap, featuring casual clothing for men as well as women. The following are some additional possibilities, in less geographically concentrated form.

Home Furnishings & Handicrafts

Galerias Gattamelata (Camino al Hotel Hacienda, across from Marina Fiesta Resort; ☎ 114/3-1166) is a branch of a larger Mexico City store that specializes in Mexican antiques and art objects—everything from *retablos* (wooden altar pieces) to Victorian-style furniture from the 19th century. **Necri** (Boulevard Marina between Madero and Ocampo; ☎ 114/3-0283), one of the earliest Cabo shops, has a particularly fine selection of Talavera pottery and tinwork picture frames. Another Cabo retail pioneer, **Mama**

Let's Make a Deal

➤ Start out with a price 75% lower than the one the vendor asks for and come up in increments. You've done well if you walk away with the item at half the original asking price.

➤ Examine an item you're thinking about buying as though you're vaguely amused by it; act terribly interested and the price immediately goes up.

➤ Be prepared to walk away if you don't get the price you want. You can always come back if you don't find the same thing elsewhere for less.

Eli's (Avenida San Lucas, 1 block west of Madero; ☎ 114/3-1616) also carries beautiful pottery and pewter. As its name suggests, **Rostros de Mexico (Faces of Mexico)** (Matamoros at Lázaro Cárdenas; no phone) specializes in masks from the antique ceremonial variety to new, solely decorative types. Another store with a name that advertises its specialty, the open-air **Cuca's Blanket Factory** (Lázaro Cárdenas at Matamoros; ☎ 114/3-1913) will let you design your own wool or cotton blanket and have it waiting for you the next day.

Clothing
Galeria Girasoles (Guerrero s/n, a few steps off Boulevard Marina; ☎ 114/3-1697) carries traditional women's clothing from all over Mexico, including beautiful appliquéd and hand-painted jackets. **Magic of the Moon** (Plaza Pericú on Hidalgo, just west of Plaza Las Glorias hotel; ☎ 114/3-3161) has both imports and locally hand-crafted fashions, from sexy bustiers to comfortable flowing outfits; custom orders are accepted. **Temptations** (Lázaro Cárdenas, between Matamoros and Boulevard Marina) carries lots of cool, gauzy cotton clothing, including the colorful Maria de Guadalajara line. Guys get their turn at the **Los Cabos Fishing Center** (Lázaro Cárdenas, at Guerrero, near the entrance to the Hotel Mar de Cortez; ☎ 114/3-3736), where, in addition to hooks, lines, and sinkers, you can find seaworthy duds.

What To Do When the Sun's Gone Down
Nightlife in Los Cabos is more than slightly askew: There's not a whole lot going on in either San José or the Corridor after dark, but in Cabo, you'll have a hard time deciding which watering hole to hit. Although Cabo's bar scene is lively—to put it mildly—there's not a big variety; many places tend to attract the "I-fear-no-beer" T-shirt–wearing fraternity crowd. You won't find lots of quieter spots in Cabo, but if you're looking to let your inhibitions down, you've come to the right place.

Unless otherwise indicated, you needn't expect to pay a cover charge at the listed places.

San José del Cabo's Best Watering Holes

Not much goes on at the **Iguana Bar and Grill** (Blvd. Mijares 24; ☎ 114/2-0266) during the week, when it's a friendly local hangout, but things loosen up a bit on the weekends with live music and dancing on Friday and Saturday nights; there's a pleasant outdoor patio, too. Just down the block, the **Tropicana Bar & Grill** (Bulevar Mijares 30; ☎ 114/5-2684) is consistently livelier, attracting tourists and townies alike to watch football on its satellite TV, listen to guitar music, and get moving to live bands on the weekends.

Cabo San Lucas Hot Spots

Cabo Wabo (Guerrero at Lázaro Cárdenas; ☎ 114/3-1188) banks not only on its rock-star owners' occasional appearances, but also on an always crowded dance floor and good acoustics. Covers for live shows run from $15 to $20 and include two drinks. The antics at the **Giggling Marlin** (Lázaro Cárdenas at Zaragoza, across from the marina; ☎ 114/3-1516) are not for the prudish or faint of heart; the club's most infamous feature is the fish scale on which singles or couples get strung up by the heels. Dancing on the

Bet You Didn't Know

Cabo Wabo is owned by Van Halen and Sammy Hagar; you never know when they—or their friends—will turn up on stage.

bar is common, and there's a small cover (about $5) when the music is live. When the Marlin shuts its doors at 1am, die-hard partiers stumble over to **Squid Row** (Boulevard Marina, opposite Plaza Bonita; ☎ 114/3-0655), which stays open 2 hours later. At this one-off link in the Carlos Anderson chain (of Carlos 'n Charlie's fame), tequila is consumed by the bucketful and women's T-shirts often end up wet. Somewhat more mellow—it closes at a sedate 12:30am—**the Rio Grill Restaurant and Bar** (Boulevard Marina 31-A at Guerrero; ☎ 114/3-1335) is renowned for its serious—and seriously long—happy hour, which runs from 4 to 8pm. The music is soft during dinner, but Thursday through Sunday, live reggae and R&B reign after 9:30pm.

Latitude 22+ (Lázaro Cárdenas, one-half block east of Moreles; ☎ 114/3-1516) caters to sporty types with its six TVs, pool tables, assorted games—and twin half-ton marlin hanging from the rafters (they've been dubbed the "Blues Brothers"). If you want to put your money where your mouth is, head over to the **Casino Real/Casino Sports Bar** (Boulevard Marina at Plaza Nautica; ☎ 114/3-1934), where you can bet on nearly any sport; the bar is attached to the Caliente Racetrack book and takes wagers on most major jock events.

Eat 'n' Rumba: Restaurants with a Musical Menu

Cabo has got the official Mexican party-town triple-crown: a **Hard Rock Cafe** (Plaza Bonita, Lázaro Cárdenas, and Boulevard Marina; ☎ 114/ 3-3779), a **Planet Hollywood** (Plaza Bonita; ☎ 114/3-3919), and a **Carlos 'n Charlie's** (Blvd. Marina 20; ☎ 114/3-2180). At all three, the focus is on fun as much as on food, although you can get a decent burger or ribs at Hard Rock and Planet Hollywood and good, if somewhat gringo-ized, Mexican fare at the home-grown Carlos 'n Charlie's. The Hard Rock sometimes features live music, and there's dancing at all three. All—surprise, surprise—also have boutiques selling logo merchandise.

Fiestas: A Taste of Mexico

You're not going to get the most authentic Mexican food, music, or dancing at a hotel fiesta, where the national culture gets a Las Vegas–style spin, but you are going to get plenty to eat and lots of lively entertainment. The venues and nights of these fiestas shift frequently; currently, you can depend on the **Palmilla** (Hwy. 100, km 27.5; ☎ 114/4-5250) to hold a fiesta every Friday night by its pool, with fireworks over the sea as a finale (cost: $30). In San José, these theme nights may be held at the **Howard Johnson Hotel** (☎ 114/2-0999) and the **Fiesta Inn** (☎ 114/2-0701). In Cabo, the **Solmar** (☎ 114/3-0022), the **Finisterra** (☎ 114/3-3333), the **Hacienda** (☎ 114/3-0123), and **Meliá San Lucas** (☎ 114/3-0420) are possibilities. Prices range from $16 (drinks, tax, and tips extra) to $35, which covers everything, including an open bar with Mexican brands. Phone the hotels or ask at your hotel travel desk (which can book these evenings for you) to find out what's on when you're in town.

Sunset Romance

It's not possible to see the sun go down everywhere in Los Cabos—only places facing the Pacific get a ringside view—but there are a few watering holes that fit the bill. On the **Corridor,** you can catch the nightly light show from **Da Giorgio II,** at the Misiones del Cabo hotel (Hwy. 100, km 5; ☎ 113/3-3988), and **Pitahayas** at Cabo del Sol (take the km 10 exit of Highway 100 and follow the signs; ☎ 114/3-2157 or 114/3-0234); both are fairly formal establishments. In **Cabo,** the more casual **Whale Watcher Bar** at the Hotel Finisterra (Blvd. Marina s/n, almost at the end; ☎ 114/3-3333) or the **cocktail lounge at the Hotel Solmar Suites** (Av. Solmar 1, at the end of Boulevard Marina; ☎ 14/ 3-3535) are equally fine options. Can't decide? At the former, you'll be elevated and have the town as a backdrop; at the latter, you're at sea level and can pretend civilization doesn't exist.

Time-Savers

To avoid disappointment, check the time that the sun sets and, in high season, book a table if you're going to either Da Giorgio II or Pitahayas.

For some quiet sounds during or after dinner, try **Edith's** (Medano Beach at Paseo del Pescador; ☎ 114/3-0801), which also offers a terrific view of El Arco. Tucked away behind the northeast side of the Plaza Las Glorias hotel, **Sancho Panza Wine Bar Cafe** (on the marina, just up from KFC; ☎ 114/3-3212) has soft lighting, the best selection of wine in town, and Latin jazz trios during the week (call ahead for the schedule). You won't go wrong if you come for dinner either (see the following chapter).

Side Trips: Getting Out of Los Cabos

As noted in earlier sections, some of the most interesting places around Los Cabos are best explored by sea or by ATV, but it's rewarding to visit both Todos Santos and La Paz by more conventional means, whether on your own or via guided tour. La Paz is a major destination in its own right; for more details, best consult a travel guide, such as *Frommer's Mexico*.

Todos Santos

Dubbed "Bohemian Baja" by the *Los Angeles Times,* Todos Santos is an agricultural town on the Pacific side of the peninsula that's becoming increasingly popular with American expats of the artistic persuasion. There's not much to do here but check out the abandoned sugar mills (the town was a sugar cane center in the mid–19th century) and walk up and down the main street, Juárez, which has are some interesting shops and art galleries. The Caffé Todos Santos, on the corner of Centenario and Topete, offers good espresso, baked goods, and prime people-watching from its sidewalk tables, and the Café Santa Fe, set in a hacienda-style building across from the main plaza and Teatro Marquéz de Léon, is one of the town's claims to culinary fame. Todos Santos is pretty sleepy (read: partially shut down) during the summer, when lots of business owners head off to cooler climes, but it comes alive again for the Festival Fundidor, held October 10 to 14 to celebrate the town's founding in 1723.

Todos Santos is some 45 miles north of Cabos San Lucas on Highway 19. If you've rented a car, it's a lovely hour's drive past wild desert scenery and seascapes, with the occasional farm (and, perhaps, burro) appearing along the side of the road. Some of the frequently running buses to La Paz also stop in Todos Santos; check with **Autotransportes Aguila** at the Cabos San Lucas bus terminal (Héroes at Moreles; ☎ 114/3-0400) for the schedule. Prices are under $10. Some tour operators also include Todos Santos on their "Explore Baja" itineraries, which take in the mining towns of El Triunfo and San Antonio, too. Travel agency schedules vary, but expect to

Bet You Didn't Know

Todos Santos is home to the 1928 Hotel California, rumored to be the model for the Eagles song of that name. There's little evidence to back that claim, but the hotel gift shop does a brisk business in T-shirts, nevertheless.

pay about $60 for a full day (7am to 4pm) trip that includes breakfast, but not lunch. Ask at your hotel tour desk for details.

La Paz

Some 110 miles north of Cabo San Lucas via Highway 19 or 122 miles northwest of San José via Highway 1, La Paz (pop. 180,000) is the capital of the southern state of the Baja Peninsula and a thriving port, but it feels like a small town. It's a good place to come for a sense of the "real" Mexico—easily acquired by sitting in a cafe along the *malecón* (seaside walkway)—as well as for cultural attractions such as the 1720 Jesuit Mission, the Anthropology Museum, and the Casa de Gobierno, which houses Baja's major historical library.

You can drive or go by bus (first- and second-class buses leave from the main bus station in both San José and Cabo, take about 2½ to 3½ hours, and cost less than $10) and wander around on your own once you get there, or take a city tour from a La Paz travel agency. They last about 3 hours and cost $25. Some of Los Cabos tour desks and travel agencies also run day trips, which depart at 7am and return at around 6pm. Prices (about $65) generally include breakfast, but not lunch.

Chapter 44

The Best of the Los Cabos Dining Scene

In This Chapter

➤ Dining in Los Cabos: The big picture

➤ Keeping costs down

➤ The best restaurants from A to Z

➤ Restaurant indexes

When it comes to dining, Los Cabos is a mixed bag. You can enjoy local cuisine or, because of the huge north-of-the-border influence, easily find something familiar to put on your plate. On the other hand, you're likely to pay prices similar to—or higher than—those at home for American-style meals that may be mediocre at best. The good news, however, is that some sophisticated chefs have begun turning the trend around, introducing more interesting recipes and looking to organic goods produced in the Baja to cater to culinarily savvy and health-conscious Californians.

A Dining Overview: Where's the Burrito?

You won't lack for restaurants in Los Cabos, no matter where you're bedding down, but you'll have a harder time locating an inexpensive meal in some parts of the resort than in others. San José is best for authentic Mexican cooking at reasonable prices, but the town doesn't have a whole lot of dining room variety. Because it's so hard to get around the Corridor and because the area's exclusive hotels tend to hire good chefs, you're most likely to dine within strolling distance of your room if you're staying on that tourist stretch. Cabo San Lucas has the best selection of eateries, but because the

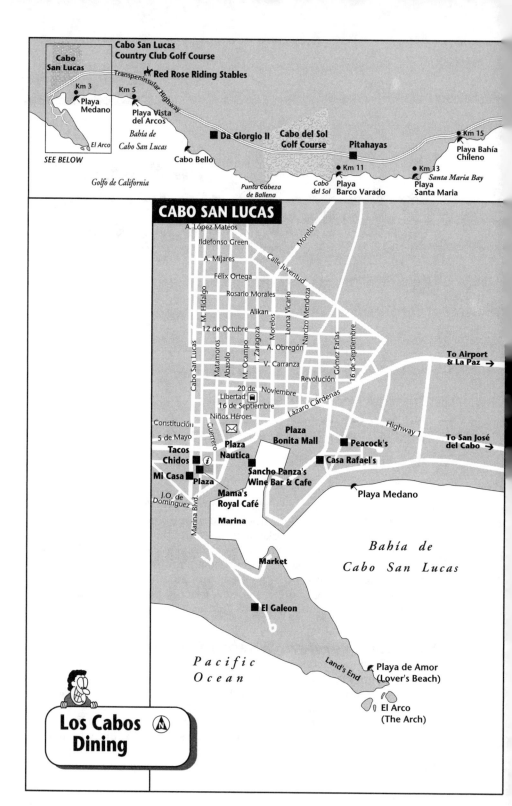

Cabo San Lucas
Country Club Golf Course

Red Rose Riding Stables

Cabo San Lucas

Km 3

Playa Medano

Km 5

Playa Vista del Arcos

Bahía de Cabo San Lucas

El Arco

SEE BELOW

Cabo Bello

Golfo de California

Da Giorgio II

Cabo del Sol Golf Course

Pitahayas

Km 11

Km 13

Km 15

Playa Bahía Chileno

Santa Maria Bay

Punta Cabeza de Ballena

Cabo del Sol

Playa Barco Varado

Playa Santa Maria

CABO SAN LUCAS

A. López Mateos
Ildefonso Green
A. Mijares
Félix Ortega
Rosario Morales
Alikan
12 de Octubre

Morelos
Calle Juventud

M. Hidalgo
Matamoros
Abasolo
M. Ocampo
I. Zaragoza
Morelos
Leona Vicario
Narcizo Mendoza
A. Obregón
V. Carranza
Revolución
Gómez Farías
16 de Septiembre

To Airport & La Paz →

Cabo San Lucas

20 de Noviembre
Libertad
16 de Septiembre
Niños Héroes

Constitución
5 de Mayo

Tacos Chidos

Mi Casa
Plaza

J.O. de Domínguez

Guerrero

Plaza Nautica

Lázaro Cárdenas

Highway 1

To San José del Cabo →

Plaza Bonita Mall

Peacock's

Casa Rafael's

Sancho Panza's Wine Bar & Cafe

Mama's Royal Café

Marina Blvd.

Marina

Playa Medano

Market

Bahía de
Cabo San Lucas

El Galeon

Pacific Ocean

Land's End

Playa de Amor (Lover's Beach)

El Arco (The Arch)

Los Cabos Dining

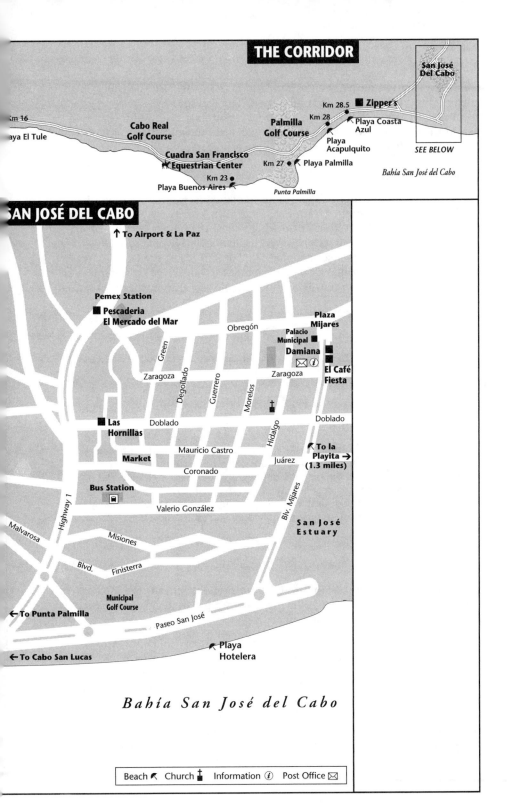

THE CORRIDOR

San José
Del Cabo

Km 28.5 ■ Zipper's
Km 28 ● ← Playa Coasta
Azul
Playa
Acapulquito

Km 16

Cabo Real
Golf Course

Palmilla
Golf Course

aya El Tule

Cuadra San Francisco
← Equestrian Center   Km 27 ● ← Playa Palmilla

Km 23 ●
Playa Buenos Aires

Punta Palmilla

SEE BELOW

Bahía San José del Cabo

SAN JOSÉ DEL CABO

↑ To Airport & La Paz

Pemex Station
■ Pescaderia
El Mercado del Mar

Obregón

Plaza
Mijares

Palacio
Municipal ■
Damiana
⊠ ⓘ

Zaragoza

Green

Degollado

Guerrero

Morelos

Zaragoza

El Café
Fiesta

■ Las
Hornillas

Doblado

Hidalgo

Doblado

Market

Mauricio Castro

Juárez

← To la
Playita →
(1.3 miles)

Coronado

Bus Station
▣

Blv. Mijares

Valerio González

San José
Estuary

Malvarosa

Highway 1

Misiones

Blvd. Finisterra

Municipal
Golf Course

← To Punta Palmilla

Paseo San José

← To Cabo San Lucas

← Playa
Hotelera

Bahía San José del Cabo

Beach ← Church ‡ Information ⓘ Post Office ⊠

level of expectation hasn't been particularly high in the past, the really top-notch places don't have much competition. The listings in this chapter reflect this division—that is, there are more restaurants reviewed in Cabo than in the Corridor, where not that many places are worth the taxi fare or the trouble to drive to. All the selections are arranged alphabetically and then, following the reviews, at-a-glance indexes break your choices down by location and by price.

Kids If you're traveling with fast food–starved kids, Cabo is your best bet; it's got KFC, Domino's, Subway, Pizza Hut, Mrs. Field's, TCBY, Baskin-Robbins, and Dairy Queen (but not the big two of the burger domain). Your teens will no doubt be happy to be taken to Planet Hollywood, Hard Rock Cafe, or Carlos 'n Charlie's (see chapter 43, "Fun On & Off the Beach"); you might not be equally thrilled by the volume of the music—or by the prices of the franchise merchandise they'll doubtless cajole you into buying for them.

Yo, Gringo!

Seafood is, not surprisingly, a specialty in Los Cabos. If you live on the West Coast or in the Southwest, you may be familiar with "Baja style" Mexican food as brought to you by California chains such as Chuy's—for example, fish tacos. Although the basics may be the same—you'll still get a piece of fish wrapped in a tortilla—you might find the preparations in Los Cabos quite different. The fish is frequently fried rather than grilled; there may be a large dollop of tartar sauce or mayonnaise added for flavor instead of just salsa; and you're as likely as not to get refried beans, not plain-cooked pintos, on the side.

Check, Please

It's easy to let a lot of pesos slip through your fingers at mealtimes in Los Cabos if you're not careful. By following a few simple strategies, however, it's possible to eat economically and still eat well.

Unlike in other beach towns, where the tax is always included in the final tab, in Los Cabos it's sometimes extra. If you see *"no incluye el I.V.A"* on the menu, expect 10% to be tacked onto your bill. Here, as everywhere else in Mexico, tips are not ordinarily tacked on, but if the words *"propina incluida"* or *"servicio incluida"* appear on your bill, then you know service has already been covered. If it hasn't, the standard in nice restaurants is 15%. Mexicans rarely tip that well in less pricey places—10% is about average—but if the service was good or you've been lingering for a long time, sticking with the 15% rule is an easy way to help the Mexican economy without going broke.

Putting Your Money Where Your Mouth Isn't

➤ Drink local. You know about good Mexican beers, but probably weren't aware that there are some decent Baja wines (see the "Got Wine?" sidebar later in this chapter).

➤ Order the catch of the day—for example, the delicious mahi-mahi—more often than expensive imports, such as shrimp and lobster.

➤ Eat somewhere other than where you've gone for happy hour. It's easy to order a lot more food than you might have intended to if you're sufficiently lubricated (restaurants bank on that).

The price categories below are arranged with the worst-case scenario in mind: They're based on a per-person dinner tab that includes appetizer, entrée, dessert, one drink, and tip. In addition, a price range for dinner entrées is included in the individual reviews. The more $ signs you see, the more money you'll be shelling out at the restaurant listed; use the following chart as a guide:

$	=	Under $15
$$	=	$15–$30
$$$	=	$30–$50
$$$$	=	Over $50

Unless otherwise noted, reservations are either not accepted or needed.

Smoke Gets in My Eyes

There are no laws against restaurant smoking in Mexico, but California has made some impact on Los Cabos when it comes to public puffing: Some dining rooms, especially the more upscale ones, have nonsmoking sections. And most places that put no restriction on their customers' nicotine use have outdoor terraces, so you're not likely to get smoked out in Los Cabos. If you're worried, however, phone ahead.

My Favorite Restaurants from A to Z

Casa Rafael's

$$$$. Cabo San Lucas. INTERNATIONAL.

It may be just down the block from Medano beach, but Casa Rafael's seems a world away, what with the candlelight, the European antiques, the piano player tickling the ivories, and the sophisticated international cuisine prepared by chef Willie Mitchell. (Well, maybe those toucans that greet you at the door are a giveaway that you're in the [semi]tropics). Meals here are intended to be taken in a leisurely fashion, the better to let you work your

Yo, Gringo!

Remember, it's considered impolite in Mexico for the waiter to bring the check before you ask for it.

way comfortably through the menu. You might start with the smoked dorado pâté or the hearts of palm with a raspberry vinaigrette dressing, and then proceed to the scampi with pasta or the New England lamb. You'll definitely need to rest up a bit before you move on to desserts, which tend toward the rich—and delicious.

Calle Playa el Medano at Camino Pescador. ☎ *114/3-0739. Reservations suggested in high season.* **Main courses:** *$24–$35.* **Open:** *Daily 6–10pm. MC, V.*

Da Giorgio II

$$–$$$. The Corridor. ITALIAN.

Sit back in a cliffside table beside a waterfall and pond and watch the sun descend over the water and El Arco; it doesn't get much more mellow than this. The food is less exciting than the view, but the salad bar is copious, the (liquor) bar well stocked, and if you stick to the simpler pastas and pizzas, you'll do fine. *Note:* don't confuse this with the Da Giorgio at the other end of the Corridor, near San José (Hwy. 1, km 25.5), which looks out over Palmilla Bay and town but doesn't catch the sunset.

Hwy. 1, km 5. ☎ *114/3-2988. Reservations suggested for sunset viewing times.* **Main courses:** *$9–$20. AE, MC, V.* **Open:** *Daily 7:30am–11pm.*

Damiana

$$–$$$. San José. MEXICAN/SEAFOOD.

Set in an 18th-century hacienda on San José's town plaza, Damiana is as Mexican as they come—almost. That is, although the food and the setting are authentic, because it's so popular with tourists (and more expensive than many townspeople can afford), you won't see many local faces here. The menu encompasses both gringo-friendly dishes, such as beef medaillons and grilled lobster tail, and more unusual specialties, such as ranchero-style shrimp with *nopalitos* (cactus strips). The backyard patio is lovely, with its flickering candles and gigantic bougainvillea, but it's small and the mariachi music and din from surrounding conversations can be overpowering on busy nights. If you want to have a quiet meal with your companion during high season, you might have to head indoors.

Plaza Mijares (Blvd. Mijares at Zaragoza). ☎ *114/2-0499. Reservations recommended during holidays and on high-season weekends.* **Main courses:** *$12–$25. AE, MC, V.* **Open:** *Daily noon–11pm.*

Most Romantic (Without Sea Views)

Casa Rafael's (Cabo San Lucas, $$$$)

Damiana (San José, $$–$$$)

El Café Fiesta
$. San José. CAFE/HEALTH FOOD/MEXICAN.

Grab a tree-shaded table on the central plaza, and settle in for a light meal and some heavy-duty people-watching. Of the available platters, salads, subs, and drinks, some are healthier than others. There's a juice bar if you want to load up on vitamins, an espresso machine for a quick caffeine fix, and everything from fruit salad and whole-wheat pitas to beef fajitas.

Plaza Mijares (Blvd. Mijares at Zaragoza). ☎ *114/2-2908.* **Main courses:** *$3–$9. MC, V.* **Open:** *Daily 7am–10:30pm.*

El Galeon
$$–$$$$. Cabo San Lucas. ITALIAN.

Both the decor and the food here are fairly traditional—lots of dark wood and ships' wheels indoors, and nothing surprising about the preparations—but from the terrace the vistas of the city and the marina are dazzling, and if you're looking for consistently dependable cooking, you won't be disappointed. There are some Mexican and American selections, but the focus is on Italian seafood. The Caesar salad is excellent, the pastas are made on the

Best Sea Views

Da Giorgio II (The Corridor, $$–$$$)

El Galeon (Cabo San Lucas, $$–$$$$)

premises, and much of the fish comes straight from the marina. A flaming Mexican coffee in the piano bar is a nice way to end the evening.

Blvd. Marina, at the turnoff to the Finisterra Hotel. ☎ *114/3-0443. Reservations suggested in high season.* **Main courses:** *$10–$30. AE, MC, V.* **Open:** *Daily 4–11pm.*

Las Hornillas
$. San José. CHICKEN/MEXICAN.

You've got only one specialty here—chicken roasted on a spit over wood— but it's a winner. Locals pile into the cheerful dining room, decked out with plants and bird cages, for the half-chicken served with tortilla, beans, and rice, or the fajitas with grilled onions and peppers, easily enough for two. Go ahead, eat with your hands; there's a sink on the side of the room to encourage you.

Calle Manuel Doblado 610, 2 blocks east of Hwy. 1. ☎ *114/2-2324.* **Main courses:** *Half-chicken $4; chicken fajitas $6. No credit cards.* **Open:** *Daily noon–10pm.*

Kids Mama's Royal Cafe
$. Cabo San Lucas. CAFE/AMERICAN/MEXICAN.

A favorite hangout for American expats and gringo visitors, Mama's is a great place to start your day or take a lunchtime shopping siesta. Sit out on the vine-covered shaded patio and enjoy a fluffy omelet with home fries, or *huevos rancheros* (a fried egg on a fried corn tortilla with tomato sauce), cream cheese–stuffed French toast, or eggs Benedict, accompanied by a large glass of fresh-squeezed juice and a bottomless cup of good, hot coffee. Lunchtime, it's burgers or enchiladas and a cold one (Corona or Negro Modelo, of course).

Hidalgo, between Zapata and Madero. ☎ *114/3-4290.* **Main courses:** *$2.50–$4 breakfast; $5–$8 lunch. No credit cards.* **Open:** *Wed–Mon 7am–2pm (closed Tues).*

Hold All Calls

Sitting smack on the busiest stretch of Medano Beach, **The Office** (☎ **114/ 3-3464**) isn't known for its food; rather, everyone turns up here sooner or later to check out the scene. Most people nurse a beer (or five) while trying to work up the nerve to go parasailing—or talk to that cute person of the opposite gender. Oh, go ahead—just don't do anything foolish like ordering the lobster here (it's overcooked and expensive).

Mi Casa
$$–$$$. Cabo San Lucas. MEXICAN.

Sit in a pretty courtyard, shaded by a thatched roof and surrounded by fuchsia flowers, and take a culinary tour of Mexico. Just across from the town square (which isn't really in the center of town in Cabo), you'll enjoy such regional dishes as *mole poblano,* the Puebla specialty famed for its complex sauce; the Yucatecan *mancha manteles,* chicken and pork cooked with tropical fruit; and Tampico-style steak served with enchiladas, rice, and guacamole. Women make fresh tortillas in front of a mural depicting the same subject (is that art imitating life or vice versa?). The menu, with its detailed explanations of the unusual dishes, is available in English, but this is still a very traditional place.

Av. Cabo San Lucas between Serdán and Lázaro Cárdenas. ☎ **114/3-1933. Main courses:** *$10–$17. AE ($45 minimum), MC, V.* **Open:** *Mon–Sat noon–10pm; Sun 4–10pm.*

Peacock's
$$$–$$$$. Cabo San Lucas. INTERNATIONAL.
Another of Cabo's colorfully decked-out patios is the venue for some of the best seafood in town, creatively prepared and beautifully presented. The handwritten menu changes every few days, but seabass Veracruz-style, mahi-mahi with grilled bell pepper sauce, or lobster tail with shrimp dijonnaise might be among your options. Don't fret if you don't like food that's spent too much time in the sea; you've got as much choice, if not more, than the fish-besotted folks. The house specialty is rack of lamb with mushrooms, and the chef does duck to perfection. And if you and your dining partner don't see eye-to-eye on the main courses, you're likely to agree on the to-die-for kahlua chocolate mousse, with taste—and calories—enough for two.

Paseo del Pescador s/n, next to the Meliá Hotel entry to Playa Medano. ☎ **114/ 3-1858. Main courses:** *$12–$32.* **Open:** *Daily 6–10pm. MC, V.*

A Diplomatic Deli

What do you do if you're a homesick U.S. consular representative and happen to be named Greenberg? Open **Señor Greenberg's Mexicatessan** (behind Plaza Nautica, off Boulevard Marina; ☎ **114/3-5630**), of course. The corned beef, pastrami, pickles, and lox are imported from home—which is San Diego, not Brooklyn, but it's as close to the real thing as you're going to get—cold cuts like turkey and cheese are local.

Pescaderia El Mercado del Mar
$$. San José. SEAFOOD/MEXICAN.
A bit off the beaten path—it's about a mile from the center of town—this casual terrace restaurant is well worth going out of your way for. It's connected to a seafood market (the "Mercado del Mar" of its name) and has its own smoker, so you know everything you eat is going to be fresh and prepared on the premises. The poblano chiles stuffed with smoked marlin is super, but beware—it'll knock your socks off. If you don't want your fish to bear even a passing resemblance to health food, go for the shrimp "Boston,"

wrapped in bacon and soaked in kahlua. Feeling indecisive? Try the seafood platter for two, piled with all kinds of delicious dishes. You'll need to walk back to your hotel after this one—it's a huge amount of food.

Mauricio Castro 1110 (just off Hwy. 1). ☎ **114/2-3266. Main courses:** *$8–$17.50. No credit cards.* **Open:** *Wed–Mon noon–10pm.*

Pitahayas
$$$–$$$$. The Corridor. PAN-ASIAN/INTERNATIONAL.
A lovely beachside setting and innovative cuisine make Pitahayas worth both the drive and the splurge. It's hard to typecast the menu: It's been described as Pan-Asian, and the ingredients and gorgeous presentations back that up, but both the hefty portion sizes and, on the downside, an occasional lack of delicacy, can be laid on the plate of the German-born chef's Teutonic culinary roots. For starters, try the coconut shrimp with a spicy chipotle cream sauce or the lobster bisque touched with lemongrass. Worthy entrées include sautéed seabass in a Thai curry-basil sauce or your classic surf 'n' turf, filet mignon and a half lobster tail. There are even a couple of interesting vegetarian dishes, a rarity in Mexico. For dessert, share a fruit pizza (sweet dough topped with seasonal fruit and marzipan and drizzled with chocolate), and you'll roll out of here more than satisfied.

Cabo del Sol Resort, Hwy. 1, km 10. ☎ **114/3-2157.** *Reservations suggested in high season.* **Main courses:** *$15–$32. AE, DC, MC, V.* **Open:** *Daily 7–11pm.*

Got Wine?

Los Cabos is a great place to check out Mexican wines. Some surprisingly good bottles are produced in Baja, and they're a whole lot cheaper than the imports. Two vineyards I'd especially recommend are Château Camou, which does a good cabernet sauvignon, and Monte Xanic, with a very decent chardonnay.

Sancho Panza Wine Bar/Cafe
$$–$$$. Cabo San Lucas. CAFE/INTERNATIONAL.
This hot new dining and drinking spot is tucked away behind the Plaza Las Glorias hotel, in back of the lighthouse on the marina, but hip expats haven't had any problem homing in on it. With its Miro-inspired decor, huge selection of California and Mexican wines by the glass, and "Nuevo Latino" food designed to appeal to both the eye and the palette, this is a place you'll want to adopt as your local hangout, too. Starters focus on tapas and salads—say a roasted garlic and warm brie appetizer, or seared tuna on a

bed of greens—while main meals run the gamut from pastas (black musroom-ricotta ravioli in vodka basil, for example) to serious meat (filet mignon in red wine). There's terrific attention to detail—the produce comes from organic farms in nearby Todos Santos, and the pecans tossed into the salad are roasted on the premises. Popular for its Latin jazz (see chapter 43, "Fun On & Off the Beach") as well as its wine and food, this spot might well outgrow its small space; stay tuned.

Marina, Loc. D 19–22 (down the alley from KFC and across from MiniGolf). ☎ *114/3-3212. Reservations suggested in high season.* **Main courses: $9–$17.** *No credit cards.* **Open:** *Mon–Sat 11am–11pm.*

Tacos Chidos
$. Cabo San Lucas. MEXICAN.

If you want to know what Baja-style fish tacos are supposed to taste like—at least in my version of the Platonic ideal—make your way to this tiny, family-run counter. Through the open kitchen, you can watch the corn tortillas being tossed and the fresh dorado being sizzled on the grill. But there are also tasty beef and pork tacos, as well as great fruit smoothies and way-cheap set-price lunch specials ($3). In the

Most Mexicano

Las Hornillas (San José, $)

Tacos Chidos (Cabo San Lucas, $)

morning, get recharged with a breakfast of eggs, beans, and rice; add some fresh-made salsa if you really want to jump-start your day.

Zapata s/n, between Hidalgo and Guerrero. ☎ *114/3-0551.* **Main courses:** *Tacos $1; combinations $2.75–$4.75. No credit cards.* **Open:** *Mon–Sat 7am–10pm.*

Tropicana Inn Bar & Grill
$$. San José. INTERNATIONAL.

Pass through the Tropicana, San José's most popular bar (see chapter 43), and you'll enter a romantic thatched-roof dining patio, all fountains, arches, and atmospheric "killer trees" (a kind of kudzu vine that wraps itself around palms). You can watch an eclectic array of dishes—Mexican, seafood, steak, and Continental fare all appear on the huge menu—emerge from the colorfully tiled open kitchen; everything is generously apportioned and well prepared. The restaurant runs many specials—for example, all-you-can-eat ribs

Best for a Gringo Fix

Mama's Royal Cafe (Cabo San Lucas, $)

Tropicana Inn Bar & Grill (San José, $$)

Zipper's (The Corridor, $–$$)

on Thursday nights, paella on Sunday—and you can eat to the beat of live Latino music come Saturday evening. The American owners import most of the meats and cheeses, as well as the coffee: It's Starbucks.

539

Blvd. Mijares 30. ☎ *113/2-1580. AE, MC, V.* **Main courses:** *$10.50–$16.*
Open: *Daily 8am–11pm.*

Zipper's
$–$$. The Corridor. AMERICAN/MEXICAN.

The quintessential surfer hangout, Zipper's sits on the south end of Los
Cabos's top surfing beach and serves up all-American fare—burgers made
with imported beef and USA catsup, deli sandwiches, mesquite-grilled steaks,
ribs, beer-battered shrimp—as well as some Mexican combos. This casual,
open-air eatery is so devoted to the basics that it's got no telephone and
takes no plastic. It's, like, just you and the waves and the food, dude.

Hwy. 1, km 28.5. No phone. **Main courses:** *Burgers and sandwiches $7–$10;
dinners $7–$15. No credit cards.* **Open:** *Sun–Thurs 11am–10pm; Fri–Sat
11am–1am.*

A Little Cafe

If you want to get away from Cabo hoi polloi and have a quiet espresso and a
muffin, try **Francisco's Cafe del Mundo** (Plaza Bonita; ☎ **114/3-2366**).
You can sit on the Plaza Bonita patio and watch the shoppers stroll by, or face
the marina and the bobbing boats.

Sound Bites: Los Cabos's Restaurants at a Glance
Restaurant Index by Price

$

El Café Fiesta (San José,
Café/Health Food/Mexican)

Las Hornillas (San José,
Chicken/Mexican)

Mama's Royal Cafe
(Cabo San Lucas, Café/
American/Mexican)

Tacos Chidos (Cabo San
Lucas, Mexican)

$–$$

Zipper's (The Corridor,
American/Mexican)

$$

Pescaderia El Mercado del Mar
(San José, International)

Tropicana Inn Bar & Grill
(San José, Seafood/Mexican)

$$–$$$

Da Giorgio II (The Corridor,
Italian)

Damiana (San José,
Mexican/Seafood)

Mi Casa (Cabo San Lucas,
Mexican)

Sancho Panza Wine Bar/Cafe
(Cabo San Lucas,
Café/International)

$$–$$$$

El Galeon (Cabo San Lucas,
Italian)

$$$–$$$$

Peacock's (Cabo San Lucas,
International)

Pitahayas (The Corridor, Pan-
Asian/International)

$$$$

Casa Rafael's (Cabo San Lucas,
International)

Restaurant Index by Location

Cabo San Lucas

Casa Rafael's $$$$

El Galeon $$–$$$$

Mama's Royal Cafe $

Mi Casa $$–$$$

Peacock's $$$–$$$$

Sancho Panza Wine Bar/Cafe
$$–$$$

Tacos Chidos $

San José del Cabo

Damiana $$–$$$

El Café Fiesta $

Las Hornillas $

Pescaderia El Mercado del
Mar $$

Tropicana Inn Bar & Grill $$

The Corridor

Da Giorgio II $$–$$$

Pitahayas $$$–$$$$

Zipper's $–$$

Hotel Preferences Worksheet

Hotel	Location	Price per night

Advantages	Disadvantages	Your Ranking (1–10)

Mexico A to Z: Facts at Your Fingertips

American Express: All the beach towns have American Express representatives. See the individual resort chapters for specific locations.

ATMs: These handy-dandy cash dispensers are available in all the beach resorts, and I suggest you use them. See chapter 7, "Money Matters," for a discussion of why, and see the individual resort chapters for the best places to find them.

Banks: You can get cash advances on your credit card in certain banks, but the process is interminable and I don't advise it. Banks give good peso-to-dollar rates, but exchange hours are limited (usually from 9 or 10am to noon or 1pm during the week) and you'll have to do quite a bit of line shuffling.

Currency Exchange: You can change money at your hotel (convenient, but exchange rates are the worst); banks (see above); or *casas de cambio* (exchange houses). At the latter, the exchange rates may not be quite as good as those at the bank, but they won't be far off, and the hours are far more convenient. I'll give you details on where to locate them in the individual resort chapters, but in general, you'll find *casas de cambio* wherever gringos congregate.

Driving Rules: In theory, driving rules are the same as they are in the United States, but if someone in front of you signals a lane change, odds are you're driving behind an American. And when a Mexican does turn on a left-hand signal, that doesn't indicate he's turning left; it means it's okay for you to pass. Usually. See chapter 9, "Tying Up the Loose Ends," for more details about the (in)advisability of renting a car in Mexico.

Drugstores: See the "Pharmacies" section in chapter 10, "Crossing the Border & What to Expect on the Other Side." See the individual resort chapters for specific locations.

Emergencies: Each of the individual resort chapters lists emergency numbers for local police, ambulances, and hospitals. As I noted in the "Playing It Safe" section in chapter 10, however, language skills tend to evaporate under stress, and unlike tourist facilities, most emergency offices don't have bilingual staff. On the other hand, hospitals and other medical facilities are repositories of highly educated and trained individuals, so they tend to have more English speakers on staff. I've listed the most reliable ones in the individual resort chapters.

Information: See chapter 3, "Getting Started," for numbers and Web sites to contact before you go, and the individual resort chapters for the locations of on-site tourist offices.

Liquor Laws: The legal drinking age in Mexico is 18. You can buy booze every day, but no sale of alcoholic beverages is permitted within 48 hours of election day (July 6 for the federal election, and November 8 for local elections). Many enterprising entrepreneurs find ways of bending the law for tourists, who aren't allowed to vote anyway.

Newspapers/Magazines: *The News,* a Mexico City–based English-language paper that reports on countrywide and international events, is usually available at all the beach resorts; sometimes you'll come across the similar *Times,* also published in Mexico City. *U.S. News and World Report* and, less often, the *International Herald Tribune* or the *L.A. Times* turn up in the tobacco shops of the larger hotels. Magazines are hit and miss, but you can usually find *Newsweek, Time,* and some fashion mags at newsstands and hotel shops. Look to the individual resort chapters for information on the English-language tourist publications available locally.

Radio & TV: Surprisingly few hotel rooms—even the luxurious ones—have clock radios, although quite a few have TV sets with radios built in. You won't have much luck trying to find English-language talk programs or classical music stations; pop and Latina sounds rule the airwaves. In contrast, you can expect any large resort hotel to have cable TV with channels such as CNN and HBO. Smaller hotels are likely to have TVs that only *habla Español.*

Rest Rooms: It's very rare to find clean public rest rooms in Mexico, although some modern shopping malls have them. Your best bet is to duck into an upscale hotel or restaurant; Mexicans are generally much nicer than Americans in allowing noncustomers access to their facilities when nature calls.

Telephone: For calling in Mexico, see "How Will Ma Bell Treat Me in Mexico?" in chapter 10. To call Mexico from your home country, dial the international service (011), then Mexico's country code (52), and then the city code of the area you want to call and the local number. If you want to call the Acapulco Convention and Visitor's Bureau from the United States, for example, you would dial ☎ 011-52-74/84-7621. The city codes for the beach towns are Cancún, 98; Cozumel, 987; Acapulco, 74; Ixtapa and Zihuatenejo, 755; Manzanillo, 333; Puerto Vallarta, 322 (329 for

Nuevo Vallarta and other locations to the north); Mazatlán, 69; and Los Cabos, 114.

Taxes: In most of Mexico, a national consumer tax of 15% known as "IVA" is levied on nearly everything. Because it's automatically incorporated into the price of most items, including restaurant meals, you're not likely to notice. The exception is hotels, which almost always list their rates exclusive of IVA—and of the additional 2% city tax that's usually tacked on. Taxes in Los Cabos and Cancún are lower than in the rest of the country: 10% rather than 15%.

Time Zones: Los Cabos and Mazatlán observe Mountain Time; Puerto Vallarta, Manzanillo, Acapulco, and Ixtapa/Zihuatenejo are in the Central Time zone; and Cancún and Cozumel are on Eastern Standard Time. Mexico observes daylight saving time.

U.S. Consuls: Acapulco, Cabo San Lucas, Cancún, Mazatlán, and Puerto Vallarta all have U.S. consular representatives; see the individual resort chapters for addresses and phone numbers.

Index

See also separate Accommodations, Restaurant, and Beach indexes, below.

553

555

Xcacel Beach - Very nice

Xaae Bay -

Chat - Xcaret better than Yel La (nice) time)

Notes

The travel experts at Frommer's, the best-selling travel guides, use their special know-how to bring you the most fun and easy-to-use guidebooks ever published.
Look for *Complete Idiot's Travel Guides* to these exciting destinations!

Available now:

Cruise Vacations

Hawaii

Las Vegas

New Orleans

New York City

Planning Your Trip to Europe

San Francisco & the Wine Country

Walt Disney World & Orlando

Coming soon:

Boston

Chicago

London

Paris

Washington, D.C.